Alice in Wonderland and the World Trade Center Disaster

Why the official story of 9/11 is a monumental lie

David Icke

First published in October 2002 by

Bridge
of Love

Bridge of Love Publications USA
1825 Shiloh Valley Drive
Wildwood
MO 63005
USA
Tel: 636-273-5951
Fax: 636-458-7823
email: bridgeloveUSA@aol.com

British Library Cataloguing-in
Publication Data
A catalogue record for this book is
available from the British Library

ISBN 0-9538810-2-4

Alice in Wonderland and the World Trade Center Disaster

Why the official story of 9/11 is a monumental lie

David Icke

dedication

*To all those who lost their lives
on September 11th and to their
loved ones left behind.*

*To all those who have lost their lives
in the "war on terrorism" and to
their loved ones left behind.*

Photograph by Thearle Photography, Ryde, Isle of Wight

Other books, tapes and videos by David Icke

It Doesn't Have To Be Like This *Green Print*

Truth Vibrations *Gateway*

Heal the World *Gateway*

The Robots' Rebellion *Gateway*

Lifting the Veil *Truthseeker*

...And The Truth Shall Set You Free *Bridge of Love*

I Am Me, I Am Free *Bridge of Love*

The Biggest Secret *Bridge of Love*

Children of the Matrix *Bridge of Love*

Turning of the Tide – a two-hour video *Bridge of Love*

The Reptilian Agenda, parts one and two video featuring David Icke
with Zulu Shaman, Credo Mutwa *Bridge of Love*

Revelations of a Mother Goddess – two-hour video with David Icke
and Arizona Wilder Bridge of Love

Speaking Out – two-hour video with David Icke Truthseeker

The Freedom Road – three-video package lasting more than five hours *Bridge of Love*

From Prison to Paradise – three two-hour videos with David Icke *Bridge of Love*

***NEW* – Secrets of the Matrix** – a three video package *Bridge of Love*

***NEW* – Satanism and the Mormon Church** – video *Bridge of Love*

Details of availability at the back of this book

This "world" is only an illusion and
we can change it any time we want.

It's just a choice right now
between fear and love.

So predictable ...

"… the plan is to engineer events, real and staged, that will create enormous fear in the countdown years to 2012. This includes a plan to start a Third World War either by stimulating the Muslim world into a 'holy war' against the West or by using the Chinese to cause global conflict. Maybe both."

David Icke, *The Biggest Secret* 1998

"Powell, like the Bushes and Cheney, is bloodline and that's why he is to be the new Secretary of State. Given that line-up and their mentality and agenda, don't be at all surprised if the United States finds itself in another manipulated war during this administration. You will see 'monsters' being created in the public mind to justify such action."

David Icke, writing on his website on the day that George W. Bush was inaugurated, January 20 2001

'twas always so...

Why of course the people don't want war. Why should some poor slob on a farm want to risk his life in a war when the best he can get out of it is to come back to his farm in one piece? Naturally the common people don't want war: neither in Russia, nor in England, nor for that matter in Germany. That is understood. But, after all, it is the leaders of the country who determine the policy and it is always a simple matter to drag the people along, whether it is a democracy, or a fascist dictatorship, or a parliament, or a communist dictatorship. Voice or no voice, the people can always be brought to the bidding of the leaders. That is easy. All you have to do is tell them they are being attacked, and denounce the peacemakers for lack of patriotism and exposing the country to danger. It works the same in any country.

Hermann Goering

Just a theory?

There exists a shadowy Government with its own Air Force, its own Navy, its own fundraising mechanism, and the ability to pursue its own ideas of the national interest, free from all checks and balances, and free from the law itself.

Senator Daniel K. Inouye

We are on the verge of a global transformation.
All we need is the right major crisis and the nations will accept the New World Order.

David Rockefeller

contents

September 11th 2001

(five-sense perspective)

We live in multi-dimensional infinity – we **are** multi-dimensional infinity. Therefore there are infinite perspectives from which to view the same events and all can be different, but equally true. It simply depends where the observer is standing at the time.

In this book I will focus for the most part on observing the shocking attacks of September 11th from within what I call the "five-sense prison" – the "world" that we see, hear, touch, smell and taste. It is from this point of observation that all but a few on this planet perceive "life". But in the final chapter I will observe the attacks of 9/11 from a much wider perspective and only then can they be seen in their greater context.

What happened on September 11th?

Ask Alice ...

Nothing would be what it is,

Because everything would be what it isn't.

And contrary-wise – what it is, it wouldn't be.

And what it wouldn't be, it would.

You see?

Lewis Carroll

In a time of universal deceit, telling the truth is a revolutionary act.

George Orwell

The real agenda behind 9/11

The Mysteries of Life speak to those who are willing to listen.

Longwalker

Since 1991 I have been uncovering the network that really controls this "world" behind the façades of "freedom", "democracy", "liberty" and "justice". In truth these exist only as illusions and delusions in the manufactured movie we are told is "life". They are figments of our perception, that's all.

Through these years there has rarely been a day in which I have not worked in some way to uncover or communicate the astonishing story of how a network of interbreeding bloodlines going back to the ancient world has expanded its control over the human population until, today, a full-blown global dictatorship is within its sight and within its grasp. To understand the true background to the horrors of September 11th 2001, you have to research and understand so many subjects, many of them considered bizarre or crazy to our conditioned reality. Once the pieces are understood then the puzzle has to be put together to allow the extraordinary picture of human existence to be revealed. So when people ask me why this information has never been made public before there are three main answers: (a) many researchers *have* uncovered aspects of it, even large swathes of it, but communicating what they know through the mainstream media has been impossible; (b) the compartmentalised secrecy behind which the truth is hidden has been extremely effective; and (c) because of the staggering amount of research over so many years that is necessary to understand the pieces even before the puzzle itself can be addressed.

Without this background knowledge the manipulators can hoodwink the global population by explaining away grotesque atrocities like September 11th with a ridiculous cover story that protects the real perpetrators and justifies the responses, like the "war" with Afghanistan, that further their goal of global dictatorship. In my last three books on these subjects, *And The Truth Shall Set You Free*, *The Biggest Secret*, and *Children Of The Matrix*, I have presented a total of 1,500 pages detailing the story of human control and how the same interbreeding bloodlines that produced the kings and queens of the ancient world now produce the presidents, prime ministers, banking and business leaders, media owners and military chiefs of the

21st century. For those who really want to know the nature of the human condition and the mental, emotional and, increasingly, physical prison in which we find ourselves, they can read those books or go to the 5,000 web pages of information at *www.davidicke.com*. Clearly, I can't detail it all again in this book because its focus is the staggering events of September 11th 2001 and their aftermath, but the information is already in print for anyone who wants more supporting evidence. Here, for those new to these subjects, I will set out a brief summary of the essential background necessary to understand what really happened on 9/11. Readers of my other books will already be well versed in this information.

Bloodlines and the "divine" right to rule

The families that covertly control the system that controls the people are spawned from ancient bloodlines that have a different DNA to the rest of the population. It has been described to me by insiders as a DNA "corruption". The differences in the DNA are tiny, but highly significant. In fact in DNA terms there is not that much difference between humans and mice, but look at the fantastic difference in how they manifest and what they can do. When you look back through history you find the theme of the "divine right" of kings and queens. What is that? It is the right to rule ... *because of your bloodline, your DNA.* I will go into the origins of these ruling families and what is really meant by "divine" at the end of the book. It is so challenging and mind-blowing to most people it is best left until much more has been said. Suffice to say that these bloodlines are not "human" in the sense that we perceive the term "human". This rule-by-bloodline still openly exists today, of course, with Queen Elizabeth II, an obvious example. She only lives in Buckingham Palace and enjoys all the power and privilege of a head of state because of her DNA. If she had a different DNA she might be cleaning the throne rather than sitting on it. The same applies to the rest of her family, which is strictly structured according to its DNA relationship to the reigning "monarch". As the ancient records confirm, it was the "royal" bloodlines (the "demi-gods") that were placed in positions of ruling royal power thousands of years ago. They were the kings and queens in Egypt, Sumer, the Indus Valley and around the world who claimed the divine right to rule because of their bloodline. What people don't realise is that the political, business, banking and media leaders are also overwhelmingly operating within a similar DNA hierarchy that decides who does what. This is because they are of the same bloodlines as the ancient royal and aristocratic families who ruled thousands of years ago. The same interbreeding "royal and aristocratic" tribe has controlled the world for all this time. Only the positions from which they operate have changed.

Fantastic cataclysms struck the earth around perhaps 11,500 to 12,000 years ago. These destroyed, in stages, vast continents in the Atlantic and Pacific that have become known as Atlantis and Mu or Lemuria. The universal stories of the Great Flood are related to this. After these literally world-shattering events, and others that followed, the "divine" bloodline installed itself again in various locations. This happened most significantly in the Near and Middle East, especially from about

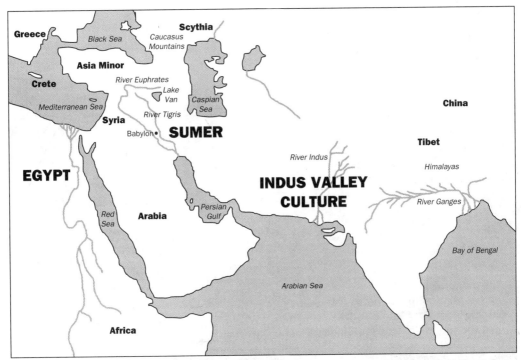

Figure 1: *The highly advanced cultures in the Middle-Near East with Sumer the most powerful and significant. From this region have come many of the bloodlines that thousands of years later continue to control the world*

4,000BC with an empire based on Sumer in what is now called Iraq, and it was located between the Tigris and Euphrates rivers. Sumer, according to official history, was the start of human "civilisation" as we know it, but in fact it was merely the re-start after the Atlantis/Mu upheavals (*Figure 1*). The bloodline was placed in the positions of royal and administrative power over the people in Sumer, Egypt, Babylon, the Indus Valley and much further afield, including the Americas and China. Over thousands of years, these bloodlines expanded out of the Middle and Near East into Europe, and the royal bloodlines of Sumer, Egypt, etc., became the royal and aristocratic families of Britain, Ireland and the countries of mainland Europe, especially France, Germany and what is now called Belgium (*Figure 2 overleaf*). Wherever they went these royal and aristocratic lines interbred obsessively with each other through arranged marriages and secret breeding programmes. You can see the same with the ruling families of today because they are seeking to perpetuate a particular genetic code, the DNA "corruption" that can be quickly diluted by breeding outside of their bloodline circle.

The bloodline empires

In ancient times Babylon was one of the headquarters of the secret society network – the "Illuminati" – through which these bloodlines manipulate humanity. Babylon was in the same region as Sumer. This Illuminati bloodline network then moved its

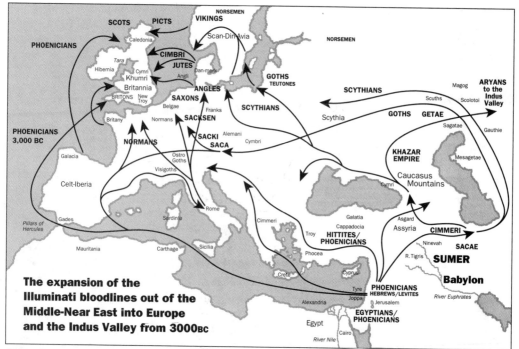

Figure 2: *From at least 3000BC, peoples of the Sumer Empire, like the Phoenicians and Egyptians, sailed to Britain and took their knowledge and symbols to those islands. Others began to move across land to settle in what we now call France, Germany, and the rest of northern Europe. Wherever they went, the Illuminati bloodlines invariably ruled as kings, queens, and nobility*

headquarters to Rome and it was during this time that we had the Roman Empire and the creation of the Roman Church or institutionalised Christianity. The headquarters eventually moved on again into northern Europe after the fall of the Roman Empire and for a period it was based in Amsterdam, The Netherlands. This was when the Dutch began to build their empire through the Dutch East India Company and they settled South Africa. In 1688, William of Orange, one of the bloodlines, invaded England from The Netherlands and took the throne as William III in 1689. William ruled jointly with Queen Mary and then by himself after her death in 1694. In that year William signed the charter that created the Bank of England, and the global banking system began to emerge. Banking and manufactured debt has always been one of the key vehicles used by the bloodlines to control humanity. From this time the bloodlines and their Illuminati secret society network moved their centre of operation to London and what followed, of course, was the "great" and enormous British Empire. This was not the Empire of the "British" in truth, but that of the Illuminati bloodlines based in Britain.

The hidden hand

This vast expansion of the British and other European empires to all parts of the world exported these bloodlines to every continent, including, most importantly today, North America. When the European empires began to recede and collapse, especially in the 20th century, it appeared that these colony continents, like the Americas, Africa, Asia and Australasia, had won their "independence". Instead the Illuminati bloodlines were merely exchanging open control for the far more effective covert control – manipulation of events by the Hidden Hand that the public has no idea even exists. While these empires were apparently being dismantled, the Illuminati left in their "former" colonies, including the United States, the bloodline and the secret society network through which they manipulate. Ever since that time they have continued to control events in these "former" colonies as part of a long-planned agenda to impose centralised control of the planet and its people. This is designed to be structured as a world government, army, central bank and currency; a micro-chipped population connected to a global computer; and a society based on constant and total surveillance of every man, woman and child. A ridiculous conspiracy 'theory'? Well have another look around and you'll see that this is happening today, now, and never more blatantly than since September 11th. We are seeing unfold by the day the very Big Brother society described by George Orwell (real name Eric Blair) in his famous book, 1984.[1] I believe that Orwell was not writing from his imagination so much as from insider knowledge of the agenda and this is the very governmental structure that is now staring us in the face – *especially* since September 11th. The need for centralisation is obvious. The greater the diversity of decision-making the less control you are going to have over those decisions. Diversity is the controllers' nightmare and they have worked constantly to centralise decision-making and increase their power. The reason that the centralisation in all areas of our lives, political, economic, business, military and media has progressed with a faster and faster pace is a simple equation. The more you centralise power the more power you have to centralise even quicker.

The bloodline presidents

The bloodlines that seek to control the world and our lives today are the same bloodlines that ruled the ancient societies. They are the presidents of the United States, the prime ministers, the leading banking and business families, the media owners and those who control the military. The US presidents are a wonderful example of this. There are some 280 million people in the United States today and many hundreds of millions more have lived in that country since the major Freemason George Washington was inaugurated more than 200 years ago. Not only that, the genetic diversity of the American people has been enormous because of the many locations from which they have come. So you would expect that the 43 presidents from Washington to George W. Bush would express some of that diversity, surely? After all, one of the mantras supporting the myth of American "freedom" is that anyone can become President of the United States. Er, sorry. The genetic diversity of the US presidents is incredibly limited and fundamentally connected to European royal and aristocratic bloodlines (see *The Biggest Secret* and *Children Of The Matrix*). Of the 43 presidents, 34 go back genetically to Charlemagne

(742–814), the most famous monarch of what we now call France and a major figure in the Illuminati story and the bloodline. He was leader of the Franks, after whom we get the name France, and Emperor of the Holy Roman Empire. From the Illuminati point of view, he was serious bloodline.

In the last weeks of the farcical 2000 US presidential election campaign, *Burke's Peerage*, the blue-blood "bible" of royal and aristocratic genealogy, confirmed the theme I am highlighting here. Four years earlier, when Bill Clinton faced Bob Dole, *Burke's Peerage* said that the candidate with the most royal genes had won every single presidential election in US history. Clinton and George W. Bush have since continued that unbroken sequence. In a Reuters report of October 17th 2000, *Burkes Peerage* confirmed that both George W. Bush and "opponent" Al Gore were of royal descent with Bush the "bluer" of the two. Purely by knowing his bloodline and watching the behind-the-scenes developments, I was able to predict three years before the 2000 election that George W. Bush would be the next President of the United States. Bush is related to every European monarch on and off the throne, including the king of Albania, and has "kinship" with every member of Britain's royal family, the report said. He is a 13th cousin of Britain's Queen Mother, who died in 2002 at the age of 101, and her daughter, Queen Elizabeth. Bush is a 13th cousin, once removed, of the heir to the throne Prince Charles, and has a direct descent from Henry III and from Henry VIII's sister, Mary Tudor, who was also the wife of Louis XI of France. Bush is further descended from Charles II of England. Harold Brooks-Baker, publishing director of *Burke's Peerage,* said in the Reuters report: "It is now clear that Mr Gore and Mr Bush have an unusually large number of royal and noble descents." But only unusual if you don't know the story. He added: "In point of fact, never in the history of the United States have two presidential candidates been as well endowed with royal alliances." Brooks-Baker said there had always been a significant "royal factor" in those who aspire to the White House with presidents George Washington, Thomas Jefferson, Franklin and Theodore Roosevelt, and Ronald Reagan, among others, all boasting blue-blood links. He said that Al Gore, a cousin of former President Richard Nixon, was a descendant of England's Edward I and has direct links to the Holy Roman Empire through Emperors Louis II, Charles II, and Louis I. This, therefore, makes him a descendant of Charlemagne, the 8th century Emperor. These Charlemagne links make Al Gore a cousin of George W. Bush.

The secret language – symbolism

The bloodlines and their Illuminati network are obsessed with symbolism and their symbols and codes going back thousands of years can clearly be found throughout American society and the rest of the world. The ancient Illuminati symbol of the pyramid with the capstone missing or the pyramid and all-seeing eye was placed on the dollar bill (*Figure 3*) in 1933/34 by President Franklin Delano Roosevelt, one of the most significant front men for the Illuminati in the United States during the 20th century. The most obvious Illuminati symbol is the eternal flame or the lighted torch and this represents the "illuminated ones", the initiates illuminated into

Figure 3: *The ancient Illuminati symbol of the pyramid and all-seeing eye on the dollar bill*

knowledge that the rest of the population is denied. The Illuminati lighted torch is held by the Statue of Liberty. This was given to New York by French Freemasons in Paris who knew what she and the torch really symbolised. There is a virtual mirror image of the Statue of Liberty on an island in the River Seine in Paris. The Statue of Liberty is, in fact, the symbolic image of Queen Semiramis, the goddess worshipped by the Illuminati bloodlines when they were based in Babylon. If you look at *Figures 4* and *5* (*overleaf*) you can see the image of Queen Semiramis on an ancient coin and her representation as the Statue of Liberty. The Babylonian trinity was: Nimrod, who was symbolised as a fish; Tammuz or Ninus, the son who died to save humanity; and Queen Semiramis, the mother goddess who was symbolised as a dove. The Illuminati use what I call reverse symbolism. They place their symbols all around us but present them with the reverse of their true meaning. For example, the dove symbolises peace to most people, but to the Illuminati bloodlines it represents their goddess, Queen Semiramis. The lighted torch means freedom and liberty to the population, but to the Illuminati it is the very symbol of their agenda and control. The Nazis reversed the ancient symbol of the swastika to symbolise the negative and Satanists have reversed the pentagram to point downwards for the same reason. Everything is symbolism and ritual to the Illuminati, and always has been. After they killed President Kennedy in Dallas in 1963, the Scottish Rite of Freemasonry placed an obelisk in Dealey Plaza with a lighted torch at the top. When they buried Kennedy at Arlington Cemetery in Washington DC they placed a lighted torch, the Illuminati eternal flame, on his grave. The spot where people leave their tributes to the murdered Princess Diana in Paris is a massive representation of the flame held by the Statue of Liberty. It is located on top of the Pont de L'Alma Tunnel where the Illuminati arranged for her to die in 1997 (see *The Biggest Secret*).

Queen Semiramis, which translates as "branch bearer", was symbolised in Babylon as a dove and when the Illuminati bloodlines moved their headquarters to Rome this goddess was worshipped as Venus Columba or Venus the Dove. The French word for dove is still colombe. This is why a man who signed his name "Colon" is known to official history as "Columbus". He was bearing the branch of the dove into the Americas in 1492 and was given this symbolic name relating to the

Figure 4: *This is how the Illuminati goddess, Queen Semiramis, the "branch-bearer", was portrayed by the ancients*

Figure 5: *Semiramis again, this time under the guise of the Statue of "Liberty"*

Illuminati "Goddess". So we have the centre of US government located in Washington "DC" – the District of Columbia, or the dove, Semiramis. We have British Columbia in Canada, Columbia Broadcasting (CBS), Columbia University, and Columbia Pictures with the symbol of the woman and the lighted torch. The symbols abound in relation to September 11th, also. The twin towers, or twin pillars, are ancient Illuminati symbols that go back at least to Atlantis. One of the foundation legends in the Mythology of the Freemasons and the Knights Templar secret societies is that of Jachin and Boaz … the "Twin Pillars" of Atlantis, which are said to have been erected at the entrance to King Solomon's Temple in Jerusalem. In the Old Testament you will find references to this:

> And he set up the pillars in the porch of the temple: and he set up the
> right pillar, and called the name thereof Jachin: and he set up the left
> pillar, and called the name thereof Boaz. **(1 Kings 7:21)**

> And he reared up the pillars before the temple, one on the right hand, and
> the other on the left; and called the name of that on the right hand Jachin,
> and the name of that on the left Boaz. **(2 Chronicles 3:17)**

You will find the symbol of the twin pillars in Freemasonic architecture and the original ones are said to have been built, according to Freemasonic legend, by inhabitants of Atlantis called "the children of Lamech". The United States is the "New Atlantis" to the Illuminati. There is a legend of the twin pillars, or twin towers, in which one represented Upper Egypt (the "north tower") and the other symbolised Lower Egypt (the south tower). There is also the mythology of the twin pillars of Hercules that he is said to have placed at the entrance to the Mediterranean. The number 11 itself, of course, consists of twin columns and first plane to hit the twin towers on September 11th was Flight 11. The recurrence of 11 in the events of that day are remarkable – but highly predictable for those who study Illuminati ritual.[2] It was 11 years to the day before 9/11 – September 11th 1990 – that Father George Bush made a speech to Congress calling for a New World Order. This is the ancient code name for the Illuminati agenda for global control that the terrorist attacks were designed to advance. The Pentagon was also targetted on September 11th. The symbol of the pentagon is the centre of the pentagram, the most obvious symbol of Satanic and Illuminati ritual and 911 is the phone number that Americans call to report emergencies. This is not a coincidence, as anyone who has studied the Illuminati's astonishing obsession with symbolism will know. In the final chapter I'll explain where this obsession comes from. The name Capitol Hill is also Illuminati symbolism and named after Capitoline Hill, a sacred place for the Illuminati outside Rome during the Roman Empire. (See *The Biggest Secret* and the symbolism archives on my website for extensive information about the Illuminati secret language that can be seen all around us.) The symbolism can also be found in their language and statements. To crack their code, you have to reverse what they appear to say. When they announce that they believe something, it means they don't. When they say they will do something, it means they won't. When they say they won't, it means they will and so on. It is a real life Alice in Wonderland. They operate with this coded symbolism in which everything is reversed. Thus killing thousands of Afghan civilians becomes "fighting for freedom, peace and justice". Reverse "theirs" to "ours" in this statement by George W. Bush after September 11th, for example, and he is actually talking about himself and those who control him:

> "Theirs is the worst kind of cruelty, the cruelty that is fed, not weakened, by tears. Theirs is the worst kind of violence, pure malice while daring to claim the authority of God. We cannot fully understand the designs and power of evil, it is enough to know that evil, like goodness, exists. And in the terrorists evil has found a willing servant."

The Illuminati

The world's "elite" families, no more than 13 at the peak of the pyramid, manipulate their control of humanity through a network of secret societies. This network and the interbreeding bloodlines it serves have become known as the Illuminati, the 'Illuminated Ones'. The Illuminati is an organisation within all significant organisations. It's like a cancer. All the major secret societies feed carefully chosen recruits into the Illuminati and these are the ones you find in positions of power throughout the world. They infest all colours, races, creeds and countries, and yet, so effective is the compartmentalised secrecy that even the vast majority of people within these secret societies have no idea what they are really part of. Most Freemasons never progress higher than the bottom three levels of degree, the so-called Blue Degrees. They have no idea what their organisation is being used for. Even most of those who make it to the apparently highest level, like the 33rd degree in the Scottish Rite, can know relatively little unless they are "chosen". Only the tiny few, all from particular bloodlines and their offshoots, progress through the official peak of their 'individual' secret society into the Illuminati degrees above that. These are the levels into which the secret societies feed the chosen ones, but at least 95% of their members have no idea that these levels exist, never mind who is in them and what happens there. Among the key secret societies within the Illuminati web are the upper levels of the Freemasons, Knights Templar, Knights of Malta, Knights of St John of Jerusalem, and the Jesuits, the network that controls the Roman Catholic Church and uses it to serve the Illuminati. The Jesuit hierarchy is extremely powerful within the Illuminati all over the world and highly significant in the manipulation of global society. Some of the family lines involved are the Rothschilds, Rockefellers, House of Lorraine, Habsburgs, and the Thurn und Taxis dynasty from Bergamo, Italy, which expanded into Belgium, Bavaria, and wider afield. The Thurn und Taxis bloodline is also highly significant to the Illuminati although not mentioned by researchers as often as some of the others.

The freemasons

Jim Shaw, a former 33rd-degree Freemason, exposes the Craft in his book, *The Deadly Deception*[3] and confirms what I have just described. He explains how Freemasonry is based on a structure of compartmentalised pyramids (*Figure 6*). Only a few make it to the top of the 33 degrees of the Scottish Rite or the 10 degrees of the York Rite and even then they still don't know the real secrets. Shaw says he was surprised when a fellow 33rd-degree Mason said that "they" had told him he was "going higher" and the guy left the temple by a different door.[4] A bigger pyramid encompasses all the major secret societies and at that point they are *one* secret society. So you have this vast web of secret societies with millions of members worldwide who think they know what they are involved in, but, in truth, only a few have any idea of what is going on and who, ultimately, is calling the shots. Albert Pike, who died in 1891, was one of the most pre-eminent figures in world Freemasonry. Among his titles were Sovereign Grand Commander of the Supreme Council of the 33rd degree and Supreme Pontiff of Universal Freemasonry. In his book, *Morals and Dogma*, written for higher-degree Freemasons, he reveals the way the lower levels are misled:

'The Blue Degrees are but the outer court or portico of the Temple. Part of the symbols are displayed there to the initiate, but he is intentionally mis-led by false interpretations. It is not intended that he shall understand them, but it is intended that he shall imagine that he understands them ... Their true implication is reserved for Adepts, the Princes of Masonry.' [5]

Exactly. Jim Shaw says that there are two kinds of Freemason. One just sits through the meetings and doesn't make much effort to understand the ritual. The other does all the work, but only keeps to the ritual, and memorises or reads the

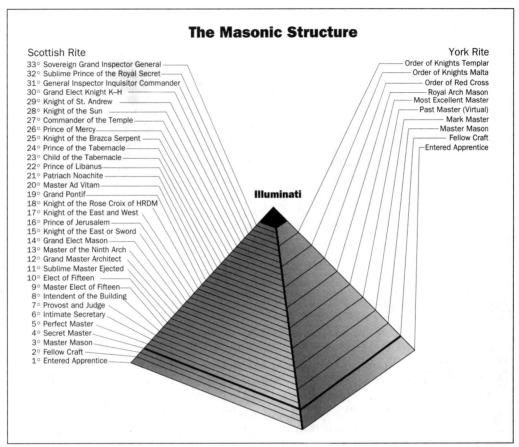

The Masonic Structure

Scottish Rite
33° Sovereign Grand Inspector General
32° Sublime Prince of the Royal Secret
31° General Inspector Inquisitor Commander
30° Grand Elect Knight K–H
29° Knight of St. Andrew
28° Knight of the Sun
27° Commander of the Temple
26° Prince of Mercy
25° Knight of the Brazca Serpent
24° Prince of the Tabernacle
23° Child of the Tabernacle
22° Prince of Libanus
21° Patriach Noachite
20° Master Ad Vitam
19° Grand Pontif
18° Knight of the Rose Croix of HRDM
17° Knight of the East and West
16° Prince of Jerusalem
15° Knight of the East or Sword
14° Grand Elect Mason
13° Master of the Ninth Arch
12° Grand Master Architect
11° Sublime Master Ejected
10° Elect of Fifteen
9° Master Elect of Fifteen
8° Intendent of the Building
7° Provost and Judge
6° Intimate Secretary
5° Perfect Master
4° Secret Master
3° Master Mason
2° Fellow Craft
1° Entered Apprentice

Illuminati

York Rite
Order of Knights Templar
Order of Knights Malta
Order of Red Cross
Royal Arch Mason
Most Excellent Master
Past Master (Virtual)
Mark Master
Master Mason
Fellow Craft
Entered Apprentice

Figure 6: *The Masonic Structure*

words without understanding what they really mean. That is correct, but there is a third kind: the very few who know the truth of who really controls Freemasonry and what the rituals and initiations are really designed to achieve. Shaw also confirms from his own experience how the Freemasons manipulate their own people into whatever positions they choose. At work, Shaw's department director, a fellow Freemason, advised him to apply for a particular job. Shaw felt he was under-qualified for the post and would fail the test paper.[6] Only through the urging of his Freemason boss did he apply. When he arrived to take the test he was amazed to see that there were only two other applicants for a job he believed would be keenly contested. When he turned over the test paper, he saw that the questions were very easy and he finished them quickly. His two rivals, however, were clearly finding the paper tough and could not complete it in the allotted time. Shaw got the job. Why? Because he was not given the same paper as the other two.

When he walked out of Freemasonry after realising the scam, the opposite happened. He found his bosses far less supportive, to say the least. This is just one small example of how the Illuminati and their secret society web ensure that their

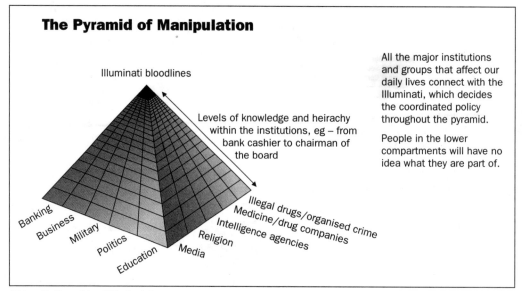

Figure 7: *Pyramids of Manipulation*

guys are in the positions that matter. It is actually astonishing how few people you need to control in order to dictate your agenda through the whole system if they are (a) in the key positions of decision-making and (b) they have the power to appoint those in the important positions below them. An example: you control the chief of police who decides the policy and he can appoint the heads of the various departments in his force. He introduces Illuminati policy and chooses his major subordinates from secret society initiates. They, in turn, can appoint the people within their departments and can thus choose more secret society initiates for the positions below them. So it goes on. Once you have control of the top man in any organisation, the pyramid is built in his, i.e. the Illuminati's, image. Governments are structured in the same way, as are "security" organisations like the FBI, CIA, British Intelligence and those who control the Pentagon. They are compartmentalised pyramids in themselves, but there is also a pyramid that encompasses all of them and can therefore coordinate a common plan of action between them, exactly as it did on September 11th.

Pyramids within pyramids

Understanding the pyramid structure is vital to understanding how the few can manipulate the many on a global scale. The pyramid structure of secret societies is mirrored in government, banking, business and every other organisation and institution. It is like those Russian dolls with one doll inside a bigger one until the biggest doll encompasses them all. The Illuminati replace the 'dolls' with pyramids (*Figure 7*). Every organisation today is a pyramid. Only the few at the top know the real agenda of the organisation and what it is trying to achieve. The further you go down the pyramid the more people are working for the organisation, but the less they know about its real agenda. They are only aware of the individual job they do every day. They don't know how their contribution (apparently innocent in isolation) connects with those of other employees in other areas of the company. They are compartmentalised from that knowledge and told only what they need to know to do their job. The only people who know how it all fits together are the very few sitting at the top – the bloodline families and their lackeys.

The smaller pyramids, like the local branch of a bank, fit into bigger and bigger pyramids, until eventually you have the pyramid that encompasses all of the banks. It is the same with the transnational corporations, political parties, secret societies, media empires and the military. If you go high enough in this structure all the transnational corporations (like the oil cartel), major political parties, secret societies, media empires and the military (via NATO, for instance), are controlled by the same families who sit at the top of the biggest pyramids. In the end there is a global pyramid that encompasses all the others, the biggest "doll" if you like. At the capstone of this you will find the most elite of the Illuminati, the "purest" of their bloodlines. In this way, they can coordinate through apparently unconnected, even "opposing" areas of society, the same policies because all roads lead eventually to them – everything from the food we eat; the water we drink; the "medical care" we receive, including vaccines; the "news" we watch and read; the "entertainment" we are given; the governments that dictate to us; the military that enforces the will of the governments; and the hard drug network aimed at destroying young people. The same families and their gofers control all of these areas and so much more. This pyramid structure is how they have manipulated the explosion of centralisation in every area of life: government, finance, business, media and military. It is not by accident or natural occurrence, it is by coldly calculated design. The outstanding Australian journalist John Pilger produced a rare and excellent exposé of globalisation for British Independent Television in July 2001 in which he pointed out that just 200 corporations are now responsible for a *quarter* of the world's economic activity. But there is another level to this that we urgently need to understand. This pyramid system means that those '200' corporations are, in effect, *one* Corporation controlled by the same force. Globalisation, which I and other "conspiracy theorists" were writing about long before it became fashionable, is just another name for the Illuminati's centralised global fascist state, which I have been exposing since the early 1990s. "Globalisation" is not just a group of greedy corporations seeking to maximise profit, it is far, far, bigger than that.

Manipulating the herd

Most people find it impossible to accept that a few people can manipulate the lives of billions and operate through all institutions and countries. I understand that; but once you have the pyramids in place and you know how to condition the mind and reality of the population, it is relatively straightforward. When a few people wish to control and direct a mass of humanity there are certain key structures that have to be in place. These are the same whether you are seeking to manipulate an individual, family, tribe, town, country, continent or planet. First you have to impose the 'norms', what is considered right and wrong, possible or impossible, sane or insane, good and bad. Most of the people will follow those 'norms' without question because of the baa-baa, herd mentality that has prevailed within the collective human mind for at least thousands of years. Second, you have to make life very unpleasant for those few who challenge your imposed 'norms'.

The most effective way to do this is to ensure that it is, in effect, a crime to be different. You make those who voice a different view, version of 'truth' and lifestyle, stand out like a black sheep in the human herd. You have already conditioned the herd to accept your norms as its reality and, through arrogance and ignorance, they ridicule or condemn those with a different spin on life. This pressurises the black sheep to conform and serves as a warning to those others in the herd who are also thinking of breaking away or challenging the prevailing reality. There is a Japanese saying that goes, "Don't be a nail that stands out above the rest because that's the first one to get hit." I could not put it better. This fear of being different and voicing a view that challenges the "norms" is overwhelmingly the fear of what other people will think of us. In reality, the fear of what the sheep around us will say and do if we seek to leave the herd and question its conditioned assumptions. This mentality creates a situation fundamental to the few controlling the many because it means that the masses are policing themselves and keeping each other in line. The sheep become the sheepdog for the rest of the herd. It is like a prisoner trying to escape while the rest of his cellmates rush to stop him. If that happened we would say the prisoners were crazy, how could they do that? But humans are doing precisely the same to each other every day by demanding that everyone conform to the 'norms' to which they blindly conform. This is nothing less than psychological fascism – the thought police with agents in every home, everywhere. Agents so deeply conditioned that most have no idea they are unpaid mind controllers. 'I'm just doing what's right for my children', I hear them say. No, what you have been programmed to believe is right for them and the belief, also, that only you know best.

We see this same theme in our daily experiences of people in uniform and others from the masses who are promoted to power over the masses. It's summed up by the satirical version of the British Labour Party song *The Red Flag*, which goes: "The working class can kiss my arse, I've got the foreman's job at last." This is all part of the divide and rule strategy so vital to ensuring that the herd will police itself. Everyone plays a part in everyone else's mental, emotional and physical imprisonment. All the controllers have to do is set the 'norms', pull the right strings at the right time, and make their human puppets dance to the appropriate tune. This they do by dictating what is taught in what we bravely call 'education' and controlling what passes for 'news' through the Illuminati-owned media. In this way they can dictate to the unthinking, unquestioning herd what it should believe about itself, other people, life, history and current events. Once you set the 'norms' there is no need to control every journalist or reporter or government official. The media and the institutions take their 'truth' from those same 'norms' and official statements, and therefore ridicule and condemn by reflex action anyone who offers another vision of reality. I turned on the text service on the UK's Independent Television to see a story that I was appearing on the Sci-Fi Channel to speak about my "bizarre" views. Whoever wrote that report has never met me, never read my books, and has never done any investigation of these subjects for his or her self. But my views must be "bizarre" to this media person because they are different to those accepted by their conditioned mind. Once you control what is considered 'normal' and possible, the whole system virtually runs itself.

Obeying the law

It is these hybrid Illuminati bloodlines, manifesting as political leaders and administrators of government, that introduce the 'laws' that will best serve their plan to keep humanity in ongoing servitude. The laws, which the masses have no say in creating, are then enforced by members of those same masses – soldiers, policemen, security guards and so on. These guys, and many women today, are mere system fodder. They are not encouraged to think for themselves and it would not be good for promotion if they did. They are paid to do as they are told, carry out orders and administer the letter of the 'law' – the law of the elite families. I remember watching a car park attendant at a botanical garden where many families were enjoying a Sunday afternoon out. He strode up and down constantly checking every car in turn looking for any that had outstayed their ticket. When he found one he was positively orgasmic. My father used to say that rules and regulations are for the guidance of the intelligent and the blind obedience of the idiot. But how many of those in the peaked caps administer the law in a sensible, every-case-on-its-merits, think-for-yourself manner? A mere fraction, and often they are far from popular with those higher up the ladder. Soldiers don't ask for justification for blowing away men, women and children they have never met and know nothing about (see Afghanistan, for example). They don't question their superiors about why they have to commit genocide. They just do it because they are told to do it and those doing the telling are themselves carrying out orders from those above them. In the end, all lines of command lead ever upwards to the 13 family bloodlines and their offshoots as they orchestrate their agenda to take over the planet.

The sheeple

The self-policing of the human herd goes far deeper than people in uniform or administrators of government. It starts with conditioned parents who impose their conditioning on their children and pressure them to follow their religious, political, economic and cultural 'norms'. One extreme example is those who insist that their offspring succumb to arranged marriages because of the rules of their ludicrous religion. There are the children of Jehovah's Witnesses who have been denied life-saving blood transfusions because their brain-dead parents insist on conducting every aspect of their lives according to the contradictory dictates of a book purveying so many stories of pure fantasy. The creation of the mental and emotional sheep pen of 'norms' that imprisons 99% of humanity goes on minute by minute in subtle and less subtle ways. There are children of Christian, Jewish, Muslim or Hindu parents who don't accept the religion, but still follow it because they don't want to upset their family. Then there is the almost universal fear of what people think of us if we speak a different version of reality or live a different kind of life. Note that the fear for those who wish to break out of the sheep pen is not the fear of what the elite families, the Illuminati or 'Illuminated Ones', will think of them. Most have no idea that such a network exists. No, the fear is of what their mother or father will think, or their friends and workmates – the very people who are conditioned by the system to stay in the pen. The sheep are keeping the other sheep in line and making life unpleasant for anyone who tries to escape.

The herd goes to war – with itself

It is so easy for a small group of interbreeding family bloodlines to control the lives (in other words, the minds) of billions, once the key institutions of 'information' are in place, as they have been for thousands of years in their various forms. There are not enough of these manipulators and their stooges to control the population physically and so they have had to create a structure in which humans control themselves through mental, emotional and, increasingly, physical imposition. Once you have the herd mentality policing itself, there is a third phase in this entrapment of human consciousness. You create factions within the herd and set them to war with each other. This is done by creating 'different' belief systems (which are not different at all) and bringing them into conflict. These belief systems are known as religions, political parties, economic theories and 'isms' of endless variety. These beliefs are perceived as 'opposites' when, as I pointed out in my book, *I Am Me, I Am Free,* they are oppo*sames*. The vision of reality and possibility within the pen is so limited that it contains no opposites and the elite have to create the perception of them to manufacture the divisions that allow them to divide and rule. I mean, what is the difference between a Christian bishop, Jewish rabbi, Muslim or Hindu priest, or a follower of Buddha, imposing their beliefs on their children and others? There is none because while the belief they seek to indoctrinate may be slightly different, often very slightly, the overall theme is exactly the same – the imposition of one person's belief on another. Look at the opposames in politics. The Far Left, as symbolised by Josef Stalin in Russia, introduced centralised control, military dictatorship and concentration camps. The 'opposite' of this was the Far Right, as symbolised by Adolf Hitler. What did he impose? Centralised control, military dictatorship and concentration camps. Yet these two opposames were set at war with each other amid propaganda that claimed they were opposites. The only difference between the Soviet Union and the so-called 'West' during the Cold War was that the Soviet Union was openly controlled by the few and the West was secretly controlled by the few. And when you get to the capstone of the pyramid you find they were the *same* few controlling both 'sides'. The same force operating through Wall Street and the City of London funded all 'sides' in the two world wars and that's provable (see *And The Truth Shall Set You Free*).

So the methods of manipulation can be summarised thus:

- You need to first imprison the human mind with a rigid belief and a fundamentally limited sense of reality – the sheep pen. It doesn't much matter what these beliefs may be, so long as they are rigid and discourage free thought and open-minded questioning. Christianity, Judaism, Islam, Hinduism and all the rest each make their contribution to human servitude while apparently claiming different 'truths'.

- You encourage those who follow these rigid beliefs to impose them on others and make life very difficult and unpleasant for anyone who does not conform.

- You bring these beliefs into conflict, so ensuring the divide and rule you so desperately need for control by the few. While the masses are busy fighting each other, and seeking to impose their beliefs and views on each other, they don't see that the Illuminati have strings attached to all of them. Humans are like moths buzzing around a light, so mesmerised by their religious belief, the football scores, the latest row on a soap opera, or the price of friggin' beer, that they fail to notice the preparations being made to smash them on the arse with a swatter.

Problem–Reaction–Solution

There are two techniques of mass manipulation that people need to understand if they are to begin to see through the game. One I have dubbed 'problem-reaction-solution' and the other I term the 'stepping-stones approach'. These have been used for thousands of years to advance the agenda and, together with fear, they remain the most effective weapons of the Illuminati. Since I first used the term problem-reaction-solution as an alternative to its previous name, the "Hegelian Dialectic", it has been constantly repeated among conspiracy researchers and others communicating the techniques of control. This is fantastic because to understand this simple, but devastating, method of human manipulation is to become so much harder to fool. Problem-reaction-solution is the key to understanding what really happened on September 11th 2001 and why. It works like this: you know that if you openly propose to remove basic freedoms, start a war or centralise power, there will be a public reaction against it. So you don't openly and honestly propose such plans, you play the P–R–S scam. At stage one you create a problem. It could be a country attacking another, a government or economic collapse, or a "terrorist attack". Anything in fact that the public will think requires a 'solution'. At stage two, you report the 'problems' you have covertly created in the way you wish the people to perceive them. Crucially you find someone to blame for the problem, a "patsy" like Lee Harvey Oswald when President Kennedy was assassinated or Timothy McVeigh in Oklahoma. You spin the background to these events in a way that encourages the people to demand that "something must be done". These are the words you want to hear because they allow you to move on to stage three, the sting. At this point you openly offer the solutions to the problems you have yourself created. These solutions, of course, involve the centralisation of power, the sacking of officials or politicians that are getting in your way, and the removal of more basic freedoms as you advance further to your global fascist state. Just ponder on the freedoms that have been removed because of 9/11. A more subtle part of the technique is to propose far more extreme changes than you expect to get away with because this allows any opposition to think you have compromised and met them halfway. But you know that you have other "problems" in the pipeline to push the agenda on.

With this technique you can so manipulate the public mind that people will demand or at least allow you to introduce what, in normal circumstances, they would vehemently oppose. The Oklahoma bomb at the Alfred P. Murrah Building on April 19th 1995 was a problem-reaction-solution classic, as I explained in *And The Truth Shall Set You Free* and will expand upon later. What followed the death and destruction in Oklahoma were "anti-terrorism" laws that sailed through Congress without challenge and removed fundamental freedoms from American people. Since September 11th this agenda has been advanced in gigantic leaps. I don't share the attitudes of people like Timothy McVeigh, nor do I defend disturbed people like Osama bin Laden, but that's not the point. Establishing the truth of what happened is the point, no matter what the views and attitudes of those involved. I think it is called justice. The two most effective problem-reaction-solutions in the 20th century were the two global wars. They changed the face of the world, as wars always do, and led to a massive centralisation of power. The United Nations, like its predecessor the League of Nations, was an Illuminati creation to act as a Trojan horse, or stalking horse, for world government.

Media poodles ... woof, woof, lick, lick

The media play their part to perfection in these 'problem-reaction-solution' scenarios. At ownership level, people like Conrad Black at the Hollinger Group and Rupert Murdoch of News International know what is going on. The editors they appoint might know something about it, as may certain columnists, but most of the journalists will have no idea. The editor is always there to block anything they write that is against the interests of the Illuminati – as directed by the owner – and if they insist on pursuing an unwelcome story they find themselves looking for another job. Most of the "information" that journalists present comes from official (Illuminati) sources anyway. In the immediate aftermath of a major event such as September 11th where are the reporters getting their information? From official sources. Name me a single piece of relevant information broadcast by the mainstream media about what happened on 9/11, how it was done, who did it and what the retaliation should be, that did not come from official sources. Exactly. Nothing. We are told that White House sources say this, FBI sources say that, and CIA or Pentagon sources say the other. This is how the Illuminati transmit through the media the version of events they wish the public to believe. These reports are blazed across the front pages of newspapers and the top of radio and television news bulletins throughout the world, and what they say becomes the 'norm', the official "history". In the weeks and months that follow, researchers who are interested in the real truth begin to dig away. Over and over they establish and document the proof of how the official version was a lie from start to finish. But where are their reports published? In small-circulation newsletters, self-published books, and on radio stations that operate with a fraction of the money and potential audience of the Illuminati empires. Therefore, years after the official version has been demolished it still prevails in the public mind. Stop anyone in London, New York, Cape Town, Sydney, anywhere, and ask them what happened on September 11th, or in Oklahoma, the Second World War, or Kosovo. Almost every time they will give you the official story because that is the only one they have heard.

Stepping stones

The bedfellow of problem-reaction-solution is the stepping-stones approach. You know where you intend to lead people, but you realise that if you gave them the true picture or went there in one giant leap, you would, once again, face substantial opposition. So you travel to your destination in little steps and each one is presented in isolation and as unconnected to all the others. It is like a drip, drip, drip, to global centralisation. This technique was used most obviously with the fascist superstate now known as the European Union. After the war if the politicians had suggested a centralised Europe with common laws and currency there would have been an outcry. People would have said they had been fighting Hitler to stop just such a European dictatorship and there was no way they were accepting another. To overcome this, the Illuminati offered a 'free trade area' and even used the problem of their manipulated world wars to encourage more cooperation between the countries of Europe. Once they had the free trade area, however, the foot in the door, they began to expand its powers until it became the fully fledged political and economic dictatorship that it is today. The same is happening with the North American Free Trade Agreement (NAFTA), and Asia Pacific Economic Co-operation (APEC), the 'free trade area' for Asia and Australia, and the same is planned for the African Union that replaced the Organisation of African Unity in 2001. I said in *And The Truth Shall Set You Free* in 1995 that the NAFTA 'free trade area' would be expanded to the whole of the Americas as the next stepping stone to a centrally controlled American Union. In 2001, George W. Bush, an Illuminati bloodline, attended the Summit of the Americas in Quebec, Canada, at which this expansion of NAFTA throughout the Americas was agreed.

Look at today's newspapers and television news bulletins and you'll see the problem-reaction-solution and stepping-stones techniques played out day after day. One extremely effective way to see through this manipulation is to keep asking yourself a simple question when faced with these daily situations: 'Who benefits from me believing this version of events, or accepting the solutions and changes being offered as a result?' The answer will be almost every time: anyone who wishes to centralise power and suppress more of our freedoms.

Blind faith

Over thousands of years, religion has brilliantly served this structure for human control. Religions have created rigid belief systems that should never be questioned. They have imposed those beliefs through fear, indoctrination, isolation, and the mass genocide of non–believers. They have fought each other for dominance of the human mind, thus producing an explosion of opportunity for the Illuminati to divide and rule for millennia. Another question: "is it more likely that an Illuminati that has its origins in the ancient past, long before these religions were created, just happened to 'get lucky' when such a perfect vehicle for human control independently emerged? … or is it rather more probable that these institutions of human enslavement were purposely created by these very same Illuminati to advance their agenda?" Look at where the major religions originated – in the very Middle/Near East where the Illuminati had its ancient headquarters. In the aftermath of 9/11 we have seen Islam used to manipulate the people, and all the religions are used in the same way when the situation suits. But religion is not *the* conspiracy, and nor are economics, politics and all the rest. They are part of a vast web of interconnected manipulation designed to persuade the masses to put themselves in prison and throw away the key. The Illuminati work through every belief system – religious, political, economic, racial and cultural – and through every side in the major 'debates'. The reason is simple. If you want to know the outcome of a game before the game has even started, you need to control all sides. The manager of a football team cannot dictate the result if he only controls one side. If, however, he is managing both sides, he can ensure the result he wants before a ball is kicked. So it is with the Illuminati, the hidden hand behind the events that affect our lives and our world every day. We should be aware when contemplating the events in New York, Washington, and Pennsylvania that the Illuminati operate through secret societies in the Near and Middle East every bit as much as they do in the United States and the so-called "West".

We see this manipulation of both sides in the protests against globalisation. To control the public perception of these gathering protests the Illuminati have organised their own agents provocateur to start the violence we see on the news broadcasts. See my website *www.davidicke.com* for more detailed background to this, including the account of how mainstream journalists watched the police lines open at a protest in Spain to allow a group with weapons and masked faces to walk through to the peacefully protesting crowd. This group then started to attack *each other*, thus 'justifying' a police charge on the peaceful gathering in which people were battered by these uniformed head cases. Once the police intervention had begun, the journalists watched the group who started the trouble walk calmly back through the police lines to be driven away in police vehicles. One was asked if he was a policeman. "Yes" was his first reply when caught off-guard, but then he denied it. The manipulation of public perception goes on before our eyes minute by minute. September 11th was the most obvious example of this I have yet seen.

Fresh air "money"

One of the most important aspects of the bloodline-Illuminati control of humanity is the money system. The Illuminati financial sting is very simple and spans the period from Sumer and Babylon to the present day. It is based on creating money that doesn't exist and lending it to people and businesses in return for interest. This creates an enormous debt for governments, business and the general population and you therefore control them. Vital to this has been permitting bankers to lend money they do not have. If you or me have a million pounds we can lend a million pounds. Very simple. But if a bank has a million pounds it can lend ten times that and more, and charge interest on it. If even a fraction of the people who theoretically have money deposited in a bank went today to remove it, the banks would slam the door in half an hour because they don't have it. Money in the bank is a myth, another confidence trick. When you go into a bank and ask for a loan, the bank does not print a single new note, nor mint a single new coin. It merely types the amount of the loan into your account. From that moment you are paying interest to the bank on what is no more than figures typed on a screen. However, if you fail to pay back that non-existent loan, the bank can come along and quite legally take your wealth that does exist, your home, land, car and possessions, to the estimated value of whatever figure was typed on to that screen – plus interest. More than that, because money is not brought into circulation by governments, but by private banks making loans to customers, the banks control how much money is in circulation. The more loans they choose to make, the more money is in circulation. What is the difference between an economic boom (prosperity) and an economic depression (poverty)? One thing only – the amount of money in circulation. Through this system, the private banks, controlled by the same Illuminati families, decide how much money will be in circulation. They can therefore create booms and busts at will. It is the same with the stock markets through which these families are moving trillions of dollars a day around the financial and banking system and deciding if they go up or down, soar or crash. Stock market crashes don't just happen – they are made to happen. Why would the Illuminati do this when they have so much money invested in these markets? Well if you know the crash is coming because you are going to cause it, you know to sell at the highest point and buy back in once the crash has happened. In this way you can increase your holdings massively by acquiring companies at a fraction of the cost before your manipulated collapse.

Most of the "money" in circulation is not physical money: cash and coins. It is represented by figures passing from one computer account to another electronically via money transfers, credit cards and chequebooks. The more money, electronic or otherwise, that is in circulation, the more economic activity can take place and the more products are bought and sold, the more income people have, and the more jobs are available. But a constant theme of this Illuminati financial coup has been to create a boom by making lots of loans and then pulling the plug, causing a depression or crash. Overpaid economists and economic correspondents, most of whom have no idea what is going on, will tell you that boom and bust is part of some natural "economic cycle". It is not. It is systematic manipulation by the Illuminati to steal the real wealth of the world. During a boom many people get themselves into more debt. The vibrant economic activity means that businesses borrow more for new technology to increase production to meet demand. People borrow more to buy a bigger house and a more expensive car because they are so confident of their economic prospects. Then, at the most opportune moment, the major banks, coordinated by the Illuminati network, raise interest rates to suppress the demand for loans and begin to call in loans already outstanding. They ensure they make far fewer loans than before. This has the effect of taking units of exchange (money in its various forms) out of circulation. This suppresses demand for products and leads to fewer jobs because there is not enough money in circulation to generate the necessary economic activity. People and businesses can no longer earn enough to repay their loans and they go bankrupt. The banks then take over their real wealth, their business, home, land, car and other possessions – in return for non-repayment of a loan that was never more than figures typed on a screen.

This has been going on in cycles over thousands of years, especially the last few centuries, and the real wealth of the world has been sucked out of the population and into the hands of those who control the banking system – the Illuminati bloodline families. The same applies to countries. Instead of creating their own interest-free money, governments borrow it from the private banking cartel and pay the interest and the capital (sometimes) by taxation of the people. A fantastic amount of the money that you pay in taxes goes straight to the private banks to pay back loans of "money" that governments could create themselves interest free! Why don't they do it? Simple. The Illuminati control the governments as much as they control the banks. What we call "privatisation" is the selling of state assets in response to bank-created debt. The world's poorest countries are handing over control of their land and resources to the Illuminati bankers because they can't pay back the vast loans made, on purpose, by the banks to ensnare them in this very situation. The world does not have to be in poverty and conflict. It is manipulated to be that way because it serves the agenda. "Third World" debt was manufactured to replace physical occupation of resource-rich or strategically situated countries under colonialism with today's financial occupation. The way they created this situation is told in detail in *And The Truth Shall Set You Free*. Once a country is indebted to foreign banks, even though the money is non-existent credit, they are forced to hand over control of their affairs to the bankers, the World Bank and the International Monetary Fund, which then dictate economic and social policy at every level. In the end all roads not only lead to the same cabal, they also lead to the same word: control.

Criminal bankruptcy

When you begin to look behind the movie screen or, more appropriately, under the stone, you see a very different world to the one portrayed on CNN. Some researchers and lawyers suggest that in the 1930s the United States, Britain, France, Germany, Italy, Spain, Portugal and many others officially declared bankruptcy, but somehow forgot to tell the people. This apparently happened during the five years of Geneva Conventions in Switzerland between 1928 and 1932, but it seems that they don't publish the volume containing details of the bankruptcy declarations. The bankers said that either the countries declared bankruptcy to the Illuminati banks or there would be no loans to get them out of the deep global depression at that time. So they accepted official bankruptcy to the global banking system and this meant, in effect, that the banks have owned those countries ever since.[7] Actually, I say countries. In fact, the United States is not a country, but a corporation, as revealed in my previous books and a stream of other published works and studies. No doubt we will find that the situation is the same in other countries too. This bankruptcy is actually in the United States Congressional Record of March 17th 1993 (Vol. 33, page H-1303). James Traficant Jr of Ohio told the House:

"Members of Congress are official trustees presiding over the greatest reorganization of any Bankrupt entity in world history, the US Government. We are setting forth hopefully, a blueprint for our future. There are some who say it is a coroner's report that will lead to our demise.

"It is an established fact that the United States Federal Government has been dissolved by the Emergency Banking Act, March 9, 1933, 48 Stat. 1, Public Law 89-719; declared by President Roosevelt, being bankrupt and insolvent. H.J.R. 192, 73rd Congress m session June 5, 1933 – Joint Resolution To Suspend The Gold Standard and Abrogate The Gold Clause dissolved the Sovereign Authority of the United States and the official capacities of all United States Governmental Offices, Officers, and Departments and is further evidence that the United States Federal Government exists today in name only.

"The receivers of the United States Bankruptcy are the International Bankers, via the United Nations, the World Bank and the International Monetary Fund. All United States Offices, Officials, and Departments are now operating within a de facto status in name only under Emergency War Powers. With the Constitutional Republican form of Government now dissolved, the receivers of the Bankruptcy have adopted a new form of government for the United States. This new form of government is known as a Democracy, being an established Socialist/Communist order under a new governor for America. This act was instituted and established by transferring and/or placing the Office of the Secretary of Treasury to that of the Governor of the International Monetary Fund. Public Law 94-564, page 8, Section H.R. 13955 reads in part: 'The US Secretary of Treasury receives no compensation for representing the United States' ...

"... Why are 90% of Americans mortgaged to the hilt and have little or no assets after all debts and liabilities have been paid? Why does it feel like you are working harder and harder and getting less and less? We are reaping what has been sown, and the results of our harvest is a painful bankruptcy, and a foreclosure on American property, precious liberties, and a way of life. Few of our elected representatives in Washington DC have dared to tell the truth. The federal United States is bankrupt. Our children will inherit this un-payable debt, and the tyranny to enforce paying it."

James Traficant was later jailed for alleged bribery and corruption. The US corporation was created behind the screen of a "Federal Government" when, after the manufactured "victory" in the American War of Independence", the British colonies exchanged overt dictatorship from London with the far more effective covert dictatorship that has been in place ever since. In effect, the Virginia Company, the corporation headed by the British Crown that controlled the former "colonies", simply changed its name to the United States and other related pseudonyms. These include, today, the United States, US, USA, United States of America, Washington DC, District of Columbia, Federal Government and "Feds". The United States Corporation is based in the District of Columbia (Queen Semiramis) and the current president of the corporation is a man called George W. Bush. He is not the president of the people or the country as they are led to believe, that's just the smokescreen. This means that Bush launched a "war on terrorism" on behalf of a private corporation to further the goals of that Corporation. It had nothing to do with "America" and "Americans" because these are very different legal entities. It is the United States Corporation that owns the US military and everything else that comes under the term "federal". This includes the Federal Reserve, the "central bank" of the United States, which is, in reality, a private bank owned by controlling stockholders (and controllers of the US Corporation) that are not even American. This is the bank from which the United States Corporation borrows "money" that is repaid with interest by the unknowing American taxpayers. The Federal Reserve was manipulated into being in 1913 and dictates the US interest rate that has a massive knock-on effect on the rest of the world. The Federal Reserve or "Fed" is currently headed by Alan Greenspan, a member of Illuminati front organisations like the Bilderberg Group, Council on Foreign Relations and Trilateral Commission. His predecessor was Paul W. Volker of ... the Bilderberg Group, Council on Foreign Relations and Trilateral Commission (see *And The Truth Shall Set You Free*). The United States Corporation is owned by families and forces in Europe and the Jesuit-controlled Vatican is very much part of this covert ownership of not only the US, but major European "countries" also.

Aye, aye, captain, er, judge

The privately owned corporation known as the United States is the holding company, if you like, and the 50 states are its subsidiaries. Therefore these states also declared bankruptcy, or had it declared for them by the holding company, the "Federal Government", but the people never knew and still don't. You can get the detail about this elsewhere and I am only summarising the situation to give people an idea of how deep this conspiracy really goes. The sting has been set up so that when you register with the "Federal Government" in any way by accepting a Social Security number, driver's licence, or any of the other official federal documents, you are, unknowingly, agreeing to become an asset-employee of the United States Corporation. From that moment you become responsible for financing the corporation's state of bankruptcy. When you pay taxes or a court or parking fine and such like, you are servicing the bankruptcy by paying that money to "government agencies" that are nothing more than debt-collecting agencies for the "creditor" banks. The US court system operates under corporate law or the Uniform Commercial Code (UCC) to administer the bankruptcy and fleece the sheep to pay back the ongoing debt. This is also known as British Maritime (military) Law and this is why the American flag always has a gold fringe when displayed in the courts of the United States, and you find the same in government buildings and federally funded schools. The gold fringe is a legal symbol indicating that the court is sitting under British Maritime Law and the Uniform Commercial Code – military and merchant law not common or constitutional law. Under the Admiralty Law of Flags the flag displayed gives notice of the law under which the ship (in this case the court) is regulated. Anyone entering that ship (court) accepts by doing so that they are submitting to the law indicated by that flag. Judges refuse to replace the flag with one without a fringe when asked by defendants who know the score because that changes the law under which the court is sitting. If you appear in a court with a gold-fringed flag your constitutional rights are suspended and you are being tried under British Maritime (military/merchant) Law. The Uniform Commercial Code was approved by the American Bar Association, which is a franchise, a subordinate branch, of the British legal system and its hierarchy. As I have been writing for many years, the power that controls America is based in Britain and Europe (very much including the Vatican) because that is where the power is located that owns the United States Corporation. By the way, if you think it is strange that a court on dry land could be administered under Maritime Law, look at US Code, Title 18 B 7. It says that Admiralty Jurisdiction is applicable in the following locations: (1) the high seas; (2) any American ship; (3) any lands reserved or acquired for the use of the United States, and under the exclusive or concurrent jurisdiction thereof, or any place purchased or otherwise acquired by the United States by consent of the legislature of the state. In other words, mainland America. All this is founded on Roman law because the Illuminati have been playing this same game throughout the centuries wherever they have gone. The major politicians know that this is how things are and so do the government administrators, the judges and lawyers, and insider "journalists".

Those who realise what is happening and ask the court for the name of the true creditor or recipients of the fines imposed by the "legal system" are always refused this information by the judge. The reason is simple. The true creditors in such cases and the ultimate recipient of the fines are the bankers to which the corporation "country" is bankrupt. This is why more and more people in the US are refusing to register in any way with the Federal Government as news and documentation of this bizarre situation continues to circulate. If the authorities can keep this fantastic deceit from the mass of the people since the 1930s you can appreciate why they were confident they could ensure that what really happened on September 11th stays comfortably under wraps. Throughout this book I will refer to what is thought to be the government of "America" as the United States or the US and, when I talk of the "US government" and similar terms, I am referring to the privately owned United States Corporation that is masquerading as the "government." It is not the government of a nation or country, it is a private corporation acting purely in the interests of the families that own and control it. The "American" president is simply the corporation's chief executive officer.

What we can do

There are two ways to meet a problem. We can look for a solution or, far more effectively, we can remove the cause. I go into these areas in detail in my other books and talks, and I will return to this at the end of this one. But one key "cause" we need to eliminate is the way we allow ourselves to be divided and ruled along the fault lines of race, religion, political persuasion, income bracket, and the other virtually endless list of human conflicts and divisions. If a major cause of human control is division then to remove it we must *unite*, simple as that. We will never agree on everything and nor should we. What a boring world it would be if we did. But that does not mean we can't unite behind what we do agree on, and come together to protect and restore the freedoms that affect us all. Right wing, left wing, black, white, Christian, Muslim or Jew, everyone is a target for the Illuminati's global fascist state. Unless people stop fighting among themselves in their arrogant and meaningless battles for superiority, we will all be divided and ruled in a global version of Nazi Germany or Communist Russia and China.

I don't care what your religion may be, or your race or political belief. Whatever it is, you are entitled to it and you can do what you like for all I care, so long as you don't seek to impose your will and belief on others. What I care about is the right of everyone to be free to follow his or her own freely chosen path through this Great Illusion we call the 'physical' world. But for each of us to be truly free, we *all* have to be truly free. The loss of another person's freedom is a loss of our own also. The murder of a child in Afghanistan is no less important than the murder of a child in New York, nor vice versa. We are in this together and we need to grow up and come together. The number of people knowingly manipulating the Illuminati agenda is a tiny fraction of the global population. They can only do it with our agreement and cooperation through self-interest, ignorance or terminal apathy. The pyramids of control are only there because we are holding them together. The power of a pyramid is at the bottom, not the top, yet we seem blind to that fact. The Illuminati are only up there because we are holding them up there.

Our response must be peaceful because to meet violence with violence and hatred with hatred makes those who protest a mirror of those they protest against. What we fight we become, and it is vital that we don't fight the Illuminati and the global agenda, but instead cease to cooperate with it. Peaceful, united, non-cooperation with the system of control and dictatorship is by far the most effective means of bringing down these networks of power. Instead of fighting the pyramids we need to walk away from them and watch them fall by themselves once our cooperation ceases to hold them together. We are watching a daily movie while believing it is real. But it's not. It is the veil behind which this highly malevolent Illuminati agenda can operate in the secrecy that is fundamental to its success. With every week the movie is being exposed for what it is, a virtual-reality illusion designed to imprison the human collective mind. We can no longer justify a lack of response by a lack of knowledge. The information is available for anyone who truly wishes to know. So what are you – we – going to do about it? That is the question that everyone must now consider if the Illuminati are going to be denied their global concentration camp, the global sweat shop, that is unfolding daily before our eyes.

I hope this short explanation has helped you to glimpse some of the astonishing manipulation that hides behind the "movie" that is sold to us by the authorities and reported by the media. If you want to know more, there are 1,500 pages of detailed information available in my last three books and 5,000 pages on my website.

Postscript: During the first printing of this book, genealogists revealed in the media the blood connections between the Bush family and British royalty, the Spencer family of Princess Diana, and Winston Churchill. Colin Powell, they said, is related to England's Edward 1st and Richard Nixon to Edward III. This is all perfectly in line with the themes of my books.

SOURCES

1   George Orwell, *1984* (Dutton/Plume, 1983). First published in 1949

2   There are some interesting websites on these subjects, including
    http://www.enterprisemission.com/tower2.htm and
    http://www.mt.net/~watcher/dollarsign.html

3   Jim Shaw, *The Deadly Deception* (Huntington House Inc, Lafayette, Louisiana, 1988)

4   Ibid, p 103

5   *Morals and Dogma of the Ancient And Accepted Scottish Rite of Freemasonry*, p 819

6   *The Deadly Deception*, pp 65 and 66

7   There is a good background article detailing this story at
    http://home.digital.net/~kenaston/Patr/Bankrupt.html

chapter 2

The Bush crime family

Liberty cannot be preserved without a general knowledge among the people, who have a right and a desire to know; but besides this, they have a right, an indisputable, unalienable, indefeasible, divine right to know that most dreaded and envied kind of knowledge, I mean of the characters and conduct of their rulers.

John Adams

Before we begin our journey through the official fairytale of September 11th, we should look at some of the background to the "world leaders" who have dictated events before and since that terrible day.

These are the men and women who have told us what happened on 9/11, who was responsible and what should happen as a result. Surely before we make decisions about what to believe we need to know if those who have peddled the official version of events can be trusted to tell us the truth. The next three chapters will be full of names and interconnecting subjects, and I can understand that some may find it overwhelming at times, but without this information it is not possible to appreciate the true context of September 11th and as this book unfolds that will become obvious. First of all, these "world leaders" are nothing like as powerful as people think they are, except over those below them in the Illuminati pyramid. Like all the personnel in government, even at apparently exalted levels, they are puppets of a higher authority in the hidden hierarchy that does not put itself on public display. The President of the United States, as with the Prime Minister of the UK and elsewhere, is a position for lieutenants of the Illuminati, not generals or colonels. They are used to play out the game in the public arena and, so long as they do that and say what they are told to say, their careers will flourish and their horrendous secrets will remain "in-house". Fail to serve the dragon, however, and you press the self-destruct button, as with John F. Kennedy and his brother Bobby. There are those, like the Bush family and Tony Blair, the British Prime Minister, who willingly and enthusiastically dance to the Illuminati tune and take the "power" and rewards that come with that. Others are caught in the web and believe there is nothing they can do except comply. Here I will present just some of the background to the famous political faces that have dominated the post 9/11 era. I emphasise the word "some" because there is far more to know than I can detail in a few chapters, and you can find more information in my other books like *And The Truth Shall Set You Free*, *The Biggest Secret*, *Children Of The Matrix*, and a long list of publications by other authors and researchers (see Bibliography).

The Bush family

The Bushes have been one of the most active Illuminati families, at a "gofer" level, for at least the last century or so. They have produced two US presidents and as both are called George Bush I will overcome the potential confusion in the text by calling George H.W. Bush either George Bush or "Father George", and I'll refer to his son, the current incumbent, as George W. Bush, "Boy George", or "Dubya". As U.S presidents go, Father George is quite high up in the Illuminati compared with most of them, but he's still small fry compared with those who really call the shots. His son, George "Dubya", of course, can just about summon the brain-cell activity to tie his shoelaces. I blame the inbreeding myself. Father George and wife Barbara are both descendants of Godfroi de Boullion (also known as Godfrey of Boullion) who, in 1099, led European noblemen in the successful Crusade to recapture Jerusalem from the Islamic faith and moved into the King's palace at Temple Mount, the alleged site of Solomon's Temple, which has been an historic obsession for the Illuminati that continues to the present time. Understanding this obsession is to understand so much about the terrible events in Jerusalem and the focus on Temple Mount by the religions of Christian, Jew and Muslim. Godfroi de Boullion was the first King of Jerusalem and the Duke of Lower Lorraine, a major region for the Illuminati bloodline to this day (see *The Biggest Secret*). So when George W. Bush, a descendant of de Boullion through both his mother and father, talked of a "Crusade" against "Islamic" terrorism after September 11th, that was no slip of the tongue or unfortunate gaffe as it was reported. He knew exactly what he was saying and why. From this "Crusade" by de Boullion came the secret society called the Knights Templar, which is widely exposed in my other books. The Knights Templar is still a major arm of the Illuminati today with top people in global politics, banking, business and media among its initiates. It was largely through the Knights Templar that the Freemasons, the world's biggest secret society, emerged.

George and Barbara Bush are from the Pierce bloodline that changed its name from Percy after fleeing England in the wake of the Gunpowder Plot led by Guy Fawkes (or so they say) to blow up the English Parliament and kill King James I in 1605. This event is still celebrated in the UK every November 5th when effigies of Guy Fawkes are burned on bonfires all over the country. The Bush ancestor Thomas Percy was one of the main plotters. George and Barbara Pierce Bush (of Merrill, Lynch, Fenner and Smith) are from the same bloodline as the US President, Franklin Pierce, who was in the White House from 1853 to 1857. Other Bush relatives include the Grosvenor families of England and America, the Tafts of Ohio, who produced William Howard Taft, president from 1909 to 1913, and the Delano-Roosevelts, who provided President Franklin Delano Roosevelt (1933–45) and Theodore Roosevelt (1901–19). The English Grosvenors are the Dukes of Westminster who own prime properties in the City of London, one of the main financial and secret society centres for the Illuminati globally. The Grosvenors of America founded the National Geographic which is notorious for removing the archaeological treasures of the world, especially those with religious significance, and relocating them at the Smithsonian Institute in Washington DC. The Institute is controlled by those Grosvenor cousins, the Smithsons, who in turn are descended from the Percys – the Pierce bloodline that produced the Bushes.[1] The ancestry of both George Bushes can also be traced to England's Alfred the Great and to Charlemagne, a highly significant figure in the Illuminati and bloodline story, and from whom 34 of the 43 US presidents are descended. With both his father and mother having such serious royal and aristocratic ancestry, this gives Baby George a mass of bloodline connections, as documented by *Burke's Peerage*. The Bushes are related to the British royal family, who are big-time Illuminati, and the two are very close. Documents apparently exist that reveal Bush family business dealings with the Queen of England through Coutts Bank in London and if anyone can give me more details about that then please let me know.

Dark secrets galore

The Bushes have long been pillars of the infamous Skull and Bones Society based in a windowless mausoleum known as "the Tomb" alongside the campus at Yale University at New Haven in Connecticut. Every year 15 bloodline students are initiated into the Skull and Bones Society and the ratio of Skull and Bones initiates who end up in positions of power in politics, banking, business, media and intelligence agencies in the United States, in front of camera and behind the scenes, is massively greater than the general student population. George W. Bush is a Skull and Bones initiate (code name "Temporary" interestingly), along with Father George Bush, and the president's grandfather, Prescott Bush, one of the funders of Adolf Hitler. Prescott Bush is most famous within the Skull and Bones "Order" for raiding the grave of the Native American Apache leader Geronimo. In May 1918 Prescott Bush and five other Skull and Bones men ransacked the grave at Fort Sill, Oklahoma. They took turns to stand guard while others robbed the grave and took away artefacts and Geronimo's skull. This was taken to the Skull and Bones headquarters at Yale where it is used in their sick rituals and ceremonies. This horrible story is told in an internal history of the Skull and Bones Society and was quoted to Ned Anderson, the Tribal Chairman of the San Carlos Apache tribe, when he was negotiating to have Geronimo's remains returned to the tribe's custody. A 1989 article in the New Yorker said: "One Bonesman … recalled during the early 70s seeing perhaps 30 skulls, not all of them human, scattered about the Tomb [at Yale]."[2] This is the mentality of the people running our world.

The Bush men also have a long association with the diabolical rituals performed by the Illuminati bloodlines every July at a place called Bohemian Grove, located in 2,700 acres of very secluded redwood forest near the hamlet of Monte Rio in Sonoma County, 75 miles north of San Francisco. This is a ritual and sexual playground for leading American and foreign politicians, mobsters, bankers, businessmen, media owners and editors, top entertainers, etc., who are initiates of the Illuminati or serve the agenda in some form. Among them are people like Presidents Jimmy Carter, Gerald Ford and Ronald Reagan; Vice President Dick Cheney; Secretaries of State Henry Kissinger, George Shultz, Casper Weinberger and Bush family crony, James Baker; Alexander Haig, the former US Defense Secretary; Alan Greenspan, the head of the Illuminati's US "central bank", the Federal Reserve; David Rockefeller, Illuminati manipulator for at least 50 years; television news anchorman Walter Cronkite; David Gergen, author and adviser to presidents for 30 years and editor-at-large at *US News and World Report*; and presidents of major media operations like CNN and the Associated Press. In July 1991, Dirk Mathison, the San Francisco bureau chief of *People* magazine, owned by the Illuminati's Time–Warner, sneaked into the Grove three times. On the third occasion he was recognised by a Time Warner executive who threw him out and his story was not allowed to appear. Mathison said that John Lehman, a former secretary of the Navy, delivered a lecture at the Grove that revealed how the Pentagon estimated 200,000 Iraqis had been killed a few months earlier in the Gulf War – a figure not made public. Another speaker at the secret Grove gathering was Al Neuharth, the founder of *USA Today*, who was identified in the official programme as chairman of the Freedom Forum – a $700-million foundation dedicated to a "free press"!

Cathy O'Brien, who was a mind-controlled slave of the Illuminati for some 30 years, tells in her book, *Trance-Formation Of America*,[3] of how she and her fellow mind-slaves were forced to serve the perversions of their abusers at Bohemian Grove. These include satanic rituals, child sacrifices, torture and blood drinking. Cathy says in her book: "Slaves of advancing age or with failed programming were ritually murdered at random in the wooded grounds of the Grove and I felt it was only a matter of time before it would be me." She says that the Grove has a number of rooms for different perversions, including a Dark Room, a Leather Room, a Necrophilia Room and one known as the Underground Lounge, spelt as U.N.derground on the sign. I know this sounds seriously far out to peoples' conditioned sense of reality, but if you read *The Biggest Secret* and *Children Of The Matrix*, as well as many other books by other researchers and victims, you will see the enormous evidence to support all this. I will explain why they are obsessed with rituals and blood drinking in the final chapter. These bloodlines can be shown to have been involved in these sickening human sacrifice rituals since Babylon and before, and it continues to this day. In *The Biggest Secret* there is a photograph of robed and hooded men at the Grove standing alongside a large fire while worshipping a 40-foot stone owl – an ancient Illuminati symbol. These world-famous Illuminati initiates at Bohemian Grove burn and sacrifice a human "effigy" under the owl at the start of their "summer camp" every year. This happens during a Babylonian-type ritual called the Cremation of Care and in the year 2000 Alex Jones, an American radio talk show host, took a hidden camera into the Grove and filmed the ritual. He was too far away to see if the sacrifice was an "effigy" or real, but the human sacrifice rituals go on among the elite of the elite in much more secret and secluded locations during the "camp". The Jones footage clearly shows the bizarre opening ritual and the sound quality is particularly good. At one point an "effigy" is floated on a boat across the lake at Bohemian Grove where it is placed under the giant owl and set on fire. At this point you hear very clearly a blood-curdling scream and one of two things are happening here. They are either sacrificing a human being in the guise of an "effigy" or they broadcast the sound of the scream of agony as part of the ceremony. Either way, these are the people running our world! President George W. Bush, like his father and grandfather, is a Bohemian Grove attendee and arrived there shortly after the video was shot. The Jones footage appeared in a television documentary on the UK's Channel 4 in 2001, a programme that skimmed the surface of what really goes on at the Grove and missed a wonderful opportunity. Alex Jones has a tendency to scream at the camera, which doesn't help his case, but he does some great work informing Americans of their plight. His own video of the Bohemian Grove footage is far better than the UK Channel 4 version and is well worth seeing. It is available through *Infowars.com*

The Bush drug network

Among the most important functions of the Bush family and the Skull and Bones Society is putting illegal drugs like cocaine and heroin on the streets of America and around the world. It was very wealthy aristocratic and other Illuminati bloodline families in Britain and the United States that launched the global drug trade and still control it. They use their government agencies to "bust" any opposition and leave the field clear for themselves. This is what is happening when you hear news reports of a "big drug find" or some villain or network being jailed for trafficking. The real players never get hit because they also control law "enforcement". The Illuminati drug-running network not only makes vast sums to fund covert projects, it also destroys lives on a massive scale, and creates fear and divide and rule through the enormous division and crime generated by those who steal, rob and mug in a desperate attempt to get the money to feed their addiction. The Skull and Bones Society is owned by the Russell Trust, an organisation controlled by the Russells, a drug-running bloodline family. They flew the skull and bones flag on their ships as they transported drugs for the British Empire from Turkey to China and elsewhere during the Opium Wars of the 19th century. The skull and bones is an ancient Illuminati symbol used in its sacrificial rituals and secret language, not least by the Knights Templar. Samuel Russell launched Russell and Company in 1823 and within seven years it had absorbed the Perkins opium syndicate based in Boston. Russell's head of operations in Canton, China, was Warren Delano Jr, the grandfather of Franklin Delano Roosevelt, the US President during the Second World War who was related to the Bush family. Roosevelt was also a cousin of his fellow wartime leader, the British Prime Minister, Winston Churchill. Other famous families (Illuminati bloodline) were partners in the Russell drug network – names like Coolidge, Forbes, Perkins, Low and Sturgis. It was Samuel Russell's cousin, William Huntington, and the Bush-related Alphonso Taft, the father of President William Howard Taft, who established the Order of the Skull and Bones in the US in 1832 and attracted America's major bloodline families to its dark rituals and grotesque agenda – families that have dominated American politics, business, banking, and covert intelligence operations. They include the Rockefellers, Harrimans, Tafts, Lords, Kelloggs, Goodyears, Whitneys, Vanderbilts, Bundys, Sloanes, Perkins, and … Bushes. The Skull and Bones men have always had a very close association with the US intelligence community and one of its most famous, or infamous, members is Father George Bush, who served the Illuminati and crimes against humanity as Director of the Central Intelligence Agency. (You'll find the detailed and sourced background to the Skull and Bones Society and the Bush connections in *And The Truth Shall Set You Free*.)

Prescott Bush, funder of Hitler

The current president's grandfather, Prescott Bush, was a Senator for Connecticut, the home of the Skull and Bones Society. He was a golf partner of President Dwight D. "Ike" Eisenhower, a military man who, like Colin Powell, enjoyed a fantastic rise to prominence because of his Illuminati sponsors. But "Ike" disappeared from view after he warned about the dangers to freedom posed by the "Military-Industrial Complex" (the Illuminati) in the closing days of his presidency. Prescott Bush was a keen and active supporter of the eugenics (master race) movement along with his bloodline associates, the Harrimans and Rockefellers. It was this clique, led by the Rockefellers, that funded the work of Adolf Hitler's race "purity" expert, Ernst Rudin, to such an extent that he could occupy an entire floor at the Kaiser Wilhelm Institute for Genealogy and Demography in Berlin.[4] Soon after Hitler had abolished elections and become dictator of Germany in 1933, the Rockefeller-funded, Bush and Harriman-supported, Dr Rudin was commissioned to write the Law for the Prevention of Hereditary Diseases in Posterity, which involved the forced sterilisation of anyone considered genetically inferior. Father George's massive funding of "population control" programmes is another modern example of this family obsession. Once again the detailed and horrific story of the master race movement supported by the Bushes, Harrimans, and Rockefellers is told in *And The Truth Shall Set You Free*. Harry S. Truman, by the way, the Freemasonic President who ordered the atomic bombing of Japan, was a Rockefeller cousin.

   Prescott Bush was involved in supporting eugenics and Hitler's crazed master race "philosophy", and he was directly involved in funding the Nazi war machine. All sides in the First and Second World Wars were funded by the same people, mainly through sources in Wall Street and the City of London (see *And The Truth Shall Set You Free*). The Illuminati use wars to change the face of society and create the opportunity to introduce their agenda of constant centralisation of power through the technique of problem-reaction-solution. They manipulate peoples and countries into conflict and fund the genocide until the status quo society is destroyed. Once that is achieved they can rebuild that society in line with their agenda. This is what the two world wars of the 20th century and the endless other conflicts have really been about – including Afghanistan and the "war on terrorism". Prescott Bush helped to finance Hitler through a company called the Union Banking Corporation (UBC). Fritz Thyssen, a German steel entrepreneur and banker, funded the Nazis from the early 1920s. His banking operation in Germany was affiliated through a subsidiary with the W.A. Harriman Company in New York (Brown Brothers, Harriman after 1933), which in turn was funded, at least in its earlier days, by the House of Rothschild. The Harriman family was prominent in supporting the Russian Revolution, Adolf Hitler and the master race insanity of the eugenics movement. A Fritz Thyssen company controlled the Union Banking Corporation in the US, which had E. Roland Harriman (Skull and Bones Society) on its board along with known Nazis and Nazi financial backers. Prescott Bush, father and grandfather of the future presidents, was also on the UBC board and owed his wealth to the Harrimans. The trio of Brown Brothers Harriman, the Sullivan and Cromwell law firm headed by Rockefeller cousin John Foster Dulles, and the Union Banking Corporation of Prescott Bush and George Herbert Walker (Father George's grandfather), represented the interests of the Nazi business cartels in the United States at the time of the Second World War. John Foster Dulles would become US Secretary of State while his brother, Allen, was the first head of the CIA! In 1942 the government seized UBC assets under the Trading With The Enemy Act, and stopped George Walker and Prescott Bush pouring money into Hitler's regime – at least in theory. Eight days later, two other Bush-managed companies, the Holland-American Trading Corporation and the Seamless Steel Equipment Corporation, were seized for the same reason. These were followed by another Bush-Harriman operation, the Silesian-American Corporation.

The Bush-Nazi connection was highlighted again more recently by John Loftus, the president of the Florida Holocaust Museum, who pointed out that Prescott Bush derived a portion of his personal fortune from his affiliation with a Nazi-controlled bank. Loftus, a former prosecutor in the Justice Department's Nazi War Crimes Unit, confirmed that Prescott Bush was a principal in the Union Banking Corporation in Manhattan in the late 1930s and the 1940s, and that leading Nazi industrialists secretly owned the bank at the time. He said they were moving money into the UBC through a second bank in Holland even after the United States declared war on Germany. The bank was liquidated in 1951, Loftus said, and President Bush's grandfather and great-grandfather received $1.5 million as part of that dissolution. He said he had a file of paperwork linking the bank and Prescott Bush to Nazi money. "That's where the Bush family fortune came from: it came from the Third Reich," Loftus said in a speech during the Sarasota Reading Festival.[5] In his book, *Unholy Trinity: The Vatican, The Nazis and the Swiss Banks*, Loftus documented the Swiss bank accounts that harboured funds confiscated from concentration camp victims, and the involvement of Italian priests in smuggling Nazi war criminals to safe havens in Canada, Central and South America, and the United States after the war. This is also detailed in *And The Truth Shall Set You Free*, which, like Loftus, exposes the Nazi connections of other prominent American Illuminati families, most notably the Rockefellers and the Kennedys. One member of the audience who heard Loftus in Florida, Nancy Krauss from Punta Gorda, said: "I am absolutely shocked. I wish this would have come out before the election. My husband voted for Bush. I don't think he would have voted for him if he would have known." [6] If people knew what the Bush family had really done, and are still doing, they would all be in jail with the key hurled into a very deep ocean.

Funding the Russian Revolution

The Harrimans and their close associate, Prescott Bush, also helped to fund the Russian Revolution. E. Roland Harriman was the brother of W. Averill Harriman (Skull and Bones Society), who was a director of a company called the Guaranty Trust when it was financing Lenin and Trotsky to trigger the Russian Revolution (another Illuminati problem-reaction-solution). Half the board members of Brown Brothers Harriman and their fellow Russian Revolution financers, J.P. Morgan, were Skull and Bones initiates. Roland Harriman, Prescott Bush and Percy Rockefeller, were in the same Bonesmen group. Averill Harriman, the Henry Kissinger of his day, would later make vast profits from Russian ventures and be appointed US Ambassador to the Soviet Union to advance Illuminati interests there. The US and Soviet governments were on different "sides" in the "Cold War"? Sure they were. It was all a game to dupe the people. Averill Harriman was also a controlling voice in the Democratic Party and dictator to President Franklin Roosevelt, he of the drug-running Illuminati bloodline related to the Bushes. Harriman's wife, Pamela, who died while US ambassador to Paris in 1997, was extremely influential in Bill Clinton's rise to the presidency, which is why he made her Ambassador to France as a pay back. In turn, her husband, Averill, a "Democrat", was very much a mentor to Prescott Bush and the Bush family in general, who are "Republicans". As one headline at the time of Bill Clinton's run for president put it: "Bush Camp Finances Clinton Campaign".[7] Like I say, the United States, as with the UK and other countries, is a one-party state masquerading as a free society. Whoever you vote for the government still gets in: the Illuminati government. Pamela Harriman was also married to Randolph Churchill, son of Britain's wartime Prime Minister, Winston Churchill (bloodline and cousin to Franklin Roosevelt) and she had affairs with the Italian Fiat boss Giovanni Agnelli (bloodline and major Illuminati major operative) and Baron Elie de Rothschild (bloodline and Illuminati operative), among a string of others. When you move in Illuminati circles, it is a very small world.

George H.W. Bush – "Father George"

This was the background into which George Herbert Walker Bush arrived in this world on June 12th 1924. He was groomed from birth to serve the Illuminati in a long list of roles, including US Ambassador to the United Nations, Chairman of the Republican Party at the time of the Watergate hearings, Director of the CIA, and Vice President and President of the United States. The Herbert Walker in his name comes from his grandfather, George Herbert Walker (Skull and Bones Society), another man heavily involved with Prescott Bush in the manipulation of the Russian Revolution, the expansion of the eugenics movement and the funding of Hitler. The golf trophy called the Walker Cup is named after him. Wherever you look in George Bush's life you find Illuminati operatives, human sacrificers, child abusers and orchestrators of genocide. George Bush himself is all of these, as my books and others have well detailed. Father George is very much a power behind the throne during the presidency of his son, who is only doing what others tell him.

I will summarise here just a few of the crimes against humanity inflicted by Father George Bush and his dominant partner, Henry Kissinger, another genocidal maniac. It will give you a flavour of the true mentality behind September 11th and the subsequent "war on terrorism". Bush served the Illuminati in China while Kissinger and the Chinese were supporting Pol Pot in the genocidal war on Cambodia that led to the systematic extermination of millions of Cambodians. Bush returned home in 1975 when he received a telegram from Kissinger saying that he was being nominated by President Ford (Kissinger in other words) to be Director of the CIA. Bush held the post in 1976 and 1977 and he is so fundamentally involved in CIA activities to this day that in 1999 its headquarters compound at Langley, Virginia, was named the George Bush Center for Intelligence. Maybe his son should join, he could do with some. The Central Intelligence Agency is part of the so-called "Inner Fed" of the secret government that consists of the CIA, the National Security Agency, FBI, NASA and the Federal Reserve "Central Bank of America". It is through "umbrella" structures like the "Inner Fed" – the pyramids – that a coordinated policy and response can be conducted between apparently unconnected agencies and organisations. Much of the funding of this cartel of manipulation comes from its involvement in the drugs trade, which the intelligence agencies and bloodline families like the Bushes control.

Father George Bush was not new to the intelligence game and his connections with the CIA would appear to go back to the 1950s or even much earlier given the Skull and Bones Society connection to the US intelligence community. In *The Immaculate Deception*,[8] Russell S. Bowen names Bush as a top CIA agent since before the agency's failed Bay of Pigs invasion of Cuba on April 17th 1961, which turned President Kennedy's attention to reforming the CIA. Bowen, a retired brigadier general who did some of the Bush family's dirty work, says that Bush worked with a man named Felix Rodriguez and other anti-Castro Cubans.[9] Intriguingly, the top secret code name of the Bay of Pigs invasion was "Operation Zapata". Bush's oil company was called Zapata Oil. Rodriguez would turn up again in the Iran-Contra arms-for-drugs scandal during the Reagan-Bush administration, which made vast quantities of hard drugs available to the young people of the United States. When you look at the personnel in the "Plumbers Group" involved in the Watergate break-in in 1972, a remarkable number of them were also involved in the Bay of Pigs debacle. William Buckley, a CIA coordinator, said that if he told what he knew about the Bay of Pigs and the Kennedy assassination "it would be the biggest scandal ever to rock the nation".[10] Buckley would later be assassinated in the Middle East. There is plenty of evidence that George Bush was a long-time CIA asset since before the Kennedy assassination when the family friend and Hitler supporter, Allen Dulles, was head of the CIA. The Dulles family are bloodline and cousins to the Rockefellers. President Kennedy sacked Allen Dulles in a purge in which JFK threatened to break up the CIA into a thousand pieces, but before he could do that he was assassinated in Dealey Plaza, Dallas, in 1963 and the same

Allen Dulles was appointed to the Warren Commission to decide who killed him! There is evidence to suggest that George Bush was far closer to the Kennedy assassination than people have believed.[11]

Father George at the CIA

From his office at the CIA headquarters in Langley, Virginia, Bush put together his team. Among them was the infamous Theodore Shackley, whom Bush named as the CIA's associate deputy director for covert operations. Shackley had been the head of the CIA station in Miami during the early 1960s, from where E. Howard Hunt and his fellow Watergate burglars would emerge. Shackley went on to head the CIA station in Saigon during the Vietnam War where he masterminded Operation Phoenix. This involved the death of tens of thousands of Vietnamese civilians who were "suspected" of working for the Viet-Cong. (Just being able to read and write was enough to invite this suspicion, apparently.) Oliver North, the "star" of the Iran-Contra affair, worked with Shackley on Operation Phoenix, which is reputed to have murdered 40,000 Vietnamese villagers. Shackley ran a huge assassination and drug operation in South-East Asia in the 1970s in which two other Bush men, Donald Gregg and Felix Rodriguez, were involved. This operation was threatened by President Kennedy seeking to withdraw from Vietnam, the Illuminati war that cost the lives of 50,000 Americans and two million Vietnamese. Bush appointed the same Theodore Shackley to an important position in his CIA and Shackley would later be recruited as Bush's speechwriter during the 1979–80 election campaign. The idea that someone like Shackley would be hired to write Bush's speeches defies the imagination. No doubt his other "talents" were the real reason for his presence. The last I heard, Shackley was living in Medellin, Columbia, home of the drug cartel. How thoroughly appropriate. Thomas Clines, a former second in command at the CIA station in Miami, was another Bush appointee at the CIA who would be involved in Iran-Contra, a scandal Bush was to say he knew nothing about.

During Bush's tenure at the CIA, the operatives knew they could do virtually as they liked because their Director had a gift for looking the other way. The power over the US intelligence operations was concentrated in Bush's hands as a result of a series of measures introduced by President Ford, a front man for the mob and an abuser of mind-controlled women (see *The Biggest Secret* and *Trance-Formation Of America*). In the words of the *New York Times*, Ford: "...centralized more power in the hands of the Director of Central Intelligence than any had had since the creation of the CIA".[12] Among Bush's CIA operatives in South America was the infamous Nazi "Butcher of Lyon", Klaus Barbie, who had escaped from Europe thanks to US (Illuminati) intelligence. It was he who masterminded the so-called "cocaine-coup" in Bolivia in June 1980 and he used the profits from CIA-supported drug networks to finance the neo-Nazi overthrow of the government in Argentina when, according to former US Drug Enforcement agent, Mike Levine, the coup was achieved by troops wearing Nazi armbands.[13] Another Illuminati front operation closely connected to Bush is Sun Myung Moon's "Moonie Church", which is connected to many prominent politicians around the world, including Ted Heath, the former Prime

Minister of the UK from 1970 to 74 (See *The Biggest Secret* and *Children Of The Matrix*). Bo Hi Pak, Moon's right-hand man, was among the first to arrive in La Paz after the Barbie-Bush "cocaine-coup" in Bolivia. Moon, it is claimed, invested $4 million in the coup and was to massively finance Bush's run for the presidency in 1988. The Washington Times newspaper, so supportive of Bush, is owned by the Moonies.[14]

The contacts George Bush made at the CIA would be invaluable when he became Vice President to Ronald Reagan on January 21st 1981. Reagan's personal fortune dates from a time shortly after becoming Governor of California when he bought some land cheaply and sold it at a vast profit to a group of benefactors who have never been publicly identified.[15] Reagan, a former B-movie actor, was a long-time member of Bohemian Grove and an initiate of the Knights of Malta. This is another a very significant strand in the Illuminati web. Reagan was 70, the oldest man to be inaugurated as President. His mind was failing and he needed long afternoon naps each day. Almost everything Reagan said, even in relatively off-the-cuff situations when greeting foreign leaders, was written for him on cue cards by his aides. George Bush was president in all, but name. After the assassination attempt on Reagan in 1981, his mind further deteriorated. This gave Bush almost complete control of affairs and in the background was the power behind the throne: his mentor, Henry Kissinger. Reagan's would-be assassin, John Hinckley, had connections to the Bush family. Father George built a network of organisations within the government with himself at the head. These were the Standing Crisis, Pre-Planning Group, the Crisis Management Center, the Terrorist Incident Working Group, the Task Force on Combating Terrorism and the Operations Sub-Group. These were subordinate to, and controlled by, the Special Situation Group chaired by Bush. If ever there was a line-up of problem-reaction-solution "organisations", then this was it. Through this network would come the arms-for-drugs operation known as Iran-Contra in which the Reagan-Bush administration illegally sold arms to the hostile regime in Iran (hostile in public anyway) and used the money they received to illegally fund and arm the Contra terrorists in Nicaragua who were fighting to overthrow the elected Sandinista government that the Illuminati wanted removed. In return for this vital support, the Contras supplied US government agencies controlled by George Bush with drugs for distribution on the streets of America and elsewhere.

Iran-contra

The now Vice President Bush hired his former CIA associate, Donald P. Gregg, as his main adviser on "national security" and Gregg brought with him a "former" CIA assassinations manager, Felix Rodriguez, whom Bush had known back to the time of the Bay of Pigs invasion and his period as head of the CIA. Gregg and Rodriguez were involved with Theodore Shackley in the assassination and drug-running operation in South-East Asia in the Vietnam War era. The two now worked out of George Bush's office! It was strictly illegal under US law for the government to supply arms to Iran or to fund and arm the Nicaraguan "freedom fighters" (terrorists) called the Contras in their war with the Sandinista government. It was certainly illegal to accept payment with drugs in return. The Reagan-Bush administration would do all of these things. One of the ways the Bush-controlled "Reagan" government secretly undermined the Sandinistas was by mining harbours in Nicaragua. A company called Continental Shelf Associates, Inc., which is based on Jupiter Island, Florida, carried out these covert operations. Jupiter Island is an interesting place. It became the fiefdom of the Harriman set, including George Bush, who has a home there. Jupiter Island has been a base for generations of Illuminati families. Continental Shelf Associates (CSA) lists many oil companies and government agencies among its clients. They include the Rockefellers' Exxon and the Bush-connected oil company Pennzoil. CSA was used by the US military for coastal mapping and reconnaissance in Grenada before the Reagan-Bush invasion in October 1983 and during US operations in the Lebanon. The company was run by Robert "Stretch" Stevens. He was a close associate of Theodore Shackley and Felix Rodriguez when they were all involved in South-East Asia and the Bay of Pigs invasion. A CSA company at the same address is Acta Non Verba, which means "action, not words". A high-level CIA officer quoted by Anton Chaitkin and Webster Griffin Tarpley, in *George Bush, The Unauthorised Biography*, said of this CSA subsidiary:

"Assassination operations and training company controlled by Ted Shackley, under cover of a private corporation with a regular board of directors, stockholders, etc, located in Florida. They covertly bring in Haitian and South East Asian boat people as recruits, as well as Koreans, Cubans, and Americans. They hire out assassination and intelligence services to governments, corporations, and individuals ..." [16]

Again, Father Bush's close friend Shackley is involved. The bombs planted in the harbours of Nicaragua caused such a row in the US that the laws against such action, the Boland Laws as they were called, were further strengthened. But at a secret meeting of the National Planning Group on June 25th 1984, Bush, Reagan and their top officials decided to ignore the law. They would fund the Contras through Honduras, just as they had used El Salvador against the Sandinistas. Bush and Oliver North, an official of the National Security Council, travelled together to El Salvador. On January 18th 1985 the Bush-appointed Felix Rodriguez is known to have met his name sake (but not thought to be a relative), Ramon Milian Rodriguez, an accountant and money launderer who worked for the Medellin drug cartel. This meeting was confirmed by Felix Rodriguez and reported in the *Miami Herald* on June 30th 1987. From his cell in Butner, North Carolina, Ramon told investigative journalist, Martha Honey:

" ...[Felix offered] ... in exchange for money for the Contra cause he would use his influence in high places to get the [cocaine] cartel US goodwill ... Frankly, one of the selling points was that he could talk directly to Bush. The issue of goodwill wasn't something that was going to go through 27 bureaucratic hands. It was something that was directly between him and Bush." [17]

This could easily be done given that Felix Rodriguez was working from Bush's office. A memo in early September 1986 sent to Oliver North by retired Army Major General John K. Singlaub, said that Rodriguez was talking of having "daily contact" with Bush's office and this, said the memo, could damage President Reagan and the Republican Party. Oliver North would also write in his notebook: "Felix has been talking too much about the VP [Vice President]".[18] In her 1987 book, *Out Of Control* former *CBS News* Producer Leslie Cockburn presents devastating evidence of Bush's involvement in Iran-Contra and drug running. She says that planes chartered by the CIA and packed with cocaine flew directly into the Homestead Air Force Base in Florida using a CIA code signal. Colonel Albert Carone, who was later murdered, said in a sworn statement that he remembered seeing Oliver North make more than 20 entries in his diary detailing how drug profits were being used to buy weapons for the Contras. He said that an entry for July 5th 1985 noted that "$14 million to buy arms came from drugs".[19]

In 1986, the Reagan-Bush administration admitted that Adolfo "Popo" Chamorro's Nicaraguan Contras, the terrorists supported by the CIA, were helping a Colombian drug-trafficker to transport drugs into the United States, and the testimony of John Stockwell, a former high-ranking CIA official, revealed that drug smuggling was an essential component of the CIA operation with the Contras. George Morales, one of South America's biggest traffickers, testified that he was approached in 1984 to fly weapons to the Contras. In return, he says, the CIA helped him to smuggle thousands of kilos of cocaine into the United States via an airstrip on the ranch of John Hull, a self-confessed CIA agent and associate of Oliver North. As Michael Ruppert, a former drugs specialist with the Los Angeles Police Department, said:

"The CIA and Ronald Reagan and [CIA Director] Bill Casey and Vice-President George Bush were running the whole operation, we know that now. They circumvented the will of Congress and there was an explosion of drug trafficking all throughout Central America, coordinated by the CIA." [20]

Meanwhile, the other aspect of Iran-Contra was continuing to illegally trade arms for hostages with Iran. Oliver North was heavily involved in the supply of arms to Iran, via Israel, in return for hostages. The release of the hostages was explained in part by the efforts of Terry Waite, the representative of Britain's Archbishop of Canterbury. Waite was being used without his knowledge by North who was quite happy for him to take the credit for the release of hostages when, in fact, they were the result of illegal arms sales. As a consequence, Waite would eventually be taken hostage himself. Throughout all of this, George Bush was telling the American people: "We will make no concessions to terrorists" – just as his son is saying today. Even before Reagan was elected, Bush negotiated with the Iranians to delay the release of American hostages until after the Presidential election of 1980 to ensure that the sitting tenant, Jimmy Carter, would not get the kudos before polling day. So well was this negotiated that 52 hostages flew out of

Iran on the day that Reagan was inaugurated after 444 days in captivity. This became known as October Surprise and no doubt the promise of arms sales to Iran by a future Reagan-Bush administration was fundamental to the deal. I know its hard for us to imagine anyone coldly ensuring that American hostages would spend months longer in captivity just to serve Bush's political agenda, but that's the mentality we are dealing with here – the same mentality that is behind September 11th and its aftermath.

In late 1986, the Iran-Contra scandal blew and Ronald Reagan had to admit some, but only some, of what was happening. He said: "A few months ago I told the American people I did not trade arms for hostages. My heart and my best intentions still tell me that is true but the facts and evidence tell me it is not."(I lied.) On October 5th a plane left the Ilopango Air Base in El Salvador with arms and ammunition for the Contra terrorists in Nicaragua. The flight had been coordinated by officials within George Bush's office. As the plane came low to make the drop, it was grounded by a Sandinista missile. Three people died in the crash, but cargo handler Eugene Hasenfus parachuted into the hands of the Sandinistas. Bush was alerted in a call to his office by drug-runner and assassin Felix Rodriguez. The truth was out. Or some of it was. The power of the Illuminati network can be the only explanation for how, despite the overwhelming evidence against him, Bush evaded prosecution even though Buz Sawyer, the pilot of the crashed plane, was found to have the private phone number of George Bush's office in his pocket! Hasenfus also stated that George Bush knew about the whole thing. But Bush denied any involvement or knowledge of what happened, and subordinates like Donald Regan, Admiral John Poindexter, Oliver North, Robert McFarlane, and Major General Richard Secord, were sacrificed and scapegoated. They were very much involved, of that there is no doubt, but Bush got away with it, as did Reagan and his Secretary of Defense Casper Weinberger. North, who was up to his eyes in the intrigue, faced hearings with other scapegoats and staggeringly emerged in the eyes of many as an American hero. On March 16th 1988 a Federal Grand Jury indicted North, Poindexter and others on charges that included conspiracy to defraud the US government. A year later, despite delays due to legal manoeuvring, North was convicted of three of the twelve criminal counts that came to court. He was fined $150,000 and was given a three-year suspended prison sentence. Poindexter, the Reagan-Bush National Security Adviser, was convicted on five counts of deceiving Congress and was jailed for six months. But both convictions would be set aside because it was claimed their testimony to Congress, for which they were given immunity, was unfairly used against them. Robert McFarlane, Poindexter's predecessor as National Security Adviser, admitted criminal charges of withholding information from Congress about the covert support for the Contras. He was fined $20,000 and given two years' probation. Others involved, like CIA Director William Casey, had "health problems". In the aftermath of the Iran-Contra revelations, Casey literally could not speak following an operation for a "brain tumour" that took away his ability to talk. Two months later he was dead. During his presidential election campaign, Bush pledged to build a "kinder, gentler, America". In July 1991

Alan D. Fiers Jr, the head of CIA covert operations in Central America between 1984 and 1986, admitted lying to Congress about the CIA's involvement in the scandal. The Tower Commission was appointed to investigate Iran-Contra and was chaired by Bush's friend, the Texas Senator John Tower. Also on the Commission were Brent Scowcroft, a Kissinger "yes man" and an executive of the Illuminati front, Kissinger Associates, and Ed Muskie, Ronald Reagan's Attorney General and a close friend since his days as Governor of California. Muskie was himself implicated in Iran-Contra. As you can see, the Commission was thoroughly independent and, predictably, cleared Father George Bush of all blame and involvement. When Bush became President he made John Tower his Secretary of Defense. Reporters asked Tower if his appointment was a pay-off from Bush. His response:

"As the Commission was made up of three people, Brent Scowcroft and Ed Muskie in addition to myself, that would be sort of impugning the integrity of Brent Scowcroft and Ed Muskie ... We found nothing to implicate the Vice President ... I wonder what kind of pay-off they're going to get?" [21]

I can tell him. Bush appointed Brent Scowcroft as his National Security Adviser. The Senate refused to accept Tower's appointment and he began to speak of the injustice he believed had been done to him. He died in a plane crash on April 5th 1991. When the Senate turned down Tower, a decision Bush probably engineered, he selected Dick Cheney as Defense Secretary. Cheney was the senior Republican member of the House Select Committee to Investigate Covert Arms Transactions with Iran and that also cleared Bush of involvement in Iran-Contra. Bush still had a problem, however, with the former Defense Secretary Casper Weinberger, who was indicted in 1992, with others, for lying to Congress over Iran-Contra. With his presidency coming to an end, this could have been disastrous for Bush and he pardoned Weinberger and the others to ensure there would be no trial. The pardon came on Christmas Eve 1992 in the dying days of his presidency after he had lost the November election to Bill Clinton and a matter of weeks before Weinberger and company were due to face a trial that would have implicated Bush. In January 1993 the presidency passed to Clinton who continued the cover-up because – as I expose in *And The Truth Shall Set You Free* – he was also involved, not least with the Contra drug operations at the Mena airstrip in Arkansas where he was Governor. It is actually possible to coordinate a drug-running and arms-running operation from the White House and get away with it. Where were the media while all this was going on? Licking arse as usual. One reporter, Gary Webb on the *San Jose Mercury News*, did have the guts to expose how the CIA and the Bush-controlled White House had poured crack cocaine into black areas to raise money for the Contras and destroy the black communities. When he did so, Webb and his newspaper were not only attacked by the authorities, but by their fellow "journalists" and major papers like the *Washington Post*, *New York Times*, and *Los Angeles Times*. How do these people sleep at night? Rather well, I would wager. In 1986 the United States was convicted by the World Court for its war crimes against Nicaragua and later faced condemnation for its actions against the people of Panama. The US response? In effect: "Piss off." As with all playground bullies, United States governments, like those in Britain, claim immunity from that which they impose upon others.

The Gulf War

Here is another example of the mentality behind the "war on terrorism" that has followed the atrocities of September 11th 2001. Today we have the Bush family in the White House, Dick Cheney as Vice President and Colin Powell as Secretary of State, and a United States international "coalition" goes to war in the Middle-Near East. In 1991 the Bush family was in the White House, Cheney was Defense Secretary and Powell was head of the US forces as Chairman of the Joint Chiefs of Staff, and a United States international "coalition" went to war in the Middle East. The Gulf War, if you add together the casualties from the initial conflict in 1991 and the sanctions and bombing that have followed, has cost the lives of more than a million Iraqi children – and rising. Already the child and civilian casualties from the "war on terrorism" are mounting as more mass murder ensues from the same source. Disputes between Iraq and Kuwait are not new. Kuwait has been under British and Illuminati control back to the days when the economic potential of oil was discovered. Iraq has one of the world's largest oil deposits and attracts the constant attention of the US and British elite. In fact, countries like Kuwait, Iraq and others in the Middle East, were created by the British and their fellow European powers drawing lines in the sand. Kuwait is a dictatorship, an unpleasant one, and the idea that the Gulf War was to "free" Kuwait is just ridiculous. If Kuwait is to be free, the dictators of the royal family elite need to give up their power and the British and US manipulation of that country and its people must end. Neither is in prospect because the way things are suits the Illuminati agenda. Kuwait is a brutal dictatorship, as is (even more so) Saudi Arabia, another country Father George Bush claimed to be protecting from the tyranny of Saddam Hussein in 1991. But after the Gulf conflict what happened? Saddam was left in power in Iraq and the Kuwaiti royal dictatorship was brought back with American and British support to continue their policy of the murder and torture of "dissidents" who campaign for little luxuries like freedom and a say in the running of their own country.

Saddam Hussein, the designated villain of the Gulf conflict, was in fact one of the gang, at least up to this point. He was a member of the elite Safari Club, which began as a consortium involving Saddam, SAVAK (the secret police of the Shah of Iran), Anwar Sadat, the later-assassinated President of Egypt, and Saudi Arabian Intelligence. It has been implicated in countless coups in Africa to further its goals and is heavily involved in arms trading and supply. Out of the Safari Club came the Pinay Circle, or Le Cercle, named after the French Prime Minister Antoine Pinay. He was a major Illuminati asset who attended the first official meeting of the elite Bilderberg Group at Oosterbeek, Holland, in May 1954. Others involved with Le Cercle included the Habsburg family, a major Illuminati bloodline. To give you an idea of its make-up and range of influence, the Le Cercle membership has included

Nicholas Elliot, a department head at Britain's MI6; William Colby, a former director of the CIA; Colonel Botta of Swiss Military Intelligence; Stefano Della Chiaie, a leading member of the Italian Secret Service; Giulio Andreotti, Henry Kissinger's friend, the former Italian Prime Minister from the notorious and terrorist P2 Freemasonry lodge, and the man who gave Mafia officials protection; Silva Munoz, a former minister for the fascist Franco in Spain and a member of the elite secret society within the Roman Catholic network, Opus Dei; Franz Josef Strauss, the German Defence Minister; and Monsignore Brunello, an agent to the Vatican. In America, one of the Le Cercle fronts is alleged to be the CIA-backed Heritage Foundation in Washington. Look at the potential for such an organisation to be a coordinating force between apparently different agencies and countries to achieve a common aim. Le Cercle and the Safari Club are basically the same entity, which is why, as the *Wall Street Journal* reported on August 16th 1990, it was the CIA that supported the Baath Party in Iraq and installed Saddam Hussein as dictator in 1968, just as they did with Colonel Gaddafi in Libya. But it is important to remember that everyone is expendable to the cause if it best serves the agenda.

Saddam Hussein was encouraged by the Americans and the British to go to war with the CIA/British Intelligence-imposed regime of the Ayatollah Khomeini in Iran in 1980. The war dragged on for eight years amid appalling suffering and loss of life. But it was good for the oil, banking and armament cartel (all controlled by the Illuminati), and for divide and rule. The British government armed both sides in this conflict and some (but only some) of this scandal surfaced through the Scott Inquiry into illegal arms sales to Iraq that reported in 1996. The Iran-Iraq War is a grotesque example of problem-reaction-solution. The CIA looked after Khomeini during his exile in Paris to ensure he was ready and waiting to take over when the Shah, another CIA puppet, had outlived his usefulness. Now Saddam would be used again, knowingly or otherwise, to start another war in the Gulf by invading Kuwait. Author and researcher George C. Andrews reported:

"A little known fact about the Gulf War is that one month before our Declaration of War on December 15, 1990, Secretary of State James Baker, signed the US Army Report from the 352nd Civil Affairs Command on the New Kuwait [unclassified, and therefore available to those interested]. This report describes in detail how extensively Kuwait will be destroyed, how the oil wells will be set on fire, and then how it will all be rebuilt 'better than before', with despotism, instead of democracy, even more entrenched than it had been before. The report includes a list of US corporations who will be assigned the profitable task of rebuilding Kuwait and extinguishing the oil fires, as well as the Arab names they will be operating under. [Exactly the same was done before the "war" in Afghanistan].

"Why have none of his political opponents thought of asking the obvious questions: How did George Bush's so-called 'blind trust' make out during the time frame of the Gulf War? Why are the huge business deals between Bush and Hussein still off-limits to the public's right to know?" [22]

To readers of my books, the answers to these questions will be obvious. The 'blind trust', by the way, is the farce that insists that presidents must hand over all their business dealings to a "trust" during their term in office. This is supposed to ensure they can't make political decisions that affect their own investments and companies. Yeah, sounds credible. Bush's 'blind trust' was controlled by his close friend William S. Farish III, the grandson of William Farish, the President of Standard Oil New Jersey when they were working with Hitler's chemical and drug cartel I.G. Farben, which ran the slave camp at Auschwitz. While William Farish was head of Standard Oil, it was supplying the Nazis through Switzerland during the war, as established by official inquiries. Today his grandson and Bush "trust manager", William S. Farish III, is the American Ambassador to the United Kingdom as Boy George Bush conducts his "war on terrorism" in conjunction with Tony Blair's British government. William Farish III is also a very close associate of Queen Elizabeth II and she keeps some of her breeding mares at his Lane's End Farm, near Versailles in Kentucky, where she has been a regular visitor.[23] (The detailed background to the involvement of the British royal family with the Illuminati can be found in *The Biggest Secret*.)

Anyway, back to the Gulf War, or Gulf Slaughter as it really was. American reconnaissance advised George Bush around July 16th and 17th 1990 that Iraqi troops were assembling along the border with Kuwait (or so the official story goes). Nothing was done. On July 25th Saddam Hussein met with the US ambassador in Baghdad, April Glaspie, who told him she was acting on the instructions of President Bush. She said the Bush government had "no opinion on the Arab-Arab conflict like your border disagreement with Kuwait". Glaspie added that she had instructions from the President to seek better relations with Iraq. She then left for a summer holiday, another indication to Saddam that the Americans were not interested in the whole thing.[24] While all of this was going on, Bush still had nothing to say in public about the troop build-ups along the Kuwaiti border. By July 31st perhaps 100,000 troops were involved. Still Bush was silent. Two days before the invasion, John Kelly, an assistant Secretary of State, was asked by a congressional hearing if the US would defend Kuwait in the event of an attack. He replied: "We have no defence treaty with any Gulf country."[25] On August 2nd Saddam invaded Kuwait. Henry Kissinger was operating behind the scenes in the form of Brent Scowcroft, the National Security Adviser, a long-time Kissinger aide back to the days of the Nixon Presidency and an executive of Kissinger Associates. Scowcroft was urging military intervention and the Bush tone began to change. The United States told the Saudi Arabians that Saddam was likely to invade their country next – utter claptrap – and Bush ordered US troops to assemble along the "threatened" Saudi border. There would be no intervention, the world was told. The US forces were only there to protect Saudi Arabia, Bush said, and economic sanctions were to be the weapon used against Saddam. The Saudi Arabians, Germans and Japanese were pressured into contributing large sums towards American costs.

But sanctions were never going to be the real weapon and the rhetoric became ever stronger. Bush labelled Saddam "the new Hitler" and said that the Second

World War had shown that appeasement of such people was not the answer. He might have added that it is also not the answer to fund both sides in a conflict and to help finance Hitler's war machine, as his father had done. For those who knew the game plan, it was easy to see what was happening. On August 23rd Kissinger's man, Brent Scowcroft, said it all: "We believe we are creating the beginning of a New World Order out of the collapse of the US–Soviet antagonisms." [26] New World Order is a very old code name for the Illuminati global agenda. The term would be used by Bush in a speech to Congress on September 11th 1990 and enter into political speak around the world to the point of tedium. He described his New World Order as "diverse nations drawn together in common cause". Lose the newspeak and this translates as world government, central bank, army and currency controlled by a Big Brother dictatorship – the very structure that 9/11 brought so much closer. Bush received enthusiastic support for his war against Iraq from Illuminati puppets Margaret Thatcher and Francois Mitterand, the 33rd degree Freemason and President of France, who had supported the Nazis during their occupation of his country. Both sent forces to the Gulf alongside the Americans and the Illuminati "coalition" was presented as a United Nations response. Bush said in that speech to Congress on September 11th 1990 – exactly 11 years to the day before 9/11:

> "Clearly no longer can a dictator count on East-West confrontation to stymie concerted United Nations action against aggression. A new partnership of nations has begun, and we stand today at a unique and extraordinary moment. The crisis in the Persian Gulf, as grave as it is, also offers a rare opportunity to move toward an historic period of cooperation. Out of these troubled times, our fifth objective – a new world order – can emerge ..." [27]

For "fifth" read "first" and, of course, this is a mirror of the rhetoric we have had to endure since the attacks on the World Trade Center. Father Bush announced on November 8th 1990 that the forces in Saudi Arabia would be substantially increased. The "defensive" force was now to switch to offensive mode. A week later Bush left on a tour of Europe and the Middle East gathering support for the invasion. He met for three hours with the late President Assad of Syria, another tool of the Illuminati, who pledged to increase his contribution to Bush's forces to 20,000 men. The Bush "UN" forces attacked on Wednesday, January 16th 1991. 120,000 air sorties were unleashed on Iraq, mostly, it turned out, against civilian areas. The operation was headed by Bush's Chairman of the Joint Chiefs of Staff, Colin Powell, who has ancestral links with many old American and British families. The number of dead and injured from the bombing of Iraq, the resulting disease and the continuing economic sanctions can hardly be comprehended. Conditions for the innocent civilians in Iraq are unimaginable under the economic stranglehold that has been imposed since the Gulf War. This is the United Nations in all its glory. It is not the promoter of freedom, peace, and justice, as its PR proclaims, it is an Illuminati stalking horse for global government. By the way, part of the propaganda to gain political and public support for the invasion of Iraq was the "evidence" given to the Senate by a teenage girl that Iraqi soldiers had thrown Kuwaiti babies from their incubators and sent the incubators to Baghdad. Later it emerged that the teenager was in fact the daughter of the Kuwait Ambassador to Washington and the whole story was a lie cooked up by public relations firm Hill and Knowlton.[28]

How Bush funded Saddam

The public were also not told that it was the Bush government that had armed and funded the very army of Saddam Hussein that Father George had now sent US troops to fight. Much of the funding was channelled through a branch of Italy's Banca Nazionale del Lavoro (BNL) in Atlanta. Congressman Henry Gonzales exposed the BNL scandal in 1991 after he noticed that this little branch of the Italian government bank had loaned Iraq *$5 billion*. This money was dispatched to Saddam after November 1989 when the Bush White House guaranteed bank loans to Iraq if they were to be used for the purchase for US farm products. If Saddam defaulted, the US taxpayers picked up the tab for the loan and, since he was always defaulting, that was obviously going to be the outcome from the start. As planned, Saddam spent the money on arms, including purchases from the Matrix Churchill machine tool company in England. This company was the subject of a court case in which the British government was implicated. Although many US investigators warned Bush that the money was being used for arms, the loans were allowed to continue. The aim was obvious when you look at the other evidence. Bush was doing the same as his father did with Hitler. He was funding an aggressor so he could start a war with him. Some of the money given to Saddam by Bush was spent on buying poison gas from a CIA front called Cardeon Industries in Chile.[29] When the war started, Saddam defaulted on the loans and the US taxpayers footed the bill for Iraq to fight their own sons and daughters. The cover-up of this, as usual, led to the targeting of the small fry. The whole thing was blamed on the bank manager at the BNL's Atlanta branch, Christopher P. Drogoul, who could never have sanctioned that sort of money without the highest authorisation. One of the network of Illuminati private "armies" is called the Wackenhut Corporation and investigative journalist John Connolly exposed in a *Spy Magazine* article[30] that Wackenhut had been involved in the arming of Iraq before the Gulf War by transporting the means to produce the very chemical weapons that Father George Bush and Co were saying posed such a threat to the world. George Wackenhut, a former FBI operative, started the company with other FBI associates in 1954 and its board has been packed over the years with recruits from the FBI, CIA and the military. It has since merged with Group 4 Falck, the world's second largest provider of Security Services. George Wackenhut is a long-time friend of Father George Bush and has contributed generously to his political campaigns and those of Boy George and Florida governor Jeb Bush. John Connolly wrote that:

"... After a six-month investigation, in the course of which we spoke to more than 300 people, we believe we know that the [Wackenhut] truck did contain equipment necessary for the manufacture of chemical weapons and where it was headed [in the Winter of 1990]: to Saddam Hussein's Iraq. And the Wackenhut Corporation – a publicly traded company with strong ties to the CIA and federal contracts worth $200 million a year – was making sure Saddam would be getting his equipment intact." [31]

A guy called Peter Kawaja said in an American radio interview that he was involved at one time with Product Ingredient Technology in Boca Raton and with Ishan Barbouti International (IBI), the builder of Pharma 150, the chemical and biological weapons complex in Rabta, Libya.[32] His experiences led him to investigate what was going on. He said he went to the CIA and FBI, and operated for the US government under a code name because they told him these people were international terrorists and that they were going to prosecute them. Kawaja said that he did his own investigation, however, which included "bugging telephone lines, buildings, and certain other locations throughout the United States". He said he intercepted communications to the Commodity Credit Corporation and the Banca Nazionale del Lavoro (BNL). Kawaja said he saw the letters of credit of the BNL, which came from Switzerland, and "a lot of other communications regarding the Gulf War that was to come." He said he recorded calls going to and coming from Baghdad, to and from the United States and London, CIA, FBI, FBI counter-intelligence, US Customs, certain politicians, and numerous other individuals. "This is my information," he said in the radio interview. "It is not second-hand." US District Judge Marvin Shoob said the claim that the Atlanta branch of the BNL could loan $5 billion to Iraq without the approval of the head office in Rome could only come out of "never-never land". The judge said that manager Drogoul and four other employees at the branch:

> "… were pawns or bit players in a far larger and wider ranging sophisticated conspiracy that involved BNL-Rome and possibly large American and foreign corporations and the governments of the United States, England, Italy and Iraq … smoke is coming out of every window. I have to conclude that the building is on fire." [33]

This is the last thing the Father Bush administration and the Illuminati wanted to hear. Judge Shoob was removed from the case and replaced by Judge Ernest Tidwell, who refused to allow any evidence to be presented about the CIA and the Bush-White House involvement in the bank. Drogoul was persuaded to plead guilty even though he wasn't. The funding of the Iraqi arms build-up before the Gulf War involved the Bush administration, the British government, the Italian government, the Soviet Union and other leading governments controlled by the Illuminati. It also involved another familiar name, Henry Kissinger. As early as 1984 his company Kissinger Associates was arranging for loans from the BNL to Iraq to finance its arms purchases from a little-known subsidiary of Fiat, which was headed by major Illuminati initiate Giovanni Agnelli. Charles Barletta, a former Justice Department investigator, was quoted about this in the US *Spotlight* newspaper on November 9th 1992. The report said:

"Barletta added that Federal probers had collected dozens of such incriminating case histories about the Kissinger firm. But Henry Kissinger seems to possess a kind of immunity. I'm not sure how he does it, but Kissinger wields as much power over the Washington National Security bureaucracy now as in the days when he was the Nixon administration's foreign policy czar. He gets the pay-off; others get the blame. Kissinger will remain unscathed until Congress finds the courage to convene a full-dress investigation into this Teflon power broker."

Home of the brave ...

It is appropriate to focus on the Gulf War before we proceed to 9/11 and the "war on terrorism", for these are mirrors of each other. Same people, same agenda, same methods, same mass slaughter of the innocent. Firstly, as with Afghanistan, the Gulf War wasn't exactly a war. My understanding of a "war" is that you need two sides, and under that definition, the Gulf War was not a "war". It was the military equivalent of putting Mike Tyson in the ring with your granny. American soldiers have described this "war" as a "turkey shoot", which is precisely what it was. The Iraqi army, mainly conscripts who had no choice, may have been armed by the US and Britain, but it was still like trying to stop an elephant with a pop gun. Iraqi men, women and children were subjected to the most intense bombing blitz in human history. Hundreds of thousands died in the bombardment and while the media were showing us pictures provided by the US military of "smart bombs" that could target a building and go through a toilet window, the truth that was being suppressed daily by the military censors was very different. At least 93% of the bombs that rained from the Iraqi skies were not "smart" and that's according to the Pentagon's own numbers, and 70% of them missed their target. Wade Frazier's excellent study of the Gulf "War" reveals the background to just one of the devices used against the Iraqi people:

"The [fuel-air] bomb works thus: there are two detonations; the first spreads a fine mist of fuel into the air, turning the area [about the size of a football field] into an explosive mix of vast proportion; then a second detonation ignites the mixture, causing an awesome explosion. The explosion is about the most powerful 'conventional' explosion we know of.

"At a pressure shock of up to 200 pounds per square inch (PSI), people in its detonation zone are often killed by the sheer compression of the air around them. Human beings can typically withstand up to about a 40-PSI shock. The bomb sucks oxygen out of the air, and can apparently even suck the lungs out through the mouths of people unfortunate enough to be in the detonation zone. Our military used it on helpless people [in the 1991 Gulf Slaughter]." [34]

These were the same weapons used in Afghanistan. The Iraqi people, living, breathing, human beings like you and me, were also subjected to a lovely piece of hardware called a "Big Blue", which produces a shock wave only eclipsed by nuclear weapons. As Wade Frazier points out, the power of the shock wave can turn a body into a hamburger. So-called "bouncing bombs" were also deployed. These are designed to "bounce" to waist height before exploding and ensure a better chance of splattering people into a thousand pieces. These are called "anti-personnel" weapons in the sanitised "newspeak" of the Illuminati front men. Then there was (and is) the "Beehive", which explodes 8,800 pieces of razor-edged shrapnel in all directions, cutting through a human body like the proverbial knife through butter. All these weapons were used against civilian men, women and children in the Gulf "War" and all the others since, including the "war on terrorism". In an oh so rare excursion into reality by the media, John Balzar of the *Los Angeles Times* reported in 1991 on the fate of Iraqi conscripts. He saw night-vision "gun sight" footage from the briefing room:

"They looked like ghostly sheep flushed from a pen – Iraqi infantrymen bewildered and terrified, jarred from sleep and fleeing their bunkers under a hellish fire. One by one, they were cut down by attackers they could not see or understand. Some were blown to bits by bursts of 30-millimeter exploding cannon shells. One man dropped, writhed on the ground, then struggled to his feet; another burst of fire tore him apart ... Even hardened soldiers hold their breath as the Iraqi soldiers, as big as football players on the television screen, run with nowhere to hide. These are not bridges exploding or airplane hangers. These are men."

The same reporter wrote:

"The mechanics of death and destruction are a grim affair. The military's scientific approach and its philosophies – for example, its preference for wounding vital organs over blowing off limbs – can be deeply disquieting to anybody who imagines such matters are left to chance. Many people would rather not know about the gruesome details".[35]

"Nuke 'em, kill 'em all"

This was not a war, it was a mass slaughter by the very forces and controllers who are now waging a "war on terrorism" against anyone they choose to demonise through their pathetic media. These protectors of "freedom" and "liberty" used the same rhetoric then as they do now to justify the mass bombing of civilians. They hide this truth because of the lies so eagerly repeated by journalists who insult our intelligence and a public that has long forgotten, not only what to think, but even how to. Then, as now, no dissent was allowed against the genocide of the innocent by the criminally insane. Talk show hosts, without two brain cells acting in unison, called for nuclear attacks on Iraq and anyone who challenged the "war" was either stupid or a supporter of evil. While the sheeple followed the fox, or Fox, the US government and their British allies were targeting civilian bomb shelters, killing hundreds of fathers, mothers and children because "Intelligence told us that the bomb shelter was actually a military headquarters". Bullshit. These are the same idiots (or coldly calculated killers more like) who bombed a town in Afghanistan a week after the Taliban had left! What people need to realise is that US surveillance satellites can read your car number plate from space; and look at how the *Airman* magazine described the capabilities of the Global Hawk unmanned surveillance plane deployed in Afghanistan:

"On an early test, for example, Global Hawk flew at 56,000 feet over the Naval Weapons Center at China Lake, California. The images it gathered were so clear that an electro-optical image stands out next to an F/A-18 fighter. An infrared image showed where concrete had cooled down from the shadow of a C-130 that had recently taken off." [36]

So there are no "mistakes" about who or what is located in a bomb shelter. It is cold-blooded murder. For the same reason there are no "mistakes" in the failure, at least officially, to establish the location of Osama bin Laden during the invasion of Afghanistan. Reporter Peter Arnett of CNN visited the civilian bomb shelter in Iraq and found it was … a bomb shelter. He also visited a milk factory bombed because it was a "chemical weapons factory" and found it was … a milk factory. In fact he had been there a year before and it was producing … milk.

The Highway of Death

On the ground thousands of Iraqi soldiers were buried alive as "UN" forces used bulldozers to fill in their trenches in fundamental contravention of international law. But nothing sums up the mentality of these deeply sick people currently waging the "war on terrorism" better than the almost unimaginable attacks on the "Highway of Death". The Iraqi army was in retreat in the wake of the air bombardment and headed out of Kuwait across the border to Basra. With them were civilians and prisoners. US pilots attacked the vehicles at the front and back of the seven-mile *retreating* human convoy, so forcing it to a standstill on the open road. They then systematically bombed the convoy, constantly racing back to their aircraft carrier to re-arm and return to continue the mass murder. As one pilot said, it was like "shooting fish in a barrel" and thousands died at the hands of the very people who now "fight terrorism" and promote themselves as morally superior to those they target. Barry McCaffrey, one of the generals involved in this mass murder, was later appointed by President Clinton to head his "war on drugs". Yet, as he conducted these crimes against humanity, Father George Bush's approval ratings soared, just as they did for his son when he continued the long, long, family association with human genocide. The blatant defiance of the Geneva Convention on the Highway of Death produced no action against the Bush administration because there is one law for America, Britain, France and Germany, etc., and a very different one for those they choose to bomb, kill, and mutilate. An International War Crimes Tribunal found President George Bush, Vice President Dan Quayle, Defense Secretary Dick Cheney, Secretary of State James Baker, and military leaders Colin

Powell and Norman Schwarzkopf, guilty of war crimes. But what was done as a result? Nothing. These are the people who have the audacity to put others on trial for war crimes, like the former Serbian leader Slobodan Milosevic.

Dark knights

The Illuminati Queen of England was most grateful to these genocidal maniacs, however, and she made Bush's military chiefs Colin Powell and "Stormin'" Norman Schwarzkopf, (the commander of Operation Desert Storm) Honorary Knights of the British Empire. Schwarzkopf has lied through his teeth about the "mystery" disease known as Gulf War Syndrome that has afflicted veterans of that slaughter. His father would have been proud of him. Norman Schwarzkopf senior had been an important player in the British-American Intelligence coup called Operation AJAX, which removed the Iranian Prime Minister Dr Mohammad Mossadegh in 1953. The Illuminati wanted him ousted after he nationalised oil production and removed the oil cartel's power over his people. The British bloodline Prime Minister Winston Churchill was also behind the coup and Mossadegh was replaced by the dictatorship of the Shah of Iran who reversed the oil nationalisation (see *And The Truth Shall Set You Free*). It is rare for the Queen to give Honorary Knighthoods and other honours to people outside the Commonwealth, but those she has chosen read like an Illuminati Who's Who. The titles are dubbed "honorary" because the American Constitution forbids the acceptance of titles from the monarch of a foreign state without the permission of Congress. So few of these honours are given because, as a British government official put it: "One must not debase the currency." I wonder if you think the following names debase the currency: George Bush, the paedophile, child killer, mass murderer, Satanist and close friend of the Windsors, was made an Honorary Knight Grand Cross of the Order of the Bath, as was Ronald Reagan, Bush's lapdog "President"; Henry Kissinger, the orchestrator of genocide on a monumental scale worldwide, was made Knight Commander of the Order of St Michael and St George at a ceremony at Windsor Castle; Brent Scowcroft, an executive of Kissinger Associates and top adviser to George Bush, was made an Honorary Knight of the British Empire; and Casper Weinberger, another Bush clone who was charged with offences in the Iran-Contra arms scandal and pardoned by Bush, is another Honorary Knight of the British Empire. After the September 11th atrocities, the insider mayor of New York, Rudolph Giuliani, was appointed an Honorary Knight Commander of the Most Excellent Order of the British Empire for doing nothing more than the job he was paid handsomely to do. So why was he such a chosen one? For some more realistic background to "hero" Giuliani and his activities see the website of Robert Lederman, a street artist in New York and a regular columnist for the *Greenwich Village Gazette*.[37]

Burying the truth

The crimes for which the Bush family and their masters and associates are responsible rarely come to light because the media, at the top level, is controlled by the Illuminati and most journalists either don't realise they are pawns in a game or they accept it to protect their careers. The accounts are legion of how evidence and footage that expose the lies, especially in wartime, are banned or confiscated. One example during the 1991 Gulf Slaughter was when the American TV networks NBC and CBS refused to air pictures shot in Iraq of the destruction of civilian areas that revealed the Bush government and military accounts to be a grotesque fiction – just as they are in the "war on terrorism". The story was blocked by the President of NBC Michael Gartner and the producers offered it to CBS, where Tom Bettag, the Executive Editor of the CBS *Evening News*, said one of them would appear on the show the following day to tell their story. That evening Bettag was sacked and the story buried. This is the real background to the TV news.[38] Footage of the Highway of Death was also suppressed and, as in the "war on terrorism", US casualties caused by the enemy were claimed to be "training accidents". Bush's lies about Iraqi troop deployments in Kuwait, provable by satellite images, were also never shown. This satellite "loophole in the lies" was the reason why the US government purchased all rights to satellite pictures of Afghanistan while that country was subjected to another insane American and British bombing onslaught. We should note, of course, that having said that the CIA-installed dictator Saddam Hussein was a threat to the world, and with the Iraqi "army" destroyed, Father George Bush suddenly called an end to the "war" and pulled the troops out leaving Saddam still intact. As Norman Schwarzkopf said with an air of disappointment: "We could have completely closed the door and made it a battle of annihilation … [it was] literally about to become the battle of Cannae, a battle of annihilation." Ah, never mind Norman, but you see your President and those who controlled him wanted Hussein to stay put, or at least appear to, so they could play that card over and over. I suspect, however, that the Saddam story is going to lead to some kind of climax eventually.

Look at this America ...

The public believe the Gulf War ended in 1991, but in fact it was only beginning. Using the "threat" of Saddam, the "threat" Bush chose not to remove when it was there for the taking, the United States and the UK, the diabolical duo of world terrorism, have led a campaign of "sanctions" against Iraq. They have also continued, unreported, the bombing of civilian targets, a policy maintained by the Clinton and Boy George Bush administrations. Investigative journalist John Pilger wrote of a woman he met in northern Iraq who had lost her husband, children and father-in-law when they were bombed by two US planes while tending their sheep on open land.[39] The sanctions against a country that imports 70% of its food have been imposed on a people already devastated by the mass bombing of their electricity, water supply, transport and sewer systems, which the British and American governments have refused to allow them to rebuild. A public health team from Harvard University went into Iraq soon after the official bombing and estimated that over 46,000 children under the age of five had already died by August 1991 because of the destruction of Iraq's infrastructure.[40] But the nightmare was only beginning. Writer Thomas J. Nagy exposed the coldly calculated way the

US military targeted the Iraqi water supply in the full knowledge of the gruesome affect this would have on the people, especially children. In an article headed "The Secret Behind the Sanctions: How the US Intentionally Destroyed Iraq's Water Supply", he wrote that "the United States knew the cost that civilian Iraqis, mostly children, would pay, and it went ahead anyway." [41] Nagy, who lectures at the School of Business and Public Management at George Washington University, uncovered documents from the US Defense Intelligence Agency that reveal a stunning disregard for human life. A document dated January 22nd 1991 says:

"Iraq depends on importing specialized equipment and some chemicals to purify its water supply ... Failing to secure supplies will result in a shortage of pure drinking water for much of the population. This could lead to increased incidences, if not epidemics, of disease." They add that the "most likely diseases during [the] next 60-90 days [include]: diarrhoeal diseases (particularly children); acute respiratory illnesses (colds and influenza); typhoid; hepatitis A (particularly children); measles, diphtheria, and pertussis (particularly children); meningitis, including meningococcal (particularly children); cholera (possible, but less likely)." [42]

This is a fundamental violation of the Geneva Convention which says:

"It is prohibited to attack, destroy, remove, or render useless objects indispensable to the survival of the civilian population, such as foodstuffs, crops, livestock, drinking water installations and supplies, and irrigation works, for the specific purpose of denying them for their sustenance value to the civilian population or to the adverse party, whatever the motive."

The US/British-led sanctions against Iraq do all of these things.

By 1995 Secretary of State Madeleine Albright was forced to admit on the US *Sixty Minutes* television programme that these sanctions had already cost the lives of *half a million* Iraqi children and that was only up to then. The figure is currently running at some 5,000 dead children a month and passing a *million* in total, while the perpetrators lead a "war on terrorism"! Albright said on *Sixty Minutes* that she thought the consequences for those children were worth it to stop Saddam. This is the mentality that controls our world. A report by Richard Garfield of Columbia University concluded that the increase in child death rates in Iraq was virtually unique in modern health studies. [43] Conditions like kwashiorkor and marasmus, the result of starvation, are now common. We are told of the horrific treatment of women by the Taliban regime in Afghanistan, but not of the same treatment by Saudi Arabia, a brutal, fascist regime, which is on the side of the "good guys" in the "war against sanity"; and we are told nothing about the plight of women in Iraq in the face of the US and British-led sanctions. Some 70% of Iraqi women are now anaemic. Denis Halliday, the coordinator of the so-called "oil-for-food" programme, resigned in September 1998 and spoke out against the genocidal affects of the sanctions. His successor, Hans von Sponeck, did the same in February 2000. The US government response was to try to discredit the two men. The "oil for food" farce provides the oil cartel with cheap Iraqi oil; 40% of Iraqi's oil, exchanged to buy food, ends up in the United States at knock-down prices because of the sanctions imposed by the United States and supported by the Illuminati front, the United Nations.

The sanctions are "justified" in part because of the "weapons of mass destruction", including biological weapons, claimed to be stockpiled by Saddam Hussein. Well, first, the Iraqi arsenal, whatever it may be, was funded by the US and British governments and their allies. Second, the biggest owner of weapons of mass destruction on the planet is the American government and by far the greatest user of them is ... the US government. Only one government has dropped nuclear weapons on another country at the time of writing ... the US government. British leaders, too, have an appalling record of genocide and as far back as 1919, when Winston Churchill was Secretary of State at the War Office, they were using chemical weapons against Iraq. Churchill said this about the use of poison gas to put down an Iraqi rebellion against colonial rule: "I do not understand this squeamishness about the use of gas. I am strongly in favour of using [it] against uncivilised tribes." [44] When Saddam Hussein offered in 1990 to destroy such weapons in Iraq if Israel did the same with theirs, the United States government said it was not willing to negotiate on that subject – not least because to acknowledge that Israel has a massive nuclear capability would make illegal the billions of dollars of US aid to that country every year.[45] They all know of Israel's nuclear stockpile, but if no one officially admits it exists they can go on with business as usual. As the former United Nations Secretary-General, Boutros Boutros-Ghali said: "It would be some time before I fully realised that the United States sees little need for diplomacy. Power is enough. Only the weak rely on diplomacy ... The Roman Empire had no need for diplomacy. Nor does the United States." [46] It appears to see no need to tell the truth, either. In early 1999, it was revealed that the Iraqis' claims about United Nations weapon inspections in their country was correct. The UNSCOM inspections were being used for spying by the United States. The *Washington Post* of March 2nd quoted US officials who described how members of the UNSCOM team had been planting spying devices for the United States during their "independent inspections". Scott Ritter, one of the weapons inspectors in Iraq, made it clear that the United States and British governments were lying about the dangers posed by Iraq – the very "dangers" they have used to justify their onslaught against Iraqi civilians, especially children. Ritter said in the June 2000 edition of *Arms Control Today*:

> "Given the comprehensive nature of the monitoring regime put in place by UNSCOM, which included a strict export-import control regime, it was possible as early as 1997 to determine that, from a qualitative standpoint, Iraq had been disarmed. Iraq no longer possessed any meaningful quantities of chemical or biological agent, if it possessed any at all, and the industrial means to produce these agents had either been eliminated

or were subject to stringent monitoring. The same was true of Iraq's nuclear and ballistic missile capabilities.

" … By the end of 1998, Iraq had, in fact, been disarmed to a level unprecedented in modern history, but UNSCOM and the Security Council were unable – and in some instances unwilling – to acknowledge this accomplishment."

Why? Because it would have destroyed the cover story necessary to continue the genocide. Add to that the voting record of the United States at the United Nations where it has consistently opposed resolutions to limit the production and testing of biological and nuclear weapons, as it has on a stream of humanitarian and freedom issues. Robert Cooper, a former diplomat and personal assistant for foreign affairs to British Prime Minister, Tony Blair, admitted in *The Post-Modern State and the World Order*: "We need to get used to the idea of double standards … [in other words] … get over it, we are hypocrites (but powerful ones)." Cooper said that the conflict with Iraq was to maintain control of oil supplies and that " … The reasons for fighting the Gulf War were not that Iraq had violated the norms of international behaviour …". Exactly. They just use any excuse to sell a lie to the people to advance their agenda – as they have with September 11th. When Saddam Hussein used chemical weapons on the Kurdish people, the United States and Britain didn't say a word because he was a US ally at the time, fighting the Iraq-Iran war in which the US and Britain were arming both sides. The forces of freedom and liberty have also been bombing Iraq with radioactive weapons and this has led to the birth of babies with horrible deformities and disease (see my website). Since this bombardment began, Iraq has developed the world's highest rate of childhood leukaemia. At the same time there has been an embargo on medicines and technology that would help to reduce the radiation. The genocidal attacks on the Iraqi population began with "Republican" George Bush, continued with "Democrat" Bill Clinton, and within a month of taking office at the start of 2001, George W. Bush, another "Republican", was ordering (being told to order) more "routine" bombing of Iraq. In truth they are just lackeys for the same one-party state and that's why the policies never change no matter who is in the White House.

The bank of crooks and criminals (BCCI)

The funding and manipulation of the Gulf War connects with another scandal, that of the Bank of Credit and Commerce International. This had close links with the Italian BNL, the bank used by the United States to bankroll Saddam Hussein. A brief summary of the BCCI debacle is necessary because of the people involved and the connections from the BCCI through to current events. The BCCI was formed in the early 1970s and expanded rapidly to boast 400 branches in 78 countries. Its name is remarkably similar to the Banque De Credit International (BCI) of the Mossad agent Rabbi Tibor Rosenbaum, which was used by the British-American Intelligence network involved in the assassination of President Kennedy (see *And The Truth Shall Set You Free*). Its "successor", the BCCI, was a major player in the drug money-laundering network and was used for this purpose by Illuminati elements within the CIA, British Intelligence and Mossad. Money to fund covert operations, terrorists groups like those of Osama bin Laden and Abu Nidal, coups and assassinations throughout the world, and the financing of Iran-Contra and Saddam Hussein, was also channelled through the BCCI. Former US Green Beret Albert Carone claimed he was a representative of the BCCI while working on covert operations. He said the bank was founded by the US intelligence community to finance covert operations worldwide without the approval of Congress.[47] In other words, to finance the Illuminati agenda. Money could be transferred between apparent enemies through this network, as with Saudi Arabian money, which found its way to Mossad. In this case, Saudi and other Gulf money was laundered through the BCCI and transferred to CenTrust in Miami, which was later seized by Federal investigators. The BCCI owned 28% of CenTrust. Allegations emerged that Robert Gates, the man Bush nominated as his Director of the CIA, had obstructed an investigation into drug money laundering by the BCCI. Gates withdrew his nomination to be CIA Director, as he had once before when implicated in Iran-Contra. The BCCI crashed amid a worldwide scandal in 1991. It was the world's biggest banking collapse and cost investors billions of dollars. Three years before the crash, Robert Gates was describing the BCCI as the Bank of Crooks and Criminals. The BCCI began to operate in Pakistan in 1972 with most of its funding provided by the Bank of America and the CIA. Bank of America also loaned money to people to buy stock in BCCI, probably to hide the scale of its control, and the B of A knew all about money laundering. In 1986, it was fined $7 million for 17,000 acts of washing dirty money. Some researchers say that the Rothschilds control the Bank of America. At the hub of the Rothschild involvement in the BCCI was Doctor Alfred Hartmann who, at the same time, was the managing director of the Swiss branch of the BCCI; the head of the Zurich Rothschild bank, AG; a board member of N.M. Rothschild in London; and a director of … Italy's BNL, the bank through which the Bush government covertly funded Saddam Hussein. The involvement of the Rothschilds at the heart of the BCCI was never mentioned or investigated by the media, nor was the alleged involvement of the financier and currency speculator, George Soros, of the Illuminati Bilderberg Group.

Here a Bush, there a Bush, everywhere a Bush, Bush

Father George Bush and his successor Bill Clinton both had considerable connections with the BCCI. Among them was Jackson Stephens. He is the owner of Stephens Incorporated, a big investment bank based in Little Rock, Arkansas, the home of Bill Clinton. Stephens was one of the founders of the BCCI. He had connections with a company called Harken Energy and arranged a loan for them from a Swiss bank affiliated with the BCCI. This would have greatly pleased George W. Bush, the then President's son, who sat on the Harken board and had a fortune invested in the company. Another investor in Harken Energy, it emerged after September 11th, was Khalid bin Mahfouz, the operations director of the BCCI and 20% shareholder who was later named by the United States government as a financial supporter of Osama bin Laden. What a coincidence. Jeb Bush, Boy George's brother and now Governor of Florida, also had numerous dealings with the BCCI. He was often seen in the bank's Miami office and Father George's deputy campaign manager, James Lake, worked for a major owner of the BCCI at the time. When Bill Clinton, Father Bush's "opponent", ran for president, his main financial backer was the same Jackson Stephens who made the donations via his Worthen National Bank, which was connected to the BCCI. Stephens was implicated in deals in which the BCCI secretly and illegally took over the First American Bank of Washington and others. This was the man who funded the Bushes and the Clintons.

Father George's involvement with the BCCI was considerable, according to the Chicago journalist, Sherman Skolnick, who made a detailed study of the bank. He has claimed publicly, including an interview on Radio Free America, that Bush, Saddam Hussein, and others, used the BCCI to split $250 billion in oil "kick backs", the skimming-off of money paid by western oil companies in the Gulf. Other researchers and insiders have said the same. Skolnick claims that the records implicating Bush in deals with Saddam and former Panama President Manuel Noriega were in the hands of the Bank of England and that the money was channelled through the BCCI and Banca Nazionale del Lavoro (BNL) branches in the USA. Henry Gonzales, the chairman of the House Banking Committee, identified links between the BCCI and BNL. Skolnick told interviewer Tom Valentine on Radio Free America:

> "[The BCCI] ... was formed in the 1970s with seed money from the Bank of America, the largest shareholders of which are the Rothschilds of Chicago, Paris, London, and Switzerland ... The bank is also linked to the financial affairs of former President Jimmy Carter and his friend, and one-time budget director, banker Bert Lance.

> "Some of the ... Democrats who have been involved in this whole affair have been published, for example, in the May 3rd issue of the Wall Street Journal. During the 1988 presidential campaign, additionally, BCCI was one of the major financiers of the Michael Dukakis campaign ... BCCI financed the Democratic Party in the United States and arranged deals for Republicans outside the United States." [48]

Jimmy Carter personally dedicated a number of BCCI branches and they made an $8.5 million donation to one of his favourite charities. Carter's foreign travel after he left the White House was paid for by the BCCI and his banker friend Bert Lance was bailed out of big financial difficulties by Gaith Pharaon, a front man for the BCCI. Andrew Young, Carter's former United Nations ambassador, and a fellow member of the Illuminati's Trilateral Commission, had a loan of $160,000 written off by the BCCI and was paid to promote the bank to individuals and governments in Africa and Central America. Orrin Hatch, the Republican Senator for Utah, was making stirring speeches in support of the BCCI even while it was being indicted for drug money laundering. This is the same Orrin Hatch who told CNN immediately after the planes struck the World Trade Center that officials believed that Osama bin

Laden could be responsible.[49] The Democrat Clark Clifford and his law partner Robert Altman, the BCCI's lawyers, were at the centre of the story, also. Pricewaterhouse, the BCCI's auditors for nearly 20 years, were giving the bank a largely clean bill of health while all the corruption was going on. Skolnick said records detailing the alleged Bush-Saddam deals were held in the Chicago branch of the BCCI, which was seized by the Federal government in 1988. Skolnick went on:

"The same bank has records showing joint business ventures between General Manuel Noriega, former dictator of Panama, and George Bush. In January of 1990, the Federal prosecutor in Tampa had former top officials of Florida's branch on trial. They were allowed to escape prison with only a slap on the wrist and a small penalty. Here's why: they told the Justice Department that if they were going to prison, they had documents from their bank showing that George Bush had private business ventures through their bank with a series of dictators including not only Saddam and Noriega, but others as well ...

"... Saddam's oil was shipped to Texas. In 1985 a Texas jury, at the behest of Pennzoil, issued the largest damages verdict in American history against Texaco. Pennzoil claimed that Texaco damaged them in a deal with Getty Oil. Who owns Pennzoil? George Bush and his friends ... as a result Texaco fell under the domination and supervision of Pennzoil. Where did the kickbacks to Saddam reportedly come from? They came from deals between Texaco and its subsidiaries purchasing oil from Iraq." [50]

You can leave your lid on ...

If you placed end to end all the questions that Father George Bush needs to answer, but won't, they would stretch from Washington to Baghdad. An official investigation was ordered to investigate the BCCI scandal and was chaired by Democrat Senator, John Kerry, of Massachusetts. It exposed nothing. Senator Kerry was chairman of the Democratic Senate Campaign Committee that received large contributions from the BCCI and he is also a member of the Skull and Bones Society. The corruption across American politics, media, banking, business and the military is simply staggering, and so it is in the United Kingdom wing of the Illuminati, where the BCCI had its main base. The British Prime Minister at the time of the cover-up was John Major who is now a business associate of Father George Bush, who was US President at the time. The British "inquiry" report on the bank by Lord Justice Bingham decided that the collapse was due to "a tragedy of errors, misunderstandings, and failures of communication". For goodness sake, it was one of the biggest drug money, terrorist-funding, and illegal arms money laundering operations the world has yet seen. It implicated some of the biggest names in global politics, banking and business, and financed terrorists, drug cartels and covert operations by British Intelligence, the CIA and others of that ilk. The Bank of England completed the cover-up through an arrangement with Abu Dhabi, the bank's principal owners at the time of the collapse. This agreement allowed important records and witnesses to leave Britain. How convenient. In his review of *Dirty Money*, a book about the BCCI, the journalist Robert Sherrill said:

"Dirty Money clearly leaves the impression that many officials are less than enthusiastic about digging deeper into the scandal. Could it be because of that rumoured list of 100 politicians that the BCCI paid off? Or because 'key investigators' have indicated that if they continued their probe it might take them 'into the highest levels of political power around the world' in ways that would dwarf even the wildest conspiracy theory. Whoa! That would never do." [51]

The invasion of Panama

Readers new to this information will no doubt be extremely surprised to see the names of Saddam Hussein and General Manuel Noriega so closely connected to Father George Bush. After all, didn't he invade both of their countries on the pretext of removing their "terrorist" regimes? Ah, but that's the movie version for public consumption. The real story, as always, is very different – just as it is with September 11th. The Bush attack on Panama on December 20th 1989 was about drugs, although not in the way it was portrayed by the government and the media. This is another fine example of how the truth of the situation is submerged in political rhetoric and media camouflage. We are told that American troops invaded Panama and abducted President Manuel Noriega because of his drug-running activities and to save American children from the evil of drugs. In fact, the opposite was the case. Noriega was on the payroll of the CIA while Bush was its Director and he was being paid some $110,000 a year for his "services", which included running drugs. When Bush was challenged about this after the invasion of Panama, he said he had never met Noriega, but then suddenly remembered the meeting. Noriega was involved in drug trafficking and rigged elections, but the Bush government and the CIA knew that when they employed him. William Tyree, a former member of the elite US Green Beret regiment, said in testimony for a law-suit against George Bush and the CIA filed in 1998 that he flew more than 100 plane loads of cocaine from Colombia to the Albrook Air Station in Panama between December 1975 and March 1976 as part of "Operation Watchtower". Looking on as the cocaine was unloaded, he said, were CIA officers, an Israeli colonel and Manuel Noriega. Tyree filed the suit in an effort to prove his innocence after being jailed for the murder of his wife, Elaine. She kept a diary of her husband's drug-running activities for the CIA and George Bush, and when Tyree began to speak out about his experiences his wife was murdered, the diary stolen, and he was framed for the killing in 1979. Tyree alleged in the suit that Father George Bush ordered the theft and destruction of his wife's diary. Another Green Beret, Colonel Albert Carone, described how he worked with Oliver North in drug trafficking during Iran-Contra. Carone was murdered in 1990 and five other Special Forces colonels also involved have died in mysterious circumstances. Carone's testimony was among the documents presented by Tyree in the lawsuit, which, of course, was covered up. [52]

Arnulfo Arias won the 1984 Panama election, but Noriega took power with a mixture of extreme violence and fraud. The US Secretary of State George Shultz, a major Illuminati operator, was dispatched to give legitimacy to Noriega and even to declare that Panama's democratic principles were a lesson to the Sandinista government in Nicaragua! According to Noriega, his relationship with Bush began to change during the Iran-Contra period when Admiral John Poindexter, the head of the National Security Council, visited him on December 17th 1985. Poindexter was prosecuted for his part in Iran-Contra. Noriega told CBS reporter Mike Wallace that Poindexter demanded that he support the illegal US war against the Sandinista government in Nicaragua. When he refused, Poindexter threatened economic warfare and the destabilisation of Panama. What Poindexter wanted was for Panama to invade Nicaragua with American support, Noriega said.[53] At no point was Noriega's alleged involvement in drugs mentioned. But the US Drug Enforcement Administration (DEA) did contact him about drugs. They wrote to congratulate him on helping them to stop Panama being used as a drug and drug money-laundering centre! Just one month later, the Reagan-Bush administration demanded that Noriega be removed on the grounds of drugs, corruption, and lack of democracy. This from a government that, through agencies like the CIA, has supported and imposed some of the most grotesque dictatorships across the world to suit its own agenda, including the financing of terrorists to murder woman and children by the thousand. The same government that said Panamanian democracy was a lesson to Nicaragua. It is not easy to establish the motivation of Drug Enforcement Administration agents because among them are both people committed to stopping the flow of drugs into America and others equally determined to increase it. A number of DEA and CIA operatives have described how some officials of the Drug Enforcement Administration are involved in expanding the availability of hard drugs on the streets of the United States. Noriega's former chief adviser, José Blandon, has claimed that the DEA has protected the biggest players in the drug empires and that DEA officials paid Noriega $4.7 million to keep quiet. Dennis Dale, who headed a DEA operation in Central America, said in testimony that "… the major targets of my investigations almost invariably turned out to be working for the CIA".[54] In February 1988, Noriega was indicted on drugs charges and all but one were related to activities before 1984 when he was on the CIA payroll. Economic sanctions against Panama followed – the economic warfare that Poindexter had promised. If Noriega had agreed to support the US with Nicaragua, or hadn't fallen out with Bush, he would still be dictator of Panama instead of sitting in a US jail.

When Bush officially became President in 1989, he made the ludicrous statement that Panama posed an "unusual and extraordinary threat" to US National Security and foreign policy. *US News and World Report* said on May 1st 1989 that Bush had authorised $10 million in CIA expenditure on projects against the Panama government. Some of the money was delivered by the CIA's Carlos Eleta Almaran, who had recently been arrested for drug trafficking. Bush ordered those charges to be dropped after Noriega was ousted. By December 20th 1989, with Noriega still there despite the CIA's best efforts, United States forces invaded Panama. Thousands of civilians, including children, were killed. This was covered up by the Bush administration, but I have seen video footage of the devastation in civilian areas caused by the US attacks – areas that housed some of the poorest people in the country. The lives of the poor had already been devastated by US economic warfare. Noriega was abducted to America for trial and jailed on drugs charges. The rest of the "free world", including Britain's Margaret Thatcher, offered not a word of protest. The judge at his trial refused to allow any CIA documents to be seen in his defence and he was sentenced to 40 years' imprisonment. What, therefore, should Bush and other government and CIA officials receive if they ever came to trial? They would have to reincarnate many times to complete the sentence. One of the key prosecution witnesses in the "trial" of Noriega was Carlos Lehder. He is a co-founder of the Medellin drug cartel in Colombia and a business partner of the Bush family, who are fundamentally involved in the Medellin operation.[55] Lehder, real name Carlos Enrique Lehder Rivas, was extradited to the US on drugs charges and gave evidence against Noriega while saying nothing about the Bush connection. He was given a much-reduced sentence for his own drug convictions and then apparently "disappeared" from the US prison system.[56] The "leaders" the Bush regime imposed on the people of Panama to replace Noriega were fundamentally connected with the money-laundering and drug-trafficking business. The new President, Guillermo Endara, was on official of at least six banks involved in drug money-laundering. The money laundered through these sources came from the Colombian drug-smuggling ring led by Augusto Falcon and Salvador Magluta, who were reported to be smuggling one ton of cocaine a month into Florida from the late 1970s until 1987.[57] The new Vice President in Panama installed by Bush was Ricardo Arias Calderon whose brother was president of the First Interamericas Bank when it was controlled by the Cali drug cartel. Official figures show that drug trafficking and money laundering in Panama after Noriega was ousted was greater than it had been when he was there. The invasion and US (Illuminati) puppet regimes that have followed also ensured that the United States would retain control of the Panama Canal zone that was officially handed back to Panama in 1999.

The truth of what really happened in Panama was suppressed – as it was in Afghanistan, Iraq, Kosovo, Bosnia ad infinitum – by the government and military control of the media. What happened in Panama happens everywhere these disturbed people take their murder machine. The media were not allowed to go anywhere that did not suit the official story and they were presented with "news" conferences in which US officials told the reporters whatever they wanted the people to believe. Other non-American journalists were arrested and a Spanish news photographer, Juantxu Rodriguez, was shot dead by US soldiers while he was taking incriminating pictures of what was really happening. There is, in fact, no independent footage of the three days of the invasion, only what the Bush government said had happened, and the Bush forces took over Panamanian television stations to broadcast their own propaganda. Can you imagine what the United States and Britain would say if any other country did this? These two are the bullies of the world. It was the same with those who campaigned for democracy or opposed the US invasion. Thousands of such people on the "dissident" lists (human rights campaigners, independent newspaper editors, union leaders and so on) were jailed without trial or even charge. Some stayed there for years. This systematic cover-up hid the fact that thousands of civilians were killed by the Bush invasion, not the 250 he claimed, and that tens of thousands were made homeless. Mass graves have since been uncovered of those who died unreported at the hands of Bush. (See the superb video, *The Panama Deception*,[58] which has pictures that Bush and his henchmen worked so hard to suppress).

Bush the child abuser

George Bush and his associate Henry Kissinger are mass murderers on a scale that beggars belief and so are those who support them and make it possible. The list of Illuminati slaughter and financial manipulation goes on and on with the manufactured wars and the CIA/British Intelligence-imposed dictators and killers placed in power across the world in Vietnam, Cambodia, Laos, Korea, Nicaragua, Panama, Grenada, Indonesia, Bosnia, Kosovo, Iraq and Afghanistan to name only a few. The dead, maimed, starving, destitute and dispossessed that have ensued can be numbered in billions of our fellow men, women and children. Now they have launched a "war on terrorism" that allows them to target any country they choose. But then why should people who sexually and violently abuse and murder little children have any emotional attachment to the suffering they daily orchestrate? Far fetched? No, no. If you read *The Biggest Secret*, *Children Of The Matrix*, and other books by researchers and victims of these people, you'll see this is no fantasy. George Bush, for example, is a notorious paedophile, torturer and killer of children among those who have researched this. In a book called *Trance-formation Of America*,[59] Cathy O'Brien, a mind-controlled slave of people like Bush and Dick Cheney for the first 30 years of her life, tells of her own and her daughter's abuse by Bush. Daughter Kelly was only a small child when Bush began his sexual and violent abuse of her, born as she was into the captivity in which her mother had long been imprisoned. This is just one of her experiences with President George Bush, father and controller of George W. Bush in the "war on terrorism. Alex Houston was her CIA handler in the US government mind-control programme known as MK Ultra:

> "Kelly became violently, physically ill after her induction into George Bush's 'neighborhood' and from every sexual encounter she had with him thereafter, she ran 104-6 degree temperatures, vomited and endured immobilizing headaches for an average of three days. These were the only telltale evidences aside from the scarring burns left on her skin. Houston forbade me to call a doctor, and Kelly forbade me to comfort her, pitifully complaining that her head 'hurt too bad even to move'. And she did not move for hours on end. Kelly often complained of severe kidney pain and her rectum usually bled for a day or two after Bush sexually abused her. My own mind-control victimization rendered me unable to help or protect her ...

"Kelly's bleeding rectum was ... one of [the] ... physical indicators of George Bush's pedophile perversions. I have overheard of him speak blatantly of his sexual abuse of her on many occasions. He used this and threats to her life to 'pull my strings' and control me. The psychological ramifications of being raped by a paedophile president are mind shattering enough, but reportedly Bush further reinforced his traumas to Kelly's mind with sophisticated NASA electronic and drug mind controlled devices. Bush also instilled the 'Who ya gonna call?' and 'I'll be watching you' binds on Kelly, further reinforcing her sense of helplessness. The systematic tortures and traumas I endured as a child now seem trite in comparison to the brutal, physical and psychological devastation that Bush inflicted on my daughter." [60]

This man was in the White House for 12 years and now his son is president. Such a mentality would not plan and execute what happened on September 11th, an event that has so massively advanced the Illuminati agenda for a global fascist state? You must be joking. It is their modus operandi in every way.

SOURCES

1   Brian Downing Quig, Who Dismantled Our Constitution?, *Grapevine* (January 2nd 1995)

2   *New Yorker* (November 27th 1989), p 108

3   Cathy O'Brien and Mark Phillips, *Trance-Formation Of America* (Reality Marketing Inc., Las Vegas, USA, 1995)

4   Anton Chaitkin and Webster Griffin Tarpley, *George Bush, The Unauthorised Biography* (Executive Intelligence Review, Washington DC, 1992)

5   See **http://serendipity.magnet.ch/jsmill/bushcrimefamily.htm** for this information and a long list of links detailing Bush family crimes

6   **http://serendipity.magnet.ch/jsmill/bushnz1.htm**

7   *Monetary and Economic Review*, December 1992, **http://www.dcia.com/campaign.html**

8   Russell S. Bowen, *The Immaculate Deception* (American West, Carson City, 1991)

9   Ibid, pp 30–31

10   Ibid

11   See Michael Collin Piper, *Final Judgement, The Missing Link in the JFK Assassination Conspiracy* (The Wolfe Press, Washington DC, 1995), pp 306-313

12   *New York Times*, February 18th 1976

13   See **http://www.disinfo.com/pages/dossier/id195/pg1/**

14   Ibid.

15   George C. Andrews, *Extraterrestrials Among Us* (Llewellyn Publications, St Paul, Minnesota, 1993), p 175

16   George Bush, the Unauthorised Biography, p 397

17   Ibid, p 399

18   *Atlantic Monthly Press*, 1987

19   Colonel Carone's statement was included in a lawsuit filed on September 4th 1998 by former Green Beret William Tyree detailing the drug-running activities of Father George Bush and the CIA

20   See Ruppert's articles on the CIA drug networks at **www.copvcia.com.http://www.fromthewilderness.com/free/ciadrugs/index.html**

21   *New York Times*, March 2nd 1989

22   George C. Andrews, *Extraterrestrial Friends and Foes* (IllumiNet Press, Lilburn, GA, USA, 1993), p 288

23   *George Bush, The Unofficial Biography*, p 515 or **http://www.lanesend.com/about/**

24   Transcript of the meeting released by the Iraqis and quoted in *The Immaculate Deception*, pp 146–147

25   Quoted in *Extra-Terrestrial Friends and Foes*, p 287

26   *Washington Post*, May 26th 1991

27   *Washington Post*, September 12th 1990

28   See **http://www.senate.gov/~rpc/rva/1032/1032147.htm** for more background

29   Rodney Stich, *Defrauding America* (Diablo Western Press, Alamo, California, 1994), p 426

30   Inside the Shadow CIA, *Spy Magazine*, September 1992

31   Ibid

32   Transcribed by Leading Edge Research Group **http://www.cco.net/~trufax**, posted at **http://www.alienobserver.com/files/text/kawa2.html**

33   *Defrauding America*, p 430

34   Wade Frazier's articles can be found at **http://home1.gte.net/res0k62m/iraq.htm** and **http://home1.gte.net/res0k62m/iraq.htm**

35   *Los Angeles Times*, February 24th 1991

36   **http://www.af.mil/news/airman/1101/hawk.html**

37   **http://baltech.org/lederman/giuliani-wtc-collapse-3-01-02.html**

38   **http://www.thirdworldtraveler.com/Project%20Censored/CensoredNews_1991.html**

39   William Thomas, *All Fall Down* (Essence Publications, 2002), p 50

40   **http://home1.gte.net/res0k62m**

41   **http://www.davidicke.net/newsroom/america/usa**

42   **http://www.progressive.org/0801issue/nagy0901.html**

43   See Richard Garfield's full report at **http://www.backflip.com/perl/go.pl?url=12664166**

44   **http://www.oneworld.net/guides/cbweapons/front.shtml**

45   *Boston Globe*, April 14th 1990

46 **http://www.zmag.org/ZMag/kosovo.htm**

47 **http://www.nexusmagazine.com/beast2.html**

48 Radio Free America, March 28th 1991. See also Sherman Skolnick's website at **http://www.skolnicksreport.com/.http://www.skolnicksreport.com**

49 *Defrauding America*, p 408–409

50 Radio Free America, March 28th 1991

51 *Washington Post* National Weekly Edition, April 13th to 19th 1992, p 34

52 See **http://www.radio4all.org/crackcia/tyree.html** for more background to this lawsuit

53 Panama: Atrocities of the Big Stick, *American Leviathan*, p 39–40

54 *All Fall Down*, p122

55 **http://www.skolnicksreport.com/ootar3.html**

56 Ibid

57 *George Bush, The Unofficial Biography*, p537

58 Panama Deception available from **http://www.amazon.com.www.amazon.com**

59 Cathy O'Brien and Mark Phillips, *Trance Formation Of America* (Reality Marketing Inc., Las Vegas, Nevada, USA, 1995)

60 Ibid, p 158. See also *The Biggest Secret* for the wider background to the Illuminati mind control and Satanic ritual networks

chapter 3

Born to be king

"It is better to remain silent and be thought a fool than to open one's mouth and remove all doubt."

Voltaire

George W. "Boy George" Bush was born on July 6th 1946 in New Haven, Connecticut, the home of Yale University and the Skull and Bones Society, but he was raised in Texas. From the moment of birth, probably even before if you read of the Illuminati "in the womb" techniques described in *The Biggest Secret*, he was, like his father, groomed and moulded to serve the Illuminati cause, and a look at his background presents September 11th and current events in a very different perspective. He attended Yale University and was initiated into the Skull and Bones Society and later Bohemian Grove before studying, at least in theory, at the Harvard Business School. Bush avoided the draft to Vietnam, a war created and perpetuated by the Illuminati who controlled his father. *Washington Post* staff writers George Lardner Jr and Lois Romano revealed in an article in 1999 how two weeks before he was due to graduate from Yale, Bush arrived at the offices of the Texas Air National Guard at Ellington Field outside Houston and said he wanted to sign up for pilot training.[1] This was on May 27th 1968 when the Vietnam War was at its peak with some 350 Americans dying every week and goodness knows how many Vietnamese. In 12 days' time he would have lost his student immunity from the draft and so he grasped, with his father's help, an escape route from combat by joining the National Guard. Father George was at this time a Congressman for Houston, and a supporter of the Vietnam conflict and the policy of sending American soldiers there to suffer and die.

Many of the American elite were trying to pull the same trick for their sons and the National Guard had a long waiting list. Not only that, Boy George had scored only 25% in a pilot aptitude test and that was the lowest acceptable grade. That will surprise no one with a brain who sees him today, and all these factors should have prevented his admission and, therefore, his avoidance of the draft to Vietnam. Yet, wait for this … Boy George was sworn in as an airman with the Texas Air National Guard on the *same day* that he applied. Colonel Walter B. "Buck" Staudt, the commander of the 147th Fighter Group, even staged a special ceremony later so he could be photographed administering the oath for Bush instead of the captain who had sworn in Bush earlier. Staudt did the same when Bush was commissioned as a second lieutenant. Lloyd Bentsen Jr, a major Texas Democrat, ensured that his son, Lloyd Bentsen III, was enlisted into the National Guard by Staudt around the same time as Bush. Both were nominated for promotion to first lieutenant on the Election Day in 1970 when Father Bentsen beat Father Bush for a seat in the Senate. Other Vietnam avoiders in the Texas National Guard included the son of Republican Senator John Tower and at least seven members of the Dallas Cowboys American football team. The *Washington Post* article revealed:

> "One address for those seeking help getting in was Ben Barnes, a Democrat who was then the speaker of the Texas House and a protégé of Governor John B. Connally. A top aide to Barnes, Nick Kralj, simultaneously served as aide to the head of the Texas Air National Guard, the late Brigadier General James M. Rose.

> "An anonymous letter addressed to a US attorney in Texas, produced in a discovery proceeding for an ongoing lawsuit, charged that Barnes assisted Bush in getting into the Guard. The suit was brought by the former director of the Texas Lottery Commission, who believes that Barnes, now a lobbyist, may have played a role in his dismissal.

> "In a deposition for the suit, Kralj confirmed that he would get calls from Barnes or his chief of staff, Robert Spelling, 'saying so-and-so is interested in getting in the Guard.' Kralj said he would then forward the names to Gen. Rose." [2]

When the obvious questions were asked about this at the time of Bush's run for the presidency, Staudt said that no favouritism had been shown to him. You are a liar Colonel Staudt, as any idiot can see. Talking of which, Bush claimed he did not join the National Guard to avoid the Vietnam War that he and his father supported, but rather because he wanted to be a fighter pilot. OK, insult my intelligence some more. Even on his National Guard application forms he ticked the box saying, "do not volunteer" when asked if he wanted to go overseas. Not only did he avoid going to Vietnam, he was even able to live in his then home town of Houston while learning to be a pilot who was never to face a conflict. He served as an F-102 pilot with the Texas Air National Guard to avoid the draft to Vietnam and became a hard-drinking, cocaine-snorting, womaniser before "discovering Jesus" (I know, I know, of course that last bit is ludicrous, but this is the official story). On November 5th 1977 the annual anniversary of the Guy Fawkes (Percy-Bush family) plot to blow up the British Parliament, Bush married former teacher and librarian, Laura Welch, who is used to smokescreen his real lifestyle, and they have two teenage daughters, Barbara and Jenna.

Snort, snort

Bush's drug habit was brought to public attention – and then buried by the media – with the publication of the book, *Fortunate Son: George Bush and the Making of a*

President, in 1999. The author J.H. Hatfield was subjected to a national campaign of character assassination after he claimed that Bush was arrested on drug charges in 1972 while serving with the National Guard, but that this had been wiped from the record by a Republican judge and friend of his father in exchange for Bush's participation in a community service programme called Project PULL in Houston's inner city. The author cites three anonymous sources to support his claim. What is for sure is that suddenly, and for no credible reason, this hard-drinking playboy felt an overwhelming desire to volunteer to work with black inner-city kids in Project PULL. After Hatfield's character was attacked by the media and pressure from the Bush camp, the publisher, St Martin's Press, withdrew the book. But in early 2000 it was republished by Soft Skull Press, a small title on New York's Lower East Side, and the publisher, Sander Hicks, released a document from the Texas Air National Guard, which reveals that Bush was suspended from flying for failure to take a medical exam in the same period that Hatfield says he was busted for cocaine possession. Bush's 175-page National Guard service records were obtained by Hicks from the Department of Defense through the Freedom of Information Act. They note the verbal orders of the "Comdr on 1 Aug 72" suspending Bush, a 27-year-old first lieutenant, for "failure to accomplish annual medical examination" while stationed at Ellington Air Force Base in Houston. Hicks, who says he knows the identity of the three unconnected Hatfield sources, writes:

> "Where was George W. Bush in 1972? Our author, J.H. Hatfield, cites three sources close to the Texas governor in the Afterword to Fortunate Son who state Bush had a cocaine arrest 'fixed' by his father in Houston in 1972. No one has adequately explained why he had a sudden charitable desire to perform community service at Project PULL, an inner-city youth center. Ironically, government documents note during the same period Bush's flying suspension for failure to take an annual medical examination, even though the Republican presidential candidate has repeatedly stated he was a healthy young man at the time. Combined with the new introduction to the book that cites an on-the-record admission by Michael Dannenhauer, former chief of staff to the elder Bush, that George W. was 'out of control' in his abuse of cocaine and alcohol and experienced 'lost weekends in Mexico' in the '70s, the Defense Department document adds further credibility to Hatfield and "Fortunate Son.'" [3]

We should also note that this medical Bush failed to take included a drug test. The London *Sunday Times* reported in April 1972 that the Pentagon had ordered drug tests at least once a year for officers on "extended active duty", including reservists like Bush. Publisher Sander Hicks quotes Michael Dannenhauer as saying: "There was cocaine use, lots of women, but the drinking was the worst." Bush lies yet again when he says that his 1972 flying suspension was because his doctor was in Houston while he was in Alabama working on a political campaign. Air Force Lieutenant Colonel (Retired) Lou Kaposta told Soft Skull Press:

"According to my background of many years as a pilot in the Air Force, you have to take the annual physical as scheduled. You do not have a choice about when, where or how. You're in the military; the individual's desires don't count. Everybody knows that." [4]

Former Staff Sergeant Mark Wilson, a veteran of the Texas Air National Guard, said there was "something fishy" about Bush's explanation. He told Soft Skull Press that Bush was stationed very near to Maxwell Air Force Base at the time and could easily have travelled there. Wilson also pointed out that Bush's initial physical exam, while still at Yale in 1968, was done at Westover Air Force Base in Massachusetts. [5] So why did Bush only want to be examined by "his doctor" at the very time that Hatfield claims he was arrested for drug offences? James Howard Hatfield, the 43-year-old author of Fortunate Son, was found dead in his hotel room in Springdale, Arkansas, on July 18th 2001. Police said he had committed "suicide" from an overdose of prescription drugs. Hatfield left a wife and a daughter. Pope John Paul II was reported to have commented on Hatfield's death to reporters outside the Basilica of St Peter after saying mass:

"I met Jim Hatfield in Chicago when Fortunate Son was getting reprinted. He shook my hand and gave me a signed copy. I gave him my blessing and told him to go forth and speak the truth. He said, 'I am already doing that, Father'. We had a laugh together. They tell me he's dead now … very tragic. He will be remembered in a series of special masses. I am sure that he is in heaven with our Lord, Jesus Christ, who said [in Matthew 5:1–2]: 'Blessed are you when they revile and persecute you, and say all kinds of evil against you for my sake. Rejoice and be glad for great is your reward in heaven, for they persecuted the prophets who were before you.'" [6]

Michael C. Ruppert, a former Los Angeles Police Department narcotics investigator, goes further in his monthly newsletter, *From The Wilderness*. [7] He says that George W. Bush and his brother, Jeb, now Governor for Florida, were filmed in a 1985 "sting" by the US Drug Enforcement Agency at Tamiami airport outside Miami. Ruppert quotes statements made by Terry Reed, who took part in drug operations for the CIA and the Bush family involving the notorious and self-confessed drug smuggler Barry Seal, who was murdered when he began to talk too much. (See *And The Truth Shall Set You Free* and Reed's book, *Compromised: Clinton, Bush and the CIA*.)[8] Ruppert says they arrived on the Bush plane King Air from the Intermountain regional airport at Mena, Arkansas, to pick up two kilos of cocaine from Seal. Mena was the location of the infamous and well-documented Mena airstrip drug operations involving the then Arkansas Governor, Bill Clinton (see *And The Truth Shall Set You Free*). There are some interesting connections between this area, the Rockefeller family, Wal-Mart stores and China highlighted on the website of researcher and investigative journalist Sherman Skolnick.[9] What's for sure there is no way that the Bush sons have not been involved in drug trafficking when their father is one of the most active drug barons in America, possibly the world. Terry Reed quotes in his book a conversation with Barry Seal about the Bush family drug operations. He says that Seal told him:

"Ever hear the old expression, it's not what ya know, it's who ya know? Well, whoever said that just hadn't caught the Vice President's kids in the dope business, 'cause I can tell ya for sure what ya know can definitely be more useful than who you know ..."

Reed asked Seal if he was saying that Father George Bush's kids were in the drug business:

"Yup, that's what I'm tellin' ya. A guy in Florida who flipped for the DEA [Drug Enforcement Administration] has got the goods on the Bush boys. Now I heard this earlier from a reliable source in Colombia, but I just sat on it then, waitin' to use it as a trump card, if I ever needed it. Well, I need ta use it now. I got names, dates, places ... even got some tape recordin's. Fuck, I even got surveillance videos catchin' the Bush boys red handed. I consider this stuff my insurance policy ... Now this is real sensitive shit inside of US Customs and DEA and those guys are pretty much under control." [10]

Barry Seal's "insurance" did not prove too effective, however, because he was silenced before he could tell his story to a bigger audience. In February 1986, soon after he began to speak out, he was murdered at Baton Rouge, Louisiana. It was blamed officially on two Colombian hitmen with Mac-10 machine guns, but while they may or may not have been the actual killers, the assassination was ordered by the highest levels of the United States government to stop his revelations about the Bush and Clinton involvement in the drug racket through Mena, Arkansas. Clinton said at a press conference at the time that he knew very little about Seal, but a number of people reported seeing them dining together at Fu Lin's, one of Clinton's favourite restaurants in Little Rock.[11] Noelle Bush, the 24-year-old daughter of Jeb Bush, was arrested in January 2001 for prescription drug fraud involving an anti-anxiety drug similar to Valium.[12] I understand her need for that after being brought up by the Bush family and living with Jeb at the governor's mansion in Florida. With stunning hypocrisy, Jeb Bush said at the time: "Unfortunately, substance abuse is an issue confronting many families across our nation ..."[13] Yes, but not every family has made billions from making those substances available on the streets of America. Stewart Webb is a private investigator who has uncovered the Bush family connections to the drugs trade and the major American financial firms who launder the money for them. He said:

"George Jr., Jeb and Neil Bush were all party to the crimes involving drugs and gun money laundering through Silverado Savings in Denver. They were all aware of 'poppy' George's schemes using CIA, Israeli Mossad, Homestead Air Force Base and Mena, Arkansas to import drugs and ship weapons." [14]

Yes, weapons to terrorists! Webb also highlights the Bush family involvement in financial fraud and murder, but his calls for a Grand Jury investigation into his findings have been ignored.

The Bush – Bin Laden connection

You will have noted earlier how Father George went to war against former business and CIA associates like Saddam Hussein and Manuel Noriega. Such people are friends while they are useful and foes when they are either a liability or more useful as enemies in the battle for control of human perception. These are fodder in a game that is far bigger than such people understand. You might expect, given this pattern, that the Bush and bin Laden families would have a history of connections and cooperation. And yes, so they have. The official story is that the bin Laden family has broken ties with Osama, their terrorist relative, but the only evidence we have for this are statements made by the bin Laden family and US Intelligence and government sources. What the hell kind of proof is that when they all have a stake in the public believing this version of events? Many others doubt these claims, and I agree. To say all ties have been severed is nonsense. The *San Antonio Express-News* quoted Yossef Bodansky, the director of the House Task Force on Terrorism and Unconventional Warfare, as saying that "Osama maintains connections" with some of his nearly two dozen brothers, but he would not elaborate.[15] The FBI must have had their doubts because it subpoenaed banks used by the bin Laden family in search of records detailing their financial activities, according to a source quoted by the *Wall Street Journal*.[16]

The BBC's *Newsnight* current affairs programme revealed that far from accepting that the bin Laden family is innocent of any criminal activity, members of their clan were being investigated by the FBI before September 11th. Reporter Greg Palast presented an FBI document with the code 1991-WF-213589, which revealed how agents of the Washington field office were investigating Abdullah bin Laden, the president, treasurer and US Director of the World Assembly of Muslim Youth (WAMY) on the grounds of national security.[17] WAMY has been suspected of funding terrorism, including the al-Qaeda* network of Osama bin Laden. His brothers, Abdullah bin Laden and Omar bin Laden, another FBI suspect, lived in the Washington suburb of Falls Church, Virginia, at 3411 Silver Maple Place. This is close to the headquarters of WAMY in the basement at 5613 Leesburg Pike, and two blocks away is the house at 5913 Leesburg where four of the alleged hijackers named by the FBI after September 11th are said to have stayed.[18] This area is close to the CIA headquarters at Langley. WAMY says it's a charity, but about the same time as the 9/11 attacks in the US, the Pakistani authorities expelled WAMY representatives. Officials in India also claimed that WAMY was funding an organisation connected to bombings in Kashmir. The Philippines military said that WAMY was funding Islamic insurgency.[19]

---

* There are several different spellings of al-Qaeda and I have chosen this version. Other spellings will appear in some direct quotes.

George W. Bush, who claims to be so determined to stop the funding of Osama bin Laden, has not frozen WAMY's assets, and Joe Trento, a "national security expert", told *Newsnight* that the FBI wanted to continue its inquiries into WAMY and Abdullah bin Laden, but was not allowed to do so. Trento said he had obtained a secret file which revealed that FBI investigations considered that WAMY fitted the pattern of organisations funding terrorism that had been bankrolled by the Saudi royal family (who are "advised" by Father George Bush) and some of the 20,000 Saudi princes. Back in the early 1990s WAMY was being named as a channel for public and private Saudi donations to hardline Islamic organisations. One recipient of WAMY support has been the Students Islamic Movement of India that supported Pakistani-backed terrorists in Kashmir and wants an Islamic state in India.[20] Reporter Greg Palast said that *Newsnight* had uncovered a long history of shadowy connections between the US State Department, the CIA and the Saudis. Michael Springman, the former head of the American visa bureau in Jeddah from 1987 to 1989, told *Newsnight*:

"In Saudi Arabia I was repeatedly ordered by high-level State Department officials to issue visas to unqualified applicants. These were, essentially, people who had no ties either to Saudi Arabia or to their own country. I complained bitterly at the time there. I returned to the US, I complained to the State Department here, to the General Accounting Office, to the Bureau of Diplomatic Security and to the Inspector General's office. I was met with silence.

"What I was protesting was in reality an effort to bring recruits, rounded up by Osama bin Laden, to the United States for terrorist training by the CIA, who then returned to Afghanistan to fight against the then Soviet Union." [21]

This was during the Soviet occupation of Afghanistan and their war with the CIA-backed Mujaheddin, including Osama bin Laden. In the period Springman is talking about here, between 1987 and 1989, Father George Bush, the former head of the CIA, officially took control of the White House after being president, in fact if not name, under Ronald Reagan. *Newsnight* also quoted "a highly placed source in a US intelligence agency" as saying there had always been "constraints" on investigating Saudis and that, under President Boy George Bush, it had become much worse. FBI agents felt that their investigations into the Saudi connection were being obstructed from the highest level in Washington, *Newsnight* reported, despite terrorism against Americans being blamed on Osama bin Laden and his Saudi-based backers. These included the bombing of the World Trade Center in 1993, which killed six people and injured a thousand, and the Khobar Towers at a US military complex in Dhahran, Saudi Arabia, three years later in which 19 Americans died and some 500 were injured. This was blamed on Osama bin Laden and yet his family business, Bin Laden Construction, was given the contract by the US to replace it![22]

Bush blocks bin Laden investigation

Newsnight reported that after George W. became president, FBI agents were told to "back off" investigations into the bin Laden-Saudi connection. Greg Palast said that just a few days after September 11th, and while Muslim "suspects" were being rounded up all over America, a special charter flight flew 11 members of the bin Laden family out of the United States to Saudi Arabia from the same Boston Airport from which the attacks on the World Trade Center had been launched. As I mentioned, Yossef Bodansky, director of the House Task Force on Terrorism and Unconventional Warfare, said that bin Laden maintains connections with some of his nearly two dozen brothers, although he would not elaborate.[23] Osama bin Laden has been ostracised and disinherited by his family? Like hell he has and the Bushes, the bin Ladens and the Saudi royal family are all extremely close. This is confirmed by Jean-Charles Brisard and Guillaume Dasquie in their French book, *Bin Laden: The Forbidden Truth*. Brisard is a private intelligence analyst who compiled a report for French intelligence in 1997 about the financing of "bin Laden's" al-Qaeda terrorist network and Dasquie is editor of *Intelligence Online*. Brisard says they prove in their book that at least until 1998 bin Laden was able to use economic and financial structures in Saudi Arabia and had contacts with various Saudi officials. After all, the Saudis were supporting the Taliban, who were protecting him in Afghanistan. "In Saudi Arabia, the left hand ignores the right hand," Brisard says, "and the FBI was fully aware of the situation."[24] Brisard reveals in his book that John O'Neill, the FBI's former deputy director and head of anti-terrorism, resigned in July 2001 because the Boy Bush State Department was blocking the investigation into the bombing in the Yemen of the *USS Cole*, an attack blamed on bin Laden. Brisard says that O'Neill told him: "The main obstacles to investigating Islamic terrorism were US oil interests and the role played by Saudi Arabia in it." When Brisard asked him why the US was unwilling to go after the states that host bin Laden, he said "because of oil". Brisard revealed in an Internet interview: "I quote [O'Neill] saying that everything about bin Laden and al-Qaida can be explainable through Saudi Arabia."[25]

In the greatest of "coincidences", John O'Neill left the FBI to become head of security at the World Trade Center and died in the attacks on September 11th. It was apparently his first day in the job. Lawyer Michael Wildes gave some 14,000 documents to the FBI implicating Saudis in the funding of terrorism. They came from a defecting Saudi diplomat represented by Wildes, but the lawyer says that FBI agents told him they were "not permitted" to read them and would not take them.[26] He said of the FBI:

> "They're cut off at the hip sometimes by supervisors or given shots that are being called from Washington at the highest levels ... You see a difference between the rank-and-file counter-intelligence agents, who are regarded by some as the motor pool of the FBI, who drive following diplomats, and the people who are getting the shots called at the highest level of our government, who have a different agenda –
> it's unconscionable."[27]

In the wake of September 11th, FBI Special Agents were furious with the way their investigations into potential terrorists and their funding were blocked. One filed an official complaint with legal representation from David Schippers, the man who led the attempted impeachment of Bill Clinton, and Judicial Watch, the private Washington organisation that investigates and prosecutes official corruption. FBI Special Agent Robert Wright, Jr, who spent four years tracking terrorist money laundering in the United States, believes that if investigations had been allowed to continue, the attacks on the World Trade Center could have been stopped.[28] Wright told the media in May 2002 that the FBI operation, code-named "Vulgar Betrayal", confiscated funds that were directly linked to Saudi Arabian businessman Yassin Kadi, also known as Yassin al-Qadi, who has since been identified as one of the "chief money launderers" for Osama bin Laden. Wright said that FBI management "intentionally and repeatedly thwarted and obstructed" his efforts to expand the investigation to arrest other terrorists and seize their assets. In August 1999 he was removed from the operation, which was then shut down. "As a direct result of the incompetence and, at times, intentional obstruction of justice by FBI management to prevent me from bringing the terrorists to justice," he said, "Americans have unknowingly been exposed to potential terrorist attacks for years."[29] Long before September 11th lawyer David Schippers tried himself to warn Attorney General John Ashcroft about the concerns of FBI agents that a terrorist attack on lower Manhattan was planned, but he never received a reply. Schippers was contacted by a number of genuine FBI agents about their concerns. He described the investigations into the funding of terrorism:

> "This agent here in Chicago filed the affidavit where he laid out the whole way that the money moves, the way that its handled, how it comes out of the Middle East into the Chicago area, not only Chicago, but into the United States, how it's covered, how the operatives are covered, and then how the money gets back, how it's transferred back, and where it's kept while it's here. And that affidavit ran like 30 pages – laid it out … He had to go through hell on earth in Washington. He had to fight like a tiger. Everybody in his own bureau and in the Department of Justice was against him and still is.[30]

Bush and bin Laden: business partners

So why would the US government want to block investigations into Osama bin Laden and other terrorist networks? Here's why. Boy George was a disastrous businessman when he followed his father, or "Poppy", into the oil and gas industry, but he was always bankrolled or manipulated out of trouble by his father and his friends. He launched his own drilling company in June 1977 in the Texas oil town of Midland. It was called Arbusto Energy and the "bust" in the name was very appropriate. "Arbusto", however, means "shrub" in Spanish (again spot on), although it seems his family believed it translated as bush. Now … one of the investors in Baby Bush's Arbusto venture was one Salem bin Laden, a close friend of King Fahd of Saudi Arabia, and brother of the "world's most wanted man,"

Osama bin Laden. The Saudi Bin Laden Group, formerly Bin Laden Brothers Construction, is one of the biggest construction companies in the Middle East with some 40,000 employees, and it has long associations with the US government and prominent American families. This was the company that helped to build American airfields in Saudi Arabia during the Gulf War and, as we shall see, built the cave and tunnel complexes with CIA funding that the United States bombed during the attacks on Afghanistan after September 11th. Charles Freeman, president of the Middle East Policy Council (funded by the bin Laden family) and former US ambassador to Saudi Arabia, says: "If there were ever any company closely connected to the US and its presence in Saudi Arabia, it's the Saudi Bin Laden Group." [31] Wayne Fagan, a San Antonio attorney who represented Salem bin Laden from 1982 to 1988, told the *San Antonio Express-News* that his client was "a good friend of the US government". [32] Salem bin Laden, investor to George W. Bush, became head of the bin Laden companies with the death in a plane crash of the family patriarch, Sheikh Mohammed bin Laden, in 1968. The Sheik left his industrial and financial empire to some 54 sons and daughters from a list of wives. Salem bin Laden, the oldest son, took over the estate in 1972.

Salem bin Laden became a business partner of George W. Bush through a middleman called James R. Bath, a close friend of the Bush family and best buddy of Boy George. They "served" in the same Texas Air National Guard unit. Indeed, the document obtained by Soft Skull Press, which reveals how Bush was suspended from flying in the same period that J. H. Hatfield said he was busted for cocaine, shows that his friend, Major James R. Bath, also failed to take his annual medical examination and was suspended from flying! It was shortly after Father George became director of the CIA in 1976 that Salem bin Laden appointed Bath, the very close friend of "Dubya", to represent his "business interests" out of the Bush family stronghold of Houston, Texas. Bill White, a former real estate partner of Bath, said that Bath told him he was an asset of the CIA and that "he had been recruited by [Father] George Bush himself in 1976 when Bush was director of the agency … he said Bush wanted him involved with the Arabs, and to get into the aviation business". During this early period as an asset of Bush's CIA, Bath was at Boy George's side when he ran unsuccessfully to be governor of Texas in 1978 and Bath (the bin Laden family?) helped to finance the campaign. Bill White's claims forced Bath to admit in sworn depositions that he represented four wealthy Saudi Arabian businessmen as a trustee and used his name on their investments in return for a 5% commission on their business deals. At the same time Bath, the buddy of Boy George, was both put on the CIA payroll by Father George to get involved with the Arabs and the aviation business, and appointed by Salem bin Laden and other bin Laden-connected Arabs as their Texas representative. This connection led to Salem bin Laden investing in George W. Bush's Arbusto oil company.

The allegations of Bill White that his former partner James Bath channelled money from Middle Eastern clients to American companies to influence the decisions of the Reagan-Bush administrations were "investigated" by the Financial Crimes Enforcement Network (FinCEN), a division of the Justice Department. But, of course, nothing came of it. White told a Texas court in 1992 that Bath and the Justice Department had "blackballed" him professionally and financially because he refused to stop revealing his knowledge of the Arab money paid into the bank accounts of American businesses and politicians. At the time of this Justice Department "review" of Bill White's evidence, a senior position in the department was held by Robert Mueller. This same Robert Mueller was appointed head of the FBI by George W. Bush and took over just two weeks before September 11th. This is the FBI from which the official story of 9/11 has come. The head of the Justice Department's criminal division under President Father George, which cleared major players in the BCCI scandal, including Bush, was also ... Robert Mueller. Having a few little doubts about Mueller's FBI version of September 11th? Yeah, me too.

Boy George, the bin Ladens, and the BCCI

By 1977, using Bath as the middleman, Salem bin Laden was investing in Dubya's Arbusto drilling company. This association continued, not least through the Illuminati's BCCI, which provided "banking services" for the Medellin drug cartel, Khun Sa (a major player in the heroin trafficking out of Asia), Manuel Noriega, Saddam Hussein, and terrorists like Abu Nidal, who, according to the former German Defence Minister and overseer of German intelligence, Andreas von Bulow, is an "instrument of Mossad", the Israeli intelligence agency.[33] The BCCI was also the main route for the funds of CIA covert operations that involved the Iran-Contra scandal and the funding of Osama bin Laden and others in Afghanistan who were resisting the Soviet Union occupation in the 1980s during the Reagan-Bush era. The result of this CIA funding through the BCCI and other sources was the creation of the Osama bin Laden network and the coming to power of the Taliban regime. The Bush family were massively involved with the BCCI and these super-rich Middle Eastern families, like the bin Ladens. Ed Rogers, Father George's White House political director, who sat in on presidential meetings, left to work for Sheikh Kamal Adham, the American representative of the BCCI and significantly a former chief of Saudi intelligence and a friend of Adnan Khashoggi, the infamous arms dealer. Khashoggi is a business associate of Father George Bush and one-time brother-in-law to Mohamed al-Fayed. When Father Bush was asked if he was concerned that a senior member of his staff had left to represent a Saudi sheikh accused of being a key player in the BCCI scandal, he said Rogers was free to do whatever he chose and Bush's only concern was that the White House was "beyond any perception of impropriety."[34] Note ... not beyond impropriety, just any perception of it. Rogers was hired to ensure good communications between the sheikh and Bush. As a Senate investigation into the BCCI revealed, Rogers left the White House and was paid $600,000 to do next to nothing. It was the same with his assistant, Haley Barbour, who would turn up later as the chairman of the National Republican Committee. The Senate investigation concluded that hiring Rogers and giving "gifts" of money to the president's son, George W. Bush, were designed to influence Father Bush's policies in relation to the BCCI.[35] Like his father, Salem bin Laden died in a plane crash near San Antonio on Memorial Day, May 29th 1988. It is amazing how dangerous flying can be when you get involved with the Bush family and their Illuminati associates. Indeed it was considered an unexplainable "freak" accident with bin Laden, a very experienced pilot, inexplicably turning his ultralight aircraft the wrong way on take-off and hitting power lines. Or so the story goes.

Bush associate finances bin Laden

Bush buddy James Bath made his fortune from commissions for investing the money of Salem bin Laden and another Saudi who becomes very significant in the tale. This is Sheikh Khalid bin Mahfouz, another investor in a George W. Bush oil company. Bin Mahfouz was the operational director of the BCCI and a controlling shareholder with a 20% stake between 1986 and 1990. He is one of the world's richest men and … a financial supporter of Osama bin Laden's terrorist network! His sister is a wife of Osama bin Laden, as revealed by CIA Director James Woolsey in his testimony to the Senate in 1998.[36] Khalid bin Mahfouz and Salem bin Laden were closely associated and Dubya's close friend James Bath worked for both of them, as he did for Gaith Pharaon, the BCCI's front man in Houston's Main Bank and a close associate of bin Mahfouz. In 1978, Bath bought Houston's Gulf Airport for Salem bin Laden and when he died in the "ultralight crash" ownership passed to bin Mahfouz. He has a big estate in Houston, the home base of Father George. Bath was also president of Skyway Aircraft Leasing Ltd, a Texas air charter company registered in the Cayman Islands, which was really owned by bin Mahfouz according to published reports in the early 1990s.[37] There was a long association between Boy George's associate James Bath and bin Mahfouz. Bath received a "loan" of $1.4 million from him in 1990.

Khalid bin Mahfouz is from the Yemen, as were the bin Ladens originally. He was for many years the banker to Saudi Arabia's King Fahd and to Father George Bush. Bin Mahfouz was known as "the king's treasurer" in Saudi Arabia. Yet after the terrorist attacks on US embassies in Kenya and Tanzania in the 1990s, which were blamed on Osama bin Laden, President Clinton's Secretary of State Madeleine Albright informed the Saudi Defence Minister, Prince Sultan, that bin Mahfouz had channelled tens of millions of dollars into terrorist groups through accounts in London and New York. According to *USA Today*, quoting "intelligence sources", bin Mahfouz and other Saudis combined to transfer $3 million to various Osama bin Laden front operations in Saudi Arabia in 1999.[38] The paper reported that a year after bin Laden was blamed for the attacks on US embassies in Africa, Khalid bin Mahfouz and other wealthy Saudis ordered the National Commercial Bank (owned by bin Mahfouz and used by the bin Laden family)[39] to transfer funds to the Capitol Trust Bank in New York City. This money was deposited with Islamic charities connected to the bin Laden network in the United States and United Kingdom.[40] The organisations alleged to have been used by bin Mahfouz and associates to fund terrorist groups, especially bin Laden, include: the London-based Advice and Reformation Committee; Blessed Relief, an African aid group whose directors included bin Mahfouz's son, Abdul Rahman Mahfouz; a Kenya branch of Help Africa People, controlled by people later convicted or indicted for the US embassy bombings in Kenya and Tanzania; the International Islamic Relief Organization, which has been linked with terrorist bomb plots in the Philippines and India; the Kenya branch of Mercy International, a war and famine relief group where evidence used to convict the embassy bombers was found; and a list of other organisations, some of which have been named by President Bush since September 11th as fronts for terrorism (he should know).[41]

Here's another example of how small the world is at this level. The Capitol Trust Bank through which at least some of these funds for Osama bin Laden are said to have been channelled is run by bin Mahfouz associate Mohammad Hussein Al-Amoudi, who is also alleged to have funded bin Laden. Al-Amoudi's lawyer has been Vernon Jordan, the close associate of Bill Clinton and friend of Monica Lewinsky. Jordan was for many years a senior executive in the law firm Akin, Gump, Strauss, Hauer and Feld in Washington, along with several close friends of the Bush family. In January 2000 Jordan moved to the New York investment bank of Lazard Freres, but retains close connections to the law firm he has served since 1982. He also sits on the boards of major corporations like American Express, the Revlon Group, Xerox Corporation and Dow Jones.[42] Akin, Gump represent some interesting combinations of people and organisations. These include bin Mahfouz and Al-Amoudi, who are alleged to have funded Osama bin Laden; they also handle the affairs of many leading Saudis through the Akin, Gump office in the capital, Riyadh; and they represent the Texas-based Holy Land Foundation for Relief and Development, which had its assets frozen by the US Treasury pending an investigation into alleged connections to the Palestinian terrorist group, Hamas.[43] Bin Mahfouz retained the services of Akin, Gump during the "investigation" into the BCCI.[44]

The National Commercial Bank in Saudi Arabia, reported to be the world's biggest private bank, was owned by bin Mahfouz, but he was forced to step back when an audit by the Saudi government revealed that $2 billion was "missing". There has, of course, been much speculation into where, or more to the point, to whom, that money went. I emphasise again, the National Commercial Bank is one of the major banks used by the bin Laden family empire and the royal family of Saudi Arabia. Bin Mahfouz was put under "house arrest" and the last I heard he was "living in luxury at a military hospital in the northern city of Taif, where he is allegedly undergoing treatment for a drug problem". Taif is only a short distance from the bin Laden family headquarters in Jeddah. Bin Mahfouz also had to hand over the Irish passports he had bought for millions of dollars for himself, ten of his wives, and business associates. Nothing really changed, however, because another family member, Mohammed bin Mahfouz, took over the National Commercial Bank along with close family business associate, Mohammed Hussein Al-Amoudi, who is based in Ethiopia and heads a vast network of companies involved in oil, banking, mining and construction. These include the Capitol Trust Bank that was named by the Clinton administration as a vehicle for funding Osama bin Laden's al-Qaeda network. The bin Mahfouz and Al-Amoudi families control three private Saudi Arabian oil companies and are partners with United States firms in a series of major oil development and pipeline projects in central and south Asia. Of course, the Bushes, Vice President Dick Cheney and many others in the US government are closely involved with the oil cartel. The Mahfouz-Al-Amoudi companies, Delta Oil, Nimir Petroleum and Corral Petroleum, formed international consortiums with United States oil giants Pennzoil (Bush family), Texaco, Unocal, Amerada Hess and Frontera Resources. Unocal is a Texas-based group that has been planning to build a massive pipeline across Afghanistan, but could not do so while the Taliban was in power. Despite their connections with Osama bin Laden, these US companies, bin Mahfouz and Al-Amoudi, have not had their assets frozen in the Bush sham to "stop money reaching terrorist organisations". The American publication, *Village Voice*, was therefore right to conclude:

> "It is most curious that the son of former CIA Director George Bush does business with the brother of Osama bin Laden in the setting up of businesses which seem very tied to the CIA – while at the same time a woman with CIA ties and who is married into the family of former CIA Director Richard Helms represents the Taliban, protector of Osama bin Laden. This coziness among the CIA and bin Laden families all suggest to me that perhaps Osama bin Laden may still very much be a CIA-protected operative, and makes me very nervous about who really orchestrated the 9/11 attacks." [45]

What a tangled web we weave ...

Once again, bin Mahfouz, the financial supporter of Osama bin Laden, was an investor in a George W. Bush oil company. Dubya's original company, Arbusto, went through changes of name with each financial failure. It became Bush Exploration when Father George became US Vice President and in September 1984 this survived only by merging with Spectrum 7 Energy Corporation. With Boy George appointed president of Spectrum, this of course also failed, and merged with Harken Energy in 1986. He was a shareholder, director and adviser to Harken and, a year later, with Harken now in trouble, along came the "investment" by Osama bin Laden supporter, Khalid bin Mahfouz.[46] He paid $25 million to acquire a 17.6% stake in the company through his US representative, Abdullah Taha Bakhsh. Mahfouz at the same time was a 20% controlling shareholder in BCCI, which official investigations revealed to be financing terrorist groups, unlawful "intelligence" operations and laundering vast amounts of drug money. Despite being a leading figure in the BCCI while it perpetrated the biggest financial fraud in history, bin Mahfouz escaped all liabilities, except for a $225-million-dollar settlement agreed with New York "prosecutors". This was pin money for him. With the Bush family so heavily involved in the BCCI it is not a surprise that it should be connected to the companies of George W. Bush.

Hey, Jack's back

Abdullah Taha Bakhsh also purchased a 9.6% stake for bin Mahfouz in the Worthen Banking Corporation in Arkansas, owned by another significant character in the story, Jackson Stephens, who funded Bill Clinton's presidential campaign and much of his political career. Bakhsh's purchase was identical to the shares in Worthen sold by three investors, Bill Clinton, Pat Robertson, the television "evangelist" (see *Children Of The Matrix*), and Mochtar Riady, the head of an Indonesian family that has close connections to the Chinese communists.[47] Jackson Stephens was a major financial supporter of Bill Clinton, but is also a close associate of the Bush family in America's one-party state. He was also closely connected with the BCCI and the Bush banker and bin Laden funder, Khalid bin Mahfouz. In a sworn statement for his lawsuit against Father George, the former Green Beret, William Tyree, said that Stephens "paid off politicians from Arkansas to look the other way and ignore the CIA cocaine operation at Mena, Arkansas." [48] In 1987, Stephens, who was also linked to the Clintons' Whitewater property scandal through the Worthen Bank, invested $25 million in … Boy George's Harken Energy. The deal was set up in Geneva and the money paid through Union des Banques Suisses and Banque de Commerce et de Placements, a Geneva branch of the BCCI. The deal was signed by Stephens and Abdullah Taha Bakhsh, the representative of bin Mahfouz. Stephen's company, Stephens Inc., donated $100,000 to Father George's re-election campaign in 1991, despite being a funder of Bill Clinton. His wife, Mary Anne Stephens, ran Father George's presidential election campaign in Arkansas in 1988 and when Boy George was manipulated into the presidency with the fixed vote in Florida in 2000, Jackson Stephens made a considerable contribution to the cost of his inauguration bash. Forget the "two-party" or "multi-party" state deal. It doesn't exist. These guys are masks on same face. When you observe the fundamental and constant connections between the Bushes, the bin Laden family, their cronies and investors, and the BCCI, including its operational director Khalid bin Mahfouz, it is sobering to note that a 400-page French parliamentary report, published on October 10th 2001, said that the Osama bin Laden financial network bore a striking resemblance to that of the BCCI.

Loser takes it all

Dubya's family and business connections made him a fortune from his failed oil company in its various incarnations. With Arbusto failing, he was made president of the company that bought it, Spectrum 7 Energy, and was given 14% of its stock while other Arbusto investors were paid 20 cents on the dollar. When Spectrum 7 lost $400,000 in six months Bush sold to Harken Energy and again received a large stock holding and a big salary as consultant and director. While Father George was US President in 1990, his son's Harken Energy was given a lucrative contract by the government of Bahrain even though Harken had never drilled a well overseas or offshore. The deal was brokered in part by David Edwards, one of Bill Clinton's closest friends, and a former employee of Stephens Inc., owned by Jackson Stephens. Clinton himself is a gofer for the Bushes and Rockefellers. The contract was awarded to Bush's company thanks to Sheikh Kalifah, the Prime Minister of Bahrain, another BCCI shareholder.[49] Jonathan Beaty and S.C. Gwynne in their book, *The Outlaw Bank: A Wild Ride Into the Secret Heart of the BCCI*, write that

"Knowledgeable oil company sources believe that the Bahrain oil concession was indeed an oblique favor to the president of the United States but say that Saudi Arabia [home of bin Laden] was behind the decision."[50] Choosing a small company with no track record was indeed a strange decision unless you know the background and personnel. Harken immediately subcontracted the work to the CIA-connected Global Marine and no oil was found. Bahrain officials say they had no idea that the President's son was involved with Harken when they awarded the contract. No, honest, they really said that.

Above the law

Insider trading – using privileged information to trade stocks – is strictly illegal and yet how can the following not be considered so? Two months before Iraq invaded Kuwait on June 20th 1990, Boy George suddenly sold two-thirds of his stock in Harken Energy, and the 121,140 shares netted him $848,560 – that's $318,430 more than they were worth according to Dr Arthur F. Ide, the author of *George W. Bush: Portrait of a Compassionate Conservative*[51] Eight days after Bush sold his stock, Harken announced second quarter losses of $23 million, Saddam Hussein then invaded Kuwait and the value of the company plummeted 75%. As Ide wrote: "George W. broke the law to [sell his shares] since the transaction was an insider stock sale."[52] Bush was cleared, however, by an investigation by the Securities and Exchange Commission (SEC), an Illuminati front dealing in financial law. It prosecutes those the Illuminati want to destroy and clears the ones they want to protect. An Associated Press report pointed out:

> "At the time of the investigation, Bush's father was President of the United States and the SEC was run by one of his biggest political supporters, Richard Breeden. The SEC's then-general counsel, James R. Doty, was another staunch presidential supporter who as a private attorney was George W. Bush's lawyer when he purchased his share of the Texas Rangers baseball team."[53]

Yet another stitch-up and there's more. Bush was defended in the investigation by the Dallas attorney, Robert Jordan. When he became US President, Boy George appointed Jordan as his ambassador to Saudi Arabia – a country that was to become extremely important a few months later when the "war on terrorism" was launched. This is, of course, the base of the bin Laden family and other Bush and terrorism funders like Khalid bin Mahfouz. Jordan has no diplomatic experience, but that's not the point. As always it is his loyalty to the Bush family that counts.

Must be genetic ...

When faced with questions about his bin Laden connections, President Dubya denied at first ever knowing his long-time friend and bin Laden family business associate, James Bath. This was an outrageous and a ludicrous lie. He then agreed that Bath had invested in Arbusto and that he knew he was a representative of Saudi Arabian interests (the bin Laden family and Khalid bin "BCCI" Mahfouz).

Bush also lied to the *Wall Street Journal* when he said he had "no idea" that the BCCI was involved in Harken Energy's finances. In fact, Harken's affairs were awash with people directly connected to the BCCI. The *Journal* quite rightly concluded that "The number of BCCI-connected people who had dealings with Harken – all since George W. Bush came on board – raises the question of whether they mask an effort to cozy up to a presidential son." [54] In fact, it goes far, far, deeper than that. The Bush family is crooked to the core and the children have been brought up to be that way. Dubya's brother Neil Bush was fined $50,000 in 1990 and banned from banking activities for his role in taking down Silverado Savings and Loans, a failure that cost taxpayers $1.3 billion and resulted from the "Reaganomics" policies of the 1980s that were orchestrated by the real power in the Oval Office, George Bush. Father George was US President when Silverado collapsed. A Resolution Trust Corporation suit against Neil Bush and other officers of Silverado was settled for $26.5 million. He voted to give $100 million in "loans" (bad ones it turned out) to two of his business partners while failing to tell his fellow board members at Silverado that they were his business partners. Federal banking investigators also followed the trail of defaulted loans to Neil Bush oil ventures like JNB International, an oil and gas exploration company that was awarded drilling concessions in Argentina even though it had no experience of international oil and gas drilling. Heard that story somewhere before? Neil Bush now runs an "educational software" company called Ignite out of Austin, Texas, and in January 2002 he was the keynote speaker at an "international forum" in Jeddah, Saudi Arabia, home of the bin Laden family, and they were the main backers of the event.[55]

The Carlyle Group – a name to remember

Khalid bin Mahfouz, the financial backer of Osama bin Laden and George W. Bush, is also an investor in the Carlyle Group, the international consulting and investment firm of Father George. It was founded in 1987 and named after the favourite New York hotel of the company's initial investors, the high-Illuminati Mellon family, the close friends of the British royal family and the force behind the lie that fluoride is good for you (see *And The Truth Shall Set You Free* and *The Biggest Secret*). The Carlyle Group also has very close links with the bin Laden family, who have been both clients and investors. Father Bush has been a paid consultant to the Bin Laden Group. Reports in the *Wall Street Journal* say these Carlyle investments have been earning the bin Laden family some 40% a year on their money since 1995.[56] So when the US boosts its military spending, as it has so massively done in the "war on terrorism", bin Laden family investments in a defence contractor like Carlyle clearly benefit. According to the *New York Times*: "Carlyle has ownership stakes in 164 companies which last year employed more than 70,000 people and generated $16 billion in revenues. About 450 institutions – mainly large pension funds and banks – are Carlyle investors …" [57] Carlyle owns a wide range of companies involved in "health care", real estate, the Internet, bottling plants, the media (including, it is reported, the French newspaper, *Le Figaro*), as well as companies producing tanks, aircraft parts and a long list of other military equipment. It is now a major player in defence contracting and telecommunications and invests in companies that do business with governments or are affected by government regulations. The *Wall Street Journal* called the Carlyle Group "… a well-connected Washington merchant bank specializing in buyouts of defense and aerospace companies." [58] Almost two-thirds of Carlyle's investments are in defence and telecommunications companies that are fundamentally affected by changes in government spending and policy because they know they can influence both, especially if one of your leading lights has his son in the White House. Dubya, himself, was an investor and board member of the Carlyle subsidiary, Caterair.

Well, well, what a line-up

Father George sat on the Carlyle board and is still very much involved as a constantly active senior consultant who nets, apparently, between $80,000 and $100,000 for every speech he makes on its behalf. He is also the senior adviser to Carlyle's Asian Partners fund.[59] Another Carlyle stalwart is James Baker, Bush's Secretary of State at the time of the Gulf War, and the man who was allocating contracts to American corporations to clear up the oil fires in Kuwait even before the conflict began. Baker is on the Carlyle board, as is former Reagan-Bush Defense Secretary, Frank Carlucci, who is the Carlyle chairman and managing director. Carlucci was number two at the CIA during the Vietnam War, assistant director of the CIA during the Jimmy Carter presidency, and both Secretary of Defense and National Security Adviser to Ronald Reagan (George Bush). He is also a past chairman of Nortel Networks Corp., which has been a partner of the Bin Laden Group in telecommunication deals. Karl Evanzz in his book, *The Judas Factor: The Plot to Kill Malcolm X,*[60] says that Carlucci's appointment as consul and second-secretary of the US Embassy in Stanleyville, the Congo, was a cover for a CIA operation that included the plot to assassinate the recently elected President Patrice Lumumba in 1961. When someone is freely elected to serve the people and not the Illuminati they must be removed. Five months after Lumumba was assassinated, Carlucci was arrested, expelled from the Congo, and returned to the US. He was expelled again in 1965, this time from Tanzania, after he was implicated in the CIA assassination of the Burundi Prime Minister Pierre Ngendandumwe. This is the man who now heads the Carlyle Group with its fundamental connections to the Bush and bin Laden families.

In relation to the agenda behind the "war on terrorism", it is important to note that Carlyle's Carlucci and James Baker are close friends and associates of the current US Defense Secretary Donald H. Rumsfeld. Baker was a classmate of Rumsfeld at Yale University and Carlucci was Rumsfeld's roommate at Yale.[61] Secretary of State Colin Powell has also described Carlucci as his "mentor". Carlucci admits that in February 2001 he met with Rumsfeld and Vice President Dick Cheney, the Gulf War Defense Secretary to Father George, to talk about military policy. This was at a time when Carlyle had several defence projects worth billions of dollars under consideration. How hilarious, therefore, are the comments of Carlucci when he said: "I've made it clear that I don't lobby the defense industry. I will give our Carlyle bankers advice on what they might do and whom they should talk to. But I do not pick up the phone and say you should fund X, Y or Z." [62] Then there are the claims of David Rubenstein, one of Carlyle's founders and a former aide to the Jimmy Carter administration that was served at the CIA by Carlucci. Rubenstein said: "Mr [Father George] Bush gives us no advice on what do with the federal government. We've gone over backwards to make sure that we do no lobbying." [63] To quote Santa Claus: "Ho, ho, ho." But even funnier was the claim by Daniel A. D'Aniello, a Carlyle managing director, that "We are greatly assisted by Baker and Bush ... [because] ... It shows that we are associated with people of the highest ethical standards." That's about as wrong as any sentence has ever been in all human history. Charles Lewis, the executive director of the Washington-based Center for Public Integrity, hit the button when he said:

> "Carlyle is as deeply wired into the current administration as they can possibly be. [Father] Bush is getting money from private interests that have business before the government, while his son is president. And, in a really peculiar way, George W. Bush could, some day [some day??] benefit financially from his own administration's decisions, through his father's investments. The average American doesn't know that and, to me, that's a jaw-dropper." [64]

The connections go on and on. Dallas attorney Robert Jordan, who defended George W. Bush against claims of insider trading and was appointed Bush's ambassador to Saudi Arabia, is a corporate lawyer in the Dallas office of Houston-based Baker Botts, lawyers to the Carlyle Group. The current "Baker" in Baker Botts is James A. Baker III, Father George's Secretary of State and a major player in the Carlyle Group. Baker Botts has an office in Riyadh, Saudi Arabia, and the firm's client list includes "more than half of the Fortune 100 companies" and the Bush oil company Pennzoil. The former UK Prime Minister, John Major, was also hired as a European consultant to Carlyle and was made chairman for Carlyle Europe in May 2001. He has travelled with Bush promoting Carlyle interests. Major was Prime Minister when the BCCI scandal broke in 1991, just as Bush was president in the United States. Lord Howe, who was Deputy Prime Minister and Home Secretary in Major's government, also sits on Carlyle's European board. Howe made a crucial contribution to the removal from office of Margaret Thatcher when the Illuminati, via its Bilderberg Group, had decided she had become a liability because of her opposition to the European superstate.

Other Carlyle directors and consultants include Fidel V. Ramos, the former Philippines President; Richard Darman, Father George's former Budget Director; Robert Grady, former assistant to Father George; Park Tae Joon, former Prime Minister of South Korea; Arthur Levitt, former chairman of the Securities and Exchange Commission (SEC); Michael Orloff, former general director of the World Health Organization; J.H. Binford Peay, retired US Army General; John Shalikashvili, former chairman of the US Joint Chiefs of Staff; Karl Otto Pohl, former president of Germany's Bundesbank; and Sami Baarma, director of Pakistan's Prime

This "world" is only an illusion and we can change it any time we want. It's just a choice right now between fear and love.

Commercial Bank in Lahore, which is owned by … Khalid bin Mahfouz. Baarma (also Baarama) is a director of Lebanon's Credit Libanaise, which is owned by the Mahfouz family. This Carlyle line-up of global influence also involves the past or present chairmen of BMW.; drug giant Hoffman-LaRoche; Nestlé; LVMH-Moët Hennessy; Louis Vuitton; and Aerospatiale, the French Airbus partner. Such connections have ensured massive growth for Carlyle. As the *New York Times* article noted of Father George's role:

"In getting business for Carlyle, Mr Bush has been impressive. His meeting with the crown prince [of Saudi Arabia] was followed by a yacht cruise and private dinners with Saudi officials, including King Fahd, all on behalf of Carlyle, which has extensive interests in the Middle East.

"And Mr Bush led Carlyle's successful entry into South Korea, the fastest-growing economy in Asia. After his meetings with the prime minister and other government and business leaders, Carlyle won a tough competition for control of KorAm, one of Korea's few healthy banks."

The article goes on:

"In a new spin on Washington's revolving door between business and government, where lobbying by former officials is restricted but soliciting investments is not, Carlyle has upped the ante and taken the practice global. Mr Bush and Mr Baker were accompanied on their trips by former Prime Minister John Major of Britain, another of Carlyle's political stars. With door openers of this calibre, along with shrewd investment skills, Carlyle has gone from an unknown in the world of private equity to one of its biggest players. Private equity, which involves buying up companies in private deals and reselling them, is a high-end business open only to the very rich." [65]

Carlyle and the bin Ladens

The Washington-based Judicial Watch, a law firm that investigates and prosecutes government corruption, has highlighted the staggering fact, reported in the *Wall Street Journal*, that Father George works for the bin Laden family through the Carlyle Group and has met with them at least twice in November 1998 and January 2000. Baker and Carlucci have also made the pilgrimage to the bin Laden family's headquarters in Jeddah, Saudi Arabia. Father George issued a statement through his chief of staff, Jean Becker, to say he only recalled one meeting with the bin Laden family – in 1998 – but when Becker was read Bush's thank you note after another meeting with the bin Ladens, she suddenly confirmed they had in fact met twice. Yes, and the rest. This connection with the bin Ladens has continued while Osama bin Laden has been the world's most wanted man and the FBI, according to news reports, subpoenaed bin Laden family business records. However, Charles Freeman, president of the Middle East Policy Council and former US Ambassador to Saudi

Arabia, says that two of the bin Laden brothers have told him since September 11th that the FBI has been "remarkably sensitive, tactful and protective" of the family because of its "long standing friendship with the US". Another former US President, the Rockefeller-funded Jimmy Carter met with ten of Osama's brothers early in 2000 on a fundraising trip for the Carter Center in Atlanta.[66] He met with Bakr bin Laden in New York in September 2000 and the bin Ladens handed over $200,000 to the Carter Center. Casper Weinberger, the former US Defense Secretary to Reagan-Bush who was charged over Iran-Contra and pardoned by Bush, is now the chairman of the New York publisher, Forbes Inc. He confirmed that Forbes executives and staff also made two visits to the bin Laden family headquarters in Jeddah.[67] The Carlyle Group, of course, is far from the only connection between the Bush and bin Laden families as we have seen, but this alone is outrageous in the circumstances. Larry Klayman, the chairman and general counsel of Judicial Watch, said:

> "This conflict of interest has now turned into a scandal. The idea of the President's father, an ex-president himself, doing business with a company under investigation by the FBI in the terror attacks of September 11 is horrible. President Bush should not ask, but demand, that his father pull out of the Carlyle Group." [68]

But of course that didn't happen because both Bushes are up to their eyes in all this and Daddy calls the shots anyway. The Carlyle Group, clients to Osama bin Laden's family and associated with bin Laden funder Khalid bin Mahfouz, was one of the major financial supporters (together with Enron) of George W. Bush's run for the presidency! Wake me up.

Looking after daddy

The London *Times* reported an investigation into the illegal investment of public funds in the Carlyle Group through a web that leads back to George W. Bush. Reporter Tom Rhodes revealed the role of Wayne Berman, a former Assistant Secretary of Commerce in the Father George administration, who represents Carlyle. His company, Park Strategies, was involved in the transfer of $800 million in 1998 from the Connecticut state pension fund into private ventures and $50 million of this was placed in a Carlyle fund. As a result of this information, Berman, who denies any wrongdoing, resigned as a "pioneer", one of 400 elite supporters selected to raise money for Boy George's presidential campaign. Rhodes goes on to explain how Dubya was also connected to investment of public funds in Carlyle. A month after he became Texas Governor, he was given a campaign contribution of $25,000 from Thomas Hicks, a multi-millionaire who Bush later placed on the Board of Regents at the University of Texas along with Tom Loeffler, a former Republican congressman and Washington lobbyist for Hicks, and Don Evans, an oil company executive, close friend of Bush, and later his presidential campaign manager. With support from Bush, Hicks used his own investment company as the university's broker and formed a corporation called the University of Texas Management Company to invest the university's assets, totalling some $13 billion. Shortly afterwards, the Hicks-controlled, Bush-appointed and supported regents handed over $10 million to the Carlyle Group, which employs his father! When Don Evans released the names of the Dubya's "pioneers" at the heart of his record-breaking presidential fundraising campaign, they included Steven Hicks (the brother of Thomas Hicks), Tom Leoffler, Wayne Berman, three partners in Vinson and Elkins (the law firm that serves as counsel to the University of Texas Management Company), and two other men who benefited from Texas University investments. Oh yes, and the Texas teachers pension fund invested $100 million with Carlyle. The board that made this decision was appointed when George W. Bush was Texas Governor.[69]

What a cheek

When you see all the connections between the Bushes and the Middle Eastern financial networks supporting people like Osama bin Laden, it is hard to even comprehend the level of pure, undiluted, bare-faced, hypocrisy that George W. Bush had to summon in the wake of September 11th when he told a White House news conference about his "crackdown" on those who do business with terrorists and the supporters of terrorists. He said in the White House Rose Garden on September 24th:

> "US banks that have assets of these groups or individuals must freeze their accounts. And US citizens or businesses are prohibited from doing business with them." He said it was "a strike on the financial foundation of the global terror network. If you do business with terrorists, if you support or succour them, you will not do business with the United States."

That applies to everyone it seems, except the Bush family, and their masters and cronies. I wonder what this means for the major British bank, Barclays plc, which is a "core investor" in a merchant bank set up on Guernsey in the Channel Islands in 1996 by Khalid bin Mahfouz, Osama bin Laden's brother-in-law? Barclays went into business with bin Mahfouz five years after he was involved in the world's biggest bank fraud, the BCCI.[70]

Saudi Arabia, a 51st state (one of many)

The endless connections between the Bushes, the Saudi Arabian royal family, elite Saudi business families, like the bin Ladens, and the terrorist networks, becomes understandable when you consider that Father George Bush, his masters and associates, control Saudi Arabia. Cathy O'Brien, a mind controlled slave to people like Father Bush and Dick Cheney for decades, saw at first hand what is really going on behind the smoke and mirrors. She writes in her book, *Trance-Formation Of America*:

> "Saudi Arabia threaded in and out of most operations in which I was involved, primarily due to their purchase and routing of weapons, drugs, and blond-haired, blue-eyed programmed children. According to George Bush's claims, Saudi Arabia was in essence

a controlled financial arm of the United States. Saudi Arabian King Fahd and his Ambassador to the US, Prince Bandar, provided a front for the unconstitutional and criminal covert operations of the US. This included the arming of Iraq and the Nicaraguan Contras; US involvement in the Bank of Credit and Commerce International (BCCI) scandal; and funding the Black Budget through purchase of our nation's children to be used as sex slaves and camel jockeys.

"Since the US 'won' control of the drug industries through the so-called Drug Wars, Saudi Arabia played an integral part in their distribution. It was my experience that Bush's claim of having Saudi Arabia King Fahd as his puppet was, in fact, reality." [71]

Cathy also tells of how she was forced by Dick Cheney, then US Defense Secretary, to have sex with King Fahd, which, to a large extent, was part of the operation to blackmail him into total compliance, should he ever think of refusing an order. Who are the financial advisers to the Saudi royal family? The Carlyle Group. Who was their banker? Khalid bin Mahfouz, funder of Osama bin Laden. Are we to believe that the Bush family and their associates who have so much control over Saudi Arabia could not have caught Osama bin Laden years ago and destroyed the business networks close to King Fahd that have funded him and others? So why didn't they do it? Because they wanted that funding to happen and they wanted bin Laden to be built up into a global monster because it suited what they had planned in New York and Washington for September 11th 2001.

Anthrax scares are good for business

Oh yes, some more facts about the Carlyle Group. As a major defence contractor, it benefits massively from wars like those in Afghanistan and others in the "war on terrorism". According to the investigative journalist Sherman Skolnick, Carlyle owns a major slice of BioPort, the company that controls the US supply of the anthrax vaccine much used in the wake of September 11th when mysterious packages containing anthrax were posted to various addresses in America. The value of the vaccine soared after the packages began to appear and one of the major beneficiaries has been … yes … yes … the bin Laden family – another investor in BioPort! [72] So, too, is Fuad El-Hibri, a Saudi businessman close to the bin Laden family, who is President and Chief Executive Officer of BioPort Corporation.[73] You could not make this up. Another beneficiary is Admiral William Crowe, former head of the Joint Chiefs of Staff when American-produced weapons-grade anthrax was being supplied to Saddam Hussein for use in the war against Iran. He served at the Pentagon for a time under Secretary of Defense Frank Carlucci, now chairman of the Carlyle Group. Admiral Crowe, a member of the Illuminati's Council on Foreign Relations and former US Ambassador to London, now owns 13% of BioPort Corporation and sits on the board. BioPort has one customer, the US Department of Defense, and one product – anthrax vaccine. It is the only US Corporation with a license to make anthrax vaccine and the licence was acquired in 1998 by buying the laboratory where the vaccine is made, the Michigan Biologic Products Institute.

President Bush is not keen for the people to know the background to BioPort and its owners. Investigative reporter Sherman Skolnick writes:

> "Under the disguise of invoking national emergency provisions, George W. Bush has ordered National Guard sentries to guard the BioPort facility in Lansing, Michigan. Bush has ordered, under pretext of 'national security', that employees and officials of BioPort are forbidden to discuss with reporters, commentators, and researchers, the nature of the ownership of BioPort Corporation. This was done to preclude details of this private corporation from being publicly disclosed. This presidential edict was quietly put through just prior to the beginning of bombing by the US of Afghanistan. Despite this clamp-down on disclosure, some very patriotic employees of BioPort have informed independent-minded commentators of the reputed ownership and operations details of BioPort Corporation." [74]

BioPort's sole customer is the US Department of Defense, which has poured millions of dollars into the company to keep it going while it has supplied only 4% of the contracted vaccine. The Defense Department advanced $18 million of taxpayers' money in 1999 and another $24 million in 2000 and yet now the investors in the company, like the Bushes and bin Ladens, make fantastic profits because of the anthrax scare. Similarly, in 1996 when the Khobar Towers US military quarters in Saudi Arabia was hit by a terrorist truck bomb blamed on Osama bin Laden, his family business made a fortune with the contract from the US military to replace it and build military barracks and airfields for US troops! [75] The anthrax drug, Cipro, which increased its sales by 600% after October 2001, is produced by the German Illuminati company, Bayer, formerly part of I.G. Farben, the very heart of Hitler's war machine and the operation that ran the concentration camp at Auschwitz (see *And The Truth Shall Set You Free*). Eberhard von Kuenheim, a former chairman of Bayer, works for the Carlyle Group. President George W. Bush has resisted all pressure to remove Bayer's patent and open the way for much cheaper generic versions, even though Bayer was apparently charging $350 for a drug you can buy in India for $10 to $20.

"Ken who?"

The Enron Corporation was the biggest financial backer of George W. Bush in his presidential election campaign and has been financially supporting his career since he was governor of Texas. You would, therefore, expect that it would be a cesspit of deceit and corruption. It was formed in 1985 by the merger of Houston Natural Gas and Internorth, and was based in the Bush home base of Houston, Texas. The following year Kenneth Lay, a member of the Illuminati Trilateral Commission, and close friend and associate of the Bushes, was made chief executive officer and later became chairman. Enron threw money like confetti at Bush and more than 250 senators and congressmen, and it bullied and manipulated a massive expansion of its global holdings helped by the nose-in-the-trough politicians on its payroll across the world. The technique was simple. The Illuminati forced the "liberalisation" and "opening up" of national energy supplies in developing countries and elsewhere, and Enron then secured the contracts to supply energy in those countries, often funded by "foreign aid" and World Bank money. Everywhere they went, power prices soared at the expense of local people and, in California, they conspired with other power companies to create false "shortages" and blackouts to justify massive multi-billion-dollar investment by the state for increasing energy supply. However, Enron was using deeply corrupt accounting administered by the Arthur Andersen Group to hide its fantastic debts and exaggerate its earnings by hundreds of millions. Eventually, like its banking "mirror" the BCCI, the house of straw came down amid a frenzy of document shredding in December 2001 in the biggest corporate bankruptcy in American history. Those responsible, like chairman Kenneth Lay and CEO Jeffrey Skilling, made multi-millions by selling their shares at the top of the market before, as they knew, the share price would collapse to the floor. Shareholders, including thousands of Enron employees who had been encouraged to buy shares by the company, lost everything, including, for thousands, their jobs. Kenneth Lay alone sold shares worth $119 million before the collapse and no wonder he could afford to donate $290,000 to the George W. Bush presidential campaign. Skilling sold some 10,000 shares a week to secure $66.9 million, and a group of 29 Enron executives and directors received $1.1 billion by selling 17.3 million shares between 1999 and mid-2001. They knew what was coming, but they cut and ran while thousands of workers and small shareholders lost billions and many their retirement pensions.

Payback

But right up to the end, George W. Bush and Dick Cheney were trying to provide Kenny Boy with value for money. Lay served on the Bush transition team after his rigged November 2000 "election", and he helped to interview candidates for the Federal Energy Regulatory Commission. This oversees the gas pipelines and electricity grids that are fundamental to Enron's business![76] Curtis Hebert, the chairman of the Commission, said he was "offended" by Lay's efforts to lobby for Enron and Hebert later resigned.[77] Enron executives were appointed to prominent positions in the Bush administration. Larry Lindsey, his Chief Economic Adviser, and Robert Zoellick, his leading trade negotiator, were both advisers to Enron and the Secretary of the Army, Thomas White, was an Enron executive before joining the Bush administration.[78] Karl Rove, Bush's senior adviser, was an Enron shareholder who took part in many government meetings about energy policy. In February and March 2000, soon after the Bush inauguration, Kenneth Lay met Vice President Cheney and energy policy was modified to suit Enron. In May, Cheney issued a statement opposing caps on energy prices in California after a memo from Lay suggesting that he do just that. In all, Lay and Enron were consulted six times before Cheney announced his energy policy.[79] Cheney has refused to make public the documents and details of what was discussed at these meetings or even allow access to the General Accounting Office, the investigative arm of Congress. The White House "energy task force" was controlled by the energy industry and part of its final report involving the policy on global warming was taken almost word for word from a policy paper issued by an energy industry trade group.[80]

When the Enron scandal broke, of course, President Boy Bush did what the Bush family always do. He lied. He played down the relationship and referred to Lay as just a "supporter". Charles Lewis, Director of the Center of Public Integrity, said there was no doubt about the very close ties between Enron and Bush: "Enron was the number one career patron for George W. Bush. There was no company in America closer to George W. Bush than Enron."[81] Then in February 2002 some two dozen letters written by Lay to the then Governor Bush were released from Texas archives after requests by the media and the watchdog group, Public Citizen. They include holiday and birthday greetings and get well notes. In one letter sent in 1997, Bush says: "Laura and I value our friendship with you." A note in the same year from Lay to Bush thanks him for his support for Enron's efforts to supply electricity for Philadelphia, then governed by Tom Ridge, who was appointed head of Homeland Security by Bush after 9/11. "I very much appreciate your call to Tom Ridge a few days ago," Lay wrote, "I am certain that it will have a positive impact on the way [Ridge] and others in Pennsylvania view our proposal."[82] Bush first met Lay in the late 1980s and yet he said he only knew him after he became governor of Texas in 1994. Eventually White House Communications Director Dan Bartlett had to admit to the *Chicago Tribune* that the relationship between Bush and Lay probably began in 1987 and 1988 when they worked on Father Bush's presidential election campaign. "He met him through his father and through his father's political activity," said Bartlett. "He does not recall specifics."[83] I bet he doesn't. Bush and Enron were one unit and both share a life-long addiction to deceit and corruption. Other "Enron"-type accounting scandals have followed with companies like Worldcom. This is, in part, a manifestation of the cesspit in which the global corporations operate, but it is also connected to the Illuminati plan to crash the world economy by destroying confidence in it. With the economy in ruins they would have a problem-reaction-solution to bring in their centralised control of everything. Incidentally, Richard Breeden, the man appointed court monitor of WorldCom after the accounting scandal broke, was the Father Bush-appointed Chairman of the Securities and Exchange Commission that cleared Boy George of insider trading with Harken Energy.

Coup on America

After Boy George's business failures in the oil industry, in which he massively benefited financially thanks to other people's money, he turned to baseball. He and a group of partners bought the franchise of the Texas Rangers in 1989. Bush was the general manager and this was part of the strategy designed to give him a positive profile in Texas with a view to him running for governor again. This he did with the money power behind him and he was elected Governor of Texas in November 1994, after which he became the most enthusiastic enforcer of capital punishment in America. The plan soon became clear – another Bush was being groomed for the presidency. He was re-elected governor on November 3rd 1998 with 68.6% of the vote. Two years later, almost to the day, he was the 43rd President of the United States, as I had predicted he would be some three years earlier. You only had to know his bloodline and see the way his political profile was being raised to realise that he was the chosen one. As a result, his presidential campaign broke all records for fundraising and, before June 2000, he had attracted donations of $37 million thanks to Enron, the Carlyle Group and the rest of the Illuminati campaign to put their man in the White House.

His "opponents" were the Arizona Republican, John McCain, in the race for the Republican nomination for president, and the then Vice President Al Gore for the presidency itself. Both of these "opponents" knew they were not meant to win because Bush was the president-in-waiting. The Illuminati had enough dirt on both of them to stop any true exposé of George W. Bush during the campaigns. Gore is also bloodline although his DNA connections are not as impressive as Bush's in the Illuminati genetic hierarchy. Again with Gore's insider knowledge of the Bush family he could have destroyed Dubya, but with Gore also heavily involved in the same horrific behaviour, and well aware of the dire consequences of crossing his masters, Bush was given an easy ride. In the same way, the Democratic "challenger" Michael Dukakis knew his role and his place when he faced Father George in the 1988 election before Bush gave way, as planned, to Clinton. But even with all the aces in his favour, George W. Bush was such an unimpressive candidate that Gore won the popular vote across the country by half a million in November 2000. In a truly representative election, that should have been enough to put Gore in the White House, but that wasn't the plan so it was not allowed to happen. The US system means that you win presidential "points" or votes for an "electoral college" based on the states you win (some states are worth more than others) and it all came down, infamously, to the result in Florida, the state governed by Bush's brother, Jeb, who, naturally being a Bush, is another monumental crook. Even though the vote in Florida was so obviously rigged (to anyone with any brain cell activity), note how meekly Al Gore accepted it in the end and slipped quietly away. He knew what had happened and he knew why, and he knew better than to cause trouble serious enough to stop Bush taking the throne. As Chicago investigative reporter, Sherman Skolnick, has pointed out, the Florida judiciary is notoriously controlled by the CIA,[84] which, in turn, is very closely associated with Father George, who had his own son, Jeb, running Florida during the "election". Sorry Al, darlin', you never stood a chance, mate. Not that he would have been any better had he won. A media consortium of the *Wall Street Journal, Washington Post, New York Times,* and CNN commissioned the National Opinion Research Council at Chicago University to inspect 170,000 disallowed votes in Florida to prove who really won the 2000 presidential election. The results were ready by the end of August 2001 and media reports suggested that the count would show that Gore beat Bush in Florida conclusively and should have been president. But after 9/11 the media consortium said that the recount had been postponed due to a "lack of resources and lack of interest" in the story after the events of September 11th.[85] Oh yes? A lack of interest in whether you have a legitimate president when he is taking you into an open-ended war across the world? "Our belief is that the priorities of the country have changed, and our priorities have changed," said Steven Goldstein, the Vice President of corporate communications at Dow Jones and Co, the owners of the *Wall Street Journal*.[86] My belief is that the media priorities actually remain very much the same – suppressing information that doesn't suit those in power. Little things, you know, like the fact that the president is an impostor.

What happened in Florida was a coup on America and yet the vast majority who watched it unfold had no idea that an unelected dictator had been imposed on their "Land of the Free and Home of the Brave" or, as someone rightly put it: "The Land of the Fee and Home of the Slave." An investigation by the US Commission on Civil Rights reported that Florida officials (controlled ultimately by Governor Jeb Bush) had been responsible for preventing citizens from voting in the election. The report called this "widespread". The commission said the officials were "grossly derelict" in the way they conducted the election. Jeb Bush and Florida Secretary of State Katherine Harris, both Republicans, were especially highlighted in the Commission's report for ignoring "mounting evidence" of problems with outdated voting technology in a number of counties, and for ignoring requests for guidance and assistance from local elections officials. These "technical problems" were used as an excuse to discount tens of thousands of votes, mostly those of black and immigrant workers most likely to vote for Gore. Remember Bush eventually "won" the state by 537 votes. Yet in Palm Beach County, 19,000 ballots were "double-punched" and discarded, and in precincts heavily populated by Haitian-Americans, there were reports of ballots that were pre-punched for Bush. Tens of thousands of other people were told they could not vote at all, even though they were carrying voter registration cards. Palm Beach County was the location of a vote fraud in the late 1990s in which the Republican mayor was forced to resign because he had benefited from an absentee vote fraud organised by his supporters. The Florida Department of Law Enforcement arrested 58 people. *Miami Herald* columnist Dave Barry wrote:

> "Florida's No 3 industry, behind tourism and skin cancer, is voter fraud. Here in Miami, we've had elections where the dead voters outnumbered the live ones. Elsewhere in the State there have been reports of irregular voting procedures, including one Palm Beach County precinct where the 'ballots' given to voters were actually pizza coupons." [87]

Bush buys the election

BBC *Newsnight* reporter Greg Palast, a rare journalist worth the name, revealed that the Jeb Bush administration in Florida paid a private company called Database Technologies (DBT) $4 million to remove from the voter lists the names of people who had committed serious crimes.[88] Palast obtained a document marked "confidential and trade secret", which says that the company was paid the money to make telephone calls to verify they got the right names. But they didn't do it. Palast said there was nothing in the State of Florida files that says these telephone calls were made and this wrongly barred thousands of Democrat voters who did not have criminal records from voting in Florida. The first list from DBT of voters they said should be barred from voting included 8,000 names supplied by George Bush's state officials in Texas! They claimed these names were all serious criminals barred from voting, but, as Palast said, it turned out that almost none were. When this was challenged, DBT issued a new list naming 58,000 felons, but one county that checked the names relevant to its voters found that this list was 95% wrong. One of those named, Reverend Willie Whiting, had never spent a night in jail in his life. Palast went to Tallahassee to question Jeb Bush's Director of Elections in Florida, Clayton Roberts. "We want to know whether George W. Bush won the election or did brother Jeb steal it for him," Palast said. Roberts agreed to talk until he realised that Palast had a copy of the secret document relating to DBT and he called the State Troopers to remove Palast and his colleagues. Palast said that he had not asked his most difficult questions before the troopers arrived. These were: Did Governor Jeb Bush, his Secretary of State Katherine Harris, and her Director of Elections, Clayton Roberts, know they had wrongly barred 22,000 black Democrat voters before the elections? After the elections did they use their powers to prevent the count of 20,000 votes for the Democrats? In Palm Beach, voting machines misread 27,000 ballots, but Jeb Bush's Secretary of State, Katharine Harris, prevented these votes from being counted by hand. She did the same in Gadstone, one of Florida's poorest and most Democrat counties, where the machines did not count one in eight ballots. This same Katherine Harris was Co-Chair of the Bush presidential campaign!

The illegitimate president

The US Commission on Civil Rights confirmed that African-American voters were ten times more likely than white voters to have their ballots rejected and that an "overzealous" state-wide campaign to reduce voter fraud resulted in disproportionately denying eligible African-American voters from casting ballots on election day. It also said that African-Americans (overwhelmingly voters for Gore if you look at history) were more likely to have been erroneously removed from voter registration rolls than Hispanic or white voters. The report criticised local election supervisors in counties hardest hit by voting problems. It said they showed a "lack of leadership" in protecting voting rights. When the official count and recount using technology gave the election to Bush by a fraction, despite those thousands of votes lost to Gore, the Democrats called for a hand count. This was the only way to count the thousands of votes that were misread by voting machines. This was the only fair way to decide an election that was deciding the president. But the Bush camp was determined that this would not happen because they knew what the outcome of a fair count would be: Bush was going to lose. So on to the scene came … oh yes, ladies and gentlemen please welcome … James A. Baker III, the Secretary of State to Father George during the Gulf War, and a major force in the bin Laden/bin Mahfouz-connected Carlyle Group. Baker told the media in Tallahassee, Florida, that he and the Bush camp were applying for a federal injunction to stop a hand count. They were doing this, he said in typical Illuminati reverse language, to ... "preserve the integrity and the consistency and the equality and finality of the most important civic action that Americans take: their votes in an election for president of the United States. We feel we have no other choice." [89] No other choice if they wanted Bush to win. They also knew that if they could have the decision made by the Bush-controlled Supreme Court they were home. In the end, the issue did indeed go to the Supreme Court where, on December 12th 2000, they gave the presidency to Bush by five votes to four, voting on party lines. The decision was utterly perverse because they agreed that in order to have equal voter protection in Florida the whole state should be recounted, but they ruled that there was not enough time to do this – even though there were still weeks to go before the electoral votes of all the states had to be officially accepted. [90] On this insane basis they gave the presidency to Bush! This is how the man who has taken the world into a "war on terrorism" came to power.

Another point about that Florida election. If you remember, the television networks that night first called Florida for Gore, then too close to call, and then for Bush. Well this is what happened. [91] In the early hours of election night, November 8th, the Fox News Channel, owned by Rupert Murdoch, declared that Florida had gone for George W. Bush and that he was the new president. The other television networks repeated this within minutes. The man at Fox who recommended this decision was John Ellis, who headed the network's decision desk. Ellis, it turns out, is the first cousin of George W. Bush and brother Jeb, the Florida Governor, and, by his own admission, he had been in constant contact with them all night. [92] Investigative reporter Kate Randall revealed:

> "Shortly after 6 p.m. two waves of exit polls from the Voter News Service (a consortium set up by the major TV networks and Associated Press) showed the Florida vote going for Democratic candidate Al Gore. John Ellis received a call from the Bush campaign in Austin and told them the bad news. At 7.52 pm the major networks, including Fox, called Florida for Gore.

> "Just after 8 pm, Jeb Bush phoned Ellis and asked him, 'Are you sure?', to which Ellis responded, 'We're looking at a screen full of Gore.' It was at this point that the Bush campaign – aided by information to which they were privy via their family connection at Fox – went into overdrive to reverse what appeared to be a Democratic victory." [93]

The Bush camp called a press conference at the Texas governor's mansion in Austin and said that, in their view, the vote was too close to call in Pennsylvania and Florida. The conference broke with previous election-night procedure in which candidates don't speak to the media until one of them has conceded. As Randall wrote:

"The actions of the Bush campaign constituted a bald-faced attempt to co-opt a servile media into stampeding public opinion in its favor. The TV networks broadcast the interview even as large numbers of voters were still heading to the polls." [94]

John Ellis, the Bush cousin at Fox, claims that exit polls by the Voter News Service showed a change in Florida in Bush's favour between 8pm and 9pm. After that, all the television networks withdrew the call for Gore and said Florida was too close to call. *Newsweek* reported that, after midnight, Bush's lead in Florida began to diminish, but despite this, at 2.16am, *Fox News* called Florida for Bush on the direction of Bush cousin, John Ellis. Again, within minutes, the other networks followed. Ellis told *New Yorker* magazine that 16 minutes before this decision he had been on the phone to the Bush brothers: "It was just the three of us guys handing the phone back and forth – me with the numbers, one of them a governor, the other the president-elect. Now *that* was cool." Randall sums up this grotesque example of media bias: "In other words, the Republican candidate, and the governor of the state where the outcome of the race would be determined, had a direct line – through their cousin – to a media outlet that would broadcast their 'victory' nationwide." [95] With this announcement by Fox, Gore called Bush to concede the election and was about to make his speech giving the presidency to Bush when he heard that, in fact, Bush's lead (even with all those lost Gore votes) was down to a few thousand and falling. Randall quite rightly asks: "Did Ellis, fearing that the networks might move Florida back into the Gore column, decide to make a pre-emptive strike in the hope of stampeding the other networks and conning Gore into making a premature concession? Did the Bush campaign have a hand in Ellis's call?" It certainly helped Bush that's for sure. Mark Fabiani, Gore's communications director, said: "To have a network like Fox call it and everybody follow suit was a tremendously damaging thing. It took literally 24 to 48 hours to convince people that Gore had won the popular vote." But, of course, Rupert Murdoch, supporter of Tony Blair in Britain, defended Ellis. No one who believes in fair play and media impartiality would do that, but this, it goes without saying, is not a problem for Murdoch.

This is only a fraction of the horrific background to the Bush family that is taking the world further and further into a war against freedom, decency, and justice. Al Martin, a retired Lieutenant Commander with the US Naval Reserves and Naval Intelligence, is the author of *The Conspirators: Secrets of an Iran-Contra Insider*.[96] Martin claims to have seen at first hand the government drug trafficking, illegal weapons deals and an "epidemic of fraud" – corporate securities fraud, real estate fraud, insurance fraud and bank fraud. He writes of the Bush family:

"You have to look at the entire Bush Family in this context – as if the entire family ran a corporation called Frauds-R-Us. Each member of the family, George Sr., George Jr., Neil, Jeb, Prescott, Wally, etc., have their own specialty of fraud. George Jr.'s speciality was insurance and security fraud. Jeb's speciality was oil and gas fraud. Neil's specialty was real estate fraud. Prescott's speciality was banking fraud. Wally's speciality was securities fraud. And George Sr.'s specialty? All of the above." [97]

This is the family of President Bush, who said after the WorldCom scandal that there must be "a new era of integrity" in American corporate life. Anyone still think these guys are telling you the truth about September 11th?

SOURCES

1   At Height of Vietnam, Bush Picks Guard, *Washington Post*, July 28th 1999, p A1

2   Ibid

3   **http://www.onlinejournal.com/Archive/Bush/SoftSkull020700/softskull020700.html**

4   Ibid

5   Ibid

6   Sander Hicks, **http://www.gwbush.com/index8-7.shtml**

7   See **www.copvcia.comwww.copvcia.com**

8   Terry Reed and John Cummings, *Compromised: Clinton, Bush, and the CIA* (SPI. Books, New York, 1994)

9   Sherman H. Skolnick, *Wal-Mart and the Red Chinese Secret Police, Part One*, August 27th 2001, **http://www.skolnicksreport.com/rcsp.html**

10 *Compromised: Clinton, Bush, and the CIA*, pp 212–213

11 **http://www.idfiles.com/globe.htm**

12 *BBC News Online*, January 29th 2001

13 Ibid

14 Uri Dowbenko, *Bush Babies in the Briar Patch*, **http://allsouthwest.com/library/mena/Steamshovel%20Press%20Offline%20Illumination.htm**

15 *San Antonio Express-News*, September 14th 1998

16 *Wall Street Journal*, September 27th 2001

17 *Newsnight*, BBC2, November 6th 2001

18 Ibid

19 Ibid

20 UK *Guardian*, November 7th 2001

21 **http://news.bbc.co.uk/hi/english/events/newsnight/newsid_1645000/1645527.stm**

22 *Air Force Magazine*, Air Force MagazineFebruary 1999

23 *San Antonio Express-News*, September 14th 1998

24 **http://www.salon.com/politics/feature/2002/02/08/forbidden**

25 Ibid

26 *All Fall Down*, p 142

27 **http://www.judicialwatch.org/1075.shtml** and
    http://www.realityexpander.com/articles/joewatson/end_justifies_means_2.html

28 **CNSNews.com**, May 30th 2002

29 Ibid

30 From the video *9/11 – The Road To Tyranny*, presented by Alex Jones and available at
    Infowars.com

31 **http://www.tenc.net/news/bushladen.htmlbid**

32 *American Free Press*, June 10th, 2001

33 **http://www.conspiracyplanet.com/channel.cfm?channelid=101&contentid=400&page=2**

34 Official Papers of the Presidents, Press Conference, October 25th 1991, George Herbert
    Walker Bush

35 **http://www.realchange.org/bushjr.htm**

36 **http://www.americanfreedomnews.com/afn_articles/bushsecrets.htm**

37 Ibid

38 Saudi Money Aiding bin Laden, *USA Today*, October 28th 1999

39 *Wall Street Journal*, September 27th 2001

40 **http://www.americanfreedomnews.com/afn_articles/bushsecrets.htm**

41 *The Ties That Bind: Barclays, a bin Laden relative, Carlyle and the BCCI boys*, by Kevin Dowling,
    http://www.onlinejournal.com/Special_Reports/Dowling110301/dowling110301.htmlis

42 **http://www.africana.com/DailyArticles/index_19991213.htm**

43 *All Fall Down*, p 144

44 Ibid

45 Ibid, p 88

46 *Intelligence* Newsletter, March 2nd 2000

47 **http://www.americanfreedomnews.com/afn_articles/bushsecrets.htm** and
    http://www.nexusmagazine.com/beast2.html

48 **http://www.nexusmagazine.com/beast2.html** and
    http://www.americanfreedomnews.com/afn_articles/bushsecrets.htm

49 Jonathan Beaty and S.C. Gwynne, *The Outlaw Bank: A Wild Ride into the Secret Heart of the
    BCCI* (Random House, New York, 1993)

50 Dr Arthur F. Ide, *George W. Bush: Portrait of a Compassionate Conservative* (Monument
    Press, Texas, September, 2000)

51 Ibid

52 *Associated Press*, September 7th 2000

53 *Wall Street Journal*, September 27th and 28th 2001

54 *Newsweek*, February 4th 2002

55 *Wall Street Journal*, September 27th and 28th 2001

56   *New York Times*, March 5th 2001

57   *Wall Street Journal*, September 27th 2001

58   Ibid

59   Karl Evanzz, *The Judas Factor: The Plot to Kill Malcolm X* (Thunder's Mouth Press, 1993)

60   *Eyes On America* by Jonathan Ashley, October 9th 2001,
     http://www.truthout.org/docs_01/0662.Bush.Saudi.htm

61   Ibid

62   Ibid

63   **http://www.truthout.org/docs_01/0662.Bush.Saudi.htm**

64   **http://www.villagevoice.com/issues/0141/gray.php**

65   *New York Times*, March 5th 2001

66   *Wall Street Journal*, September 27th 2001

67   Ibid

68   Statement issued October Ist 2001, **http://aztlan.net/judwatch.htm**

69   The Carlyle Group: ex-government officials cash in, by Shannon Jones, May 16th 2001,
     World Socialist Website, **http://www.wsws.org/articles/2001/may2001/carl-m16.shtml**

70   The ties that bind: Barclays, a bin Laden relative, Carlyle and the BCCI boys, by Kevin Dowling,
     http://www.onlinejournal.com/Special_Reports/Dowling110301/dowling110301.htmlis

71   *Trance-Formation Of America*, p 215

72   See the Skolnick Report,
     http://www.makethemaccountable.com/2002/01/index_020129.html

73   Ibid

74   **http://www.makethemaccountable.com/2002/01/index_020129.html**

75   *Wall Street Journal*, September 27th 2001

76   **http://abcnews.go.com/sections/politics/DailyNews**

77   Ibid

78   Ibid

79   **http://www.corpwatch.org/issues/PID.jsp?articleid=2278**

80   **http://www.bushnews.com/bushlies.htm**

81   **http://abcnews.go.com/sections/politics/DailyNews**

82   Bush-Lay letters suggest close relationship, CNN, February 17th 2002,
     http://www.cnn.com/2002/US/02/17/bush.lay

83   *Chicago Tribune*, March 6th 2002

84   **http://www.skolnicksreport.com**

85   *Daily Telegraph*, October 21st 2001

86   Ibid

87   World Socialist Website, **http://www.wsws.org**

88 *Newsnight,* February 16th 2001
    http://news.bbc.co.uk/hi/english/events/newsnight/newsid_1174000/1174115.stm

89 Common Dreams News Center **http://www.commondreams.org/headlines/111100-01.htm**

90 **www.bushwatch.com**

91 Kate Randall, November 17th 2000, World Socialist Website,
    www.wsws.org/articles/2000/nov2000/fox-n17.shtml

92 *New Yorker,* November 2000

93 Kate Randall, November 17th 2000, World Socialist Website,
    www.wsws.org/articles/2000/nov2000/fox-n17.shtml

94 Ibid

95 Ibid

96 National Liberty Press LLC, 2001

97 **www.almartinraw.com**

chapter 4

"Big Dick" Cheney

"Planet Earth is the asylum to which the rest of the universe sends it's lunatics."

Voltaire

The Bushes have always surrounded themselves with crooks, killers, and deeply disturbed friends and associates. It makes them feel at home, see. There are few better examples of this than their fellow Bohemian Grove attendee, Dick Cheney, the White House Chief of Staff to President Ford; Father George's Defense Secretary at the time of the Gulf conflict; and Vice President to George W. Bush during the "war on terrorism".

Cathy O'Brien in her book, *Trance-Formation Of America*, tells of her horrific experiences of Cheney when she was a victim of the Illuminati/CIA mind-control programmes and Cheney was Defense Secretary to Father George, who sexually and violently abused her and her little daughter, Kelly. Cathy details in her book how she was involved in drug running operations under instructions from Cheney, some of which involved Bandar bin Sultan (Cheney called him "the Sultan"). Bin Sultan was the deeply corrupt US ambassador to King Fahd of Saudi Arabia, the George Bush puppet and close associate of the bin Laden family and terrorist financiers like Khalid bin Mahfouz. Cathy also describes the constant and sickening brutality that she and her daughter suffered from Cheney and Bush. This was just one occasion:

"Bush attempted to sell Cheney on the idea of pedophillia through graphic descriptions of having sex with Kelly. Both were already sexually aroused from drugs and anticipation. Cheney demonstrated to Bush why he did not have sex with kids by exposing himself to Kelly and saying: 'Come here.' Upon seeing Cheney's unusually large penis, Kelly reeled back in horror and cried 'No!' which made them both laugh. Bush asked Cheney for his liquid cocaine atomizer as he got up to take Kelly to the bedroom. When Cheney remarked how benevolent it was of Bush to numb her with it before sex, Bush replied: 'The hell it is. It's for me.' He described his excited state in typical vulgar terms and explained that he wanted to spray cocaine on his penis to last longer.

"Cheney said: 'I thought it was for the kid'.

"Bush explained: 'Half the fun is having them squirm.' He took Kelly's hand and led her off to the bedroom.

"Cheney told me that since I was responsible for Bush's assault on my daughter … I would 'burn' (in hell). He burned my inner thigh with the fireplace poker and threatened to throw Kelly in the fire. He hypnotically enhanced his description of her burning to traumatize me deeply. As he sexually brutalized me, I heard Kelly's whimpers coming from the bedroom. As her cries grew louder, Cheney turned on classical music to drown out her cries for help." [1]

Another time, Cathy tells of what happened when she asked Cheney, amid yet another brutal beating session, if she could go to the toilet:

"Cheney's face turned red with rage. He was on me in an instant, slamming my back into the wall with one arm across my chest and his hand on my throat, choking me while applying pressure to the carotid artery in my neck with his thumb. His eyes bulged and he spit as he growled: 'If you don't mind, I will kill you. I could kill you – kill you – with my bare hands. You are not the first and you won't be the last. I'll kill you any time I goddam well please.' He flung me on the cot-type bed that was behind me. There he finished taking his rage out on me sexually." [2]

This is the same Dick Cheney who is US Vice President telling the world who we must bomb and slaughter to win the "war on terrorism". It is also worth noting the unbelievable hypocrisy involved when Boy George, the son of a paedophile and associate of Cheney, announced an initiative in August 2002 to "protect America's children". Richard Bruce Cheney was born in Nebraska in 1941 and was brought up in Casper, Wyoming. He is yet another of the clique to hail from Yale, home of the Skull and Bones Society, but he dropped out before eventually securing a degree in political science at Wyoming University. Cheney then headed for Washington where he joined the Nixon administration as a special assistant to … Donald Rumsfeld, the Defense Secretary today in the "war on terrorism". Rumsfeld at that time was the first director of the Office of [Illuminati] Economic Opportunity. When Nixon resigned over the Kissinger-engineered Watergate scandal in 1974 (see *And The Truth Shall Set You Free*), Rumsfeld joined the White House staff as assistant to the new president, Gerald Ford, another abuser of Cathy O'Brien, and a man who, thanks to Watergate, never had to be elected and never would have been if the voters had been given a say. That was another coup on America. Ford's intellectual capacity was akin to that of George W. Bush and the famous saying that he couldn't walk and chew gum at the same time was right on. Cheney moved with Rumsfeld and eventually became Ford's Chief of Staff between 1975 and 1977 when he was still in his early thirties. After the first of several heart attacks, he was elected as Congressman for Wyoming and remained in office until Father George made him Defense Secretary when he was elected president in 1988. Cheney is yet another of the bloodline cliques which are keen to send others into battle, so long as they never have to go. He also avoided the draft to Vietnam when he was given deferments because he was a student and a "registrant with a child". Just like President "Dubya", he told his Senate confirmation hearing that he "would have been obviously happy to serve had I been called". Funny how they never are, though. In 1964, Cheney married his wife, Lynne, another Washington insider. She was head of the National Endowment of the Humanities from 1986 to 1993 under Reagan and then Bush (or, in truth, Bush and then Bush). She later became a senior fellow at the American Enterprise Institute (where Cheney was also involved between 1993 and 1995) and was co-host of CNN's appalling "debate" show *Crossfire Sunday* for three years until 1998. Mrs Cheney was on the Lockheed Martin board from 1994 until January 2001 – the very company that the then Texas Governor George W. Bush tried to contract to run the Texas welfare system. Fortunately, public protests stopped him. Bruce Jackson, the Lockheed Martin Vice President, was a finance chair of the Bush for President campaign.

Dick Cheney became best known during the Gulf Slaughter in 1991 when he worked to ensure the mass murder of hundreds of thousands of Iraqi civilians, now more than a million when you include the sanctions. Alongside him in that administration were President Father George (Carlyle Group), Secretary of State James Baker (Carlyle Group) and Colin Powell, Chairman of the Joint Chiefs of Staff. Cheney stated that his "defence" policy was "Arms for America's friends and arms control for its potential foes." Which, of course, was baloney. The policy was "Sell second-rate arms to countries that we can then demonise for being armed and dangerous, thus giving us the excuse to use our state-of-the-art weapons to blow the shit out of their civilian population."

Big Dick and big business

After Bush's pre-arranged defeat to his subordinate associate Bill Clinton in 1992, Cheney moved into "private business" to serve the Illuminati in another way pending his return to Washington with Little George nine years later. Cheney became fantastically wealthy as a director of elite companies like Morgan Stanley, Union Pacific, Procter & Gamble, and Ross Perot's Electronic Data Systems Corporation. His most important appointment, however, came in 1995 when he became the Chairman and Chief Executive of the (yet again) Texas-based Halliburton Oil. This was founded in 1919 and owns a highly significant subsidiary called Brown & Root. Cheney had no experience in the oil industry, but that's not why Halliburton offered him the job. He had other "qualities" that would expand their business. While Cheney was Defense Secretary (and before and afterwards), Brown & Root has been awarded hundreds of millions of dollars' worth of construction contracts in war zones like Bosnia, Somalia and Haiti after they had been devastated by US bombing and manipulation. In the same way, in July 1999, a Balkan Assistance and Reconstruction Conference in Washington DC was arranged for Balkan government officials to meet with executives from Cheney's Halliburton/Brown & Root and other US corporations to plan the financial and political needs for the occupation and operation of the Balkans. The technique is this: you control the political decisions to start wars that suit your agenda; you lend the governments money to buy armaments from you and they use your oil to fight the wars; then, when all this has devastated the target country and its population, you get yourself awarded the contracts to rebuild what you have destroyed. Cheney is the biggest shareholder in Halliburton with a stake of some $45.5 million and the company's board includes Lawrence Eagleburger, who held State Department posts under President Father George and is an executive of the notorious Kissinger Associates (see *And The Truth Shall Set You Free*).

Paying for the privilege

Halliburton and Brown & Root have long used political patronage and funding to expand business and profits. Brown & Root's ticket to the top came through its political contributions to President Lyndon Johnson from the time he ran for Senate in 1948. The *Austin Chronicle* once called him "the candidate from Brown and Root" [3] Thanks to Johnson they made billions on government contracts, including those relating to the Vietnam War after Johnson reversed the policies of the assassinated JFK and plunged America deeper into the conflict. During Vietnam, Johnson gave his personal funders contracts for airports, pipelines and military bases.[4] According to biographer Ronnie Dugger, author of *The Politician: The Life and Times of Lyndon Johnson,*[5] much of the money he was paid by Brown & Root came in cash. "It was a totally corrupt relationship and it benefited both of them enormously," says Dugger, "Brown & Root got rich, and Johnson got power and riches." Using the same tactics, the contracts have flowed from government ever since. Michael C. Ruppert, a former Los Angeles police officer, wrote in a study of Brown & Root:

> "From Bosnia and Kosovo, to Chechnya, to Rwanda, to Burma, to Pakistan, to Laos, to Vietnam, to Indonesia, to Iran to Libya to Mexico to Colombia, Brown & Root's traditional operations have expanded from heavy construction to include the provision of logistical support for the US military. Now, instead of US Army quartermasters, the world is likely to see Brown & Root warehouses storing and managing everything from uniforms to rations to vehicles." [6]

Both Halliburton and Brown & Root were funders of a now infamous company called Permindex, a British Intelligence front organisation headed by the Canadian Louis M. Bloomfield, which, it is now well documented, was the central coordinating network behind the assassination of President Kennedy in Dallas (Texas again) in 1963. (See *And The Truth Shall Set You Free* for the detailed background.) Permindex also ran death squads in Europe, Mexico, Central America, the Caribbean and the United States. Clay Shaw is the only man to be tried for involvement in the assassination, but the New Orleans District Attorney, Jim Garrison, failed to secure a conviction because the key prosecution witnesses had this strange habit of dying from less than natural causes. Shaw, a British intelligence operative who worked for Churchill during the Second World War, ran a division of Permindex in New Orleans. After the assassination, Halliburton purchased Brown & Root. The connections from Permindex involved a stream of famous companies, banks and personalities, including the Bush family and the Bronfman gangster family in Canada through its Seagram liquor operation.[7] Halliburton, at Cheney's say-so, bought and merged with Dresser Industries in an $8 billion deal in 1998 to create the biggest oil-drilling services company in the world. George W. Bush's grandfather Prescott Bush was on the board of Dresser Industries for 22 years in his capacity as a partner in Brown Brothers, Harriman, the funders of Hitler and the eugenics movement, which owned Dresser. The President and Chairman of the Dresser board was Henry Neil Mallon, Prescott's Skull and Bones buddy, who was among those involved in raiding the grave of the Apache chief Geronimo at Fort Sill, Oklahoma, in 1918 to steal his skull and take it back to Skull and Bones headquarters at Yale. It was Mallon, apparently, who burned the flesh and hair off the skull after Bush and friends had stolen it. Father George's crooked son, Neil Mallon Bush of Silverado Savings and Loans fame, was named after the Dresser President, and Father George began his oil career with the company. There is, researchers suggest, a photograph that includes Prescott Bush, and George and Barbara Bush holding an infant George W. in front of the Dresser Industries executive plane.[8]

Snouts in the trough

Cheney says he stands for small government and against government handouts. What he means, naturally, is he believes in that for everyone else, not himself. Halliburton received in five years some $4 billion (at least) in government contracts and loans insured by the taxpayer. The government, through the US Export-Import Bank, also guaranteed credits worth $489 million to a Russian oil company to the benefit of Halliburton, through Brown & Root. This company, according to Russian and American sources and documents, is connected to drug trafficking and organised crime.[9] Before Cheney took over at Halliburton, its business with the US Defense Department was worth around $300 million a year. When Cheney, the former Defense Secretary, arrived their government contracts soared to more than $650 million, according to the *Baltimore Sun*.[10] It's the same story with loans and guarantees from the government's Export-Import Bank and the Overseas Private Investment Corporation: $100 million in the five years before Cheney, but at least $1.5 billion under his leadership. In return for political support and loan guarantees, Halliburton donated vast sums to political candidates and parties after Cheney's arrival, and the lobbying budget doubled: $300,000 a year on lobbying politicians before Cheney and $600,000 with him at the helm. Halliburton has also benefited from US "aid" to various countries, which was then spent by the recipients on hiring Halliburton. The *Los Angeles Times* obtained State Department documents that showed how government officials helped Halliburton to win major contracts in Asia and Africa.[11] This is the way the Illuminati families and agents operate. They control the government decisions through the Illuminati one-party state and operate companies, like Halliburton and the Carlyle Group, which benefit from those government decisions and policies. This is how, once Cheney took over, Halliburton was able to expand so rapidly and become the fifth largest defence contractor in the US, so benefiting enormously from conflicts like the "war on terrorism". It has a worldwide operation involving 130 countries and is America's biggest non-union company.[12] No wonder Cheney was given a $34 million "retirement package" when he left in the summer of 2000 to be the running mate of Boy George. This was after five years on a salary of $1.3 million a year, plus bonuses of millions more, stock options worth some $45 million,[13] and his sale of 100,000 Halliburton shares that netted him $5.1 million.[14] The "retirement package" also included 400,000 unvested stock options due to "vest" over three years. This means that the higher the value of Halliburton stock in this period the more money the Vice President will accrue, and the oil industry depends very much on government policy. The *Baltimore Sun* of June 10th 2002 reported that Halliburton was being investigated by the Securities and Exchange Commission for accounting irregularities. An "aggressive accounting practice" at Halliburton approved by the (Enron/Worldcom) accounting firm Arthur Andersen was said to be behind the investigation, and involved allegations of counting $100 million in revenue that had not yet been received.

Working with terrorists

Cheney's Halliburton has worked closely with some of the most appalling terrorist dictatorships on the planet. He talks of "constructive engagement" in which you work with such regimes and pass on American values. No need. The values of successive US and British governments are a mirror of those employed by these very terrorist dictatorships. For Cheney, this is nothing to do with "values" – he doesn't have any – it is about working with anyone at any price to ensure more money and power, and the advancement of the Illuminati agenda. Dick Cheney was the Defense Secretary in the Gulf Slaughter supposedly aimed at Saddam Hussein in 1991. Yet he made big profits for himself and Halliburton after 1998 through deals with … Saddam Hussein's Iraq. The London *Financial Times* reported that Cheney oversaw $23.8 million worth of contracts for the sale of "oil industry" technology and services to Iraq. He used Halliburton subsidiaries in France, Italy, Germany and Austria to hide the Cheney-Halliburton connection. Among these companies were Dresser Rand and Ingersoll-Dresser Pump.[15] These contracts together were worth more than any other US company doing business with Iraq. The *International Herald Tribune* reported that "Dresser-Rand and Ingersoll-Dresser Pump Co., joint ventures that Halliburton has sold … have done work in Iraq on contracts for the reconstruction of Iraq's oil industry, under the United Nations' Oil for Food Program." [16] A Halliburton spokesman admitted in the *Tribune* article that the Dresser subsidiaries had sold oil-pumping equipment to Iraq via their European agents. So get this: staggeringly, these Halliburton group contracts were helping to rebuild the oil infrastructure of Iraq destroyed by the bombs dropped by United States planes commanded from the Pentagon by the then Defense Secretary Dick Cheney! At the same time Cheney was supporting sanctions against Iraq that have so far produced around a million dead children. (What happened there to "constructive engagement"?)

The oil cartel benefits enormously from cheap oil pumped by Iraq in the United Nations' (Illuminati) "oil-for-food programme". Many Illuminati companies and front men are benefiting from contracts with Iraq and other brutal dictatorships while supporting sanctions that are killing thousands of Iraqi children every month. John Deutsch, the former head of the CIA, is a director of Schlumberger, the second largest US oil services company, which also does business, through subsidiaries, with Iraq. Halliburton has struck deals in Iran and Libya, even though they were on the State Department's list of terrorist states. The Halliburton subsidiary Brown & Root was fined $3.8 million for violation of US sanctions against Libya. Cheney, incidentally, lied on US television (it comes so easy to him) when he was asked during the 2000 presidential campaign on ABC's *This Week* programme about Halliburton's deals with Iraq while he was in charge. He had this brief exchange with interviewer Sam Donaldson, who then just let the matter drop:

> Donaldson: "I'm told, and correct me if I'm wrong, that Halliburton, through subsidiaries, was actually trying to do business in Iraq?"

> Cheney: "No. No. I had a firm policy that I wouldn't do anything in Iraq – even arrangements that were supposedly legal."

What's that they say? Liar, liar, pants on fire? The Gore camp didn't raise this explosive information because they were up to their eyes in corruption too.

Anything goes

A number of pressure groups have sought to expose the support by Halliburton under Cheney's leadership of the brutal military dictatorship in Burma through their involvement in pipeline construction. Among Halliburton's partners, according to published reports, has been the British company Alfred McAlpine. Readers of my other books, like *The Biggest Secret*, will need no introduction to the McAlpine family. EarthRights, the human rights group based in Washington DC, condemned Cheney's Halliburton for two pipeline projects in Burma, the building of which led to rape, murder, indentured labour, the forced relocation of villages and other crimes against humanity.[17] The regime in Burma (also known as Myanmar) has been condemned constantly by the U.N. General Assembly, the International Labor Organization, Amnesty International, the European Union and the US government, which withdrew its ambassador and imposed sanctions. Funnily enough, these sanctions laws specifically exempt the work that Halliburton does. Katie Redford, a human rights lawyer for EarthRights, said: "Halliburton partners and subsidiaries, both before and during Dick Cheney's tenure as CEO, have been contractors for pipeline projects that have led to crimes against humanity in Burma."[18] The International Labor Organization said the junta in Burma is guilty of "an international crime", possibly "a crime against humanity", through its exploitation of forced child labour. Tens of thousands of people have been abused, murdered and driven from their homelands by the Burmese army, thousands have been tortured, and the jails are full of political prisoners. The junta is also one of the world's major producers and traffickers of heroin. All this matters not a jot to Dick Cheney. In fact to him it will be all the more reason to get involved. Also working with the Burmese terrorists on the oil pipelines has been Unocal (Union Oil of California) – the company that proposed a pipeline across Afghanistan, but said the Taliban had to go before it could happen.

Cheney sought to overcome any obstacles to his company's business dealings with one of the world's most oppressive regimes by using USA-Engage, the lobbying group that opposed investment sanctions against Burma. He was also on the board of the National Foreign Trade Council that helped to pressure the Supreme Court to overturn a Massachusetts state law that imposed penalties on companies trading with Burma. When it suits Cheney's agenda he is against even financial sanctions against an oppressive terrorist regime. When it suits him another way, he is in favour of blitz bombing the country and killing thousands of civilians, as in Iraq and Afghanistan.[19]

Halliburton has both denied involvement in Burma and said that it has not tried to hide its involvement. Go figure. *Wall Street Journal* reporter Peter Waldman points out that when Halliburton proclaimed its "success story" in December 1996 with a press conference to announce several big contracts in Asia and Europe there was no mention of one of their biggest deals of the year – in Burma.[20] A spokeswoman for Halliburton said she was not able to establish why the company failed to mention the Burma contract for its subsidiary, European Marine. I think I can help her there. She also declined to explain the massive revenue increase – some 77% – for European Marine in 1997, the year that most of the Burma work was done. I'm sure I can be of some assistance to her there, too. The Halliburton contract was mostly for work on the pipeline offshore and the company claimed that it had no dealings with the Burmese people or the military. This is simply not true. A 1996 report by the U.N. Special Rapporteur on Burma, Judge Rajsoomer Lallah of Mauritius, revealed that people were forced to work offshore as well. He found that in 1995 the military ordered about 200 villagers to go to Heinze Island, an uninhabited shoal in the Andaman Sea where Burmese forces set up a base camp to guard construction work on the offshore pipeline. Peter Waldman told the story in his *Wall Street Journal* report:

> "On Heinze Island, Judge Lallah found, the villagers were required to work for two weeks without pay, clearing land, building bamboo barracks and constructing a helicopter pad high atop a steep hill – probably for later use by the Western companies that built the pipeline, according to Burmese human-rights monitors. The villagers were forced to pay their own transportation costs to the island; those who refused to go were arrested and sent into rebellious areas to serve as porters for the military, Judge Lallah wrote." [21]

... and there's more

Burma is only one in a long list of Cheney-Halliburton deals with dubious and terrorist regimes. Human rights activists point to Halliburton's role in Algeria, Angola, Bosnia, Croatia, Haiti, Iran, Iraq, Rwanda, Somalia, Indonesia, Libya and

Nigeria. Halliburton's partner in Russia, Tyumen Oil, has been accused of committing massive fraud to gain control of a Siberian oil field. EarthRights revealed that a Halliburton contract with Indonesia was cancelled by the government when they investigated those that had been corruptly awarded. One corporate watchdog organisation in Indonesia said that Halliburton's engineering division, Kellogg Brown & Root, was among 59 companies that used "collusive, corruptive and nepotistic practices" with the family of the former president Suharto, a vicious and corrupt dictator installed by British and American intelligence to serve the interests of the corporate giants owned by the Illuminati.[22] That's why Indonesia is now one of the sweatshop capitals of the world where people living in abject poverty work a fantastic number of hours a week for pitiful pay so that big-name clothing and sportswear companies can accrue staggering profits by making the products there for next to nothing while selling them for high prices in the West. It's called "globalisation" and "free trade".

In Nigeria, Halliburton worked with Shell and Chevron, which were both implicated in gross violations of human rights and the environment. (British Petroleum, Esso, Du Pont, ERAP, Texaco, and Total also have interests in Nigeria.) Cheney's firm increased its involvement there after the military dictatorship executed several environmental activists and violently prevented protests against the oil industry. Halliburton was accused of complicity in the shooting of a protestor by Nigeria's Mobile Police Unit. In another incident, highlighted by the New York-based pressure group, Human Rights Watch, soldiers using a Chevron helicopter and Chevron boats attacked villagers in two small communities in Delta State, Opia and Ikenyan. They killed at least four people and burned most of the villages to the ground. More than 50 people were still missing, Human Rights Watch reported. Chevron, who merged with Texaco a month after 9/11, claimed it was a "counterattack" resulting from a confrontation between local youths and soldiers at a Chevron drilling rig. Community members denied there was any such confrontation. Condoleeza Rice, the current US National Security Adviser to Bush and Cheney, was a director of Chevron from 1991 and she took charge of public policy for the board. She even had a Chevron oil tanker named after her. Rice was involved in negotiating Chevron investments in the vast untapped reserves of oil in the Caspian Sea region before leaving to join her long-time buddy, George W. Bush. As National Security Adviser she is very much involved in the "war on terrorism", which has removed the Taliban regime and opened the way for oil and gas pipelines across Afghanistan. These are the very pipelines designed to tap the vast gas and oil reserves around ... the Caspian Sea.

It's the oil, stupid

Before we can understand one (of many) reasons for September 11th and the "war on terrorism" we have to understand the plans of the Illuminati with regard to the fantastic oil and gas reserves of the Caspian Sea region. Cheney's Halliburton does major business in Kazakhstan, Azerbaijan, and Iran, which are all in the same crucial region as Afghanistan (*Figure 8*).[23] Specialists suggest that the Caspian area might

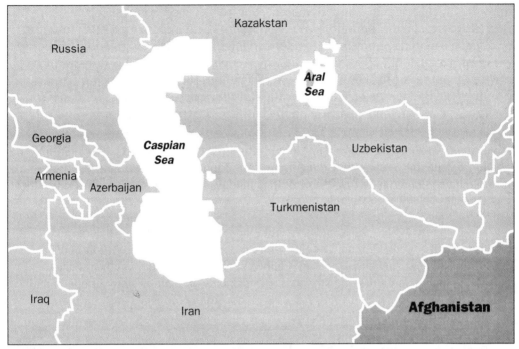

Figure 8: *The Caspian Sea region the Illuminati (indeed different factions of them) are desperate to control*

contain the world's third largest oil and natural gas reserves after the Gulf region and Siberia, and it has been the number one target of the oil cartel and its political representatives since the manufactured break-up of the former Soviet Union aided by Illuminati front man, Mikhail Gorbachev (see *And The Truth Shall Set You Free* and *The Biggest Secret*). The *San Francisco Chronicle* estimated the proven and projected reserves in the region to be more than 800 billion barrels of crude petroleum and its equivalent in natural gas.[24] The combined oil reserves in the Americas and Europe are reckoned to be fewer than 160 billion barrels. The biggest Caspian fields are in Kazakhstan and Azerbaijan (both in Halliburton's portfolio, and Cheney sat on the state of Kazakhstan's Oil Advisory Board). Lesser reserves are located in Georgia, Uzbekistan, Turkmenistan and Armenia. The projected value of this, based on average prices in the 1990s, is $5 trillion, a very conservative estimate. This is the region in which the United States is locating troops in the name of the "war on terrorism". The real reason is to secure control of the oil and gas reserves and the pipelines that will take them to market. William Ramsay, a US Deputy Assistant Secretary of State for Energy, Sanctions and Commodities, said that Caspian oil is "crucial to the world energy balance over the next 25 years." He also revealed that: "… there already exists a kind of outline of a new Silk Road running through the Caucasus and beyond the Caspian. We think oil and gas pipelines, roads, railways and fiber optics can make this 21st century Silk Road a superhighway linking Europe and Central Asia."[25] The manufactured wars in the Balkans that have caused so much death and suffering, were also engineered, in part, for this same reason – oil from the Caspian region. Doug Bereuter, Chairman of the US House [of Representatives] Sub Committee on Asia and the Pacific, confirmed that American policy goals in this region are the "independence" of the new states and their ties to the West (yeah, right), breaking Russia's monopoly over oil and gas transport routes, encouraging the construction of East–West pipelines that do not transit Iran, and denying Iran dangerous leverage over the central Asian economies.[26] Researcher George Draffan wrote in an article on the battle for Caspian oil:

"The 1995 Dayton Accords led to a major NATO military operation to 'pacify' Bosnia-Herzegovina. For the multinational corporations working alongside NATO, one of the most important rewards will be the construction of a trans-Balkan pipeline to bring oil from the Caspian Sea region to Europe.

"The European Union, the US government, and a gang of multinational corporations (including BP, Amoco, Exxon, Unocal, Caterpillar, Halliburton/Brown & Root, and Mitsubishi) are using all the military, political, and economic tools at their disposal to destroy and recreate the infrastructure and economy of south-eastern Europe in their own image. The conflicts of interest between government officials and corporate executives are blatant and revealing.

"Recent NATO military action in Yugoslavia is part of a long strategic (economic) battle to control the Balkans. The current focus is to secure oil and gas pipeline routes from the oilfields of the Caspian Sea to the consumers of Europe. Multinational oil corporations from the US, Britain and other European countries, and Russia are signing multibillion-dollar contracts with Kazakhstan." [27]

This includes Cheney's Halliburton and, incidentally, all the US Army camps in Bosnia for the "peacekeeping" operations are built and run by Halliburton's major subsidiary Brown & Root. War is so great for business. Condoleezza Rice's ChevronTexaco is leading a Caspian Pipeline Consortium developing Caspian-Kazakhstan oil deposits. Others in the trough are BP-Amoco, Exxon-Mobil and Unocal. They are seeking to access these reserves from Azerbaijan, Kazakhstan and Turkmenistan, the three countries that surround the Caspian together with Russia and Iran. The Russians want a pipeline north from the Caspian into their territory to the Black Sea. Russian military action, claimed by President Putin to be a response to Chechnya and al-Qaeda terrorism, has "coincidentally" taken place near the projected routes of the pipelines. Putin is a "former" KGB operative and head of the Federal Security Service (FSB) and anything he says should be disbelieved by reflex action. When you look at the frenzy to control and access these oil and gas reserves, the pattern of conflict and terrorism across this whole Middle East and Caspian region starts to make coordinated sense. Author Michael Griffin wrote in *Reaping the Whirlwind*[28] that the Taliban's rise to power in Afghanistan can be linked to a "single, golden theme", which he identified in places like Chechnya, Nagorno-Karabakh, Abkhazia and Turkish Kurdistan:

... "each represented a distinct, tactical move, crucial at the time, in discerning which power would ultimately become master of the pipelines which, some time in this century, will transport the oil and gas from the Caspian basin to an energy-avid world." [29]

Different place, same names

The oil cartel and its political cronies and associates are working together to maximise their power and profits. One example is the Azerbaijan International Operating Company (AIOC), which is a consortium involving the country's state oil company together with Pennzoil (Bush), Unocal, Exxon, British corporations BP-Amoco and Ramco Khazar, Lukoil (Russia), Den Norske Stats Olieselscap (Norway), Turkie Petrollari (Turkey), Itochu (Japan) and Delta Nimir Khazar (Saudi Arabia). Note that Pennzoil, a major player in the project, was created when Father George Bush's Zapata Oil took over Penn Oil in 1963. Baker and Botts, the law firm now headed by James Baker, Bush's Carlyle Group associate, handle Pennzoil's legal affairs. Thomas Petzinger, a business journalist on the *Wall Street Journal*, would later write: "For 25 years, the internal legal department at Pennzoil had been almost indistinguishable from Baker and Botts." [30] Pennzoil's partner in the project, Delta Nimir, is controlled by our old friends Mohammed Hussein Al-Amoudi and Khalid bin Mahfouz, both of whom have financial ties to "Osama bin Laden's" al-Qaeda. Bin Mahfouz has funded George W. Bush's oil company and the Carlyle Group of Father George. Other business partnerships involving bin Mahfouz, Al-Amoudi, and leading US oil giants include the following: the Nimir Petroleum (Mahfouz family) deal with ChevronTexaco to develop massive oil fields in Kazakhstan that are said to contain up to 1.5 billion barrels of oil; the Delta Oil (Al-Amoudi family) partnership with Amerada Hess to develop oil fields in Azerbaijan; and Delta-Hess is part of a consortium hoping to build a $2.4 billion oil pipeline from Azerbaijan to Turkey.

One of the directors of the US and Saudi-dominated Azerbaijan International Operating Company is Brent Scowcroft, a former US National Security Adviser, an executive of Kissinger Associates, and a very close associate of Father George Bush. The plans of this consortium involve a thousand-mile pipeline from Baku on the Caspian across Azerbaijan and Georgia to the Turkish port of Ceyhan on the Mediterranean, which was projected to cost $3 billion. Oil is a main reason (along with drugs) for the Turkish and other attacks on the lands of the Kurds and the massive expansion of the Turkish armed forces. Turkey has already murdered thousands of Kurds, destroyed thousands of villages and produced millions of refugees. The horrors of September 11th have provided the excuse for both British and American forces to be dispatched to the very region necessary to secure control of the Caspian oil reserves and pipeline projects and for enormous increases in spending on "defence" and "security". As I was writing this chapter, President Bush announced a $48 billion increase in US defence spending to $379 billion and said he would spend whatever it takes to keep the American people safe. What's that about there being no money for the poor and hungry? These vast increases have nothing to do with protecting Americans, and everything to do with protecting and advancing the interests of Bush, those who fund and control him, and the global agenda that he serves.

Trading with terror

Azerbaijan, like the other oil-rich or pipeline-significant countries in the Caspian, has an appalling human rights record. Ethnic cleansing of Armenians in Nagorno-Karabakh, a mountainous region of Azerbaijan, has led to sanctions and restrictions on US aid to the country. This was made law through section 907 of the 1992 Freedom Support Act. Cheney has pressed for the repeal of this section to release funds for the oil cartel's operations in Azerbaijan and has lobbied constantly for sanctions to be lifted on Iran and other countries to ease through the Illuminati oil agenda he represents. He is also among those lobbying for the Azerbaijan–Turkey pipeline on behalf of the Azerbaijan International Operating Company. His fellow lobbyists include James Baker, Father George's Secretary of State, oil company lawyer, and director of the Carlyle Group; Zbigniew Brzezinski, National Security Adviser to Jimmy Carter and founder of the Illuminati's Trilateral Commission; Lloyd Bentsen, former US Secretary of the Treasury; John Sununu, former White House Chief of Staff to George Bush; Tim Eggar, the former British Energy Minister and now CEO of Britain's Monument Oil; Malcolm Rifkind, the former British Foreign Secretary and now a director of the British oil corporation, Ramco; oh yes, and Richard Secord, the former US Air Force Major General charged for his part in Father George's Iran-Contra affair, has been helping to train the Azerbaijani army.

By 1997, Pennzoil, Unocal, Amoco and Exxon had invested $5 billion in Azerbaijan and, as we have seen so many times, forcibly controlling the population to ensure unchallenged control for the oil cartel is a constant strategy. Compliant dictatorships are good for business and I include "democracies" in that also. The Azerbaijan government is now serving the interests of this American and British takeover of the Caspian region by selling off ports, railroads, the national airline, airports and other state-run enterprises to "foreign investors". It is an identical story in the Balkans where the same thing is happening. Governments are installed after manipulated wars that will sell off major state assets to the Illuminati corporations and award contracts to their companies for "reconstruction". Contracts for the Balkan region, are estimated to be worth £30 billion. Then there is the money (taxpayers money) paid out for "reconstruction" and "aid" by the World Bank and the International Monetary Fund (IMF), both of which are 100% Illuminati (see *And The Truth Shall Set You Free*). Most of this money also ends up with the corporations and this is why the projects funded by this diabolical duo are designed to benefit business interests and not local populations. NATO, the world army in all but name, is nothing more than the means for the Illuminati cartels to bully and bomb their targets into submission so this process can unfold – that's the real reason for the Balkan occupation by foreign troops.

This strategy was promoted by Zbigniew Brzezinski, the founder of the Trilateral Commission and major Illuminati insider, in his 1997 book *The Grand Chessboard*. He said that control of Uzbekistan was the key to dominating the region and its oil and gas reserves. This is why the US has had "military advisers" in Uzbekistan for a long time and this "support" has been increased still further in the "war on terrorism". Writing of the need for the United States to dominate the region, Brzezinski says: "The three grand imperatives of imperial geostrategy are to prevent collusion and security dependence among the vassals, to keep tributaries pliant and protected, and to keep the barbarians from coming together." [31] I think divide and rule would put it more succinctly. An article by writer Nicholas Lemann in the *New Yorker* also revealed that after the collapse of the Soviet Union in 1989 Dick Cheney formed a group to plan a strategy for the 1990s and beyond.[32] This group included the current Secretary of Defense Donald Rumsfeld, the current Deputy Secretary of Defense Paul Wolfowitz, the current Secretary of State Colin Powell, and Lewis "Scooter" Libby, currently Cheney's chief of staff. The aim was to "shape" the world in their desired image or, as another member, Zalmay Khalilzad, put it … to "preclude the rise of another global rival for the indefinite future". Lemann says he was shown a copy of the document Cheney's group put together called *Defense Strategy for the 1990s: The Regional Defense Strategy, Secretary of Defense, Dick Cheney, January 1993.* This was the month that Bill Clinton was inaugurated, and Cheney and Father Bush left the White House. This "strategy", planned in the early 1990s, is pretty much what the Bush and Cheney government is doing today – a government that includes the key people who put the document together. The "war on terrorism" was a response to September 11th? Ha, ha, ha. Whoop, whoop, whoop. It's the way they tell 'em.

So why Afghanistan?

All of this brings me to Afghanistan and the Texas-based oil giant Unocal, one of the world's leading independent natural gas and crude oil exploration and production companies. It has been a project-partner many times with Cheney's Texas-based Halliburton. The Burma pipeline is one example of this and as Cheney said in his 1998 speech to the "Collateral Damage Conference" presented by the Washington "think tank", the Cato Institute: "About 70 to 75% of our business is energy related, serving customers like Unocal, Exxon, Shell, Chevron and many other major oil companies around the world." Both Halliburton and Unocal have business and crony connections to the Bush family, as indeed do Chevron, Shell, and Exxon come to that. In October 1997, Unocal led an international consortium that beat off competition from the Argentine company, Bridas, to sign a $2 billion contract with Turkmenistan for the CentGas project (Central Asia Gas), a massive pipeline that included 750 metres across western Afghanistan. It would connect the vast natural gas reserves of Turkmenistan (possibly the world's biggest) to a plant and ports on the Arabian Sea coast of Pakistan – yet another military dictatorship controlled by the "West" (Illuminati). An oil version was also planned and extensions into India were being considered. How fascinating that in that same month, on October 27th 1997, a press release from Cheney's Halliburton announced that the company had received a Letter of Intent from Petronas Carigali (Turkmenistan) to provide

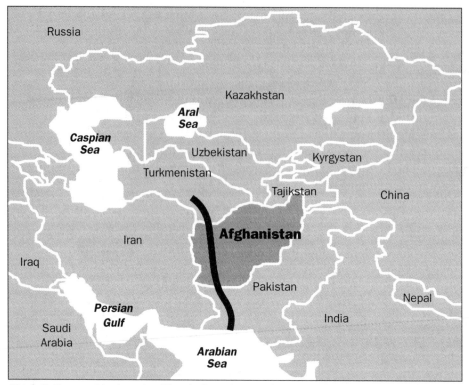

Figure 9: *The approximate route of the pipelines planned across Afghanistan to carry oil and gas to world markets*

integrated drilling services worth an initial $30 million for an exploration and appraisal programme in the Caspian Sea beginning in late 1997. It went on: "Halliburton, in conjunction with alliance partners, Dresser Industries and Western Atlas, will provide a combination of 10 services … Halliburton will be the lead contractor and project manager in addition to providing technical services. The value of the award is estimated to be US $30 million for the total project." This no doubt was Halliburton's contribution to the Unocal pipeline across Afghanistan (*Figure 9*).

Taliban we love you

Turkmenistan's dictator President Niyazov said he had a promise of support for the pipeline from both the ruling Taliban and from anti-Taliban factions in Afghanistan. Turkmenistan's official negotiator on the pipeline project was Yosef Maiman, a "former" agent with the Israeli intelligence agency, Mossad, which, at the highest level, is the same organisation as the CIA, British intelligence, and so on. The Taliban were keen to go ahead because it would net them some $100 million a year, but to make the project work Unocal needed the US State Department to formally recognise the Taliban government that had seized power with it's usual extreme violence in 1996 from the factions of the Mujahadin that had fought, with CIA support, to remove the Soviet Union from the country. The Taliban killed and castrated the former president Najibullah, and hung his body and that of his brother from traffic lights at the entrance to the Presidential Palace. In September 1996, a day after the Taliban took power in Kabul, a US State Department spokesman, Glyn Davies, said that the United States saw "nothing objectionable" in the Taliban inflicting its strict interpretation of Islamic law. Unocal and partners hired some big names to press the case for a deal with the Taliban. Among them were Henry Kissinger, the former Secretary of State and one of the major Illuminati manipulators of the past 40 years; Robert Oakley, the US Ambassador to Pakistan during the Reagan and Bush administrations; and the Afghan-born Zalmay Khalilzad, a former adviser on Afghanistan in the Reagan (Bush) State Department. This is the same man appointed by President George W. Bush as Special Envoy to Afghanistan and Khalilzad is a former adviser to Unocal on the pipeline project! The journalist and cartoonist, Ted Rall, says that Khalilzad worked for the Reagan Administration in arming the CIA-funded Mujahadin during the Soviet occupation of Afghanistan. This was the period when the Osama bin Laden network was formed with American government money and it eventually led to the coming to power of the Taliban. Khalilzad was also part of Dick Cheney's "strategy group" in the early 1990s and argued that it was "vital" to prevent a rival to the United States' supremacy from emerging and "to be willing to use force if necessary."[33] When the Taliban were removed by the "war on terrorism" following 9/11, the head of the new government in Afghanistan was named as Hamid Karzai who, according to the French publication *Le Monde*, is a former consultant to … yes … Unocal.[34] Robert Oakley was also Ambassador to Somalia and Zaire, a head of "counterterrorism" for Reagan and Bush, and one of the US government officials ensuring that CIA funds reached the Afghan resistance groups, including that of Osama bin Laden, during the Soviet occupation between 1979 and 1989. Oakley later worked for Delta-Nimir, the joint operation of the bin Mahfouz and Al-Amoudi families, the funders of Osama bin Laden and associates of the Bushes. Delta-Nimir was a partner of Unocal in the Afghan pipeline project and was already a major investor with Unocal in the oil fields of Azerbaijan, as I have outlined. At the same time as working for the Unocal consortium, Oakley and Khalilzad were also advising the US State Department.[35] Another of those hired to "advise" and lobby on behalf of the Turkmenistan government in the early 1990s was Alexander Haig, the Knights of Malta initiate and formerly a Reagan-Bush Secretary of State, commander of NATO forces, and one-time military assistant to Henry Kissinger.

Unocal gave the Taliban a fax machine to speed communications and funded a job training programme through the University of Nebraska in the Taliban stronghold of Kandahar to train people to work on the pipeline. Unocal flew Taliban officials to the United States for talks in early December 1997 and spent several days at their headquarters in Sugarland, Texas, enjoying star treatment. Sugarland is part of Houston, the home of the Bush family operations. The visit also included meetings with the State Department in Washington. There was no talk whatsoever about Taliban support for terrorism and Osama bin Laden, and no talk of handing him over. Instead Unocal "offered them a generous cut of the profits", according to journalist John Pilger.[36] Dick Cheney was in Texas at this time as head of Halliburton, which stood to gain enormously from the Unocal-Taliban pipeline.

Oops, sorry, Taliban we hate you

What scuppered the Unocal deal, among other things, was the mounting outrage among women's groups at the Taliban's unbelievable abuse of women and their basic human rights. American women's groups began to organise protests against Unocal and the Feminist Majority Foundation in Los Angeles petitioned the California State Government to revoke Unocal's charter in response to their negotiations with the Taliban. It became impossible for the Taliban regime to be recognised. Then, in 1998, came the bombings of US Embassies in Kenya and Tanzania, which killed 224 people, 12 of them American. Osama bin Laden was blamed for these outrages and President Clinton ordered the bombing of targets in Afghanistan and Sudan, two countries said to be protecting him. He also froze bin Laden's assets (it says here) and banned US firms from doing business with him. The Bush family must have been out of the country at the time and didn't hear that one. With these developments Unocal's plans were in ruins and they pulled out of the pipeline deal on December 4th 1998. John J. Maresca, Unocal's Vice President for International Relations, had told the House Committee on International Relations that the "Taliban government in Afghanistan is an obstacle" to the pipeline project and that "construction of the pipeline cannot begin until a recognized government is in place in Kabul that has the confidence of governments, lenders, and our company." In the wake of September 11th, that is *exactly* what has happened, and the Afghanistan pipeline is now going to be built! This is all just a co-incidence, of course, and nothing to worry about. As the US Government Energy Information fact sheet on Afghanistan said in December 2000:

> "Afghanistan's significance from an energy standpoint stems from its geographic position as a potential transit route for oil and natural gas exports from Central Asia to the Arabian Sea. This potential includes proposed multi-billion dollar oil and gas export pipelines through Afghanistan, although these plans have now been thrown into serious question ..."

Not, however, for long, it seems, thanks to September 11th and the bombing into oblivion of the Taliban. This invasion was ordered by the Bush administration, including Vice-President Dick Cheney. In May 2002, Mohammad Alim Razim, the Minister for Mines and Industries in the Interim government of "Unocal's" Hamid Karzai, announced plans to build the pipeline and he said that Unocal was the "lead company".[37] The BBC reported that the pipeline was expected to be built with "funds from donor countries for the reconstruction of Afghanistan". Put another way, the people that made a fortune from the invasion of Afghanistan through their arms sales will now have much of the cost of their pipeline met by taxpayers, er, sorry, "aid to help the poor people of Afghanistan rebuild their country".[38] Before this announcement, the BBC had reported how "oil experts" had dismissed the suggestion that the "war on terrorism" in Afghanistan was in any way about oil. It is so comforting to know that the academics understand what is happening in the world and thus can pass on their stunning insights to their students. Paul Stevens, Professor of Petroleum Policy and Economics at Dundee University, said: "There was discussion of the pipeline to carry gas to Pakistan, but it was abandoned way before current events because of political, economic and stability problems. So the idea that oil is now driving this war is totally unrealistic. It would be more sensible to be considering a pipeline on the moon." [39] Which is where, on this evidence, Professor Stevens might choose to relocate. It's made of cheese you know.

The drug connection (naturally)

Anyone who has done even basic research into the Bush family and their network of placemen will always look for the drug connection, such is the enormous involvement they have with the global drug cartel. So it is with Vice President Dick Cheney, the long-time Bush crony and beneficiary. Michael C. Ruppert is a former officer with the Los Angeles Police Department (LAPD) who also worked for its Organized Crime Intelligence Division. He now produces an excellent newsletter called *From the Wilderness*.[40] In his edition of October 24th 2000, headed "Halliburton Corporation's Brown & Root is one of the major components of the Bush-Cheney drug empire", Ruppert highlights the role played in the Bush-Cheney drug network by the Halliburton subsidiary Brown & Root. This company is fundamentally connected to the US military, the intelligence agencies and their operations around the world, including Bosnia, Kosovo and Macedonia, and employs 20,000 people in more than 100 countries. The Kosovo Liberation Army (KLA) was a CIA-backed operation and was used, in part, as the excuse for the US and British-controlled NATO to bomb and invade Serbia and Kosovo in support of Illuminati drug and oil pipeline interests. According to the *Christian Science Monitor* and *Jane's Intelligence Review*, the Kosovo Liberation Army controls 70% of the heroin entering western Europe. At the same time Cheney's Brown & Root was making billions with its US government supply and support contracts in the same region, as it still does today.[41] It is amazing how the location of Brown & Root operations for the government and the drug running by government agencies tend to synchronise again and again, and this was highlighted in a report by the Center for Public Integrity (CPI)[42] which suggests that drug money was involved in the financial success of Halliburton under Dick Cheney's leadership between 1995 and 2000 and, in particular, through its subsidiary Brown & Root. Then there are those "loans" given by US government agencies that paid for Brown & Root contracts abroad. Michael Ruppert writes:

"The loans had been granted by the Export-Import Bank and the Overseas Private Investment Corporation. According to [CIA operative] Ralph McGehee's [publication] 'CIA Base' both institutions are heavily infiltrated by the CIA and routinely provide NOC [non official cover] to its officers. One of those loans to Russian financial/banking conglomerate, The Alfa Group of Companies, contained $292 million to pay for Brown and Root's contract to refurbish a Siberian oil field owned by the Russian Tyumen Oil Company.

The Alfa Group completed its 51% acquisition of Tyumen Oil in what was allegedly a rigged bidding process in 1998. An official Russian government report claimed that the Alfa Group's top executives, oligarchs Mikhail Fridman and Pyotr Aven, 'allegedly participated in the transit of drugs from Southeast Asia through Russia and into Europe.' These same executives, Fridman and Aven, who reportedly smuggled the heroin in connection with Russia's Solntsevo mob family, were the same ones who applied for the ... [US government] ... loans that Halliburton's lobbying later safely secured. As a result Brown and Root's work in Alfa Tyumen oil fields could continue – and expand.

"After describing how organized criminal interests in the Alfa Group had allegedly stolen the oil field by fraud, the [Center for Public Integrity] story, using official reports from the FSB (the Russian equivalent of the FBI), oil companies such as BP-Amoco, former CIA and KGB officers and press accounts, then established a solid link to Alfa Tyumen and the transportation of heroin. In 1995, sacks of heroin disguised as sugar were stolen from a rail container leased by Alfa-Echo and sold in the Siberian town of Khabarovsk. A problem arose when many residents of the town became 'intoxicated' or 'poisoned'." [43]

The Center for Public Integrity (CPI) story also says that the Russian FSB ("FBI") report stated that within days of this incident, agents from the Ministry of Internal Affairs raided Alfa-Echo (or Eko) buildings to discover drugs and other "compromising documentation", and it was claimed that Alfa Bank has laundered drug funds from Russian and Colombian drug cartels. The CPI reported that the lead Washington attorney for the Russian Tyumen Oil Company was James C. Langdon, Jr of Akin, Gump, Strauss, Hauer and Feld. This is the same Akin, Gump which, as I highlighted earlier, represents the bin Laden financers Khalid bin Mahfouz and Mohammed Hussein Al-Amoudi, and the Texas-based Holy Land Foundation for Relief and Development, which had its assets frozen by the US Treasury pending an investigation into alleged connections to the Palestinian terrorist group Hamas. Bin Mahfouz retained the services of Akin, Gump during the "investigation" into the BCCI. [44] The most famous name at Akin, Gump is Vernon Jordan, the associate of Bill Clinton and friend of Monica Lewinsky, and the firm is awash with cronies of the Bush family. The Center for Public Integrity report highlighting the drug connection to Cheney's Halliburton and Brown and Root also says that the Akin, Gump attorney James C. Langdon Jr "helped coordinate a $2.2 million fund raiser for [George W.] Bush ... He then agreed to help recruit 100 lawyers and lobbyists in the capital to raise $25,000 each for W's campaign." What a web.

A personal story

Michael Ruppert also tells of his own experience with the government, Brown & Root, and drugs in 1977 while he was with the Los Angeles Police Department. He said he travelled to New Orleans in June of that year to try to salvage his relationship with Nordica Theodora D'Orsay, or "Teddy", a CIA contract agent, who had suddenly disappeared. She had wanted him to participate in her operations from within the Los Angeles Police, but he said: "I had refused to get involved with drugs in any way and everything she mentioned seemed to involve either heroin or cocaine along with guns that she was always moving out of the country." [45] The Director of the CIA at this time was … Father George Bush. Ruppert said he knew that Teddy's "work" involved the CIA, Los Angeles Police Department, the royal family of Iran, the Mafia and drugs. Ruppert says he found Teddy living in an apartment in Greta, New Orleans, equipped with "scrambler phones, night vision devices and working from sealed communiqués delivered by naval and air force personnel from nearby Belle Chasse Naval Air Station". Teddy, he writes, was involved in "something truly ugly" – arranging for large quantities of weapons to be loaded onto ships for Iran and working with associates of New Orleans Mafia boss Carlos Marcello to coordinate the boat service delivering major shipments of heroin to the city. The boats arrived at Marcello-controlled docks, he says, "unmolested by even the New Orleans police she introduced me to, along with divers, military men, former Green Berets and CIA personnel". He continues:

> "The service boats were retrieving the heroin from oil rigs in the Gulf of Mexico, oil rigs in international waters, oil rigs built and serviced by Brown and Root. The guns that Teddy monitored, apparently Vietnam era surplus AK 47s and M16s, were being loaded onto ships also owned or leased by Brown and Root. And more than once during the eight days I spent in New Orleans I met and ate at restaurants with Brown and Root employees who were boarding those ships and leaving for Iran within days. Once, while leaving a bar and apparently having asked the wrong question, I was shot at in an attempt to scare me off." [46]

Disgusted with what he saw, Ruppert says he returned to California and reported all he had seen, including the Brown & Root connection, to the Los Angeles Police Department. As a result, he says, he was forced to leave the LAPD at the end of 1978 under threat of death. He says he complained to the LAPD's Internal Affairs Division and to the LA office of the FBI under the command of Ted Gunderson, a man who has become part of the "conspiracy exposure" movement in more recent times. Ruppert says he and his attorney wrote to the politicians, the Department of Justice, the CIA, and contacted the *Los Angeles Times*. The FBI and the Los Angeles Police Department claimed he was crazy. Where have I heard that before? In 1981 a two-part news story in the Los Angeles *Herald Examiner* revealed that the FBI had taken "Teddy" into custody, but released her with no further action. Aaron Cohen, a former New Orleans Crime Commissioner, told the paper that after 30 years of studying Louisiana's organized crime operations he found Ruppert's description of events to be "perfectly plausible". [47] Ruppert says that, to this day, a CIA report prepared as a result of his complaint remains classified and exempt from release "pursuant to Executive Order of the President in the interests of national security and because it would reveal the identities of CIA agents". His written testimony to the Senate Select Committee on Intelligence, dated October 1st 1997, can be found at *http://www.copvcia.comhttp://www.copvcia.com/ssci.htm*. He says that on October 26th 1981 he reported what he saw in New Orleans to his friend and University of California classmate, Craig Fuller, in the basement of the West Wing of the White House. (Fuller became Chief of Staff to Vice President Father George Bush from 1981 to 1985.) Ruppert says he later learned more of the background to what he witnessed in New Orleans:

> "In 1982, then UCLA [University of California] political science professor Paul Jabber filled in many of the pieces in my quest to understand what I had seen in New Orleans. He was qualified to do so because he had served as a CIA and State Department consultant to the Carter administration. Paul explained that, after a 1975 treaty between the Shah of Iran and Saddam Hussein, the Shah had cut off all overt military support for Kurdish rebels fighting Saddam from the north of Iraq. In exchange, the Shah had gained access to the Shat al-Arab waterway so that he could multiply his oil exports and income. Not wanting to lose a long-term valuable asset in the Kurds, the CIA had then used Brown and Root, which operated in both countries and maintained port facilities in the Persian Gulf and near Shat al-Arab, to rearm the Kurds. The whole operation had been financed with heroin. Paul was matter-of-fact about it. In 1983 Paul Jabber left UCLA to become a Vice President of Banker's Trust and Chairman of the Middle East Department of the Council on Foreign Relations." [48]

What Michael Ruppert says fits with my own full-time research since 1991, which has listed endless examples of what he describes all over the world as Illuminati governments, corporations and organised crime inter-connect. Ruppert suggests that ..."the relationships between key institutions, players and the Bushes themselves suggest that under a George "W" administration the Bush family and its allies may well be able, using Brown & Root as the operational interface, to control the drug trade all the way from Medellin to Moscow". Brown & Root, the company ultimately controlled by Vice President Dick Cheney from 1995 to 2000, had no presence in Colombia apparently until 1997 when it suddenly began to acquire nearly a million square feet of warehouse space. "Watch that space" would seem to be the best advice going on past experience. What do they know about Colombia that the public do not? One of the most obvious Bush-US Government drug operations was the already discussed Iran-Contra period in the 1980s in which Oliver North was a major figure. Cathy O'Brien tells in *Trance-Formation of America* of attending drugs parties in which the drug-running North was among the guests.[49] Cheney was a vehement defender of North's Iran-Contra activities while serving on the House Intelligence Committee, and supported his election campaign for a Senate seat in Virginia in 1994. Fortunately North didn't make it.

So there you have some of the appalling background to Dick Cheney who, with Father George, is the immediate power behind the throne, or high chair, of President Bush. It would not surprise me in the least if Boy George was assassinated in a staged "terrorist attack" to dramatically increase the problem-reaction-solution possibilities of the "war on terrorism". After all, his code-name in the Skull and Bones Society was "Temporary" and if Bush were to go, who would be president? Dick Cheney.

SOURCES

1   *Trance-Formation Of America*, p 196

2   Ibid, p 100

3   **http://www.austinchronicle.com/issues/dispatch/2000-08-25/pols_feature2.html**

4   See *The Candidate From Brown and Root* by Robert Bryce, August 28th 2000,
     http://multihome.www.desert.net

5   Ronnie Dugger, *The Politician: The Life and Times of Lyndon Johnson* (Norton, 1982)

6   **http://www.nexusmagazine.com/bushcheney.html**

7   You can find a lot of detail about these connections at
     http://a-albionic.org/assassination/cheney_bush_jfk.txt

8   *George Bush: The Unofficial Biography*, p 140–142

9   Michael C. Ruppert, *Wilderness* Publications (October 24th 2000, PO Box 6061-350,
     Sherman Oaks CA 91413), or **www.copvcia.com**

10   Quoted in the *Austin Chronicle*, August 28th 2000

11   *Los Angeles Times*, March 23rd 1991

12   **http://www.halliburton.com**

13   *Associated Press*, July 26th 2000

14   See Halliburton's filings with the Securities and Exchange Commission

15   More details at **http://www.truthout.org/docs_01/02.01E.Cheney.Hussein.htm**

16   *International Herald Tribune*, July 2000

17   See *Halliburton's Destructive Engagement: How Dick Cheney and USA-Engage Subvert
     Democracy at Home and Abroad*, by Kenny Bruno and Jim Valette, a report by EarthRights
     International, October 2000, **http://www.earthrights.org/pubs/halliburton.html**

18   **http://www.earthrights.org/halliburton/pr100400.html**

19   *Guardian*, July 28th 2000

20   *Wall Street Journal*, October 27th 2000

21   Ibid

22   **www.earthrights.org/halliburton/hallintro.html**

23   Halliburton annual report, March 2000

24   *San Francisco Chronicle*, September 26th 2001

25   *Pipeline Superhighway Replaces The Silk Road* by Stuart Parrott (London, November 19th
     1997)

26   See article by George Draffan at **www.endgame.orgwww.endgame.org**

27   Ibid

28   Michael Griffin, *Reaping the Whirlwind* (Pluto Press, January 2000), p 115

29   Ibid

30   **http://www.onlinejournal.com/Archive/Bush/Oiligarchy1-1/Oiligarchy1-3/oiligarchy1-3.html**

31   Zbigniew Brzezinski, *The Grand Chessboard, American Primacy And its Geostrategic Imperatives* (Basic Books, 1997)

32   The Next World Order, The Bush Administration may have a brand-new doctrine of power, *New Yorker*, April Ist 2002

33   Ibid

34   **http://www.rense.com/general18/ine.htm**

35   *Washington Post*, November 5th 2001, p A01

36   *All Fall Down*, p 86

37   *BBC News*, May 13th 2002

38   Ibid

39   Ibid

40   Available from PO Box 6061-350, Sherman Oaks, CA 91413, or **www.copvcia.com**

41   *Christian Science Monitor*, October 20th 1994; *Jane's Intelligence Review*, February 1st 1995

42   *Cheney Led Halliburton To Feast at Federal Trough*, by Knut Royce and Nathaniel Heller, Center for Public Integrity, August 2nd 2000, **www.public-i.org**

43   Halliburton Corporation's Brown and Root is one of the major components of the Bush-Cheney drug empire, *From the Wilderness* Newsletter, October 24th 2000

44   *All Fall Down*, p 144

45   Halliburton Corporation's Brown and Root is one of the Major Components of the Bush-Cheney Drug Empire, *From the Wilderness* Newsletter, October 24th 2000

46   Ibid

47   Los Angeles *Herald Examiner*, October 11th and 18th 1981

48   Halliburton Corporation's Brown and Root is one of the major components of the Bush-Cheney drug empire, *From the Wilderness* Newsletter, October 24th 2000

49   *Trance-Formation Of America*, p 149–150

chapter 5

The rest of the gang

He does not preach what he practises until he has practised what he preaches.

Confucius

I could continue for chapters detailing the fantastic web of interconnected corruption that underpins the entire global government, banking, business, military and media structure. It is almost impossible to exaggerate what is really going on behind the "movie screen" and it is vital to understand this if we are going to see September 11th in its true context. Before I focus specifically on the events of that day and their aftermath I will briefly summarise some essential information about the other famous names that have sold us the lie about 9/11 and used it to justify the "war on terrorism". Used car, anyone?

Colin Powell and Richard Armitage

I put these two together because they are so close to each other and they now head the US State Department in the "war against sanity". George W. Bush named Powell as his Secretary of State and Powell chose Armitage as his deputy. Colin Luther Powell is seen by most Americans as some kind of "war hero", a man you can trust. In fact, like those around him in the Bush administration, he is a terrorist under any accepted definition of the word. Colin Powell moralising about the need to "stop terrorism" is like Bill Clinton delivering a lecture on celibacy. The Bush family has sponsored his career and he was Chairman of the Joint Chiefs of Staff, the military head of U.S forces, when Father George and Dick Cheney launched the Gulf War in 1991. It was obvious that when the Bushes, Cheney and Powell got together again at the start of 2001, with Boy George as the voice of his father, that the United States would find itself in another war. I wrote on my website *davidicke.com* on Bush's inauguration day, January 20th 2001:

> "Powell, like the Bushes and Cheney, is bloodline and that's why he is to be the new Secretary of State. Given that line-up and their mentality and agenda, don't be at all surprised if the United States finds itself in another manipulated war during this administration. You will see "monsters" being created in the public mind to justify such action."

It took only months.

The rise and rise of Colin Powell

Father George appointed Powell as the Chairman of the Joint Chiefs of Staff, US Department of Defense, in 1989. At 52, Powell became the youngest head of the Joint Chiefs and the first African-American. In this position he would serve the Bush Illuminati agenda in the manufactured "wars" not only in Iraq, but also in Panama, Somalia and elsewhere. Many researchers have demolished the Powell myth and some are detailed in the sources at the end of this chapter.[1] They have exposed his long record of breaking international human rights legislation – and worse – in the Iran-Contra scandal, the invasions of Grenada in 1983 and Panama in 1989, the Gulf War, and others. His confidants and sponsors say it all, really. Apart from Father George, these include Casper Weinberger and Frank C. Carlucci, both former Secretaries of Defense; Richard L. Armitage; Vernon E. Jordan, Jr; and Dick Cheney.[2] Weinberger was charged over Iran-Contra, but was pardoned by George Bush in the last days of his presidency; Carlucci is a former number two at the CIA and now chairman of the Bush-and-Baker-dominated Carlyle Group; Dick Cheney speaks for itself; Vernon E. Jordan is the friend of Bill Clinton and Monica Lewinsky and a lawyer with Akin, Gump, et al, which represents the Osama bin Laden backers and Bush family business associates, Khalid bin Mahfouz and Mohammad Hussein al-Amoudi. Jordan is a serious insider with more than 50 honorary doctorates at U.S universities including Yale and Harvard, and is connected to a stream of Illuminati organisations like the Bilderberg Group, the Trilateral Commission, the Council on Foreign Relations, Joint Center for Political Studies, Brookings Institution, Ford Foundation, American Express, Bankers Trust, and Dow Jones. Powell described Richard Armitage in his book, *My American Journey*,[3] as "my brother and my bodyguard". According to a *Los Angeles Times* article by John Broder: "Some of Powell's advice comes from others through Armitage, thus insulating Powell from directly consulting people who might then be identified as his 'advisers'." In short, Powell and Armitage are real close.

The other drug-running "Dick"

Interesting, then, that Armitage is another Bush family clone and confidant who served under Father George and Ronald Reagan, and has been widely implicated in some deeply unpleasant activities. Armitage has been accused by many sources of involvement in drug running, hit squads, and CIA dirty tricks on behalf of US administrations (the Illuminati). James 'Bo' Gritz, a former Operations Colonel in the Green Berets, says he investigated claims that US prisoners of war from Vietnam were still being held many years after the end of the conflict when they should have long been released. In his 1991 book, *Called To Serve*, and an accompanying video,[4] Gritz named Richard Armitage, Powell's close friend and deputy Secretary of State in today's "war on terrorism", as a major middleman between the US government and General Khun Sa, then the leading "warlord" operating in the Golden Triangle of the international opium trade. Gritz wrote:

"If Richard Armitage was, as Khun Sa avowed, a major participant in parallel government drug trafficking, then it explained why our efforts to rescue POWs had been inexplicably foiled, time after time ... If it was true, Richard Armitage would be the last man in the world who would desire to see prisoners of war come home alive." [5]

Gritz said that Khun Sa told him the United States government had purchased all of the opium supply for 1989 – some 900 tons. When Gritz returned to Burma five months later, Khun Sa agreed to be interviewed on video and name the names of the US government agents he worked with, although he said the names were old ones and not the current operatives. He said the government official in charge of buying the opium crop was Richard Armitage and that he was working with the notorious Mafia boss in Florida, Santos Trafficante. Khun Sa said he was paid $300,000 a ton for the opium while officials of the US government were selling it on the streets of America and elsewhere for $1 million a ton. This is a major way that the Illuminati fund their covert projects without using traceable sources. Gritz approached President Father George Bush to reveal what he had discovered, but Bush didn't want to know for a simple reason – he was heavily involved himself. These claims of involvement in drug running and arms trafficking by Armitage have reportedly been supported by staff at the US Embassy in Bangkok and his appointment was ended by the United States Ambassador to Thailand at the time, Morton Abramowitz. Among those who have exposed the gruesome activities of Armitage is the excellent researcher and writer, David Guyatt, and you can read his comprehensive article about Bush, Armitage, and the CIA-sponsored cocaine and heroin network in South-East Asia on his website.[6] Guyatt writes:

"Behind the scenes, a virtual war was in progress as the department of Justice and the FBI fought to indict Armitage for his narcotics and other criminal activities. Attorney General Thornburg, a political appointee of President Bush, powerfully resisted these measures. Significantly, however, Armitage was also under scrutiny by Federal Investigators working for the President's Commission on Organized Crime, with a focus on foreign organized criminal activity in gambling and drug trafficking.

"Meanwhile, yet another investigator who believed Armitage was 'dirty' was frustrated in his investigations by Frank Carlucci, the Secretary of Defense [now chairman of the Carlyle Group], and other powerful patrons. In 1975 during Armitage's CIA tour in Vietnam, Carlucci was number two at the CIA. Because of the numerous high level obstructions, investigations into Armitage's criminal activities were curtailed, but not before some damaging information had been gathered ... Such was the strength of the information developed on Armitage that he was forced to abandon his nomination for Secretary of the Army, and, in fact, all other official US government posts. Subsequently, Defense officials stated privately that Armitage would never again be permitted to darken the doors of the Department of Defense. [Instead he darkens the doors of Colin Powell's State Department.]

"Known as 'Mr Phu' (literally meaning 'Mr Rich') amongst the Vietnamese community, Armitage, despite his disgrace, was still able to count on the enormous power of his political patrons and avoided criminal prosecution. Knowing far too much about US government 'dirt' during the previous three decades provided him with an instant 'do not go to jail' card." [7]

Armitage withdrew from his nomination by Father George to be Secretary of the Army in 1989 because he would have faced a confirmation hearing amid reports that organisations representing US war veterans were preparing to oppose him in the light of his activities in South-East Asia. Armitage has also been linked, along with characters like Theodore Shackley and Thomas Clines, to Project Phoenix, the CIA mass-murder unit in South-East Asia that I mentioned earlier. Former CIA officer Ralph McGehee, who has since tried to tell some truth about the agency, says that between 1968 and 1972, the Phoenix, or Phuong Hoang, Operation rounded up hundreds of thousands of Vietnamese and them turned over to the Vietnamese police for "questioning" (brutal torture).[8] Tens of thousands (at least) were murdered through Project Phoenix, most of them perfectly innocent civilians. By late 1975, Armitage is reported to have been working out of Bangkok and reports suggest that in the period 1976 to 1979 he was involved with Shackley, Clines and Iran-Contra operative Richard Secord, in setting up a number of corporations and subsidiaries around the world including Lake Resources, Stanford Technology Trading Group, Companie de Services Fiduciaria, CSF Investments and Udall Research Corporation. During this time, Secord was in Iran coordinating the sale of US military aircraft and weapons to Middle Eastern countries.[9]

Oil, drugs and the upper reaches of politics constantly go together. After Armitage did not become Secretary of the Army, Father Bush made him a personal envoy holding the rank of Ambassador and under this guise Armitage went to the former Soviet Union to assist it with its "economic development" in 1989. This was just as the race for control of the Caspian oil and gas fields was really getting under way after the "fall" of Soviet Communism and new drug routes were being organised, which include Azerbaijan. Interestingly, Armitage is a member of the United States Azerbaijan Chamber of Commerce along with ... Dick Cheney. They are also both members of the Illuminati "think tank", the Aspen Institute, which is mentioned in some of my other books. Armitage is reported to have visited Burma in 1997 on a trip sponsored by the Burma/Myanmar Forum, a group in Washington DC that enjoys major sponsorship from Unocal.[10] This is the same Richard Armitage who is now Deputy Secretary of State to his extremely close friend, Colin Powell; the same Armitage who tells the world who is responsible for September 11th and who should be bombed and murdered in response. Armitage knows the Afghanistan region well. He was an American "adviser" during the war between the Afghanistan Mujahadin and the Soviet Union when Osama bin Laden's network was funded and armed into existence by the CIA. Armitage and Powell apparently first met in 1981 and a Powell profile in *USA Weekend* in 1993[11] said that after Powell became Chairman of the Joint Chiefs of Staff under Bush, he and

Armitage ... "started to call each other daily to share information and bounce ideas off each other ... They have become sounding boards for just about anything the other guy wants to discuss. Often they talk, if only briefly, two or three times a day." *Newsweek* reported that Armitage "may be Powell's closest friend".

Frankie's everywhere

The guy who protected Armitage from prosecution for crimes against humanity in both South-East Asia and on the streets of the United States was Frank C. Carlucci III, the former Assistant Director of the CIA during the Jimmy Carter presidency and both Secretary of Defense and National Security Adviser to Ronald Reagan (i.e. George Bush). He is now chairman of the Carlyle Group. Colin Powell has referred to Carlucci many times as his "mentor"!!! This does not surprise me a bit given Carlucci's background and the desperate company that Powell chooses to keep. Karl Evanzz says in his book, *The Judas Factor: The Plot to Kill Malcolm X,*[12] that Carlucci's appointment as Consul and Second-Secretary of the US Embassy in Stanleyville, the Congo, was a cover for a CIA operation that included the plot to assassinate the recently elected President Patrice Lumumba in 1961. Five months after Lumumba was assassinated, Carlucci was arrested, expelled from the Congo, and returned to the US. He was expelled from Tanzania in 1965 after he was implicated in the CIA assassination of the Burundi Prime Minister Pierre Ngendandumwe. Carlucci would later be appointed to major positions, including Secretary of Defense, by Bush and Reagan because, clearly, he was just the sort of character they needed for their agenda. This is the man that Colin Powell calls his "mentor" while lecturing the world on the outrages and dangers of terrorism!

Colin Powell, this is your life

With a line-up of characters like these supporting Colin Powell it is clear that he is bloodline and that he would, by definition, have an interesting "history". Colin Powell was born in 1937 into a family of Jamaican immigrants and was brought up in the South Bronx area of New York City. He decided to make the Army his career and was commissioned as a lieutenant in 1958. It was Colin Powell who "investigated" the infamous My Lai Massacre. This was when members of the US Army's Americal Division entered the hamlet of My Lai 4 in South Vietnam on March 16th 1968, tortured and murdered hundreds of civilians, and raped countless women and young girls. The horror was reported by Tom Glen, a soldier who told of his own involvement at My Lai in a letter to General Creighton Abrams, the commander of US forces in Vietnam, but his claims were dismissed and covered up. Major Colin Powell, the Deputy Assistant Chief of Staff for Operations, G-3, at Americal Division headquarters, was ordered to investigate the claims and "report within three days with a suggested reply to Glen", according to an article in *The New Republic*.[13] Powell's report decided that Glen's story was not true except, possibly, for "isolated instances". He added: "In direct refutation of this portrayal is the fact that relations between American soldiers and the Vietnamese people are excellent." *The New Republic* article concluded that a proper investigation of the charges made by Tom Glen may have led to a legitimate inquiry into the My Lai Massacre and into others that "included a company that had gone along with Tom Glen's on March 16th 1968 and committed a separate massacre of ninety people at My Khe, for which no one was ever punished". However, Powell did not choose to investigate the My Lai massacre and it was only later when a second soldier, Ron Ridenhour, gave details to a congressman that the army was forced to investigate publicly and Powell's original "investigation" was shown to be a sham and a cover-up of the atrocities against Vietnamese civilians. But Powell, who knows how to fall in a bog and come out clean, even managed to secure a Legion of Merit citation during the Ridenhour investigation. Clearly from early in his military career, Colin Powell's desire to see justice done and terrorism punished would not appear to be his guiding light.

When he returned to the United States, Powell's career began to progress rapidly under the Illuminati sponsorship of characters like Weinberger and Carlucci. He attended George Washington University and thanks to his powerful backers he progressed through the hierarchy at the Pentagon. He became National Security Adviser in 1987 to Reagan-Bush, a post previously held by people like Henry Kissinger and Zbigniew Brzezinski, who are both extremely significant players in the Illuminati web (See *And The Truth Shall Set You Free*). National Security Adviser, like Chairman of the Joint Chiefs of Staff and Secretary of State, is a major Illuminati appointment and Powell has been all three. While he was Senior Military Assistant to Secretary of Defense Weinberger during the Reagan years, he played a major role in operations like the invasion of Grenada and the US bombing (based on false "evidence") of Libya. It was also during this period with Weinberger that Powell was implicated in the Iran-Contra affair in which Weinberger was fundamentally involved. Weinberger kept details of the illegal transfer of arms to Iran in a personal diary that he compiled at meetings of the National Security Council. Yet Powell supported Weinberger in denying the existence of the diary before later having to admit the claims were true. Powell told the Iran-Contra investigation under oath:

"The Secretary, to my knowledge, did not keep a diary. Whatever notes he kept, I don't know how he uses them or what he does with them. He does not have a diary ..."

But in a later sworn statement, he said:

"During the period I worked with Secretary Weinberger ... I observed on his desk a small pad of white paper ... I viewed it as his personal diary ... Knowing Secretary Weinberger as I did and knowing the routine way he would jot down notes on these pads ... I considered them a private diary."

Iran-Contra prosecutor Lawrence Walsh said Powell's testimony was "at least misleading", but "did not warrant prosecution." Funnily enough, the Iran-Contra Special Counsel's report said virtually the same about Powell's best buddy, Richard Armitage: "Independent Counsel declined to prosecute Armitage because the OIC's limited resources were focused on the case against Weinberger and because the evidence against Armitage, while substantial, did not reach the threshold of proof beyond a reasonable doubt." From the National Security Archive comes this account of Powell's involvement:

"Weinberger testified before the [Senate Select] Committee [on Intelligence] that later that day he received a call from Poindexter informing him of the President's action [to send weapons to Iran]. Weinberger … instructed military aide, Major General Colin Powell, to arrange the transfer of the weapons … to the CIA, and that the matter was to be closely held at the direction of the President. General Powell had had previous discussions with North about the program and about Israel's problems in getting replacement TOW's [missiles] … According to Armitage and a CIA official, Powell worked with Major General Vincent Russo of the Defense Logistics Agency to provide the material securely and without any loss of funds for the Army." [14]

Powell's best buddy Richard Armitage was also involved with Oliver North. According to North's book, *Under Fire,*[15] they served together on a secret CIA "anti-terrorism unit" that North chaired. Powell, as National Security Adviser to Reagan, threatened to stop all US aid to South American countries that would not support the Contra terrorist war in Nicaragua and he would have been further drawn into the investigative web of Iran-Contra had George Bush not outrageously pardoned Powell's boss, Casper Weinberger and others involved in the scandal in the closing days of his presidency. Powell would have been very relieved. His career has included leading US forces in George Bush's drug-related invasion of Manuel Noriega's Panama in 1989 after he became Chairman of the Joint Chiefs of Staff. Thousands of Panamanian civilians were killed and whole areas of civilian homes were destroyed. This was covered up by controlling where the media could go, incinerating bodies and dumping corpses in mass graves before they were identified, and taking control of all registration by taking over hospitals and mortuaries. Two years later, Powell led US forces in the Gulf War in which at least 200,000 Iraqis died, according to a speech at Bohemian Grove shortly after the conflict by John Lehman, Reagan's first Navy Secretary. Under Powell's leadership in Iraq, civilian areas were targeted, conscripts were buried alive in their trenches by bulldozers, more than 40 tons of radioactive material was scattered across the desert by bombs using depleted uranium, oil refineries were set on fire, and thousands of civilians, prisoners and retreating Iraqi soldiers were coldly and systematically murdered on the infamous "Highway of Death". This, and so much more, under the leadership of "war hero" Colin Powell, the friend of so many deeply disturbed people, and now the US Secretary of State helping to dictate the "war on terrorism". Powell claims he never once received an illegal order during his military career (utter claptrap) and yet the actions of his troops in those Iraqi massacres alone should have prompted charges relating to war crimes. Colin Powell's record of serving the Illuminati interests – and taking the rewards – with invasions and massacres of poor and defenceless peoples in Grenada, Panama, Iraq,

Haiti and elsewhere is grotesque, and this is the man, like the Bushes, Cheney and the rest of them, who is moralising about freedom and justice while systematically destroying both throughout the world.

Apart from sending others to the battlefield and orchestrating the slaughter of the innocent, Powell has also had a career in business. He has served on the boards of America Online (AOL) and Gulfstream Aerospace, which makes planes for governments like Kuwait and Saudi Arabia, and for Hollywood movies stars. The current Defense Secretary, Donald Rumsfeld, also served on Gulfstream's board and had stock worth $11 million when US defence contractor, General Dynamics in 1999, bought the company. I don't know what Powell made from the deal, but he is reported to have earned $4 million in increased stock value when AOL merged with that Illuminati front, TimeWarner. His son, Michael K. Powell, was the only commissioner at the Federal Communications Commission (FCC) who said the merger deal should be allowed to go through without scrutiny. He denied any conflict of interest with his father's shareholding in AOL at the time, which was worth some $13 million according to newspaper reports. The FCC calls itself an "independent" United States government agency (I love it), which regulates "interstate and international communications by radio, television, wire, satellite and cable"... [in the] ... "50 states, the District of Columbia, and US possessions".[16] In fact, Michael K. Powell, a 1999 Henry Crown Fellow of the (Illuminati) Aspen Institute, does not appear to be in favour of much regulation of media corporations, an attitude that suits the gang perfectly. Two days after his inauguration in January 2001, President George W. Bush appointed a new chairman of the FCC ... Michael K. Powell. The man he replaced, William Kennard, now works for the Carlyle Group.

Donald Rumsfeld – Mr Aspartame

Bush's Defense Secretary in the "war on terrorism" is Donald Rumsfeld, a long-time insider with an impeccable record of service to the global agenda. After attending Princeton University and serving in the Navy, he began his career in Washington DC as an administrative assistant. He was elected to Congress from his home state of Illinois in 1962 and joined the Richard Nixon administration (controlled by Illuminati Secretary of State Henry Kissinger) in 1969. Rumsfeld was a member of the Nixon cabinet from 1971 to 1972 – the year of the Watergate break-in, the sting on Nixon orchestrated by Kissinger (see *And The Truth Shall Set You Free*). In 1973 as the Watergate storm unfolded, Rumsfeld went to Europe as US Ambassador to NATO before returning the following year when Nixon had been ousted. He became chairman of the transition to the presidency of the unelected, Watergate-imposed Gerald Ford and his Vice President Nelson Rockefeller. Rumsfeld joined the Ford cabinet as Chief of Staff at the White House (which means he must have been very acceptable to Kissinger) and he became US Secretary of Defense for the first time between 1975 and 1977.

Rumsfeld moved into private business after that while maintaining a close involvement in politics. During his time as Chairman and Chief Executive of G D

Searle, the pharmaceutical company now owned by the appalling Monsanto, he was given a stream of appointments in and by government. These were: member of the President's General Advisory Committee on Arms Control – Reagan Administration (1982 – 1986); Reagan's Special Envoy on the Law of the Sea Treaty (1982 – 1983); senior adviser to Reagan's Panel on Strategic Systems (1983 – 1984); member of the US Joint Advisory Commission on US/Japan Relations – Reagan Administration (1983 – 1984); President Reagan's Special Envoy to the Middle East (1983 – 1984); member of the National Commission on the Public Service (1987 – 1990); member of the National Economic Commission (1988 – 1989); member of the Board of Visitors of the National Defense University (1988 – 1992); member of the Commission on US/Japan Relations (1989 – 1991); Federal Communications Commission High Definition Television Advisory Committee (1992 – 1993); chairman, Commission on the Ballistic Missile Threat to the United States (1998 – 1999); member of the US Trade Deficit Review Commission (1999 – 2000); and chairman of the US Commission to Assess National Security Space Management and Organization (2000).[17]

How helpful all these government connections proved when as head of G D Searle, he used his Washington insider contacts to ensure that the Food and Drug Administration (FDA) gave the go-ahead to market the infamous artificial sweetener, aspartame. Rumsfeld was to Searle what Cheney was (is) to Halliburton. (I describe the manipulation of the FDA decision in *Children Of The Matrix*.) Aspartame consists of two synthetic amino acids, phenylalanine (50%) and aspartic acid (40 %) bound in methanol (10%). FDA documents released under the Freedom of Information Act in 1995 reveal that the consequences of this horrendous substance include blindness and death. Others, according to scientists, are brain tumours, brain lesions, headaches, mood swings, skin polyps, insomnia, depression, suppression of intelligence and effects on short-term memory. Investigative author and food specialist Carol Guilford calls aspartame a "molecular holocaust".[18] This is the mind suppressant (sorry "sweetener") for which Donald Rumsfeld was hired by Searle in 1977 to win government approval. In January 1981, with the Rumsfeld's friends in power under Bush and Reagan, he told a sales meeting, according to one attendee, that he would "call in his markers" and get aspartame approved by the end of the year. Immediately the then commissioner of the Food and Drug Administration had his authority suspended and the job was given to Dr Arthur Hull Hayes, a professor and contract researcher for the Defense Department. His first major decision was to approve the use of aspartame in dry foods and his last, in 1983, was to approve it for soft drinks. This was despite all the evidence of its consequences and the opposition of his own board of inquiry. Hayes then left the FDA to become a senior adviser to the public relations firm of … Rumsfeld's G D Searle. Rumsfeld earned millions for manipulating a truly horrible substance into widespread use and he picked up a $12 million bonus when Searle was bought by the Nazi-connected Monsanto, the promoter of genetically modified (GM) food. Orrin Hatch, the Mormon senator from Utah, also took money from Searle for pressing their case on aspartame, and he worked to suppress independent studies into its safety. Hatch was also the man who promoted the BCCI and said immediately after 9/11 that the authorities believed that Osama bin Laden could be responsible. The Food and Drug Administration in America, like its equivalent in other countries, is an Illuminati front to block products that are good for humanity and to push through, without proper testing, those that suit the agenda. This happened with aspartame thanks to Rumsfeld. First, the FDA approved its use on the basis of ridiculous data and then had to withdraw that permission in the face of studies showing that it caused seizures and brain tumours in animals. But the FDA restored approval in 1981 thanks to Dr Arthur Hull Hayes, despite the unanimous opposition of a Public Board of Inquiry, which had reviewed the scientific data and recommended a delay. Dr Ralph G. Walton, a Professor of Psychiatry at North Eastern Ohio University College of Medicine, reviewed all the studies on aspartame and found 166 with relevance for human safety. All of the 74 studies funded by the aspartame industry gave it the all-clear, but 92% of those independently funded revealed safety problems. Which ones would you believe?

The reason this poison was approved against all the evidence is simple corruption. A commissioner of the Food and Drug Administration, an acting commissioner, six other operatives, and two attorneys assigned to prosecute NutraSweet for submitting fraudulent tests, left the organisation to work for ... NutraSweet, a trade name for aspartame. One genuine scientist working for the FDA wrote to a US senator: "It's like a script for Abbott and Costello. It works like this: 'approve our poison, and when you stop being a bureaucrat we'll make you a plutocrat! After it's licensed we'll pay off the American Dietetics, the American Diabetes Association, the American Medical Association and anyone we need who's for sale'." The man orchestrating all this was Donald Rumsfeld, now US "Defense" Secretary in the "war on terrorism". Clearly a man you can trust. By the way, the Monsanto Corporation of St Louis, Missouri, expanded the accredited uses for aspartame after taking over Rumsfeld's G D Searle in 1985. Monsanto is an Illuminati company to its fingertips and the promoter of genetically modified food, another part of the Illuminati assault on the human mind and body. It is using the same methods to win approval for genetically modified food as it did for aspartame. The current Bush administration is awash with people connected to Monsanto.

A few other "characters"

John Ashcroft, George W. Bush's Attorney General, is one of the Monsanto funded insiders in Boy George's US government. Ashcroft is another with his snout in the corporate trough with Microsoft and Enron among his benefactors. When the Enron scandal broke, with President Bush's biggest funder collapsing amid document shredding and fantastic corruption, we had the farcical situation in which Attorney General Ashcroft could not take part in the subsequent investigation because he had taken money from them! In the November 2000 election for the Senate, Ashcroft failed even to beat a dead man. His opponent, the Missouri Governor Mel Carnahan, died in a plane crash with his son and campaign adviser while flying in a Cessna to a campaign rally. Carnahan's name stayed on the ballot paper and more people voted for him than Ashcroft. It was the first time anyone had posthumously won election to the Senate. He couldn't do any worse than the live ones, that's for sure. Ashcroft was soon back in Washington, however, when the incoming President Bush named him as US Attorney General. This is the man who has been dismantling basic human freedoms in the United States since September 11th with an enthusiasm and glee that can only be described as orgasmic. He was appointed by Boy George to replace the deeply corrupt Janet Reno, she of Waco mass murder fame. Attorney General is another big Illuminati-nominated post. Ashcroft is a member of the "Religious Right" that has spawned Bush family clones like the monumental hypocrite Pat Robertson (see *Children Of The Matrix*) who has used his "ministry" and massive public donations to his "humanitarian projects" to expand his business empire in places like the Congo when it was ruled by his friend, the vicious and corrupt dictator, Mobuto Sese-Seko. Show me a member of the "Religious Right" and I'll show you a hypocrite, or, at least, it has never failed yet. Anyway, this is the "spiritual" home of John Ashcroft, the freedom-destroying Attorney General, who has seized on the deaths of thousands in New York and Washington to cast aside basic human freedoms.

Ashcroft describes himself as a Christian conservative who doesn't smoke, drink or dance. He is against abortion because it takes a human life created by God, and yet supports the death penalty and the murder of men, women, and children, in their thousands every month in Iraq, and mass murder in many other parts of the world like Afghanistan. Ashcroft's claim to fame before he became an official freedom-buster for the Bush administration was his "war on drugs" and addictive substances (like the many Father George Bush headed while running drugs himself). Ashcroft demands the death penalty for such offences. Bad news, eh, Georgie? At the same time Ashcroft has taken $44,500 from liquor companies since 1993, including $20,000 from the St Louis-based Anheuser-Busch. He has also been lauded by the booze industry in a video tribute produced by the Beer Institute of America. When *Mother Jones* magazine questioned this contradiction, Ashcroft said: "It is a product that it is in demand [yes, like drugs] and when it's used responsibly it's like other products." Ashcroft also accepted money from the tobacco industry for his 1994 Senate race and said of tobacco that people should be free to make bad choices. Unless Ashcroft decides otherwise, that is. Here you have another hypocrite with a selective morality that changes by the sentence to meet the needs of the moment. This is the guy, people of America, who is taking your freedom away.

The "anti-terrorism" terrorist

John Negroponte is President Bush's Ambassador to the United Nations, clearly a vital role in the "war on terrorism". Negroponte knows all about the subject from his days as US ambassador to Honduras between 1981 and 1985 where he helped to coordinate America's covert war against the Sandinista government in Nicaragua. During his spell in Honduras, US aid to that country soared from $3.9 million in 1980 to $77.4 million in 1984. This funded so many US bases and so much weaponry that the country became known as *USS Honduras*. A four-part series in the *Baltimore Sun* in 1995 exposed the widespread murder and torture there by Battalion 316, a "secret army" trained and funded by the CIA. The outstanding Australian journalist (a real one), John Pilger, wrote in the UK's *New Statesman* magazine:

> "How appropriate that John Negroponte is Bush's ambassador at the United Nations. This week, he delivered America's threat to the world that it may 'require' to attack more and more countries. As US ambassador to Honduras in the early 1980s, Negroponte oversaw American funding of the regime's death squads, known as Battalion 316, that wiped out the democratic opposition, while the CIA ran its 'contra' war of terror against neighbouring Nicaragua. Murdering teachers and slitting the throats of midwives were a speciality." [19]

I can see why Bush chose him, then.

Wendy "pathet lao" Chamberlain

The US Ambassador to Pakistan who has played a pivotal role in the vital relationship between Pakistan and the United States since September 11th is Wendy Chamberlain, who is described innocently in an official profile I read as a "mother of two". The lady is rather more than that, as you would expect as an appointee of George W. Bush, or, more accurately, of those who control him. (Forgive me if I find it hard to believe that Boy George is making the foreign policy decisions when, during his election campaign, he thought Nigeria was a continent, failed to name the presidents of Chechnya, Pakistan and India, confused Slovakia and Slovenia, and asserted that Greeks were called 'Grecians' and East Timorese were East Timorians.) [20] Before Bush sent Wendy Chamberlain to Pakistan in the weeks before 9/11, she was Deputy Assistant Secretary at the International Narcotics and Law Bureau of the State Department. But she is best known for her period as US Ambassador to Laos while that country was controlled by the terrorists of the Pathet Lao regime. She got along with these terrorist dictators extremely well, it would appear. Philip Smith, director of the Lao Veterans of America, led the opposition to Chamberlain's appointment to Pakistan from the 350,000-strong Lao and Hmong exile community in the United States. "The freedom-loving people in Pakistan, Afghanistan and South Asia need to be informed and aware that Wendy Chamberlain has a deplorable track record of utter and total appeasement," he said. "She has never met a military general or dictatorship that she did not like." A letter circulated on the Internet by the Lao Veterans, dated June 29th 2001, urged confirmation hearings to block Chamberlain's appointment to Pakistan and revealed some of the "highlights" of her period in Laos:

> "The Laotian and Hmong-American community is overwhelmingly opposed to the confirmation of Wendy Chamberlain as Ambassador to Pakistan given her deplorable track-record of total appeasement in Laos (see news report from Washington, DC, in Agence France Press, June 26th 2001). We will "never forget" the deaths of our people, and relatives, in Laos under her terrible and arrogant reign. She worked to strengthen

the hands of the generals and the military dictatorship. We, therefore, ask that you put an immediate "hold" on her confirmation on the Senate floor to send a powerful message that State Department officials involved in countenancing crimes against humanity and gross human rights violations against the relatives of Lao and Hmong-Americans will not be rewarded with promotions – especially a promotion to such an important position. Moreover, by putting a "hold" on Chamberlain on the Senate Floor, it will send an important message that a new policy toward Laos is needed–not the weak and pandering policy of appeasement that Chamberlain so vigorously promoted and that cost so many innocent people their lives.

"Clearly, Ambassador Chamberlain has never met a military general or dictatorship that she did not like – and did not work to appease. She is utterly unfit for a senior Ambassadorship in Pakistan, a country of immense importance to US national security interests, compared to the tiny, third-world nation of Laos, which she, somehow, totally bungled at the cost of many lives. It should be noted that Ms Chamberlain served disgracefully as US Ambassador to Laos where she "went native" (dressing in native costumes at late-night parties with Pathet Lao communist generals where she frequently drank excessively and submissively catered to every whim of the military junta at the expense of the United States and its citizens). Indeed, Chamberlain worked overtime to appease the military generals in Laos – while the relatives of Lao and Hmong-Americans died at the cruel hands of the regime. She also countenanced the massacre of thousands of Hmong and Lao civilians and opposition leaders in Laos during her deplorable tenure. Moreover, she did nothing to gain access or intervene to reopen Xeng Khouang (Xieng Khouang), Sysamboun "Special Zone," and other often-closed areas of Laos – including the Lao gulag system in Sam Neua and elsewhere – where military crackdowns and ethnic cleansing operations occurred against thousands of Hmong and Lao people." [21]

She sounds like a perfect Bush appointment. In fact, Chamberlain's behaviour in Laos was so disgraceful that the US House of Representatives took the unprecedented step of introducing legislation in response.[22] House Resolution 332 cites Chamberlain's behaviour and methods that included the collaboration with communist Pathet Lao officials (terrorists) over the disappearance of two Hmong-Americans. This was the lady appointed by Bush to the key post of Ambassador to Pakistan months before 9/11 and the "war on terrorism" in which Pakistan would be of major importance. Bush, or rather his masters, also appointed Christina Rocca as US Assistant Secretary of State for South Asia weeks before 9/11. Her bureau is responsible for US foreign policy and relations with Afghanistan, Bangladesh, Bhutan, India, the Maldives, Nepal, Pakistan and Sri Lanka. Rocca is a career officer of the CIA going back through the Father Bush and Reagan years at least to 1982. She, like Deputy Secretary of State Richard Armitage, was involved in CIA operations relating to the war between Afghanistan and the Soviet Union when Osama bin Laden's terrorist network was funded and armed into being by the CIA. Rocca has shown a keen interest in Afghanistan and Pakistan affairs for many years.

The Queen's buddy

Coordinating communications between Washington and London since September 11th has been the American Ambassador to Britain (or the Court of St James's to be accurate), one William Stamps Farish III. This is the grandson of William Stamps Farish, the president of the Rockefellers' Standard Oil, New Jersey, (now Exxon), when they were supplying Hitler and the Nazis with fuel during the Second World War. A letter written by Standard Oil Vice President Frank A. Howard, to William S. Farish was released by the US Justice Department at the time. Remember that I.G. Farben was at the very core of the Nazi war machine and ran concentration camps like the one at Auschwitz. The letter to Farish said:

"… In England I met by appointment the Royal Dutch [Shell Oil] gentlemen from Holland and … a general agreement was reached on the necessary changes in our relations with the I.G. [Farben], in view of the state of war … the Royal Dutch Shell Group is essentially British…I also had several meetings with the [British] air ministry …

"I required the help to obtain the necessary permission to go to Holland … After discussions with the [American] Ambassador [Joseph Kennedy, JFK's father] … the situation was cleared completely … The gentlemen of the Air Ministry … very kindly offered to assist me in re-entering England.

"Pursuant to these arrangements, I was able to keep my appointment in Holland (having been flown there on a British Air Force bomber), where I had three days of discussion with the representatives of I.G. They delivered to me assignments of some 2,000 foreign patents and … we did our best to work out complete plans for a modus vivendi which could operate through the term of the war, whether or not the US came in."

William S. Farish refuelled Nazi shipping and submarines in Spain and Latin America during the war and it was the Standard Oil/I.G. Farben enterprise that opened the Auschwitz Camp on June 14th 1940, and used the slave labour of Jews, political opponents, gypsies, and others to produce artificial rubber and gasoline from coal. Farish was very close to Hermann Schmitz, the chairman of I.G. Farben. Standard Oil hired the Illuminati publicist Ivy Lee to promote I.G. Farben and the Nazis in the United States (see *And The Truth Shall Set You Free* for the detailed background). In this same period, Prescott Bush, President Bush's grandfather, was helping to fund the Nazis and so you would expect the Bushes and the Farish family to be close. Farish's grandson, William S. Farish III, became a very close friend and associate of Father George and a bosom buddy of the Queen of England. She has visited his Lane's End ranch in Kentucky many times, taking her horses to breed with Farish's prize stallions. She apparently travels by Royal Air Force plane to the Blue Grass Airport in Lexington on these occasions.[23] As I said earlier, when Father George Bush became Vice President to Reagan, he had to (officially) hand over his business affairs and investments to a "blind trust" and the man chosen to run it was the same William S. Farish III, the US Ambassador in London and the middleman in the "war on terrorism" between the Bush, Blair, and the Queen. Wherever you look it is clear that what has followed September 11th has been coordinated throughout by the Bush cartel.

Tony Blair

Since the election of Tony Blair as UK Prime Minister on May 1st 1997, a coup has taken place in Britain. Blair, who should by law be an accountable Prime Minister running the country in cooperation with his cabinet, has become "President Blair", running his own agenda in league with unelected "advisers". Mo Mowlam was Blair's former Secretary for Northern Ireland and she was the only member of his sycophantic, spineless, bunch of shady main-chancers (his "cabinet") that I would trust to tell me the time. After she left the government, she told the BBC documentary, *Cabinet Confidential*: "Tony's acting more like a president than a prime minister and in that situation the cabinet itself is dead". Mowlam suggested that the unelected advisers have more power than the cabinet in relation to the prime minister. "They seemed to be operating instead of the cabinet," she said, and she continued:

> "He makes decisions with a small coterie of people, advisers, just like the president of the United States. He doesn't go back to cabinet, he isn't inclusive in terms of other cabinet ministers and if he really wants to get the support of the public and the support of Parliament there has to be more people included." [24]

As in Nazi Germany, you are not allowed to speak out against Herr Blair. Freedom of speech and having a right to an opinion is only accepted if Blair agrees with what you say. The difference is that in Nazi Germany they assassinated you for challenging the Fuhrer and in Blair's Britain they assassinate your character. Mowlam was "Our Mo" when she was in the Blair cabinet and "Mad Mo" when she started challenging high command. One of Blair's "BIGs" – Buffoons in Government – who has dismissed her in such terms is the punch-throwing and in my view oaf of a Deputy Prime Minister, John Prescott. Along with Foreign Secretary Jack "straw man" Straw, Prescott is perhaps the number one "BIG" in the Blair cabinet from where I'm sitting. Blair, in truth, has become a dictator masquerading as a democratic prime minister and since September 11th he has been a law unto himself. The BBC documentary showed how Blair's "war cabinet" included his unelected director of communications and strategy, Alistair Campbell, and the newly appointed head of government relations, Sally Morgan. Campbell, a former tabloid journalist, is paid by a Civil Service that is supposed to be politically impartial and yet he is a Labour supporter whose role in the Blair circle is to spin news and events to present his "boss" in the best light and to get the people to see the world in a way that suits Blair's agenda. None of this is a surprise to me because to my eyes Blair has always had a large notice on his forehead warning: "Not to be trusted". I felt this long before he became Prime Minister. I have said in previous books and talks that he was an Illuminati place man put in power to serve the cause, which included taking the UK into the European single currency, dropping the pound sterling, and absorbing British independence into the European fascist superstate. I wrote that years ago and that is precisely what he is doing, helped by the pathetic Liberal Democrats of Charles Kennedy. Anyone who supports the Euro single currency is supporting their own financial imprisonment by unelected bankers working to the Illuminati agenda for global control.

The chosen one

Tony Charles Lynton Blair was born in Edinburgh, Scotland, on May 6th 1953. His father, Leo, was a law lecturer at Edinburgh University, a major educational centre for the Illuminati. Blair grew up in the industrial city of Durham, which is most famous for its cathedral, and also lived in Australia for three years. He was educated at the Durham Choristers School before returning to Edinburgh to attend the prestigious (if you like that sort of thing) Fettes College. Blair went on to Oxford University and then took a legal apprenticeship at the chambers of Alexander Irvine, a Queens Counsel and influential in the Labour Party. Blair became a barrister specialising in industrial and employment law, and met his lawyer wife, Cherie, during his apprenticeship. They married in 1980 and have four children, Euan, Nicky, Kathryn and Leo (who, on May 20th 2000, became the first child to be born to a sitting prime minister in 152 years). Blair's brother, William James Lynton Blair QC, also went into law from this "ordinary family" and has been a consultant with the World Bank and the International Monetary Fund. In 1983, Blair was elected to Parliament as the Labour MP for Sedgefield, near Durham in the north-east of England, and began a rapid rise the top. He was given a number of jobs in the Labour shadow cabinet during the long years of Labour opposition to Margaret Thatcher's Conservative government and her successor, John Major, who is now European representative of the Carlyle Group.

At some point in the Blair story he clearly became the chosen one for some powerful forces and within 24 hours of the sudden death of the then Labour Party leader John Smith from a heart attack, the whole of the British media had already decided that Blair was his successor. I still think there is more to know about Smith's death. The wave of support for Blair within a Labour Party that had been out of government for so long was fuelled by the media message that here was the only person who could lead them back to Downing Street. Blair was elected leader of the party in July 1994, a year after he had been invited to attend his first meeting of the Illuminati's secretive Bilderberg Group in a hotel at Vouliagment, Greece. Blair took control of the Labour Party at every level and has transformed it into a fiercely centralised dictatorship, a personalised, customised vehicle for his (the Illuminati's) agenda. It has become a vacuum of principle in which Blair's word is law. And Blair is controlled by the shadowy figures that decide what his word will be. With the media propaganda machine behind him, Blair, at 44, became the youngest British Prime Minister since Lord Liverpool in 1812 when he was elected by a landslide on May 1st 1997. Months earlier I had said in public talks that not only would Blair be the next UK prime minister, but that he would be elected on May Ist – an extremely important date in the Illuminati ritual calendar (see *The Biggest Secret*). In the UK it is the sitting prime minister who decides the date of the general election. In this case that was John "Carlyle Group" Major, the Conservative leader. Major chose May 1st.

Dancing for Rupert

One of Blair's most significant supporters is the major Illuminati media tycoon Rupert Murdoch. His News Corporation has some 800 subsidiaries and owns the UK *Times*, *Sunday Times*, and the downmarket tabloids the *Sun* and *News of the World*. His holdings also include Sky Global Networks, which owns the satellite television company BSkyB. Murdoch controls Twentieth Century Fox, the Fox TV network, *New York Post*, and close to 200 newspapers worldwide, to name only some of his holdings. Murdoch had always thrown his UK newspapers behind the Conservative candidate in UK elections, but when Blair became Labour leader, all that suddenly changed. Blair was now his man. This has been incredibly beneficial for Blair and it also ensures access on demand to the UK Prime Minster for Murdoch. It was alleged that after the 1997 election win Blair rang the Bilderberger Italian Prime Minister Romano Prodi to help Murdoch to expand his empire in Italy by buying into the Mediaset empire. This was owned by another Illuminati media and political front man, the convicted crook Silvio Berlusconi, who became, staggeringly, Italian Prime Minister. Murdoch's daughter, Elisabeth, a News Corporation executive, is a close friend of Blair's long-time spinner Peter Mandelson.

One major example of this Blair-Murdoch relationship came in May 2002 when Blair's government announced plans to change the rules on media ownership to allow Murdoch to expand his holdings in Britain against all the principles of media diversity. A year earlier Murdoch visited Blair at Downing Street to "discuss his concerns over Britain's cross-ownership laws".[25] These "concerns" were related to rules that prevented him from owning a terrestrial television station because his newspapers have a 33% share of the UK market and he also owns the satellite TV network BSkyB. But with all of his newspapers supporting Blair during election campaigns, Murdoch has no problem telling the Prime Minister what to do, and the easing of media regulations means that Murdoch can now buy the terrestrial station Channel 5 if he wishes. Blair also opened the way for corporations outside of Europe to own British television companies. The major ITV network, once owned by many companies in the various regions of the country, will be allowed to become one centrally owned operation. The rules will now permit this network to be bought by Illuminati corporations like Disney and AOL/TimeWarner and it also allows the ITV network and Channel 5 to be owned by the same people. Channel 5 is currently controlled by the Illuminati media giant Bertelsmann, which is reported to have ambitions to dominate the UK commercial television market. Bertelsmann is a Germany-based company whose American printing operation suddenly, without any warning, refused to print my books in early 2002. Something I said chaps? Blair also plans to allow the same people to own more than one national radio station, and newspaper groups can buy radio stations. The rules preventing one radio group owning more than 15% of the market are scrapped. All these changes by Blair are precisely in line with the Illuminati agenda for centralisation of media power. Like I say, Blair is a 100%, wholly owned subsidiary of the Illuminati.

We are full of sleaze if you please ...

From the moment Blair walked into Downing Street he has slavishly pursued the Illuminati agenda, pressing for further centralisation of the European Union and conceding more and more power to the Brussels bureaucrats over British law and society. He has all along been preparing to replace the pound sterling with the euro as I said in my books back in the 1990s and he has backed every Illuminati military intervention by deploying British forces and supporting the American government at every turn in the former Yugoslavia, Afghanistan and the "war on terrorism" in general. He has also showered government jobs and patronage on his friends, supporters and associates in the same way the Bushes do in America. "Tony's Cronies" has become a common phrase in British political life. Also like the Bushes, he enjoys massive support from the top business leaders and corporations as the gap between rich and poor (which the Labour Party was formed 100 years ago to close) gets wider and wider under Herr Blair. On May 14th 2001, before Blair won his second term, 58 business leaders wrote a letter to Rupert Murdoch's *Times* newspaper urging business to support a Blair victory. They were chairmen or chief executives and a number had been knighted or given other "honours" by Blair, who has turned the United Kingdom political scene into a mirror of that headquarters of political slush and sleaze, the United States. Indeed Blair insists that he and President Bush think alike.[26]

Blair's Downing Street "Chief of Staff" Jonathan Powell is supposed to be an impartial civil servant who is paid by the taxpayer. Yet he once worked for the Labour Party raising money through "donations" from business. Clearly he's still working for the Labour Party, it's just that they aren't paying for him – the people are. The deeply corrupt Enron Corporation donated money to Blair's Labour Party and saw changes unfold in government energy policy that suited their agenda. Blair says the two were not connected. Then there was the bizarre story of Lakshmi Mittal, the Indian steel tycoon and one of the richest men in Britain. At the end of May 2001, Mr Mittal gave £125,000 to the Labour Party shortly before the general election in which Blair won his second term. After his victory Blair sent a letter to the Romanian Prime Minister Adrian Nastase supporting the takeover of Sidex, its nationalised steel company, by Mr Mittal's firm, LNM. Days later Romania awarded the £300 million sale to Mr Mittal in the face of French competition. Mr Blair said he sent the letter because he was supporting a "British company" and not because of the very large cheque Mr Mittal had given his party. This is a lie. Mittal's LNM is a multi-national corporation registered in the Caribbean tax haven of the Dutch Antilles and of the 125,000 people it employees worldwide, fewer than 100 live in the UK![27] Not only that, but Mr Mittal's empire is in direct competition with British firms that do employ British people. When the story broke, the lies poured out of

Downing Street as always. They said that Mittal's donation was made after the general election (lie); they said his company was British (lie); that Blair had only signed the letter drafted by the Foreign Office as a matter of routine (lie – the letter was amended and rewritten by Blair's office); they said it was only a letter of congratulation and did not affect the deal (lie – the British Embassy in Bucharest said it was an important factor in clinching the contract). Mittal's wife also gave £5,000 to the constituency fund of Keith Vaz, Blair's former Minister for Europe, who faced a major Parliamentary investigation into his financial activities and behaviour that led to him being suspended from Parliament for a month. I cannot stress it enough – these are the people telling you what happened on September 11th and who was responsible! A website called Red Star Research keeps tabs on the Herr Blair Bunch of special advisers and business leaders that influence government policy and pay the Labour Party bills.[28]

The cynical nature of Blair and his government was highlighted in May 2002 in a *Panorama* documentary on BBC television. This revealed how Blair had spent record sums of taxpayers' money on "government information" advertisements in the weeks before the general election that gave him a second term. In the 12 months before the election the government was the UK's biggest buyer of advertising with a record £192 million being spent – up 70% on the previous year – and almost half of that money was used between January and March 2001 in the run-up to the election. A record £49 million was spent in the March alone. Government advertising is purchased through a government department called COI Communications, which is supposed to be independent of party politics. The advertising itself is supposed to be used to inform the public about changes in the law and policy. Instead, as *Panorama* clearly demonstrated, Blair used this taxpayers' money to promote his government in an effort to increase his support at the coming election. What cynical corruption of the system, what contempt for the people he claims to represent. Tony Blair, again like Bush, is one of the most blatantly and transparently insincere politicians I have ever seen in a profession that is largely insincere by reflex action. His "off the cuff" remarks are carefully rehearsed and worded – as with his "spontaneous" tribute to Princess Diana on the day she was murdered in Paris in 1997 (see *The Biggest Secret*). It turned out he had been rehearsing the "spontaneity" all morning with his spinner Alistair Campbell. You can always tell when Blair has been rehearsing an "emotional, heartfelt, statesmanlike" and "spontaneous" response because he keeps pausing between words and looking down in the contrived manner of some C-movie actor. Blair also strenuously denied that Diana's death was anything more than an accident, and resisted an independent investigation.

Tony two–tongues

Journalist John Pilger highlighted a classic example of Blair double-speak when he wrote of … "the grotesque hypocrisy of Tony Blair weeping for the children of Dunblane, then sending machine guns that mow down children in East Timor …"[29] With Blair and his ministers and officials working as the sales and marketing team, Britain is the second biggest exporter of arms in the world (second to guess who?)

and the single biggest arms manufacturer on the planet is British Aerospace. These weapons are used by terrorists of all kinds in the Middle East and across the world.[30] In 1975, Britain sold arms abroad worth $470 million. By 1995 it was *4.7 billion*.[31] Ironically, but appropriately in the circumstances, on the morning of September 11th 2001 as those planes were hijacked, a protest was under way in the Docklands area of London against the biggest "arms fair" – death and terror market place – yet held in Britain. While Tony Blair was in front of the cameras condemning terrorism, British arms manufacturers were down the road in Docklands seeking to sell weapons for terrorism with the full support of Tony Blair. Nothing captures the cold, calculating, heartless approach of the Blair government better than the case of Jo Moore, the Blair crony and adviser to the former Transport Secretary Stephen Byers. Within an hour of the second plane crashing into the World Trade Center, and while the rest of the world looked on in stunned horror, Jo Moore was sending an e-mail to Blair government colleagues saying that the disaster had provided a good opportunity that day to "bury" controversial stories they did not want to be publicised. Blair and Byers both had a very public opportunity to stand for common decency in their government by sacking Ms Moore. They refused to do so despite the public outrage that followed, and it was only much later after another storm broke in her department that she was told to go. I'll take no lectures on morality from Tony Blair, thank you very much.

What a fantastic cesspit of sleaze, corruption, mass murder, drug running and terrorism we have had to wade through in these last five chapters. And pinch yourself: these are the same honest, fair, just, peace-loving, big-hearted, thoroughly trustworthy characters that have told us what happened on September 11th, who was responsible, and what should happen as a consequence. Somehow, you know, I don't think I'll take their word for it. Imagine being their speechwriter. What a breeze of a job. They just have to repeat the same line over and over:

"Lies, lies, lies, lies, lies, lies, lies, lies, lies, lies, lies, lies, lies, lies. Thankyou."

Talking of which, let us now consider the background to 9/11…

SOURCES

1   An American Tale: Colin Powell is Only One Chapter in a Remarkable Immigrant Story, Steven V. Roberts, *US News & World Report*, August 21st 1995; Boring Details (Iran Contra Case Cover-ups) Robert Parry, *Mother Jones* magazine, July–August 1993; Bosnia Betrayed (United States Policy on Intervention), June Jordan, The Progressive, September 1993; Colin Powell Just One More Warlord: Like General Schwarzkopf Before Him, This Man Knows the

Art of Self-Lionization, by Colman McCarthy, *National Catholic Reporter*, October 15th 1993; Ellen Ray, William Schaap, Karl Van Meter and Louis Wolf, Dirty Work 2: The CIA in Africa (Lyle Stuart Inc., 1979); Goldwater: Powell a Shoo-in, Associated Press, October 12th 1995; GOP Bid Won't be easy For Powell, Experts Say, by Ronald Brownstein, *Los Angeles Times*, October 16th 1995; Powell Cites Mixed Feelings About Washington Rally, Reuters, October 16th 1995; Presidential Eugenics … Guess Who's Got Royal Genes, Reuters, October 16th 1995; Report Rips Powell On Somalia, Associated Press, October 1st 1995; The Demobilization of Colin Powell, Life Magazine, July 1993; The Legend of Colin Powell: Anatomy of an Establishment Career, *The New Republic*, April 17th 1995

2   Powell's Intimates Urge Against White House Run, *Los Angeles Times*, October 7th 1995

3   *Colin Powell, My American Journey* (Random House, 1995)

4   *Called To Serve* and the video, *A Nation Betrayed*, are available from **http://www.bogritz.com/books.htm**

5   *Called To Serve*

6   **http://www.deepblacklies.co.uk/main_page.htm**

7   **http://www.copi.com/articles/guyatt/deep_black2.html**

8   **http://prorev.com/bush3.htm#armitage**

9   Ibid

10   Online Journal, Players on a Rigged Grand Chessboard: Bridas, Unocal and the Afghanistan Pipeline, March 6th 2002, **http://www.onlinejournal.com/Special_Reports/Chin030602/chin030602.html**

11   **http://prorev.com/bush3.htm**

12   Karl Evanzz, *The Judas Factor: The Plot to Kill Malcolm X* (Thunder's Mouth Press, 1993)

13   The Legend of Colin Powell: Anatomy of an Establishment Career, *The New Republic*, April 17th 1995

14   The National Security Archive, *The Chronology: The Documented Day-by-Day Account of the Secret Military Assistance to Iran and the Contras* (Warner Books, 1987), p 262

15   Oliver North, *Under Fire* (Harper Collins, 1991)

16   FCC website, **http://www.fcc.gov**

17   U.S Department of Defense biography

18   See **http://www.change-links.org/Crimie.htm**

19   **http://www.change-links.org/Crimie.htm** *New Statesman*, October 15th 2001

20   **http://www.jang.com.pk/thenews/columnists/furrukh/furrukh1.htm**

21   **http://www.laosfreedom.com/doc7tosenator.html**

22   H. Res. 332/H. Res. 169; in the 106th Congress

23   *George Bush: The Unofficial Biography*, p 515

24   **http://news.bbc.co.uk/hi/english/uk_politics/newsid_1660000/1660330.stm**

25   *Guardian*, June 13th 2001

26   *The Day That Shook The World* (BBC Worldwide Ltd, 2001), p 181, a pathetic BBC publication slavishly repeating the official story of 9/11

27   *Daily Mail*, February 14th 2002, p 7

This "world" is only an illusion and we can change it any time we want. It's just a choice right now between fear and love.

28 **http://www.red-star-research.org.uk/index.html**

29 **http://pilger.carlton.com/print/19220**

30 *Addicted To Arms, A Will Self Investigation*, BBC2, April 28th 2002

31 Ibid

chapter 6

Play it again, scam

The individual is handicapped by coming face to face with a conspiracy so monstrous he cannot believe it exists.

J. Edgar Hoover, the most infamous head of the FBI – and he should know!

History is ablaze with examples of engineered terrorism and war that mirror the events and aftermath of September 11th. I guess if the technique keeps working, why change it? In my other books you will find many of these recounted in detail, but here are some of the problem-reaction-solutions of enormous relevance to the events of September 11th. For those who are new to this information the parallels will be startling.

The Oklahoma bomb

There was a "rehearsal" for what happened on September 11th. It came some six years earlier on April 19th 1995 when a massive bomb, or bombs in truth, destroyed the Alfred P. Murrah Building in Oklahoma City and 168 people, many of them children at a day care centre, were killed. All the classic features were there: the problem of a "terrorist attack" on a US federal building; the villain or "patsy" named immediately as Timothy McVeigh; the reaction of understandable outrage from the people as they saw the devastation and believed the government's version of events; and the solution, with a series of measures that removed civil liberties and targeted the so-called Christian Patriot or militia movement that had been having considerable success exposing the global conspiracy in the years before. It was claimed that McVeigh was connected to the militia underground and his alleged accomplice, Terry Nichols, was also portrayed as some white supremacist and racist even though his two marriages had been to a Mexican and a Filipino. McVeigh was executed and Nichols is currently serving a life sentence. "Anti-terrorism" bills were rushed through Congress in days and at least some had clearly been written and printed before the bombing. They included all the elements of destroying civil liberties that have been still further extended as a result of 9/11. Within 24 hours of the carnage, President Bill Clinton was calling for " ...an easing of restrictions on the military's involvement in domestic law enforcement". Once again this was achieved to an even greater extent after September 11th.

Clinton also used the bombing to urge the media to ban "anti-government extremists" from their papers, screens and microphones, and he attacked the alternative talk radio shows that are designed to give the public a rare opportunity to hear and communicate information that differs from the official line. The bombing was said to have been a response by McVeigh to the murder of men, women and children by the United States government at Waco, Texas, on April 19th 1993. One of the government agencies blamed for Waco was the Bureau of Alcohol Tobacco and Firearms (ATF), which had offices in the Murrah Building and the official story says that they were the target. In "response" to the bombing, one bill[1] proposed by the Democrat Charles Schumer, now the Senator for New York State, included five-year prison sentences for publicly engaging in "unseemly speculation" and publishing or transmitting by wire or electronic means "baseless conspiracy theories regarding the Federal government of the United States". Naturally, the government would decide if it was "baseless". Schumer had also vehemently dismissed evidence of the mass murder in Waco in a way that beggared belief. His fascist bill never became law, but you watch them try again whenever they think they can succeed. Already the FBI "Joint Anti-Terrorism Task Force" has issued flyers urging the public to call with information about possible "terrorists" within the United States. The flyers say that among the people to watch for are "'defenders' of the US Constitution against the federal government and UN"; people who make "numerous references to the Constitution"; those who "attempt to police the police"; and "Lone individuals".[2]

Oklahoma fantasy

There is another tell-tale sign with these set-ups and stings, be it Oklahoma, the Kennedy assassination or September 11th. The official story is so full of untruths and glaring contradictions that anyone with half a brain could take it apart. The US government claimed that a fertiliser and fuel oil bomb left by McVeigh in a Ryder truck destroyed the Murrah Building. He was executed by lethal injection on June 11th 2001 and became the first federal execution for 38 years. Actually, I say he was executed; there are those who question even that. Susan Carlson, a reporter for WLS-AM Radio in Chicago, witnessed the "execution" at Terre Haute, Indiana, and says that McVeigh "… appeared to be still breathing or what appeared to be shallow breathing, even after being pronounced dead and his eyes remained open".[3] McVeigh had said he was micro-chipped while serving in the US forces and to understand, perhaps, why he would not vigorously defend himself when he could not possibly have been responsible for that scale of death and devastation we would need to know what was going on and being said or threatened behind the scenes. Significantly when McVeigh was first arrested he was given a "mental assessment" by Louis Jolyon West from the University of California. What the newspaper reports of this did not say is that West is one of the most notorious CIA mind controllers in America, as my books and many others have revealed (see *And The Truth Shall Set You Free* and *The Biggest Secret*). Another interesting coincidence is that two years before the Oklahoma bomb, Martin Keating, the brother of

Oklahoma Governor Frank Keating, wrote a book called *The Final Jihad*. This was a novel about a terrorist attack on the "Oklahoma City Building" by a man called Thomas McVeigh. Keating dedicated the book to the "Knights of the Secret Circle".

The provable lie

The FBI said the Murrah Building was destroyed by a single ammonium nitrate truck bomb in a 20-foot Ryder rental truck parked outside by McVeigh. The problem is that this is provably impossible. You have only got to look at the small crater left where the truck was standing to see that the explosive power could never have brought down the Murrah Building and there are other little details like the fact that while some pillars closer to the truck bomb did not fall, others further away did. Retired Brigadier General Benton K. Partin said from the start that the fuel-fertiliser device in the Ryder truck could not possibly have brought down the Murrah Building. Too many facts, he said, simply didn't add up. Partin is no anti-government "extremist", although that was the way he was portrayed in order to discredit his devastating information. He was chairman of the Republican Party in Fairfax County, Virginia, for four years and among a long list of US Air Force appointments he was Commander of the Armament Laboratory, the top research and development facility at Elgin Air Force Base in Florida. During his 31 years of active duty he became a highly acclaimed expert in weapons systems and explosives, and his Air Force and civilian career record is extremely long and impressive. Partin's detailed assessment of the bombing has been widely quoted in the alternative media, but virtually ignored in the mainstream even though it destroys the official story. Actually, make that *because* it destroys the official story. Partin's report, dated July 30th 1995, says that the serious damage and demolition to supporting columns inside the building could only have been caused by devices attached to, or placed within, the columns. It was simply not possible for that to be achieved by an explosion from outside the building. Yes, the truck bomb could have shattered windows and scattered considerable debris, but the laws of physics mean that it could not bring down concrete pillars that distance away. Partin pointed out that " …most people fail to appreciate how inefficient a blast is in air and how dramatically its destructive potential drops off just a few feet from the explosion".[4] The main columns in the Murrah Building were made to survive pressure of more than 3,000 pounds per square inch. There is no way, as Partin's report points out, for a fuel-fertiliser bomb that far from the building to generate more than a fraction of that pressure. However, Partin says that the fantastic damage to the Murrah Building could have been caused by a total of just 150 pounds of explosive if it was located in the right places on the right support columns.[5] Dr Rodger Raubach, a PhD in physical chemistry and member of the research faculty at Stanford University, said: "General Partin's assessment is absolutely correct. I don't care if they pulled up a semi-trailer truck with 20 tons of ammonium nitrate; it wouldn't do the damage we saw there."[6] Faced with these facts about the impossibility of a truck bomb causing the damage, the "McVeigh bomb" began to miraculously increase in size. The Bureau of Alcohol, Tobacco and Firearms, and other government agencies originally said the bomb contained 1,200 pounds of ammonium nitrate and fuel oil (ANFO). But, as if by magic, it was to become 4,000 pounds and eventually 4,800. I even heard 7,000 pounds quoted in the media around the time of McVeigh's execution in 2001. But a study by the US Air Force confirmed that even at 4,800 pounds, the story does not make sense:

> "It is impossible to ascribe the damage that occurred on April 19th, 1995, to a single truck bomb containing 4,800 pounds ... In fact, the maximum predicted damage of the floor panels of the Murrah federal building is equal to approximately 1% of the total floor area of the building.

> "It must be concluded that the damage at the Murrah federal building is not the result of the truck bomb itself, but rather due to other factors such as locally placed charges within the building itself." [7]

This report was not presented at McVeigh's trial, together with 4,000 pages of other evidence that the FBI claimed to have "lost". The FBI, the same FBI now "investigating" 9/11, also interviewed General Partin but did nothing when he showed that the official story was impossible. He sent copies of his detailed engineering analysis, including colour photographs, to every member of Congress and more than 1,000 media organisations. Only a handful of replies came back. They would rather the orchestrators of mass murder remain at large than reveal that the government and its agencies are lying at every turn. Yet people still say to me that if the conspiracy I am exposing were true the media would tell us about it! Researcher J. Orlin Grabbe and others have revealed that a secret Pentagon report on the bombing came to basically the same conclusions as Partin. Grabbe says the Pentagon commissioned nine explosives experts to write reports and accepted two of them as the "official" report.[8] He says he spoke to both experts, but they declined to be interviewed because of "confidentiality agreements with the Pentagon". Grabbe says that sources familiar with the Pentagon report told him that the conclusions were the same as those of General Partin, except that the Pentagon report concluded there were demolition charges placed on five columns, not the four suggested by Partin.

These findings are not only supported by the science, but by witness accounts. Many said they heard more than one explosion. A 500-page report by the Oklahoma City Bombing Investigation Commission said that many witnesses "have testified to hearing a second bomb" and that "explosives experts contend that the extent of the damage to the building could not have resulted from a single truck bomb ..." [9] The seismographic record at the Oklahoma Geological Survey (OGS) at the University of Oklahoma recorded two "seismic events" at the time the Murrah Building was hit and a geophysicist at the OGS, Dr Raymon L. Brown, told *New American* magazine that the simplest explanation for this was that there were "two separate explosions".[10] Witnesses support this. After rescuers arrived on the scene there were many reports of other bombs being found and defused, and the area was evacuated several times. Volunteers at the site and television viewers remember how the police and fire authorities warned that another device, or devices, had been found in the rubble. If you watch recordings of stations like KFOR-TV, Channel 9 News, and Channel 4 News from that morning you see the reporters and witnesses talking of other bombs on the site that had not exploded. (You can see this footage in the video *911 – The Road To Tyranny*, presented by Alex Jones. It is available through ***Infowars.com***) Oklahoma Governor Frank Keating tells one interviewer: "Reports that I have is that one device was deactivated, apparently there's another device …" A television presenter quotes the FBI as saying that the explosion was caused by a "very sophisticated device and had to have been done by an explosives expert". A spokesman for the rescue teams says that they are not able to get into the wreckage to retrieve the injured because of the unexploded bombs still in the building. A reporter with KWTV said that he had just seen a bomb squad truck going towards the Murrah Building to defuse another device. Senator Charles Key's Oklahoma Bombing Investigation Committee confirmed these reports. It concluded: "There is sufficient evidence to confirm that law enforcement agencies in Oklahoma City, as well as Washington DC, had sufficient prior knowledge of the impending disaster, yet took minimum measures to avert the bombing. Documents and witnesses support this conclusion." The report said there were at least four sightings of other bombs in the building.[11] According to police logs and firefighter witnesses, it was the Bureau of Alcohol, Tobacco and Firearms (ATF) that removed these unexploded bombs from the scene. This is the organisation that was supposed to have been McVeigh's target in the official cover story. We were told at different times that other bombs were found, no other bombs were found, and that bombs were found, but they were "dummies" used for training by the ATF. Soon all of this was forgotten and the official version of what happened dominated the media.

Rubble trouble

The rubble from the Murrah Building contained the proof of where the bombs were really located, what they were, and how many there were. All that was required to establish what had happened beyond doubt was for explosives experts to go in and do their analysis. General Partin made this very point and requested that the site be protected so this investigation could take place. He wrote to the Oklahoma Senator Don Nickles and delivered the letter personally to his Washington office and those of some 23 other senators and around 30 congressmen on May 18th 1995. He wrote:

"I am concerned that vital evidence will soon be destroyed with the pending demolition of the Federal Building in Oklahoma City. From all the evidence I have seen in the published material, I can say with a high level of confidence that the damage pattern on the reinforced concrete superstructure could not possibly have been attained from the single truck bomb without supplementing demolition charges at some of the reinforced column bases. The total incompatibility with a single truck bomb lies in the fact that either some of the columns collapsed that should not have collapsed or some of the columns are still standing that should have collapsed and did not."[12]

Instead of listening to General Partin, the government hired a company called Controlled Demolition to bring down the rest of the building and take the rubble to a private landfill site operated by BFI Waste Systems. Here the remains of the Murrah Building were kept under guard by the Wackenhut Corporation, one of the Illuminati's private armies, which I mentioned earlier in relation to the chemical weapons equipment shipped by Wackenhut to Saddam Hussein before the Gulf War. George Wackenhut, a former FBI operative, started the company with other FBI associates in 1954, and recruits from the FBI, CIA, and the military have dominated its board. George Wackenhut is a long-time friend of Father Bush and has funded his political campaigns along with those of Boy George and Florida governor Jeb Bush. McVeigh's defence team and independent explosives experts were refused access to the rubble that would have revealed all. If that is not the most blatant admission that there is something to hide, I don't know what is. Ironically, on its own website Controlled Demolition says of the Murrah contract: "When a crime scene involves the detonation of explosives, and the possibility of undetonated materials exist, an experienced contractor is needed to preserve evidence critical to ongoing investigations while dealing with any explosives discovered." [13] So why was McVeigh's defence not allowed access to any virgin remains to conduct such investigations? Controlled Demolition says it was hired to work at the Murrah Building and instigate a "timely implosion" of the ruins. The company says on its website:

> "[At the request of] ... the General Services Administration (GSA), and subsequently that of the Federal Bureau of Investigation (FBI), Controlled Demolition Incorporated (CDI), was able to assist in analysing the integrity of the unstable Alfred P. Murrah Federal Building in Oklahoma City. Controlled Demolition's team coordinated with rescue and body retrieval efforts by authorities, salvaged evidence for the FBI's investigation, prepared the building for implosion, and completed the demolition sequence in a continuous work program. Controlled Demolition Incorporated is equipped to work closely with governmental agencies under complex project scenarios that demand professionalism and attention to detail while working under difficult site, political and emotional conditions." [14]

The company is owned by the Loizeaux family and headed by Mark Loizeaux out of Baltimore, just a short drive from Washington DC. In February 2000, a Federal Grand Jury indicted Mark Loizeaux, Douglas Loizeaux and Controlled Demolition on charges of falsely reporting campaign contributions by asking family members and employees to donate to the campaign of Elijah E. Cummings, a Democrat Representative for Maryland. The *Baltimore Sun* reported that the illegal contributions allegedly occurred between 1996 and 1998, but the Loizeaux brothers and the company were acquitted in September 2000. Controlled Demolition certainly seems to be well respected by the United States government and its agencies because it has been awarded federal contracts worth billions. Six years after it carried away the remains of the Alfred P. Murrah Building in Oklahoma and took it to a safe place guarded by Wackenhut, Controlled Demolition was hired by the government again for an even bigger job … removing the remains of the World Trade Center.

Same old story

As with 9/11 the government's version of the Oklahoma bombing is a mass of lies and manipulation. The Bureau of Alcohol, Tobacco and Firearms, or the ATF as it is known, was supposed to be McVeigh's target. How convenient and strange, therefore, that no ATF agents were killed or injured because they were miraculously not in the office that morning. There were no badge-carrying federal agents in the building, only civilian workers.[15] When these facts became known, the ATF wheeled out agent Alex McCauley who told of the heroic efforts to help to rescue victims by himself and a fellow agent, who was said to have fallen three floors in an elevator and survived. But Duane James, the building maintenance supervisor, proved technically and logistically that the story was a lie. It was "pure fantasy", he said, and the ATF had to retract the story and admit that McCauley was nowhere near the building let alone in it. They will not, however, say where he or any of their other personnel were.[16] Federal Judge Wayne Alley was not in his chambers across the street from the Murrah Building either. He told the *Oregonian* newspaper that he had decided not to go to work that day because "there had been talk". He said:

> "Let me just say that within the past two or three weeks, information has been disseminated … that indicated concerns on the part of people who ought to know, that we ought to be a little more careful … My subjective impression was there was a reason for a dissemination of these concerns." [17]

In other words, he was warned off and took the advice. Witnesses who spoke with ATF agents at the scene have confirmed this. When asked if any of their men were injured they said they were not in the building because they had been tipped off through their pagers not to go into work that day. Tiffany Bible, a paramedic who was at the Murrah Building within minutes of the blasts, swore in an affidavit that she found the ATF in full combat gear (which apparently takes half an hour to put on) and they said they had been warned not to go to work that day.

Why was the bomb squad on site *before* the bombing?

Glenn and Kathy Wilburn, who lost two small children in the bombing, worked constantly and passionately for years to uncover the truth of what happened. They conducted and documented more than 300 hours of interviews, and persuaded people to talk who had remained silent for fear of the consequences. They established beyond question that a heavily armed bomb squad had been in downtown Oklahoma near the Murrah Building that morning before the bombs exploded. Many people saw them, including Oklahoma lawyer Daniel J. Adomitis, who was heading for a charity board meeting at 7.30am, an hour and a half before the explosion:

"There was this fairly large truck with a trailer behind it. It had a shield on the side of the door that said 'bomb disposal' or 'bomb squad' below it. And I really found that interesting. You know, I'd never seen anything like that in person." [18]

Some parents saw these people in their bomb squad uniforms as they dropped their children off at the day care centre at the Murrah Building, children they would never see alive again. Eventually, after months of denial by the FBI and other government agencies, the Sheriff's Department had to admit that the bomb squad had been there. The Wilburns were bitterly attacked by other bereaved families as they challenged the government story and they were denounced as "conspiracy theorists". But in the end other families also became convinced that the authorities had prior knowledge of the bombing – just as they had about 9/11. The Wilburns and many other families filed legal claims against the US government alleging they had "detailed prior knowledge of the planned bombing of the Murrah Building yet failed to prevent the bombing from taking place" and claimed that ATF agents were "alerted not to go to work on April 19th 1995".[19]

A few more little gems about the Oklahoma bombing. In early April, shortly before the attack, a Ryder truck was photographed from the air within the concrete walls of a military compound near Camp Gruber-Braggs, Oklahoma, and you can see these pictures on the Internet.[20] Danny Colson, the FBI's director of the terrorist task force, told *Time* magazine in 1999 that when he heard of the blast he had driven to Oklahoma from his home in Dallas at speeds of 100 miles an hour to support the rescue operation and the "investigation". Oops, Danny boy, caught by the round ones there darlin'. Colson checked into the Embassy Suites Hotel in Oklahoma at 12.20am on April 19th ... just 9 hours before the bomb went off.[21] Why? The FBI said it found McVeigh's truck rental agency from a vehicle identification number (VIN) on the Ryder truck's rear axle. This axle was somehow found both in the bomb crater (Mayor of Oklahoma press statement) and three blocks away (FBI). Must be one hell of an axle. Wherever it was found, the FBI story is another provable lie. Rear axles of vehicles manufactured in America were not imprinted with a VIN and the Ryder rental company did not add them to the axles either. The FBI also says that McVeigh rented the truck with both his real ID and a false ID. This same FBI had to admit shortly before McVeigh's first scheduled execution that they had withheld 4,304 documents from his defence team and he was given a month-long stay of execution because of this. The FBI's "star witness" against McVeigh was Michael Fortier, who admits doing a deal to testify for the prosecution in return for lighter sentences for gun offences. He told the court that he and McVeigh had made themselves familiar with the Murrah Building weeks before the bombing to establish the location of the ATF offices. Well in that case why did McVeigh stop at a gas station in the Ryder truck that morning and ask the way to the building? Why would he do that anyway when he knew he would be recognised and reported after the bombing? In that one moment he connected himself to the Ryder truck and the Murrah Building. Why? If he had spent so much time locating the ATF offices, why did he park the truck on the side of the Murrah Building furthest away from the

ATF section when he could have left it directly underneath? We are also asked to believe – and depressingly many do – that having connected himself with the Ryder truck and the Murrah Building before the bombing by stopping at the gas station, he then proceeded to "get away" undetected in a highly visible yellow car travelling at nearly 100 miles an hour with expired licence plates, and that when he was stopped by the police for a traffic violation a man who had just murdered 168 people and maimed hundreds made no attempt to avoid arrest even though he was armed and a highly trained soldier. It's nonsense, of course it is, but these are the people telling us what happened on September 11th, who did it and who we should bomb in retaliation.

McVeigh was arrested so conveniently for a traffic offence immediately after the bombing for the same reason that Lee Harvey Oswald was arrested in a cinema immediately after the Kennedy assassination and Osama bin Laden was named as the culprit after 9/11. They are the patsies required by problem-reaction-solution to hide the real orchestrators. Just as 9/11 was a massive version of what happened in Oklahoma, so Oklahoma was a repeat of the Kennedy assassination. Lee Harvey Oswald was a US agent who was placed in the right place at the right time without being told exactly why he was there. He realised this after Kennedy was shot and ran. When he was arrested he said he was a patsy, a stooge, and would have said so in court. That's why he was paraded in public to allow another government agent, Jack Ruby, to shoot him and kill the evidence (see *And The Truth Shall Set You Free*). In the same way, very possibly, McVeigh was a government stooge who parked the Ryder truck without knowing the full story. This would explain why he saw no problem in stopping at the gas station to ask the way to the Murrah building and why he made such a "getaway" and offered no resistance to the police officer. McVeigh apparently said that he was not told what the project was really all about and had been trapped, "framed", and made a patsy to cover up high-level US government complicity.[22]

Father Bush and the Iraqi connection

I almost completed a section without mentioning the Bush family, but naturally that couldn't last. It will stagger Americans to learn that at the end of the Gulf War in 1991 President Father George Bush arranged for around 4,000 officers from the military and intelligence agencies of Iraq, mostly from the Republican Guard, to relocate in the United States; 2,000 of these officers became resident in … Oklahoma. Another 500 went to Lincoln, Nebraska. Father Bush arranged for their funding, housing and employment, and this has been continued by Bill Clinton and Baby Bush. Jayna Davis, a former reporter with NBC affiliate KFOR-TV in Oklahoma, has worked tirelessly since the bombing to uncover the true story. In 1996 the *New York Times* Company bought her television station and stopped her reports, but she has continued to uncover devastating information. She has established that more than 70 witnesses saw McVeigh with other men and that more than 20 of these sightings involved men with Middle Eastern features. A sketch of a man with "olive skin" seen with McVeigh was released by the FBI immediately after the bombing and he became known as "John Doe 2". But the FBI has withheld at least 12 surveillance camera videos showing what happened and who was there that morning, and 1,034 fingerprints taken by the FBI have never been checked.[23] Jayna Davis' lawyer is David Schippers, who led the impeachment proceedings against Bill Clinton and represents FBI agents who had their investigations into terrorist suspects blocked by their superiors before 9/11. Schippers said of the FBI's manipulation of witness evidence relating to Oklahoma:

> "Some of these people who gave affidavits were interviewed by the FBI during the course of the investigation. They were interviewed about the second person they saw and the agents tried to make them say that the second person was Nichols. Every single one of these people said absolutely not, it was a Middle Eastern type individual. Now, listen to this, none of those 302s, none of those investigative reports, have ever surfaced." [24]

Jayna Davis has produced a detailed dossier and interviewed witnesses who have said they will testify that they saw McVeigh with a former Iraqi soldier who lived in Oklahoma City at the time of the bombing. This man surrendered during the Gulf War and was resettled in the United States from a detention camp in Saudi Arabia.[25] Immediately after the blast, the FBI put out an All-Points Bulletin for Middle Eastern-looking suspects seen fleeing the scene in a brown Chevrolet pickup with tinted windows and a bug shield.[26] As James Patterson, an editorial writer on the *Indianapolis Star*, remarked: "Something here doesn't pass the smell test." [27] The FBI has refused to release the videotapes collected from surveillance cameras around the Murrah Building because they are "part of the investigation" (the traditional excuse), but TV reporter Brad Edwards located a source who had seen parts of them. Edwards presented a reconstruction for viewers on News Channel 4 of what his source claimed to have seen:

> "The source said that the tapes show two men inside [the Ryder truck]. One strongly resembling Timothy McVeigh gets out of the driver's side, steps down, he then appears to have dropped something on the step up into the truck. He bends down and appears to pick something up off the step. Then he turns and walks directly across this street towards the General Electric building. All this time John Doe number two is still inside the Ryder truck's cab sitting on the passenger side. Time passes. The surveillance tape is time-lapse photography. Without knowing exactly the time interval between shots our source can't be sure how long John Doe number two sat in that cab. What was he doing all that time? Then the tape shows John Doe number two getting out of the passenger side of the Ryder truck. Again the tape shows that a bombing witness accurately described what happened next to News Channel 4 … the tape shows John Doe two getting out, shutting the passenger side door. He steps towards the front of the truck and is momentarily out of the frame of the surveillance camera. But shortly he appears back in frame walking towards the rear of the truck, still on the sidewalk in the front of the Murrah Building." [28]

The source said that "John Doe" wore a baseball cap, was taller than the man resembling McVeigh, and had an olive complexion. This was supported by many witnesses, including a man interviewed with a blacked-out face and featured in the report by Brad Edwards:

"I was standing in the building and I looked out the window and I seen the Ryder truck and I seen a man get out of the Ryder truck. He was olive complexion and he was ... he had black curly hair. He was wearing a baseball cap but his curls were sticking out of his hat. It was very short in the back but you could still see the curls in his hair. He was not American, he was foreign, you could tell by his skin, his face, and the way his face was ..."

Senator Charles Key, who helped to produce a report on Oklahoma, said his understanding was that there is a video showing McVeigh and John Doe 2 getting out of the Ryder Truck and into another pick up. "Where is that video ... are we going to get to see it?" he asks. Er, you must be joking, the FBI replies. Incidentally I was on a radio show in America in May 2002 talking about the way the FBI had refused to release these surveillance camera tapes. A former FBI agent came on the line saying loudly and vehemently that he worked on the case and there were no surveillance tapes. It took a member of the public to come on tell him that not only did the tapes exist, the FBI had admitted this on the national news! In 2001 the FBI said it was not going to release the tapes at all because of "national security" (the security of the official lie). When McVeigh went on trial the FBI did not use the tapes in prosecution because they would have destroyed its story. If only McVeigh and no one else had been on the tapes, the world would have seen them within hours of the blast. Rule number one of cover stories: if letting the public see something would support your cover story you let them see it. If the public seeing something would destroy your cover story you don't let them see it. Surveillance cameras are part of the Illuminati system of control, but they are also a problem for them when they carry out their public operations. Therefore we have a clear red flag test on these occasions – are we allowed to see the surveillance camera tapes of the scene in question? There are 17 surveillance cameras working 24 hours a day along the route of the last journey taken by Princess Diana between the Ritz Hotel and the Pont de L'Alma tunnel in Paris. But at that time, of all times, every single one of the 17 cameras was "not working" – or so we are told. James Patterson of the *Indianapolis Star* wrote that critical evidence that several Middle Eastern men may have been connected to the Oklahoma bombing appeared to have been kept from the public by the FBI. He added:

"Officially, the FBI has dismissed the possibility of a John Doe No. 2, an olive-skinned man whose sketch they released immediately after the bombing, or other suspects. But current and former FBI agents in Oklahoma City say they received documents pointing to another person or even a cell of Middle Eastern operatives. At a minimum, Congress should question one former FBI agent who says he obtained 22 affidavits and more than 30 witness statements describing sightings of Middle Easterners with McVeigh." [29]

Hoppy Heidelberg, a prominent Oklahoma horse breeder, was dismissed from the grand jury "investigating" the case when he went public with his complaints that the "investigation" was a sham. He said he was not allowed to ask for witnesses, even though it was his lawful right, and one of the areas he wanted to explore was the reports of the "John Doe 2". He said he was visited by FBI agents brandishing guns who said that if he knew what was good for him he would shut up. Apparently state, local and federal police detained dozens of Middle Eastern men after the bombing as they tried to leave the United States, and these included "former" members of the Iraqi Republican Guard. It has been reported that in their possession were bomb-making materials, but President Clinton insisted they were released. David Schippers, the Chief Investigative Counsel for the House Judiciary Committee Impeachment Hearing of Bill Clinton, said that the same team that carried out the Oklahoma bombing also carried out the September 11th attacks. He said that he understood a former Iraqi Republican Guard officer called Al-Hussaini Hussain, who had been mentioned by reporter Jayna Davis as a possible John Doe 2 in her investigations into Oklahoma, later worked at Boston Logan Airport where two of the 9/11 flights took off.[30] Larry Johnson, a former Deputy Director of the State Department's Office on Counterterrorism, told *Fox News* the same. He said he believed that Al-Hussaini Hussain was John Doe 2 in Oklahoma and he added: "The thing that really concerns me relative to 9/11 [is that] when he left Oklahoma around 1996 and 1997, he went to work at Logan Airport in Boston. We don't know where he is now."[31] Jayna Davis has testified under oath before a grand jury, and in 1997 she attempted to hand over a large part of her evidence to the FBI, but those in control were not interested.[32] They have shown a similar lack of interest when offered information about Osama bin Laden, which would have dismantled the official story. Former FBI agent Dan Vogel offered to testify at a hearing of Terry Nichols, the man convicted with McVeigh, that he had received from Jayna Davis 22 affidavits from witnesses who had seen McVeigh with Middle Eastern men in the months, weeks and days before the attack and on the morning it happened. He wanted to testify that he had sent the package to FBI agent Henry C. Gibbons, but the witness statements were not made public. However, Judge Linder ruled that Vogel could not make this devastating testimony because the [In]Justice Department did not want the evidence to be heard and would not authorise the testimony.[33]

Waco revisited

The FBI and the ATF were, with others, responsible for the mass murder of men, women and children at Waco, Texas, on April 19th 1993. If they had something on David Koresh, the leader of the Branch Davidians, they could have arrested him months earlier when he often left the compound. But these people are mentally disturbed and the plan was for a ritual murder by fire. Adolf Hitler and the Nazis, who were serious black occultists (see my previous books) chose the same day, April 19th, to burn the Jewish ghetto in Warsaw in 1943. The Nazis torched the ghetto block by block and then flooded and smoke-bombed the sewers when the

Jews tried to use them to escape. What the ATF and FBI did at Waco was virtually identical. According to the occult law followed so slavishly by the Illuminati and their agents, April 19th and 20th are dedicated to their god Baal and demand blood sacrifice. The Columbine High School shooting at Littleton, Colorado, was on April 20th 1999 and also involved the ATF and the FBI; so did Oklahoma – on April 19th. I cannot stress enough the obsession these people have with occult ritual and I explore this in detail in *The Biggest Secret*. Two brilliant documentaries, *Waco: The Rules of Engagement* (1997) and *Waco: A New Revelation* (1999) devastatingly expose the mass murder by the FBI and ATF, and the involvement at the highest levels of the US government.[34] The *Rules of Engagement* won an Emmy for best investigative journalism. The follow-up, *A New Revelation*, is actually narrated by former FBI Special Agent Dr Frederic Whitehurst. It was Dr Whitehurst who exposed the criminal manipulation of evidence and the stunning "incompetence" at the FBI crime laboratory. The documentaries reveal how the authorities used "flash-bang" devices to start the fire that engulfed the Mount Carmel compound at Waco after filling the compound with high explosives and poisonous gas. The devices were found at all locations where the fires started, but were claimed to have been silencers and gun parts. They also show how "shape" charges were placed by military operatives at the top of a concrete walk-in-cooler that became a "bunker" where the women and children sought to escape from the lethal concentrations of CS gas. The "shape" charges blew a hole in the concrete roof, killed everyone inside, and caused the partial disintegration and fusing together of some of the bodies of the women and children because of the pressure and heat from the blast. Military explosives expert General Benton Partin supports this version of events, and shape charges have also been identified by some researchers in relation to the Murrah Building in Oklahoma and the World Trade Center towers on September 11th. Gene Cullen, a CIA service officer, is among the sources that confirm how Delta Force, the elite (and brain dead) unit of the US military, was at the compound during the "siege". Delta Force fired on anyone who tried to flee the compound through the only escape route, and they either died this way or in the inferno. The FBI claims to have tapes of the Davidians planning to set the compound alight, but they have never produced them because they are lying. The FBI, the source of the official story of September 11th, has some very decent, dedicated people working at the foot soldier levels. But the FBI and related agencies are controlled higher up the pyramid by some of the most unbalanced and corrupt people currently resident on planet earth. What was the outcome for the FBI and ATF after Waco? Their funding was increased. After Oklahoma? Same. After September 11th? What do you think?

The FBI, like the ATF, is a deeply corrupt organisation – and the FBI is the source through which the official version of September 11th has been sold to the world. The Illuminati elements within the United States government and others, not least the British, have a long and horrendous history of terrorist activity. They often use foreign front men to carry out the attacks, but it is they who plan and orchestrate them. One example occurred on March 8th 1985 when Lebanese intelligence operatives trained by the Reagan-Bush CIA exploded a car bomb outside a mosque in Beirut to assassinate Sheikh Mohammed Hussein Fadlallah, the Shiite Muslim cleric who some believed to be the "spiritual" leader of the terrorist group Hezbollah. He survived, but more than 80 worshippers were killed. Robert "Iran-Contra" McFarlane, Reagan's National Security Adviser, said that the bombers "may have been trained by the US, but the individuals who carried it out were rogue operatives" and the CIA in no way sanctioned or supported the attack.[35] Sure they didn't and, by the way, spaghetti grows on trees.

Pearl Harbor

George W. Bush called the events of September 11th "Our Pearl Harbor" and for once he was right, although not in the way he wanted us to believe. Interestingly, months earlier a blockbuster movie had been released by Hollywood amid massive promotion about this very attack by the Japanese Air Force on Pearl Harbor, Hawaii, in 1941. It was the attack that took the United States into the Second World War. To this day popular accounts of history portray President Franklin Delano Roosevelt, a Bush family relative, as a man who "strove in vain to ward off war".[36] This is yet another gross misrepresentation. Both the Roosevelts and the Delanos are bloodline and I mentioned earlier that his grandfather, Warren Delano, was a major operator in the drug networks operated by the Russell family, the founders of the Skull and Bones Society. Delano also worked in the drugs network of the British government in Asia, China and the Far East in general. When Roosevelt was seeking re-election as president in 1940 he repeated the same mantra: "… while I am talking to you, mothers and fathers, I give you one more assurance. I have said this before but I shall say it again and again and again; your boys are not going to be sent into any foreign wars!"[37] He even had the nerve to add that: "You can therefore nail any talk about sending armies to Europe as deliberate untruth."[38] This is what people wanted to hear and he was re-elected. Roosevelt, however, an Illuminati stooge to his fingertips, knew that the sons and many daughters of America were going to war again very soon. What he needed was an event of such magnitude that America would go to war while, at the same time, Roosevelt would be cleared of any responsibility for going back on his clear and constantly repeated pledge of the election campaign. The Illuminati plan, long known by Roosevelt, was to engineer an attack on the United States that would so anger public opinion that people would agree to go to war against the aggressor and join the European conflict also. As a member of Woodrow Wilson's administration in the First World War, Roosevelt would have been well schooled in manipulating public opinion with engineered events. In 1939, Senator P. Nye of North Dakota said that he had seen a series of volumes called *The Next War*. These included one entitled *Propaganda in the Next War* and these were written before there was any talk of a Second World War. As Senator Nye revealed, the material included the plan for manipulating public opinion into accepting American involvement in another global conflict, which these documents revealed was coming. The propaganda document, which originated in Britain, said:

"To persuade her [the United States] to take our part will be much more difficult, so difficult as to be unlikely to succeed. It will need a definite threat to America, a threat moreover, which will have to be brought home to every citizen, before the Republic again take arms in an external quarrel …

"The position will naturally be considerably eased if *Japan were involved*, and this might and probably would bring America in without much further ado. [My emphasis.] At any rate, it would be a natural and obvious effect of our propagandists to achieve this, just as in the Great War, they succeeded in embroiling the United States with Germany …

"Fortunately with America, our propaganda is on firm ground. We can be entirely sincere, as our main plank will be the old democratic one. We must clearly enunciate our belief in the Democratic form of government, and our firm resolve to adhere to … the old Goddess of Democracy." [39]

Sound familiar in the months since September 11th? The Council on Foreign Relations (CFR) is an Illuminati front in the United States formed and dominated by the Rockefeller family. It is part of a web that includes the Bilderberg Group, Trilateral Commission, and the London-based Royal Institute of International Affairs. This network is described in detail in *And The Truth Shall Set You Free* and *The Biggest Secret*. It was the Council on Foreign Relations that devised the plan to antagonise Japan to such a degree that it would attack the United States. At the forefront of this was Roosevelt's Secretary of War, Henry Stimson, a founder of the CFR. In his diary he wrote, "We face the delicate question of diplomatic fencing to be done so as to be sure that Japan is put into the wrong and makes the first bad overt move." [40] The CFR's War and Peace Studies Project sent a memo to Roosevelt suggesting that aid be given to China during her conflict with Japan and that Japanese assets in the US be frozen, a trade embargo imposed and Japan refused access to the Panama Canal. I can recommend an excellent book called *Pearl Harbor, The Story of the Secret War*, by George Morgenstern, which sets out how the Japanese were goaded into the attack on Pearl Harbor on December 7th 1941. [41] Roosevelt, an Illuminati bloodline wholly owned by the Council on Foreign Relations, set about provoking Japan into an attack with a number of measures, including the targeting of Japanese oil supplies. For four years before the attack the Roosevelt administration had been intercepting and decoding secret Japanese messages. They knew that the Japanese intended to alert their diplomatic centres around the world of a decision to go to war through a false weather report during the daily Japanese-language short-wave news broadcast. The forecast of "east wind rain" indicated war with the United States; "west wind clear" would mean a decision to go to war with Britain, and British and Dutch colonies in the east; "north wind cloudy" meant war with Russia.

As a Congressional investigation heard in 1945, the messages indicating a decision to go to war with the United States and Britain, though not with Russia, were intercepted and decoded on December 3rd 1941 – four days before Pearl Harbor. [42] These messages subsequently went "missing" from Navy files. Other decoded messages gave Roosevelt prior warning of the attack, but the public were not told and nor were the sitting targets in Hawaii. On January 27th 1941, Joseph Grew, the US Ambassador to Tokyo, had written to Roosevelt to say that in the event of war, Pearl Harbor would be the first target.[43] In all, Roosevelt had information from eight different sources indicating a probable attack.[44] The historian Robert Stinnett revealed the results of 17 years of research into the Pearl Harbor conspiracy in his book, *Day of Deceit: The Truth About FDR and Pearl Harbor* [45] His research included more than a million documents obtained under the Freedom of Information Act, which show that knowledge of the Japanese plans was kept from commanders in Hawaii – the very same men who were later made scapegoats for what happened. Stinnett uncovered a memo written on October 7th 1940 by Lt Commander Arthur McCollum, who headed the Far East section of US Naval Intelligence. McCollum confirms the policy of systematically provoking the Japanese to attack the United States in order to provide the political and public motivation for the declaration of war. The attack was purely to manipulate American public opinion into agreeing to take part in another Illuminati war that had long been planned, and no one was more duped than the Japanese. They had been tricked into attacking the US both by the Americans and the Germans. The German Foreign Minister, Joachim von Ribbentrop, had been pressing the Japanese to attack the United States. On December 6th 1941 Hitler had added to the Japanese resolve by indicating that German forces were about to enter Moscow. On December 8th, the day after Pearl Harbor, the Germans were found to be in retreat from the Russian front. More than 3,000 people were killed at Pearl Harbor, about the same as the official death toll on September 11th, and they were yet more victims of the Illuminati agenda. The day after Pearl Harbor, Allen Dulles, an Illuminati agent, Hitler supporter and cousin to the Rockefellers, was appointed to the staff of the Office of the Coordinator of Information. This later became the Office of Strategic Services (OSS) and then the CIA. It was he who was sacked by John F. Kennedy as head of the CIA and then served on the Warren Commission to "investigate" the JFK assassination. The Pearl Harbor plan worked brilliantly as public opinion reacted exactly as required to the attack on American soil. The United States was involved in another war in Europe and "our boys" who, according to Roosevelt, were not going to be sent into another European conflict, were now on their way, many of them to die. Winston Churchill, the Illuminati bloodline Prime Minister in Britain and a relative of Roosevelt and the Bushes, said of the news: "That is what I have dreamed of, aimed at, and worked for, and now it has come to pass".[46] He might have added: "and I always knew it was going to". The influence on Roosevelt of the Council on Foreign Relations, with its membership throughout the government, banking, commerce, media and military, cannot be overestimated. Roosevelt's son-in-law, Curtis Dall, said:

"For a long time I felt that [Roosevelt] … had developed many thoughts and ideas that were his own to benefit this country, the USA. But he didn't. Most of his thoughts, his political 'ammunition', as it were, were carefully manufactured for him in advance by the Council on Foreign Relations – One World Money Group. Brilliantly, with great gusto, like a fine piece of artillery, he exploded that 'ammunition' in the middle of on unsuspecting target, the American people – and thus paid off and retained his internationalist support." [47]

The Roosevelt mansion on East 65th Street in New York was actually next door to the Council on Foreign Relations and it was a committee known as the Informal Agenda Group, packed with members of the CFR, which wrote the proposal for the United Nations and handed it to Roosevelt who made it public on June 16th 1944 as if he was the architect.[48] Henry Louis Mencken writes in *The American Language*[49] that the term "United Nations" was first mentioned by Roosevelt in a meeting with Churchill at the White House in December 1941 – the month of Pearl Harbor.[50] Some 74 members of the Council on Foreign Relations were in the US delegation at the founding meeting of the United Nations, which was created from the start as a vehicle for eventual world government. The Rockefellers donated the land on which the UN building in Manhattan is built, as they did the site of the headquarters of the earlier League of Nations in Switzerland. This was their first attempt to create a stalking horse for the global centralisation of political power. The Rockefellers were also responsible for the building of two other famous buildings in Manhattan … the twin towers of the World Trade Center. The Council on Foreign Relations, founded in 1921, has its members in key positions throughout the US government, military, and media today, and many of the people telling us what happened on September 11th and who was responsible are from the ranks of the CFR – just as they were with Pearl Harbor, the Oklahoma bombing and so many other problem-reaction-solutions of the last 80 years.

Operation Northwoods

In April 2001, just four months before September 11th, a book was published by James Bamford, who was formerly the Washington Investigative Producer for *World News Tonight* with Peter Jennings on ABC Television. It was called *Body of Secrets*[51] and revealed a plan hatched 40 years ago by America's top military leaders, the Joints Chiefs of Staff at the Pentagon, to commit acts of terrorism in US cities, kill civilians and blame it on the Cuban president Fidel Castro. The plan was called Operation Northwoods, and was designed to win public and international support for an invasion of Cuba that would remove Castro. Bamford quotes military leaders as writing: "We could blow up a US ship in Guantanamo Bay and blame Cuba", and "casualty lists in US newspapers would cause a helpful wave of national indignation". The Joint Chiefs of Staff also proposed to kill the astronaut John Glenn during the first attempt to put an American into orbit and blame that on Cuba, the documents reveal. If Glenn's rocket exploded, "the objective is to provide irrevocable proof … that the fault lies with the Communists et all Cuba [sic]," say the Northwood documents. Bamford writes:

> " … the plan, which had the written approval of the Chairman and every member of the Joint Chiefs of Staff, called for innocent people to be shot on American streets; for boats carrying refugees fleeing Cuba to be sunk on the high seas; for a wave of violent

terrorism to be launched in Washington DC, Miami, and elsewhere. People would be framed for bombings they did not commit; planes would be hijacked. Using phoney evidence, all of it would be blamed on Castro, thus giving Lemnitzer [the Chairman of the Joint Chiefs of Staff] and his cabal the excuse, as well as the public and international backing, they needed to launch their war." [52]

The plan was to stir up so much hatred for Cuba in the United States that the people would support an invasion and even demand that this was done. They intended to explode plastic bombs, arrest Cuban agents and release previously prepared documents falsely substantiating Cuban involvement. The plan included attacks on the now infamous US base at Guantanamo Bay on Cuba where, since the invasion of Afghanistan, the "Land of Freedom" has kept untried and uncharged "terrorists" in disgraceful, inhuman, conditions. These attacks on the base would be blamed on Castro. The documents speak of "a series of well co-ordinated incidents … in and around Guantanamo to give genuine appearance of being done by hostile Cuban forces".[53] A Memorandum of July 27th 1962 says that the operation would mean an enormous increase in Cuban and American casualties.[54] The techniques to be used included: starting rumours; using clandestine radio; landing friendly Cubans in uniform "over the fence" to stage "attacks" on the base; capturing (friendly) Cuban saboteurs inside the base; starting riots near the base main gate using friendly Cubans; blowing up ammunition inside the base and starting fires; burning aircraft on the base and blaming Cuba; throwing mortar shells into the base; capturing assault teams approaching from the sea or Guantanamo City; capturing a militia group which storms the base to sabotage a ship in harbour; sinking a ship near the harbour entrance; blowing up an unmanned vessel in Cuban water and blaming it on Cuban aircraft that would naturally come and investigate what had happened; issue false casualty lists to the US media to whip up public opinion against Cuba; and, look at this … "conduct funerals for mock victims." [55]

The Northwoods documents also call for the use of Soviet Union MIG-type lookalike aircraft flown by US pilots to harass civil aircraft, attack surface shipping and destroy US military "drone" (remotely controlled) aircraft to give the impression it was all done by Communists. "An F-86 properly painted would convince air passengers that they saw a Cuban MIG …" one document says.[56] It was further planned to stage the mock shooting-down of a US Air Force plane in international waters by simply getting the pilot, using a made-up name, to report that he was under attack and then stop transmitting. He would then fly back to his base where the plane would be repainted with a new tail number and the pilot would resume his real name. A US submarine would send aircraft to search for wreckage in the sea and this would be found to confirm the attack and blame it on Cuba. James Bamford's book is a history of the biggest intelligence operation in America, the National Security Agency (NSA), which makes the CIA look like a whimpering poodle. Bamford says the NSA was not involved in Operation Northwoods, but I don't agree. I don't buy the "it was just the Pentagon" line at all. Of course the NSA would be involved in such an operation, as it would have been in 9/11. Bamford says the plans for these terrorist acts against American targets had the written approval of all the Joint Chiefs of Staff, headed by Eisenhower's appointee, Army General Lyman L. Lemnitzer, and were presented by Robert McNamara, the [Illuminati] Defense Secretary, to President Kennedy in March 1962. Eventually the "civilian leadership" rejected them and three days later President Kennedy told Lemnitzer there was virtually no chance of ever using overt force to take Cuba. Operation Northwoods remained secret for 40 years until these documents came to light. Bamford told his former employers at *ABC News*:

> "These were Joint Chiefs of Staff documents. The reason these were held secret for so long is the Joint Chiefs never wanted to give these up because they were so embarrassing. The whole point of a democracy is to have leaders responding to the public will, and here this is the complete reverse, the military trying to trick the American people into a war that they want but that nobody else wants." [57]

Why, one is right to wonder, do they allow the public to hear of this these only months before a very similar plan unfolded on September 11th 2001? Bamford writes that even after the original plans were rejected, others continued to be developed, such as creating a war between Cuba and another Latin American country that would allow the US to intervene. It is no good people claiming their leaders could not have been behind the horrors of 9/11 when the documents exist to show that the Pentagon had planned in detail something very similar 40 years ago. And wait for this … Operation Northwoods also planned the hijacking of civil aircraft. The documents say it was possible to create an incident that would convince the people that the Cuban aircraft had shot down a chartered civil airliner on a flight from the United States to Jamaica, Guatemala, Venezuela or Panama. The destination would be chosen so the route would cross Cuba and the plan was to replace the civil airliner with an identical one remotely controlled from the ground and painted in the same colours. The real plane would be landed at an Air Force base and the passengers, boarded under aliases, would be taken off. The remotely controlled replacement would then be flown over Cuba, send a distress signal and be destroyed by radio signal. And all this was planned 40 years ago. Imagine what the technology is like today by comparison? James Bamford writes in *Body of Secrets*:

> "An aircraft at Elgin AFB would be painted and numbered as an exact duplicate for a civil registered aircraft belonging to a CIA proprietary organization in the Miami area. At a designated time the duplicate would be substituted for the actual civil aircraft and would be loaded with the selected passengers, all boarded under carefully prepared aliases. The actual registered aircraft would be converted into a drone [a remotely controlled unmanned aircraft]. Take off times of the drone aircraft and the actual aircraft will be scheduled to allow a rendezvous south of Florida.

> "From the rendezvous point the passenger-carrying aircraft will descend to minimum altitude and go directly into an auxiliary field at Elgin AFB where arrangements will have

been made to evacuate the passengers and return the aircraft to its original status. The drone aircraft meanwhile will continue to fly the filed flight plan. When over Cuba the drone will be transmitting on the international distress frequency a "May Day" message stating he is under attack by Cuban MiG aircraft. The transmission will be interrupted by destruction of the aircraft, which will be triggered by radio signal. This will allow ICAO [International Civil Aviation Organisation] radio stations in the Western Hemisphere to tell the US what has happened to the aircraft instead of the US trying to 'sell' the incident."

Forty years later, in New York and Washington, something remarkably similar happened on 9/11 and, for Fidel Castro, read Osama bin Laden. Also it was clearly possible 40 years ago for transmissions to be made from an aircraft in which there were no pilots or passengers on board. You can see from these examples, and I could quote so many more, that the problem-reaction-solution techniques that were employed on September 11th are nothing new. Like I say, if it keeps working, why change it?

SOURCES

1   H.R. 2580

2   **http://www.rense.com/general17/fly.htm**

3   MSNBC, video streaming, June 11th 2001; see also
    http://www.skolnicksreport.com/claffair2.html

4   Oklahoma City Bombing, Expert Analysis: **http://www.cowan70.freeserve.co.uk/
    miscellaneous/oklahoma_bombing_expert_analysis.html**

5   **http://www.brasscheck.com/OKBOMB**

6   Oklahoma City Bombing, Expert Analysis: **http://www.cowan70.freeserve.co.uk/
    miscellaneous/oklahoma_bombing_expert_analysis.html**

7   Case Study Relating Blast Effects to the Events of April 19, 1995. Alfred P. Murrah, Federal
    Building, Oklahoma City, Oklahoma. For the detailed background to this report see
    http://thenewamerican.com/tna/1997/vo13no07/vo13no07_blasts.htm

8   See J. Orlin Grabbe's report at **http://www.aci.net/kalliste/okcbomb.htm**

9   *WorldNetDaily.com,* **http://www.wnd.com/news/article.asp?ARTICLE_ID=22874**

10 **http://www.thenewamerican.com/tna/1995/vo11no12/vo11no12_bombs.htm**

11 **http://serendipity.magnet.ch/wot/psyopnews2.htm#seven_wtc**

12 **http://www.cowan70.freeserve.co.uk/miscellaneous/oklahoma_bombing_
    expert_analysis.html**

13 **http://www.controlled-demolition.com/controlled.html**

14 Ibid

15 Thirty Oklahoma City Bombing Questions that Demand an Answer NOW! **http://www.parascope.com/articles/0697/30quest.htm**

16 Ibid

17 *Oregonian*, April 20th 1995

18 Daniel Adomitis is quoted by many different sources and this is one of them: **http://home.kscable.com/mholter/tim04.htm**

19 Bomb Squad Seen Before Blast; Ambrose Evans-Pritchard: Federal Judge Said Many Were Warned of Danger, *WorldNetDaily* **http://wnd.com/news/article.asp?ARTICLE_ID=23016**

20 **http://members.aol.com/bardsquill/truck.htm** and **http://www.whatreallyhappened.com/RANCHO/POLITICS/OK/TRUCK/truck.html**

21 *9/11 – The Road To Tyranny*

22 You can find this report in many places on the Internet. This is one of them: **http://www.darkconspiracy.com/conspiracies/bomb/okla/usgov.txt**

23 There is a very good summary of the evidence compiled by Jayna Davis at **http://c1.zedo.com/ads2/i/3853/172/152009261/0/i.html?e=i;s=141;b=%23ffffff; d=1;z=0.7631069367268365**

24 *9/11 – The Road To Tyranny*

25 *Indianapolis Star*, April 6th 2002 **http://www.starnews.com/article.php?ecolpatterson06.html,opinion**

26 Ibid

27 Ibid

28 You can see this presentation on the video *9/11 – The Road To Tyranny*

29 Missing Evidence From Oklahoma City, *Indianapolis Star*, November 17th 2001

30 *9/11 – The Road To Tyranny*

31 Anti-terror Prober: OKC Bombing Suspect Worked at 9/11 Airport, **NewsMax.com**, May 7th 2002, **http://www.newsmax.com/showinsidecover.shtml?a=2002/5/7/215007**

32 **http://www.financialsense.com/stormwatch/geo/pastanalysis/2001/110501.htm**

33 **http://www.newsmakingnews.com/archives/archive8,19,01.htm**

34 You can get these documentaries from MGA films at 1-877-GET-WACO or at **www.waco-anewrevelation.comwww.waco-anewrevelation.com**

35 **http://www.pbs.org/wgbh/pages/frontline/shows/target/etc/cron.html**

36 *Pears Cyclopaedia*, 85th edition, p 852

37 Boston, October 30th 1940, Public Papers and Addresses of Franklin D. Roosevelt

38 Ibid, December 29th 1940

39 Congressional Record, 76th Congress, Vol. 84, No. 82, P:6597-6604

40 Jim Keith, *Casebook On Alternative 3* (IllumiNet Press USA, 1994), p 25

41 George Morgenstern, *Pearl Harbor, The Story of the Secret War* (Costa Mesa, USA, 1991 edition). First published in 1947

42   Joint Congressional Committee of the investigation of the Pearl Harbor attack – largely a cover-up

43   Jan van Helsing, *Secret Societies And Their Power in the 20th Century* (Ewertverlag, Gran Canana, Spain, 1995), p 210

44   *Casebook On Alternative 3*, p 26

45   Robert Stinnett, *Day of Deceit: The Truth About FDR and Pearl Harbor* (Simon & Schuster), May 2001

46   February 15th, 1942. Radio Address Reported in the *New York Times* of February 16th

47   *Casebook On Alternative 3*, p 25

48   James Perloff, *The Shadows of Power: The Council On Foreign Relations and the American Decline*, p 71

49   Henry Louis Mencken, *The American Language* (New York, 1919)

50   Eustace Mullins, *The World Order, Our Secret Rulers* (self-published, USA, Second Edition, 1992), p 2

51   James Bamford, *Body Of Secrets* (Doubleday, April 2001)

52   Ibid, p 82

53   **nara.gov** Document 138, March 9th 1962

54   **nara.gov** Document 63

55   Documents 138–142, September 4th 1962

56   **nara.gov** Document 141

57   **http://more.abcnews.go.com/sections/us/dailynews/jointchiefs_010501.html**

chapter 7

Problem-Reaction-Solution

"If the freedom of speech is taken away, then dumb and silent we may be led, like sheep to the slaughter."

George Washington

The attacks of September 11th and their consequences for freedom are a textbook example of the problem-reaction-solution technique. This becomes obvious when you observe both the attacks and their aftermath. In this chapter I will outline the official story of what happened and the response that followed. I should stress that many of the "facts" in this official version depend on which spokesman or agency you speak to because they often contradict each other.

The US government and its "security" agencies like the CIA and FBI say they had no idea that a terrorist attack was planned on that beautiful east coast morning as tens of thousands of people began their working day in the office complexes of Manhattan and at the headquarters of the American military at the Pentagon in Washington DC. These "security" agencies employ together perhaps 100,000 people in the United States and worldwide, and devour some $35 billion from US taxpayers every year (and that's only the official funds). Yet they claim not to have uncovered one single piece of information to suggest that some "19 Arab terrorists" (part of a network of perhaps 50, it is suggested) were planning to simultaneously hijack four US commercial aircraft in American airspace and crash them into the very symbols of US military and financial power. The first they knew, so the story goes, was when it was far too late to respond. That is an outrageous lie to be filed with all the rest and has been revealed as such.

The Problem

At 7.59am that Tuesday morning, American Airlines Flight 11, a Boeing 767, took off from Logan International Airport in Boston heading for Los Angeles. On board were 81 passengers, two pilots and nine flight attendants. Following along the runway soon afterwards was United Airlines Flight 175, another Boeing 767, which departed at 8.14am, also for LA. It was carrying 56 passengers, two pilots and seven flight attendants. At 8.01am, and 150 miles to the south, United Airlines Flight 93 pulled back from the gate at Newark, New Jersey, and the Boeing 757 began its routine journey across America to San Francisco with 38 passengers, two pilots and five attendants. But for some reason, which United Airlines could not explain when I asked them, the take-off was delayed and it did not leave the ground until 8.42. Meanwhile, at 8.10, American Airlines Flight 77 left Washington's Dulles International Airport for Los Angeles with 58 passengers, two pilots and four attendants aboard a Boeing 757.

American Airlines flight 11

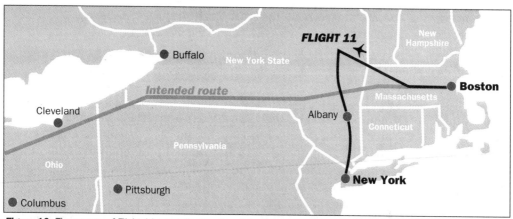

Figure 10: *The course of Flight 11 according to aircraft tracking company Flight Explorer*

The official story claims that shortly after American Airlines Flight 11 took off from Boston at 7.59 bound for Los Angeles, Arab terrorists hijacked the plane using small knives and box cutters. The pilot and co-pilot of Flight 11 were John Ogonowski and Tom McGuinness, a former F-14 Navy Tomcat pilot described as "big and burly". Around 14 minutes into the flight they were instructed by air traffic control to make a 20-degree turn to the right, according to a "federal official familiar with transcripts of the air-traffic-control conversations of all four flights".[1] The pilot replied in the normal way of ground to air communications by repeating the instruction and giving the flight code: "20 right, AAL11". Very soon after this, the pilot was asked to climb to 35,000 feet, but there was no response. The following is claimed to be a transcript of the exchange that took place at about 8.13am, 14 minutes into the flight:

> *Boston Control Center:* "AAL11 turn 20 degrees right."
> *AAL11:* "20 right AAL11."
> *Controller A:* "AAL11 now climb maintain FL350 [35,000 feet]."
> *Controller A:* "AAL11 climb maintain FL350."
> *Controller A:* "AAL11 Boston."
> *Controller A:* "AAL11, ah, the American on the frequency how do you hear me?"
> *Controller B breaks in:* "This is Athens."

Controller A: "This is Boston. I turned American 20 left and I was going to climb him; he will not respond to me now at all."
Controller B: "Looks like he's turning right."
Controller A: "Yeah, I turned him right."
Controller B: "Oh, O.K."
Controller A: "And he's only going to, um, I think 29."
Controller B: "Sure that's fine."
Controller A: "Eh, but I'm not talking to him."
Controller B: "He won't answer you. He's nordo [no radar] roger. Thanks." [2]

So the first sign of a problem that morning was shortly after 8.13am and it is claimed that only at 8.40 – 27 minutes later – did the Federal Aviation Administration (FAA) inform NORAD, which guards North American airspace, that Flight 11 had been hijacked. Why? We shall see that this is against all procedures detailed in the Federal Aviation Administration and Pentagon instruction manuals. The FAA is the civilian government operation that runs the air traffic system in the United States while NORAD, the North American Aerospace Defense Command, is an American and Canadian military organisation that is supposed to protect North America against attacks by "aircraft, missiles, or space vehicles … ensuring air sovereignty and air defense of the airspace of Canada and the United States".[3] I will have a great deal more to say about these organisations in due course. It is claimed that after contact was lost with Flight 11, a controller heard a voice from the cockpit at 8.24am that said: "We have some planes. Just stay quiet and you will be OK. We are returning to the airport. Nobody move." The controller is said to have replied: "Who's trying to call me?" But there was no response. Another "radio transmission" said to have been heard by controllers at 8.33am was: "Nobody move please. We are going back to the airport. Don't try to make any stupid moves." Two minutes later another instruction is said to have been: "Everything will be OK. If you try to make any moves, you'll endanger yourself and the airplane. Just stay quiet." If that's true, the pilots had time to switch on the microphone in the cockpit, which, the official version says, allowed air traffic controllers to hear the hijackers. Either that or the hijackers were confusing the aircraft radio with the intercom. Strangely, the secret four-digit alert code that warns the ground that a plane has been hijacked was never sent and that's the first thing a pilot is supposed to do in such circumstances. It was the same story with all four aircraft. There was only one other contact between Flight 11 and air traffic control, the official story goes. That was when controllers were asked for a route, or air corridor, to JFK Airport in New York, although by whom is not stated by officials. I asked the media office of the Federal Aviation Administration who in the cockpit made this request and they said they did not have that information. Why? The transponder, or IFF beacon, which allows an aircraft to be more easily tracked on radar and supplies other information, was switched off at 8.20 over the Hudson River and the plane turned sharply and headed for New York. Losing the transponder would have made it harder to track the plane, but, I emphasise, it was still very much trackable by conventional radar.

"Attendants call from plane"

We are told that flight attendant Madeline Amy Sweeney, a 35-year-old mother of two, made a call from the plane to American Airlines Flight Services Manager Michael Woodward at Boston Logan Airport and said there were four hijackers on board (the FBI claims there were five). She said they had stabbed two flight attendants, we are told. She is claimed to have said: "A hijacker cut the throat of a business class passenger and he appears to be dead." The terrorists, Sweeney said, "had just gained access to the cockpit." [4] This begs the question of why the pilots had not sent the hijack code if things were happening on the plane before the hijackers gained access to the cockpit. The FBI report to the media on this alleged conversation says that even as Sweeney was relating details about the hijackers to Woodward, the men were storming the front of the plane. I ask again: if all hell was breaking lose in the plane and passengers were being attacked why no hijack code from the cockpit and why wasn't the cockpit door immediately secured from the inside? According to Woodward, when the plane changed direction and began to descend Sweeney called the cockpit, but there was no reply. Sweeney is said to have told Woodward the seat numbers of the hijackers and that the plane was going down. Her final words were given as: "I see water and buildings. Oh my God. Oh my God." American Airlines later released an account of a conversation it says took place during the flight between attendant Betty Ong and airline officials. They say that Ong pressed number 8 on a seatback GTE Airfone and got through to an American Airlines reservations agent who called the system operations control centre in Fort Worth, Texas. The time was 8.27am, around 12 minutes after the cockpit first failed to respond to air traffic instructions. Craig Marquis, the manager on duty, said that Betty Ong told him that two flight attendants had been stabbed and one was being given oxygen. A passenger had been slashed in the throat and looked dead and the hijackers were in the cockpit. She said that the passengers had been sprayed with something that made her eyes burn and she was having difficulty breathing. She said there were four hijackers (again not the five the FBI claims) and she said they were in the first-class seats, 2A, 2B, 9A, and 9B. These numbers were slightly different to those given by the other attendant, Madeline Amy Sweeney, and both were different to those given by the FBI. I asked the FBI why there was such a discrepancy, but they said they could not answer questions because of the "ongoing investigation" and I would have to apply through the Freedom of Information Act in years to come to find the information I wanted! (See *Appendix 1* and *2*.) Betty Ong is claimed to have said that the wounded passenger was in seat 10B. Marquis asked Betty Ong if the plane was descending. "We're starting to descend. We're starting to descend," she is said to have replied. At 8.46am, 48 minutes after leaving Boston, Flight 11 crashed into the north tower of the World Trade Center at the 96th of the 110 floors.

The FBI later listed five hijackers on Flight 11, thus ignoring the fact that calls, apparently from two separate flight attendants actually on the flight, both said four. I will use the names and spellings from the indictment of Zacarias Moussaoui, who was accused of involvement in the planning of the attacks. The indictment relates to his appearance before the United States District Court for the Eastern District of Virginia, Alexandria Division, in December 2001. Among those named by the FBI as a hijacker of Flight 11 was Mohamed Atta, an Egyptian, who it says was at the controls when the plane struck the World Trade Center. The FBI also claims he was the overall leader of the 9/11 terrorists. The other hijackers on Flight 11 were named on the indictment as Satam al-Suqami, from the United Arab Emirates, and Abdul Alomari, Wail al-Shehri, and Waleed al-Shehri, all from Saudi Arabia. Al-Suqami, the FBI tells us, was the only one of the five who was not a trained pilot.

United Airlines flight 175

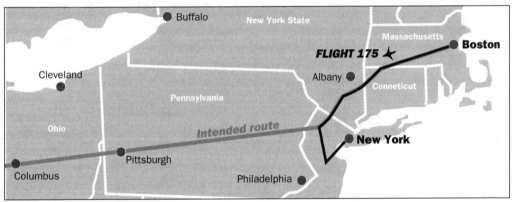

Figure 11: *The route of Flight 175*

Captain Victor J. Saracini, aged 51, and 38-year-old first officer Michael R. Horrocks were at the controls of Flight 175 when it pushed back from Gate 19 at Boston's Logan Airport. This was seven gates along from Flight 11, which had left from Gate 26 about 15 minutes earlier. The official stories of what happened to the two planes are very similar. Flight 175 took off about 8.14am and nothing seemed amiss in the initial climb. At 8.37, with AA Flight 11 now known to be in trouble, a controller is said to have asked Saracini and Horrocks if they could see American Flight 11 ahead of them.

Controller: "Do you have traffic? Look at, uh, your twelve to one o'clock at about, uh, ten miles south bound to see if you can see an American seventy six seven out there please."

UAL175: "Affirmative we have him, uh, he looks, uh, about twenty yeah about twenty nine, twenty eight thousand."

Controller: "United 175 turn five turn thirty degrees to the right I [want to] keep you away from this traffic." [5]

We are then told there were no further communications between the ground and Flight 175 until 8.41, that's just five minutes before Flight 11 crashed into the World Trade Center. At this time one of the pilots on Flight 175 is claimed to have called the controller and said, using the pilot code for Boston: "We heard a suspicious transmission on our departure from B-O-S. Sounds like someone keyed the mike and said, 'Everyone stay in your seats'." [6] Again I asked the Federal Aviation Administration for more information on this exchange, but they said they could not comment. Just 90 seconds after that exchange between cockpit and controller, Flight 175 veered off-course over northern New Jersey and headed south before turning back in a U-turn towards New York at some 400 miles an hour, aiming for the World Trade Center.[7] That is just 90 seconds between no problem and the plane being taken over by hijackers and flown off-course? Once again the transponder was switched off and there was no hijack code from the pilots, as with all four aircraft involved. Howard Dulmage, an aviation attorney and pilot, said: "You think four times in one morning one of those crews would have done that. That means they had to be upon them before they could react." [8] Well that's one way of explaining it, anyway, but there are others. A female flight attendant is said to have spoken to a mechanic at an airline maintenance centre in San Francisco that takes in-flight calls from attendants reporting items that need replacing or repairing. The mechanic, we are told, reported the conversation about 8.50am to Rich "Doc" Miles, the manager of the United Airlines System Operations Center in Chicago. He says the mechanic told him that the attendant had said: "Oh my God. The crew has been killed; a flight attendant has been stabbed. We've been hijacked." [9] The line then went dead. If this is all true then, according to the official timeline, the hijackers stormed the cockpit, killed the crew, took over the controls, a flight attendant rang the airline mechanic, and he called Rich "Doc" Miles to report what she said, all in the space of around seven minutes. Messages were sent to the cockpit computer without reply. Passenger Peter Hanson, a software salesman, apparently used his cellphone to ring his parents in Easton, Connecticut, at about 9am, some 45 minutes after take-off, and said that hijackers with knives had taken over the plane and stabbed a stewardess. Soon after, he called again and before the line was lost he is said to have told his father Lee that the plane was "going down". Hanson's wife Sue, son Peter, and their two-year-old daughter Christine were also on the plane. Around this time, it is claimed, an unidentified stewardess rang an emergency number from the back of the plane and described how colleagues had been stabbed. At 9.03am Flight 175 smashed into the south tower of the World Trade Center on live television amid a fireball that no one who saw it will ever forget.

The FBI says the hijackers of Flight 175 were led by Marwan al-Shehhi of the United Arab Emirates, a close friend and associate of Mohamed Atta. FBI statements claim that Al-Shehhi piloted the aircraft into the south tower. Also on the plane, the FBI tells us, were Fayez Ahmed (also Banihammad Fayez) and Mohald al-Shehri, both Saudis who had undergone flight training, and Ahmed al-Ghamdi and Hamza al-Ghamdi, also from Saudi Arabia.

American Airlines flight 77

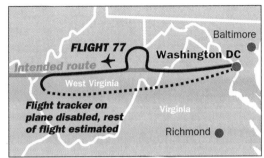

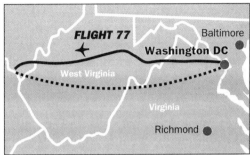

Figure 12: *The* USA Today *version of the route of Flight 77*

Figure 13: *The other version of Flight 77 published elsewhere in the media*

In the cockpit that morning as Flight 77 took off from Washington Dulles at 8.20am were 51-year-old Captain Charles F. "Chic" Burlingame III and first officer David Charlebois, who was 39. Burlingame was a graduate of the "Top Gun" fighter pilot school and was such a perfectionist that one colleague said that he would carry a set of small paint brushes to dust the instruments. He had once worked at the Pentagon while a Navy reservist not far from where his flight would crash that morning. His father was in the Navy and Air Force for 23 years and he and his wife are buried in the Arlington National Cemetery close to the Pentagon. Among the passengers was a former American Airlines pilot called Wilson "Bud" Flagg, a retired Navy Admiral once posted to the Pentagon; Brian Jack, a head of fiscal economics in the office of Defense Secretary Donald Rumsfeld at the Pentagon, where he had worked for 25 years; three engineers from plane makers, Boeing; and Barbara Olson, wife of the US Solicitor General, Theodore "Ted" Olson, and a contributor to CNN.

Flight Explorer is a company that tracks commercial flights in real time using data provided by the Federal Aviation Administration, and can be accessed on the Internet.[10] There are, however, two published versions of the route of Flight 77, both sourced to Flight Explorer. The version published in *USA Today* (*Figure 12*) includes a very strange "loop" deviation from its course as it turned north over West Virginia, then west, before turning south and returning to its authorised route.[11] This loop is not included in the course data published by other media organisations, and this serious deviation happened well before the transponder was is said to have been turned off and the plane turned around to head back for Washington. If this did happen, what on earth were the air traffic controllers doing in that time and what was the reason given by the cockpit before the aircraft returned to its agreed route? I asked the Federal Aviation Administration that very question, but it wouldn't comment. I contacted Flight Explorer to ask for confirmation that the *USA Today* version was correct and I was sent the route in *Figure 13*. About 8.50am we are told that the cockpit stopped responding to controllers and six minutes later the transponder was turned off. A controller is said to have called the aircraft repeatedly asking: "American 77 indy radio check, how do you read?" At 9.02am, still nearly 40 minutes before impact, a controller is said to have told American Airlines: "We lost track control of the guy, he's in coast track [no transponder] but we haven't – we don't really know where his target is and we can't get a hold of him." [12] An "unidentified" aircraft was then picked up on radar headed for Washington at some 500 miles an hour. Some reports say that a military C130 (Golfer 06) took off from the Andrews Air Force Base near Washington to identify the plane and reported it was a Boeing 767 (it was a 757) moving low and very fast. This was Flight 77, we are told, with the Pentagon as its target.

It is said that one of the terrorists told the passengers that they were going to die and they should phone their families. We are told that former federal prosecutor and CNN contributor Barbara Olson rang her husband, Ted Olson, US Solicitor General, at his office in the Justice Department at about 9.25, according to media reports. Olson says he was watching television coverage of the World Trade Center when his secretary told him: "Your wife is on the phone." Olson said that Barbara, his third wife, told him that her plane had been hijacked using box cutters and knives. She said nothing about the number of hijackers or their nationality. [13] There appear to be several published versions of their conversation and in one she said the pilots were with her. Ted Olson told her about the World Trade Center and she said: "What should I tell the pilot?" before the line went down. Olson said he called the Justice Department command centre who told him they had no idea the plane had been hijacked. His wife rang back and said the plane was circling, but the line was lost again, he said. [14] Olson was the lawyer who argued the case before the Supreme Court for George W. Bush to be elected president after the Florida fiasco and has been a vehement advocate of Bush's anti-terrorism laws since September 11th. On March 17th 2002, Ted Olson was defending the United States before the Supreme Court against charges of murder by the CIA. Olson said that day:

> "It's easy to imagine an infinite number of situations where the government might legitimately give out false information. It's an unfortunate reality that the issuance of incomplete information and even misinformation by government may sometimes be perceived as necessary to protect vital interests."

By 9.42, some 80 minutes after take-off, Flight 77 was seen approaching Washington DC, it is claimed. The plane is said to have made a sharp turn and descended very steeply from 7,000 feet to near surface level. It is reported to have crossed a highway, clipping street lamps, before striking a helicopter pad and exploding into a five-storey section of the Pentagon, one of the world's biggest buildings, at 9.43. Defense Secretary Donald Rumsfeld was in an office at the opposite end of the building to the impact and such is the size of the Pentagon he felt only a "jarring thing". A total of 190 people died in the plane and the Pentagon, we are told. The FBI announced to the media that five hijackers were on board Flight 77 led by Hani Hanjour. He had a commercial pilot's license and was said at first to have been at the controls when the plane struck the Pentagon until it was clear from his flight instructors that he was a terrible pilot even in small planes. He is a Saudi and so were the others named by the FBI as being on the plane. They were Majed Moqed, Salem al-Hamzi, Khalid al-Midhar and Nawaf al-Hamzi. The latter two were the only accused who appeared on the terrorist alert list.

United Airlines flight 93

Figure 14: *The route of Flight 93*

Flight 93 left Gate 17 at Newark International Airport at 8.01am, bound for San Francisco, and took off at 8.42am after a long and unexplained delay. At the controls were the 43-year-old captain Jason Dahl, from Littleton, Colorado, and the 36-year-old first officer LeRoy Homer of Marlton, New Jersey. They flew west over Pennsylvania and into northern Ohio where they received a message from United Airlines warning all pilots of a potential "cockpit intrusion". The cockpit of Flight 93 confirmed receipt of the message and because of its late departure this was the only one of the four planes that had prior warning of possible trouble. It is said that Flight 93 was hijacked some 30 minutes after take off, that's around 9.10am, and after the two planes had crashed into the World Trade Center. We are told it was 9.16 when the Federal Aviation Administration told its military colleagues at NORAD that Flight 93 may have been hijacked, but the official story says that it was not until 9.40 that the transponder signal was lost. The hijackers are said to have forced their way into the cockpit wearing red bandanas around their heads and one of them warned he had a bomb attached to his waist. The official version says the hijackers told the passengers they were taking the plane to another airport. Air traffic controllers apparently claim that they heard two short radio transmissions around the time the "cockpit was stormed" and in one they heard a pilot say: "Get out of here". An unnamed government official quoted in the media said there were at least four radio transmissions in which the phrases "bomb on board", "our demands" and "keep quiet" were heard.[15] A lot of these alleged conversations remind me of a low-budget movie. *ABC News* claimed to have secured a tape of these transmissions in which a hijacker says: "We'd like you all to remain seated. There is a bomb on board. And we are going to turn back to the airport. And they had our demands, so please remain quiet." [16] Passengers used their cellphones and seat-back phones to call their friends and family, we are told, and they heard about the planes crashing in New York and Washington. This, it is claimed, led to passengers getting together to challenge the four hijackers, who were armed once again with small knives and box cutters, the official story goes. At 9.45 Todd Beamer, a 32-year-old employee of the computer software company Oracle, is said to have spoken to airphone supervisor Lisa Jefferson after his credit card was refused when he tried to call his family. A summary of the 15-minute conversation was faxed by the Verizon phone company to his wife in which he said that the pilot and co-pilot appeared to be dead and the hijackers were flying the plane. But another passenger, Lauren Grandcolas, is reported to have phoned her husband Jack in San Francisco to say: "We have been hijacked. They are being kind. I love you." [17] Beamer is said to have stated that one hijacker was guarding 27 passengers at the back of the aircraft with what he was told was a bomb around his waist. He is reported to have said that two other hijackers were in the cockpit and another was guarding first class. Beamer sent love to his wife, who was five months pregnant, and his two small sons. The last words the phone supervisor is said to have heard him say were: "Are you guy's ready? Let's roll." [18] His wife Lisa, who never spoke to him directly, said she recognised the phrase as one he used with their sons. A contact that knows members of the Illuminati High Council in the United States told me that Verizon is a major Illuminati operation. At 9.42 Mark Bingham, a 31-year-old rugby player and an enormous man at six feet five, called his mother Alice Hoglan from the plane. "Mom, this is Mark Bingham," he said, sounding very nervous. "I want to let you know that I love you. I'm calling from the plane. We've been taken over. There are three men that say they have a bomb." [19] The FBI and Beamer said there were four. Jeremy Glick, a former national judo champion, talked to his wife, Liz, on an airphone and asked if it was true about planes crashing into the World Trade Center. He said the passengers were taking a vote over whether they should try to take back the plane. "Honey, you need to do it," she told him. Glick's mother-in-law told CNN that he also called her and said that "one of the hijackers had a red box he said was a bomb and one had a knife of some nature". [20] She said he asked her if reports about attacks on the World Trade Center were true and she told him they were. He left the phone for a while, she said, returning to say: "The men voted to attack the terrorists." Thomas Burnett Jr, a 38-year-old father of three girls, called from the plane four times and in his last call he told his wife that they planned to challenge the hijackers. "I know we're all going to die," he told her, "There's three of us who are going to do something about it. I love you, honey." [21] Flight attendant Sandy Bradshaw called her husband Phil, a US Airways pilot. "Have you heard what's going on?" she said. "My flight has been hijacked. My flight has been hijacked with three guys with knives." Note again that the FBI says four, just as it names five for Flight 11 when the attendants were reported to have said four. Sandy said she was in the galley filling jugs with boiling water and she ended: "Everyone's running to first class. I've got to go. Bye." [22] The official version is that passengers attacked the hijackers and the plane smashed into a field at Shanksville, Pennsylvania, at 575 miles an hour. The time given for the crash varies considerably. NORAD, the official military defenders of North American airspace, told me it happened at approximately 10.03, many other reports say 10.10, and still others 10.37. This last time is some two hours and 38 minutes after the first hijacked plane left Boston. By now thousands of people were dead and the world was in trauma at the unspeakable horror of what had happened. The FBI said the four hijackers on Flight 93 were Saeed al-Ghamdi, Ahmed al-Haznawi, Ahmed al-Nami, and Ziad Jarrah.

Television brought the shocking scenes to hundreds of millions of people as the north tower burned from the collision with Flight 11. Then, 18 minutes later, as people were watching those pictures, Flight 175 careered into the south tower amid an enormous explosion of flame. It is estimated that some 20,000 people could have been working in each of the towers at that time in the morning and the official death toll was a little under three thousand. At 10am, less than an hour after the impact from Flight 175, the south tower collapsed as a horrified world looked on. Half an hour later the north tower went the same way. The official explanation for the imploding collapse was that the fuel fire had weakened steel supports and the floors above the impact began to fall, creating an ever more powerful chain reaction as floors crashed upon floors until the whole building fell like some enormous house of cards. Among the dead were 341 fire fighters together with other rescuers who had rushed into the buildings to help and been killed in the sudden collapse.

The President and the pet goat story

President Bush was in Florida on the morning of September 11th for a long-standing photo opportunity at the Emma E. Booker Elementary School at Sarasota. The official story says that he began the day with a four and a half mile jog, two laps of a golf course on Longboat Key.[23] There are inexplicably conflicting reports of what Bush did that morning and when he knew about the first plane to strike the World Trade Center. I will go into these strange events in Sarasota in some detail later. One of the official reports was that Bush was told about Flight 11 by his White House Chief of Staff Andrew Card on the way to a classroom where he was scheduled to promote his "education" policy.[24] The official tale is that Bush went to a private room and spoke on the phone with his National Security Adviser Condoleezza Rice. We are told that at this point the crash of Flight 11 could have been considered just a "terrible accident", but this is a lie, as we shall see. After hearing about Flight 11 crashing into the north tower of the World Trade Center, President Bush acted decisively. He went into the classroom to hear children reading a story about a pet goat. Bush entered the classroom at about 9am with Education Secretary Ron Paige and Florida Lieutenant Governor Frank Brogan. They paused for media photographs and Bush sat down in front of the 18 children from the second grade. As the children read to him he said: "Really good readers – whew!" Bush interrupted at one point, saying, "This must be Sixth Grade."[25] This is a guy who has just been told that a commercial airliner has smashed into one of the two biggest buildings in America in the heart of downtown New York. Chief of Staff Andrew Card then appeared in the classroom and whispered into Bush's ear to tell him about the crash of the second plane, Flight 175. This was the picture seen all over the world along with headlines like: "The Moment Bush Knew". Yet still he

This "world" is only an illusion and we can change it any time we want. It's just a choice right now between fear and love.

stayed in the classroom listening to children reading about a pet goat. It was only around 9.30 – *26 minutes* after hearing of the second crash and some 45 after the first – that Bush reacted. He went into the school library to announce:

> "Ladies and gentlemen, this is a difficult moment for America. Two airplanes have crashed into the World Trade Center in an apparent terrorist attack on our country. I am going to conduct a full-scale investigation and hunt down and find those folks who committed this act. Terrorism against our nation will not stand." [26]

Those folks? *Those folks?* Bush's behaviour that morning was, at the very least, criminally inept and incompetent, but it was more than that, as I shall highlight later. Bush was taken to the presidential plane, Air Force One, and it was naturally believed that he would head for Washington at this time of terror and chaos for his country. Instead he embarked on a day-long tour of the skies that included stops at Barksdale Air Force Base, Louisiana, and the US Strategic Command at Offutt Air Force base in Nebraska. He did not arrive in Washington until 7pm – ten hours after Andrew Card walked into the classroom and told him of the second crash. Even the official story says that Bush did not call Vice President Cheney to put the US military on high alert status until 10 o'clock that morning when he was in Air Force One. Between 9.05am when he was told of the second crash in New York and the moment when he picked up the phone to put the US military on high alert status an astonishing *55 minutes* had elapsed. It was in this period that Flight 77 crashed into an unprotected Pentagon. When understandable questions were being asked about Bush's unexplained dash to Louisiana and on to Nebraska after his nation had suffered such a massive terrorist attack, White House spokespeople said that they had received a phone call giving a secret code to say that Air Force One was the next target. Like most of the 9/11 story this turned out to be a solid gold lie and later had to be admitted as such.

I have seen reports that Father George Bush was in the White House with Cheney while the attacks were happening[27] and an Air Force source also said that this was true. These reports say that Bush left Washington by private jet at 10am that morning while other air traffic was being grounded. This is not that far from the official story, which says that he and wife Barbara were at the White House the night before and flew out of Washington on the morning of 9/11. Father Bush told CNN that they were flying to St. Paul, Minneapolis, when the first news was flashed to their Secret Service detail about the attacks. Their plane was diverted to Milwaukee, Wisconsin, and they were taken to a motel beyond the city limits where they could only follow events on television like everyone else, it is claimed.[28] If Father George Bush was not actively involved in events then I have a seafront home in the Gobi Desert.

Herr Blair hears the news

From the start, President Bush and British Prime Minister Tony Blair were singing, as always, from the same song sheet. Blair was in Brighton on the south coast of England when the World Trade Center was struck. He was due to make what was going to be a difficult and less than well-received speech to trades unionists, but this was cancelled and he headed back by train for London. According to media reports, Blair called his Foreign and Defence Secretaries, Jack Straw and Geoff Hoon. The three agreed, the reports say, to build "… an international alliance which included the rest of Europe, Muslim nations, China and Russia." [29] But why would Blair and his yes-men do this immediately after the American attacks when they should have had no idea who was behind them according to the CIA and FBI? Not even the Americans had officially mentioned any suspects at that stage. We are talking of actions taken immediately after the attacks and Blair is already preparing for what became known as the "war on terrorism". Back in London, Blair told a news conference that Britain would stand "shoulder to shoulder" with the United States. This was, in effect, a blank cheque speech, as events were to confirm. In the hours and days that followed, the culprit or "patsy" was already being dusted down – Osama bin Laden. His name would be repeated like a mantra by Bush, Powell and Blair until he became guilty, not by evidence, but by constant repetition. During his summer holiday a month before 9/11 Blair had read security reports on Osama bin Laden and Islamic fundamentalism, and read parts of the Koran to "… try and understand aspects of the faith and fathom out whether a justification for terrorism could really be found, as often argued, in its pages".[30] What a coincidence.

Once upon a time in fairyland …

The television networks were naming Osama bin Laden as the likely culprit in the hours after the planes struck the World Trade Center and Colin Powell, the Secretary of State, first mentioned that Osama bin Laden was a "prime suspect" two days after 9/11. Powell told the media: "We are looking at those terrorist organisations who have the kind of capacity to conduct the kind of attack that we saw." Really? Did he mean the CIA and the Pentagon? No, as it turns out. Asked whether he was referring to Osama bin Laden, he answered: "Yes." Once bin Laden's name was in the ring, the "evidence" began to emerge in support of the theory that the attack was carried out by extreme Islamic fundamentalists. An official "investigation" was launched by two Bush family gofers: Attorney General John Ashcroft and the two-weeks-in-the-job FBI chief, Robert Mueller. The FBI immediately named 19 Arab men as responsible for the hijackings. This was remarkable in itself because this same agency, along with the CIA, had told us it did not have even a glimmer of an idea that the biggest terrorist attack in American history was being put together for months before September 11th and, in Mueller's words, almost certainly years. But now the names and pictures of those involved were suddenly produced. What fantastic detective work! The problem was, as we shall discuss later, that more than a third of the names on the FBI "hijacker" list were found to be still alive! Maybe they parachuted just before impact? Anything becomes possible when the official story needs propping up.

The "biggest investigation in American history" with 4,000 officers and 3,000 support personnel apparently deployed by the FBI alone was helped by some staggering good fortune. This included the fact that the bag of "mastermind"

Mohamed Atta failed to make it on to Flight 11 and this presented the FBI with "incriminating evidence" together with the contents of abandoned hire cars in airport car parks. The FBI said it found a Saudi passport, an international driver's license, a copy of the Koran, "some kind of religious tape", and, yes, yes, a videotape on how to fly Boeing 757s and 747s.[31] What a piece of luck. But even this was eclipsed by the miraculous find, widely reported in the media, of a passport from one of the hijackers that was discovered in the street a few blocks from the World Trade Center. Somehow, while some two thousand bodies have never been found, a paper passport that had been in the pocket or bag of a hijacker had survived the impact of a commercial airliner at some 400 miles an hour and the fireball that followed. It had fallen from the plane and wafted down to be found, still recognisable and identifiable, in the street. If that is possible, maybe the still-alive hijackers did parachute after all. We were also told, again despite two thousand bodies disappearing without trace, that a stewardess with her hands tied behind her back was discovered soon after the attacks – just as the official story was being heavily promoted.[32]

The Reaction

These miracle finds and the constant repetition of the official story served to support the script to which Bush, Blair and their "teams" were all working. Arab hijackers had stormed the cockpits, the trained pilots among them had taken over the controls, and the planes were deliberately aimed at their targets in a mass suicide and murder attack on America. What's more, the hijackers were working for Osama bin Laden who was based in Afghanistan and protected by the Taliban regime. Once this cover story was established immediately after September 11th nothing was allowed to challenge its supremacy. This is how it was and this is how it is. End of story. If you question anything we tell you then clearly you are supporting terrorism. Or, as Bush put it: "You are either with us or against us." (Roughly translated that means: "You either don't have a brain or you do.") This was the story parroted hour after hour, week after week, by the mainstream media across the world. The media is a megaphone for the official version of events. Official sources tell the media what happened and the media repeat this slavishly and call it "news". The BBC and its like, for example, reported the "hijacker passport" story without any reference to the fact that it was clearly ridiculous. No, really, the FBI told us, so it must be true.

Timothy Lee Harvey bin Laden

Colin Powell attended a meeting of the National Security Council at the White House after 9/11 and it was agreed that he, Bush and deputy Secretary of State Richard Armitage would work to build an "international consensus" against terrorism. What a trio to lead the world in a moral crusade against those who pursue crimes against humanity! Pinch me, please. The message was: Osama bin Laden is the Mr Big behind 9/11 and as the Taliban are protecting him in Afghanistan they would have to be removed as well if they did not hand him over.

By Tony Blair's own admission, no evidence whatsoever was produced that would have stood the test of a courtroom. But that mattered not. Bush, Blair, and their handlers and henchmen had decided that was the story and that was the end of it. When the Taliban asked for evidence against bin Laden before handing him over, Bush replied: "They are harbouring a terrorist and they need to hand him over. There's no need to discuss innocence or guilt. We know he's guilty." [33] What a perfect summary of the arrogant dictatorship that runs America and the wider world. Don't do as I do, do as I say. Powell and Blair embarked on their "whirlwind diplomacy" to gather support for the Anglo-American "war on terrorism". This "diplomacy", as usual, involved telling their hosts around the world about the consequences for them and their countries of not doing what was demanded. Powell publicly warned Pakistan: "... as we gather information and as we look at possible sources of the attack, it would be useful to point out to the Pakistani leadership at every level that we are looking for and expecting their fullest cooperation and their help and support".[34] Pakistan President General Pervez Musharraf knew the score and Pakistan's military dictatorship, with a horrendous record of supporting terrorist groups, joined the "war on terrorism". This involved handing over decision-making to Bush, Powell and the rest of American government mafia, but then that was no problem for the Pakistan authorities and their intelligence network because that is a branch of the CIA anyway. Musharraf "won" five more years in office in a "referendum" in late April 2002, which was described by the Human Rights Commission in Pakistan as a "humiliating fraud".[35] Obviously they moved the gang in from Florida to ensure the right result.

Terrorists "fight" terrorism

The criteria for joining the anti-terrorism "coalition" was not your record of supporting terrorism because on that basis the United States and Britain would have been denied membership before anyone. No, the criteria was: will you do what the United States and Britain tell you to do? If yes, you're in and against terrorism; if no, you are a supporter of terrorism. These guys really are the bullies of the world. They had the nerve to wheel out the "first ladies", Laura Bush and Cherie Blair, within 24 hours of each other to condemn the Taliban for their treatment of women. Yes, the Taliban's sick ideology was horrible, but not a word was said about the appalling treatment of women by Saudi Arabia, where I lived for some months in the late 1970s. The difference between the condemnation of the Taliban and the silence about Saudi Arabia was simply that the Taliban was the target to be demonised to justify the invasion of Afghanistan while the Saudis who joined the "war on terrorism" are an arm of the United States and the Carlyle Group of Daddy Bush, Baker and Carlucci. This is the peace-loving, justice-supporting, Saudi Arabia that is the home of Osama bin Laden and much of his funding; the Saudi Arabia that conducts a terrorist war against its own people to keep the tyrants and hypocrites in the Saudi "royal" family in power as poodles of the US government; and the Saudi Arabia that continues to chop off people's heads and hands according to their Nazi religious "law". Saudi Arabia is controlled by a deeply disturbed terrorist regime – the "royal" dictatorship – and hypocrisy rules, OK? This becomes even more blatant when you consider that it was Saudi and US support that underpinned the Taliban. Who are the "advisers" to the Saudi royal family? Father George's Carlyle Group. Who are very close to the "royal" House of Saud? The bin Laden family. Who owned the National Commercial Bank the Saudi royal family uses to conduct its business affairs? Khalid bin Mahfouz, funder of Bush family businesses, 20% shareholder in the BCCI, and named by the US government as a funder of Osama bin Laden. Who controls that bank now? Mohammed Hussein Al-Amoudi, a close business associate of bin Mahfouz, and another man named as a funder of Osama bin Laden's network. What was the bank named by the US government as a source of the funding for bin Laden? The National Commercial Bank of Saudi Arabia. Who were part of the consortium with Unocal to build the pipelines across Afghanistan? Delta (Al-Amoudi) and Nimir (bin Mahfouz). No wonder Saudi Arabia was considered one of the good guys by Bush and Blair while the Taliban were condemned and bombed into oblivion. I think, however, that demonising Saudi Arabia to advance the agenda may be part of the plan also sometime in the future. Everyone and everything is expendable to these people when it suits the agenda.

Secretary of State Colin Powell, reading from the script, pledged "to make sure that we go after terrorism and get it by its branch and root".[36] That did not, of course, include his own involvement in terrorist activity on behalf of the United States government or anyone who took orders from that government. Sanctions against Pakistan in response to its nuclear weapons programme were removed by President Bush when the Pakistani leadership agreed to play ball. Funny how Pakistan and India having nuclear weapons was so dangerous that sanctions were imposed, but suddenly, when they agreed to follow orders from Bush and his masters after 9/11, that "nuclear threat" immediately diminished. The next thing you know they are both threatening to use them against each other. But what arrogance to say that the US and Britain can have nuclear weapons by right, but any lesser political and economic power must not. NATO and the United Nations also played their parts in the 9/11 movie. The UN Security Council has only five permanent members – the United States, Britain, China, France and Russia. These five have the power of veto over "substantive issues". The Security Council has, in truth, been dominated by Britain and America, so naturally it would follow the party line after September 11th with a call for "all necessary means" to be used to overcome the threat of terrorism. NATO rolled over and purred, not least because the NATO Secretary General was Lord Robertson, a close associate of Tony Blair and his former Secretary of Defence. Like Blair, Robertson attends meetings of the Illuminati's Bilderberg Group and was invited to the one at Turnberry in Scotland shortly before being named Secretary General of NATO in 1999. The last six heads of NATO have been from the Bilderberg Group. The day after September 11th, the 19-member NATO Council, "encouraged" by Robertson, invoked for the first time Article Five of its founding charter. This says that an attack on one member is an attack on all of them. Clearly copies of the script had been widely distributed.

Puppet parliaments

Both Houses of Congress authorised Bush to "use all necessary and appropriate force" against those responsible, including any nations supporting them, and the UK parliament gave Blair similar unquestioned backing to do the same (when he even bothered to ask). This meant that within days of the attacks the Bush-Blair Illuminati-serving Axis of Evil (the real one) had all it needed to wage a war that had been years in the planning. While both the US and UK governments had long failed the poor, homeless, and deprived through a "lack of money to do everything we would like", suddenly, as with all wars, money was no object. Funny how there is a shortage of money to keep people alive and help them achieve a decent quality of life, but there is never a shortage of funds to spend on killing and maiming them. There is a simple reason for this: when there is something the Illuminati want to happen to advance their agenda, the Illuminati produce the funds to make happen. Congress immediately sanctioned $40 billion for the "war on terrorism" and within months Bush announced a $48 billion increase in defence spending to "fight the war on terror". This was an increase of almost 15%, the biggest in 20 years, and it brought U.S military spending to *$379 billion*. The money has been assigned, so we are told, to salary increases for military personnel (dictators always look after their soldiers) and the latest precision weapons, missile defences, unmanned vehicles and high-tech equipment for ground troops. A large chunk will also go to "homeland defence" (control of the people) and Bush called for the hiring of 30,000 airport security workers and an extra 300 FBI agents – an FBI which, with 4,000 operatives already, did not, we are told officially, have the slightest clue that the biggest terrorist attack in history had been in the planning for years. The CIA budget is also due to increase by an estimated $1.5 billion or $2 billion by 2003, although we can't know the true figure because the CIA budget is classified.[37] "I have a responsibility to prepare the nation for all that lies ahead," Bush said. He was right, too. A responsibility to the Illuminati hierarchy to prepare the nation for what they have already planned will lie ahead.

Forever John Wayne

President Bush, like Reagan and all American leaders, has a massive built-in advantage in his pursuit of a dictatorship at home and mass murder abroad. It is the collective mind of America. Individually Americans are overwhelmingly wonderful people and a joy to know and be with. They are almost always helpful, kind, and friendly. But the collective mind, the national mind if you like, can be barely one-dimensional when it falls for the manipulations of its government. There is a part of the American collective psyche that is forever John Wayne. It sees only good guys and bad guys, cowboys and Indians, black and white. Many Americans (though it is changing) see the world in these terms and their access to foreign news and events is so sparse and slanted in the US media that they have virtually no idea what is happening beyond the American borders, or even inside them come to that. Instead they let their leaders tell them what is happening and they are sold a fantasy based on the clichéd script of a movie starring John Wayne or Sylvester Stallone. Rocky and Rambo have long had desks in the PR offices at the White House, the State Department and the Pentagon. Bush's speechwriters targeted exactly this response after 9/11 by providing quotes like: "I can hear you and the rest of the world hears you and the people who knocked these buildings down will hear all of us soon." Get on yer horse Big Jaaahn. This planet ain't big enough for the both of us. The Rambo response – no subtleties, no shades of grey, shoot first and ask no questions – is used to manipulate the emotions of the American psyche and to activate macho man and macho woman. Mainstream radio talk show hosts are classic expressions of this with their mindless calls to "nuke 'em" whenever the bullies in government pick yet another fight with a country that has no means of credible defence. Among the public responses quoted in the media in the aftermath of September 11th was that of Joan Renshaw, a grandmother in Atlanta: "I'm angry. I'm hoping we wipe these people out, and if we need to, wipe out the country that is hosting them. Just get rid of them all." [38] Then there was Phil Beckwith, a former Navy Chief Petty Officer from Wyoming: "I know just what to do with these Arab people. We have to find them, kill them, wrap them in pigskin and bury them. That way they will never go to heaven. Bury Osama bin Laden with a pigskin, donate blood for the people in New York and God bless this great country." [39] We have the same collective mentality in Britain, although there appears to be a much greater outbreak of scepticism here among the general public. Calls in America and elsewhere for a peaceful response to September 11th were lost in the clamour and lust for revenge. One banner encapsulated the situation when it said, "An Eye for An Eye Makes the World Blind". But such sentiments were dismissed as weak and cowardly, or even, as support for the terrorists. Add all these political and public responses together and it meant only one thing: thousands of civilians in Afghanistan who had never seen Osama bin Laden, including children who had never even heard of him, were now doomed to die from bombs dropped on their already devastated settlements by the forces of "freedom" and "justice".

The Solution

"War" with Afghanistan

As in Iraq, the "real men" of the American and British Air Forces bravely flew out of range of the ancient technology that passed for the Afghanistan air defences while dropping state-of-the-art bombs and missiles on civilians. Once again this was not a war; that needs two sides. This was the playground bully at work, and it was just another cold-blooded slaughter. The US government bought the rights to all satellite images of Afghanistan before the bombing started in order to hide where their bombs were really being targeted. The following are some of the reports of civilian deaths that were made public. The vast majority were not.

- **October 11th:** Two US jets bombed the mountain village of Karam. The death toll was estimated at between 100 and 160.

- **October 13th:** Bombs fell on the Qila Meer Abas neighbourhood, two kilometres south of Kabul airport. Four civilians were reportedly killed.

- **October 18th:** 47 civilians were said to have been killed when a central marketplace near Kandahar was bombed.

- **October 23rd:** More than 90 civilians were reportedly killed when low-flying US gun ships fired on the farming villages of Bori Chokar and Chowkar-karez, north of Kandahar.

- **October 31st:** An F-18 attacked a Red Crescent clinic in a pre-dawn raid killing between 15 and 25 people.

- **November 10th:** Villages in the Khakrez district were reportedly bombed, killing more than 150 civilians.[40]

On that terrible morning of September 11th 2001 it is estimated that 2,998 civilians died in New York, Washington and the crash of Flight 93 in Pennsylvania. They called it the worst terrorist attack in history. Yet a study by Professor Marc Herold of the University of New Hampshire concluded that between October 7th and December 7th 2001 at least 3,800 Afghanistan civilians (men, women, and children with no connection whatsoever to 9/11) died from American and British attacks. This figure was a "very, very conservative estimate," Professor Herold said. "I think that a much more realistic figure would be around 5,000," he suggested, "You know for Afghanistan, 3,700 to 5,000 is a really substantial number."[41] Professor Herold's figures were based only on deaths reported in the mainstream media and did not include those in remote areas of Afghanistan and those unreported in the press (God only knows how many that would be). Nor does the figure include those who died because the air strikes prevented their access to hospitals, food or electricity, or those who were injured and died later. Add together all of the Afghan civilians who died as a result of the US-British bombardment and you will have a figure of many, many, thousands more than those who died on September 11th. If 9/11 was the "worst terrorist act in history" what does that make the attacks on civilians in Afghanistan, never mind Iraq? They said that what happened in America was "evil" and then responded by killing even more civilians in a far-away country. In the newspeak of the Illuminati they called this mass murder of the innocent "Operation Infinite Justice" and then "Operation Enduring Freedom". A group of Americans who lost relatives in the attacks of September 11th showed more humanity and understanding in one day than Bush has shown since he first came under his father's spell. They flew to Kabul to meet Afghans who lost members of their own families in the Bush-Blair bombing. Derrill Bodley, a music professor from California, lost his 20-year-old daughter Deora, who was on United Airlines Flight 93, which went down in Pennsylvania. He met the father of a five-year-old Afghan girl who died when an American bomb landed on a residential area of Kabul. Bodley said: "This trip is about respect and love for all human beings – regardless of where they come from." [42] That is the real voice of America speaking. The voice I see in the vast majority of Americans I meet once they have stopped, taken a breath and cleared their minds of their government's propaganda and life-long conditioning.

Massacre in the moonlight

As I cannot say too often, those who claim to lead America have no love for their country or their people. Whether the dead are Americans or Afghans or Iraqis makes no difference to the Illuminati. They see them as the same cattle, the same cannon fodder, on the road to global control. One of the few news reports to tell any truth about the calculated attacks on Afghan civilians was written by Catherine Philip in the *Weekend Australian* of November 3rd–4th 2001. Filing from Quetta in Pakistan, she told a chilling story of what so many Afghan villagers experienced. Under the headline "Massacre in the Moonlight – Alarm of a Different Kind", she reported:

"When Zamina Ahmed was awakened by the warplanes roaring overhead and heard the deafening boom of a bomb dropping close by, her first thought was to get out of the house. Grabbing her son, Sabir, 5, she ran into the courtyard of the sprawling family compound, searching for a safe place to hide.
"Behind her in the house, her daughter, Shaida, 14, cowered in her bed, too terrified to run. As the door banged shut, she heard the deafening rattle of gunfire from the sky. She looked out of the glassless window in time to see her mother slump lifeless to the ground. 'The moon was shining and in the light, I saw her fall to the ground with Sabir still in her arms,' Shaida said. 'I knew she had been shot'.

"Naseer Mohammed, 20, and his niece, Najia, 14, had nearly made it out of the compound when the bullets started raining down. One bullet caught Najia squarely in the chest, killing her instantly. Mr Mohammed ran on to find cover, leaving her body sprawled on the dusty ground.

"Hiding in the entrance to a nearby cave, he watched as the gunships – believed to be American AC130s, deployed to hunt down and kill Taliban forces and terrorists from the al-Qaeda network – circled over the village firing repeatedly at the people as they fled their homes.

"'When they dropped the first bomb, everyone ran out and then they began firing on the people,' Mr Mohammed said. 'I was very frightened and confused. I wondered why are they doing this to us.' The attack lasted an hour. By the time it was over, 18 members of the family were dead, five of them children. All were killed by gunfire after they ran into the open.

"'Just because I hid in a room, I am alive,' Shaida said. 'Those who ran into the yard were killed.' Survivors arriving across the border in Quetta, Pakistan, say as many as 17 other civilians died in the attack on Chowkar Karez village on the evening of October

22, bringing the total of dead to 35. The accounts they give of the attack are strikingly consistent. Without exception, they say the first bomb was dropped around 11pm, that most people immediately ran outside in fear and were then mown down by gunfire from the circling gunships. 'They were huge planes,' Mr Mohammed said. 'If the Taliban and Osama bin Laden are the targets then why were they shooting at us?'

"Whatever happened in Chowkar Karez, it does not appear to be a simple case of a bomb going astray. The gunners who strafed the village clearly believed that there was something there that they had to destroy. On the night of October 23, the day after the first attack, the planes returned, circling overhead and firing into the houses. That time, the people stayed inside. In the morning, they left. None of the villagers seem sure if they would return. For those who survived, the wounds go as deep as shrapnel." [43]

This is just another every-day story of America and Britain making war on terrorism. It was Iraq revisited with many more like it destined to come until the people of this world emerge from their comatose state. Andrew Gumbel, writing in the UK *Independent* of November 3rd, also reported the massacre of Chowkar Karez. He wrote that "Western journalists and human rights organisations published the clearest evidence yet of mass civilian casualties caused by the American bombing campaign yesterday". He went on:

"Visiting journalists counted 18 fresh graves but were told the villagers had not been able to sort out the many severed limbs and body parts to give each person their own final resting place. 'As we buried the dead, the planes came again,' said an old farmer called Mangal, who claimed to have lost 30 relatives including 12 women and 14 children. 'We had to work quickly. Not everyone got their own grave' ..." [44]

The Pentagon confirmed that an AC-130 Spectre gunship attacked the village (several were involved, not only one, the villagers said), but a spokesman claimed it was a "legitimate target". However, anything is deemed a legitimate target to these disturbed people. "There was a positively identified Taliban encampment, which included al-Qa'ida collaborators, in the vicinity of Chowkar that was struck in October," a Pentagon parrot told the *Washington Post*. "The encampment was fully developed and was a legitimate military target under the law of armed conflict." [45] The same law, I take it, that says that those who defend themselves against such attacks from a foreign aggressor cannot be called prisoners of war because they weren't wearing uniforms. In other words, America's law, Britain's law, Illuminati law, which constantly changes to fit the moment and has no regard for life.

Intellectual prostitutes

The reports of Afghan casualties and the targeting of civilians I have featured here are rare because of the media management orchestrated through the political and military network and the Illuminati-owned media like CNN, a subsidiary of AOL-

Time Warner. The New York-based organisation called FAIR (Fairness and Accuracy in Reporting)[46] highlighted the extraordinary comments by Walter Isaacson, the chairman of CNN or, as I call it, Claptrap No News or the Criminal News Network. As reported by the *Washington Post*,[47] Isaacson " … ordered his staff to balance images of civilian devastation in Afghan cities with reminders that the Taliban harbors murderous terrorists, saying it 'seems perverse to focus too much on the casualties or hardship in Afghanistan'." Isaacson had the nerve to tell the *Washington Post*: "I want to make sure we're not used as a propaganda platform." [48] No kidding. These guys have no shame. Howard Kurtz, the *Post*'s media reporter, quoted a memo from Isaacson to CNN's international correspondents that admonished reporters covering civilian deaths not to "forget it is that country's leaders who are responsible for the situation Afghanistan is now in". He suggested that journalists should put the responsibility for civilian deaths with the Taliban, not the American military. Kurtz also quoted a memo from Rick Davis, CNN's head of "standards" and practices, which recommended the following sample comments for news presenters to say after reports of Afghan civilian casualties:

"We must keep in mind, after seeing reports like this from Taliban-controlled areas, that these US military actions are in response to a terrorist attack that killed close to 5,000 innocent people in the US' or, 'We must keep in mind, after seeing reports like this, that the Taliban regime in Afghanistan continues to harbor terrorists who have praised the September 11 attacks that killed close to 5,000 innocent people in the US' or 'The Pentagon has repeatedly stressed that it is trying to minimize civilian casualties in Afghanistan, even as the Taliban regime continues to harbor terrorists who are connected to the September 11 attacks that claimed thousands of innocent lives in the US'" [49]

Davis added that "even though it may start sounding rote, it is important that we make this point each time". During its US broadcasts CNN "quickly switched to the rubble of the World Trade Center" after showing images of the damage in Kandahar and the news anchor "reminded viewers of the deaths of as many as 5,000 people whose biggest crime was going to work and getting there on time".[50] So what was the biggest crime of Afghan children then? Appalling as CNN may be, this outrageous manipulation of news can be found all over the world. The *New York Times* reported that such policies were being implemented at other television networks. "In the United States television images of Afghan bombing victims are fleeting, cushioned between anchors or American officials explaining that such sights are only one side of the story", the *New York Times* said.[51] While the mainstream media spews out the official story of 9/11 those who question or expose it are virtually denied access. Investigator Mike Ruppert had his scheduled appearance on the Murdoch Fox channel cancelled at the last minute in May 2002. The *Geraldo Rivera* programme said that there was no time for him because the *New York Times* was breaking a story of newly intercepted communications from al-Qaeda that suggested another attack was imminent. Well how come they didn't intercept communications before 9/11 then? Of course the reason for the cancellation was that someone higher up said no. The same has happened to me when presenters and reporters have asked me to appear and then the invitation is withdrawn close to airtime accompanied by one of those "Er, um, er," stuttering "explanations" that insult the intelligence.

How does anyone believe the media is going to tell us the truth when the very forces that are desperate to deny us the truth own the press and broadcasting? The three major US television networks, CBS, NBC and ABC, are an excellent case in point. The giant Westinghouse owns CBS, and NBC is controlled by General Electric. These are both companies that make a fortune from wars and the Illuminati agenda as a whole. In 1996 Disney bought ABC. This has been an Illuminati operation since Mickey Mouse and is constantly named in relation to mind-control programmes (see *The Biggest Secret*). The "Watergate" journalist Carl Bernstein has written that hundreds of prominent US media owners and journalists have knowingly worked for the CIA, including William Paley of CBS, Arthur Sulzberger of the *New York Times*, Henry Luce of *Time-Life*, William Buckley of the *National Review*, and Ben Bradlee of the *Washington Post*.[52] Journalist Deborah Davis also reveals the CIA-media connection in her book, *Katherine the Great*, an investigation into the long-time publisher of the *Washington Post*, the late Katherine Graham.[53] The book was apparently "pulled from bookstores and pulped" after objections from Graham, but Davis took her publishers to court for censorship and won. It was republished with Sheridan Square Press in 1991.[54] Davis writes that by the 1950s the CIA "owned respected members of the *New York Times*, *Newsweek*, CBS, and other communications vehicles, plus at least four to six hundred reporters, according to a CIA analyst."[55] What must it be today? As Robert Lederman, a New York writer, artist and campaigner, put it: "The media is not influenced by the CIA – the media is the CIA."[56] A man behind this media takeover was Frank Wisner, who orchestrated Project Paperclip, the CIA operation that arranged for a long list of Nazis to escape from Germany at the end of the war to continue their work for the Illuminati in the United States, South America and elsewhere. If the media is telling you something it is because that is what the authorities want you to believe. As someone once said in a television drama: "A lie can go around the world before the truth has got its boots on." This is possible because of media owners like Katherine Graham, publisher of the *Washington Post* and a member of the Illuminati's Bilderberg Group, Council on Foreign Relations and Trilateral Commission. She said in a speech at CIA headquarters in 1988:

> "We live in a dirty and dangerous world. There are some things the general public does not need to know and shouldn't. I believe democracy flourishes when the government can take legitimate steps to keep its secrets, and when the press can decide whether to print what it knows." [57]

This is the mentality that is telling you what happened on September 11th, who was responsible, and what should happen as a result. These are also the people who are "reporting" the wars and giving you the government propaganda to justify them. Comforting, isn't it?

Bye, bye freedom

Across the world, the deaths of those 3,000 Americans and citizens of 80 nations have been used to promote the destruction of basic freedoms. Even when I was in New Zealand two months after 9/11 they were proposing new "anti-terrorism" laws to "protect the public". How on earth anyone in New Zealand is in any more danger now than they were on September 10th 2001 would defeat anyone with a modicum of intelligence. Enough to move your eyelids would be sufficient to see what a nonsense that is. But common sense is not the motivation here. The aim and the game is for the Illuminati to activate its operatives and unthinking stooges to use the excuse of the World Trade Center disaster to further imprison the human cattle. Gary Hart of the Council on Foreign Relations talked of "a continuing trade off between security and liberty and freedom going forward into the 21st century".[58] US Attorney General John Ashcroft set about his task with undisguised relish, and the dismantling of freedoms and the increase in government surveillance has been introduced with what the American Civil Liberties Union calls "dizzying speed".[59] Ashcroft and the Bush administration rushed through the "USA Patriot Act" in response to the 9/11 attacks and I have no doubt it was already drafted well before those planes took off from Boston airport. In fact James X. Dempsey and David Cole reveal in their book, *Terrorism and the Constitution: Sacrificing Civil Liberties in the Name of National Security*,[60] that the most extreme elements of the "anti-terrorism" laws introduced after Oklahoma and September 11th were developed "long before the bombings that triggered their final enactment." Dempsey is a former assistant counsel to the House Judiciary Subcommittee on Civil and Constitutional Rights, and Cole is a professor of law at Georgetown University and an attorney with the Center for Constitutional Rights. They document how it was the Reagan-Bush and Bush-Quayle administrations that first proposed some of the "most troubling provisions" that were to become law after Oklahoma and September 11th, but Congress had rejected them as unconstitutional. These included giving power to the Secretary of State to designate groups as terrorist organisations without judicial or congressional review. But then came the Oklahoma bombing and attitudes began to change as people like Senator Orrin Hatch from Mormon Utah aggressively supported the introduction of the Bush proposals. Hatch is the man who dismissed any suggestion that the authorities were responsible for Waco; who took money from Rumsfeld's Searle pharmaceuticals to support aspartame; who made stirring speeches in support of the BCCI; who called those who questioned the "anti-terrorism" laws after 9/11 as nothing more than "Senate egos"; who told the media immediately after the September 11th attacks that Osama bin Laden was the likely suspect. Nice man. "Senator Hatch wanted to make it more difficult for federal courts to order retrials of prisoners where state courts had violated the US Constitution", according to Dempsey and Cole. In the wake of Oklahoma the dismantling of basic freedoms first proposed by Father George Bush became law and even more so after September 11th. A coincidence? Not a chance.

As I mentioned earlier, whenever the Illuminati use words the real meaning is the very opposite of how they are presented. For example, the control of the world economy by a few global corporations owned by the same people is called "free trade" and a dictatorship is called a democracy or a "democratic front". In this case, removing the very freedoms on which the United States claims to have been founded is called an act of patriotism or a "USA Patriot Act", a term that derives from the very deliberate naming of the legislation as "Uniting and Strengthening America by Providing Appropriate Tools Required to Intercept and Obstruct Terrorism Act". The government demonises "patriots" and "patriotism" when the American Patriot movement challenges the tyranny of government and the global conspiracy, but "patriotism" is promoted when it means doing whatever the government tells you. This is an old, old, trick. Theodore Roosevelt defined patriotism in far more sensible and mature terms. He said:

> "Patriotism means to stand by the country. It does not mean to stand by the president or any other public official, save exactly to the degree in which he himself stands by the country. It is patriotic to support him insofar as he efficiently serves the country. It is unpatriotic not to oppose him to the exact extent that by inefficiently or otherwise he fails in his duty to stand by the country. In either event, it is unpatriotic not to tell the truth, whether about the president or anyone else."

As Samuel Johnson said: "Patriotism is the last refuge of the scoundrel." The Patriot Act, and other legislation and presidential decrees, have basically given those that control the American government the legal right to do whatever they like. Many of these new "laws" have been implemented through a scam introduced by the Boy George administration called the "emergency rule-making authority", which exempts the Attorney General from respecting the normal notice and comment period for such changes. Crucially for Americans, the definition of a terrorist in the Patriot Act is designed to apply to them also. The act defines terrorism as activities that "involve acts dangerous to human life that are a violation of the criminal laws of the United States or of any State; or appear to be intended 'to intimidate or coerce a civilian population' and "to influence the policy of a government by intimidation or coercion". That could be defined as almost anything, including legitimate peaceful protest. President Bush issued a "Military Order" on November 13th 2001 that makes legal the potentially indefinite detention of any "non-citizen" accused of terrorism, and permits the "trial" of such defendants by a secret military commission with no provision for judicial review.[61] The person can therefore be chosen by the President to go before a secret tribunal, which can "try", convict and sentence him, including imposing the death sentence, without making any of its evidence or the defence case available to the public. Indeed the public would not have to be told the tribunal had even happened. Christopher Pyle, Professor of Politics and Constitutional Law at Mount Holyoke College, says that military tribunals do not need to establish guilt beyond a reasonable doubt or even "a preponderance of evidence pointing to guilt". He adds: "The court just needs to convince the majority of the military officers present – all of whom see themselves as being 'at war' with this prisoner ... that he has been involved in a terrorist act." [62] This Presidential Order was issued without a formal Congressional declaration of war and without Congressional authorisation to use military tribunals. Professor Pyle said he has no idea how Bush even had the power to make such laws. "Where does the President get the right to do this?" he says. "He claims the right to do this as President, as commander in chief, pursuant to the resolution passed in Congress after the September 11th attacks and pursuant to several statutes in US code. But there's nothing in either the Congressional resolution or federal law that allows the President to override the legislative process." [63]

This fascist order from Bush for secret military "trials" applies to any individual the President claims to have "reason to believe" is: (a) a member of al-Qaeda; (b) in any way involved in "acts of international terrorism" (a term that is not defined by the order); or (c) has "knowingly harbored" either of the above. Administration officials have announced that they intend to use President Bush's "Military Order" in any case in which *they* decide that an open public hearing would not be consistent with the needs of security. Bush spokesmen say the order applies only to those accused of war crimes, but the jurisdiction of the order does not include any such restriction. [64] The order therefore gives a liar, crook and promoter of capital punishment like George W. Bush, and his successors, the right to ignore the United States criminal justice system whenever it suits him or the agenda he serves. Watch for these laws being extended to include US citizens when an excuse for that can be manufactured. Yet the vast majority of Americans stand by and watch this happen, even cheer in support while believing they live in the "freest country in the world". You have almost got to laugh. Almost. The following are some of the other powers included in the "Patriot Act" and related new laws that were introduced only because of the September 11th attacks. Much of the information is supplied by the American Civil Liberties Union. [65]

The Patriot Act allows federal agents to search a person's home secretly; monitor anyone's Internet browsing whenever they choose; expand wiretaps without any need for permission from a judge (not that this would be hard to get, to say the least); seize voicemail messages; and give secret grand jury testimony to the FBI and intelligence agencies. Law enforcement officers now have the legal right to share intercepts of telephone conversations and Internet communications with the CIA, National Security Agency, Department of Defense and other federal agencies with no court order required and there are, in effect, no restrictions on the subsequent use of recorded conversations. The Act does not prohibit the CIA and other agencies from sharing with foreign governments the surveillance information gleaned from a criminal investigation, even if this could put at risk a person's family living abroad. This information can include medical records, mental health records, financial records, video rental records, fingerprints, DNA samples from a person's hair, employment records, "employment-based" drug-testing records and immigration records maintained by non-profit agencies. Before this, FBI agents had to seek such permission from a judge or through a grand jury subpoena issued in connection with a criminal investigation. These safeguards are no longer necessary. They can do what they want.

Section 215 of the Patriot Act grants FBI agents authority to obtain an order from a "FISA" court or any federal magistrate requiring any person or business to produce any books, records, documents or items. FISA is the US Foreign Intelligence Surveillance Act of 1978 that was "updated" across the millennium to allow wiretaps of American residents who would otherwise be beyond the FBI's authority. Under the Patriot Act a judge has no discretion with these FBI requests. He or she must issue the order after receiving an FBI application that claims to be involved in a foreign intelligence investigation. It doesn't have to be true; they just have to say it. This means that the FBI can secretly conduct a physical search or wiretap to obtain "evidence of a crime" without proving the probable cause of a crime. All they need to do is claim "intelligence authority", even when the person whose home they wish to break into, or whose telephone they want to tap, is an American. Given the FBI's horrific and well-documented history of investigating people merely because of their race or political views, it is easy to see how these powers will be used. The *New York Times* also reported that Attorney General Ashcroft was considering a plan to relax restrictions on the FBI by giving them greater freedom to spy on religious and political organizations.[66] All these new laws make the FBI and the CIA, in effect, the same organisation – exactly what the Illuminati want in their agenda of centralisation and globalisation. The Patriot Act means that the CIA can now easily spy on American citizens, a role it has been forbidden to take, at least in law, since the Church Committee exposed appalling abuses of its surveillance of American citizens in the 1970s. But now the Patriot Act allows disclosure to the CIA of "foreign intelligence information" obtained in connection with a domestic criminal investigation, without defining "foreign intelligence information". This, says the American Civil Liberties Union, represents "extraordinary extensions of the previous powers of the foreign intelligence agencies, including the CIA, to obtain information about Americans".[67] All this will happen without a court order.

Ashcroft's Department of "Justice" can now monitor conversations between "suspects" and their lawyers (when they can get one). All "Justice" Department officials require is "reasonable suspicion" (and they decide what that means) to believe that a prisoner "may" use communications with attorneys or their agents "to further or facilitate acts of terrorism". The regulation requires that the Director of the Bureau of Prisons "shall … provide appropriate procedures for the monitoring or review of communications between that inmate and attorneys or attorneys' agents who are traditionally covered by the attorney-client privilege. This includes pre-trial detainees who have not been convicted of any crime and are therefore presumed innocent, and material witnesses and individuals who are being held on suspected immigration violations and are not accused of any crime.

Under the Patriot Act, financial institutions now monitor daily financial transactions even more closely than before and are required to share this information with federal agencies, including intelligence agencies like the CIA. These provisions go far beyond searching for terrorist funds or money laundering (like the Bush-connected BCCI) and involve snooping on perfectly innocent financial transactions by American citizens. Once again the "fight against terrorism" is being used to massively increase surveillance of the very population these new laws are supposed to be "protecting" from terrorism. Section 358 allows law enforcement and intelligence agencies to gain easy and secret access to credit reports. These agencies would not have to ask a judge for permission and the person involved would never know what had happened. It is another "do what you like" invasion of privacy, with the agencies having no requirement to justify their actions with evidence of a crime, suspicious activity, or even relevance to an investigation.

When it comes to the government being open to the same scrutiny, however, that's another story. Ashcroft has sought to undermine the American Freedom of Information Act with a change of policy that encourages federal agencies to resist Freedom of Information Act requests whenever they have legal grounds to do so. He has told them to withhold information whenever they could argue a "sound legal basis" for doing so. On one hand, they are introducing laws to gather more information about people while, on the other, seeking to prevent them knowing, under Freedom of Information, what is on government files.

"Homeland security" (homeland control)

The Patriot Act was claimed to be the result of two weeks of "closed-door negotiations" between Congress and the Bush administration. Bullshit. Congressman Ron Paul said they were not even allowed to read the Patriot Bill before they were asked to vote on it, and the "sunset clauses" that people were led to believe limited the period the laws are in force turn out not to apply to the most important areas that remove basic freedoms. The legislation, as always in these cases, was already drafted and waiting before those planes struck the World Trade Center. Coordinating this invasion of privacy and the vast expansion of surveillance under the guise of fighting terrorism is the Office of Homeland Security, more accurately known in my house as the Office of Homeland Control. It is amazing how often that, by swapping the word "security" for "control", you get the truth about an organisation or situation. In fact you can do this with all the Illuminati statements. Reverse them and you see what they really mean. The Office of Homeland Security – a classic Big Brother title – was created by Bush immediately "after" September 11th and is headed by the President's pal Tom Ridge, the former Governor of Pennsylvania. After he was elected Governor in 1993 he introduced new anti-crime laws, some of which were ruled unconstitutional.[68] Ridge campaigned for all juveniles to be tried as adults and for them to serve adult sentences in adult prisons. He reversed a three-to-one ratio of granting parole to a three-to-one ratio against.[69] Under Ridge's leadership, the state police were ordered to raid the headquarters of people preparing to protest at the 2000 Republican National Convention in Philadelphia. Some 500 people were arrested before they could protest and most were never convicted of any offence. Ridge and Bush both have the same approach to "law enforcement". Ridge presided over the first state execution in Pennsylvania since 1960 and then embarked on a policy of signing a stream of execution warrants, just as Bush did as Governor of Texas. It was Ridge who pressed for the legislation that introduced the "three-strikes law" and a faster death penalty process. The three-strikes law was a stunning piece of insane stupidity that mandated life prison sentences for anyone convicted of three felonies. This treats a murder as a "strike" in the same way as filling out a false driver's licence application. I can see why Bush chose Ridge to head "Homeland Security". Ridge's role is to create an ever more centralised pyramid of government agencies that will allow even fewer people to dictate the policy and actions of what are supposed to be "independent" organisations like the FBI and CIA. As Bush said when he announced the appointment of Ridge:

> "Today, dozens of federal departments and agencies, as well as state and local governments, have responsibilities affecting homeland security. These efforts must be coordinated at the highest level." [70]

In short, centralise and solidify the pyramid to ensure ever more control over ever more people by ever fewer. Dick Cheney appointed Admiral Steve Abbot as Ridge's number two. Abbot was Deputy Commander-in-Chief of the US European Command during the conflict in Kosovo and was Deputy Director of Operations for the Chairman of the Joint Chiefs of Staff (Colin Powell) at the end of the Father George Bush administration. In May 2001, four months before September 11th, Dick Cheney launched a review to "strengthen preparedness against an act of domestic terrorism, particularly one using a weapon of mass destruction".[71] Admiral Abbot was appointed to lead this Cheney group as Executive Director of the Vice President's National Preparedness Review. Abbot is a Rhodes Scholar. These are carefully chosen overseas students, like Bill Clinton, who are sent to England to study at Oxford University. These elite scholarships are named after Cecil Rhodes, one of the most infamous Illuminati operatives of the last 200 years (see *And The Truth Shall Set You Free* and *The Biggest Secret*). The Office of Homeland Security is dominated and controlled by the military through the Pentagon and it is the Illuminati goal to have domestic "law enforcement" conducted by the military, just as any fascist or communist state would do. Airport security is already controlled by the military because of 9/11 and that is designed to get the people used to having soldiers around calling the shots in public places. The military running the airports is just the start. As Timothy Edgar, a Legislative Counsel with the American Civil Liberties Union, says: "The military's mission is not to respect constitutional liberties. Its mission is to use overwhelming force to defeat and kill the enemy." [72] But then that's the idea. To the Illuminati and their henchmen like Bush, Cheney, et al., the people *are* the enemy. Herr Bush announced in April 2002 another strand in America's centralised fascist state. It is Northern Command, or NORTHCOM. This is headed by a four-star general and will "coordinate" with the Office of Homeland "Defense". The first head of NORTHCOM was widely predicted in the media to be

Ralph Eberhart, the head of NORAD and Space Command at Cheyenne Mountain, whose inaction on September 11th was a disgrace. NORTHCOM will coordinate "homeland defence" for North America and Mexico and this is the first time that Mexico comes under a Pentagon command as the global state continues to unfold. General Richard Myers, the head of the Joint Chiefs of Staff, said NORTHCOM would "streamline the Pentagon's various agencies and commands now assigned to support homeland defense roles, putting them under one commander." [73] Take away the Orwellian language and you are left with: "It will further centralise the military control of the United States."

Most sinister of all is the "Citizen Corps initiative", the Bush (Illuminati) plan to recruit a million workers as informants who will report any suspected "terrorist activity" among their colleagues, friends, and clients. These informants will be drawn from "truckers, letter carriers, train conductors, ship captains, utility employees and others". The American Civil Liberties Union said the Orwellian "Terrorist Information and Prevention System" (TIPS) threatened to turn local cable or gas or electrical technicians into government-sanctioned peeping toms. What was that I was saying about the masses policing each other? Now it's official. This is the whole thrust of the Illuminati agenda – to get the people to keep the people in line and act as a global intelligence gathering network in which no one will know who is a "friend" and who is a government spy. Like I say, they want a global version of Nazi Germany. Read George Orwell's book, 1984, if you want to now what they have planned.

Federal evil malevolent agency (FEMA)

One of the key organisations in the Illuminati armoury for their domestic dictatorship and homeland control in the United States is the Federal Emergency Management Agency, or FEMA. It is supposed to be there to respond to disasters and emergencies, but in truth that is only a tiny part of its operation, the part that is officially funded through government agencies. The real role of FEMA is the one financed covertly by the profits from the multi-billion-dollar Illuminati-intelligence agency drug racket. Former Green Beret William Tyree launched a lawsuit against the CIA and Father George Bush in September 1998 claiming that they had allowed the drug profits to fund FEMA's covert activities without the knowledge of Congress.[74] FEMA was created through a presidential Executive Order, an undemocratic, dictatorial outrage, in which the President introduces laws without debate in Congress. An Executive Order issued by the President only has to appear in a legal newspaper called the *Federal Register* to become law, and great swathes of the Illuminati's fascist-state-in-waiting has been put together in this way. Among the founders of FEMA was Zbigniew Brzezinski, the man behind the Trilateral Commission at the behest of David Rockefeller. Brzezinski predicted years ago in his book *Between Two Ages*,[75] that a tiny elite would use its political and financial power and surveillance technology to control the population and dominate the masses. He could say that with confidence because he knew what was planned.

Another famous name involved with FEMA was Oliver North, the drug-running gofer from Iran-Contra. Ben Bradlee Jr writes in *Guts and Glory: The Rise and Fall of Oliver North*[76] that the Iran-Contra "star" helped FEMA to stage a national emergency rehearsal in April 1984 known as Rex-84 Bravo. This was a practice exercise in readiness for martial law and a FEMA takeover in the event of a "national emergency". The *Miami Herald* reported in 1987 that North was involved with FEMA in exercises involving the rounding-up of refugees and "troublemakers". Former Green Beret Colonel Albert Carone, who was murdered in 1990, said in a sworn statement for the William Tyree lawsuit that he worked with North in CIA-Mafia drug operations and he also confirmed North's use of drug profits to create and fund FEMA. He said that FEMA violated the United States Constitution and "established a succession to the Office of the President in the event of an emergency that circumvented the Vice President and the Speaker of the House of Representatives".[77] Colonel Carone added: "Colonel Ollie North worked on developing a plan known as FEMA, which would in an ill-defined national emergency, allow the US Military to take control of the United States to ensure National Security." According to Carone's statement, the term "FEMA" originally meant "Federal Emergency Military Action", but was renamed "Management Agency" because the public would more easily accept it. Carone said that a National Security Council directive issued in 1981 states: "Normally a state of martial law will be proclaimed by the President. However in the absence of such action by the President, a senior military commander may impose martial law in an area of his command where there had been a complete breakdown in the exercise of government functions by local authorities." That directive, which allows a military takeover inside the borders of the United States, was signed by … Frank Carlucci, now chairman of the Carlyle Group.

FEMA and associated agencies have been given sweeping powers by presidential executive orders to take control of all areas of life during a "national emergency" – whenever the Illuminati front men in government decide to invoke them. In such circumstances FEMA can force the population to live and work wherever they are told. People can be moved from their homes and have their property seized, including farms and businesses. Their children can be taken away from them and FEMA has the power to take over all communications, food and energy sources, health care, finance, education, welfare and transportation, including your personal vehicles. The Postmaster General can order that all men, women and children are registered.[78] It is also FEMA that controls the network of concentration camps, or "detention centers", in the United States that are in place and waiting for the dissidents and "troublemakers" when the Illuminati fascist takeover is complete. Yes, concentration camps in America, of which more later.

Foreigners today, Americans tomorrow

By observing the treatment of foreign nationals since September 11th we can see the future for Americans in their own land and for the rest of the world also. The authorities have been detaining people across America without charge or trial on no grounds whatsoever except for the colour of their skin and country of origin. Some cases have come to light, but most have not. Anser Mehmood, a Pakistani truck driver in New Jersey, was allowed no contact with his family for three months after he was arrested without charge in early October 2001. His wife and four children were forced to sell virtually every possession because they no longer had any income and were heading back to Karachi simply to survive while their husband and father awaits his fate. Mohammed Rafiq Butt, another man detailed, died of heart failure at the Hudson County Jail in Kearny, New Jersey, on October 23rd.[79] The *Washington Post* reported how two Pakistani immigrants were held for 49 days before being charged with overstaying their visas and an Israeli was held for 66 days before being charged with entering the country illegally.[80] A Saudi national Dr Al Bader Al-Hazmi, a radiologist at the Texas Health Science Center, was held without access to either his lawyer or his family for seven days. After nearly two weeks in detention, Dr Al-Hazmi was released with no charges against him. The *Wall Street Journal* featured the case of Tarek Mohamed Fayad, an Egyptian national and a dentist in California. He was detained by the FBI on September 13th and transferred to the Brooklyn Detention Center in New York City. The *Journal* said it was a month before his lawyer was able to locate and talk to him.[81] Some seven months after 9/11 Judge Shira Scheindlin ruled that a Jordanian student had been "unlawfully detained" by Ashcroft's Injustice Department because, like so many, he had been jailed purely to ensure that he gives evidence to a grand jury. The judge said that "… since 1789, no Congress had granted the government the authority to imprison an innocent person in order to guarantee that he will testify before a grand jury conducting a criminal investigation".[82] Ashcroft, of course, said he would appeal. Not to me he doesn't. We don't know how many innocent people have been detained in America without trial or charge since 9/11 because Ashcroft's operation has refused to say how many have been jailed without charge or trial, and on what basis. The public have no idea who they are, where they are or in what conditions they are being kept. A look at the disgraceful, inhuman, treatment of the uncharged, untried, inmates at the US military base at "Camp X-Ray" at Guantanamo Bay in Cuba, however, will probably give you a fair idea of the indignity to which they are subjected. As Groucho Marx said: "Military justice is to justice what military music is to music." This is America, the "Land of the Free"? What an illusion. All this when members of the bin Laden family were allowed to leave Boston Airport for Saudi Arabia just days after 9/11 with no problem at all because of their friends in high places like President Bush.

Britain's fascist state rolls on

In Britain, the Blair government and his "socialist" Home Secretary David Blunkett have also been sweeping away still more freedoms and civil liberties. Blunkett, the one-time "left-wing radical" on Sheffield council, is now just another cap-touching establishment puppet. How the mighty fall. Following the Illuminati script after 9/11, the Blair government now allows foreign-born "terrorist suspects" to be detained without trial, a move described by the civil rights group Liberty as "a fundamental violation of the rule of law".[83] Internment without trial breaches the

European Convention on Human Rights and this can only be overridden if a state of emergency is declared. So what did Blair and Blunkett do? They declared a state of emergency, thus bypassing Article 5 of the Convention. The UK has jailed "terrorist suspects" on no evidence whatsoever. Lotfi Raissi, a 27-year-old Algerian pilot, was arrested days after September 11th and accused by the FBI – yes, them again – of training pilots involved in the attacks. He was jailed by the British authorities in a high-security prison for five months while extradition proceedings took place to hand him over to the American government. But on February 12th 2002, a judge released him because the FBI had produced nothing to back up its ludicrous claims. The FBI said he was an Islamic fundamentalist when he is married to a white Roman Catholic! His wife and brother lost their jobs because of this criminal injustice and his brother Mohammed said: "They've destroyed his life, his future and his dream." [84] But rather than accept they were wrong, apologise and pay him compensation, the American government announced that they would still continue to pursue his extradition on two counts of falsifying an application for a United States pilot's licence. One of these involves failing to declare an old tennis injury! My God, these are the people "investigating" 9/11 and telling us what happened. Fortunately a judge later dismissed the US claims, and Raissi and his family were left to pick up the pieces of their shattered lives.

Tony Blair has long targeted civil liberties. He has sought to reduce the number of trials for UK citizens that are heard by a jury, and laws were passed long before 9/11 to erode rights to data privacy and other freedoms. Blair is an Illuminati gofer. They put him in power and they have kept him there, so obviously you would expect him to slavishly pursue their agenda, as he has on every front. New "anti-terrorist" laws mean that telecommunications companies are instructed, under the guise of "national security", to keep data on phone calls, faxes and e-mails. Britain already has more surveillance cameras per head of population than anywhere else in the world and I saw one school featured in a BBC children's television documentary that had installed nearly 40 cameras and the children couldn't move without being followed on a TV screen. All this is ensuring that children grow up surrounded by surveillance and accept the Big Brother society as part of everyday life. New laws have increased the rights of government agencies to spy on the population's financial transactions and freeze "suspected" terrorist funds. Who decides who is "suspected"? They do of course.

Freedom, R.I.P

Nine months after September 11th it emerged that the Blair government was planning devastating advances in the Big Brother fascist state through something called the Regulation of Investigatory Powers, or R.I.P, Act. The *Guardian* newspaper revealed that ministers proposed to dramatically expand the number of people and organisations who could demand to be given personal data on the population. The police, intelligence services, Customs & Excise and the Inland Revenue already had these powers, but the Blair government planned to increase the list to include seven government departments, every local council in the country, any fire authority, the

National Health Service in Scotland and Northern Ireland, and 11 other public bodies. These organisations would be able to demand, without a court order, that phone companies, Internet service providers and postal operators give them details of a person's phone calls, the source and destination of e-mails, the identity of websites they have visited and the location of their mobile phones, which would reveal the location of the user to within a few hundred yards.[85] The government said these expanded powers were needed to "fight terrorism". Clearly this is an outrageous lie. John Wadham, director of the human rights organisation, Liberty, said: "This list demonstrates an issue that many people may not have realised: it is not just the police who will be looking at our communications records, it is practically every public servant who will be able to play this game." [86] Ian Brown, director of the Foundation for Information Policy Research, said he was appalled at "this huge increase in the scope of government snooping" and how these powers were being handed to "a practically endless queue of bureaucrats in Whitehall and town halls".[87] Simon Davies, director of Privacy International, said:

> "The Home Office has absolutely breached its commitment that this law would not become a general surveillance power for the government. The exhaustive list of organisations who will be able to access data without a court order proves that this amounts to a systematic attack on the right to privacy." [88]

The laws have fundamental implications for journalists and Internet users and servers. Steve Rawlinson, Chief Technical Officer of Claranet, said it dealt with a lot of requests from the police for private information, but many of these were a "fishing expedition" and they told the police they were not satisfied there were sufficient grounds. The new laws meant they would have no choice but to hand over private data. Journalists complained that they would no longer be able to keep their sources private, but most of them should have thought of that when they were ridiculing those who were telling them this was coming. Maybe they will now wake up to the fact that the fascist conspiracy they have been ridiculing and claiming does not exist is targeting them and their children as much as anyone else. Home Secretary David Blunkett had the nerve to propose these new laws after pledging in the wake of September 11th that he would not give anyone the power to routinely monitor phone calls or e-mails between individuals. In the summer of 2002 Blunkett also announced laws that force airlines to provide the government with details of every passenger they check-in on an international flight, including the name, address and passport number. The airlines said this would create chaos and massively increase the queues for check-in. But why should Blunkett and company care? While the people are queuing, they'll be in the VIP lounge.

"Airy fairy" freedoms

The response of the Ashcrofts and Blunketts to legitimate concerns about the loss of basic freedoms has been depressingly predictable. It's an old, old, technique: don't address the concerns in an adult way as part of your duty as a public servant – seek to discredit those who question and challenge your role as a public dictator. Blunkett called the concerns of civil rights campaigners "airy fairy" and, employing the usual technique of painting a polarised picture of black vs white, he said in a television interview on London Weekend Television: "We could live in a world which is airy fairy, libertarian, where everybody does precisely what they like and we believe the best of everybody and then they destroy us." [89] That, of course, is not what freedom campaigners are suggesting, and Blunkett knows it. But he says that simply to discredit those who challenge his decisions and to present a false picture of the situation to the public. The UK Foreign Secretary Jack "straw man" Straw, a man I would not trust to run a market stall, said that "naïve" campaigners against stronger Internet surveillance laws have hurt the anti-terrorism campaign. If you don't support what we demand and accept without question the erosion of your own freedoms, you are helping terrorists. Straw also sought to justify the dismantling of freedom when he told the media: "The most fundamental civil liberty is the right to life and preserving that and sustaining that must come before others." [90] This is the same Straw who was a vehement supporter of the bombing of Afghanistan that killed thousands more civilians than the attacks in America. Brain-cell activity never was an essential criteria for being a politician, in fact it can be a serious handicap to career advancement. Then there was one Kevin Hughes, a member of Blair's Labour Party, who said during the steam-rollered parliamentary "debate" on the anti-terrorism laws that opponents of the plan were from the ... "yoghurt-eating, muesli-eating, *Guardian*-reading, sandal-wearing fraternity".[91] What a prat. In the US, of course, Attorney General Ashcroft takes the same line. When challenged on his attacks on basic freedoms, he told the Senate Judiciary Committee:

> "To those who pit Americans against immigrants, citizens against non-citizens, to those who scare peace-loving people with phantoms of lost liberty, my message is this: Your tactics only aid terrorists for they erode our national unity and diminish our resolve ... They give ammunition to America's enemies and pause to America's friends. They encourage people of good will to remain silent in the face of evil." [92]

More black is white, more smoke and mirrors. Orrin Hatch, the aspartame supporter and senator for the Illuminati Mormon stronghold of Utah, told his colleagues on the committee that criticism of White House plans was nothing more than "Senate egos". He said: "I would implore my colleagues, let's keep our focus where it matters: on protecting our citizens." [93] Yeah, yeah, OK, Orrin, you've done your job and I'm sure they will be very pleased with you. Senator Russell Feingold was the lone vote in the Senate against this silent invasion by federal and state dictatorship. He provided confirmation that at least some common sense and principle still survives – just, only just – in Washington. He said:

> "If we lived in a country that allowed the police to search your home at any time for any reason, if we lived in a country that allowed the government to open your mail, eavesdrop

on phone conversations, intercept your e-mail communications, hold people in jail indefinitely on suspicion that they were up to no good, then the government would no doubt discover and arrest more terrorists. But that would probably not be a country in which we would want to live. That would not be a country in which we could, in good conscience, ask our young people to die for. In short, that country wouldn't be America." [94]

Such voices of sanity are so few. In the US Congress, the British Parliament, and their like across the world, fundamental attacks on freedom went through with hardly a murmur of serious challenge from politicians or public – all thanks to 9/11. Coincidence?

Bush hides daddy's secrets ... and his own

But get this: while the Bush government was issuing an explosion of new laws and directives to gather ever more information about the population and impose ever greater surveillance, he took time out on November 1st 2001 to issue an Executive Order that gives Bush and former presidents (like his father) the right to veto requests to open any presidential records. Even if a former president wants his records to be released, the Executive Order permits President Bush or any sitting president to assert executive privilege to stop this, and Boy George and former presidents are now given an indefinite amount of time to ponder any requests. This is a blatant move to hide the grotesque secrets of his father, other presidents and himself, particularly, in his case, in relation to 9/11. How coincidental, too, that this was invoked just as records of the Reagan-Bush administration were due for release under the Presidential Records Act, a post-Watergate law intended to ensure the release of administration records 12 years after a president leaves office. [95]

So who benefits?

What happened on September 11th was the most glaring and obvious example I have seen of the technique I have dubbed problem-reaction-solution. 9/11 had every element in enormous abundance. First you covertly create the problem and immediately name the person or people "responsible" to divert attention from any open-minded speculation or questioning about who was really behind it. Second, you report the problem through the media in the form that you wish the public to believe. Third, you offer the solution to your problem amid the manipulated public clamour for you to "do something". The atrocities in America, and their aftermath, have provided an excuse for an open-ended problem-reaction-solution in the form of the "war on terrorism". How can you tell when you have won a war on terrorism? You can't. They have launched a war without end in which they can attack any country or target they can demonise as either "terrorists" or "supporters of terrorists". That was the idea. As British Prime Minister Tony Blair said immediately after September 11th:

> "This is a moment to seize. The kaleidoscope has been shaken, the pieces are in flux, soon they will settle again. Before they do, let us reorder this world around us."

And on September 12th, at a televised event organised by the Rockefeller-Illuminati Council on Foreign Relations, the former presidential candidate Gary Hart said:

"There is a chance for the President of the United States to use this disaster to carry out … a phrase his father used … and that is a New World Order."

That phrase was delivered in a speech by Father George in relation to the Gulf "War" on September 11th 1990 – 11 years to the day before 9/11. As I said in the opening chapter, the antidote to P-R-S is the question: "Who benefits?" This always reveals the force behind the "problem". Who benefits from 9/11? One group and one group alone – anyone who wants a massive increase in surveillance and control of the people, individually and collectively; the further centralisation of global power; a systematic destruction of basic freedoms and civil liberties; an excuse to invade, devastate and take over any country they choose to target; and a fantastic increase in public spending on the military for operations at home and aboard. Whoever was behind 9/11 has achieved all of these aims and so much more. Who wants such a society? The Illuminati and their agents in government, as I have been exposing for more than a decade. They want centralisation of power in all areas of our lives until the world government, central bank, currency, army, police force, intelligence agency, and micro-chipped population are in place. They want an excuse to send their armies into any country whose regime is not playing ball, or whose land and resources they desire to control. One event has given them all of these things since September 11th 2001. Are we really to believe that those two facts are not connected, that all this is all mere "coincidence"? Are we really?

I was interviewed on a Los Angeles radio station in the days after 9/11 by a couple of hosts who were not the sharpest pins in the box to say the least. I said that the attacks had been organised within their own borders by Illuminati groups that control the federal government and the military, and that they would soon see new laws introduced by that same federal government that would remove fundamental freedoms from American society. The idea that agencies of the United States government could have been involved in the attacks against American people was more than their neuron pathways could process and the hosts decided that I must either be "mad" or "on something". So I made them an offer to come back on the show a month later and I said that if massive erosions of freedom had not occurred in America by then I would hold my hand up and say I was wrong. They said OK, it was a deal; they would call me in a month. The erosions of freedom duly took place.

They never called.

SOURCES

1   *Boston Globe*, September 23rd 2001 **http://www.boston.com/news/packages/ underattack/news/planes_reconstruction.htm#aa11**

2   **http://professor2222.tripod.com/Flight-93/Flight93.htm**

3   NORAD website: **http://www.spacecom.af.mil/norad**

4   *Boston Globe*, September 23rd 2001

5   **http://professor2222.tripod.com/Flight-93/Flight93.htm**

6   *Boston Globe*, September 23rd 2001

7   Ibid

8   Ibid

9   Ibid

10   **http://www.flightexplorer.com/** and **http://www.flightexplorer.com/FastTrack.asp**

11   **http://www.usatoday.com/graphics/news/gra/gflightpath2/frame.htm**

12   See alleged transcript of air traffic communications with Flight 77 in *Appendix 3*

13   *Washington Post*, September 12th 2001

14   Ibid

15   *Boston Globe*, September 23rd 2001

16   Ibid

17   **http://timesargus.nybor.com/Story/33577.html** reporting the original story in the Boston **Globehttp://timesargus.nybor.com/Story/33577.html**

18   Ibid

19   Ibid

20   Ibid

21   Ibid

22   Ibid

23   *The Orlando Sentinel*, September 11th 2001 **http://www.dominionpost.com/af/terrorstrikesus/2001/09/11/0w**

24   Ibid

25   Ibid

26   Ibid

27   **http://hometown.aol.com/estrellaberosin/page1Analysis911Facts.html**

28   **http://www.cnn.com/ALLPOLITICS/time/2001/10/01/bush.family.html**

29   When Our World Changed Forever, *Observer*, September 16th 2001

30   Ibid

31   Ibid

32   http://www.dal.net/wtc/victims.html

33   Bush Says No to New Taliban Offer for Talks, *Los Angeles Times*, October 15th 2001

34   US Department of State Office of the Spokesman, September 12th 2001, Washington, DC, on-the-record Briefing by Secretary of State Colin L. Powell

35   Musharraf Easily Wins Five More Years, *International Herald Tribune*, May 3rd 2002, p 3, quoting Associated Press

36   The *Chronicle Review*, September 28th 2001,
      http://chronicle.com/free/v48/i05/05b00701.htm

37   Associated Press, February 4th 2002

38   **http://www.observer.co.uk/Print/0,3858,4258258,00.htm**

39   Ibid

40   BBC News Online, January 3rd 2002

41   Ibid

42   Global Exchange press release, January 9th 2002,
      http://www.globalexchange.org/september11/gx010902.html

43   Catherine Philip, *Weekend Australian*, November 3rd-4th 2001

44   UK *Independent*, November 3rd 2001

45   **http://www.globalpeaceandjustice.org/nws/afg11-03a.htm**

46   FAIR (Fairness & Accuracy In Reporting), 112 W. 27th Street, New York, NY 10001

47   *Washington Post*, October 31st, 2001

48   Ibid

49   Fairness and Accuracy In Reporting, November 1st 2001
      http://www.fair.org/activism/cnn-casualties.html

50   *New York Times*, November 1st 2001

51   Ibid

52   The CIA and the Media, *Rolling Stone*, October 20th 1977

53   Deborah Davis, *Katherine the Great: Katherine Graham and her Washington Post Empire* (republished by Sheridan Square Press in 1991)

54   **http://www.afn.org/~iguana/archives/2001_07/20010710.html**
      All Fall Down, p 160. See also John M. Crewdson and Joseph B. Treaster, The CIA's 3-Decade Effort to Mold the World's Views, *New York Times*, December 25th 1977, pp 1, 12; Terrence Smith, CIA Contacts With Reporters, *New York Times*, p 13; Crewdson and Treaster, Worldwide Propaganda Network Built by the CIA, *New York Times*, December 26th 1977, pp 1, 37; Crewdson and Treaster, CIA Established Many Links to Journalists in US and Abroad, *New York Times*, December 27th 1977, pp 1, 40–41.

55   **http://www.baltech.org/lederman/915apology.html**

56   Daniel Brandt, Journalism and the CIA: The Mighty Wurlitzer, Public Information Research, Namebase Newsline, April – June 1997,
      http://www.geocities.com/CapitolHill/8425/CIAPRESS.HTM

57   *9/11 – The Road To Tyranny*

This "world" is only an illusion and we can change it any time we want. It's just a choice right now between fear and love.

58 American Civil Liberties Union, **http://www.aclu.org**

59 James X. Dempsey and David Cole, *Terrorism and the Constitution: Sacrificing Civil Liberties in the Name of National Security*, available from the First Amendment Foundation, 3321-12th St NE

60 Washington DC 20017

61 **http://www.aclu.org**

62 Ibid

63 Ibid

64 Ibid

65 Ibid

66 *New York Times*, December 1st 2001

67 **http://www.aclu.org**

68 **http://www.guerrillanews.com/civil_liberties/doc172.html**

69 **Ibidhttp://www.guerrillanews.com/civil_liberties/doc172.html**

70 **http://www.whitehouse.gov/news/releases/2001/09/20010920-8.html**

71 White House press release, Office of the Press Secretary, October 29th 2001

72 ACLU press release, February 6th 2002

73 **http://ww2.pstripes.osd.mil/02/apr02/command.pdf**

74 *All Fall Down*, p. 166 and **http://www.nexusmagazine.com/beast1.html**

75 Zbigniew Brzezinski, *Between Two Ages: America's Role in the Technetronic Era* (The Viking Press, 1970)

76 Ben Bradlee Jr, *Guts and Glory: The Rise and Fall of Oliver North* (Donald I. Fine Inc., 1988)

77 I. Case No. 98CV11829JLT United States District Court – Boston Tyree vs Bush, CIA, Celluci, Harshbarger et al., **http://www.radio4all.org/crackcia/tyree.html**

78 **http://www.mt.net/~watcher/fema.html**

79 The Disappeared, by Andrew Gumbel, UK *Independent*, February 26th 2002. See **http://www.commondreams.org/views02/0226-08.htm**

80 **http://www.aclu.org/news/2002/w011502a.html**

81 **http://www.commondreams.org/views02/0226-08.htm**

82 US Detention Tactic Is Illegal, Court Rules, *International Herald Tribune*, May 3rd 2001, p 3, quoting a report in *The Washington Post*

83 *Guardian*, November 12th 2001

84 **http://news.bbc.co.uk/hi/english/uk/england/newsid_1815000/1815903.stm**

85 *Guardian*, June 11th 2002

86 Ibid

87 Ibid

88 Ibid

89 UK to Detain Terrorism Suspects Without Trial, Reuters, November 12th 2001

90 Net Freedom Fears 'Hurt Terror Fight', BBC News Online, September 28th 2001
    http://news.bbc.co.uk/hi/english/uk_politics/newsid_1568000/1568254.stm

91 Britain: Parliament Overwhelmingly Approves Anti-Terrorism Bill, by Chris Marsden
    and Julie Hyland, November 23rd 2001, World Socialist Website,
    http://www.wsws.org/articles/2001/nov2001/bill-n23.shtml

92 **http://www.cnn.com/2001/US/12/06/inv.ashcroft.hearing**

93 Ibid

94 Senate speech, October 11th 2001,
    http://feingold.senate.gov/releases/01/10/101101at.html

95 *USA Today*, November 11th 2001

chapter 8

House of cards

"Let us never tolerate outrageous conspiracy theories concerning the attacks of September the 11th."

George W. Bush

The official story of what happened on that horrific day in the autumn of 2001 is an obvious and transparent fantasy, and the atrocities of September 11th were yet another version of Oklahoma and Pearl Harbor.

All of these attacks (and so, so, many more) were not only *made* to happen they were *allowed* to happen and this is the combination you see in all these Illuminati stings. They arrange for their agents in government, the intelligence network, the military, and terrorist groups to execute the plan. At the same time they ensure that the plan is allowed to happened through lax security, and that those who are truly responsible are never named, let alone caught. Ideally you want both the execution of the plan and the "failed security" to involve the same organisation because that provides optimum efficiency and potential for cover-up. So, often, you find that the perpetrators and those protecting the perpetrators are actually the *same* people. The evidence is clear that the attacks of September 11th were allowed to happen. Colonel Leroy Fletcher Prouty spent a long career in the US Air Force and special operations in which he was heavily involved with the CIA, then led by its notorious first director Allen Dulles. Prouty later wrote and lectured about some of these clandestine operations and authored the book, *JFK, The CIA, Vietnam And The Plot To Assassinate John F. Kennedy*.[1] The Donald Sutherland character called "X" in the Oliver Stone movie *JFK* was apparently based to an extent on Prouty. This guy operated for decades in the shadowy world from which came the real orchestrators of 9/11. Fletcher Prouty said:

> "No one has to direct an assassination – it happens. The active role is played secretly by permitting it to happen. This is the greatest single clue. Who has the power to call off or reduce the usual security precautions?" [2]

If you look at the evidence detailed in books by myself and others, Fletcher Prouty's words are true in the assassinations of John F. Kennedy, his brother Bobby,

Martin Luther King, Princess Diana, Israeli Prime Minister Yitzhak Rabin, Swedish Prime Minister Olaf Palme … the list could go on for pages. The same is also true of September 11th.

NORAD and Cheyenne Mountain

The organisation charged with the task of protecting North American airspace in both the United States and Canada is NORAD, the North American Areospace Defense Command, headquartered at the Peterson Air Force Base in Colorado with its operational centre in the nearby Rocky Mountains. This was the organisation that did nothing to prevent the attacks while all hell was happening in the skies over America on September 11th , and it is important to look in some depth at its background and capabilities. NORAD was created by an agreement signed by the US and Canadian governments on May 12th 1958. NORAD's brief, to quote its own website, involves:

> "… the monitoring of man-made objects in space, and the detection, validation, and warning of attack against North America whether by aircraft, missiles, or space vehicles, utilizing mutual support arrangements with other commands. Aerospace control includes ensuring air sovereignty and air defense of the airspace of Canada and the United States." [3]

NORAD has an agreement with the civilian Federal Aviation Administration (FAA) to respond to civil aviation emergencies when commercial aircraft are hijacked, lose contact with air traffic controllers, or stray off-course. What happened on 9/11, therefore, was exactly what NORAD is there to deal with. The President of the United States and the Prime Minister of Canada officially appoint NORAD's commander. This means, of course, that the President of the United States appoints him. Again quoting the NORAD website: "Cheyenne Mountain serves as a central collection and coordination facility for a worldwide system of sensors designed to provide … the leadership of Canada and the US with an accurate picture of any aerospace threat." [4] Ah yes, Cheyenne Mountain. It was not long into my research of the global conspiracy in 1992 that I first came across Cheyenne Mountain in Colorado. There have been many mysterious animal mutilations in that area, including some at the nearby Cheyenne Mountain Zoo, and researchers into "UFO" activity have long had their eyes on the Cheyenne Mountain complex. What we do know for sure is that this is the vast super-secret headquarters for the "defence" of North America and was the early warning and response centre during the (manufactured) "Cold War" with the Soviet Union. It is also the location of so much more that we are not told about.

The complex is mounted on more than 1,300 half-ton springs that allow it to sway up to a foot horizontally in any direction should it be struck by an earthquake or nuclear attack. The two main doors consist of 25 tons of baffled steel, three feet thick, and the complex is located 2,000 feet inside the granite mountain. In the same region are other major military and technology centres like Ent Air Force Base, Fort

Carson Army Base, Peterson Airfield, Lowry Air Force bombing range, the US Air Force Academy, the Buckley Air National Guard and Naval Air Station, and the Rocky Mountain Arsenal. A Scripps Howard News Service survey reported in 1998 that about 7,000 people were employed within Cheyenne Mountain and that spending on the facility was substantially increased by the best part of $2 billion after the "Cold War" was over.[5] This would seem to be a strange contradiction if you didn't know that the massive network of underground bases and the tunnel systems that connect them across the United States are not there primarily to protect the population at all. Their role is to control the population. Inside Cheyenne Mountain are some of the most brilliant technological minds in the world using and developing technology that is light years ahead of anything you will see in the public arena. It is a big mistake to judge what is possible only on the basis of technology you know about. These guys aren't working with that.

The following information comes from the official Cheyenne Mountain website[6] and represents only a fraction of what really goes on there. The excavation of Cheyenne Mountain near Colorado Springs began in May 1961 and was completed in around a year, according to the official story. The NORAD command centre was located here and became fully operational on April 20th 1966 when its duties were transferred from Ent Air Force Base, also in Colorado. NORAD has since been joined inside Cheyenne Mountain by other "early warning and response" organisations with the responsibility for defending North America from air attack. One is the Air Force Space Command that is supposed to provide protection from space and missile attack, and this operates the Space Defense Operations Center. Personnel at the Space Defense Operations Center and "their worldwide sensors, under the direction of Air Defense Command", supported the first flight of the space shuttle in April 1981.[7] Cheyenne Mountain has continued to support every shuttle mission since. General Ralph E. Eberhart, the commander of NORAD at the time of 9/11, was also commander of Space Command and he took over on February 18th 2000 from General Richard B. Myers who became Deputy Chairman of the Joint Chiefs of Staff at the Pentagon, and Chairman immediately after 9/11. Eberhart and Myers also both served at the "CIA" Air Force Base at Langley, Virginia, from where, it is claimed, jets were scrambled (far too late) to intercept Flight 77 as it headed for Washington. Eberhart was Commander, Air Combat Command, from June 1999 to February 2000 when he replaced Myers at NORAD. More about Myers' behaviour on September 11th in due course. I am going to detail at some length the capabilities of the Cheyenne Mountain complex for reasons that will become very clear. This is what its official website says about the NORAD operations today, and the information is highly revealing in the light of the events – or non-events – of September 11th:

"The Air Defense Operations Center uses its air defense network to provide surveillance and control of air operations to North America and unknown traffic. Today the NORAD Combat Operations Center has evolved into the Cheyenne Mountain Operations Center that collects data from a worldwide system of satellites, radars, and other sensors and processes that information on sophisticated computer systems to support critical NORAD and US Space Command missions. The Cheyenne Mountain Operations Center provides warning of ballistic missile or air attacks against North America, assists the air sovereignty mission for the United States and Canada, and, if necessary, is the focal point for air defense operations to counter enemy bombers or cruise missiles.

"In support of the US Space Command mission, the Cheyenne Mountain Operations Center provides a day-to-day picture of precisely what is in space and where it is located. The Cheyenne Mountain Operations Center also supports space operations, providing critical information such as collision avoidance data for space shuttle flights and troubleshooting satellite interference problems. Since the Persian Gulf War, the Cheyenne Mountain Operations Center has continued to play a vital and expanding role in supporting our deployed forces with warning for short-range ballistic missiles such as the Iraqi Scuds. Cheyenne Mountain operations are conducted by six centers manned 24 hours a day, 365 days a year. The centers are: Command Center, Air Defense Operations Center, Missile Warning Center, Space Control Center, Combined Intelligence Watch Center, and the Systems Center."

And it goes on:

"The Command Center is the heart of operations in Cheyenne Mountain. In this center, the Command Director and his crew serve as the NORAD and US Space Command Commander in Chief's direct representatives for monitoring, processing, and interpreting missile, space or air events which could have operational impacts on our forces or capabilities, or could be potential threats to North America or US and allied forces overseas. The Command Center is linked directly to the National Command Authorities of both the US and Canada as well as to regional command centers overseas. When required, the Command Director must consult directly with the NORAD and US Space Command Commander in Chief for time-critical assessments of missile, air, and space events; he takes action to ensure the Commander in Chief's response and direction are properly conveyed and executed ...

"... The Air Defense Operations Center provides command and control for the air surveillance and air defense network for North America. In 1994, they monitored over 700 'unknown' radar tracks entering North American airspace. Many of these were subsequently identified as friendly aircraft that had erred from flight plans or used improper procedures. Yet nearly 100 were identified as illegal drug-carrying aircraft that were subsequently prosecuted by the US and Canadian Drug Enforcement Agencies." [8]

The technology located within Cheyenne Mountain is the state of the state of the state of the art. Its website explains how the Missile Warning Center employs a "worldwide sensor and communications network to provide warning of missile attacks, either long or short range, launched against North America or our forces overseas". So much so that its technology provides information "regarding missile launches anywhere on earth which are detected by the strategic missile warning system and which could be a potential threat to Canada or the US". The Space Control Center at Cheyenne Mountain, opened in March 1994, has the highly sophisticated technology that "supports the space control missions of space surveillance and protection of our assets in space" and its primary objective is to perform "the surveillance mission … to detect, track, identify, and catalog all man-made objects in space". The Center has a computerised catalogue of "all orbiting space objects, charts objects, charts present position, plots future orbital paths, and forecasts times and general locations for significant objects re-entering the Earth's atmosphere." The website tells us that the Space Control Center is currently tracking some 8,000 "on-orbit objects", and this information is used to provide NASA with collision avoidance information during space flights. Cheyenne Mountain is also home to the Combined Intelligence Watch, which serves as North America's "indications and warning center for worldwide threats from space, missile, and strategic air activity, as well as geopolitical unrest that could affect North America and US forces/interests abroad".[9] Put another way, they have a satellite surveillance network that could read your licence plate from space wherever you may be. The Combined Intelligence Watch "gathers intelligence information to assist all the Cheyenne Mountain work centers in correlating and analyzing events to support NORAD and US Space Command decision makers".[10] There is a Systems Center that "ensures continuity of operations throughout the Cheyenne Mountain Operations Center by providing communications and computer systems management for over 100 computer systems and 600 communications circuits in support of NORAD and US Space Command missile warning, space control, and air defense missions".[11]

"Most unique installation"

Cheyenne Mountain calls itself one of the most unique installations in the world and is the likely command centre for the "Star Wars" satellite network so beloved of both the Bushes and Reagan (the Bushes). The complex has the potential for massive cooperation and coordination between apparently unconnected organisations because it employs staff from the Army, Navy, Marine, Air Force and Canadian Forces. Cheyenne Mountain operates military communication and navigation satellites that direct and guide "western" armies during their bombardments of Iraq, Afghanistan and elsewhere. Major Mike Birmingham, an Army spokesman for the Colorado base, said: "Space support basically allowed US forces to perform that famous 'left hook' operation [employed during the Gulf War]. The Iraqis assumed no one could navigate that well in the desert."[12] But, despite all of this amazing technology and response capability, four commercial airliners hijacked in American airspace proved too much for them on September 11th. Why? If anyone is still in any doubt about the technological and coordination capability we are talking about here and its instant communications network throughout the United States government, military and air traffic surveillance, the official Cheyenne Mountain website says:

"The Cheyenne Mountain Operations Center comprises the largest and most complex command and control network in the world. The system uses satellites, microwave radio routes, and fiber optic links to transmit and receive vital communications. Two blast-hardened microwave antennas and two underground coaxial cables transmit the bulk of electronic information. Most of this information is data sent from the worldwide space surveillance and warning network directly to computers inside the Mountain. Redundant and survivable communications hotlines connect the Command Center to the Pentagon, White House, US Strategic Command, Canadian Forces Headquarters in Ottawa, other aerospace defense system command posts, and major military centers around the world." [13]

Now take a deep breath and consider the following. This was the very organisation that failed to respond in time to the hijacking of four commercial airliners in American airspace over densely populated areas between 8.13am, when communication was lost with Flight 11, and at least 9.38 when Flight 77 crashed into the Pentagon. That's around *an hour and a half* and not one NORAD plane was able (so they tell us) to intercept any of the hijacked aircraft in the very airspace its fantastic technology is specifically there to monitor and protect. Flight 77 alone, the one that hit the Pentagon, was in the air for 80 minutes and is officially reported to have performed a U-turn from its authorised course more than 40 minutes before impact.

The Federal Aviation Administration (FAA)

Another point to emphasise is that the civilian (US government) Federal Aviation Administration, which has a joint response procedure with NORAD to respond to hijackings, is a monumentally corrupt organisation steeped in the culture of the cover-up. I am not referring to most of the employees, nor even those who tell the media what the high-ups tell them to say. I am speaking of the controlling core of the FAA. Rodney Stich, a former navy and airline pilot and crash investigator with the FAA, has widely documented some of the corruption that he experienced directly and through his own investigations. He is the author of the book *Unfriendly Skies*[14] and he reveals the following:

- FAA management personnel have refused to take action when faced with major air safety and criminal violations reported by air safety inspectors.
- FAA management warns federal air safety inspectors not to report air safety problems or air safety violations.
- Official government air safety reports of major air safety problems and air safety violations filed by federal air safety inspectors are destroyed.
- FAA management harass, threaten and retaliate against federal air safety inspectors who try to report or carry out the federal government's air safety responsibilities.
- Key federal air safety inspectors are removed from their government air safety duties to stop them from reporting and taking actions on serious air safety problems or air safety violations.

- FAA management encourages inspectors to ignore major air safety problems by providing outstanding performance ratings, financial bonuses and promotions to those inspectors who don't report these problems, while doing the opposite to those inspectors who do report the problems and try to address them.
- FAA management has covered up crash-causing air safety misconduct exposed by FAA inspectors who have produced official government reports of corruption within the FAA in relation to a series of fatal airline crashes. More than 4,000 pages of hearing transcript exist supporting charges of corrupt and criminal activities within the FAA with regard to a series of fatal airline crashes.[15]
- An FAA administrator covered up testimony and dozens of government documents supporting charges of corruption within the FAA relating to fatal airline crashes, including a United Airlines DC-8 crash into New York City.

Stich is also particularly scathing about the management of United Airlines. He says that the information about FAA corruption has repeatedly been given to the "politically appointed" National Transportation Safety Board, but it had been covered up and "fraud-related" air disasters were allowed to continue. He accused the Board of "falsifying accident reports that covered up for their own duplicity in the crashes and deaths".[16] Stich cites the FBI, US attorneys and "the main Justice Department personnel" as other people and government agencies who have been given the facts about FAA corruption involving major aircraft disasters, but ignored it and even retaliated against him and other former federal agents who tried to expose what was happening. He names the federal judges he says have blocked his efforts to expose FAA corruption through the courts.[17] He tells the same story about members of Congress who, he says, ignored the documented evidence of "hard-core corruption" within the FAA:

> "These are the same members of Congress, and the secretary of the Department of Transportation, whose crocodile tears cover up for the fact that they were repeatedly offered evidence of the corruption that resulted in a series of fatal airline crashes, fatal hijackings, and who helped insure the success of the September 11, 2001, terrorist hijackers. The cover-up of these matters by members of Congress following the September 11 tragedies will insure the protection of the guilty and continuation of the tragic consequences, as documented for the past 40 years in the books described at this site." [18]

This is the same corrupt network that is telling you what happened when those planes were hijacked on September 11th. It is also the organisation that, with NORAD and the Pentagon, was responsible for responding to what happened that day.

The case of Payne Stewart

An example of the FAA-NORAD reaction procedure can be seen in the case of the private Learjet carrying the golfer Payne Stewart and his friends on October 25th 1999. Air traffic controllers lost contact with Stewart's plane after it took off from

Orlando in Florida heading for Dallas. When air traffic controllers realised all was not well, the FAA contacted NORAD and fighter jets were scrambled to check out what was happening. The Learjet had suffered a pressurisation failure and was flying on autopilot while the real pilot and passengers were unconscious. An *ABC News* report, quoting the Air Force but differing slightly from the findings of the official investigation, said that after contact was initially lost, two F-15s from Tyndall Air Force Base in Florida were sent to track the Learjet. The F-15s pulled back and two F-16s in the air from Florida's Eglin Air Force Base took over. When the Learjet reached the Midwest, the Eglin F-16s withdrew and four F-16s and a mid-air refuelling tanker from the Tulsa National Guard replaced them. Finally, two F-16s from Fargo, North Dakota, moved in close to look into the windows to see if the pilot was slumped over and to help clear airspace. "Officials hoped that the F-16s could provide assistance to anyone on board who might have helped land the plane safely", said ABC.[19] When the Learjet ran out of fuel, the F-16 pilots said they saw the plane fall to the ground. White House spokesman Joe Lockhart said the National Security Council monitored the doomed flight, fearing the jet might crash in a populated area. President Bill Clinton could have ordered fighters to shoot down the Learjet to avoid that potential tragedy, but Lockhart said no such recommendation had been made. Clinton told reporters at the time: "I am very grateful for the work the FAA did, and for the two Air Force pilots, and the others in the Air Force that monitored this plane and made every effort to try to make contact with it."[20]

Another important point to note. If you were "highly trained" Arab terrorists from this "brilliantly organised" network of Osama bin Laden, a network we are told was capable of hijacking four commercial aircraft at the same time in American airspace, one of your obvious and fundamental calculations would be the possible NORAD reaction time once it was known that the planes had been seized. So why did they choose to hijack the planes that hit the World Trade Center in Boston with a flight time to New York well in excess of possible NORAD reaction time and why would they have Flight 77 and 93 fly way out towards the Midwest before turning around and going all the way back? In the case of Flight 77 it meant that they had to fly for 45 minutes from the time the plane was known to be hijacked to the moment it struck the Pentagon. By any criteria, and the most minimal study of NORAD and FAA procedures on the Internet, they would have known that Air Force jets would be scrambled. They would also have known that these procedures involved the possible shooting down of aircraft that threaten US cities. Any idiot putting this plan together, with the aim of crashing planes into the World Trade Center and the Pentagon, would have known that under NORAD's normal, every-other-day, reaction times, they would have to complete the mission as soon as possible. Taking off from New York and Washington, and crashing them immediately into those buildings would have been the ideal plan for them, surely? Instead, Flight 77, which actually took off from Washington, was allowed to fly away from the city for around three quarters of an hour before the hijack happened and then had to be flown all the way back! This is clearly ridiculous. But, of course, if those behind the attacks knew that NORAD would not be reacting that day, these details would no longer be a problem or have to be taken into account when planning the operation.

NORAD's no-show

With the fantastic technology available to NORAD and the Cheyenne Mountain operation in general, reacting to what happened on September 11th should not have been a problem. In the past 20 years the technology has been introduced that allows aircraft to be safely navigated and communicated with from almost anywhere on or above the earth, thanks to the satellite network known as the Global Positioning System (GPS). This was created for use by the US military and, says one article, provides "incredibly accurate position information to end users".[21] I'll just give you that again: it provides "incredibly accurate position information to end users". Who controls this system? NORAD and the rest of the gang at Cheyenne Mountain. Yet they could not track those hijacked planes and follow what was going on? Besides all the ground-based and satellite based sensors and surveillance, NORAD also directs the AWACS aircraft which are in the air 24 hours a day, refuelling from flying tankers. AWACS (airborne warning and control system) are a modified Boeing airframe from a 707/320 with the 30-foot rotating radar dome on the top. They are the premier "air battle command and control" aircraft in the world today. They provide surveillance to NORAD from the earth's surface to the stratosphere over land and water, and one was involved in the Payne Stewart case.[22] The AWACS radar has a range of more than 250 miles (375.5 kilometres) for low-flying targets and further for those at higher altitudes. It has a "friend or foe" identification system that can detect, identify and track friendly or "enemy" low-flying aircraft by eliminating "ground clutter" that can confuse other radar systems.[23] There is, to put it mildly, no credible excuse imaginable for what happened – or rather didn't – on 9/11.

What should have happened

The system for what should have happened is made very clear in the official regulations and procedures of the Federal Aviation Administration (FAA).[24] Chapter 7 of the procedures deals with the "escort of hijacked aircraft". It says that an FAA "hijack coordinator" on duty at the Washington DC headquarters will request the military to provide an escort aircraft for a confirmed hijacked plane to: (a) assure positive flight following (that's staying on the authorised course to you and me); (b) report unusual observances; and (c) aid search and rescue in the event of an emergency. The escort service, say the regulations, will be requested by the FAA hijack coordinator by direct contact with the National Military Command Center (NMCC) at the Pentagon. Normally NORAD escort aircraft will take the required action, it says. "The center/control tower shall coordinate with the designated NORAD … military unit advising of the hijack aircraft's location, direction of flight, altitude, type of aircraft and recommended flight plan to intercept the hijack aircraft", the document instructs. Escort aircraft are told to position themselves five miles directly behind the hijacked plane and to approach it from the rear to avoid the possibility of being observed. The escort plane should take the same altitude, speed and heading as the hijacked aircraft. When a hijacking happens within the continental United States, say the procedures, the "appropriate NORAD … Senior Director" is forwarded reports of the aircraft's call sign of position of latitude and longitude, heading, speed and altitude. An escort mission can be terminated by FAA headquarters, the National Military Command Center at the Pentagon or major military command authority – in other words NORAD.[25] Air traffic controllers can, through the Federal Aviation Administration, call for military planes to escort or "intercept" a commercial aircraft if contact is lost with the pilot, the plane strays from its designated course or anything inexplicable is happening. In 2000, NORAD scrambled jets 125 times in such circumstances. An intercept does not require the approval of the President or some high-up government official. It is a routine response to check what is going on and who is flying the plane. The intention is not to blow the plane from the sky, which would have needed presidential approval or, since 9/11, the approval of the head of NORAD and other designated military chiefs. There is an agreed procedure and code for communicating between intercepting NORAD jets and the commercial aircraft. For example:

> "Rocking wings from a position slightly above and ahead of, and normally to the left of, the intercepted aircraft and, after acknowledgement, a slow level turn, normally to the left, on to the desired heading = You have been intercepted, follow me; circling aerodrome, lowering landing gear and over flying runway in direction of landing … = Land at this aerodrome."[26]

There is, likewise, a series of coded replies for the other aircraft. If the hijacked plane does not follow these orders, the interceptor can "make a pass in front of the aircraft" and eventually "fire tracer rounds in the airplane's path" or "down it with a missile", according to Marine Corps Major Mike Snyder, a NORAD spokesman quoted in the *Boston Globe*.[27] He also confirmed that fighters' intercepting aircraft was "routine". For example, after 9/11 when a small private Cessna flew near to President Bush's ranch at Crawford, Texas, the Federal Aviation Administration activated a response through NORAD and two jets were dispatched immediately. They tuned to the pilot's frequency and ordered him to land. Another similar incident was reported in Wood County, Texas, where Rodney Mize, the Sheriff's senior Dispatcher, confirmed that a private plane carrying four reporters from the *Houston Chronicle* was forced down by two military pilots in A-10 Warthog jets. They flew above and below the plane and it landed at Wisener Field near Mineola.[28] Bush's ranch, it seems, is far more important than the Pentagon and the World Trade Center. Such incidents are happening week after week as the Federal Aviation Administration and NORAD activate the response system.

The hijack procedure

If a problem with an aircraft is considered a possible hijack by the air traffic controller a much higher level of command is activated. FAA spokeswoman, Alison Duquette, explained: "The air traffic controller would notify the supervisor on the floor, who would then immediately notify the FAA's regional operation center who would notify NORAD, as well as others."[29] In these cases, according the regulations: "The escort service will be requested by the FAA hijack coordinator by direct contact with the National Military Command Center (NMCC) [based at the Pentagon]."[30] The Defense Department (DOD) manual covering plane hijackings says: "In the event of a hijacking, the NMCC will be notified by the most expeditious means by the FAA. The NMCC will, with the exception of immediate responses … forward requests for DOD assistance to the Secretary of Defense for approval."[31] It was because of this procedure that, according to CNN "… officers on [sic] the Joint Chiefs were monitoring the [Payne Stewart] Learjet on radar screens inside the Pentagon's National Military Command Center".[32] Federal Aviation Administration regulations leave air traffic controllers in no doubt that they must never take chances. They are told that if there is an unexpected loss of radar or radio communication they must consider that "an aircraft emergency exists"…[33] and … "If … you are in doubt that a situation constitutes an emergency or potential emergency, handle it as though it were an emergency."[34] Within Cheyenne Mountain at the NORAD headquarters is the Air Defense Liaison Officer, a top FAA official, who is there to coordinate between the FAA and NORAD in these situations. All these personnel and procedures were in place on September 11th. Yet look at what happened.

The NORAD timeline

I asked both NORAD and the FAA for the sequence of events and the timeline for what occurred that morning. Both say that only at 8.40am did the FAA notify NORAD that American Airlines Flight 11 had been hijacked. Yet contact was lost with the aircraft at 8.13 and at the very latest, by 8.20, it was clear that something serious was wrong. We should know why it took up to 27 minutes, according to the official story, for Air Traffic Control through the FAA to alert NORAD. The *New York Times* reported that Flight 11 maintained its authorised course for only 16 minutes after take-off and "just past Worcester, Mass., instead of taking a southerly turn, the Boeing 767 swung to the north at 8.15. It had been taken over …"[35] Let's give the controllers another five minutes before they were sure the aircraft was in trouble. This still means that the FAA waited 20 minutes from the point of confirmed lost contact to report that a commercial airliner was not responding to instructions and had changed course with a deactivated transponder over an area of high population and in skies criss-crossed by intensive air traffic. I asked the FAA to confirm when exactly it was known that Flight 11 was in trouble and why it took so long to contact NORAD. The FAA spokesman would not answer.

I repeat, the Federal Aviation Administration regulations instruct air traffic controllers that if there is an unexpected loss of radar or radio communication they must consider that "an aircraft emergency exists"… and …"If … you are in doubt that a situation constitutes an emergency or potential emergency, handle it as though it were an emergency." This could not be clearer. For goodness sake, the official story says that at 8.24am the controller heard from the cockpit of Flight 11: "We have some planes. Just stay quiet and you will be OK. We are returning to the airport. Nobody move." That is said to have happened 16 minutes before we are told the FAA alerted

NORAD that the plane had been hijacked! The transponder was switched off at 8.20 – 20 minutes before NORAD was informed, we are asked to believe. Let us not forget that through all of this the Air Force was constantly monitoring the commercial air traffic system as it does 24 hours a day. This has to be done to prevent collisions between commercial and Air Force planes. Flight attendant Betty Ong is said to have used a seatback phone to call an American Airlines reservations agent, who contacted the system operations control centre in Fort Worth. Betty is said to have made that call at 8.27 – 13 minutes before NORAD says it was told of the hijack. Even five minutes before the first alleged contact with NORAD, controllers are claimed to have heard another cockpit transmission that said: "Nobody move please. We are going back to the airport. Don't try to make any stupid moves." This FAA-NORAD timeline therefore is simply ridiculous. NORAD says it scrambled fighter jets from the Otis Air National Guard Base on Cape Cod in Massachusets at 8.46, six minutes after it says it was told of the hijack. At the very time they were taking off, according to the NORAD timeline, Flight 11 was crashing into the north tower. An F-15 departing from Otis can reach New York City in 10 to 12 minutes, according to an Otis spokeswoman, and can fly three times the speed of a 767.[36] If you take it to be 10 minutes that means the jets would be flying at around 918 miles per hour, well within their top speed. A NORAD spokesman, however, quoted the speed of the scrambled F-15s to me at only between 603 and 675 miles per hour. Why not faster? One of the pilots, named only as "Duff", told the BBC "documentary" *Clear The Skies* on September 1st 2002 that they did fly supersonic and this statement added to the contradictions emerging from different spokesmen for the US military.

But wait. It gets sillier. The Pentagon told CNN that NORAD was "informed of the plane striking the World Trade Center at 8.47". *Informed?* We are talking about the most sophisticated military surveillance operation on the planet which, in its own words, is "the largest and most complex command and control network in the world", utilising a vast network of satellites and cutting-edge-air tracking and surveillance technology. Cheyenne Mountain can tell you if a missile has been launched on the other side of the world and it has to be "informed" that a commercial airliner it claims it has already belatedly scrambled jets to intercept has hit the World Trade Center? It's insane. We are told that at 8.52, two F-15 Eagles took off from Otis base on Cape Cod, Massachusetts, 185 miles from New York, to intercept the second hijacked plane from Boston: Flight 175. About ten minutes later, at 9.03, Flight 175 smashed into the south tower with the F-15s still 70 miles away, so they tell us. One other point is that the World Trade Center is said by one of its first tenants to be a "No Fly Zone". If that is so, there has to be a system of air response very close to New York, otherwise the No Fly Zone would be unenforceable. What would be the point of it? Ken Smith, a tenant of the World Trade Center back in 1979, said on Radio Free America that when he was there it was well known by tenants that the WTC was a No Fly Zone. Smith said that any plane off-course within 12 miles of the WTC was given a warning to change direction and he added: "If you came within five miles they would threaten to shoot you down. If you came within three miles, they could shoot you down."[37]

The Pentagon "No Fly Zone"

This just gets crazier and crazier when you look at Flight 77. The official timeline says that the FAA notified NORAD at 9.24am (usually reported as 9.25) that United Airlines Flight 77 from Dulles Airport at Washington DC to Los Angeles may have been hijacked. Yet it was known before 9 o'clock that there was a problem with the plane. As I've mentioned earlier, radar reports published by *USA Today* suggest that Flight 77 took a massive detour off-course in a north to west to south loop over West Virginia before returning to course for a short time (*Figure 15*). This course is very different from the routes published by the rest of the media and could, I guess, be a mistake. If it was, however, it was a massive one. *USA Today* source their route to Flight Explorer, a company that tracks commercial aircraft in real time on the Internet using data supplied by the Federal Aviation Administration. I contacted Flight Explorer and asked for confirmation, or otherwise, of the *USA Today* graphic.

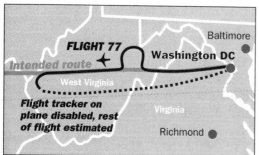

Figure 15: *The* USA Today *version of the route of Flight 77*

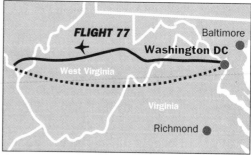

Figure 16: *The other version of Flight 77 published elsewhere in the media*

They sent me a course that did not include such a blatant detour (*Figure 16*), so take your pick. If the "*USA Today*" detour did happen, it would have been at around 8.36 going by the Flight Explorer timeline. This was at least 16 minutes after it was known that Flight 11 had been hijacked, but no action was taken about Flight 77 deviating wildly from its course, if that is what occurred. This continued to be the case even after Flight 11 had smashed into the World·Trade Center and it was known that Flight 175 had also been hijacked and crashed into the other tower. I asked the FAA what happened when, according to *USA Today*, Flight 77 looped off course before returning to the scheduled route because, obviously, I wanted to establish the truth about the course taken by the plane. Did it loop or did it not? If it did, what action had been taken at that time? What communications were made with the cockpit to establish what was going on? The FAA would not answer me, saying I had all the information it could give. The *New York Times* published what it claimed was a partial transcript of the communication tapes between Flight 77 and air traffic controllers. Air traffic controllers failed to make contact with Flight 77 from 8.56 according the transcript and at 8.58 Jim McDonnell, a representative of American Airlines (AAL), is on the line. The airline also tries and fails to make contact with the plane. The following is an exchange on the transcript that is said to have taken place from about 9.02; that's 17 minutes after AA Flight 11 had crashed into the World Trade Center and little more than a minute before United Airlines 175 would do the same:

9:02:07 AAL: American Airlines dispatch Jim McDonnell [on the line].

9:02:09 Indianapolis Control, Henderson Sector Radar Associate: Yeah this is Indianapolis center, we, uh, I don't know if I'm talking to the same guy about American 77.

9:02:13 AAL: Yeah I cell called him but I did not get a reply back from him.

9:02:17 Indianapolis Control, Henderson Sector Radar Associate: We, uh, we lost track control of the guy he's in coast track but we haven't, we don't where his target is and we can't get a hold of him um, you guys tried him and no response.

9:02:26 AAL: no response (background noise).

9:02:28 Indianapolis Control, Henderson Sector Radar Associate: Yeah we have no radar contact and uh no communications with him so if you guys could try again.

9:02:35 AAL: We're doing it.

9:02:37 Indianapolis Control, Henderson Sector Radar Associate: All right thanks a lot.

9:02:38 AAL: We're doing it thank you.

9:03:07 Indianapolis Control, Henderson Sector Radar: American 77 Indy.

[Around this point United Airlines Flight 175 crashed into the World Trade Center.]

9:06:20 Indianapolis Control: override line beeping.

9:06:21 Indianapolis Control, Dacos Radar Associate: Falmouth Dacos.

9:06:22 Indianapolis Control, Henderson Sector Radar Associate: This is Henderson American seventy seven do you guys have radar on him is he over Falmouth or –

9:06:25 Indianapolis Control, Dacos Radar Associate: No we just moved the track there we never you know.

9:06:27 Indianapolis Control, Henderson Sector Radar Associate: O.K. all right you just have the track out there.

9:06:29 Indianapolis Control, Dacos Radar Associate: You guys never been able to raise him at all.

9:06:31 Indianapolis Control, Henderson Sector Radar Associate: No, we called [the] company, they can't even get a hold of him so there's no, no, uh, no radio communications and no radar.

9:06:36 Indianapolis Control, Dacos Radar Associate: And his last clearance as far as you know is on course to Falmouth and then jay one thirty four right, well we're just gonna treat him like non radar and we've already told the next sector they're gonna have to sterilize for him until we find out.

9:06:49 Indianapolis Control, Henderson Sector Radar Associate: O.K. thanks.

9:06:50 Indianapolis Control, Dacos Radar Associate: ID.

9:08:43   Indianapolis Control, Henderson Sector Radar Associate: override line beeping.

9:08:54   Indianapolis Control, Henderson Sector Radar Associate: line ringing.

9:09:27   AAL: And it was a Boston-L.A. flight and 77 is a Dulles-L.A. flight and uh we've had an unconfirmed report a second airplane just flew into the World Trade Center.

9:09:00   AAL: American dispatch Jim McDonnell.

9:09:02   Indianapolis Control, Henderson Sector radar associate: Indianapolis Center did you get a hold of American 77 by chance?

9:09:05   AAL: No sir but we have an unconfirmed report the second airplane hit the World Trade Center and exploded.

9:09:10   Indianapolis Control, Henderson Sector Radar Associate: Say again.

9:09:11   AAL: You know we lost American eleven to a hijacking American was off … Boston to Los Angeles flight.

9:09:17   Indianapolis Control, Henderson Sector Radar Associate: It was all right I can't really I can't hear what you're saying there you said American eleven.

9:09:23   AAL: Yes we were hijacked.

9:09:25   Indianapolis Control, Henderson Sector Radar Associate: And it –

9:09:27   AAL: And it was a Boston – L.A. flight and 77 is a Dulles – L.A. flight and, uh, we've had an unconfirmed report a second airplane just flew into the World Trade Center.

9:09:42   Indianapolis Control, Henderson Sector Radar Associate: Thank you very much good-bye.

9:10:30   Indianapolis Control, Henderson Sector Radar Associate: calls Indianapolis Control, Dacos Radar Associate line beeps.

9:10:32   Indianapolis Control, Dacos Radar Associate: Indianapolis Control, Dacos.

9:10:34   Indianapolis Control, Henderson Sector Radar Associate: All right this is Henderson, there was an American eleven departed off of, uh, New York going to L.A. got hijacked. American 77 departed off of Dulles is going to L.A. dispatch doesn't know where he's at and confirmed that two airplanes have been uh, they crashed into, uh, the World Trade Center in New York, so as far as American 77 we don't know where he is but they say uh American eleven was hijacked off of a New York airport going to LAX [Los Angeles] and uh.

9:11:07   Indianapolis Control, Dacos PA: But we don't have a track on him.

9:11:07   Indianapolis Control, Henderson Sector Radar Associate: Affirmative.

9:11:10   Indianapolis Control, Dacos Radar Associate: You mean like they just took off without a clearance.

9:11:13   Indianapolis Control, Henderson Sector Radar Associate: No, you mean American eleven.

9:11:14   Indianapolis Control, Dacos Radar Associate: Yep.

9:11:15   Indianapolis Control, Henderson Sector Radar Associate: He, he's depart well I guess he did because he was going to L.A.

9:11:17   Indianapolis Control, Dacos Radar Associate: But nobody ever tracked American eleven is what I'm asking.

9:11:20 Indianapolis Control, Henderson Sector Radar Associate: Don't know that, I don't.

9:11:22 Indianapolis Control, Dacos Radar Associate: Oh O.K.

9:11:23 Indianapolis Control, Henderson Sector Radar Associate: Know just where he left from or uh?

9:11:25 Indianapolis Control, Dacos Radar Associate: There's no flight plan in the machine right now and –

9:11:28 Indianapolis Control, Henderson Sector Radar Associate: Yeah I just looked at that, too.

9:11:29 Indianapolis Control, Dacos Radar Associate: I'm …

9:11:30 Indianapolis Control, Henderson Sector Radar Associate: As far as what we know that's, that's all we know I talked to dispatch and that's what they relayed and they confirmed it here that I guess two airplanes about crashed into the Trade Center.

9:11:37 Indianapolis Control, Dacos Radar Associate: Huh?

9:11:39 Indianapolis Control, Henderson Sector Radar Associate: All right.

9:11:40 Indianapolis Control, Dacos Radar Associate: Oh.

9:13:54 Indianapolis Control, Henderson Sector Radar Associate: override line beeping.

9:14:04 Indianapolis Control, Henderson Sector Radar Associate: line ringing.

9:14:37 AAL: American dispatch Jim McDonnell.

9:14:39 Indianapolis Control, Henderson Sector Radar Associate: Indy center here.

9:14:40 AAL: Yes sir.

9:14:42 Indianapolis Control, Henderson Sector Radar Associate: American eleven you guys said he departed off of uh New York.

9:14:45 AAL: Boston.

9:14:46 Indianapolis Control, Henderson Sector Radar Associate: Boston, he was going to L.A. and it was a hijacked airplane.

9:14:49 AAL: Yes.

9:14:50 Indianapolis Control, Henderson Sector Radar Associate: And have you heard anything from American 77.

9:14:52 AAL: No.[38]

The whole transcript published by the *New York Times* can be read in *Appendix 4*, but it ends soon after the segment above and does not continue to the time when NORAD was at long last alerted. It is worth emphasising that during this exchange, if it is genuine, they acknowledged that two flights bound for Los Angeles had crashed into the World Trade Center and that contact with Flight 77, another Los Angeles-bound plane, had been lost for some *29 minutes* by that point. But it would be another *ten minutes* before NORAD was informed, according to the timeline agreed by both NORAD and the FAA. Staggering. On air safety grounds alone there should have been an immediate response to Flight 77 because of the lethal dangers to other aircraft of flying off-course. Then soon after the *"USA Today* loop" was completed, if that was the case, and it returned to its course the transponder signal disappeared from the screens of air traffic control and yet still NORAD was not alerted according to the official story agreed by both NORAD and the Federal Aviation Administration. The plane then did a 180-degree turn near the Ohio border and headed back towards Washington, but *still* no alert even with two hijacked planes buried in the World Trade Center and with controllers apparently unable to locate Flight 77 on their radar screens for ten minutes. Only at 9.24 was NORAD told by the FAA that Flight 77 was in serious trouble, both organisations told me. As a *New York Times* report said: "By 9.25am the FAA, in consultation with the Pentagon, had taken the radical step of banning all take-offs around the country, but fighters still had not been dispatched." [39] This was some 40 minutes after Flight 77 dramatically changed course and Flight 11 crashed into the World Trade Center; it was at least 35 minutes after air traffic controllers knew that Flight 77 had been hijacked; 24 minutes after the transponder signal was lost; 22 minutes after Flight 175 hit the World Trade Center; and 18 minutes after air traffic control facilities throughout the country knew that Flight 77 had likely been hijacked. Yet look at the FAA regulations again for air traffic controllers: "Consider that an aircraft emergency exists … when: … There is unexpected loss of radar contact and radio communications with any … aircraft" [40] and "If … you are in doubt that a situation constitutes an emergency or potential emergency, handle it as though it were an emergency." [41] MSNBC reported the day after 9/11 on how seriously air traffic controllers and their bosses at the FAA are supposed to take aircraft that deviate from their agreed route:

"If a plane deviates by 15 degrees, or two miles from that course, the flight controllers will hit the panic button. They'll call the plane, saying 'American 11, you're deviating from course.' It's considered a real emergency, like a police car screeching down a highway at 100 miles an hour. When golfer Payne Stewart's incapacitated Learjet missed a turn at a fix, heading north instead of west to Texas, F-16 interceptors were quickly dispatched." [42]

It was at 8.50am that contact was lost with the cockpit of Flight 77. At that moment the flight would have been under the control of the Indianapolis Air Route Traffic Control Center, one of 20 regional centres that track flights between airports. [43] At 9.02, still 40 minutes before impact with the Pentagon, a controller is reported to have told American Airlines the latest news on Flight 77: "We lost track control of the guy, he's in coast track but we haven't – we don't really know where his target is and we can't get a hold of him." [44] Yet it was only at 9.24 that NORAD was told that Flight 77 "may" have been hijacked? Oh do come on, this is the land of clouds and cuckoos. As a *Newsday* report pointed out: "The record suggests that teenagers on instant-message networks communicate faster than some federal officials did during the crisis." [45] Or as the *New York Times* put it:

"… despite elaborate plans that link civilian and military efforts to control the nation's airspace in defense of the country, and despite two other jetliners' having already hit the

World Trade Center in New York, the fighter planes that scrambled into protective orbits around Washington did not arrive until 15 minutes after Flight 77 hit the Pentagon." [46]

But even beyond all this, there is a more fundamental question that needs to be answered. Why, when two hijacked airliners had been crashed into the World Trade Center weren't fighter jets deployed immediately to guard the skies over Washington? Surely the first thing you would do after what happened in New York is to instigate air defence for your other most likely targets – Washington being the most obvious.

Air traffic controllers mystified

The *Miami Herald* talked to air traffic controllers who said they could not understand why there was no reaction to what was happening in the skies that morning.[47] Why no reaction from the FAA and the military? "That's a question that more and more people are going to ask," one controller in Miami told the *Herald*. "What the hell went on here? Was anyone doing anything about it? Just as a national defense thing, how are they able to fly around and no one go after them?" [48] The *Herald* quoted controllers who said that even with the transponder silent, the plane would have been visible on radar both to controllers who handle cross-continent air traffic and to a Federal Aviation Administration command centre outside of Washington. The FAA would not discuss with the *Miami Herald* the track of Flight 77 or what happened in air-control centres while it was in flight, and nor would American Airlines. Air traffic controllers told the *Herald* that the trouble should have been instantly noticeable. Flight 77, like all such planes, would have first showed up on radar screens as a short solid line, the *Herald* reported, with a readout that identifies the plane and gives its altitude and speed. When the transponder shuts down, the short line vanishes. The speed number goes away too. "It's just something that catches your eye", one controller said.[49] The first move when a transponder goes down would be to contact the pilot and tell him the transponder wasn't working. But even if the plane remained silent, controllers could still find it – by switching their screen display to the old-fashioned radar that bounces a signal off the plane's metal skin, the *Herald* said. The report went on:

> "Military jets are routinely scrambled in the case of hijackings and "runners," planes that do not answer or do not heed air traffic controllers. But FAA officials would not say when controllers detected the errant Flight 77 or whether any fighter jets were able to get into the air to confront it. Fighter jets are based nearby, in Virginia, and could have reached the White House within minutes, aviation sources say ...

> "... The FAA has a detailed hijacking manual: Supervisors are notified. The FAA command center near Washington and the FBI are put on alert. Military jets are scrambled to follow the plane. Air-traffic controllers try to figure out where the hijacker wants to go and, if necessary, clear an air space of other traffic." [50]

Big Dick reveals all

Vice President Dick Cheney told NBC's *Meet the Press*[51] that from the time that Flight 11 struck the World Trade Center the secret service travelling with President Bush in Florida had "open lines" with the Federal Aviation Administration. He said: "The secret service has an arrangement with the FAA. They had open lines after the World Trade Center was ..." He didn't finish the sentence, no doubt because he realised he had said too much, and it is worth pondering the wider implications of that statement. The FAA had open lines with the secret service after the World Trade Center was hit? That happened at 8.46, about the time that Flight 77 was known to be in trouble, and yet the FAA said they did not tell NORAD and the Pentagon Command Center about Flight 77 until 9.24 when they had already established open lines to the secret service. Are we being told that the Pentagon and NORAD did not have open lines also with the FAA and were able to follow in real time the communications and non-communications from the cockpits long before a single fighter jet was deployed? Indeed the FAA and NORAD have both confirmed to me that they had open lines to discuss Flights 77 and 93, the one that crashed in Pennsylvania. I asked the FAA when exactly these open lines were established, but its spokesman would not say. Surely in any sane system these would have been established, as Cheney indicated, at least from the moment the first plane struck the World Trade Center. So, again, why the delay in responding?

We are told that after contact was lost with Flight 77 and its transponder was deactivated, an "unidentified" aircraft was eventually picked up on radar heading for Washington at some 500 miles an hour and this turned out to be Flight 77. Unidentified? Have you seen the tracking technology available to NORAD and Cheyenne Mountain? Even when a transponder is turned off the plane can still be tracked by conventional radar, let alone by the technology those guys have. At around 9.27, NORAD says it ordered jets scrambled from Langley Air Force Base in Virginia (the base of the CIA's own fleet of military aircraft) to intercept Flight 77. Before becoming head of NORAD, General Ralph Eberhart was Commander, Air Combat Command, at Langley. At 9.35, it is said, three F-16 Fighting Falcons took off from Langley for Washington. Note the approximately eight minutes' response time before they were in the air in this official story when the Air Force apparently claims response times of scramble to 29,000 feet in two and a half minutes.[52] An F-16 has a top speed of some 1,800 miles an hour, twice the speed of sound. At 9.37, Flight 77 was "lost from radar screens", the story goes, and a minute later hit the Pentagon, precisely 60 years to the day since construction of that building began on September 11th 1941, the year of Pearl Harbor. The NORAD jets arrived at 9.49, so we are told. Shucks, just missed again. What terrible bad luck. These jets flew at speeds of about ".9 mach" or just below the speed of sound, according to information given to me by NORAD spokesman Barry Venable, who, I must say, was extremely thorough and efficient in his dealings with me.[53] He said that .9 mach is between 603 and 675 miles per hour depending on the altitude the planes were flying. The higher they fly the faster they go. Of course, their top speed of 1,800 miles an hour is not possible over land at lower altitudes, but less than the speed of sound for aircraft capable of twice the speed of sound might legitimately be questioned here when they were pursuing a hijacked airliner heading for the US capital after two others had been crashed into the World Trade Center. Barry Venable quoted similar speeds for the planes NORAD says were scrambled from Otis Air Force Base, but an Otis spokesman quoted by the local *Cape Cod Times* said the 153 miles from there to New York can be made by an F-15 in as little as ten minutes – that's around 918 miles per hour. At that speed the 130 miles from Langley to Washington would be completed in around eight minutes. This speed would have put jets from Langley over the Pentagon at about 9.38/39 – just as Flight 77 was turning in to crash and not "12 minutes [or] 105 miles" away as the NORAD timelines says they were at the time of impact.

A commercial airliner can fly from Washington to Ohio, turn back and fly all the way from the Midwest to cross a No Fly Zone and crash into the headquarters of the most powerful military force on earth without a military response worth the name? Vice President Dick Cheney even told the NBC *Meet the Press* programme[54] that: "It doesn't do any good to put up a combat air patrol if you don't give them instructions to act, if, in fact, they feel it's appropriate." He says this to divert attention from the fact that this is precisely what is happening every week in the skies of North America. You can check out and intercept ("stop, deflect, or interrupt the progress or intended course of")[55] an aircraft without shooting it down, for goodness sake. Again this was Cheney's attempt to mislead people from the central questions that will unleash the genie.

Why not Andrews?

Langley is around 130 miles from Washington so why did NORAD say it scrambled jets from that far away when Andrews Air Force Base, the one designated to defend Washington DC, is only a little over ten miles from the capital and pilots from there could have had breakfast and still intercepted Flight 77 with time to spare? This is even allowing for the fact that NORAD only activated interception procedures some 34 minutes after contact with the plane was lost. Andrews Air Force Base is a minute or so by fighter jet from Washington DC and that's why it is the capital's first line of air defence (see map, *Figure 17 overleaf*). In the name of sanity, the airspace above the Pentagon and the White House is a No Fly Zone and of course there are going to be squadrons on standby at the nearest Air Force base to defend that. Andrews is one of the most famous bases in America because it is the home of Air Force One, the President's plane, and foreign heads of state often pass through there. Again, are you going to locate the presidential plane at a base that does not have fighters that are ready to move at a moment's notice? Andrews, in fact, has two major squadrons on what are officially termed the highest possible state of readiness. These are the 121st Fighter Squadron of the 113th Fighter Wing and the 321st Marine Fighter Attack Squadron of the 49th Marine Air Group. Thousands of

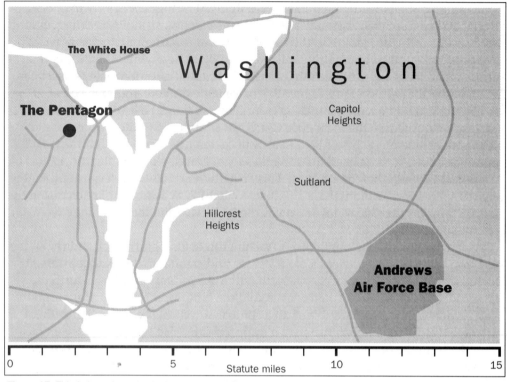

Figure 17: *This is how close the Andrews Air Force Base is to The Pentagon. So why no reaction until after the building was hit?*

people are employed at the base and they have at their disposal the very F-16s that NORAD says it deployed from 130 miles away at Langley, plus F/A-18 fighters. The sidewinder missiles carried by F-16s have a range of 18 miles and they would only have to get off the ground, lock in and fire to stop a plane crashing into the Pentagon. The fact that these planes were not scrambled from Andrews at any time before impact with the Pentagon is stunning. The Andrews AFB website went down immediately after September 11th and did not reappear until around mid-November.[56] When it came back online it no longer had a link to the Air Force web pages describing the capabilities and mission of 113th Fighter Wing of the Air National Guard at Andrews – the capability of reacting immediately to any threat by air to Washington.[57]

A website called dcmiltary.com is authorised to supply information to those employed by US forces. It reported before 9/11 (although I haven't been able to find the web page since) that Andrews is the base for the 121st Fighter Squadron, 113th Fighter Wing, and it confirmed its role: "… as part of its dual mission, the 113th provides capable and ready response forces for the District of Columbia in the event of a natural disaster or civil emergency. Members also assist local and federal law enforcement agencies in combating drug trafficking in the District of Colombia. [They] are full partners with the active Air Force." [58] Of the 321st Marine Fighter

Attack Squadron of the 49th Marine Air Group at Andrews, it says: "In the best tradition of the Marine Corps, a 'few good men and women' support two combat-ready reserve units at Andrews AFB. Marine Fighter Attack Squadron (VMFA) 321, a Marine Corps Reserve squadron, flies the sophisticated F/A-18 Hornet. Marine Aviation Logistics Squadron 49, Detachment A, provides maintenance and supply functions necessary to maintain a force in readiness." [59] These units are operated by the District of Colombia National Guard, headquartered at Andrews, and its official website has this to say about its capabilities:

"The DC Air National Guard is located on Andrews Air Force Base, in Camp Springs, Maryland. We are home to the 113th Wing: the 121 Fighter Squadron (including the F-16 Fighting Falcons) and the 201 Air Lift Squadron; the 121 Weather Squadron; and the 231 Combat Communications Squadron.

"The DC Air National Guard has called Andrews AFB home since the unit's post-war reorganization in 1946. We draw our members from throughout the District of Columbia metropolitan area, as well as from more distant points in Maryland, Virginia, and neighboring states.

"The unit has about 1,400 people, most of whom spend one weekend each month at Andrews for scheduled training. A smaller, full-time contingent maintains the day-to-day operations as a framework that supports the full-time flying training mission.

"We presently fly the F16-C and F16-D Fighting Falcon jet fighters, after conversion from the F4-D in January 1990. The F16 is the ninth different type of fighter in the wing's 44-year history."

And look at how it completes this piece of self-congratulation:

"Throughout its existence, the men and women of the DC Air National Guard have been and will continue to be a vital part of the community and the total force. They stand ready to respond to the needs of the District of Columbia – and the nation – should the need arise." [Except on September 11th] [60]

The DC Air National Guard even calls itself the "Capital Guardians"! Before 9/11, although not it seems afterwards, they made their mission crystal clear when they claimed to …"provide combat units in the highest possible state of readiness". So where on earth were they on September 11th when a commercial airliner flew back towards Washington, for 45 minutes after Air Traffic Control lost contact, to crash a minute's flying time from Andrews AFB? It was not the fault of the pilots who, I'm sure, are utterly bewildered at what happened. It is the highest level of the military and government that we have to focus on – those with the power to decide not to deploy from Andrews. NORAD spokesman Barry Venable told me that NORAD fighters were "not standing alert, nor even stationed, at Andrews AFB on

11 September. The USAF did indeed have fighters stationed at Andrews AFB on 11 September, but not for the purpose of standing air sovereignty alert – a role NORAD performs."[61] Then how come fighters from Andrews were in the sky over Washington immediately after the Pentagon was hit? *USA Today*, America's national newspaper, also sought to explain away the "Andrews mystery" by reporting that "Andrews Air Force Base, home to Air Force One, is only 15 miles [sic] away from the Pentagon, but it had no fighters assigned to it. Defense officials won't say whether that has changed."[62] Not even NORAD claims there were no fighters at Andrews, and what kind of journalism is it that prints this story when the truth is only a "Netfind" away? The same *USA Today* edition also said in direct contradiction: "The District of Columbia National Guard maintained fighter planes at Andrews Air Force Base, only about 15 miles [sic] from the Pentagon, but those planes were not on alert and not deployed."[63] The *San Diego Union-Tribune*, however, told the truth about Andrews when it reported:

> "Air defense around Washington is provided mainly by fighter planes from Andrews Air Force Base in Maryland near the District of Columbia border. The DC Air National Guard is also based there and equipped with F-16 fighter planes, a National Guard spokesman said. But the fighters took to the skies over Washington only after the devastating attack on the Pentagon ..."[64]

Other media sources also reported that fighters from Andrews AFB were deployed over Washington. NBC *Nightly News* said: "It was after the attack on the Pentagon that the Air Force then decided to scramble F-16s out of the DC National Guard Andrews Air Force Base to fly a protective cover over Washington, DC."[65] The UK *Daily Telegraph* said: "Within minutes of the attack [on the Pentagon] American forces around the world were put on one of their highest states of alert – Defcon 3, just two notches short of all-out war – and F-16s from Andrews Air Force Base were in the air over Washington DC."[66] A "former Pentagon Air Traffic Controller" quoted, but not named, is said to have commented:

> "All those years ago when I was in the Pentagon, this wouldn't have happened. Air Traffic Control Radar images were (and are) available in the understructures of the Pentagon, and any commercial flight within 300 miles of DC that made an abrupt course change toward Washington, turned off their transponder, and refused to communicate with ATC, would have been intercepted at supersonic speeds within a max of 9 minutes by a fighter out of Andrews. Period. Why these planes weren't, baffles me. If we could get fighters off the ground in two minutes then, we could now."[67]

And yet a Pentagon spokesman, Rear Admiral Craig Quigley, made this astonishing statement: "Planes come up and down the Potomac all the time. You can hear them in the building. There was no warning."[68] John A. Koskinen, the Washington DC City Administrator, said the District was "largely helpless" to stop such attacks.[69] Utter garbage.

What happened to flight 93?

United Airlines Flight 93 from Newark, New Jersey, to San Francisco was, we are told, reported to NORAD as a possible hijack at 9.16am. This was about around 16 minutes after the aircraft is thought to have been taken over. At 9.35am Flight 93 filed a new flight plan and headed for Washington. I asked the FAA who in the cockpit filed that plan and what exchange took place between air traffic control, but the spokesman said he could give me no information on this. At 9.40, it is claimed, the transponder signal stopped and "radar contact was lost". This is nonsense. We are talking NORAD and Cheyenne Mountain here and, like the FAA system, they can still track a plane after the transponder has been switched off. At approximately 10.03 according to the NORAD timeline (anything up to 10.37 according to others), Flight 93 "crashed" near Shanksville, Pennsylvania, and the NORAD timeline says that no fighter jet was within 100 miles of the plane when it went down. By 10.03, if we take the NORAD version, it was an hour and 11 minutes since fighters are said to have been scrambled from Otis AFB to New York and 50 minutes since Flight 93 was reported to NORAD as a possible hijack. My own feeling is that at least one jet did get to Flight 93 on this occasion and may well have shot down the aircraft. I will elaborate on the background later.

What a shambles

The FAA-NORAD-Pentagon response procedure in these circumstances could not be clearer in the official regulations. Equally clear is that on September 11th, on that day of all days, that response was a disgrace. I do not believe for a second that this is unconnected to the fact that the Illuminati, working through US government agencies, wanted the attacks of September 11th to happen as they did. Somewhere in that normal line of response from the FAA's air traffic control through to the Pentagon and the scrambling of NORAD jets a spanner was thrown in the works to slow down the reaction times. If you accept that the FAA and NORAD timelines are correct, the FAA is an organisation that has some serious questions to answer, but won't. I asked the FAA media spokesman Fraser Jones the following questions:

1. I have been going through the timeline you sent to me and I have some questions. I asked when there was first known to be a problem with the four flights and in answer to that you gave me the times that the FAA informed NORAD. These are not the same times as when a problem was first identified. Could I have the times when problems were first identified?

2. Flight 11 failed to respond to the air traffic controller at 8.13 and yet both the FAA and NORAD say that the FAA did not inform NORAD of a problem until 8.40. Why a delay of 27 minutes?

3. Flight 77 failed to respond to air traffic control at 8.50am and six minutes later the transponder was turned off … yet both NORAD and the FAA say that the

FAA did not inform NORAD of a problem until 9.24. Why the delay of 34 minutes, especially when, by 9.03am, two planes had crashed into the World Trade Center?

4. Before Flight 77 turned around it made a detour off course in a north-west-south loop over West Virginia [according to *USA Today*] before returning briefly to its agreed route. Why was this ignored?

5. At what time exactly did the FAA and NORAD establish open lines to discuss Flight 77 and Flight 93?

6. NORAD has told me that the FAA is responsible for policing No Fly Zones like the one over Washington and New York. What is the procedure the FAA has for doing this, what aircraft does it use and where are they based, and what happened on September 11th when there was no response? If the FAA doesn't have planes, then who does? What is the point of a No Fly Zone if there is nothing to defend it?

Mr Jones replied that he had already provided "all the info" he had for questions one to five (none of which gave me an answer to any of them). For question six he said: "The FAA monitors prohibited airspace and would be aware if a pilot blundered into such an area. Our mission is not civil defense. We would help coordinate the appropriate response given the circumstances".[70] What on earth does that mean? NORAD told me that it is not responsible for policing the No Fly Zone over Washington and it was a matter for the civilian FAA. The FAA tells me it "monitors prohibited airspace" and would be aware if a pilot blundered into such an area and would then help to coordinate the appropriate response in the circumstances. Oh really well take your time, no rush. How long does it take for a plane to enter restricted airspace over Washington before it parks itself in the White House, Capitol Hill, or the Pentagon? Seconds. So where would the immediate air or ground-to-air response come from? Langley AFB 130 miles away? What the hell use would that be? Now the FAA and NORAD are either not telling me the truth or there is no system for protecting No Fly Zones. One or the other must be the case given what they have both said. I asked Fraser Jones whom the FAA would contact when the No Fly Zone threatened to be breached and they "coordinate the appropriate response in the circumstances", but I received no reply. Couldn't be Andrews AFB and the DC Air National Guard could it?

Military special operations commander was head of FAA "security"

The head of security for the FAA on September 11th was Michael Canavan, who resigned after only 10 months in the job shortly after the attacks. Canavan is a retired US Army lieutenant general, who had been Chief of Staff of the US European Command in Stuttgart, Germany. Canavan has a considerable background in US Special Operations, which, according to the Department of

Defense's Dictionary of Military and Associated Terms, are defined as: "Operations conducted by specially organized, trained, and equipped military and paramilitary forces to achieve military, political, economic or psychological objectives by unconventional means in hostile, denied or politically sensitive areas." In short: operations that are above the law and off the record. Canavan was Commanding General, Special Operations Command, Europe, and Commanding General, Joint Special Operations Command, at Fort Bragg, North Carolina. In July 2002, the military announced that four soldiers with Special Forces based at Fort Bragg had murdered their wives and three of the men had recently returned from Afghanistan. Two had also killed themselves and the other two had been charged with murder. The military said the murders were "not stress related". This is the same Fort Bragg that provided several officers from its US Army 4th Psychological Operations (PSYOPS) Group to work in the news division at CNN's headquarters in Atlanta in the final days of the Kosovo War, according to media reports, and also staffed the National Security Council's Office of Public Diplomacy (OPD), a shadowy government propaganda agency that planted stories in the US media supporting the Reagan-Bush Administration's policies in Central America. The *Miami Herald* of July 19th 1987 quoted a "senior US official" as describing the OPD as a "vast psychological warfare operation of the kind the military conducts to influence a population in enemy territory." These are the sorts of operations that Michael Canavan, the head of FAA security on September 11th, would have been involved with in his high positions in Special Operations Command.

What is absolutely clear is that the FAA's response to the hijackings that morning was bizarre, and this happened in what must be the best-defended airspace in the world. Let us consider again the capabilities detailed in the official websites of the FAA's partners in policing US airspace, NORAD and Cheyenne Mountain:

- The NORAD Command Center at Cheyenne Mountain is responsible for "monitoring, processing, and interpreting missile, space or air events which could have operational impacts on our forces or capabilities, or could be potential threats to North America or US and allied forces overseas." *So why not on September 11th?*

- Cheyenne Mountain serves as a central collection and coordination facility for a worldwide system of sensors designed to provide … the leadership of Canada and the US with an accurate picture of any aerospace threat." *So why not on September 11th?*

- The Command Centre is linked directly to the National Command Authorities of both the US and Canada as well as to regional command centres overseas. When required, the Command Director must consult directly with the NORAD and US Space Command Commander in Chief for time-critical assessments of missile, air, and space events; he takes action to ensure the Commander in Chief's response and direction are properly conveyed and executed … *So why not on September 11th?*

- "... The Air Defense Operations Center provides command and control for the air surveillance and air defense network for North America. In 1994, they monitored over 700 'unknown' radar tracks entering North American airspace. Many of these were subsequently identified as friendly aircraft that had erred from flight plans or used improper procedures." *So where was the monitoring on September 11th?*

- There is also a Systems Center that "ensures continuity of operations throughout the Cheyenne Mountain Operations Center by providing communications and computer systems management for over 100 computer systems and 600 communications circuits in support of NORAD and US Space Command missile warning, space control, and air defence missions. *So why not on September 11th?*

- Cheyenne Mountain is responsible for "... the monitoring of man-made objects in space, and the detection, validation, and warning of attack against North America whether by aircraft, missiles, or space vehicles, utilizing mutual support arrangements with other commands. Aerospace control includes ensuring air sovereignty and air defense of the airspace of Canada and the United States." *So why not on September 11th?*

The standing rule of NORAD officals is to apparently give unknown airplanes approaching US airspace two minutes to identify themselves. If this does not happen fighter-intercepts are scrambled in two minutes without exception. The head of the Russian Air Force, Anatoli Kornukov, said: "As soon as something like that [the hijackings] happens here, I am reported about that right away and in a minute we are all up." [71] The response to what happened on September 11th was a total shambles, but what was it that Colonel Leroy Fletcher Prouty said? "No one has to direct an assassination – it happens. The active role is played secretly by permitting it to happen. This is the greatest single clue. Who has the power to call off or reduce the usual security precautions?" He could not have put it better in relation to 9/11. The FAA and NORAD are not the only ones who have some serious questions to answer. So do President Bush, the Commander-in-Chief of US forces; Donald Rumsfeld, the Secretary of Defense; and Air Force General Richard B. Myers, the then Acting Chairman of the Joint Chiefs of Staff. What a trio this is ...

SOURCES

1   Leroy Fletcher Prouty, *JFK, The CIA, Vietnam And The Plot To Assassinate John F. Kennedy* (Birch Lane Press, 1992)

2   Jim Marrs, *Crossfire: The Plot That Killed Kennedy* (Carrol and Graf Publishers, New York, 1989), p 382

3　http://www.peterson.af.mil/norad/about_us.htm

4　Ibid

5　There is more background from the Scripps Howard News Agency at **http://www.trnonline. com/archives/2001archives/07022001/regional_news/25818.shtml**

6　**https://www.cheyennemountain.af.mil**

7　Ibid

8　Ibid

9　Ibid

10　Ibid

11　Ibid

12　**http://www.fas.org/news/usa/1998/08/index.html**

13　**https://www.cheyennemountain.af.mil**

14　Rodney Stich, *Unfriendly Skies*. This book can be ordered through **http://www.unfriendlyskies.com**

15　**http://www.unfriendlyskies.com/faa_hearing.html**

16　**http://www.unfriendlyskies.com/faa_corruption.html**

17　**http://www.conspiracyplanet.com/channel.cfm?channelid=54&contentid=173**

18　**http://www.unfriendlyskies.com/faa_corruption.html**

19　**http://abcnews.go.com/sections/us/DailyNews/plane102599.html**

20　Ibid

21　Thwarting Skyjackings from the Ground, published in *Quill* magazine, February 1998. Posted to FACSNET, October 2nd 2001, **http://www.facsnet.org/issues/specials/terrorism/aviation.php3**

22　**http://www.cnn.com/US/9910/26/shootdown**

23　**http://www.af.mil/news/factsheets/E_3_Sentry__AWACS_.html**

24　**http://www.faa.gov/Atpubs/MIL/http://www.faa.gov/Atpubs/MIL**

25　Section 5: Mission Termination 7-5-1

26　**http://www.faa.gov/ATpubs/AIM/Chap5/aim0506.html#5-6-4**

27　*Boston Globe*, September 15th 2001, third edition, p A1

28　AP *Associated Press*, September 13th 2001

29　*Cape Cod Times*, September 16th 2001

30　FAA Order 7610.4J

31　Chairman of the Joints Chiefs of Staff Instruction, Aircraft Piracy (Hijacking) and Destruction of Derelict Airborne Objects, dated June 2001 **http://www.dtic.mil/doctrine/jel/cjcsd/cjcsi/3610_01a.pdf1**

32　**CNN.com**, Pentagon Never Considered Downing Stewart's Learjet, President Would Have to Make Decision, October 26th 1999

33　FAA Order 7110.65M

34 Ibid

35 A Plane Left Boston and Skimmed Over River and Mountain in a Deadly Detour, *New York Times*, September 13th 2001.

36 Did Hijackers Fly Through Holes in US Air Defense?, *Cape Cod Times*, September 16th 2001.

37 Stated on Radio Free America and quoted by William Thomas in *All Fall Down* (Essence Publications, Canada, 2002), p 5

38 I found this at **paulboutin.weblogger.com/discuss/msgReader$80**

39 Pentagon Tracked Deadly Jet but Found No Way to Stop It, *New York Times*, September 15th 2001

40 FAA Order 7110.65M 10-2-5

41 FAA Order 7110.65M 10-1-1-c

42 MSNBC, September 12th 2001, **http://www.msnbc.com/news/627524.asp#BODY**

43 Who Watched as Flight Plan was Aborted? *Miami Herald*, September 14th 2001.

44 See the full published section of the alleged transcript of Air Traffic communications with Flight 77 in *Appendix 4*

45 Air Attack on Pentagon Indicates Weaknesses, by Sylvia Adcock, Brian Donovan and Craig Gordon, *Newsday*, September 23rd 2001

46 Pentagon Tracked Deadly Jet but Found No Way to Stop It, *New York Times*, September 15th 2001

47 Who watched as flight plan was aborted? *Miami Herald*, September 14th 2001

48 Ibid

49 Ibid

50 Ibid

51 *Meet the Press*, NBC, September 16th 2001

52 **http://www.spiritofmaat.com/messages/oct7/strike.htm**

53 E-mail to the author, May 31st 2002

54 *Meet the Press*, NBC, September 16th 2001

55 *American Heritage Dictionary*

56 Guilty for 9/11: Bush, Rumsfeld, Myers, by Illarion Bykov and Jared Israel, posted November 14th 2001; updated November 17th 2001, **http://www.tenc.net/indict/indict-1.htm**

57 Ibid

58 **dcmilitary.com** DC Military

59 Ibid

60 **http://www.dcandr.ang.af.mil/aboutDCANG.htm**

61 E-mail to the author, May 20th 2002

62 *USA Today*, September 17th 2001

63 Ibid

64   *San Diego Union-Tribune*, September 12th 2001

65   NBC *Nightly News*, September 11th 2001

66   *Daily Telegraph*, September 16th 2001

67   http://www.flight93crash.com/flight93_military_faq.html

68   Attack Shatters Beefed-up Security Without Knowledge of Terrorists' Intent, Barriers and Bills Useless, Experts Say, *Washington Post*, September 12th 2001, p. B01.

69   *Washington Post*, September 12th 2001

70   E-mail to the author June 3rd 2002

71   **http://emperors-clothes.com/news/airf.htm**

chapter 9

Where were you on 9/11?

Without censorship, things can get terribly confused in the public mind.

General William Westmoreland, Commander US forces in Vietnam

Two weeks after the attacks on America, General Richard B. Myers officially took over as the Chairman of the Joint Chiefs of Staff. Before his appointment to the Pentagon as Deputy Chairman in 2000, he was the Commander of NORAD. Myers, therefore, knew precisely what the procedures were for reacting to unexplained happenings with planes in North American airspace.

As we have seen, Federal Aviation Administration regulations say: "The escort service will be requested by the FAA hijack coordinator by direct contact with the National Military Command Center (NMCC)". The NMCC is based at the Pentagon, headquarters of the Joint Chiefs, and the Department of Defense's own manual says that: "In the event of a hijacking, the National Military Command Center will be notified by the most expeditious means by the Federal Aviation Administration. The NMCC will, with the exception of immediate responses … forward requests for DOD [Department of Defense] assistance to the Secretary of Defense for approval." This is the same National Military Command Center that claims it had no warning that an airliner was about to crash into its own building some 45 minutes after it deviated off course! Where was General Myers while all this was going on and what were the top brass in the Pentagon doing all this time? What was Defense Secretary Rumsfeld doing? Where was President Bush? Myers knew the response procedures. He knew that Andrews AFB around ten miles down the road had all that was necessary to respond to Flight 77 as it headed for Washington. Yet nothing was done. The *New York Times* tried to explain what was happening at the Pentagon that morning:

> "During the hour or so that American Airlines Flight 77 was under the control of hijackers, up to the moment it struck the west side of the Pentagon, military officials in a command center on the east side of the building were urgently talking to law enforcement and air traffic control officials about what to do."

(No, you didn't misread that.)

"But despite elaborate plans that link civilian and military efforts to control the nation's airspace in defense of the country, and despite two other jetliners' having already hit the World Trade Center in New York, the fighter planes that scrambled into protective orbits around Washington did not arrive until 15 minutes after Flight 77 hit the Pentagon." [1]

What? Military chiefs in the Pentagon command centre were "urgently talking about what to do?" Uh? These are the guys who are supposed to protect the United States from nuclear attack! "Er, now there's a missile heading for us gentlemen that will end life in America as we know it. This is due to land on this building in two minutes, now what do you think we should do?" If they were talking to air traffic officials (FAA) during the hour in question why no response from NORAD? Why are we told that NORAD, which is under Pentagon command, was not alerted about Flight 77 until 9.24 when the Pentagon command centre was "urgently talking to law enforcement and air traffic control officials about what to do" for "the hour or so that American Airlines Flight 77 was under the control of the hijackers"? Given what had happened in New York why weren't planes scrambled to patrol the skies over Washington as a matter of course anyway? General Myers told his Senate confirmation hearing when he became Chairman of the Joint Chiefs of Staff that he pledged "…to keep our armed forces at that razor's edge"! A Pentagon spokesman, Air Force Lieutenant Colonel Vic Warzinski, even had the audacity to tell *Newsday* that: "The Pentagon was simply not aware that this aircraft was coming our way …" [2] The Cheyenne Mountain official website says of the NORAD Command Center: "Redundant and survivable communications hot lines connect the Command Center to the Pentagon, White House, US Strategic Command, Canadian Forces Headquarters in Ottawa, other aerospace defense system command posts, and major military centers around the world." [3] And the Pentagon didn't know that a hijacked plane heading for its own city for more than 45 minutes was coming its way?? CNN reported that while Payne Stewart's plane was flying on auto pilot "… officers on [sic] the Joint Chiefs were monitoring the Learjet on radar screens inside the Pentagon's National Military Command Center". [4] Of course they were, that's what they are supposed to do. Why are we told they did not do this on September 11th when four planes were hijacked, and that they didn't know one was heading in their direction? It is an insult to the intelligence. CNN also quoted officials at the Pentagon as saying they were never made aware of the threat from hijacked United Airlines Flight 93 until after it crashed in Pennsylvania. [5] Reports say that the Federal Aviation Administration informed NORAD at 9.16am that Flight 93 may have been hijacked and the transponder was turned off at 9.40, although NORAD and the FAA both told me that open lines between them were established to discuss Flight 93. There is no way that the Pentagon's National Military Command Center with open lines to the FAA and NORAD was not told of the hijack of Flight 93 until it crashed after 10am. The Pentagon's entire story is nonsense, of course it is, and it is designed to hide the simple truth – at the highest levels of power within the US government and military these attacks were being allowed to happen.

Flight 77 crashed into the Pentagon on the west side of what is the biggest office complex in the world. This is the opposite side of the building to where the main offices of Donald Rumsfeld and the military top brass and the National Military Command Center are located. The targeted section had been the first of five to undergo renovations and strengthening to protect the Pentagon from terrorist attacks. Yet this is the very section these "highly trained, highly professional" terrorists aimed for?? Such is the size and strength of the Pentagon that Rumsfeld said that he only felt a "jarring thing" when the plane hit.[6] If you were really a crazed Islamic fanatic dedicated to attacking the "Great Satan America", why would you aim the plane at the very opposite side of a 29-acre, six million-square-foot building to where your real targets are? The same reason why Timothy McVeigh parked the Ryder truck as far away as possible from his alleged target, the offices of the ATF, I guess.

Where was Myers?

General Myers was Acting Chairman of the Joint Chiefs of Staff on September 11th in the absence abroad of the outgoing General Hugh Shelton. Myers would be confirmed as Shelton's successor at a Senate hearing only two days later. Chairman of the Joint Chiefs is the highest-ranking uniformed military post and third in command of US forces with only the president and the defense secretary above him in the line of command. Surely this is a man who would have been at the centre of events with America "under attack" from terrorists. Where was Myers while all hell was breaking loose in those two horrific hours? It turns out, and I'm not kidding, that he was having a meeting with Senator Max Cleland of Georgia on Capitol Hill. I think its best if you sit down while you read the following, and breathing deeply might help too. This is Myers' account of his movements that morning described in an interview with the Armed Forces Radio and Television Service:

> "I remember it was like watching a bad movie. I was on Capitol Hill. I was about ready to meet with Senator Cleland. I was meeting with him in preparation for my hearing, my confirmation hearing to be the Chairman of the Joint Chiefs of Staff. And I remember before we walked in there was a TV that was playing and somebody has said, 'An airplane has hit one of the World Trade Center towers'. They thought it was an airplane, and they thought it was a small airplane or something like that. So we walked in and we did the office call with Senator Cleland."

The highest-ranking uniformed officer in the US military on American soil that day hears that a plane has hit the World Trade Center and instead of checking it out he goes into a routine meeting with a senator about confirmation hearings? Come again? And it gets worse:

> "Sometime during that office call the second tower was hit. Nobody informed us of that. But when we came out, that was obvious. Then right at that time somebody said the Pentagon has been hit." [7]

Hold on, let me sit down here and strap in. No one informs the Acting Chairman of the Joint Chiefs of Staff, the top military man on American soil that day, that a second airliner has hit the World Trade Center when, down in Florida, the White House Chief of Staff, Andrew Card, is telling President Bush that "America is under attack", according to the official story? General Myers' account makes no rational sense whatsoever. Do they really think we are all so stupid that we would believe that the Acting Chairman of the Joint Chiefs of Staff is not contactable at all times and that he would not have been told of the second plane – indeed the first also – as a matter of course by the Pentagon? If he wasn't, why the hell not? Myers then says that "right at the time" when he and Cleland came out of their meeting "somebody said the Pentagon has been hit". We can therefore add a timeline to his story. Myers' account puts him in the meeting with Cleland at no later than around 9am before the second plane crashed and he did not come out until the Pentagon was struck, that's no earlier than 9.38 – 9.40. How amazing that this meeting took place across precisely the time that the attacks were happening. The *New York Times* tells us that "during the hour or so that American Airlines Flight 77 was under the control of hijackers, up to the moment it struck the west side of the Pentagon, military officials in a command center on the east side of the building were urgently talking to law enforcement and air traffic control officials about what to do." [8] All this was happening and they didn't inform their ultimate boss that day who was in a meeting down the street on Capitol Hill? Smell a rat? I smell a whole species. General Myers says that when he emerged from the meeting to be told what most of the world already knew, he launched into action:

> "Immediately, somebody handed me a cell phone, and it was General Eberhart out at NORAD in Colorado Springs talking about what was happening and the actions he was going to take. We immediately, after talking to him, jumped in the car, ran back to the Pentagon." [How do you do both?] [9]

I have detailed the fantastic technology and communications network at the disposal of NORAD and the Pentagon, and yet NORAD contacts the acting military head of US forces only *after* three planes have crashed over nearly an hour and when somebody handed him a cell phone? The NORAD commander General Eberhart – the man who replaced Myers at Cheyenne Mountain – is telling him "the actions he is *going* to take" after three airliners are embedded in three of America's biggest buildings and 3,000 people are dead? What in God's name had Eberhart and his NORAD operation been doing all this time? If you feel you can stand any more, General Myers also told Armed Forces Radio and Television:

> "The Chairman [General Shelton] had left that morning to go to Europe, so he was somewhere over the Atlantic. As I got to the Pentagon I noticed a lot of people were coming out of the Pentagon. Of course they'd been told to evacuate. My concern was where can you best discharge your duties? … [My] battle station was in the National Military Command Center. I asked if it was still running, they said it sure is, so I went

back in the building to the Command Center and was joined shortly thereafter by the Secretary of Defense. The Deputy Secretary actually went to another location at that point. We did what had to be done in terms of the command and control of the day ..."

The interviewer asked Myers if he could believe that it was actually a terrorist attack:

"I didn't know what to believe at the time. That was the problem. We had these events, and then subsequently the airplane went down in Pennsylvania. We were trying to tie this together, what does this mean? General Eberhart was working with the Federal Aviation Agency trying to figure out the logical steps at this point. We had some fighters airborne at that time in case we had some hijacked airplanes that were possibly a threat to other institutions or structures, but it was initially pretty confusing. You hate to admit it, but we hadn't thought about this."

Given what is claimed to have happened, the voices said to have been heard from the cockpit radios, and reports by passengers and attendants on cellphones and airphones that morning, to say they didn't know this was a "terrorist attack" is an unbelievable misrepresentation of events. Only with three planes down, thousands dead, and a fourth soon to crash in Pennsylvania, did the top military officer on duty that day walk into the command centre at the Pentagon which, as we have seen, has clear and set procedures for reacting to hijackings or aircraft anomalies and would have had open lines to the Federal Aviation Administration and NORAD throughout. Only then did the Defense Secretary Donald Rumsfeld appear and he was in the building from about the time that Flight 11, the first hijacked plane, was leaving its gate at Boston Logan. More about Rumsfeld shortly, but let us stay with General Myers because this guy really is something else. You may have seen him: a grey-haired chap in uniform giving news conferences at the Pentagon while his forces bombed innocent civilians in Afghanistan and elsewhere. Two days after 9/11 Myers appeared before the Senate Armed Services Committee hearing that confirmed his appointment as Chairman of the Joint Chiefs of Staff. Committee Chairman Senator Carl Levin questioned him about what had happened while the attacks were taking place:

Levin: Was the Defense Department contacted by the FAA or the FBI or any other agency after the first two hijacked aircraft crashed into the World Trade Center, prior to the time that the Pentagon was hit?

Myers: Sir, I don't know the answer to that question. I can get that for you, for the record.

Levin: Thank you. Did the Defense Department take – or was the Defense Department asked to take action against any specific aircraft?

Myers: Sir, we were ...

Levin: ... And did you take action against – for instance, there have been statements that the aircraft that crashed in Pennsylvania was shot down. Those stories continue to exist.

Myers: Mr Chairman, the armed forces did not shoot down any aircraft. When it became clear what the threat was, we did scramble fighter aircraft, AWACS, radar aircraft and tanker aircraft to begin to establish orbits in case other aircraft showed up in the FAA system that were hijacked. But we never actually had to use force.

Levin: Was that order that you just described given before or after the Pentagon was struck? Do you know?

Myers: That order, to the best of my knowledge, was after the Pentagon was struck.[10]

Well, well, well. The highest-ranking military man in America, third only in military authority to the President and the Defense Secretary, and himself a former Commander of NORAD, does not know two days after 9/11 if his own Defense Department was contacted by the FAA or the FBI or any other agency after the first two hijacked aircraft crashed into the World Trade Center and before the Pentagon was hit? You mean he didn't ask at any time after he claims to have rushed to his "battle station", the National Military Command Center in the Pentagon, where they would have known everything that had happened? What utter tripe. He knew exactly the procedure and lines of communications as both the Acting Chairman of the Joint Chiefs of Staff and a former head of NORAD. He knew that the Defense Department, NORAD, and the FAA work closely in hijack situations and that the Pentagon would have been notified before the first plane crashed, never mind after the first two had done so. He knew that fighters are deployed as a matter of course to seek out rogue aircraft. General Myers you are a liar and the question that follows is why are you lying? Myers says that "to his knowledge" no order was given to scramble jets in response to the attacks until after the Pentagon was hit. "To his knowledge"? You mean he didn't ask that question either when he "ran" to the Pentagon or for two days afterwards? In that time no one told him? This question of whether jets were indeed scrambled before the Pentagon was struck is interesting because not only did Myers say that to his knowledge this was the case, this appeared to be NORAD's position for several days also, although NORAD spokesman Barry Venable says this is not the case and sent me an Associated Press report of September 11th in which NORAD spokesman Colonel Mike Perini is quoted as saying "NORAD controllers did track one of the hijacked planes, but it crashed into the World Trade Center even as fighters were scrambling." However, other NORAD spokesmen said the very opposite, as did General Myers. Two Cape Cod pilots, named only as Duff and Nasty, spoke to the BBC programme *Clear The Skies*, which slavishly and unquestioningly repeated the official story from start to finish. The pilots said they did scramble to New York, but could not get there in time.

Cue Dan

The "we did scramble planes" story only began to circulate after a report by Dan Rather, the Council on Foreign Relations member and CBS News "anchor". Rather is the man who told talk show host David Letterman: "George Bush is the President. He makes the decisions. Wherever he wants me to line up, just tell me where." [11] It was Rather who announced to the nation on September 14th that jets had been scrambled while quoting no sources. From this "Rather exclusive" the "we scrambled jets, but they were just too late" story became the official history. In fact on September 12th, Rather himself had asked the CBS Military Consultant, Colonel Mitch Mitchell, why the Pentagon didn't have a system in which fighters were used to defend against attacks like 9/11. [12] Rather's revelations that jets were deployed on September 11th before the Pentagon was hit came the day after the disastrous testimony of General Myers to the Senate Armed Forces Committee in which he had made the shocking statement that no fighters had been ordered to intercept the first three hijacked airliners over a period of nearly an hour and a half. Myers made no mention of planes scrambling from Otis or Langley, the CIA Air Force base where he was stationed for three years in the late 1980s. Then, hey presto, the following day the scrambled fighter jets story suddenly appeared on CBS. Dan Rather said that night:

> "CBS News has learned the FAA alerted US Air Defense units of a possible hijacking at 8.38 Tuesday morning, and six minutes later, at 8.44, two F-15s received a scramble order at Otis Air Force Base on Cape Cod. But two minutes later, at 8.46, American Airlines Flight 11, the first hijacked jet, slammed into the World Trade Center. Six minutes later, at 8.52, the F-15s were airborne and began racing towards New York City, but the fighters were still 70 miles away when the second hijacked jet, United Airlines Flight 175, hit the second Trade Center tower. Shortly after that blast, the F-15s reached Manhattan and began flying air cover missions over the city.

> "But to the south, a new danger and a new response. At 9.30, three F-16s were launched out of Langley Air Force base in Virginia, 150 miles [130] south of Washington. But just seven minutes later, at 9.37, American Airlines Flight 77 hit the Pentagon. The F-16s arrived in Washington just before 10am and began flying cover over the nation's capital." [13]

The contradictions can be clearly observed in two reports in the *Boston Globe* just four days apart. On Saturday, September 15th, reporter Glen Johnson highlighted the opposing accounts of CBS and NORAD. [14] After repeating Rather's CBS "exclusive" the night before, he writes that NORAD at this stage still denied scrambling any jets before the Pentagon was attacked, even though a NORAD spokesman, Marine Corps Major Mike Snyder, said they "routinely" intercept aircraft. Go figure. The *Globe* quoted Snyder as saying: "We scramble aircraft to respond to any aircraft that we consider a potential threat. The hijacked aircraft were normal, scheduled commercial aircraft on approved flight plans and we only had 10 minutes prior notice to the first attack, which unfortunately was not enough notice." [15] But he also confirmed that none were scrambled for the next hour either! The *Globe* story says:

" ... Snyder, the NORAD spokesman ... said the command did not immediately scramble any fighters even though it was alerted to a hijacking 10 minutes before the first plane, American Airlines Flight 11 from Boston to Los Angeles, slammed into the first World Trade Center tower at 8.45am Tuesday.

"Never before had a hijacked airliner been steered into a skyscraper, Snyder noted, in trying to explain the lack of immediate response.

"The spokesman said the fighters remained on the ground until after the Pentagon was hit by American Airlines Flight 77 at 9.40am, during which time the second trade center tower was struck by United Airlines Flight 175, which also originated in Boston and was destined for Los Angeles.

"By that time, military authorities realized the scope of the attack, Snyder said, and finally ordered the jets aloft." [16]

Vice President Cheney was still telling this same story on September 16th on the NBC show *Meet the Press* when he said it was Bush who personally made the decision to send up interceptors and he suggested this was only done after the Pentagon was hit. [17] How does that square with having fighters in the air heading for hijacked airliners before that time? [18] But then suddenly the story changed, new song sheets all round at Cheyenne Mountain and the Pentagon. By September 19th, eight days after 9/11, Glen Johnson and the *Boston Globe* were now reporting a very different version of events from NORAD. Johnson wrote that:

"Two fighter jets dispatched from Otis Air National Guard Base on Cape Cod had closed to within 71 miles of New York last week when the second of two hijacked airliners slammed into the World Trade Center towers, the military confirmed Tuesday.

"Similarly, two F-16 fighters that had scrambled from Langley Air Force Base in Virginia streaked toward Washington as a third airliner bore in on the Pentagon, but both were still about 12 minutes away when the commandeered plane struck the nation's military headquarters." [19]

This timeline, provided by NORAD, had miraculously changed. As Johnson rightly pointed out: "The account contradicted earlier statements from a defense command spokesman and the incoming chairman of the Joint Chiefs of Staff [General Myers]. Both said the military did not launch its planes until after the Pentagon had been hit." Now a "different defense command spokesman", Army Major Barry

Venable, said the previous statements were based on "inaccurate information".[20] I met Glen Johnson in Boston and he told me he had called the public affairs office at Otis Air Force Base to ask them to confirm that they did scramble planes that morning, but they refused to comment for reasons of "operational security" even though their bosses at NORAD had now issued a press release saying that they had. Johnson told me that eventually they would not return his calls. What goes on? I asked NORAD if I could speak with the pilots of the planes that were said to have been scrambled from Otis, but I was told they had "elected not to speak with the media".[21] They had no problem, however, speaking with the BBC programme *Clear The Skies* that unquestioningly repeated the official line and enjoyed great cooperation and access to Cheyenne Mountain and other military establishments as a result. I am not saying that the Otis and Langley jets were not scrambled, albeit way too late, but the blatant contradictions in the official story are constant and obvious.

Anyway, even according to this new timeline of NORAD and the Pentagon, no fighter jet got within 100 miles of even the fourth aircraft, Flight 93, before it crashed in Pennsylvania. Johnson highlights the obvious point that these "scrambled" jets flew to their targets at well below their potential speed. Why? We had the same contradictions with Flight 93 almost two hours after the problem was first identified with Flight 11. Major General Paul Weaver, director of the Air National Guard, said that "No Air National Guard or other military planes were scrambled to chase the fourth hijacked airliner, United Airlines Flight 93." [22] This is a staggering statement in itself. But Rumsfeld's Deputy Defense Secretary Paul Wolfowitz was quoted in the *Boston Herald* telling a very different story. He said that "… the Air Force was tracking the hijacked plane that crashed in Pennsylvania on Tuesday after other airliners slammed into the Pentagon and World Trade Center and had been in a position to bring it down if necessary".[23] The whole official story is a mess. During his "evidence" to the Senate Committee on September 13th, General Myers was questioned by Senator Bill Nelson, who clearly exposed how ridiculous the earlier explanations had been:

Nelson: The second World Trade tower was hit shortly after 9am. And the Pentagon was hit approximately 40 minutes later. That's approximately. You would know specifically what the timeline was. The crash that occurred in Pennsylvania after the Newark westbound flight was turned around 180 degrees and started heading back to Washington was approximately an hour after the World Trade Center second explosion. You said earlier in your testimony that we had not scrambled any military aircraft until after the Pentagon was hit. And so, my question would be: why?

Myers: I think I had that right, that it was not until then. I'd have to go back and review the exact timelines. *[He **thinks** that's right?]*

Nelson: Perhaps we want to do this in our session, in executive [secret] session. But my question is an obvious one for not only this committee, but for the executive branch and the military establishment. If we knew that there was a general threat on terrorist activity, which we did, and we suddenly have two trade towers in New York being obviously hit by terrorist activity, of commercial airliners taken off course from Boston to Los Angeles, then what happened to the response of the defense establishment once we saw the diversion of the aircraft headed west from Dulles turning around 180 degrees and, likewise, in the aircraft taking off from Newark and, in flight, turning 180 degrees? That's the question. I leave it to you as to how you would like to answer it. But we would like an answer.

Myers: You bet. I spoke, after the second tower was hit, I spoke to the commander of NORAD, General Eberhart. And at that point, I think [think?] the decision was at that point to start launching aircraft.
[Pardon? In his interview with Armed Forces Radio and Television he said that when he came out of his meeting on Capitol Hill with Senator Max Cleland he was told of the second plane crashing into the WTC and that the Pentagon had just been hit. Only then, he said, did he talk to Eberhart. Myers is changing his accounts in response to Nelson's questions as they expose the inexplicable non-reaction of NORAD and the Pentagon. What Myers is therefore saying here again is that no planes were scrambled until after the Pentagon was hit.]

Myers: One of the things you have to understand, senator, is that in our posture right now, that we have many fewer aircraft on alert than we did during the height of the Cold War. And so, we've got just a few bases around the perimeter of the United States.
[What about the fighters a minute's flying time from Washington at Andrews AFB, which were deployed after the Pentagon was hit?]

Myers: So it's not just a question of launching aircraft, it's launching to do what? You have to have a specific threat. We're pretty good if the threat's coming from outside. We're not so good if the threat's coming from inside.
[Two planes have hit the WTC and another hijacked aircraft is heading for Washington and he says you have to have a "specific threat" before scrambling fighters? And "launching to do what?" Launching to do what they do every week of the year and as a former commander of NORAD he well knows that. Why were planes not deployed over Washington as soon as the World Trade Center was attacked? If it was felt right to do that after the Pentagon was hit why not before?]

Myers: In this case, if my memory serves me – and I'll have to get back to you for the record – my memory says that we had launched on the one that eventually crashed in Pennsylvania. I mean, we had gotten somebody close to it, as I recall. I'll have to check that out. *[Remember this is the top-ranking uniformed military officer in America speaking.]* I do not recall if that was the case for the one that had taken off from Dulles. But part of it is just where we are positioned around this country to do that kind of work because that was never – it goes back to Senator Collins' issue. Is this one of the things that we'll worry about. You know, what's next? But our posture today is not one of the many sites and the many tens of aircraft on alert. We just have a handful today.

Let us not forget that General Myers said that he headed straight for the command centre in the Pentagon after he came out of his meeting on Capitol Hill. The idea that he did not know that morning, never mind two days later, what fighter jets had been, or not been, scrambled is simply laughable. Of course he knew and what he said until he was faced with uncomfortable questions is that they did not scramble jets until the Pentagon was hit. When you have someone presenting such a travesty of the truth and dithering around unable to answer the most basic of questions – answers he would clearly have known – the alarm bells begin to explode. Later, Senator Nelson emphasises his point again to the committee:

> "Mr Chairman, may I, just for the record? Commenting from CNN on the timeline, 9.03 is the correct time that the United Airlines flight crashed into the south tower of the World Trade Center; 9.43 is the time that American Airlines Flight 77 crashed into the Pentagon. And 10.10am is the time that United Airlines Flight 93 crashed in Somerset County, Pennsylvania. So that was 40 minutes between the second tower being hit and the Pentagon crash. And it is an hour and seven minutes until the crash occurred in Pennsylvania." [24]

NORAD or snorad?

General Ralph Eberhart, Commander in Chief of NORAD and Space Command at Cheyenne Mountain, appeared on October 25th 2001 before the Senate Armed Services Committee Holds Hearing on the Role of Defense Department in Homeland Security. By now the new song sheets had been circulated all round. Eberhart said that the Federal Aviation Administration did not notify NORAD or the Department of Defense that Flight 77 was "probably hijacked" until 9.24am, even though it had changed course and turned back at about 8.55 – after the first plane had already crashed into the World Trade Center. So the plane was "probably hijacked"? Can it get any sillier? Eberhart said: "I show it as 9.24 that we were notified, and that's the first notification that we received. I do not know, sir, why it took that amount of time for FAA. I hate to say it, but you'll have to ask FAA." He was asked if they had now improved the communication system:

> "Sir, I assure you that we have, and we practice this daily now, and now it takes about one minute from the time that FAA sees some sort of discrepancy on their radar scope or detects a discrepancy in terms of their communication before they notify NORAD. So that certainly has been fixed.

> "I think at that time, the FAA was still thinking that if they saw a problem it was a problem that was a result of a mechanical failure or some sort of crew deviation. They weren't thinking hijacking. Today, the first thing they think is hijacking, and we respond accordingly." [25]

You can see from the evidence presented in the last chapter about the normal reaction procedures of the FAA and NORAD before September 11th that we are being seriously misled here. If you look at what happened to those planes it was clear to air traffic controllers that the aircraft were not suffering a "mechanical failure or some sort of crew deviation" and so why is Eberhart talking such nonsense? Senator Warner asked Eberhart if the FAA and NORAD had not rehearsed the possibilities of an aircraft being seized by terrorists. Eberhart replied:

"… although we practice this, day in and day out, the FAA sees on their scopes scores of problems that are a result of mechanical problems, switch errors, pilot errors, et cetera, and that's what they think when they see this".

Oh do come on. Contact was lost with the cockpits, transponders were turned off, there were massive changes of course, and planes were crashing into buildings. Then we are told there were calls from passengers on the planes and "terrorists" heard in the cockpits. Nothing to worry about, Ralph, must be a mechanical fault. Note also that he says they "practice this, day in and day out … " using the pre-September 11th tense if you read the sentence. Eberhart continued:

"Although we have exercised this, we have practiced it, in most cases it's a hijacking like most of the hijackings, all of the hijackings I'm aware of, where we have plenty of time to react, we get on the wing, and we follow this airplane to where it lands and then the negotiations start. We were not thinking a missile – an airborne missile that was going to be used as a target – a manned missile if you will.

"And in most cases when we practice this, regrettably we practiced it – the origin of this flight was from overseas and we did not have the time-distance problems that we had on that morning. We had plenty of time to react. We were notified that for sure there was a hijacking and we were notified that they were holding a gun to the pilot's head and telling him to fly toward New York City or Washington, DC. So that's how we had practiced this, sir.

"I certainly wish we had practiced it differently, but I really think that, for sure in the first two instances, and probably in the third, the time and distance would not have allowed us to get an airplane to the right place at the right time." [26]

What is this man saying? His operation has access to the most sophisticated tracking and surveillance technology on earth – and in space – known to man. Two planes hit the World Trade Center and he claims they don't have the time to intercept a plane that turned back 45 minutes before it struck the Pentagon? He says that they "were not thinking a missile – an airborne missile that was going to be used as a target – a manned missile if you will", but two such "missiles" had already crashed into the World Trade Center before the non-reaction to Flight 77 in Washington by the FAA-NORAD system. Then out came the song sheet when

Senator Wayne Allard asked him if they had aircraft "at least up in the air with the second plane to hit the twin towers". Eberhart replied, "Yes sir." The following exchange then took place:

Allard: And so what I'm interested in knowing is, what was the process there and then, how was that followed-up with the other aircraft that you identified that were coming or heading toward Washington, and how you responded? And how was the FAA interacting with NORAD in that whole situation, starting with that first plane that you deployed heading toward New York City?

Eberhart: Yes, sir. The first flight I think was American Flight 11. *[He **thinks**?]* The FAA, once they notified us and we issued a scramble order almost simultaneously to the first crash, tragically. That flight of two out of Otis Air Force Base, out of Cape Cod ...

Allard: Let me understand – so right at the time the first aircraft was hitting the twin towers, you were being notified by FAA that you had another plane headed toward the towers, you just routinely brought another aircraft ...

Eberhart: No, they notified us of the first hijacking just about the time that that airplane was hitting the tower.

Allard: OK.

Eberhart: And at that time, we issued a scramble order for the two F-15s out of Otis Air Force Base *[even though NORAD was denying this for a week]*. We continued to send those airplanes toward New York City because initially, as we worked with the FAA, we weren't sure if that was the hijacked airplane *[a ludicrous statement]*. I mean, I hate to admit this, but I'm sitting there hoping that someone has made a mistake; there has been an accident; that this isn't the hijacked airplane, because there is confusion. We were told it was a light commuter airplane. It didn't look like that was caused by a light commuter airplane. *[With NORAD's technology they would have known exactly what it was, so why is he saying this?]* So we were still trying to sort this out, so we're moving the two F-15s and we continue to move them. They're flying toward New York City. In fact, they are eight minutes away from New York City when the second crash occurs. We didn't turn around. We didn't send them back.

Allard: They hadn't made a sighting of that ...

Eberhart: Again, it's time and distance. It took them only six minutes to get airborne. *[The US Air Force claims a potential response time of 2.5 minutes from scramble to 29,000 feet.]* Once we told them to get airborne, it took them six minutes to get airborne. I think this talks about the professionalism and training of these individuals. Tragically, there was just too much distance between Otis and New York City to get there in time to ...

Allard: Did FAA then notify you that you had a second hijacked plane somewhere in there, and the planes up there were ...

Eberhart: During that time, yes, we were notified, and again we'll provide the exact time line for the record.

Allard: I'm not interested in exact time lines as much as I am just how the FAA reacted with NORAD during this time period. And then you had the other two planes heading out. Then FAA continued to notify NORAD that you had two other potential hijackings, these headed for Washington; is that correct?

Eberhart: Yes, sir. The initial hijacking of the one, I think *[think?]* it's 77 that crashed into the Pentagon, we were working that with the FAA and we launched the airplanes out of Langley Air Force Base as soon as they notified us about hijacking. At that time it took those airplanes, two F-16s, again, six minutes to get airborne. They were approximately 13 minutes away from Washington, DC, when that tragic crash occurred. Six minutes to get airborne, but still 13 minutes to it.

I don't want to worry you, but this guy is the head of the operation that is supposed to protect the United States from attacks from air and space. Better get that shelter dug smartish. Eberhart also revealed that NORAD helped to provide the radars used by the FAA to track aircraft in US airspace and that NORAD has "moved manpower on the order of about 200 people over the years to the FAA to operate these radars". I wonder if any NORAD staff were on FAA duty that day? We can't know because no one is saying and if they did, would you believe them? Eberhart also said that he could not discuss in an open session who had the authority to order a commercial plane to be shot down, even though the White House had confirmed it was the President before 9/11 and that the head of NORAD and a list of other named military men could now issue such an order. Oh, by the way, at the end of Senator Allard's questioning in which Eberhart's answers were pathetic to anyone who has looked at what should have happened on 9/11, the Senator said: "Well, I just want to thank you and your people for, I know, I think a tremendous effort in light of some totally unexpected circumstances. And at least, I, for one, appreciate, you know, the readiness that was displayed." I know, incredible isn't it? But these are the people running our world.

Where was Rumsfeld?

OK, we have established where General Myers was that morning – nowhere to be seen. But what about the Defense Secretary Donald Rumsfeld, the number two in the United States military command structure? It turns out he was working on the east side of the Pentagon from before the time that Flight 11 took off from Boston. He told the CNN talk show *Larry King Live* on December 5th that he was in his office and was given no warning whatsoever that Flight 77 was heading for Washington before it crashed into the Pentagon.[27] Can the official story get any more insane? Unfortunately it can. This is the headquarters of the US military with open lines to NORAD at Cheyenne Mountain with all its satellites, AWACS and ground-based surveillance, and with open lines by now with the FAA. Two planes had already crashed into the World Trade Center and the US Defence Secretary was given no warning that an aircraft was about to crash into the building he was in, albeit a long, long, way from impact? This is an extraordinary statement and more transparent tosh. Larry King failed to ask a single question about the Defense Secretary's ridiculous story, but that, of course, will surprise no one. Rumsfeld related to King that earlier that morning he had told a congressional delegation in his office at the Pentagon: "Sometime in the next two, four, six, eight, ten, twelve months, there would be an event that would occur in the world that would be sufficiently shocking that it would remind people, again, how important it is to have a strong, healthy Defense Department that contributes – that underpins peace and stability in our world. And that is what underpins peace and stability." [28] How prophetic. Then came another outrageous statement that Rumsfeld made to King. He said that during this meeting in his office …

"… someone walked in and handed me a note that said that a plane had just hit the World Trade Center. And we adjourned the meeting. And I went in to get my CIA briefing right next door here, and the whole building shook within 15 minutes. And it was a jarring thing." [29]

Now hold on here. The first plane hit the World Trade Center at about 8.46. The Pentagon wasn't hit until around 9.38. Yet Rumsfeld tells King he was handed a note saying a plane had "just" hit the WTC and within 15 minutes Flight 77 crashed into the Pentagon? Are we being asked to believe that the Defense Secretary wasn't told about the first plane hitting the WTC until some 40 minutes after it happened when he is sitting in his own office at the Pentagon all this time? This is the only way that the "within 15 minutes" can be explained. Most of America and hundreds of millions across the world were watching events unfold live on television before 9am and yet the Defense Secretary, number two only to the President in the US military command, didn't know until about 9.20? Where does that leave the "just" hit the World Trade Center in the Rumsfeld story and why was he not told about the second hit on the WTC at the same time? Rumsfeld's own Department of Defense manual says: "In the event of a hijacking, the [National Military Command Center at the Pentagon] will be notified by the most expeditious means by the FAA. The NMCC will, with the exception of immediate responses … forward requests for DOD assistance to the Secretary of Defense for approval." [30] Given this procedure alone the Secretary of Defense would surely have been told immediately the first plane hit the north tower – 50 to 55 minutes before the Pentagon was hit, not 15. In fact, he would have had to be told under the Pentagon's own procedures immediately it was known that the first plane had been hijacked. That would have been around 8.20 – an hour and 20 minutes before the Pentagon was hit. The lies are just so blatant.

The *Washington Post* reported that after Rumsfeld was informed of the World Trade Center attack by his Chief of Staff he "stayed in his office on the east side of the Pentagon for a scheduled CIA briefing" – note "scheduled" – while "several of his senior aides rushed to the Pentagon's command center deep within the five-sided complex, where a crisis action center [no-action center] was being set up." [31] If you only believe the ludicrous official version that Pentagon officials were given 12 minutes' warning of the plane heading their way, why would no one tell the Defense Secretary before he felt his "jarring thing"? And, according to the official story from Rumsfeld's own military, jets were dispatched from Langley at 9.30 to intercept the plane and yet Rumsfeld and others in the Pentagon had no warning that the building was likely to be hit? Nowhere, but nowhere, do their pieces fit and there is a very good reason for that. It's a pack of lies. I contacted the Pentagon with the following list of questions, but officials chose not to answer them.

1. With the capability of United States air defence, how can a hijacked airliner, Flight 77, be allowed to fly for 45 minutes towards Washington, with communication lost with air traffic control and the transponder turned off, approach a No Fly Zone and hit your headquarters without any challenge whatsoever?

2. Why was the Defense Secretary Mr Rumsfeld unaware that the plane was approaching until the Pentagon was actually struck?

3. Why was Secretary Rumsfeld not told of the first plane striking the WTC until around 15 minutes before Flight 77 struck the Pentagon (thus about 9.20am to 9.25am)? Why was he not told at this time that a second plane had struck the World Trade Center?

4. Why was Richard Myers, the acting chairman of the Joint Chiefs of Staff, not informed that two planes had struck the WTC and that another was heading for Washington while he was in a scheduled meeting on Capitol Hill and available throughout? Why did he only learn of what was happening when he emerged from the meeting to be told that the Pentagon had been hit? Is there not a constant communication link between the Chairman and the Pentagon?

5. Why were the ground to air defences at the Pentagon and the White House not activated when Flight 77 approached?

6. Why is there no survelliance camera footage of Flight 77 from much closer to the point of impact? The pictures released by the Pentagon seem to be a long way away for a building that must be guarded by a very large number of cameras, many of them looking outwards.

Dan Philbin from the Office of the Assistant Secretary of Defense (Public Affairs) Directorate for Public Inquiry and Analysis merely referred me to transcripts of Pentagon press briefings on the Internet that did not address these questions.[32] I told him so and asked for direct answers, but he did not respond. Mind you, if I were the Pentagon I wouldn't want to be faced with answering these questions either because to do so credibly is simply not possible.

Where was Bush?

So to George W. Bush. Where was he when his country needed a decisive President? He was not in Washington that morning, which doesn't surprise me at all. Instead, as I have already mentioned, he was back in brother Jeb's state of Florida for a pre-publicised photo opportunity at the Emma E. Booker Elementary School in Sarasota. What he did that morning, and when and how he heard of Flight 11 striking the World Trade Center, depends very much on which official account you want to hear. There are several from people like Bush, Cheney and Ari Fleischer, the President's press secretary. Sonya Ross, an Associated Press reporter, said she knew of the first crash even before Bush had reached the school that morning:

> "My cell phone rang as President Bush's motorcade coursed toward Emma E. Booker Elementary School in Sarasota, Florida. A colleague reported that a plane had crashed into the World Trade Center in New York. No further information.

> "I called the AP desk in Washington, seeking details. Same scant information. But I knew it had to be grim. I searched for a White House official to question, but none was on hand until 9.05am." [33]

If her office knew and enough time had passed for them to call her on a cellphone, Bush must have known well before he arrived at the school that the aircraft had crashed into the WTC, and he must have known even earlier that there was a hijack in progress on Flight 11. Contact was lost with the aircraft at 8.13am and the President travels with a staff that is in instant contact with the National Military Command Center (NMCC) at the Pentagon, which coordinates with NORAD, the FAA and the government intelligence network. John Cochran, an ABC journalist, was reporting Bush's visit to Florida that day. He told Peter Jennings on ABC:

> "Peter, as you know, the President's down in Florida talking about education. He got out of his hotel suite this morning, was about to leave, reporters saw the White House Chief of Staff, Andy Card, whisper into his ear. The reporter said to the President, 'Do you know what's going on in New York?' He said he did, and he said he will have something about it later. His first event is about half an hour at an elementary school in Sarasota, Florida." [34]

How do you explain the report that when Card whispered in the President's ear outside his hotel that Bush "did not respond"? Would he not have been utterly shocked and insisted on cancelling the school visit to handle the situation? After all, at that time he was the only one who could give permission for a civilian airliner to be shot down. How could he be ready to react to events sitting in a classroom listening to children reading? One reason why someone would not be stunned to hear such information, of course, is if they already knew what was going to happen. At the very least from about 8.46am when Flight 11 crashed, the secret service that looks after the safety of the President had "open lines" with the Federal Aviation Administration. This was confirmed by Vice President Dick Cheney on NBC's *Meet the Press*.[35] In truth, the open lines would surely have been activated earlier than that when Flight 11 began to act very strangely and dramatically change course. The Bush team in Florida knew precisely what the FAA knew by that time – indeed suspected from about 8.20 – that Flight 11 had been hijacked. It would have been the most basic security response to keep the President away from a pre-arranged, publicised, event at a school, especially as it is only five miles from the Sarasota-Bradenton International Airport. Especially after Flight 11 struck the World Trade Center the thought that the President could be a target of a similar attack must have occurred to them, yet there appears to have been no discussion about the President's security given these circumstances and off he went to the school as planned. Did they know something we didn't?

"There's one terrible pilot"

Despite the eye-witness reports of when Bush must have known that Flight 11 was in trouble, he completely contradicted this – and the earlier accounts of his own officials – in an extraordinary performance on December 4th at a "town meeting" at the Orange County Convention Center in Orlando, Florida, where he was answering non-challenging questions from a sycophantic audience. I actually watched this happen live on CNN in a hotel bar. As I sipped my beer and despaired at the hero worship being enjoyed by a village idiot, Bush made a startling statement about September 11th. For the next two days I scanned the newspapers, the Internet "news" sites, including CNN, but there was no mention of the amazing statement he had made. Weeks later a Belgian visitor to my website sent me the words that Bush had said. They were posted on the White House website, hidden away in the full and long transcript of the meeting.[36] Bush was talking about what happened on September 11th and how he heard of the atrocities in New York, in answer to a question from a young boy called Jordan:

> "Well, Jordan, you're not going to believe what state I was in when I heard about the terrorist attack *[well it didn't show]*. I was in Florida. And my Chief of Staff, Andy Card – actually, I was in a classroom talking about a reading program that works. I was sitting outside the classroom waiting to go in, and I saw an airplane hit the tower – the TV was obviously on. And I used to fly, myself, and I said, well, there's one terrible pilot. I said it must have been a horrible accident. But I was whisked off there; I didn't have much time to think about it. And I was sitting in the classroom, and Andy Card, my Chief of Staff, who is sitting over here, walked in and said, 'A second plane has hit the tower, America is under attack.'"

Figure 18: *"Mr President, America is under attack."*
"OK Andy, as soon as I've heard what happens to this goat, I'll be right out."

A few facts. There was no live television coverage of the first plane hitting the tower – how could there be? The recorded footage of the first crash did not air until long after Bush went into the classroom where he was told of the second crash by Card (*Figure 18*). The live pictures were of the second plane when the television networks were already broadcasting shots of the burning north tower. How could he, therefore, claim to have seen the first plane strike? This is simply not possible, so what on earth is he talking about? What about his reaction of "there's one terrible pilot"? Uh? A passenger jet crashes into a 110-storey building full of people and all the President of the United States can say is "there's one terrible pilot"! We have already seen that Bush must have known about the first crash before he even arrived at the school and he wants us to believe that the President of the United States, the Commander-in-Chief of US forces and "homeland" defence, would not be told before that time how contact with Flight 11 had been lost, its transponder had been turned off, and that it had veered sharply off-course? Contact was lost at 8.13 and the plane did not hit the north tower until about 8.46. The Federal Aviation Administration, NORAD and the National Military Command Center at the Pentagon were tracking the plane from soon after contact ceased. Bush, remember, said before leaving his hotel for the school that he would "have something" later about what was happening in New York and the Associated Press reporter said she knew of the first crash before Bush had even arrived at the school. Yet he says that he saw the plane crash on a television at the school (not possible) and his reaction was: "I used to fly myself, and I said, well, there's one terrible pilot. I said it must have been a horrible accident." Lies, lies, lies again. Bush's story is also in direct contradiction to the earlier official version that he was told about Flight 11 in a call from his National Security Adviser Condoleezza Rice before he went into the classroom.[37] This, in turn, contradicts the accounts of reporters who make it clear that Bush must have known what was happening before he arrived at the school.

Then, knowing what had happened and knowing the plane had been hijacked, how does the President of the United States react to these monumental events? He walks into a classroom to read to children from the second grade and hear them read him a story about a pet goat! As the children read to him he said: "Really good readers – whew!" Bush interrupted at one point, saying, "This must be Sixth Grade." God help us. There has just been a catastrophe in New York, Mr President, involving thousands of people and you know the cause is a hijacked airliner. Hello? When Andrew Card came into the classroom and whispered in his ear that a second plane had hit the World Trade Center and that "America is under attack", what does the President do then? He continues to sit there listening to a story about a pet goat. If you were writing this as fiction they'd say it was a ridiculous story. Associated Press reported on September 12th:

> "In Sarasota, Florida, Bush was reading to children in a classroom at 9.05am when his chief of staff Andrew Card whispered into his ear. The president briefly turned somber before he resumed reading. He addressed the tragedy about a half-hour later." [38]

He "briefly" remained somber, or sombre, as we spell it in Britain? He's just been told that a second commercial airliner has struck the World Trade Center. Death and destruction on a massive scale was already obvious and the President knew the first plane had been hijacked before he went into the classroom. Yet he turned "briefly somber" before continuing to focus on the adventures of a pet goat. Jenna Heath of Cox Newspapers' Washington Bureau reported that Bush "did not appear preoccupied" as he introduced Education Secretary Rod Paige inside the classroom and shook hands with teacher Sandra Kay Daniels. "There was no sign that [Condoleezza] Rice had just told Bush about the first attack on New York's World Trade Center during a telephone call," Heath wrote.[39] Look at his reaction when Card "whispered in his ear" before he left his hotel? "He did not respond," said witnesses. Is this really a natural response from a man who has just been told of such events in the country he is supposed to be leading? Or is it the response of someone who knew full well what was going on and why? Bush told the Florida town meeting on December 4th:

> "But I knew I needed to act. I knew that if the nation's under attack, the role of the Commander-in-Chief is to respond forcefully to prevent other attacks from happening. And so, I've talked to the Secretary of Defense; one of the first acts I did was to put our military on alert." [40]

Bush says he knew he needed to act, but the indisputable truth is that he didn't. What's all this about calling Defense Secretary Rumsfeld? When did he do that? Rumsfeld told Larry King that even though he was in his office in the Pentagon he didn't know anything was happening until he was handed a note while meeting a congressional delegation in his office little more than 15 minutes before the Pentagon was struck at about 9.38. We are being told here that although the President knew well before 9am, the Defense Secretary was not told until at least half an hour later even though he was in the Pentagon. Wherever you look there is a deluge of lies and contradictions. Bush says that he put the military on alert, but he could not have done this until he was finished with the goat story and left the classroom shortly before 9.30 – more than 40 minutes after the first plane hit. As I mentioned, the official tale (official version 99933/S11/666/update/triplicate) is that Bush was taken to a private room before he went into the classroom and spoke on the phone with his National Security Adviser Condoleezza Rice, who told him about Flight 11. We are told that at this point the crash of Flight 11 could have been considered just a "terrible accident" – an obvious lie. If Bush talked to his National Security Adviser before 9am, how come Defense Secretary Rumsfeld says he didn't know anything for another 25 minutes? Why was Rice not in immediate contact with Rumsfeld? Why wasn't the President? Why wasn't anyone? It was 9.30 – 26 minutes after hearing of the second crash – before Bush went into the school library to announce:

> "Ladies and gentlemen, this is a difficult moment for America. Two airplanes have crashed into the World Trade Center, in an apparent terrorist attack on our country. I am going to conduct a full-scale investigation and hunt down and find those folks who committed this act. Terrorism against our nation will not stand."

No, Mr Bush, you were about to name the patsy and the target that suited the agenda of those who control you. The "folks" are much closer to home, as you well know.

The lie about scare force one

Bush was taken to Air Force One, the presidential plane, and even the official story says that he did not call Vice President Cheney and put the US military on high alert status until at least 10am, by which time the Pentagon had been hit. Bush headed for Barksdale Air Force base, Louisiana, and the US Strategic Command at Offutt Air Force base in Nebraska, and did not arrive at the White House, via the Andrews Air Force Base, until shortly before 7pm. This was more than ten hours after the first strike on the World Trade Center. When understandable questions were being asked about why Bush did not head straight for Washington to lead his country at such a terrible time, the White House said that they had received a phone call giving a secret code to say that Air Force One was the next target. No they didn't, that was yet another lie. John Ashcroft, the Attorney General and the man who delivers "justice" to others, also said the "government has credible evidence that the White House and Air Force One were targets".[41] Lie again. Reports were circulated through the news agencies on September 12th that quoted a White House spokesman as saying: "There was real and credible information that the White House and Air Force One were targets of terrorist attacks and that the plane that hit the Pentagon was headed for the White House." Ari Fleischer, the White House Press Secretary, confirmed this the same afternoon. The Secret Service had "specific and credible information" that the White House and Air Force One were potential targets, he said. Bush's chief political strategist, the Enron shareholder Karl Rove, was quoted the following day as confirming that the threat came in language that proved the terrorists had knowledge of the President's "procedures and whereabouts".[42] So why did they allow him to attend a publicised appearance at a school in the circumstances of that morning and why, if there was a specific threat to Air Force One, was Bush taken straight to the airport to take off in that plane after he had finished with the pet goat story? Maureen Dowd wrote in the *New York Times* that Karl Rove had "called around town, trying to sell reporters the story."[43]

But two weeks later the White House was forced to back down on the whole fantasy and on September 25th the CBS *Evening News* reported that the call "simply never happened".[44] Most newspapers did not even report this fantastic exposure of the lies spewed out daily by the Bush administration, and the *Washington Post* only ran the story on an inside page.

It was this same White House press spokesman, Ari Fleischer, who repeated the lies about Air Force One, which told us how Flight 77 was heading for the White House before it "veered off" and aimed at the Pentagon. Vice President Cheney said the same on NBC's *Meet the Press*. He confirmed that the plane was being tracked (so why no response?) and "when it entered the danger zone and looked like it was headed for the White House was when they grabbed me and evacuated me to the basement ..."[45] They waited, he claims, until the aircraft was "in the danger zone" before evacuating the Vice President when they had been tracking a hijacked plane's progress towards Washington for some 40 minutes after two planes had already crashed into the World Trade Center. The *CBS News* Transportation Correspondent Bob Orr reported that the recorded flight path of Flight 77 does not support what Cheney and Fleischer claim:

> "Eight minutes before the crash, at 9.30am EDT, radar tracked the plane as it closed to within 30 miles of Washington. Sources say the hijacked jet continued east at a high speed toward the city, but flew several miles south of the restricted airspace around the White House."

Once again I sent a list of questions to the White House media office relating to these events. They were faxed in May 2002, but they chose not to answer.

1. When did the President know that Flight 11 was in trouble or there could be a problem? When did the FAA, NORAD, and the Pentagon communicate this information to the President's support team in Florida that morning?
   Would not respond.

2. Why, when he was told of the first plane striking the WTC, did the President continue with his engagement and go into a reading class at the Emma Booker School?
   Would not respond.

3. Why when told by Andrew Card in the classroom that a second plane had struck the WTC and that "America is under attack", did he continue to stay in the classroom for some time?
   Would not respond.

4. When did the President put the United States military on high alert?
   Would not respond.

5. Why did the President not go back to Washington immediately when we now know that the story of the telephone warning that Air Force One was the next target never happened?
    Would not respond.

6. Why did the President tell a public meeting that he saw the first plane strike the WTC and said "There's one a terrible pilot", when he could not possibly have seen that happen before he entered the classroom? That footage was not aired until much later.
    Would not respond.

7. Why was the President not considered to be in danger when the attacks began, and thus removed from the school and a pre-announced visit when the school was only a short distance from an airport?
    Would not respond.

Why no evacuation?

Another piece of criminal negligence – in truth more than that – was the failure to evacuate the Pentagon, the White House and other major Washington symbols until the Pentagon was struck. This was despite a warning apparently issued to the Pentagon by the Federal Aviation Administration. CNN, quoting "Defense Department officials", said that no action was taken for at least 12 minutes despite warnings that an airliner "appeared" to be heading towards Washington.[46] (In fact the aircraft must have been tracked heading in that direction for more than 40 minutes.) American Forces Press Service reported that personnel at the Pentagon realised they could be a target long before they were hit: "We were watching the World Trade Center on the television," said a Navy officer. "When the second plane deliberately dove into the tower, someone said, 'The World Trade Center is one of the most recognizable symbols of America. We're sitting in a close second.'"[47] The top people in the Pentagon, apparently, could not see what everyone else could. Or maybe, I would suggest, some of them could see very clearly, but did nothing. Retired General Wesley Clark, a former NATO Supreme Commander, said, "We've known for some time that some group has been planning this, obviously, we didn't do enough to prepare for such an attack."[48] Officials at the Pentagon, quoted by CNN, said, "no mechanism existed within the US government to notify various departments and agencies under such circumstances". No mechanism to evacuate the Pentagon with a flying bomb heading in its direction?? In contradiction of this, Pentagon spokesman Glenn Flood said "to call for a general evacuation, at that point, it would have been just guessing … We evacuate when we know something is a real threat to us."[49] Clearly something is only considered a "real threat" when it smashes into the building. Oh, it was a real threat then; better evacuate, I guess. *Newsday* reported that many of the building's 20,000 workers were still sitting at their desks when the plane struck, and some said they heard the crash but didn't know the plane had hit the

Pentagon until they saw it on TV![50] "The first thought everyone had was that it had been a bomb," said Victoria Clarke, a spokeswoman for Defense Secretary Rumsfeld.[51] Only with a hole in the side of the building and 125 employees and workers dead was the building evacuated followed by the White House, Capitol Hill and elsewhere. None of the Pentagon top brass were killed or injured because they did not work in the part of the building that was struck. General Richard Myers, the Chairman of the Joint Chiefs of Staff, had the unbelievable nerve to say at a memorial ceremony for the victims that they were "serving their country" in the course of doing their jobs at the Pentagon, "and on September 11 were called to make the ultimate sacrifice".[52] Sacrifice, I think, was the only appropriate word. They were allowed to die, as the recorded facts make so plain. All this was coldly calculated by those running the 9/11 operation because the more death and destruction they could cause, the bigger would be the problem, the bigger the reaction and therefore the bigger the solution that could be offered – a war without end and the dismantling of basic freedoms. The families of those who died in the Pentagon have an open and shut case for a lawsuit against the US government for the gross negligence that cost the lives of their loved ones. It is, however, as I continue to stress, far more than "negligence" that is behind all this.

And where was "Big Dick"?

Representatives of government, "security" agencies and the military at the highest levels constantly lied over and over about what did and did not happen. Which brings me to Dick Cheney. Where was the Vice President all this time? He told the media on September 12th that a clerical secretary watching television in his Washington office alerted him to the attacks.[53] Oh really, Dick. The Cheyenne Mountain official website says of the NORAD Command Center: "Redundant and survivable communications hotlines connect the Command Center to the Pentagon, White House, US Strategic Command, Canadian Forces Headquarters in Ottawa, other aerospace defense system command posts, and major military centers around the world."[54] Yet Cheney, sitting in the White House, says he learned of the attacks when a clerical secretary comes in and says, "Hey, you'll never guess what I've just seen on the telly." The whole story is a joke. But look at the common denominator here between Bush, Rumsfeld and Myers, the 1, 2, 3, in the military command structure, and Cheney. Their stories and actions all ensured that they were not in a position to react immediately to events until after the Pentagon was hit. Or rather they had an excuse not to do so. Bush was occupied with the goat story until shortly before the Pentagon was hit and then went straight into another room to make a statement to the media. Rumsfeld gave Larry King a tale that he knew nothing about the World Trade Center until 15 minutes before the Pentagon was hit, and claims no one told him that plane was coming. "So how could I order a response?" is the obvious implication. Myers says that he was in a pre-arranged meeting with a senator throughout the period between the first strike on the World Trade Center and the crash, almost an hour later, into the Pentagon. Isn't that all so terribly convenient? Another key question is where was Father George Bush, the orchestrator, with Cheney, of the Boy George "Presidency"? He admits himself that he was at the White House the night before, but says he flew to St Paul, Minneapolis, the next morning. What time the next morning? The first plane to be hijacked was Flight 11 at about 8.15. Two planes had crashed into the World Trade Center by 9.03 and, if Flight 93 had not been delayed well over half an hour before take-off, it is highly probable that all four aircraft would have hit their targets by around 9.40. What were Father Bush and Cheney doing while all this was going on?

Where were the ground-to-air defences?

There is one other massive red flag also, which provides yet more confirmation, as if it were needed, that the attacks of September 11th were allowed to happen by the very authorities that are, in retaliation, waging a global war on terrorism. While I was on a speaking tour in Australia a few weeks after 9/11, I was told by a man who is involved with the computer systems of the Australian military that his country's forces were on full alert status immediately the World Trade Center was hit. That makes it more than an hour before America, the target of the attacks, was put on the same status by George Bush once he had finished with the pet goat and arrived at Air Force One. But the Australian contact told me something else. He said that the Australian Parliament building in Canberra is protected from air attack by hidden ground-to-air missiles. He said that the procedure is as follows: when an aircraft enters the protected airspace around the parliament building the pilot is contacted immediately by a computer system that demands he or she punch in a code authorising the plane to fly into that airspace. If this is not done in seconds, the contact told me, the computer launches a missile to blow the plane from the sky. Even at the G-8 Summit in Genoa, Italy, in July 2001 airspace was closed over the city and defended with ground-to-air missiles. My Australian contact said he knew for a fact that the Pentagon and Washington DC in general are defended by an even more sophisticated missile system than Canberra, but works in basically the same way. It is obvious that this would be the case and it has been openly accepted that a ground-to-air system is in place to defend the White House. The *Globe and Mail* newspaper in Canada provided one of the rare mentions of the Pentagon system. It reported: "Meanwhile, there was no explanation of how four airliners could be hijacked and flown – in at least two cases hundreds of kilometres and for nearly an hour – without being successfully intercepted. That one ploughed into the Pentagon, supposedly protected by surface-to-air missiles, dramatically demonstrated US vulnerability." [55] Why weren't those missiles launched to stop the Pentagon crash? The same reason that the FAA, NORAD and the Defense Department did not scramble fighter jets, or at least not in time. They weren't meant to.

An insider speaks

After I had originally completed this chapter I came across an investigative website that claims to have conducted a phone interview on December 9th 2001 with a member of the US Air Force based in New York. It was said that this source was ordered to the crash sites in New York, Pennsylvania and the Pentagon within days of 9/11 as part of an Air Force investigation. What he and others discovered, the website claims he told them, was that the standard response procedures were fully in effect that morning and were followed to the letter as usual by Air Traffic Control and that Air National Guard and Air Force units were alerted immediately it was clear that something was amiss with the four aircraft. But he said that after these alerts and requests for action were received from Air Traffic Control and the FAA, orders from the "highest level of the executive branch of the federal government were received, demanding that the Air Force stand down and not follow through with established scramble-intercept procedures that morning until further notice".[56] This Air Force contact was unnamed, but then, to be fair, how could he have been? People will just have to decide for themselves if what he is claimed to have said rings true. But it is a scenario that does fit what happened that morning and makes sense of the apparently nonsensical lack of response.

No planes were scrambled to intercept the hijacked planes (either at all or in time) and no ground-to-air defences were activated to save the lives of those who died inside the Pentagon and the World Trade Center. Some would call this incompetence. But staggering as that alone would be, what happened on September 11th is far more than that. It was calculated mass murder. The first position taken by the authorities is that there was nothing they could have done. That is what they really want you to believe. The second, when that doesn't work, is to let you think they were incompetent. Both positions are designed to hide the truth – the truth that what we are looking at here amid the explosion of lies and diversions is not incompetence at all. This was orchestrated incompetence in which forces at, and behind, the highest levels of the United States government and military were intervening to stop the system working as it normally would. To stop thousands of people going home to their families that September day because it suited the sick agenda for those people to die and for the world to watch it all live on television.

But these same forces did not only allow the atrocities to happen. They made them happen, too.

SOURCES

1   *New York Times*, September 15th 2001

2   *Newsday*, September 23rd 2001

3   **https://www.cheyennemountain.af.mil**

4   **CNN.com**, Pentagon Never Considered Downing Stewart's Learjet, President Would Have to Make Decision, October 26th 1999

5   CNN, September 17th 2001

6   *Larry King Live*, CNN, December 5th 2001,
     http://www.cnn.com/transcripts/0112/05/lkl.00.html

7   US Armed Forces Radio and Television Service, October 17th 2001. Transcript can be found
     at **http://www.dtic.mil/jcs/chairman/AFRTS_Interview.htm**

8   *New York Times*, September 15th 2001

9   **http://www.dtic.mil/jcs/chairman/AFRTS_Interview.htm**

10   Senate Arms Services Committee, September 13th 2001. You can read a full transcript at
     http://www.emperors-clothes.com/9/11backups/mycon.htm

11   *All Fall Down*, p 181

12   *CBS News Special Report*, September 12th 2001, "Aftermath of and investigation into
     attacks on World Trade Center and the Pentagon."

13   **http://emperor.vwh.net/9/11backups/changes.htm**

14   *Boston Globe*, September 15th 2001, third edition, p A1

15   Ibid

16   Ibid

17   (1a) *Meet the Press*, NBC, September 16th 2001

18   CNN, September 17th 2001

19   *Boston Globe*, September 19th 2001

20   Ibid

21   E-mail to the author from NORAD spokesman Barry Venable, May 20th 2002

22   *Seattle Times*, September 16th 2001

23   *Boston Herald*, September 15th 2001

24   Senate Arms Services Committee, September 13th 2001

25   Senate Armed Services Committee Holds Hearing on Role of Defense Department in
     Homeland Security, October 25th 2000

26   Ibid

27   *Larry King Live*, December 5th 2001

28   Ibid

29   Ibid

30   Chairman of the Joints Chiefs of Staff Instruction, Aircraft Piracy (Hijacking) and
     Destruction of Derelict Airborne Objects, dated June 2001.
     http://www.dtic.mil/doctrine/jel/cjcsd/cjcsi/3610_01a.pdf1

31   At the Pentagon: Response Hampered by Confusion, Lack of Preparedness, *Washington
     Post*, September 16th 2001, p A01

32   E-mail to the author, June 4th 2001

33   Associated Press, September 12th 2001. AP 12 September

34   *ABC News Special Report*, September 11th 2001

35   *Meet the Press*, NBC, September 16th 2001

36   **www.whitehouse.gov/news/releases/2001/12/20011204-17.html**

37   Bush Vows to Punish Attackers and Those who Harbored Them, *Cox Newspapers*, September 12th 2001

38   Associated Press, September 12th 2001

39   Bush Vows to Punish Attackers and Those who Harbored Them, *Cox Newspapers*, September 12th 2001

40   Town meeting at the Orange County Convention Center in Orlando, December 4th 2001

41   *Washington Post*, September 13th 2001,p A01

42   White House Lied about Threat to Air Force One, by Jerry White, September 28th 2001, World Socialist Website, **http://www.wsws.org/articles/2001/sep2001/bush-s28.shtml**

43   *New York Times*, September 23rd 2001

44   White House lied about threat to Air Force One, September 28th 2001, World Socialist Website, **http://www.wsws.org/articles/2001/sep2001/bush-s28.shtml**

45   *Meet the Press*, NBC, September 16th 2001

46   CNN, September 17th 2001

47   *Defenselink News*, September 13th 2001

48   Air Attack on Pentagon Indicates Weaknesses, *Newsday*, September 23rd 2001

49   Ibid

50   Ibid

51   At the Pentagon: Response Hampered by Confusion, Lack of Preparedness, *Washington Post*, September 16th 2001, p A01

52   Bush, Rumsfeld speak at Pentagon Memorial, CNN, October 11th 2001, **http://www.cnn.com/2001/US/10/11/rec.pentagon.memorial**

53   **http://www.whitecloud.com/wag_the_dog.htm**

54   **https://www.cheyennemountain.af.mil**

55   *Globe* and *Mail*, US Prepares for a New Kind of War, September 14th 2000

56   **http://www.indymedia.org:8081//front.php3?article_id=103406**

chapter 10

The "hijackers"

Many are destined to reason wrongly, others, not to reason at all; and others,
to persecute those who do reason.

Voltaire

Accepted versions of "truth" and "history" are rarely the result of factual
information. They are formed by simple repetition. Tell people something often
enough and they will believe it. Thus it has become the accepted truth and the
official history that 19 hijackers working for Osama bin Laden hijacked four
commercial aircraft, took over the controls, and flew them into the World Trade
Center and the Pentagon while the fourth crashed when passengers attacked the
Arab pilots. These hijackers, we are told, learned to fly at schools in the United
States where they trained on small light planes like the Cessna. Keep that in mind
as you read the next two statements. First a report on what happened when Flight
77 is said to have crashed into the Pentagon:

> "The hijacker-pilots were then forced to execute a difficult high-speed descending turn.
> Radar shows Flight 77 did a downward spiral, turning almost a complete circle and
> dropping the last 7,000 feet in two-and-a-half minutes. The steep turn was so smooth,
> the sources say, it's clear there was no fight for control going on. And the complex
> maneuver suggests the hijackers had better flying skills than many investigators first
> believed. The jetliner disappeared from radar at 9.37 and less than a minute later it
> clipped the tops of street lights and plowed into the Pentagon at 460 mph." [1]

Now the remarks of Rick Garza, a flying instructor at Sorbi's Flying Club in San
Diego, who remembers trying to teach Khalid al-Mihdhar and Nawaq al-Hamzi,
two of the Arab "pilots" alleged to have been on Flight 77:

> "It was like Dumb and Dumber. I mean, they were clueless. It was clear to me they
> weren't going to make it as pilots." [2]

A third "pilot" who is said to have been on board Flight 77 was Hani Hanjour.
The FBI announced at first that he was in the captain's seat performing that highly

skilled manoeuvre to approach the Pentagon and yet instructors at the Freeway Airport in Bowie, Maryland banned him from renting a plane, because he was such a poor pilot only *six weeks* before 9/11. Clearly there's something seriously wrong here with these stories. But, no problem, no worries, because what happened on those four flights and who was in the cockpits can be revealed by the information secured by the black boxes that contain the flight data and cockpit voice recorders. Er, well, perhaps not. Even though there were two in each plane we are told that most of them did not survive the crashes in a condition to provide this data and that others did not reveal information that would prove what happened. So many fatally damaged black boxes is rather strange to say the least, given that they are designed precisely to survive intact, as we have seen so many times in other air crashes all over the world year after year. The voice recorders, for example, were recovered from Egypt Air Flight 990, which crashed into the ocean, and TWA Flight 800, which exploded in mid air after leaving New York. A few facts to ponder from a report by *ABC News*:

> "Although investigators look for an entire black box, sometimes the only parts of the device that survive are the recorder's crash-survivable memory units (CSMU). The CSMU is almost indestructible. It is housed within a stainless-steel shell that contains titanium or aluminum and a high-temperature insulation of dry silica material.

> "It is designed to withstand heat of up to 2,000 degrees Fahrenheit for one hour, salt water for at least 30 days, immersion in a variety of liquids such as jet fuel and lubricants, and an impact of 3,400 Gs. By comparison, astronauts are typically exposed to up to six Gs during a shuttle takeoff." [3]

With a beacon transmitter the black boxes can be, and have been, located deep under the ocean and under piles of rubble when buildings have been struck. The *ABC News* information is confirmed by the United States National Transportation Safety Board on its official website. It also says that "both the Flight Data Recorder and the Cockpit Voice Recorder have proven to be valuable tools in the accident investigation process. They can provide information that may be difficult to obtain by other means".[4] What a pity, then, that so many black boxes were destroyed from four aircraft in four separate crashes. FBI spokesman Bill Crowley said the cockpit voice recorder of Flight 93 found at the Pennsylvania crash site was in "fairly good condition", but had been sent to the manufacturer for help in extracting information after officials with the National Transportation Safety Board could not get sound from the device.[5] The FBI later claimed to have played this cockpit recording to relatives of those who died on Flight 93, but was it the real one? What was heard certainly appeared to be inconclusive and unclear. The FBI said that the voice recorder on Flight 77, recovered, we are told, from the rubble of the Pentagon, could yield no information because it was too severely burned.[6] A black box can survive heat of 2,000 degrees Fahrenheit for an hour! I asked the FBI for details of the black boxes and their condition, but I was told that this information could not be given because of the "ongoing investigation". Every other question about the official story was met with the same response.

Life's little miracles

How amazing that black boxes made of virtually indestructible material can fail to survive and yet, according to the always-truthful New York Police Department and the FBI, the paper passport of one of the hijackers was found in a New York street even though it was in a plane that crashed in a fireball into the World Trade Center. Ain't life just incredible? The "passport" was found a few blocks from the WTC "in the vicinity of Vesty Street".[7] Away from the ruins of the building, then, and away from any prying eyes when it was "found". How about this for a laughable contradiction so typical of the official fairytale. FBI Assistant Director Barry Mawn told a news conference that the passport was found "several blocks" from the World Trade Center and it was possible (I love it) that other personal effects from the hijackers might have been expelled from the crash scene when the planes made impact. No, really. Mawn said they had launched a "grid search" of the whole area in the hope of finding other important evidence. Yet at the same news conference it was said that it was unlikely that the remains of the hijackers would be conclusively identified since nothing was likely to be available for use as a DNA match. What a joke. No bodies survive, just a passport one of them was carrying. I rang New York Police Department to request more details about this "passport" and their press office put me on to a Detective Burns, a man who, shall we say, was less than helpful. I asked him for the name of the "hijacker" to whom the passport belonged:

"I don't think that information has ever been given out."

"Why not?"

"Because it is part of our investigation and that investigation is still ongoing."

"How would that affect the investigation?"

"I don't know why, it's part of the investigation, I don't know why it would affect the investigation, it has never been given out and the reason it's never been given out is because it's part of the investigation." [Go figure.]

"So anything that's part of the investigation, the public's not allowed to hear?"

"Not until the investigation is complete."

"Which is when do you think?"

"I have no idea. You know, information may compromise the investigation, so that information was not given out."

"Who knows it and could give it out?"

"It is not going to be given out until the investigation is completed and the Chief of Detectives gives it out."

"So we have got to believe it happened, even though we don't know whose passport it was?"

"OK."

Detective Burns is another pawn caught in the game. Like airline and airport media spokespeople, he can only say what he is told to say from his compartmentalised prison. If knowing who owned the passport might prejudice the investigation, why announce that you have found one at all? The answer is obvious. Saying that you have found the passport supports the story of who the "hijackers" were and that they were on the aircraft. Telling us who owned the passport would prejudice, not the "investigation", but the cover story masquerading as an investigation. They won't tell us that "information" because the story is nonsense and if there is no passport there can be no "hijacker" owner. There is a simple equation we might consider here – those who tell the truth do not need to lie. Or, as Mark Twain once said: "When you tell the truth you don't have to remember anything." The official story tells so many lies so often that it has to remember everything it has previously said. This being impossible, given the different voices and departments (and the intellect of people like Bush), it is easy to see why there are so many holes and contradictions. Given a mainstream media with a modicum of basic intelligence and an ounce of will and courage to establish the truth there would be famous people in jail by now – and they would not be Arabs.

The CIA and FBI claimed they had no prior warning of the September 11th attacks even though that is what they are paid to establish. Clearly this is nonsense and has been shown to be so, but let's run with it for a moment. Let's say it was really true that they didn't know. This incompetence in failing to trace any orchestration of such a massive and long-planned attack on US soil would, in any sane society, lead to wholesale sackings and inquiries. But what happened? Bush has rewarded the CIA and FBI for their "incompetence" by vastly increasing their budgets. Again the contradiction can be explained by the realisation that these agencies were not supposed to stop the attacks before they happened, just as the FAA, NORAD and the Pentagon were not supposed to stop them while they were under way. Having failed, so they say, to track any sign whatsoever of the "terrorists" and their plans before September 11th, the FBI was able to name the 19 men it claims were responsible immediately afterwards. What brilliance. The problem was that seven, maybe more, of the 19 named by the FBI were found to be still alive! Now that is some trick, to fly planes into buildings and crash them into fields, and turn up thousands of miles away within days still very much in this world. You've got to hand it to these Arab guys, they're so cunning. Saudi Arabian Foreign Minister, Prince Saud Al-Faisal, revealed through the Arabic Press in New York that at least five Saudi men named were not dead and an official at the Saudi Arabian Embassy in Washington DC confirmed to the *Orlando Sentinel* that four of these still-alive hijackers were Saeed al-Ghamdi, Mohald al-Shehri, Abdulaziz Alomari and Salem al-Hamzi.[8] The list of the "guilty 19" was released by an FBI led by the Bush clone and appointee Robert Mueller, who took over the organisation only two weeks before September 11th. The following names and spellings appeared on an indictment presented by the US government to the United States District Court in Virginia in December 2001.

This "world" is only an illusion and we can change it any time we want. It's just a choice right now between fear and love.

American Airlines Flight 11

Mohamed Atta: an Egyptian national who is said to have been the leader of the hijackers and, says the FBI, the "pilot" who directed Flight 11 into the World Trade Center. The FBI also says that he once met with "Islamic extremists" at the Spanish resort of Salou, although no evidence is produced. Given the staggering untruths told by the FBI and other government agencies decade after decade, and never more so than since 9/11, you'll understand if I don't take the official information released on these matters at face value. Such "information" is so often of two-faced value. Atta is said to have used the name Mohamed El-Amir when he was an electrical engineering student at the Technical University in Hamburg, Germany, where he lived with his cousin Marwan al-Shehhi, who is said to have been on Flight 175. The FBI says that Atta arrived in the US with al-Shehhi in May 2000 and lived in Florida at Coral Springs, Hollywood, and Venice, where they attended the flying school run by Huffman Aviation before, we are told, training on flight simulators for the Boeing 727 at SimCenter in Opalacka, Florida. Atta and al-Shehhi are reported to have been seen in a bar in Hollywood five days before September 11th drinking and playing video games. Oh, fundamentalist Muslims, then?

Abdulaziz Alomari: said to have been a Saudi national, who gave an address in Jeddah. Alomari was described as a pilot and flight engineer and is claimed to have once worked for Saudi Flight Ops, a flight maintenance company at New York's JFK Airport. He is reported to have lived with his wife and four children in a rented house in Vero Beach, Florida, before leaving on September 3rd and telling his landlord he was returning home to Saudi Arabia. Video footage from surveillance cameras at the airport at Portland, Maine, is said to show Alomari with Atta boarding a flight to Boston on the morning of September 11th. Or rather it doesn't. Alomari was found to be still alive, as confirmed to the *Orlando Sentinel* by the Saudi Arabian Embassy in Washington. Abdulaziz Alomari, a pilot with Saudi Airlines, walked into the US Consulate in Jeddah to demand why he was being reported as a dead hijacker by the American media.[9] That whole FBI story outlined above is nonsense. Another Abdulaziz Alomari, a Saudi electrical engineer, said he lost his passport while studying in Denver, Colorado, and someone could have stolen his identity. He said: "I couldn't believe it when the FBI put me on their list. They gave my name and my date of birth, but I am not a suicide bomber. I am here. I am alive. I have no idea how to fly a plane. I had nothing to do with this."[10] It seems that the profile of the "hijacker" Alomari was a fusion of these two people. Robert Fisk, writing in the UK *Independent*, said it was possible that the hijacker adopted Alomari's identity, but, as Fisk rightly points out, if he had been using the same false name while training as a pilot in the US, he would presumably have been uncovered.[11]

Waleed M. al-Shehri: a "possible Saudi national", who the FBI says it believes lived in the US from at least 1994 and had both a social security number and a Florida driver's licence. He is said to have been a graduate from the Embry-Riddle Aeronautical University in Daytona Beach, Florida, and owned a commercial pilot's licence. A neighbour in Florida described him as a "nice guy" who supported the Florida Marlins baseball team. Until 14 months before 9/11 he lived at a boarding house three blocks from the CIA headquarters in Virginia, across the river from Washington DC, says the FBI, and when he left he told the landlord he was going home to Saudi Arabia. As it turns out, that is what he did. Waleed is still alive. He is a pilot with Saudi Airlines now taking further training in Morocco, according to an official of Royal Air Moroc, and his father says that he is alive and well and living in Morocco. So where does that leave the report by Kay Nehm, Germany's Chief Federal Prosecutor? He said that Waleed M. al-Shehri belonged to a terror group formed "with the aim of carrying out a series of crimes together with other Islamic fundamentalist groups abroad, to attack the United States in a spectacular way through the destruction of symbolic buildings".[12]

Wail al-Shehri: also said to have been a pilot by the FBI and "may" have lived in Florida and Massachusetts. Sorry chaps, it seems he is still alive. The *Los Angeles Times* reported that a man of the same name is the son of a Saudi diplomat in Bombay. "I personally talked to both father and son today," said Gaafar Allagany, the head of the information centre at the Saudi Embassy.[13]

Satam al-Suqami: believed to be from the United Arab Emirates. It is said that he had a Florida driver's licence with an address in Boynton Beach and also held a Saudi Arabian licence. Note that while the two flight attendants who are claimed to have made calls from Flight 11 both said there were four hijackers, the FBI claims five.

United Airlines Flight 175

Marwan al-Shehhi: the cousin of Mohamed Atta. The FBI claims that he and Atta had connections in Hamburg with an Islamic group planning attacks on American targets. Al-Shehhi was born in the United Arab Emirates, but while in Germany his mother said he told her he would not be returning home.[14] She felt someone was listening to their calls and using threats to stop him returning to his family. Al-Shehhi is said to be alive and living in Morocco according to some reports, but I have seen no confirmation of this.

Fayez Ahmed (also Banihammad Fayez): "may" have lived in Florida at Delray Beach and although his pilot's licence lists the address of the Spartan School of Aeronautics, Tulsa, Oklahoma, there is no record that he ever attended the school.

Ahmed al-Ghamdi: "may" have lived in Delray Beach and is reported to have lived at a boarding house near CIA headquarters in Virginia. Waleed M. al-Shehri is also reported to have lived in that same Vienna house.

Hamza al-Ghamdi: "may" have lived in Delray Beach.

Mohald al-Shehri: "may" have lived in Delray Beach. Plenty is known about these two, then. Al-Shehri was yet another who was not on the plane because he's still alive, according to the Saudi Embassy.

American Airlines Flight 77

Hani Hanjour: believed to have been the pilot who crashed the plane into the Pentagon, according to the FBI in its first "hijacker" list. But instructors at the Freeway Airport in Bowie, Maryland, where he took lessons just six weeks before 9/11, said that he was so poor they refused to rent him a plane. Hanjour took flying lessons at CRM Airline Training in Scottsdale, Arizona, in 1996 and 1997, we are told, but left before completing the classes he had paid for. The FBI says that he was given a commercial pilot's licence in 1999 and gave an address in Taif, Saudi Arabia, where, interestingly, the United States Military Training Mission to Saudi Arabia operates a joint training mission under the command of United States Central Command at MacDill Air Force Base, Florida. It is claimed that Hanjour joined the Sawyer School of Aviation flight simulator club in Phoenix, which gives members unlimited use of a flight simulator. He is said to have lived in Phoenix and San Diego, taking English lessons at the University of Arizona in 1991 and might have lived in Oakland, California in 1996. He stayed with a family in Miramar, Florida, for several weeks and they described him as a "kind and gentle man" who liked children. All in all the perfect profile of a fanatical Islamic kamikaze pilot with brilliant flying skills intent on mass murder.

Khalid al-Midhar (also Mihdhar): The FBI told us there was surveillance videotape showing al-Midhar meeting in Malaysia with one of the suspects in the bombing of the *USS Cole* in October 2000, but this is now open to serious question. Al-Midhar is said to have lived in San Diego in 2000, "may" have lived in New York, and joined Gold's Gym in Greenbelt, Maryland, weeks before 9/11. The FBI says he had two expired visas. Rick Garza, an instructor at Sorbi's Flying Club in San Diego, described the flying abilities of al-Midhar and his friend Nawaf al-Hamzi, as like "Dumb and Dumber". Al-Midhar would become so afraid during lessons that he would start praying to Allah, so he was just the man for a kamikaze plane hijacking.[15] Garza said they called from the Middle East to arrange lessons and paid with credit cards in their own names. Plenty to hide then. Al-Midhar was listed as "alive" in yet another list of FBI hijackers circulated to American banks,[16] and Arab newspapers also reported that he was still alive. This was the man that UK Prime Minister Tony Blair linked to terrorist attacks against US embassies and the *USS Cole* in his "evidence" against bin Laden. But the UK *Guardian* reported that his identity is the subject of much confusion because it was believed that he was using several aliases and, the paper said, American investigators "are not even certain that his name is really Khalid al-Mihdhar".[17] How can the FBI be so certain that

Khalid al-Mihdhar or Midhar was on Flight 77, and how can they say he was caught on video in Malaysia, if they don't really know who he is? According to *Arab News*, a young Saudi computer programmer called Khalid al-Mihammadi was confused with al-Mihdhar and had "the shock of his life when he saw that his picture was among the suspects who had hijacked American Airlines Flight 77 that crashed into the Pentagon in Washington on Sept. 11." [18] Al-Mihammadi had studied English in the United States for nine months, but had returned to Saudi Arabia earlier in the year. Associated Press reported that "officials, speaking on condition of anonymity", said they were exploring several possibilities: al-Midhar never entered the country and his name was used as an alias by one of the hijackers; he allowed his name to be used on the flight by another hijacker to kid US officials that he died; he did in fact die in the crash as a hijacker.[19] There is a fourth possibility, of course: the whole story is bollocks.

Nawaf al-Hamzi: we are told that, with al-Midhar, he bought a Toyota Corolla bearing California licence plates. He was the other half of "Dumb and Dumber". Al-Hamzi's San Diego landlord said he helped him to open an account at the Bank of America and showed him how to write an advertisement in English on the Internet looking for a Mexican wife. Yep, sounds like we have another Islamic fundamentalist on our hands here. The manager of his apartment block in Clairemont, San Diego, says he was a model tenant who often dropped in for coffee and cookies.[20] Flying instructor Rick Garza described al-Hamzi as charming. He had a "great, great personality", and was "someone you could become attached to very quickly," Gaza said. "They [came] back to say goodbye, that's how nice they were." Garza remembered how they said: "We'll come see you once our English improves." [21] Al-Hamzi's father says that the photograph of his son released by the FBI looks nothing like him and had been fabricated. He apparently issued a picture of his son that was clearly different from the one circulated by the FBI.[22]

Salem al-Hamzi: brother of Nawaf and believed to have lived in Fort Lee and Wayne, New Jersey. The FBI says he was one of the group that attended Gold's Gym in Greenbelt, Maryland. Well he had a long way to travel just to keep fit because the Saudi Embassy in Washington confirmed he is still alive and works at a petrochemical plant in Yanbou, Saudi Arabia.[23] Once again his father says that the picture issued by the FBI bears no resemblance to him, and produced his own picture to prove it.[24]

Majed Moqed: also said to have attended Gold's Gym in Greenbelt between September 2nd and 6th with Khalid al-Midhar, Nawaf al-Hamzi, Salem al-Hamzi and Hani Hanjour. An employee at the gym said they refused long-term membership and paid for the sessions with "a wad of cash". He was seen on a surveillance camera with Hani Hanjour using an ATM machine in Laurel, Maryland, on September 5th, or so it is claimed.

United Airlines Flight 93

Saeed al-Ghamdi: The FBI says he "may" have lived in Delray Beach, but the Saudi Embassy revealed that he is still alive and has been working for Tunis Air. He said: "I was completely shocked. For the past 10 months I have been based in Tunis with 22 other pilots learning to fly an Airbus 320. The FBI provided no evidence of my presumed involvement in the attacks." [25]

Ziad Jarrah: "may" have been a pilot says the FBI, but his mother, Nafisa Jarrah, told the London *Daily Mirror* that her son was no Muslim fanatic. He had attended an evangelical Christian school in Lebanon and later said he "wouldn't mind marrying a non-Muslim". He enjoyed dancing, loved his family, immersed himself in western culture and loved to socialise. He was planning to marry his Turkish girlfriend two weeks after September 11th. She was a student at the American University in Beirut, which has a reputation for attracting the children of the westernised elite of the Arab world. They later moved to university in Germany and she reported him missing after the 9/11 attacks. His uncle, Jamal Jarrah, was quoted in the UK *Independent* of September 16th as saying:

> "He was so normal. His personality and his life bore no relation to the kind of things that happened. He led a very normal life. He had girlfriends, he went to nightclubs, he went dancing sometimes."

The article says that everyone who knew Ziad Jarrah said he was a happy, secular youth, who liked women and that he never showed any interest in religion and never visited the mosque for prayers. The media claimed that his Turkish girlfriend Asl had said that he disappeared for a while and went to Afghanistan. But in a telephone conversation witnessed by Ibrahim Awadh of the Saudi Arabian *Arab News* Staff, Jamal Jarrah, the alleged "hijacker's" uncle, asked Asl if she had made such a statement to the media. She angrily replied: "From where they get all this? It is all lies. I did not speak with anyone. The police did not allow me to talk with anyone, even on the telephone. I am speaking to you now in the presence of police." She was also asked if she had ever seen Mohamed Atta or anyone else who appeared on the list of suspected hijackers, but she said emphatically no. She added: "Listen, Jamal. You know we were about to get married. Ziad was a jovial and kind-hearted gentleman. I loved him with all my heart, and we were preparing to return to Lebanon for our wedding." [26] Ziad Jarrah's tutor at Greifswald's Arndt University, Gudrun Schimpfky, said: "He was just a lovely, kind young man." [27] If you read the background to Jarrah, the idea that he was an Islamic extremist who would carry out such attacks cannot be sustained.[28] So what has happened to him? Why did he go missing?

Ahmed al-Nami: "may" have lived in Delray Beach, says the FBI. Oops, sorry, but old Ahmed is still with us and he was shocked to see himself named as a hijacker.

He had never lost his passport and said it was "very worrying" that the FBI could name him without any checks being made. I'm afraid that's par for the course, Ahmed. Another man mentioned by the FBI as a hijacker suspect, a Saudi national called Ameer Bukhari, was dropped from its wanted list when it was found that he had died a year before. Good decision, boys. Muhammad Bukhari, another Saudi Airlines pilot, was arrested because he was apparently mistaken for a Saudi suspect called Adnan Bukhari, who was himself found by the FBI and is no longer a suspect. Even so, reporters gained access to his home in Vero Beach and broadcast live reports from his living room!

Ahmed al-Haznawi: "may" have lived in Delray Beach, Florida. Wow, massive dossier on him I see.

This is pretty much all the FBI can tell us and Director Robert Mueller was twice forced to admit on CNN that there is "no legal proof to prove the identities of the suicidal hijackers".[29] Mueller also admitted in a speech to the Commonwealth Club in San Francisco on April 19th 2002: "In our investigation, we have not uncovered a single piece of paper – either here in the United States or in the treasure trove of information that has turned up in Afghanistan and elsewhere – that mentioned any suspect of the September 11 plot." This after what Attorney General John Ashcroft described as "perhaps the most massive and intensive investigation ever conducted in America".[30] Mueller said that 4,000 special agents and 3,000 support workers, some 25% of FBI employees, had been assigned to the case. These included more than 400 FBI crime lab experts who were sent to the crash sites. Ashcroft said that investigators had received more than 100,000 tip-offs and Mueller said there were "over 200,000 leads we are investigating". So why have they found bugger all? Why does the official story, so confidently delivered as "fact", turn out to be just a ludicrous pile of mights, mays, maybes and "suicide hijackers" who are still alive? Mueller claimed that some of the suspected hijackers and their accomplices had ties to several terrorist groups, but he "declined to provide details".[31]

The first FBI list of "hijackers" was released on September 14th and then a new list was issued on the 27th with slightly different spellings, and additional names and aliases.[32] Either way, at least seven of the 19 named by the FBI were found to be alive and the first FBI list names seven as pilots and the second only six. Hani Hanjour was no longer listed as a pilot, no doubt because given his flying record the idea that he flew a commercial airliner for 45 minutes and then executed that fantastic turn into the Pentagon is insane even by FBI standards. Nationals of Saudi Arabia dominate the list and they were led, it is claimed, by Mohamed Atta, an Egyptian, on behalf of Osama bin Laden, who is a member of a Saudi Arabian family. There is not one name on the list from Afghanistan. Yet the "war on terrorism" was launched against Afghanistan with Saudi Arabia paraded as one of the countries in the US "anti-terrorist coalition"! In December 2001, after those alleged hijackers were found to be alive, the FBI and the United States government were still naming the same men in the indictment against an alleged accomplice,

Zacarias Moussaoui, in the District Court for the Eastern District of Virginia, Alexandria Division.

Where are the "hijackers"?

American and United Airlines released "partial" passenger lists for the four hijacked planes and not one contained any of the "terrorists" named by the FBI, nor even anyone with an Arabic name. The airlines said that some passengers were not listed because their next of kin had yet to be informed. That would not have applied to the hijackers, though, surely, so why were they not there? I met with Michael Woodward, the American Airlines Flight Services Manager at Boston Airport, who says he took the call from attendant Madeline Amy Sweeney shortly before Flight 11 crashed. I must say he didn't seem very at ease as we spoke, especially when I said the government's version of events was clearly ludicrous. He told me that when he took the call from the plane he punched up the passenger list for Flight 11 on his computer screen and Atta's name was there in the seat that Sweeney had mentioned. But a BBC report, *The Last Moments of Flight 11*, points out that Sweeney said there were only four hijackers while the FBI says there were five and that "the seat numbers she gave were different from those registered in the hijackers' names".[33] Another attendant, Betty Ong, gave different seat numbers for the hijackers in her call. I asked the FBI to explain these inconsistencies, but it would not give me an answer. In fact five passengers are missing from the list released for American Airlines Flight 11 and eight for AA Flight 77. It is the same story with the lists issued by United Airlines. Nine names were absent from UA Flight 175 and 12 from UA Flight 93.

If the "hijackers" were on those planes then surely check-in staff would remember them. After all, when you travel by air inside America you don't tend to see that many Arabic people and as these guys were supposed to have flown in business class and first class they would have had their own check-in desks and attendants with far fewer passengers to deal with than those checking in economy passengers. There were very light passenger loads on all four planes anyway. We are told that Atta was in first class and if he was on board there is no way the first-class check-in attendant would not have remembered him, especially as he would have had to present a photo ID that matched his face and name with his ticket. When my wife later asked Michael Woodward if he could put me in contact with the check-in staff that dealt with Atta and company that morning, he paused and said: "Mmmm, I don't know who that would be." Maybe it's just me, but I found that a strange statement five months after the attacks. If you had taken a call from someone on a hijacked airliner that then crashed into the World Trade Center, wouldn't you want to know from your colleagues who did what and what exactly happened that morning? Was there never any conversation between staff in five months about who checked in these guys, what happened and what they were like? I find that bewildering. He said he would find out the name of the check-in person for me, but when he did not reply over the next three days I returned to Boston Airport in search of the person who checked in Atta and his fellow hijackers. I talked to a check-in staff supervisor on duty at American and asked him about speaking to the check-in staff in business and first class on September 11th. But he became very agitated and would not even tell me his name. He went over to a check-in computer, refusing to enter into any conversation, to find the number of the American Airlines media centre in Texas. Asked why he couldn't, or wouldn't, speak to me, he replied, "It's for personal reasons", and would say no more.

The airline response

I asked the American Airlines corporate headquarters in Fort Worth, Texas, if they could confirm that the alleged hijackers passed through their check-in systems at Boston Logan and Washington Dulles. Tim Kincaid, Manager of Communications Planning, American Airlines Corporate Communications, replied that I would have to ask the FBI![34] I asked if I could speak with the check-in staff that dealt with the "hijackers" to confirm that they went through. Kincaid replied: "Sorry, no." Rich Nelson, the media spokesman for United Airlines based in Chicago, told me the same. When I asked if he could confirm that the men named as hijackers passed through United's normal check-in procedures at Boston Logan and Newark, New Jersey, Nelson also referred me to the FBI. I could not speak with the check-in staff involved, he said, out of respect for their privacy.[35] However, I heard a very different story from Stanley Hilton, the San Francisco lawyer who has filed a $7 billion lawsuit against Bush and other members of his government on behalf of families who lost loved ones in the attacks. The lawsuit alleges that the government knew the attacks were coming and I'll talk more about this later. Hilton told me that clients who work for American Airlines, flight attendants and pilots, had been subjected to "very tough gag orders" and were threatened with "immediate termination if they talk about any of this publicly". That would certainly explain my own experience with AA staff at Boston Logan and why should we think it would be any different at United?

I said to Tim Kincaid at American Airlines that when they released passenger lists for Flights 11 and 77 there were five names missing on Flight 11 and eight for 77. I said I understood the original reason given for some of the passenger names not being there – next of kin not yet notified – but why were there no names for the hijackers on those lists? Kincaid's reply: "Sorry, you'll need to contact the FBI." I said that given that the next of kin for all the passengers will now long have been informed, could I have complete passenger lists for Flights 11 and 77? Kincaid referred me to the American Airlines website for news releases for September 2001, which merely had the original lists with the names missing. I went back to ask if the incomplete passenger lists released on September 12th were the only ones they had published. He said that the news release "is the only one we put out and is as complete as we could make it". He explained that "some families asked that their loved one's name not be listed, and [they had] honored their wishes".[36] But this is not the reason originally given for the missing passengers, which was that next of kin had not been informed. Are we to believe that by some fantastic coincidence the very same next of kin who had not been informed soon enough for their loved ones to be included in the first list are the very same next of kin who decided they did not want the names of their loved ones to be published? And where are the hijackers? I contacted Kincaid again: "What do you mean by "as complete as we could make it? Why no hijackers anywhere?" His reply: "That's as much as we can share. Call the FBI." [37] All this time later we have still not had a full passenger list for the 9/11 flights and not seen the airline ticket and boarding pass documentation of the "hijackers" who are claimed to have been on those planes. I asked Kincaid, a pleasant guy merely doing his job, if I could I see copies of the paperwork detailing the calls made by Betty Ong and Madeline Amy Sweeney to AA ground staff from Flight 11, but it was the usual reply: "Contact the FBI." [38] Rich Nelson, the media spokesman for United Airlines, told me that they only released the names of those whose families authorised them to do so. [39]

Then there is the matter of the passenger numbers on the four flights involved. OK, it was a Tuesday, the slowest day of the week I understand, but these were pan-American flights leaving at a time to coincide with the start of the business day on the west coast in major cities, Los Angeles and San Francisco. Yet Flight 11 had only 81 passengers on a plane that can carry 158 (American Airlines figures); Flight 175 had 56 passengers on a plane with a capacity of 168 (United Airlines figures); Flight 77 was carrying 56 passengers when the capacity was 176 (American Airlines figures); and Flight 93 had just 38 on a plane capable of holding 182 (United Airlines figures). We have four aircraft leaving from three airports, all hijacked in well under two hours, all left to their fate with no effective reaction from the FAA-NORAD response system, the Pentagon or government, and all remarkably low on passengers. I asked American Airlines for the average number of passengers on Flights 11 and 77 throughout the year 2000. They told me: "This information is proprietary and not available, sorry." [40] At least I wasn't told to contact the FBI. Rich Nelson at United Airlines said that, beyond saying that Tuesdays are typically light days, he couldn't tell me the average passenger numbers for those flights because it was considered to be "proprietary information." [41]

Even with the small number of passengers we are still told that between four and five hijackers without guns could overpower and control two pilots in each plane, and between 43 and 90 passengers and flight attendants, using box cutters and knives. On Flight 77 alone was attendant Michelle Heidenberger who had been "trained to handle a hijacking", reported the *Washington Post*. "She knew not to let anyone in the cockpit. She knew to tell the hijacker that she didn't have a key and would have to call the pilots. None of her training mattered." [42] There were some big guys on these planes, in the cockpit and among the passengers. Mark Bingham, a 31-year-old rugby player, was an enormous man who stood six feet five and Jeremy Glick, a former national Judo champion, were both on Flight 93, for example. Judo is an art of self-defence, not least against people with knives.

The cover-up technique

I contacted the FBI and was advised to fax a list of my 47 questions to Rex Tomb, a representative for the FBI's Fugitive Publicity and Internet Media Services Unit.

Many of these questions were the ones I had asked the two airlines and other organisations involved in September 11th, which they told me could only be answered by the FBI. (You can read them in *Appendix 1*.) A few days later I received a faxed reply from Ernest J. Porter at the Office of Public and Congressional Affairs saying that Mr Tomb had given my questions to him. Mr Porter said that he regretted being the bearer of disappointing news, but it was not possible for the FBI to answer any of my questions. The news was not, in fact, "disappointing", just depressingly predictable. Mr Porter told me: "It will be some time, perhaps years, before the FBI's investigative files on this case may be available through vehicles such as the Freedom of Information Act. The answers to your questions may be found in the files at that time." [43] One of my questions was "When did Robert Mueller officially become head of the FBI! If information is considered dangerous to "national security" (and the authorities decide that) those files can be withheld under the Freedom of Information Act and, when you look at the way freedoms are being destroyed by the week, what is going to be left of that Act by the time the 9/11 files are up for release? It's a smokescreen, of course it is. When you look through the questions I faxed to Rex Tomb you can see how basic some of them are and how many relate to FBI statements made immediately after 9/11 when its leadership was telling the public the official story of what happened. The propaganda and cover-up technique comes clearly into focus. It is the same technique used with all such set-ups: (1) you give the media the "information" about the event that tells the public the story you want them to believe; (2) you tell everyone with any knowledge or relevant information about the event that they must pass all inquiries to the FBI; (3) the FBI then says it cannot answer questions about its official story because of the "ongoing investigation". Funny how the "ongoing investigation" did not prevent the FBI from announcing its version of what happened. It only becomes a problem when the FBI is questioned about that version. There are many decent, dedicated people working for the FBI, but when it comes to the positions of power the bureau is not there to uncover the truth, but to prevent it ever being known.

Mind games

Before I continue to explore the fantasies of the official story, it is important to stress the potential the Illuminati have for mind control. This could well have been employed as part of the 9/11 operation. Within the Illuminati network going back beyond the start of conventional human history they have held the knowledge of how to control a person's mind and manipulate its reality. In my other books I have detailed the background to government mind control projects in which children are taken at a very early age and turned into traumatised zombies with their minds no longer their own. The foundation of these projects worldwide is a technique called trauma-based mind control, and this is another way that the satanic networks of the Illuminati fit into the picture. The mind has a defence mechanism that shuts out, or "compartmentalises", the memory of extreme trauma. This is why people cannot remember the moment of impact in a serious road accident. Their mind creates an amnesic barrier around the event so they don't have to keep reliving that horrible memory. From ancient times this has been understood by the Illuminati. In the concentration camps of Nazi Germany the method of exploiting this potential for mind control was further perfected. Joseph Mengele, the infamous "Angel of Death", and his fellow Nazis realised that if you could systematically traumatise someone through torture, sexual abuse, and by sacrificing and torturing others as they watched, you could shatter a person's mind into a honeycomb of self-contained compartments or amnesic barriers. Satanic rituals are widely used to do this. The mind's unity shatters into these various compartments or "altars" as they are called in the mind-control business. Each compartmentalised "altar" is unaware of the existence of the others. Each one thinks it is the whole mind when, in truth, it is only a fragment detached from the rest of itself.

Once in this compartmentalised state the fragment, or "altar", can be programmed for various tasks or experiences. The victim is given a programmed "front altar", as they call it. This is the day-to-day personality that people interact with, and their friends and acquaintances think is "them". Using trigger words or hypnotic keys, sounds or signals, the compartments can be pulled forward or pushed back like a mental filing cabinet, replacing the front altar for a task or experience – anything from having sex with a famous person to assassinating an Illuminati target. When this task or experience is over, the manipulators bring back the "front altar" to resume its role as the conscious mind once again. This means that after the victims have performed a task, they forget what they have done and who with. In this way, world-famous people have sex with children, but the children can't remember it has happened. It is only many years later – often not even then – that they remember their experience as the compartments start to break down and flood those memories into the conscious level as "flash-backs" of what happened (see *The Biggest Secret* and *Children Of The Matrix*). This compartmentalised condition has become known as Multiple Personality Disorder (MPD) or Dissociative Identity Disorder (DID). The latter is more accurate because the compartments are not "personalities" as such; they are fragments of mind that have "disassociated" – become detached from – the rest of the consciousness. It is like moving a radio dial across the stations, the compartments, tuning into one and then another. Even this technique is primitive compared with the latest methods using technology. All this must be taken into account when making judgements about September 11th. Suicide bombers around the world are overwhelmingly multiple-personality-mind-controlled stooges and once they are given the trigger to activate the programming they will do anything that the programmed responses command.

Many soldiers become multiples when they experience unimaginable slaughter. Their minds suppress the memory and they have no recollection of what they saw. Traugott Konstantin Oesterreich, a professor at Tubingen University in Germany, wrote a classic study of Multiple Personality Disorder (MPD) and "demonic possession" in 1921 called *Possession, Demonical and Other*. This revealed that trauma-based mind control was being used in France, Germany, and Belgium long before the dawn of the 20th century. Survivors and professionals have told of how the British used agents programmed through MPD in the First World War. Although the trauma may be forgotten, the subconscious memory is still affecting them and their lives, physically, mentally and emotionally. Many people who are sexually abused and systematically traumatised as children appear mentally and physically unstable, especially if the programming has stopped and the compartment walls begin to dismantle. I have sat in on sessions with the British therapist Vera Diamond and seen people switch between vastly different personalities one after the other by the use of a single word or sentence. It is incredible to experience. One of her clients has to be attached to a plastic bag that collects her urine because her bladder has been destroyed by torture. Her medical records are so enormous it shocked a doctor who saw them. This lady was just … 30 years of age. Mind control can also put people in the wrong place at the wrong time so they can be blamed for something they didn't do. You can also mind control a pilot to do what you programme him to do and he would have no idea that this was so until the trigger word or code was given and the programmed compartment took over his thinking processes. I would urge you to read the lengthy and detailed section on the mind-control programmes in *The Biggest Secret* because they open up so many other possible explanations of events and behaviour convenient to the Illuminati. The number of people under mind control of this kind today is simply staggering.

I must say that, along with many others, I have great doubts that Zacarias Moussaoui, the so-called "20th hijacker", is in control of his own mind. People who met him as part of his legal defence described him as "confused" and in need of a psychological examination. Lead defence lawyer Frank Dunham said Moussaoui's behaviour "caused us to question his mental status". As I completed this book, Moussaoui was in the process of going to trial for his involvement in the September 11th attacks. He was in custody on that day for immigration offences, but the authorities claim that he was part of the plot and had he not been arrested he would have been on Flight 93. He appeared in court in Alexandria, Virginia, on July 18th 2002 and entered a plea of guilty, but the judge rejected that and asked him to think about it further. "I am guilty", he said, and he added: "I am a member of al-Qaeda. I pledge bayat to Osama bin Laden." (Bayat is apparently the loyalty oath taken by members of al-Qaeda.) He told the judge that he had been involved in the plot since 1995 and had "many, many information [sic] to give to the America [sic] people about an existing conspiracy". Moussaoui was in court to face a "superseding indictment" by the government that made adjustments to make him eligible for the death penalty. The charges involving a potential death sentence were conspiracy to commit acts of terrorism transcending national boundaries, conspiracy to commit aircraft piracy, conspiracy to destroy aircraft and conspiracy to use weapons of mass destruction. Moussaoui, a French citizen of Moroccan descent, told the judge: "I want to enter a plea today of guilty, because this will ensure to save my life." He said that he had "certain knowledge about September 11" and he went on: "I know exactly who done it, I know which group, who participated, and I know when it was decided." Here was a guy who claimed allegiance to Osama bin Laden and was supposed to be willing to die, in his eyes gloriously, in a suicide terrorist attack against the "Great Satan", the United States. Yet now he was saying that he would tell all, reveal details of an "existing conspiracy" and admit to everything, so long as the US government would spare his life. He had previously entered pleas of not guilty while, at one hearing, publicly praying for the destruction of the United States and Israel and for the death of his yet-to-be-selected jurors. But now "not guilty" became "I admit everything".

Moussaoui was representing himself after submitting a staggering 94 hand-written motions declaring his wish to do so. Standby defense attorney Frank Dunham told CNN that he didn't believe Moussaoui was agreeing to plead guilty to the charges he faces. "If someone went over the indictment with him line by line I don't believe he'd agree to all of the charges," he said, "What he's admitting to is not consistent with what he's charged with." US District Judge Leonie Brinkema told Moussaoui it might be in his best interest to enter into plea bargain negotiations with the government. "You cannot plead guilty and then say, 'But I didn't do this and I didn't do that and somebody else did that,'" she said. Moussaoui became agitated by this and replied: "For the guilt phase, I'm guilty, but for the death penalty, we will see." He said that a jury "will be able to evaluate how much responsibility I have in this." A week later, on July 25th 2002, Moussaoui pleaded guilty to four of the six charges against him – the ones that carried the death penalty. Judge Brinkema explained that this meant he accepted responsibility for involvement in the planning or execution of the attacks. The judge questioned him about his involvement and it became obvious that he was not, in fact, admitting that he had taken part in the 9/11 conspiracy. After a recess, he withdrew his guilty plea and quoted Hamlet: "'To be or not to be, that is the question.' I say: To plead guilty or not to plead guilty, that is the question". Judge Brinkema said it was "absolutely right" and "not an unwise decision" to withdraw his guilty plea. She had already indicated that she would be unlikely to accept it. I think it is worth remembering here that the bumbling, confused, bizarre and contradictory behaviour of Moussaoui comes from a man that the US government claims was fundamentally involved in the planning of the hijack of four planes in American airspace and part of a plot that is claimed by the authorities to have been brilliantly hatched and carried out by highly skilled and highly professional terrorists. How ridiculous it all is. Just before the court hearing closed, Moussaoui said that a British agent was "an important part of the conspiracy", and he would reveal more when he had his day in court. Moussaoui's trial was set for late September 2002 and you may well be aware of the outcome by the time you read this. Moussaoui is a pathetic pawn in a game he doesn't even begin to understand and no doubt his "trial" will be designed to be a platform to yet again sell the official version of September 11th. Maybe the FBI will use the trial to present some of the "evidence" it has refused to reveal or talk about in the year since the attacks, although it certainly didn't do that in the trial of Timothy McVeigh.

The "ringleader"

Most of those who met the alleged hijackers appeared to be astonished that they could have carried out such attacks. They were "ordinary" people or, as one article put it: "Friendly neighbors, serious students and model dads: the men suspected of hijacking the jets that carried out history's deadliest terror strikes looked a lot more like the guy next door than the incarnation of the devil." [44] The focus has been on 33-year-old Mohamed Atta as the "ringleader" of the "hijackers". His father, Mohamed al-Amir Atta, a retired Cairo lawyer, said: "Oh God! He is so decent, so shy and tender. I used to tell him 'Toughen up, boy!'" [45] In a statement to the London-based *al-Sharq al-Awsat* newspaper on September 22nd 2001, his father said that Atta was in Germany and that he had phoned him after the attacks. [46] He claims that on September 12th he was at his holiday home on the Mediterranean coast without radio or television and unaware of the attacks in America the previous day. He says his son called him there and they talked about "normal things". Only later that day did he hear what had happened in the United States, he said. [47] He also dismissed the suggestion that Atta was a supporter of al-Qaeda: "Mohamed, my son, hates Osama bin Laden like he hates the sinner. Do not forget that Osama bin Laden is behind the attack on our embassy in Pakistan. Mohamed is a real Egyptian. All this talk is nonsense." [48] He said he believed that his son's identity had been stolen. Given that so many of the alleged hijackers are still alive, that is not such a fantastic statement. If, in fact, he didn't die on the plane, it is highly likely he was killed soon afterwards to protect the official story or he may be an intelligence asset of some kind playing his part in orchestrating the cover story. Who knows? His father said that Atta doesn't know how to fly a plane and in fact is frightened of flying, always vomiting when he travelled by air. "He was a donkey when it came to politics. I advised him, like my father advised me, that politics equals hypocrisy," he said. [49] He said his son was brought up to limit social contact to concentrate on his education.

Atta grew up in a middle-class home in Cairo and had two sisters. One is a university lecturer and the other a doctor. He became an architect and urban planner, and from 1992 studied at Hamburg's Technical University in a city that is home to around 80,000 Muslims of various nationalities. Professors apparently remember him being quiet, but not a radical thinker. Ralph Bodenstein, a fellow student who spent three months with him on a field study in 1995, said: "I knew him as an idealist who had great dreams about people living together." [50] Others remember him as intelligent, polite and tolerant of other religions. [51] Dittmar Machule, his German professor, told the *Wall Street Journal*: "I never heard any anti-Zionist, anti-American or anti-Christian statements from him." Others recalled how he condemned terrorist attacks on tourists in Egypt. In 1999 he presented his thesis on the restoration of the old quarter of the city of Aleppo in Syria and his 152-page study argued that urban planning should reflect the traditional coexistence of Muslims and Christians. [52] Atta appears to have registered with Bab Souria, formerly known as Syria Online, in 1997 under the name Mohamed El-Amir asking for information about Aleppo. The story goes that he had disappeared from the university from mid-1997 to October 1998 and when he returned, according to the *New York Times*, he had changed. He now wore a beard and persuaded the university to provide a prayer room for himself and other Arab students, including al-Shehhi and one other "suspected hijacker", a Lebanese student named Ziad Jarrah or Jarrahi, who studied aircraft design. He was the one who liked nightclubs and was due to marry his Turkish girlfriend two weeks after September 11th. Atta was outspoken, we are told, about the government of Egyptian President Hosni Mubarak and sympathised with the Muslim Brotherhood, Egypt's most established religious political organisation, and intellectuals facing persecution by Egyptian authorities. (Must be a terrorist then, I guess?) He also criticised the "fat cat" families and officers close to the Mubarak regime, enriching themselves while the larger community suffered.[53] (So do I.) A restoration project around Cairo's old city gates, Bab Al-Nasr and Bab Al-Futuh, which involved knocking down the homes and workshops of the poor, "made him angry" and he said it was a completely absurd way of developing the city to turn it into Disneyworld, recalled fellow student Ralph Bodenstein.[54] (Quite right too.) Some recalled that Atta criticised the United States for the Gulf War, its domination of the United Nations and Israel's treatment of the Palestinians.[55] (So do I) Another "fellow student" was quoted by the German newspaper *Die Zeit* as saying that Atta was "very sceptical about the achievements of the Western world" and "the ever accelerating Americanisation of his homeland [and] the entry of modernisation into the Arab world did not please him." Big deal. I am far more than just sceptical about the achievements of the western world and the rampant imposition of its "culture", but that does not mean I want to kill myself in an airplane crash and take thousands of people with me.

The FBI says it believes that Atta first arrived in the United States in 2000 with al-Shehhi and, in November and December of that year, it claims that Atta purchased flight deck videos for the Boeing 747 Model 200, Boeing 757 Model 200, Boeing 767 Model 300ER, the Airbus A320 Model 200 and other items from a pilot store in Ohio. This is thought to be Sporty's Pilot Shop at the Clermont County Airport about 20 miles from Cincinnati, although the owners won't confirm this except to say they have spoken with the FBI. Nawaf al-Hamzi, who is alleged to have been on Flight 77, is said to have bought similar videos from an "Ohio Pilot Store" and so is Zacarias Moussaoui, a 33-year-old (at the time of arrest) French national, who was indicted after 9/11 for being involved in the plot.[56] Officials say that Atta was given his visa at the US Consulate in Berlin on May 18th 2000 and landed at Newark, New Jersey, on June 3rd on a flight from Prague in the Czech Republic. He overstayed his visa by more than 30 days, but was allowed back for another six months when he returned to the US with no questions asked by immigration.[57] This is not normally the case when previous visas have been overstayed. Some who claim to have met him and rented him rooms in America have been quoted in the media as saying he was cold, distant and secretive. They talk of his stare, like the one portayed in the picture distributed to the media by the FBI. We need to be very careful about those "remembering" someone after an event has happened in which a person has been named as responsible. I learned years ago as a journalist that in such circumstances "witnesses" often have "memories" that fit the situation they have been told has happened. Others have said that Atta was mild-mannered, attentive and courteous. Over a period of time most of us would be described in different ways by different people, depending on the mood we were in when we met them and whether we liked them or they pissed us off.

There have been many false or unsubstantiated claims against Atta and much "information" has been presented as "proof" when it is nothing of the kind. He was said to be wanted for the bombing of an Israeli bus in Jerusalem in 1986 and one newspaper report said: "He was so brazen that he crisscrossed US and European borders under his own name while listed as a suspect in a 1986 Israeli bus bombing." But Brigadier General David Tsur, the Chief of Staff of the Israeli Ministry of Public Security, said that Atta was not the man suspected of the bombing.[58] The wanted man was Mahmoud Mahmoud Atta (also known as Mahmoud Abad Ahmad), a 33-year-old (in 1986) Jordanian who ambushed a bus in the West Bank.[59] Mohamed Atta was said to have met with an official of Iraqi intelligence in Prague in April 2000 and this was used to implicate Iraq with the attacks. Iraq denied this and, once again, no evidence was produced except for Secretary of State Colin Powell saying the information came from Czech Prime Minister Milos Zeman. In May 2002 the *International Herald Tribune* reported a senior Bush official as saying there was no evidence that Atta met the Iraqis in Prague.[60] The whole story is claimed to have come from Czech "intelligence" thinking that a man seen on surveillance camera footage was Atta, but this turned out not to be true. The *Herald Tribune* further revealed that no evidence whatsoever had been found that Atta had left the United States and visited Prague at that time.[61] See how "history" and "truth" are created from utter crap? But what the people retain is not the detail that destroys the story, but the "image" that the sum total of the lies and false statements presents to them. Atta was reported by "witnesses" to have been at the Professional Aviation Flight Training University in Punta Gorda, California, but when the FBI checked the story he had never attended that flying school.

Atta is claimed to have been seen in Norfolk, Virginia, in the winter of 2000 where he "might" have been surveying the US naval base as a possible target. Who says so? The FBI through *Newsweek*. He "might" have been "casing" Boston's Logan Airport more than six months before. Who says so? *Newsweek*. Sources? The usual. The *Chicago Tribune* said that he was a member of the Egyptian Jihad group with ties to Osama bin Laden. Who said so? "Sources".[62] The FBI said that Atta flew from Miami, Florida, to Madrid, Spain, on July 9th 2001 and picked up a rental car ordered through the Internet.[63] The *Observer* newspaper in London claims to have seen hotel records confirming that Atta spent at least one night at the Montsant hotel in the resort town of Salou on Spain's eastern coast during this trip and he returned his Hyundai Accent rental car to Madrid airport on July 18th, less than two months before the attacks.[64] It is claimed that he went to Salou to meet with four unidentified Muslim extremists. Who says so? A Spanish newspaper. Sources? "Investigators." Oh, them again. Now I am not saying that any of this is true or not true, just that all the "evidence" we have is from agencies with a genetic condition widely known as "lying through your teeth". The FBI claims that Atta met an "al-Qaeda" operative called Ramzi bin Shibh in Salou. Shibh is claimed to have once shared an apartment with Atta and "the authorities believe" he may have been involved in the planning of 9/11 from Germany.[65] But the *International Herald Tribune,* reporting the *New York Times,* said that investigations in Salou by the FBI and Spanish intelligence had found no one who saw the two together at the resort. Another point to note here: Atta and Marwan al-Shehhi were alleged by the FBI in a court indictment in December 2001 to have bought a knife in Zurich, Switzerland, on July 8th 2001. How could Atta do that if, as the FBI also claims, he didn't fly from Florida to Spain until July 9th?[66]

The official story says that Atta drove some 3,200 miles in rental cars in America between August 6th and September 9th, a period of more than a month. This is seen as significant, but I have driven that distance in half the time in rental cars in America. Is that significant? He and al-Shehhi apparently walked into Warrick Rent-A-Car in Pompano Beach, Florida, on August 6th. Brad Warrick, the owner, said that Atta carried a briefcase, was polite and looked like a businessman. "He didn't spend money like there was an unlimited source. He squabbled a little bit over mileage", Warrick remembers, and after renting a Chevy Corsica for a week, Atta switched to a Ford Escort because it cost ten dollars less. Yet Atta was said by other "witnesses" to have unlimited funds and wads of notes in his pocket. Warrick said the two Arabs were always "uncommonly polite" and always "… had a briefcase and books in the trunk".[67] This description of Atta's demeanour is at odds with reports from the flying schools where he is described very differently. Warrick said that on one occasion Atta phoned from Venice, Florida, to say that the oil light had flickered on and when he returned the car on September 9th, just two days before the attacks. Atta had reminded him about the problem. "The only thing out of the ordinary was that he was nice enough to let me know that the car needed an oil change," Warrick said. "That was odd since he was planning to die in a matter of days."[68] Or was he? Warrick said he found it odd that Atta had been concerned about the condition of the car when he returned it just two days before the hijacking. "I mean, if you're going on a suicide mission, why not leave the car at the airport?"[69] Precisely. You'll never get a job with the FBI, Mr Warrick. Atta was lucky not to be stopped by a traffic cop (very easy, as I know, when travelling those distances in cop-happy America) because in the April he had been given a ticket for driving without a licence and didn't show for a court hearing. The bench issued a warrant for his arrest, but the police failed to act on it.[70] He overstayed his visa, but no action was taken. He skipped a court appearance and had an arrest warrant issued, but nothing was done. Lucky man. Atta is said to have rented a Piper Archer single-engine plane at Palm Beach County Park Airport in Lantana on August 16th, 17th and 20th or on three consecutive days from August 19th, depending on which report you read. The manageress told the media that he said he had wanted to complete 100 flying hours. On August 28th he is said to have used a Visa card to buy two one-way tickets on the Internet for Flight 11 … quoting a frequent flyer membership number obtained only three days before! Anyone who has frequent flyer membership knows how long it takes to build up enough free miles to make it worthwhile – in Atta's case it would have been long after September 11th had passed. Why is he collecting the miles if he plans to kill himself days later? The other ticket, we are told, was in the name of Abdulaziz Alomari, or whoever that was because Alomari is still alive.

On September 7th, Atta was said to have been at Shuckums Oyster Pub and Seafood Grill in Hollywood, 30 miles from Miami, with Marwan al-Shehhi and another man, according to the night manager, Tony Amos, and they stayed from around 4.30pm until about 7pm.[71] Waitress Patricia Idrissi told the media that one of them went to play a video machine at one end of the restaurant while Atta and al-Shehhi sat drinking and arguing. Al-Shehhi drank rum and coke, she said, while Atta downed five Stolichnaya vodkas with orange juice. The bill was $48 and Atta argued with the manager about it. This is a guy with a pocketful of notes who, we are told, was only four days from driving a plane into the World Trade Center? "You think I can't pay my bill?" Atta is said to have shouted. "I am a pilot for American Airlines. I can pay my fucking bill." Mmmm. Did he really mention American Airlines? Seems very convenient to me. He paid the bill from a "thick wad" of $50 and $100 bills, staff said, so why the argument about the cost only days before September 11th? This is just silly. Islamic law strictly forbids drinking alcohol. Atta's father said: "If my son sees you with a beer, he'll cross the road" and he was "very shy, very polite, would never swear".[72] He said it was "… like accusing a decent, veiled religious girl of smuggling prostitutes into Egypt. It is nonsense, imagination!"[73] Other reports have said that al-Shehhi did all the boozing, which, if true, casts still more doubt on the "American Airlines" statement that Atta is said to have made according to the same witness who claims he drank five vodkas. But whether it was al-Shehhi or both of them hitting the bottle, these people are claimed to be Islamic fanatics willing to kill themselves and thousands of others for their faith. Yet they drink such a fundamentally banned substance in public or anywhere else? It just doesn't add up. Azzan Ali, a friend of Atta and al-Shehhi when they were students at a Florida flying school, said: "They were very religious."[74] Then there were the reports of other "Islamic fundamentalists" drinking in a strip bar the night before September 11th. Associated Press reported on September 13th: "Three men spewed anti-American sentiments in a bar and talked of impending bloodshed the night before the terrorist attacks." John Kap, a strip club manager in Daytona Beach, told FBI investigators that the men in his bar used credit cards to spend $200 to $300 each on lap dances and drinks, the report said. "They were talking about what a bad place America is," Kap is quoted as telling the FBI. "They said 'Wait 'til tomorrow. America is going to see bloodshed.'" It's all so convenient. Kap said that he gave the FBI the men's credit card receipts, photocopied driver's licences, a business card left by one of the suspects, "a copy of a Koran that one of the men had left at the bar", the Associated Press report claimed. Pardon me? A Muslim "fanatic" would take a Koran into a strip bar and leave it there? Oh do let's be sensible here. These alleged "hijackers" and "accomplices" seem to have left copies of the Koran everywhere they went – how perfect for the cover story. What were these guys, the Islamic version of the Gideons? The Associated Press article says that the FBI told Kap not to reveal the names of these men. The *Arab News* of Saudi Arabia asked:

> "How could the hijackers themselves have been 'Islamists' if they frequented bars, drank in some cases beer and wine, and one even attended an evangelical Christian school and stated that he would not have minded marrying a non-Muslim? How can we have faith in the investigations when almost half of the original list of hijackers have turned out either to be dead [before the event] or alive and well in other parts of the world?" [75]

A writer on the Liberty of Freedom website said:

> "Ziad Jarrahi, the alleged Lebanese hijacker of the plane which crashed in Pennsylvania, had a Turkish girlfriend in Hamburg and enjoyed nightclubs and drinking. Yet at the same time, we are being told that these same hijackers spent the night before the attack getting drunk in bars, making noise, screaming insults at the "infidels", and doing everything they could to attract attention to themselves. They used the credit cards issued in their stolen names, allowed their driver's licenses with the stolen names to be photocopied, and used public library computers to send emails back and forth using their stolen names signed to unencrypted messages about their plans to steal aircraft and crash them into buildings, then decorated their apartments with absurdly obvious props such as a crop dusting manual to the point where the whole affair reads like a low budget "B" detective movie from the 1930s. In short, these men did everything they could to make sure everyone knew who they were, or more to the point, who they were pretending to be." [76]

Yes, who they were *pretending* to be is the crucial point, I would suggest. What we are seeing here are the staged events designed to build the cover story and hide what really happened and who was really responsible. This is very easy because the mainstream media simply accepted this fairy story without question. I remember seeing a television "documentary" about Mohamed Atta on the UK channel, ITV, in which Jonathan Dimbleby, one of Britain's best-known current affairs presenters, repeated the FBI cover story without question from start to finish. Unbelievable.

Miracle journey

The day after Atta was apparently seen at the bar in Florida, a man of Middle Eastern appearance walked into the control tower at Boston's Logan Airport, say some reports, and it was believed this could have been him. Well if it was, that was a bloody quick flight from Florida to Boston and where are the details of his ticket? Also, Atta returned his rental car to Warrick Rent-A-Car in Florida the following day, the 9th. So for that to have been Atta, he must have flown from Florida to Boston on the 8th, walked up to the control tower at the airport, and then flown back again to Florida to take the rental car back. Then he must have flown back to Boston again to rent another car and drive to Portland, Maine, if the story is to be believed. This is how silly it gets. Several hours before this "Atta" figure showed up at the Boston Airport control tower, it is said that four "Middle Eastern men" had asked a controller how to get into the tower. This begs the question of what "Atta" and these other men expected to gain by getting into the tower. What would it have told them? It wouldn't have helped them hijack the planes three days later in any way. What it would have done is attract attention to them and suspicion, the last thing they would have wanted so close to their "big day" at the very airport where they were acting suspiciously. But, on the other hand, if you were setting up a cover story for September 11th you would want "Middle Eastern men" acting suspiciously at the airport where the first two planes were to be hijacked. I asked the FBI about the "Atta" man and the other four at the control tower, but officials refused to answer my questions.

The official story cannot explain, it would seem, what happened to Atta after he returned his rental car to Warrick in Florida on September 9th until he hired another car at Boston Airport on the 10th. "It is unsure how he travelled north," said one report I read.[77] Well let's just look at it logically, just for the benefit of the FBI leadership. He was in Florida one day and Boston the next, and the distance between them is 1,673 miles. So, er, he didn't walk and, er, he didn't drive, and, er, he didn't sail. Ah, got it. He must have flown then. So where are the flight details and ticket bookings that would be simple to find? Exactly. I asked the FBI about this and officials refused to answer. The FBI tale is that after arriving in Boston on September 10th Atta and Abdulaziz Alomari rented a Nissan Altima from the Alamo company at Boston Logan Airport and drove just over 100 miles to Portland, Maine. They are said to have stayed overnight at a Comfort Inn before heading the next morning for Portland Airport and a plane back to Boston to pick up Flight 11. In Maine, investigators claim that Atta and Alomari met up with other hijackers who came into the United States from across the Canadian border.[78] These other men are said to have driven back from Maine to Boston Airport while Atta and Alomari flew to Boston the next morning. In Portland, on September 10th, five Arab men, "believed" to be the "hijackers" and including Atta, tried to buy or rent cellphones from a store, investigators say.[79] They were refused at first because they did not have the proper identification, but that all changed when the men paid $3,000 in cash.[80] Why would you not pay cash anyway if you had "wads of notes" and knew you were going to die the next morning? If they did not have proper identification to buy cellphones, how did Atta manage to hire a car that same day? How did they manage to buy air tickets because that is what they now tried to do, we are asked to believe.[81] You have just got to hear this next bit. The men are reported to have used their new phones to call the airport at Bangor, Maine, to get a flight to Boston, but they could not get one with the right times. They then allegedly called the Portland International Jetport where two made reservations – clearly this is supposed to be Atta and Alomari. The other three men are believed, according to some reports, to have returned to Boston in Atta's rented Nissan, but police say they found this car at Portland Airport.[82] If they did, how did these other "hijackers" get to Boston Logan to connect with Flights 11 and 175? If they didn't use Atta's rental car they must have hired another or gone by plane. Where is the documentation? No one seems to ask these questions. Let's just take a breath here. Highly trained terrorists with the brains and organisation to hijack four commercial airliners within the same hour in American airspace, take over the controls and direct them to their target, wait until the day before to book seats on planes to connect with the flights they have planned meticulously for years to hijack? And they only buy cellphones at that time also? What? But hold on, there's more.

Atta and Alomari are said to have been caught on video at Portland as they boarded a USAir flight for Boston on that morning of September 11th. Well for a start that wasn't Alomari on the videotape as we were told because he is still alive. But, despite this, we are asked to accept without question that the other guy was Atta. Maybe it was, but we don't know for sure. Atta's father said: "The man in the video is bigger than my son".[83] Some more questions arise here. Why would the leader of the biggest plane hijack in history, an attack years in the planning, risk flying into Boston that morning and giving himself only an hour and a quarter between landing in Boston from Portland and taking off on Flight 11? Why would he wait until the day before to book his ticket? And wait for this. On the videotape released by the FBI of "Atta" and "Alomari" getting on the plane at Portland is the time code 05-53-41 (*Figure 19*). That's just 19 seconds short of six minutes to six. I know you can work that out, but it is worth emphasising because the flight they took from Portland to Boston that morning, USAir Flight 5930, was scheduled to depart at … 6am. That's only *six minutes* after "Atta" and "Alomari" were "captured" on videotape passing through security! No wonder they were described as "rushing" for the plane. The FBI timeline says that Atta and Alomari checked out of their hotel in Portland at 5.33am, just 27 minutes before their plane was due to depart and they then had to park their rental car, check in and get to the gate. One airline employee told reporters: "The girl that checked Atta said he was sweating bullets, that he was running late. His forehead was drenched." [84] Anyone who travels by air knows that if you leave it that late you are highly likely to miss the flight. Not only did the leader of the biggest plane hijacking in history take the chance of flying into Boston from a connecting flight that morning, he arrived so late that the Portland plane left only minutes after he got to the gate. And he only secured a seat the day before? All that planning and he took those risks of not even getting to Boston? What was that the *Washington Post* said about the "… astonishing degree of organization and planning undertaken by the terrorists"?[85] Hilarious. "Astonishing degree of organization and planning? It was more like the Keystone Cops. No, sorry, that's the FBI (or what decent and intelligent agents in the FBI are forced to be by their superiors). I asked the FBI about all these anomalies and contradictions, but officials refused to answer my questions.

On the Portland airport security video a second time code appears in the centre of the screen – the last place you would put a time code on a surveillance video. This code reads 05.45 and appears to be only there to hide the ridiculous

Figure 19: *"Mohamed Atta" and "Abdulaziz Alomari" caught on an airport security camera rushing for their plane at Portland, Maine, on the morning of September 11th. Note the difference between the time code in the centre of the frame (which is the last place you would put it) and the one at the bottom (where you would put it) that shows that there are only six minutes before the plane leaves*

contradiction of a highly professional leader of the hijackers running to his plane at six minutes to departure. The way the shot is framed by most of the media only the second time code in the middle of the screen is included, not the true one at the bottom of the frame. If this second, centre-of-the-screen, time code was correct, it means that Atta and friend must have checked out of their hotel, taken their car to the airport car park, checked in and passed through security to the gate all in 12 minutes! I rang Ruth Dudley, a very nice lady, who is Head of Security at Portland Airport. I asked her why there were two time codes – one of them slap bang in the middle of the screen. She said she didn't know and would have to see it to give me an opinion. Unfortunately, she said, they didn't have those tapes anymore because they were immediately confiscated by the FBI. I asked the FBI why there were two time codes on the video and why one was in the middle of the screen, but officials refused to answer.

Other "hijackers" arrived at Boston Airport at about 7.15am in a white Mitsubishi Mirage with Virginia licence plates, we are told.[86] The car contained "five" Arab men (three in other reports) and in one window was a pass allowing access to restricted areas at the airport, the FBI says. Media reports (official statements) claimed that another (unidentified) "witness" remembered the five men because there was an argument over a parking space. Note that time again. They arrived at 7.15am for flights taking off just before 8am and they are still in the car park, yet to reach the check-in desk and go through security to the gate. Anyone who has travelled in the United States will know that queues for check-in can be long at that time in the morning and the "five Arab men" left it ridiculously late to arrive at the airport on that day of all days. Then they also wasted more time arguing about a parking space? Why are they leaving it so tight when they have planned these attacks for years, according to the FBI, and what are they doing worrying about a car space when they are about to kill themselves? What this story does, however, is place "Middle Eastern men" in the Boston Airport car park that morning. But hey, not only did these guys leave it so late, they were said in one report to have bought their tickets in cash when they arrived at the airport. The "Mitsubishi" hijackers are reported to have "paid $4,500 each for their last-minute first-class tickets …" when they arrived at Boston Airport on the morning of September 11th.[87] David Boeri on *NewsCenter 5* in Boston reported: "Sources say at least four suspects, described as Middle Eastern men, arrived late to the airport, purchased one-way tickets and paid in cash for them, all of those factors being known security risk flags".[88] He said security personnel were trained to question late-arriving passengers who pay in cash for tickets. Surely "highly trained" hijackers would know this?

They arrive in the Boston Airport car park only 45 minutes before departure, let alone actual boarding, and according to these reports, they still don't have tickets for the flights they intend to hijack. Why did they not secure places on the flights long before to ensure that years of planning would not be destroyed by "sorry sir, the flight is full"? I asked American Airlines to confirm how Atta booked and paid for his tickets on Flight 11, but I got the usual reply: "Contact the FBI". I asked when and how others named as hijackers by the FBI booked and paid for their tickets on Flights 11 and 77 – "Contact the FBI".[89] Rich Nelson, media spokesman for United Airlines, told me the same: "We have not commented on that. Only the FBI, which is leading the investigation, could or would answer that." [90] I asked the FBI to confirm how each of the men named as hijackers had purchased their tickets, but officials refused to answer. The Boston Channel, however, reported how "FBI investigators detained and interviewed Logan Airport ticket takers who may have been the last people who came into contact with the hijackers before they boarded the two flights to New York." The report said that a Gismond Pepin was behind the ticket counter but didn't notice anything unusual when the two flights boarded, she told the FBI. She is quoted as saying:

> "They asked me if I seen anything out of the ordinary, but it would have been something I would have called to my manager's attention if I would have seen it at the moment, but unfortunately, nothing caught anybody's eye that was suspicious." [91]

However, the indictment in the case against alleged terrorist Zacarias Moussaoui presented to the United States District Court for the Eastern District of Virginia,

Alexandria Division, in December 2001, claims that 14 of the 19 named by the FBI purchased their tickets in the following way. Khalid al-Midhar and Majed Moqed bought tickets with cash for American Airlines Flight 77 "on or about" August 25th 2001, but it doesn't say where. Waleed al-Shehri and Wail al-Shehri made reservations on American Airlines Flight 11 "on or about" August 26th, listing a telephone number in Florida as a contact number. The next day, the indictment claims, Fayez Ahmed and Mohald al-Shehri made reservations for electronic, one-way tickets on Flight 175, listing the same Florida phone number, and Nawaf al-Hamzi and Salem al-Hamzi booked flights on American Airlines Flight 77. On or about August 28th, Satam al-Suqami paid cash for a ticket on American Airlines Flight 11, the FBI say, and Mohammed Atta and Abdulaziz Alomari booked two seats on Flight 11, listing the same Florida number. The following day Ahmed al-Ghamdi and Hamza al-Ghamdi reserved one-way tickets for Flight 175 and Ahmed al-Haznawi purchased a ticket for Flight 93 from Newark, but the indictment does not say how or where. Clearly many of these people didn't do that because they are still alive.

Camera shy

I have noticed that many people seem to believe they have seen video footage of Atta and friend getting on to Flight 11 at Boston. This is because people tend to get an impression from a news item, not the detail. The only pictures we have seen of two "hijackers" getting on a plane anywhere were recorded as they went through security at Portland, Maine, not Boston, because it turns out that, despite being an international airport, Boston Logan had no surveillance cameras in the departure lounge. As one newspaper article put it: "In perhaps the most stunning example of Massport's lax security safeguards, Logan International Airport is missing a basic tool found not only in virtually every other airport, but in most 7-Elevens" (a chain of small food stores for those not familiar with America).[92] Massport runs Boston Logan Airport and almost every other transport operation in the city it would seem. I went to see its media spokesman when I was speaking in Boston in February 2002 and he said that Massport was not responsible for security. He confirmed there were no video cameras in the departure lounge, but they did now have face-recognition cameras taking still pictures to ensure that the person who checked in was the person getting on the plane. The US military is also all over the airport and now controls the operation since September 11th, giving orders to the civilian authorities. The *Boston Herald* article pointed out that this lack of cameras in the departure lounge has prevented the FBI from definitively identifying the men who boarded the planes. How strange that in these times when you cannot move without being watched by a camera somewhere around you, they did not have them at an international airport, but they did have them at a small regional one at Portland. Such cameras had been in widespread use in airports for some 15 years before 9/11. Michael Taylor, President of American International Security Corp. of Boston, said: "It's not rocket science, convenience stores employ them, why wouldn't Massport?" The absence of cameras where you will find them at almost every other similar airport is another one of those endless coincidences that continue to surface. This means that the evidence is simply not there to prove that the "hijackers" named by the authorities were on the Boston planes. Charles Slepian, a New York security consultant, said:

> "You have names, but the FBI has said it hasn't been able to match the faces of those who were on the flights. Who boarded at Logan? You don't have pictures, and that's a problem. And are those suspects the ones who actually got on at Logan or are they still alive? Who knows? That's one of the big questions the cameras would have been able to answer." [93]

How convenient that at Boston Airport of all places they can't do that. Funny, too, how there are 17 surveillance cameras constantly filming the roads between the Ritz Hotel and the Pont de L'Alma tunnel in Paris and they would have proved beyond question what happened to the car in which Princess Diana died in 1997. Unfortunately, for reasons never explained, none of them was working the night she died (see *The Biggest Secret*). Sometimes cameras are useful to the Illuminati when they want to see us, but they can be a real problem when they wish to hide themselves and their activities. Still, hold on: we may not be able to confirm that the FBI "names" boarded the flights from Boston Logan because there are no cameras, and the airlines won't let me speak to the check-in staff, but they do have cameras in parking garages, ramp areas and on Logan's roadways to monitor traffic. Why haven't we been shown video pictures of these "Middle Eastern men" who arrived in the car park at 7.15 and had the argument with the unnamed driver about the car parking space? What about the men we are told arrived at the car park in their vehicle several times in the days before September 11th? Where is the footage of the other hijackers arriving that morning? If five came in the Mitsubishi, and Atta and friend arrived on the flight from Portland, what happened to the three other men the FBI says were on the two Boston aircraft? Surely the "Middle Eastern men" who asked how to get into the control tower must be on tape somewhere as well as the one who seems to have got in "unaccompanied". Indeed, the *Boston Globe* reported on September 13th:

> "When they reviewed videotape of the parking lot's surveillance camera, investigators found that the car had entered the lot up to five times between last Wednesday and Tuesday, according to sources. Those sources said the constant presence of the car over the last week suggested that the terrorists had scouted the airport, or performed dry runs for the daring attack." [94]

Who was seen on the tape getting in and out of the car on these "videos", then? If they have footage of that, where is the recording of the "Middle Eastern men" arriving in the white Mitsubishi on the morning of September 11th and having the argument over a parking space with an unidentified driver? [95] I asked the FBI all these questions, but officials refused to answer. Another thing. Michael Taylor, president of American International Security Corp., says he has worked for the Port

Authority of New York and New Jersey, and he confirmed that Newark, New Jersey, from where Flight 93 departed, has video cameras in the departure lounge. Why haven't we been shown footage of the "hijackers" boarding that flight?[96] Dulles International Airport in Washington DC, the starting point for Flight 77, also has cameras in the departure lounge, so same question. I put this very point to Tara Hamilton, a very pleasant woman, in the media office at Washington Dulles Airport. She replied:

> "I've checked with our airport police department and they inform me that the FBI is in charge of all information regarding September 11th and the specifics about the men who came to Dulles Airport. In regard to questions about our airport cameras, those are part of our security system and we're not able to discuss that. I'm sorry we're not able to provide the information you are seeking but am sure you understand our situation." [97]

Well actually, no I don't. If releasing video footage of "Atta" and friend at Portland airport is OK, what is the problem with letting us see other "hijackers" boarding planes at other airports? Like all of these media spokespeople, Tara Hamilton was just saying what she was told to say, and the idea that asking for confirmation that the "hijackers" were caught on camera would in any way affect the airport security system is ridiculous. They don't want to discuss it, that's the truth. I asked the FBI why these pictures had not been released, but officials refused to answer.

Even without the cameras at Boston, however, the gods clearly wanted to help the FBI and other government "investigators" to find those responsible. Of all the luggage of all the passengers on all the airlines in all the world on that day of all days, it was Atta's bag or bags that didn't make it on to Flight 11.[98] Inside, the FBI says, was a note dated five years earlier in which he said he was willing to martyr himself in a holy war against infidels. Yeah, course he did.[99] Yawn. It is claimed to give instructions for Atta's burial and what should be done with his possessions "when I die". The *Los Angeles Times* reported: "Authorities said Atta instructed that he be buried 'next to good Muslims,' with his body pointed east toward Mecca, that strict Muslim traditions be followed for his burial and that no women be allowed at his funeral. The document is dated April 11th 1996, "suggesting that Atta may have been considering a suicide attack for several years before he carried it out." [100] This included the fact, apparently, that he wanted to "go to heaven as a martyr".[101] How they can say this without laughing is beyond me. It's not even a B-movie script. But hold on what's this? Oh my God! They only found in Atta's bags a copy of the Koran, a Saudi passport, and … oh no… a video of how to fly a commercial airliner. Bingo! Game, set, and match, all sorted, doubles all round. After the attacks, police say they found Atta's red 1989 Pontiac Grand Prix in the parking lot of Logan Airport and the rented Altima in Portland. Why would Atta rent the Altima at Boston Airport to drive to Portland if he had another car already at Boston? Where did this car come from when he had been at the other end of America, in Florida, with another rental car until September 9th? Florida police understandably appealed for anyone who might find the Grand Prix in the area where Atta was said to be living.[102] Instead it turned up in a Boston car park 1,673 miles away and yet Atta went to car rental companies in Florida on the 9th and Boston on the 10th, according to the official story. Do the sums and you find that even if Atta maintained a speed of 100 miles an hour for the entire journey (no chance, he would have had so many speeding tickets) with no hold ups or stops whatsoever, it would take nearly 17 hours to complete the journey. Not worth even going there, it's so stupid. Yet the *Chicago Tribune* said: "Sometime before the attack, Atta, perhaps accompanied by al-Shehhi, made his way up the Eastern Seaboard. After Tuesday's attack, police found Atta's Grand Prix in the parking lot of Boston's Logan International Airport." [103] If they had only stopped to think instead of taking the official story without question, the reporters would have seen how ridiculous that is.

Another point. Why the hell a man who is about to fly an airliner into the World Trade Center would take bags with him and check them into the hold is beyond anyone with a neuron pathway even partially active. But, like I say, miracles do tend to happen with government cover stories. In fact miracles are essential. And, would you believe it? The Mitsubishi in the car park at Boston Airport was found to contain a ramp pass allowing access to restricted areas, a copy of the Koran, a fuel consumption calculator and a flight training manual written in Arabic on how to fly a 767.[104] Wow. What synchronicity. All this was "discovered" at the very time the Bush government was preparing to pin the blame on Arab terrorists working for Osama bin Laden. Shit, thank you God. Just a thought, though: maybe a note signed by Osama bin Laden saying "all the best with your mass murder on my behalf today by flying those planes into the World Trade Center and the Pentagon" might have been a nice touch, just to cover all bases. Perhaps they could have placed the note inside the hijacker's passport that was "found" a few blocks from the World Trade Center. Nicely charred at the edges, you know the sort of thing. Add all this to the 757 manuals and "eight inch stack of East Coast flight maps" that were claimed to have been found in hotel rooms rented by some "hijackers" and the story is complete.[105] Oh yes, not to forget the reports that al-Shehhi and Atta were spotted in Switzerland that summer buying pocket knives and box cutters the day before the FBI says Atta flew from Florida to Spain! "Hey Mohamed, we need box cutters and pocket knives, better fly to Switzerland to buy them, eh?" But one point that occurs to me, not being too bright and all, is why an Islamic kamikaze terrorist would have checked in bags on the plane and left his Koran inside. In fact these guys seem to have left Korans everywhere in bars, cars and baggage. Why would "Muslim fanatics" do this? Better call the FBI, they'll know. And what they don't they'll make up. Simple.

Thy will be done

The letter and "will" "found" in the baggage of Mohamed Atta that miraculously did not make it on to Flight 11 was claimed to include a five-page message to his fellow hijackers. The FBI says that essentially the same letter was found in the wreckage of Flight 93 in Pennsylvania. "Essentially" the same document? Did Atta, or whoever, hand-write basically the same five-page instruction to every one of them then? Had he not heard of photocopiers? Attorney General John Ashcroft also told a "Justice Department" news conference on September 28th that another copy of the "letter" had been found at Washington Dulles Airport "in a vehicle used by Nawaf al-Hamzi, one of the hijackers on American Airlines Flight 77". The letter, said Ashcroft, "is a disturbing and shocking view into the mindset of these terrorists. The letter provides instructions to the terrorists to be carried out both prior to and during their terrorist attacks." Yeah, yeah.

The FBI released "extracts" of the letter "found" in "Atta's luggage" via the *Washington Post* on September 28th. It was claimed to be originally written in Arabic by someone alleged to be an Islamic fanatic. The full and original Arabic text has not been released by the FBI and nor has the version "found" in the wreckage of Flight 93. "Atta", or one of his "accomplices", begins with these words: "In the name of God, the most merciful, the most compassionate … In the name of God, of myself, and of my family." It is claimed to say: "The time of fun and waste is gone"…"Be optimistic … Check all your items – your bag, your clothes, your knives, your will, your IDs, your passport … In the morning, try to pray the morning prayer with an open heart." It also tells the "hijackers" to "make sure that nobody is following you." Blimey, this lot were highly trained professionals weren't they? Under a heading of "Last Night", it tells each hijacker to "remind yourself that in this night you will face many challenges. But you have to face them and understand it 100 per cent … Obey God, his messenger, and don't fight among yourself [sic] where [sic] you become weak … Everybody hates death, fears death …" But Muslims, and an excellent article by British journalist, Robert Fisk, reveal some major problems with these alleged words of a "Muslim fanatic".[106] They point out that no Muslim, never mind a fanatical one, would include his family in the opening statement of prayer and nor would he ever do it without mentioning the Prophet Mohammed immediately after "God". The line that "everyone hates death, fears death" is ridiculous. A Muslim, especially one who is prepared to give up his life to the cause, is not someone who hates and fears death. This is the moment that they believe they are starting a new life in paradise. Who writes this stuff? Certainly not a Muslim. As Fisk says in his analysis:

"If the handwritten, five-page document which the FBI says it found in the baggage of Mohamed Atta, the suicide bomber from Egypt, is genuine, then the men who murdered more than 7,000 [later said to be about 3,000] innocent people believed in a very exclusive version of Islam – or were surprisingly unfamiliar with their religion."

"… What Muslim would urge his fellow believers to recite the Morning Prayer – and then go on to quote from it? A devout Muslim would not need to be reminded of his duty to say the first of the five prayers of the day – and would certainly not need to be reminded of the text. It is as if a Christian, urging his followers to recite the Lord's Prayer, felt it necessary to read the whole prayer in case they didn't remember it … Lebanese and Palestinian suicide bombers have never been known to refer to 'the time of fun and waste' – because a true Muslim would not have 'wasted' his time and would regard pleasure as a reward of the after-life." [107]

Here are some of the other instructions for the hijackers in the "letter":

Pray during the night and be persistent in asking God to give you victory, control and conquest, and that He may make your task easier and not expose us.

Shouldn't we take advantage of these last hours to offer good deeds and obedience? *[Nah, let's just get pissed.]*

Bless your body with some verses of the Qur'an (done by reading verses into one's hands and then rubbing the hands over whatever is to be blessed), the luggage, clothes, the knife, your personal effects, your ID, passport, and all your papers. *[Why would they need luggage and why would fanatical Muslims have to be told how to bless something?]*

Check your weapon before you leave and long before you leave. You must make your knife sharp and must not discomfort your animal during the slaughter. *[Oh yes, and don't sleep in so you have to run your arse off to get on the Portland plane.]*

Tighten your clothes, since this is the way of the pious generations after the Prophet. They would tighten their clothes before battle. Tighten your shoes well, wear socks so that your feet will be solidly in your shoes. *[Didn't your mum ever tell you that? Mine neither.]*

When the taxi takes you to (M) *[we are told this initial could stand for matar, airport in Arabic, or it could always be McDonald's, of course]* remember God constantly while in the car. Remember the supplication for entering a car, for entering a town, the supplication of place and other supplications. *[I think it is more important to remember that the FBI says these guys went to the airports in cars, not taxis.]*

When you have reached (M) and have left the taxi, say a supplication of place ('Oh Lord, I ask you for the best of this place, and ask you to protect me from its evils'), and everywhere you go say that prayer and smile and be calm, for God is with the believers. *[Say a prayer, smile and be calm? I thought they were supposed to have had an argument with a guy over a car space immediately they arrived! They ought to listen more.]*

In his "will" Atta also asks that his body be washed and buried. What, after flying a plane with 20,000 gallons of fuel into the World Trade Center? Hell of an embalming job that one. These "documents" are pathetic and should be filed away under "L" for ludicrous or "P" for pull the other one. In the same file should go the hijacker passport "found" in New York, the bin Laden "video confession" and all the other juvenile examples of make-believe that the FBI and the authorities in general have had to put before us to sell their fairytale of what happened, who did it and what the consequences should be. It should also be noted that while they produced this "letter" to the hijackers, which talks of everyone fearing death, the FBI also said that 11 of the 19 hijackers named did not know they were on a suicide mission, but believed themselves to be preparing for a conventional hijack.[108]

The "pilots" and heeere's Jackie – again

A key strand of the official story is that several of the 19 named by the FBI had learned to fly at American pilot schools in preparation for hijacking four commercial airliners and taking over the controls. They did this, we are told, by practising on single-engine planes and mostly incompetently at that. The main centre for this flying tuition was the little airport at Venice, a small town in Florida, not far from Sarasota where Bush visited the school on the morning of 9/11. Venice is a seaside resort on the Gulf of Mexico on Florida's south-western coast and known as the "shark tooth capital of the world". The city of Venice has a population of fewer than 30,000 and it's a retirement centre, home to the blue rinse-brigade. Venice Airport was mentioned during the Iran-Contra hearings when Oliver North was being questioned and the subject involved gun running from the airport to the Contras. Funnily enough, small as Venice may be, our old friend from earlier, Jackson Stephens, has long had a presence there.[109] Stephens, you may recall, was an investor in George W. Bush's Harken Energy together with Khalid bin Mahfouz, the man named by the US State Department as a financial backer of Osama bin Laden. These two have something else in common, too, – their involvement in the BCCI in which the Bush family was also fundamentally implicated. Stephens is a close friend and financial backer of Father George and funded Bill Clinton's campaigns to be governor of Arkansas and US President. He has also been linked by researchers to the National Security Agency, the major overseer of the US intelligence network and boss to the CIA. Some government officials have accused the NSA of destroying data relevant to the 9/11 investigation.[110] Stephens was also a roommate of President Jimmy Carter at the US Naval Academy. To put it mildly, this guy has massive "connections" and has been named in relation to a number of scandals, including the Whitewater land deals that involved the Clintons, and the Iran-Contra gun-running and cocaine smuggling operation through Mena, Arkansas, while Clinton was governor and Bush and Reagan were in the White House. A block away from Venice Airport and the "hijacker's" flying school is the former national headquarters of the Stephens company, Beverly Enterprises.[111] Today it is home to his former law firm, Boone, Boone and Boone, and a Stephens executive still has an office there.[112] Boone, Boone and Boone, it seems, pretty much run the place. Venice is a "Boone town", you might say.

The FBI says that two flying schools at Venice Airport were attended by all the alleged "hijacker-pilots" who passed through Florida even though the state has some 200 flying schools to choose from. The Venice schools had both changed hands shortly before Atta and Co arrived there and both were purchased by Dutch nationals. Rudi Dekkers bought Huffman Aviation, and Arne Kruithof from

Rotterdam bought the Florida Flight Center. Not long before the "hijackers" were said to have arrived at Huffman Aviation, Dekkers launched an aggressive European 'marketing' campaign, as reported in the local paper, the *Venice Gondolier* at the time. "The world is my working place," Dekkers told to the paper. "I won't forget Venice, but I'm going to market throughout the world, Germany, France, Belgium. That's our goal, to get people to come in here from all over the world." [113] So it proved. Foreign nationals soon made up 80% of the student pilots at the school. Hundreds a year were paying thousands of dollars while Dekkers, it is reported, was falling behind with the rent.[114] Daniel Hopsicker, author of *Barry and the Boys: The CIA, the Mob, and America's Secret History*,[115] says that Huffman Aviation is one of the schools authorised by the Immigration and Naturalization Service to issue I-20M immigration forms.[116] These help foreign students to secure US visas as vocational students. Hopsicker quotes an "observer" at Venice Airport as saying of Dekkers:

> "I've always had some suspicions about the way he breezed into town out of nowhere. Just too many odd little things. For example, he has absolutely no aviation background as far as anyone can tell. And he evidently had no use for, nor knowledge of, FAA rules and regs." [117]

Dekkers claimed to have extensive aviation experience, but Richard Boehlke, a former business associate who fell out with him big time it seems, said: "He was an oxymoron the day I met him. I can't believe anyone handed him millions of dollars to run a business he had no experience in." [118] Given Boehlke's business background, however, something very similar might apply to him. Mohamed Atta, who is alleged to have piloted Flight 11, and Marwan al-Shehhi, the man the FBI says was at the controls of Flight 175, attended Dekkers' school, we are told. Ziad Jarrah, the alleged pilot of Flight 93 and the guy who was due to marry his Turkish girlfriend was a student at Kruithof's operation, the FBI claims. However, reports in the national and local media reveal a familiar trend in the 9/11 "story". Different people tell a different tale about the same events and personalities. Ivan Chirivella was an instructor at Jones Aviation Flying Service Inc. at Sarasota Bradenton International Airport, which is just half an hour from Venice and five miles or so from the Emma E. Booker Elementary School where President Bush was on the morning of September 11th. Chirivella told Associated Press that Atta and al-Shehhi went to his school in September or October 2000 and asked for flying instruction.[119] He said they came to him from Huffman Aviation and he claimed to have given them lessons virtually every morning in that period. Dekkers, however, says they were with his school between late July and December or January, paying, according to Dekkers, $20,000 each. They are remembered for stalling a Piper Warrior on a Miami area runway and then abandoning the aircraft, walking across another active runway, and making controllers in the tower furious, it is reported.[120]

We are told that Atta and al-Shehhi rented a room for a short time in the house owned by Charlie Voss, a former Huffman Aviation employee, in Venice. Voss apparently is also a former C130 pilot with the US military, according to researcher

Daniel Hopsicker.[121] Voss said they hardly spoke and left their room a mess. He asked them to leave after a few days, Voss told reporters. One of the Huffman Aviation instructors told the media he had taught Atta and al-Shehhi in a single-engine Cessna 172. This was "Mark Mickart", whose real name is Mark Wierdak.[122] Daniel Hopsicker says he traced a half-sister of Mickart/Wierdak who works for the British Consulate in Venezuela. She told them that she and Wierdak "... used to share the same father". Hopsicker says he established that Mickart/Wierdak also flies out of the Sarasota-Bradenton Airport for Agape Flights. This is a Christian missionary group who call themselves an independent ministry fighting disease, poverty and illiteracy. For more than 20 years they have been running a flight every week to and from the Dominican Republic in the Caribbean, Hopsicker says he established. Florida is a major centre of drug trafficking and CIA, Mafia, and military activity, all of which so often go together. I have seen the Saudi royal family mentioned for its connection to the Florida elite and criminal networks. Hopsicker says that the son of Alvin Malnik of the Miami Mafia is married into the Saudi royal family through a daughter of a Saudi prince. The king of Saudi Arabia would regularly send his private 747 to Florida to allow Malnik and gang to do business with the Saudis away from public view, Hopsicker reports.[123]

Trained by the United States?

Florida is also home to the Naval Air Station in Pensacola, where the US military operates exchange programmes for overseas officers. Within days of September 11th there were reports in *Newsweek*, the *Washington Post*, and the Knight Ridder newspapers, that five of the hijackers named by the FBI were trained at secure US bases in the 1990s, including three at Pensacola. *Newsweek* quoted a "high-ranking US Navy source" as saying that three of the alleged hijackers listed Pensacola Naval Air Station as their address on driver's licences and car registrations.[124] The report said these men were believed to be Saeed al-Ghamdi and Ahmad al-Nami, who were allegedly on Flight 93, and Ahmed al-Ghamdi, who is alleged to have hijacked Flight 175. Al-Ghamdi and al-Nami are apparently both still alive. It is claimed that their training at Pensacola was paid for by Saudi Arabia, the ally of the United States, and associates and clients of the Carlyle Group. *Newsweek* claimed that military records showed that the three used the address of 10 Radford Boulevard, a base roadway where the residences of foreign-military flight trainees are located. In March 1997, Saeed al-Ghamdi listed the address to register a 1998 Oldsmobile, *Newsweek* said, and five months later used it to register a late-model Buick. The report says that driving licences were believed to have been issued to the other two suspects in 1996 and 1998, and also list the barracks as their residences. An FBI spokesman is quoted as saying the hijackers could have stolen the identities of people who trained at the bases. Mohamed Atta was reported by *Newsweek* to have attended the Maxwell AFB in Montgomery, Alabama.[125] In response to the *Newsweek* report, the Florida Democrat Senator Bill Nelson faxed a request to Attorney General John Ashcroft demanding confirmation or otherwise of this story. A spokesman for the senator said:

"In the wake of those reports we asked about the Pensacola Naval Air Station but we never got a definitive answer from the Justice Department. So we asked the FBI for an answer if and when they could provide us one. Their response to date [five months later] has been that they are trying to sort through something complicated and difficult." [126]

A Pentagon spokesman responded on September 16th by saying that "name matches may not necessarily mean the students were the hijackers, and that discrepancies in biographical data indicate, "We are probably not talking about the same people." [127] *"May not necessarily?" "Probably"?* You mean they don't know? Of course they do, and so why don't they simply point out the background to those foreign trainees with, coincidentally, the same names as those claimed to be hijackers? But they won't do that. A Pentagon spokesman, for example, denied that the Mohamed Atta who attended the International Officer's School is the same man who is claimed to have been the leader of the hijackers. Yet he refused all requests for the biographical background of the Mohamed Atta at the school. The spokesman told reporters: "I do not have the authority to tell you who [which hijackers] attended which schools." Did some of the alleged hijackers, including Atta, attend military training schools in the United States? [128] I asked the FBI this question, but officials refused to answer. Daniel Hopsicker, who has written extensively on the Florida flying schools and the military-CIA connection, said: "We know of at least one woman in Montgomery, Alabama, who has credibly insisted to local reporters that she met Atta at a party on the base. She remembers because she then introduced him to her friends." He writes that he was told that Arab pilots, mostly Saudis, occupied most of one of the most elite upscale apartment complexes in Montgomery. [129] The *Los Angeles Times* also quoted a "defense official" as saying that two of the hijackers were former Saudi fighter pilots who had attended two prominent US military programmes, the Defense Language School at Lackland Air Force Base, Texas, and the Air Force's Air War College at Maxwell Air Force Base, Alabama. [130] Also, in Taif, Saudi Arabia, the last known location of the bin Laden-funding Khalid bin Mahfouz, the United States Military Training Mission operates a joint training mission under the command of United States Central Command at MacDill Air Force Base in Florida. Could some of these guys have been trained by the United States? It certainly wouldn't be the first time this has happened. Michael Springman, the former head of the American visa bureau in Jeddah from 1987 to 1989, told the BBC *Newsnight* programme:

"In Saudi Arabia I was repeatedly ordered by high level State Department officials to issue visas to unqualified applicants. These were, essentially, people who had no ties either to Saudi Arabia or to their own country. I complained bitterly at the time there. I returned to the US, I complained to the State Department here, to the General Accounting Office, to the Bureau of Diplomatic Security and to the Inspector General's office. I was met with silence." [131]

The BBC also quoted "a highly placed source in a US intelligence agency" as saying there had always been "constraints" on investigating Saudis and that under President George W. Bush it had become much worse.[132] It is worth noting that the Kennedy assassination was blamed on a US-trained CIA operative called Lee Harvey Oswald. The Oklahoma bombing patsy was a highly trained US soldier (and what else?), Timothy McVeigh, together with Iraqi Republican Guard officers who were relocated to the United States, and Oklahoma in particular, by Father George Bush after the Gulf War. Al Martin, a retired Navy Lt. Commander, says that one of the Iranians involved in the bombing of the World Trade Center in 1993 was trained at the Redstone Arsenal in Huntsville, Alabama, and completed an explosives course in the guise of a Pakistani officer. Not just anyone can qualify to attend these US military training schools. You need connections with foreign governments "friendly" with the United States. In other words, governments in league with the Illuminati elements that control the United States. If Atta did not have this high-level backing, he could not have gained admission to the Maxwell AFB training school. If we look at an example of a foreign student who qualified for US military training you can see the sort of background we are looking at here. Colonel Mohammed Ahmed Hamel al Qubaisi became a Defense Military Naval and Air Attaché at the United Arab Emirates Embassy in Washington DC and was previously Chief of Intelligence in the Embassy and Security Division and in the Security Division-Air Force Intelligence and Security Directorate Security Officer-Air Force Intelligence and Security Directorate.[133] This is no squaddie, foot soldier or guy off the street. Nor could Atta have been if he did attend such a school at Maxwell. In the *Newsweek* article, a former Navy pilot at the Pensacola base in Florida was quoted as saying:

> "We always, always, always trained other countries' pilots. When I was there two decades ago, it was Iranians. The Shah was in power. Whoever the country du jour is, that's whose pilots we train."[134]

The American military's country of choice for such trainees in the 1990s turns out to be … Saudi Arabia. Well, well, hello again. Almost from the start of this book Saudi Arabia has been a constant theme, together with the Bush family. Father George's Carlyle Group are "advisers" to the Saudi royal family and control them, according to insiders. James Baker of the Carlyle Group also has a base in Saudi Arabia for his law firm, Baker and Botts, legal advisers to the Bushes. The bin Laden family, investors in the Carlyle Group and Boy George's Arbusto Energy, are based in Saudi Arabia and at least 11 members of that family, some report many more, were allowed to fly home from Boston Airport immediately after September 11th. Then there are those other Bush family investors who have been named as financial backers of the Osama bin Laden network, our old friends, Mohamed Hussein Al-Amoudi and Khalid bin Mahfouz. The latter was a major player in the BCCI, the drug money laundering operation and a front for intelligence agency manipulation, including the CIA funding of Osama bin Laden. Another BCCI player was Jackson

Stephens who apparently has a liking for the little town of Venice where the flight schools are located that are supposed to have "trained" Atta and company. The overwhelming majority of those named as "hijackers" by the FBI were Saudi nationals. Even Atta, an Egyptian, was reported to have a Saudi passport. To put the cherry on the cake, men of the same name as some alleged hijackers, including Atta, attended US military training schools at secure bases in the 1990s at the very time when Saudi Arabia was the country of choice for such training. Oh, and people do not qualify for such training unless they are well connected or supported by high levels of authority in the country they are representing, in this case … Saudi Arabia.

The *Newsweek* article quotes a "Pentagon source" as saying that at least two of those trained were former Saudi Air Force pilots. Apparently, some of the "hijackers" had pilot's licenses connecting them to the Saudi Arabian national airline, which is owned by the government of Saudi Arabia. Were the formerly German-based Mohamed Atta and some of his alleged colleagues assets of the CIA or the CIA-associated German intelligence, British intelligence and Mossad? Former German Defence Secretary Andreas von Bulow told me that the CIA, German intelligence, and Mossad, were extremely closely connected and the same certainly goes for British intelligence. Were Atta and company knowingly or unknowingly constructing the cover story, but never boarded the planes? Were they set up to be in the wrong place at the wrong time? Are these stories of the "hijackers" trained at US military establishments simply a diversion? Any of these situations is possible. In fact, the story that is truly *im*possible is the one told by the FBI and the US government. Terrorist patsies and stooges are frequently set up by the intelligence agency network, which then protects its own operatives from exposure. The FBI assistant director James Fox named the man responsible for planting the explosives in the 1993 bombing of the World Trade Center as Mohammed Salameh, a follower of a CIA asset called Omar Abdel Rahman. It was claimed that Salameh left the bomb in a rented Ford Econoline van. But the *International Herald Tribune* reported that the telephone number and apartment listed on the rental agreement for the van belonged to Josie Hadas, a long-established Mossad operative.[135] The *Washington Post* revealed: "A search of the Hadas apartment Thursday afternoon had discovered among other things, a letter addressed to the defendant [Salameh], tools and wiring, and manuals concerning antennae, circuitry and electromagnetic devices." The *Post* said the FBI had concluded that this constituted evidence of a bomb maker at the location. So why was Josie Hadas, Mossad operative, not arrested? Whatever happened to him? Salameh rented the Ford Econoline, but reported it stolen to the police before the bombing, and even returned to the rental company to hand over police documents detailing the reported theft and asked for his $400 deposit to be returned. Salameh was clearly set up and something very similar happened when the World Trade Center was attacked again in 2001.

Larry Johnson, the former deputy director of the State Department's office on counterterrorism, told *Fox News* that the paths of alleged hijackers Mohamed Atta and Marwan Al-Shehhi, and alleged accomplice, Zacarias Moussaoui, had crossed on more than one occasion with that of Al-Hussaini Hussain, the man Johnson believes was the John Doe 2 with McVeigh outside the Murrah Building in Oklahoma.[136] He is not alone in this belief. Johnson said that the motel in Oklahoma City where the Murrah bombing is said to have been planned was visited by Atta, al-Shehhi and Moussaoui five weeks before 9/11. Johnson said:

> "I've spoken to the owner of the motel. After the 9/11 attacks he called the FBI, the FBI came out and interviewed him – and he identified Mohamed Atta, Marwan Al-Shehhi and Zacarias Moussaoui."

Al-Hussaini Hussain was one of Saddam Hussein's Republican Guard officers who were relocated to the United States, especially Oklahoma, by Father George Bush after the Gulf War and some of these people have also been connected by researchers to the World Trade Center bombing of 1993, which strongly appears to have involved Mossad operative, Jose Hadas. Johnson says that after leaving Oklahoma, Al-Hussaini Hussain secured a job at Boston Logan Airport where Flights 11 and 175 departed before being flown into the World Trade Center by, it is claimed, Mohamed Atta and Marwan al-Shehhi. It is possible that Atta, al-Shehhi and a few of the others could have been intelligence assets who did not know the true picture, but I think most of those on the FBI list are fake identities used to hide what really happened. I believe their role was in constructing the cover story, knowingly or unknowingly. Clearly this is true of many of those named by the FBI because they are still alive. We should keep in mind the technique of compartmentalisation in which different groups and people within these intelligence networks have no idea what other groups and people in the same network are doing, or what the big picture might be. They only know what they need to know to do their jobs. I'll come back to possible scenarios in a later chapter.

Why not Indian Point?

Here's another puzzling question if you buy the "Arab terrorists hated Americans and wanted to destroy the infidels in the home of Satan" story. Why did Flight 11 fly almost directly over the massive nuclear power installations at Indian Point, around 24 miles from New York City, and why did Flight 175 fly past only a few minutes away? Why didn't they both target Indian Point and have the potential to turn that whole region of the United States, including New York, into an uninhabitable wasteland and in the process kill millions of "infidels" through radiation poisoning in the months and years to come? There are three nuclear plants at Indian Point, two of them active apparently, and apart from the power stations themselves the complex has an enormous store of radioactive waste. Why fly over this nuclear complex on the way to New York when devastation beyond belief would have been caused by aiming the two planes at Indian Point? But, of course, the question again answers itself. Attacking the World Trade Center does not affect the elite that control the United States, except in positively advancing their agenda. Targeting Indian Point would mean that the headquarters and lives of the US elite would also be threatened and fundamentally affected. See how these "hijackers" were so understanding and aware of the needs of the very US elite they were supposed to hate? They showed the same consideration when they targeted the side of the Pentagon that was furthest away from the offices of the Defense Secretary, the Joint Chiefs of Staff, and the other leaders of the US military. So kind, so thoughtful. Not only that, these highly professional hijackers directed the plane at the very section of the building that had just undergone rebuilding and reinforcement to protect it against terrorist attack! Or, as CBS put it on November 28th, 2001: "In an astonishing stroke of luck, the terrorists had hit the only section of the Pentagon designed to resist a terrorist attack." Hey Abdul, you sure this map is the right way up?

Expert scepticism

Andreas von Bulow, the former German Minister of Defence and Minister for Research and Technology in the government of German Chancellor Helmut Schmidt, told the German daily newspaper *Der Tagesspiegel* that the official story of September 11th was nonsense.[137] During official government investigations he learned about the methods of German and American intelligence and security agencies, and he wrote a book on the subject, *Im Namen des Staates* (In the Name of the State). He says that 95% of the work of intelligence agencies is deception and disinformation communicated through the mass media to create an "acceptable 'virtual' version of events".[138] Von Bulow told *Der Tagesspiegel* that the planning of the 9/11 attacks was technically and organisationally a master achievement. To hijack four huge airplanes within a few minutes and, within one hour, to drive them into their targets, with complicated flight manoeuvres, was unthinkable, he said, without years of support from "secret apparatuses of the state and industry". He said there are 26 intelligence services in the United States with a budget of $30 billion – more than the German defence budget – and yet they were not able to prevent the attacks and "for 60 decisive minutes the military and intelligence services let fighter planes stay on the ground". But within 48 hours, he said, the FBI had presented a list of suicide attackers, seven of which turned out to be alive. He went on:

> "If this Atta was the decisive man in the operation, it's really strange that he took such a risk of taking a plane that would reach Boston such a short time before the connecting flight. Had his flight been a few minutes late, he would not have been in the plane that was hijacked. Why should a sophisticated terrorist do this? One can, by the way, read on CNN (Internet) that none of these names were on the official passenger lists. None of them had gone through the check-in procedures. And why did none of the threatened pilots give the agreed-upon code 7700 over the transponder to the ground station?

> "In addition: The black boxes which are fire and shock proof, as well as the voice recordings, contain no valuable data ... [and] ... assailants ... in their preparations, leave tracks behind them like a herd of stampeding elephants. They made payments with credit cards with their own names; they reported to their flight instructors with their own names. They left behind rented cars with flight manuals in Arabic ... They took with them, on their suicide trip, wills and farewell letters, which fall into the hands of the FBI,

because they were stored in the wrong place and wrongly addressed. Clues were left behind like in a child's game of hide-and-seek, which were to be followed!" [139]

Eckehardt Werthebach, the former chief of German domestic intelligence, agrees with this assessment. He told the *American Free Press* that the magnitude of the planning and the "deathly precision" could not have been achieved without support from a state intelligence organisation. The lack of prior warning would also indicate such an involvement, he said.[140] Horst Ehmke, the man who supervised German intelligence in the 1970s, says the same – an intelligence organisation had to be involved. He said the events of September 11th looked like a "Hollywood production".[141]

"Evidence" to die for

It is staggering to think that at least 5,000 Afghan civilians died in just the first phase of the "war on terrorism" when the only justification for this mass murder was the "evidence" outlined here for who was responsible for the attacks of September 11th. The authorities named a group of "hijackers" overwhelmingly dominated by Saudis with not a single Afghan on the list. The FBI's "list" of "hijackers" was utterly discredited with at least seven, possibly more, of the 19 named found to be still alive. The passenger lists as issued by the two airlines do not include the names of the "hijackers" or anyone with an Arab name and the seat numbers for them given by two flight attendants on Flight 11 and by the FBI do not match. There are no cameras in the Boston Airport departure lounge to prove that Atta and his alleged accomplices even got on the planes. I was denied access to the American and United Airlines check-in staff on duty that day to confirm that they remembered checking them in. Video footage showing the alleged hijackers boarding at Newark, New Jersey and Washington Dulles, where they do have surveillance cameras, has not been made public when it would add substance to the official story's collapsing credibility. Why don't they release them if they really exist when they have long released the pictures from Portland, Maine? Why have we not seen footage of the "Middle Eastern men" in the car park at Boston Airport where they have surveillance cameras recording the comings and goings? Despite this complete lack of evidence and with FBI chief Robert Mueller saying they have "no legal proof to prove the identities of the suicidal hijackers", Bush and Blair stampeded the world into a war that has already killed thousands of civilians and will go on to kill millions unless these lunatics are stopped. How can you blame the attacks on Osama bin Laden when you can't even say who the hijackers were, never mind link them to bin Laden, which, even with their spectacularly discredited "list", they have demonstrably failed to do?

There are ridiculous contradictions between the pilot skills required to manoeuvre and navigate those planes to find and strike those buildings, and the reports from flying instructors of the limited, often non-existent, abilities of those claimed to have been hijacker-pilots. One effort to overcome this has been the story of how Atta and al-Shehhi practiced on a Boeing 727 simulator at SimCenter Inc. in

Opa-locka, near Miami, owned by Henry R. George. He said the two men had spent three hours each in the school's 727 jet simulator on December 29th and 30th 2000. "They did not seem to have enough skill to pilot real jet airliners, although they had sufficient skills to turn and drive an airplane," George said.[142] They spent most of their time practising manoeuvres and turns, he said, but they did take off and land on the simulator as well. It was not a formal training programme for flying jets, George pointed out, and it was "a mini, mini introduction".[143] What about the claims that they were highly trained pilots who carried out the 9/11 attacks? Note that he says they practised take offs and landings while the media only emphasised that they wanted to practise turns because it fitted with the government's story. George also added: "To me, they acted like normal human beings, nothing abnormal. They were polite, maybe even shy."[144] The FBI says that Hani Hanjour joined the Sawyer School of Aviation flight simulator club in Phoenix, which gives members unlimited use of a flight simulator, and yet his flying ability was so limited according to instructors at the schools he attended that even the FBI had to withdraw the claims that he was flying Flight 77 when it is said to have struck the Pentagon. One other question: if these men who attended US flying schools were part of the al-Qaeda network that has, we are told, unlimited funds and a fantastic global web of contacts, operatives, and supporters, why did they take the risk of learning to fly (or not as it turned out) in the United States before September 11th? Why not learn at a safe location somewhere else in the world under the tutelage of flying instructors who were part of their network?

If you have evidence to prove that your story is true then you have no need to invent "evidence" like passports miraculously falling from fireballs and Islamic "letters" that any Muslim can see were not written by followers, never mind fanatics, of their religion. If what you say is correct, you don't prevent witnesses being interviewed, you release videotapes to back up your claims, you answer basic questions, and you don't keep contracting yourself day after day. You do all of those things only when you don't have evidence and when you are seeking to mislead. The official story does not make sense, none of it adds up, and for a very good reason. It's not true.

Postscript: During the first print run of this book the FBI said that the "hijacker passport" story it had called a news conference to reveal was now a "rumour that might be true". No kidding.

SOURCES

1   *CBS News*, September 26th 2001

2   San Diegans See Area as Likely Target, *Washington Post*, September 24th 2001, p A7

3   *ABC News*, **http://abcnews.go.com/sections/scitech/TechTV/techtv_blackboxes 010917.html**

4　http://www.ntsb.gov/aviation/CVR_FDR.htm

5　*St Petersburg Times*, September 16th 2001

6　Ibid

7　http://asia.cnn.com/2001/US/09/17/inv.investigation.terrorism/index.html

8　*Orlando Sentinel*, September 20th 2001

9　http://www.whatreallyhappened.com/who.html

10　UK *Daily Telegraph*, September 23rd 2001

11　UK *Independent*, September 17th 2001

12　*Chicago Tribune*, September 16th 2001

13　*Los Angeles Times*, September 21st 2001

14　CBS, September 27th 2001

15　http://www.cbsnews.com/htdocs/america_under_attack/terror/team3_right.html

16　http://www.abqtrib.com/archives/news01/092001_news_trail.shtml

17　UK *Guardian*, October 7th 2002

18　*Arab News*, September 27th 2001

19　*Associated Press*, September 20th 2001

20　http://www.cbsnews.com/htdocs/america_under_attack/terror/team3_right.html

21　*Associated Press*, September 18th 2001

22　*Arab News*, September 22nd 2001

23　CBS, September 27th 2001

24　*Arab News*, September 22nd 2001

25　UK *Daily Telegraph*, September 23rd 2001

26　http://www.newsmedianews.com/wtc.htm

27　*Los Angeles Times*, http://www.latimes.com/news/nationworld/nation/la-102301jarrah.story

28　Ibid

29　CNN, September 20th and 27th 2001

30　*Washington Post*, September 13th 2001, pA01

31　Ibid

32　http://www.fbi.gov/pressrel/penttbom/penttbomb.htm

33　The Last Moments of Flight 11, BBC News Online, September 21st 2001

34　E-mail reply to the author from Tim Kincaid, Manager of Communications Planning, American Airlines Corporate Communications, March 14th 2001

35　E-mail to the author from United Airlines media spokesman, Rich Nelson, on March 20th 2002

36　E-mail to the author, March 15th 2001

37　Ibid

38 E-mail to the author, March 14th 2001

39 E-mail to the author by United Airlines media spokesman, Rich Nelson, on March 20th 2002

40 E-mail reply to the author from Tim Kincaid, the manager of Communications Planning, American Airlines Corporate Communications, March 14th 2001

41 E-mail to the author from United Airlines media spokesman, Rich Nelson, on March 20th 2002

42 On flight 77: Our Plane Is Being Hijacked, *Washington Post*, September 12th 2001, pp A 1, 11

43 Fax to the author on May 11th 2002, see *Appendix 2*

44 *Hindustan Times*, September 18th 2001

45 *Kansas City Star*, September 18th, 2001

46 **http://www.arabicnews.com/ansub/Daily/Day/010922/2001092213.html**

47 *Newsweek*, September 24th 2001

48 *ABC News*, September 2001

49 *Kansas City Star*, September 18th 2001

50 Ibid

51 Ibid

52 Ibid

53 Ibid

54 Ibid

55 Ibid

56 Indictment of Zacarias Moussaoui, United States District Court for the Eastern District of Virginia, Alexandria Division, December 2001

57 *Kansas City Star*, September 18th 2001

58 **http://www.gopbi.com/partners/pbpost/news/924_terrorist.html**

59 Urban Legends Reference Pages **http://www.snopes2.com**

60 No Link Between Hijacker and Iraqi, *International Herald Tribune*, May 2nd 2002, p 3. This was quoting a report in the *Washington Post*

61 Ibid

62 *Chicago Tribune*, September 16th 2001

63 UK *Observer*, September 23rd 2001

64 Ibid

65 Manhunt for Shadowy Figure in Sept. 11 Plot, *International Herald Tribune*, May 2nd 2002, p 3, quoting a report in the *New York Times*

66 Indictment against Zacarias Moussaoui, United States District Court for the Eastern District of Virginia, Alexandria Division, December 2001

67 **http://www.thedailycamera.com/news/terror/sept01/0914profiles.html**

68 Ibid

69 *Kansas City Star*, September 18th 2001

70   Ibid

71   **http://www.orlandosentinel.com/news/nationworld/orl-asecflorida14091401sep14.story**

72   *ABC News*, September 2001

73   *Kansas City Star*, September 18th 2001

74   *St Petersburg Times*, September 14th 2001

75   **http://www.westerndefense.org/articles/SaudiArabia/october01.htm**

76   **http://www.inlibertyandfreedom.com/hoax.htm**

77   **http://www.smh.com.au/news/0109/18/world/world14.html**

78   *Chicago Tribune*, September 16th 2001

79   *Kansas City Star*, September 18th 2001

80   Ibid

81   Ibid

82   Ibid

83   Al-Ahram Weekly Online, September 27th to October 3rd 2001

84   *All Fall Down*, p 45

85   *Washington Post*, September 13th 2001, p A01

86   **http://www.observer.co.uk/Print/0,3858,4258186,00.html**

87   *Kansas City Star*, September 18th 2001

88   *NewsCenter 5*, September 12th 2001
     http://www.thebostonchannel.com/News/957448/index.html

89   E-mail reply to the author from Tim Kincaid, the manager of Communications Planning, American Airlines Corporate Communications, March 14th 2001

90   E-mail to the author from Rich Nelson, media spokesman for United Airlines, March 20th 2002

91   **http://www.thebostonchannel.com/News/957059/index.html** The Boston Channel, September 12th 2001, **http://www.thebostonchannel.com/News/957059/index.html**

92   Logan Lacks Video Cameras, *Boston Herald*, September 29th 2001

93   Ibid

94   *Boston Globe*, September 13th 2001

95   Ibid

96   *Boston Herald*, September 29th 2001

97   E-mail reply to the author on March 14th 2001

98   *Los Angeles Times*, October 6th 2001

99   *New York Post*, September 21st 2001,
     http://www.warroom.com/nyterrorism/proberstrace.htm

100 *Los Angeles Times*, October 6th 2001

101 *Kansas City Star*, September 18th 2001

102 **http://www.click10.com/mia/news/stories/news-95639520010911-090905.html** and
http://www.observer.co.uk/Print/0,3858,4258186,00.html

103 *Chicago Tribune*, September 16th 2001

104 Associated Press, September 12th 2001

105 *St Petersburg Times*, September 16th 2001

106 UK *Independent*, September 29th 2001

107 Ibid

108 UK *Guardian*, quoted in *All Fall Down*, p 35

109 **http://www.madcowprod.com/index8.html**

110 *Boston Globe*, **http://www.boston.com/dailyglobe2/300/nation/Spy_agency_destroys_
data_angering_others_in_probe+.shtml**

111 **http://www.madcowprod.com/index8.html**

112 Ibid

113 **http://www.madcowprod.com/index.x.html** New owners of Huffman Aviation have global
presence

114 Ibid

115 Daniel Hopsicker, author of *Barry and the Boys: The CIA, the Mob, and America's Secret
History*, available through his website at **http://www.barryandtheboys.com**

116 **http://www.madcowprod.com/index6.html**

117 **http://www.madcowprod.com/index8.html**

118 **http://www.kpam.com/cgi-local/arch.read.pl?exclusive-2001.101614.31.00**

119 **http://www.madcowprod.com/index7.html**

120 *Kansas City Star*, September 18th 2001

121 **http://www.madcowprod.com/index.3.html**

122 **http://www.madcowprod.com/index7.html**

123 Ibid

124 Alleged Hijackers May Have Trained at US Bases, *Newsweek*, September 15th 2001

125 Ibid

126 **http://www.realityexpander.com/articles/joewatson/end_justifies_means_2.html**

127 **http://www.madcowprod.com/index6.html**

128 Ibid

129 **http://www.madcowprod.com/index9.html**

130 *Chicago Tribune*, September 16th 2001

131 **http://news.bbc.co.uk/hi/english/events/newsnight/newsid_1645000/1645527.stm**

132 **http://news.bbc.co.uk/hi/english/events/newsnight/newsid_1645000/1645527.stm**

133 **http://www.madcowprod.com/index6.html**

134 *Newsweek*, September 15th 2001

135 *International Herald Tribune*, June 8th 1993

136 *Fox News*, May 7th 2002

137 *Der Tagesspiegel*, January 13th 2002

138 Ibid

139 Ibid

140 *All Fall Down*, p 204

141 *All Fall Down*, p 205

142 *Kansas City Star*, September 18th 2001

143 Ibid

144 Ibid

chapter 11

Prior knowledge

Whenever you find that you are on the side of the majority, it is time to pause and reflect

Mark Twain

Many questions remain about what happened on September 11th, but there is much that we do already know. We know that the Bush family has business and other associations with the bin Laden family. We know that President Boy George Bush ordered the FBI to back off investigations into the bin Laden family's involvement in funding the al-Qaeda network and other terrorist groups. We know that at least 11 members of the bin Laden family were allowed to fly out of America from Boston Logan days after 9/11 at a time when everyone else with an Arab face in America was considered a suspect. We know that only months before September 11th John O'Neill resigned as deputy director of the FBI and head of counter-terrorism because he was not allowed to investigate the bin Laden network. We know that Father George Bush has made visits to the bin Ladens in Saudi Arabia and has been an adviser to the family business. We know that Bush family members are business associates of people like Khalid bin Mahfouz who has been named by the US State Department as a funder of Osama bin Laden. We know that Father George arranged for thousands of officers and troops from Saddam Hussein's Republican Guard to settle in the United States after the Gulf War, most of them in Oklahoma. We know that reporters have linked some of these people to the Oklahoma bombing and the 1993 bombing of the World Trade Center. As I will outline later, we know that the invasion of Afghanistan was being planned long before September 11th and that the bombing of a stone-age country in the middle of a famine had nothing to do with 9/11 – except that it provided the public excuse. We know that the removal of the Taliban has opened the way for the crucial oil and gas pipelines the Bush family and their Illuminati associates are desperate to build to open the floodgates to the Caspian Sea reserves they have long coveted. We know that the bin Laden network in Afghanistan was funded into existence by the CIA and that the tunnel systems bombed by US and British forces were paid for by the CIA and built by the bin Laden family construction empire, as I will highlight in a later chapter. We know that the lack of response to the 9/11 attacks that morning was utterly bizarre, as was the behaviour of the top three commanders of the US military, Bush, Rumsfeld and Myers. We know that in the months before September 11th Bush was given many warnings about possible attacks on the American mainland using commercial aircraft, but nothing was done. We know that the official story is intelligence-insulting nonsense and that the attacks have massively advanced the very Illuminati agenda for a centralised, militarised, fascist state that I and others have been warning about for so long.

Air Force insider says Bush knew

Lieutenant Colonel Steve Butler, a US Air Force veteran and vice chancellor for student affairs at the Defense Language Institute in Monterey, California, said that Bush knew the 9/11 attacks were coming, but did nothing. Butler sent a letter setting out his claims to the *Monterey County Herald* and it was published on May 26th 2002. "Of course Bush knew about the impending attacks on America," Butler said in the letter. "He did nothing to warn the American people because he needed this war on terrorism." Butler is a former combat pilot who took part in the Gulf War in 1991, and he said that Boy George was using Osama bin Laden in the same way that his father used Saddam Hussein and Iraq. After the letter appeared, Butler was relieved of his duties at the language school and assigned to temporary duty at Travis Air Force Base pending an investigation into his conduct. I understand that Butler is not just making wild allegations, but has definite knowledge that Bush and the Pentagon were well aware that the attacks were coming and when. Butler's assertions are supported by a stream of other evidence and I'm not surprised they wanted to shut him up fast.

Bush "warned" of attacks

It is indicative of where you find the real investigative journalism that months before the mainstream media published the story, Internet websites were detailing the reports that President Bush was told of possible hijackings in the United States before September 11th and did nothing to warn people. Before I detail some of this background, however, a warning of my own. We need to be careful about the double-spin technique or what I call "the fallback position". When these Illuminati operations are played out there is always a number one cover story that they want the people to believe – and most do. In this case it is that Osama bin Laden organised the entire operation with "his" al-Qaeda network and it was so brilliantly done that the US agencies had no idea what was going on until the planes crashed. But they know that not everyone will believe that and will look for some kind of conspiracy behind the official version. So they give them one to keep them happy and occupied. When Princess Diana was assassinated in Paris in 1997 the number one cover story was that it was all a terrible accident caused by a drunk driver. The fallback position was that she was murdered because the British royal family did not want her to marry a Muslim, Dodi Fayed. Both stories are untrue, but together they provide alternative explanations accepted by the vast majority of people. The 9/11 fall back position for conspiracy researchers and others who question the official line is that (a) the Bush administration knew the attacks were coming, but were so incompetent that they did nothing or (b) the Bush administration knew the attacks were coming, but did nothing because allowing them to happen would give them the excuse to launch a war on terrorism for reasons of oil and advancing their fascist agenda. What these two versions and the number one cover story all have in common is very significant: no matter what the background detail might be, Osama bin Laden and al-Qaeda were responsible for organising the whole thing and the plan involved "terrorists" trained at US flying schools. This suits the Illuminati because it hides the most important truth, I would suggest, that the core organisation behind the attacks was not based in a cave in Afghanistan, but in the headquarters of the US government, intelligence "community", the military, and at the highest level of the Illuminati hierarchy. I would advise that we keep that in mind when we hear the stories that "Bush was warned". Incompetence is often used as a screen to cover up calculated involvement, and this "incompetence" can be used, as in this case, to justify the "reorganisation" (centralisation) of intelligence and security agencies to put the power in even fewer hands. Yes Bush was warned, but it was more than that, much, much, more.

In May 2002 the story broke widely in the mainstream media (big red flag) of the number of warnings given to, and circulating within, the Bush administration and its agencies. The White House admitted eight months after the attacks that Bush was told by US intelligence before September 11th that Osama bin Laden's terrorist network might hijack American airplanes, we are told. The White House press secretary Ari Fleischer said the administration notified the "appropriate agencies" in the summer of 2001 that hijackings were possible, but the Massport organisation that runs Boston Logan Airport told the *Boston Globe* it was told nothing about this.[1] Fleischer would not say when or how Bush was given the information, but it emerged that it was during an intelligence briefing on August 6th 2001 – or so we're told. These are the same US intelligence agencies that said they had no idea that the September 11th attacks were being planned. The CIA would only say in response to these reports that the subject of airline hijackings was among a number of terrorist methods raised to US government officials at the time. In fact, Congressional correspondent David Welna said on National Public Radio on the morning of September 11th: "I spoke with Congressman Ike Skelton – a Democrat from Missouri and a member of the Armed Services Committee – who said that just recently the Director of the CIA warned that there could be an attack, an imminent attack, on the United States of this nature. So this is not entirely unexpected."[2]

Federal ban on investigation (FBI)

It was also reported that a classified memo written by an FBI agent in Phoenix at that same time urged FBI headquarters to investigate Middle Eastern men enrolled in American flight schools and said that terrorist groups like the bin Laden group could be sending students to the schools as part of terrorist plans. Law enforcement officials said the memo was received at bureau headquarters in late July and was reviewed by counterterrorism staff. But no action was taken in response to the memo's urgings to compile information on the visa applications of foreign students seeking admission to aviation schools. On August 17th a flight instructor at the Pan Am Flying Academy in Eagan, Minnesota, called the local FBI office to report his suspicions about a 33-year-old French-Moroccan called Zacarias Moussaoui, who was later charged with being involved. But the *New York Times* reported that senior FBI officials repeatedly denied requests by agents at the Minnesota office for a detailed investigation into his background.[3] One of the facts that interested the agents was that Moussaoui was attending flying schools and yet since 9/11 the FBI Director Robert Mueller has constantly claimed the FBI had no idea that potential terrorists were training to be pilots in the US. He said it was "news, quite obviously," and added: "If we had understood that to be the case, we would have – perhaps one could have averted this." This is clearly another monumental lie, but I stress again that we need to be very careful that these stories are not circulating to underpin the "hijackers attending flying schools did it" scenario. For me the agents were in danger of thwarting the cover story rather than exposing the real plot and that's why their efforts were blocked. Information from FBI agents in Minnesota was included in an internal FBI document warning that Moussaoui "might be planning on flying something into the World Trade Center".[4] The agents asked for a warrant to search Moussaoui's personal computer, but these were refused by the Justice Department of Bush Attorney General John Ashcroft. Coleen Rowley, an FBI agent for more than 21 years and Minneapolis Chief Division Counsel, sent a memo in May 2002 to FBI Director Robert Mueller condemning the way the bureau headquarters had blocked terrorist investigations before 9/11. She said that certain facts about this had been "omitted, downplayed, glossed over and/or mis-characterised in an effort to avoid or minimise personal and/or institutional embarrassment on the part of the FBI and/or perhaps even for improper political reasons." She went on:

"In the day or two following September 11th, you, Director Mueller, made the statement to the effect that if the FBI had only had any advance warning of the attacks, we (meaning the FBI), may have been able to take some action to prevent the tragedy. Fearing that this statement could easily come back to haunt the FBI upon revelation of the information that had been developed pre-September 11th about Moussaoui, I and others in the Minneapolis Office, immediately sought to reach your office through an assortment of higher level FBIHQ contacts, in order to quickly make you aware of the background of the Moussaoui investigation and forewarn you so that your public statements could be accordingly modified.

"When such statements from you and other FBI officials continued, we thought that somehow you had not received the message and we made further efforts. Finally when similar comments were made weeks later, in Assistant Director Caruso's congressional testimony in response to the first public leaks about Moussaoui we faced the sad realization that the remarks indicated someone, possibly with your approval, had decided to circle the wagons at FBIHQ in an apparent effort to protect the FBI from embarrassment and the relevant FBI officials from scrutiny. Everything I have seen and heard about the FBI's official stance and the FBI's internal preparations in anticipation of further congressional inquiry, had, unfortunately, confirmed my worst suspicions in this regard." [5]

In straightforward terms, Mueller was knowingly lying and allowing his associates to lie. Rowley revealed how "in a desperate 11th hour measure to bypass the "FBIHQ roadblock" the Minneapolis Division directly notified the CIA's Counter Terrorist Center, but FBI headquarters "chastised" the Minneapolis agents for making the direct notification without their approval! Rowley told Mueller that in the early aftermath of September 11th when she was recounting the pre-September 11th events concerning the Moussaoui investigation to other FBI personnel in other divisions or FBI headquarters, "almost everyone's first question was 'Why? –Why would an FBI agent(s) deliberately sabotage a case?'" If they would care to read this book they might see the answer to that question and the fact that it was so widely asked shows how the compartmentalisation works so effectively. FBI Special Agent Robert Wright, Jr, who investigated the laundering of money for terrorism in the United States for four years, was equally livid at how his efforts were blocked by superiors. He told the media on May 30th 2002:

"I truly believe I would be derelict in my duty as an American if I did not do my best to bring the FBI's dereliction of duty to the attention of others. I have made it my mission … to legally expose the problems of the FBI to the President of the United States, the US Congress, and the American people." [6]

FBI agents were so angry at the way they were blocked by their own superiors that they gave their information to Chicago lawyer David Schippers, the man who led the legal efforts to impeach President Clinton. Schippers said he contacted the office of Attorney General John Ashcroft to urge an investigation, but his pleas were ignored. Schippers says he was given information by FBI agents and intelligence sources that a massive terrorist attack was being planned for lower Manhattan and he had tried in vain for six weeks to communicate this information to Ashcroft. He said he had also tried in the past to tell Ashcroft about the connection between the Oklahoma bombing and the Iraqi officers and soldiers that were brought to Oklahoma after the Gulf War by Father George Bush, but got the same response.[7] He said of the Iraqi officers: "The word is out even today that the Oklahoma City police are not allowed to touch them." Schippers described his efforts to warn Ashcroft:

"I was trying to get people to understand that [the terrorist group] Hamas had infiltrated the United States. I tried the House, I tried the Senate, I tried the Department of Justice, these were the very people who put up roadblocks on the attack against the terrorists under Clinton and are still there. They still constitute almost like a moat between the people with information and the people who should hear the information.

"I used people who were personal friends of John Ashcroft to try and get him. One of them called me back and said right I've talked to him, he'll call you tomorrow morning. This was like a month before the bombing [9/11 attacks].

"The next day I got a call from a lower ranked official of the Justice Department who said they don't start their investigations at the top. He would look into my information and get back to me. He never did." [8]

Stansfield Turner, a former head of the CIA, said on US television that the FBI had been closely following up to six bin Laden "cells" in the months before 9/11 and had tapped every phone line and computer communication. The FBI could not move in, he said, because the men had not done anything illegal.[9] The FBI and CIA were not aware of what was going on? Sure. How come an Urban Search and Rescue Team from the Federal Emergency Management Agency (FEMA), a massive Illuminati front, was deployed to New York City the night *before* the attacks. On September 11th, Tom Kennedy, a FEMA official, told Dan Rather on *CBS News*: "We're currently one of the first teams that was deployed to support the City of New York in this disaster. We arrived on late Monday night and went right into action on Tuesday morning." [10] Now I have heard of being clairvoyant, but ...?? As long ago as December 1996 the German paper *Die Welt* and *Agence France Presse* reported that the CIA and other intelligence agencies had learned of plans to crash commercial airliners into the twin towers. The reports claimed that the information was found on the computer of al-Qaeda operatives arrested in the Philippines. The plan, called "Operation Bojinka", was also revealed in 1997 during the trial in New York of Ramsi Youssef who was jailed for his part in the 1993 World Trade Center bombing (with enormous help from the FBI). Other sources for warnings of the attacks are claimed to include the following:

The German Intelligence agency BND warned both the CIA and Israel in June that Middle Eastern terrorists were "planning to hijack commercial aircraft to use as weapons to attack important symbols of American and Israeli culture." The story referred to an electronic eavesdropping system called Echelon that is used by US-connected countries to tap cellphone and electronic communications, and the information shared with each other. The BND warnings were also passed to the United Kingdom, it is reported.[11]

Russia's President Putin said that before September 11th he had ordered Russian intelligence to warn the US government "in the strongest possible terms" of imminent assaults on airports and government buildings.[12]

The German newspaper *Neue Presse* reported how a 29-year-old Iranian held in custody in Hanover warned US intelligence officials of an attack planned in America the week of September 10th. He pleaded to be allowed to talk with the authorities in America, but US officials hung up on him when he said he was awaiting deportation from Germany. Hours before the 9/11 attacks the Iranian begged to fax a letter to President Bush, but was not allowed to do so. On September 14th officials from the US Justice Department and intelligence agencies interviewed him.

Vice President Dick Cheney said that political criticism of the Bush government's failure to react to warnings was "thoroughly irresponsible and totally unworthy of national leaders in time of war". He also tried to deflect these headlines by saying that "Without a doubt, a very real threat of another perhaps more devastating attack still exists." You should know, Dick. Just as the questions were being asked about what the president knew and when, it was announced with perfect timing that an American citizen had been arrested without charge for plotting a "dirty bomb" attack in the United States. A "dirty bomb" is made of conventional explosives, but contains radioactive material. Donna Newman, the lawyer of Abdullah al-Muhajir, formerly Jose Padilla, called the government case "weak" and filed a petition challenging the legal basis for classifying her client as an "enemy combatant" – a term that allows his indefinite detention without trial. Bush in typical style said: "This guy, Padilla, is a bad guy and he is where he needs to be detained." Such is the world we live in since September 11th.

It happened before at the WTC

It is obvious that many people knew to a larger or lesser extent that the attacks were coming, and for the FBI and CIA to claim they had no warning is to insult the mind of a five year old. The fact is that all this has happened before. The *New York Times* revealed how the FBI had the chance to stop the carnage in the bombing of the World Trade Center on February 26th 1993, but failed to do so. The *Times* published conversations secretly recorded by FBI informer Emad Ali Salem, a one-time Egyptian army officer, which show how the FBI knew the attack was coming and planned to substitute the explosives in the truck bomb for harmless powder. But Salem said an FBI supervisor called John Anticev stopped the plan, and six people died and 1,000 were injured. Emad Ali Salem says on the tape: "Guys, now you saw this bomb went off and you both know we could avoid that." [13] He said that the FBI agents were paid to "prevent problems like this from happening" and in a conversation with an agent Floyd, Salem says to him: "Do you deny your supervisor is the main reason of bombing the World Trade Center?" Salem said Mr Anticev did not deny it. "We was handling the case perfectly well until the supervisor messed it up, upside down," Salem says. [14] So Salem, an FBI informant, built the bomb that exploded at the World Trade Center; he was paid a million dollars by the bureau; and he was under the witness protection programme when he was the chief prosecution witness in the trial of those blamed by the FBI! Ron Kuby, an attorney for one of the defendants, said of the article revealing the tapes:

"The article on the FBI being involved in the World Trade Center bombing actually understated the evidence, believe it or not. The informer, Emad Salem, is actually on tape saying that he built the bomb that ultimately blew up the World Trade Center ... In addition, we have received information that he was visually observed at the scene of the bombing shortly after the bombing took place. Shortly after that, he was admitted to the hospital, suffering from an ear problem that was consistent with exposure to blast ... The mastermind is the government of the United States. It was a phoney, government-engineered conspiracy to begin with. It would never have amounted to anything had the government not planned it." [15]

So here we have the bomb that exploded at the World Trade Center in 1993, built by an informant on the FBI payroll and planted in a truck with a rental agreement that included the phone number and address of a notorious Mossad agent, Josie Hadas! But there's more. Sheikh Omar Abdel-Rahman, the "spiritual leader" of the Egyptian extremist group Gamaa Al-Islamya, was convicted in January 1996 of "seditious conspiracy" and sentenced to life imprisonment for his part in planning the 1993 World Trade Center bombing. He was put on the State Department's "watch list" in 1987, but recruited by the CIA in support of Osama bin Laden and the Mujahadin in Afghanistan during the Soviet occupation in the 1980s. American foreign correspondent Mary Anne Weaver revealed that in Peshawar, Pakistan, in the late 1980s Sheikh Omar became involved with US and Pakistani intelligence officials who were orchestrating the war against the Soviets and that the "sixty or so CIA and Special Forces officers based there considered him a 'valuable asset'." [16] They overlooked his anti-western message and his incitement to holy war, she wrote, because they wanted him to help unify the mujahadin groups. Sheikh Omar was given a one-year visa to enter the United States on May 10th 1990 from a CIA agent posing as an official at the US Consulate in Khartoum, Sudan, and he arrived in New York in July 1990. [17] The visa was revoked in November that year and the State Department warned the Immigration and Naturalization Service to watch for him. Instead, within months, they granted Sheikh Omar a green card (work permit) and two years later came the World Trade Center bombing for which he and others were convicted. [18] A CIA asset was convicted of conspiracy to plant a bomb that was made by an informant of the FBI and left in a rental truck connected to a Mossad agent. Unbelievable. We are supposed to believe these guys when they tell us what happened on September 11th and who was responsible? Or that the CIA and FBI had no connection to what happened and who did it? It was also later revealed, in keeping with the FBI's appalling history of lies and cover-ups, that "evidence" was changed to support the prosecution of people the FBI claimed to be responsible for the 1993 World Trade Center bombing. On August 14th 1995, FBI special agent Dr Frederic Whitehurst testified in the trial that the FBI concocted misleading scientific reports and pressured two of their scientists to lie to support its prosecution of the defendants. He was asked if during his examination of bomb residue materials and chemicals connected with the defendants, he became aware that the FBI agents investigating the case had developed a preliminary theory that the bomb that blew up the World Trade Center was a urea nitrate bomb? "That is correct," he replied. The questioning continued as follows:

"Did there come a time when you began to experience pressure from within the FBI to reach certain conclusions that supported that theory of the investigation?"

"Yes, that is correct."

"In other words, you began to experience pressure on you to say that the explosion was caused by a urea nitrate bomb?"

"Yes, that is correct."

"And you were aware that such a finding would strengthen the prosecution of the defendants who were on trial, who were going on trial in that case, correct?"

"Absolutely." [19]

Special agent Frederic Whitehurst, the senior FBI explosives expert, found himself demoted to paint analysis. A Boston court released two men in January 2001 who had spent 30 years in jail for a murder they did not commit because the FBI rigged the "evidence". Two other innocent men also jailed for the killing had already died in prison. The FBI was protecting an informant known as Joseph "the Animal" Barboza, who had been named to agents as one of those responsible for the murder. Barboza even gave testimony against the convicted men and was protected from prosecution by his FBI handlers, agents H. Paul Rico and Dennis Condon. Agent Condon testified at the time in support of killer Barboza's credibility and even after the trial when Barboza said that he had falsely named the four men, the FBI kept quiet and the courts denied a new trial.[20] The FBI had the Algerian pilot Lotfi Raissi jailed for five months amid claims that he trained some of the 9/11 "pilots", but then produced no evidence whatsoever to support that allegation. This is the same organisation that is telling you what happened on September 11th and who did it.

The "spy who knew", but no one listened?

More than a month before September 11th, Delmart Edward Joseph "Mike" Vreeland, who claims to be an operative with US Naval Intelligence, says he warned from his Canadian prison cell that the attacks were going to happen. Vreeland gave a note to prison guards listing potential targets including the World Trade Center, the White House and the Pentagon, and it said: "Let one happen, stop the rest." Vreeland was in prison on what he says were manufactured charges relating to credit card fraud that were designed to keep him out of circulation. He says he was in Moscow working for Naval Intelligence in the closing months of 2000 on a mission related to the "Star Wars" defence system, and flew to Toronto in December of that year. He said he had a sealed pouch containing intelligence documents that he was supposed to hand over, but when his contact didn't turn up he opened the pouch and read some of the contents. Vreeland says the documents gave warnings of the planned attacks on the World Trade Center. This was nine months before they happened. Vreeland told investigator Mike Ruppert what the documents said:

> "One document was written in English by a US agent, who had picked up a copy of a document that had been sent to V. Putin by K. Hussein, Saddam Hussein's son. This is what the translation of the doc indicates. The Iraqis knew in June 2000 that I was coming [to Russia]. I didn't get my orders until August. The letter said that Bastien [a Canadian embassy official later found dead] and Vreeland would be dealt with 'in a manner suitable to us.' The letter specifically stated on page two, 'Our American official guarantees this.'" [21]

Vreeland was held by the Canadians at the request of the United States and he says he told the Canadian authorities on December 6th 2000 that he needed to contact the Canadian military immediately, but he said they "… turned blue, walked away, and I never saw them again". Vreeland said he thought he was dealing with idiots who had no clue about what was about to happen, but he added: "It's been put to me that there were certain officials who wanted the attacks to happen." US officials have denied that Vreeland is Naval Intelligence operative and say he was thrown out of the Navy after a few months in 1986. But in January 2002 his lawyer called the Pentagon switchboard from an open court and asked the operator for the office of Lieutenant Delmart Vreeland. The operator confirmed Vreeland's rank as a Lieutenant O-3, his room number, and gave his direct-dial number. The people who lied about Vreeland are the same people telling you what happened on September 11th. With no one willing to listen to him Vreeland wrote his warning on a piece of paper, sealed it in an envelope, and handed it to jail guards a month before the attacks. They opened the letter on September 14th and told the authorities. Vreeland would not reveal who gave him the document pouch because it would "jeopardise the lives of active agents, and … violate the National Security Act of 1947". Mike Ruppert's questioning of Vreeland included the following exchange.

Q: Your written warning contains the statement, "Let one happen, stop the rest." Who was going to let one happen? Who was going to stop the rest?
A: I can't comment on the advice of counsel.
Q: Does that statement imply that the US or some other intelligence agency had achieved complete penetration of the terrorist cells?
A: That goes without question. Sometimes certain governments design, create networks like al-Qaeda, which was really the government in Afghanistan. Those entities create specific problems at the creating government's direction. *[Problem-reaction-solution.]*
Q: Do you know who had achieved this penetration?
A: I cannot comment on that.
Q: Is it possible that the terrorist cells were being "run" without knowing by whom?
A: Absolutely.[22]

This is the compartmentalisation I keep emphasising in which those lower down the pyramid, even very high up, do not know who is the ultimate "Mr Big" and what the agenda really is. Most al-Qaeda supporters see bin Laden as the top man because they know no better and have been told no different. Vreeland was eventually freed from jail and charges dismissed, but he still faced extradition proceedings by the US government to take him back to the United States and he believed he would not survive very long if that were to happen. If he is an asset of Naval Intelligence, one of the major strands in the Illuminati web in the US, we have to be careful about what he says, but that does not mean it isn't true. Interestingly, contacts with connections into the Illuminati High Council in the United States tell me that the Office of Naval Intelligence was fundamentally involved in the organisation of the September 11th attacks.

More confirmation

Evidence of prior knowledge of the attacks is clear from other information. The day before, the investment company Goldman Sachs circulated a memo warning of a possible terrorist attack and advising employees to stay away from American government buildings. Willie Brown, the Mayor of San Francisco, said he was warned at 10pm the previous night by what he called "My security people at the airport" to be especially cautious about travelling by air on September 11th.[23] Why were the FBI and CIA not aware that something was bubbling? The fact is they were. On August 28th the Federal Aviation Administration had issued a warning to airlines and airports that people connected to terrorist networks were planning to fly on US airlines, it is reported. Author Salman Rushdie, who has been targeted by Arab extremists for his book *The Satanic Verses*, told the London *Times* that he believed the US authorities knew of an imminent terrorist strike when they banned him from taking internal flights in Canada and the US just a week before the attacks. "On September 3 the Federal Aviation Administration made an emergency ruling to stop Rushdie from flying unless airlines complied with strict and costly security measures," the *Times* reported.[24] Rushdie said the airlines would not upgrade their security. "The FAA told the author's publisher that US intelligence had given warning of 'something out there' but failed to give any further details," the *Times* said. "The FAA confirmed that it stepped up security measures concerning Mr Rushdie but refused to give a reason." [25]

On September 18th, the Israeli newspaper *Ha'aretz* reported that five Israelis had been "detained for what the Federal Bureau of Investigation has described as 'puzzling behaviour' following the terror attack on the World Trade Center in New York". These people were not named, but the paper quoted one of their mothers. She said they were arrested around four hours after the attacks when they were filming the scene from the roof of the building where they worked. "They thought that because he has citizenship of a European country as well as of Israel that he was working for the Mossad," she added. Mossad is the Israeli intelligence agency that grew from the intelligence arm of the Rothschild family that was formed back in the 18th/19th centuries. Police were called to the scene and then the FBI because it is claimed they were seen "videotaping the disaster and shouting in what was interpreted as cries of joy and mockery". The UK *Daily Telegraph* claimed that Mossad had "warned their counterparts in the United States the previous month that large-scale terrorist attacks on highly visible targets on the American mainland were imminent." The FBI denies this. The *Washington Post* reported, as did Ha'aretz, that a New York-based instant-messaging firm called Odigo, which has offices in Israel, had confirmed "that two employees received text messages warning of an attack on the World Trade Center two hours before terrorists crashed planes into the New York landmarks".[26] Micha Macover, the Odigo CEO, said two workers received the messages and had told the company's management about the warnings after the attacks. Why hasn't this blatant prior knowledge been investigated and followed up by the media? The *Washington Times* revealed the day before the attacks the existence of an official 68-page report by 60 officers at the US Army's School for Advanced Military Studies, which warned that Mossad was capable of targeting the United States. The report described Mossad as "ruthless and cunning" and "a wildcard".[27]

Casino prophets

Then there was the stock trading immediately before September 11th involving airlines and companies involved in the attacks. This provides spectacular evidence of prior knowledge. Again the "government story is true" mindset has led to media speculation that this trading must have been the work of Osama bin Laden. But who is more likely to have been behind this, a guy in a cave in Afghanistan or those who run both the government and the banking/stock market system? These include the CIA, which has long and fundamental connections to the financial elite. Many of the CIA's leading personnel over the years have come from this very background, starting with its first director, Allen Dulles, the Nazi supporter and business associate. The CIA claims to constantly monitor unusual financial transactions on the markets to track evidence of possible terrorist and criminal activity. What does it call "unusual" when you consider what happened in the days before 9/11? The stock markets are not there to benefit the people. They are casinos. A news report from Wall Street or the London Stock Exchange is little more than a report from Las Vegas on how the blackjack or roulette tables are going. They bet with people's lives and livelihoods. Two ways of doing this are "put" and "call" options. A "put option" is when you bet that the stock in a company will go down in value. If it does you can make big money. A "call option" is when you bet that the stock price will go up. Clearly the stock price in the airlines involved in the hijackings, American Airlines and United Airlines, would fall immediately after the attacks, as would that of companies with a major operation in the World Trade Center. How fascinating, then, that 4,744 put options were placed on United Airlines against only 396 call options at the Chicago Board Options Exchange between September 6th and 7th. Three days later, 4,516 put options were purchased on American Airlines on the exchange and only 748 call options. This represented six times the usual number of put options, and trading in other airlines did not follow this pattern. The same trading can be seen in major companies at the World Trade Center like Morgan Stanley Dean Witter and Merrill Lynch, both of whom occupied 22 floors, and in major insurance companies that would face enormous claims as a result of the attacks. When these highly unusual trades were reported, revealing as they do blatant prior knowledge of the attacks, more than $2.5 million in put option profits on United Airlines went unclaimed. Michael Ruppert, the researcher and former Los Angeles Police Department drug investigator, makes a CIA connection to this evidence of insider trading in the days before September 11th:

> "That evidence also demonstrates that, in the case of at least one of these trades - which has left a $2.5 million prize unclaimed – the firm used to place the 'put options' on United Airlines stock was, until 1998, managed by the man who is now in the number three Executive Director position at the Central Intelligence Agency. Until 1997, A.B. 'Buzzy' Krongard had been Chairman of the investment bank A.B. Brown. A.B. Brown was acquired by Banker's Trust in 1997. Krongard then became, as part of the merger, Vice Chairman of Banker's Trust-A.B. Brown, one of 20 major US banks named by Senator Carl Levin this year as being connected to money laundering. Krongard's last position at Banker's Trust (BT) was to oversee 'private client relations'. In this capacity he had direct hands-on relations with some of the wealthiest people in the world in a kind of specialized banking operation that has been identified by the US Senate and other investigators as being closely connected to the laundering of drug money." [28]

In 1998 Krongard was appointed as counsel to CIA Director George Tenet and was promoted to Executive Director of the CIA by George W. Bush in March 2001. After Krongard left for the CIA, Bankers Trust-A.B.-Brown was taken over in 1999 by Deutsche Bank to form the biggest bank in Europe. Deutsche Bank was also used for the highly unusual pre-9/11 trading and its London branch is frequented, apparently, by the bin Laden family. Thus the question may be asked again. Who is more likely to have been behind these "prior knowledge" stock trades, Osama bin Laden from a cave in Afghanistan or the vast financial network connected to the CIA? The same CIA that failed to respond to these highly unusual stock movements just as US air defences failed to respond to four hijacked airliners. The same CIA and "intelligence community" that, despite a more than $30 billion annual budget (and that's just the official one), claimed like the FBI that it had no idea that the attacks were going to happen until it switched on TV with the rest of the nation. When news of the stock trades broke, the CIA announced there would be an investigation, and media reports said that market regulators in the US, UK, Germany, Switzerland, Italy and Japan were to be involved. Have you ever heard another word about this "investigation", even though the transactions must be traceable? No, me neither. The trail did not lead to bin Laden or the Islamic world, or sure as hell we would have seen it blazed across the front pages a long time ago.

Bush sued by families over 9/11

Eight months after the attacks, a $7 billion lawsuit was filed against President Bush on behalf of families who lost loved ones. It was filed by San Francisco lawyer, Stanley Hilton, a former aide to presidential candidate, Bob Dole. It alleges that Bush and other government officials allowed the attacks to happen for political gain and that Osama bin Laden has been used as a scapegoat. Hilton said he had information that bin Laden died some years ago of kidney failure. He told the media: "I hope … [the lawsuit] … will expose the fact that there are numbers of people in the government, including Bush and his top assistants, who wanted this to happen." The class action suit, which represents the families of 14 victims and involves 400 plaintiffs, names ten defendants, including Bush, Vice President Dick Cheney, Defense Secretary Donald Rumsfeld, National Security Adviser Condoleeza Rice, and Transportation Secretary Norman Mineta. Hilton said he has sources within the FBI, CIA, National Security Agency and Naval intelligence, and these made it clear that the official story was a lie. I called Stanley Hilton and we had a long talk about the lawsuit and his information. He told me that the government had offered each of the families of 9/11 victims $1.8 million if they waived the right to sue the government, security companies and the airlines etc., for what happened, but only 400 had accepted this at the time we spoke in July 2002. Hilton described the offer as a "bribe" and "hush money". He said he was in touch with other lawyers representing 9/11 families and the vast majority of them were extremely sceptical about the official tale. "The families feel basically that there's something mysterious, there's pieces of the puzzle missing."

Hilton told me that he had contacts that had been in several meetings with the "top Pentagon brass" before September 11th, at which the attacks were discussed. "They all knew this was being planned and they all had prior knowledge", he said. "They all facilitated this to go through and, in my opinion, not only facilitated it, but instigated it." He said that US and Israeli intelligence had infiltrated al-Qaeda and other terrorist groups and knew precisely what was going on. He said that Air Force personnel had told him that when Flight 77 entered the No Fly Zone over Washington it gave the top secret code to indicate that it was the President's plane, Air Force One, and this was why there was no response from the capital's ground-to-air defense system. Hilton said that a flight attendant with American Airlines, who knew many of the attendants who died on September 11th, told him that a pilot on the American Airlines Airbus A300, which mysteriously crashed after take-off from New York two months after 9/11, had some knowledge of what had happened during the attacks. She told Hilton that the pilot had been in the control tower at New York's Kennedy Airport while the hijackings were taking place and he knew the official story was not true. She said he was having qualms about keeping quiet about what he had seen and Hilton said the "unofficial rumour" at American Airlines was that the plane was sabotaged so that the pilot would be killed. Hilton said he had learned that many "top Bush officials" flew on American Airlines commercial planes, but a few weeks before the attacks this stopped.

Stanley Hilton said his experience since filing the suit had left him shocked at the behaviour of the mainstream media, who were clearly just "foot soldiers for Bush". People had been urged to press for him to be disbarred, he said, and he had been attacked as "unpatriotic". What better confirmation can there be that he is on to something?

SOURCES

1   **http://truthout.com/docs_02/05.24A.Political.Terror.htm**

2   Report on Morning Edition, National Public Radio, September 11th 2001

3   **http://www.thenewamerican.com/tna/2002/03-11-2002/vo18no05_didweknow_print.htm**

4   **http://arizona.indymedia.org/front.php3?article_id=3401&group=webcast**

5   **http://www.cnsnews.com/ViewNation.asp?Page=\Nation\archive\200205\NAT20020530d.html**

6   *9/11 – The Road To Tyranny* and **http://www.thenewamerican.com/tna/2002/03-11-2002/ vo18no05_didweknow_print.htm**

7   Ibid

8   CNN, October 3rd 2001

9   *CBS News*, September 11th 2001

10 German daily *Frankfurter Algemeine Zeitung* (*FAZ*), September 14th 2001

11 MSNBC interview, September 15th 2001

12 Tapes Depict Proposal to Thwart Bomb Used in Trade Center Blast, by Ralph Blumenthal, *New York Times*, October 28th 1993

13 Ibid.

14 **http://www.newsmedianews.com/wtc.htm**

15 *Atlantic Monthly*, May 1996, quoted in the New American **http://www.thenewamerican.com/tna/1997/vo13no05/vo13no05_assets.htm**

16 **http://www.thenewamerican.com/tna/1997/vo13no05/vo13no05_assets.htm**

17 Ibid

18 Official court transcript, p 16337

19 **http://www.thebostonchannel.com/News/751977/detail.html**

20 You can read the full interview at **http://www.rise4news.net/vreeland_interview.html**

21 Ibid

22 *All Fall Down*, p 14

23 Rushdie's Air Ban, London *Times*, September 27th 2001

24 Ibid

25 *Washington Post*, September 27th 2001

26 *Washington Times*, September 10th 2001

27 Michael C. Ruppert and FTW Publications at **www.copvcia.comhttp://www.copvcia.com**

chapter 12

Searching the maze (with smoke and mirrors)

The elementary principle of all deception is to attract the enemy's attention to what you wish him to see, and to distract his attention from what you do not wish him to see.

General Sir Archibald Wavell,
Memorandum to the British Chiefs of Staff, 1940

The technique so clearly used on September 11th has been played over and over to advance the Illuminati agenda. The suggestion that government leaders and agencies were involved in the horrific events of 9/11 (under the instructions of their masters) to create an enormous problem to which they could offer a fascist solution is not fantastic at all. History is ablaze with such events.

Burning the Reichstag

The German Nazis burned down the Reichstag, the parliament building, using this very technique. Hitler became Chancellor of Germany on January 30th 1933, and on February 27th the parliament building was torched and the attack blamed on Marinus van der Lubbe, a mentally challenged Dutch Communist who was later executed for a crime he did not commit. The day after the fire, Hitler invoked Article 48 of the Weimar Constitution that allowed civil liberties to be suspended during a "national emergency". This Decree of the Reich President for the Protection of the People and State brought an end to freedom of speech and the press, right of assembly and association, right to privacy in postal and electronic communications, protection against unlawful searches and seizures, individual rights to property, and the rights for states to be self-governing. Another decree created the federal "police" agencies, the SS or "special security" and the SA or "storm troops". The rest, as they say, is history and look at what has happened as a result of 9/11. What Hitler introduced to fight "Communist terrorism" was a mirror of what Bush has signed into law since the attacks in America. The sinking of the Lusitania, which brought the US into the First World War, the attack on Pearl Harbor, which brought them into the Second, the list of P-R-S examples goes on and on, and you can read about countless more in *And The Truth Shall Set You Free*.

"Chechnya terrorists"

While I was writing this book the former Kremlin insider Boris Berezovsky publicly accused the Russian State Security Service (FSB) of organising the bombings of apartment blocks in Moscow and Volgodonsk in September 1999 to provide the excuse for war against the separatist republic of Chechnya. President Putin was Prime Minister of Russia at the time. Berezovsky was once one of the most powerful men in Russia and belonged to the inner circle of the former Russian president Boris Yeltsin, which was known as "The Family". But he fell from favour with Putin and the state arbitration court ordered the closure of Berezovsky's TV6, the country's last independent national television station. In an interview broadcast on the Ekho Moskvy radio station, Berezovsky said he was preparing a package of documents to prove that it was the special services that organised the explosions and they had been preparing another in Ryazan. "The authorities are simply afraid to hear the truth about their crimes," he said. The Moscow bombings killed 228 people, including 21 children, and in Volgodonsk 199 died, two of them children. In the autumn of 2000, officials from the FSB (the equivalent of the FBI and formerly headed by Putin) said they had proof that the blasts had been organised and financed by Chechens, but failed to secure convictions. (In the autumn of 2001 officials from the FBI said they had proof that the attacks had been organised and financed by Osama bin Laden, but failed to produce the evidence.) On September 23rd 1999, only a week after the second bomb in Moscow, residents in an apartment block in Ryazan found bags in the basement containing a substance that looked like hexogen, the explosive used in the Moscow blasts. The local FSB said that an "act of terrorism" had been prevented, but the federal FSB later said it was just a training exercise. A training exercise? Remember the excuse for the bomb squad's presence around the Murrah Building in Oklahoma before the bomb went off was that they were on a "training exercise". This after they had first denied the bomb squad was even there. A former FSB colonel, Alexander Litvinenko, now in exile in London, says the federal FSB office was not on a training exercise in Ryazan (and nor was the one in Oklahoma). Litvinenko says in his co-authored book, *The FSB Blows Up Russia*,[1] that the planned blast involved federal FSB and was only prevented by the local FSB. This is all classic problem-reaction-solution to justify a response against Chechnya, which just happens to be in the Caspian Sea region and significant in the control of oil.

Gulf of Tonkin

The "incident" that exploded as the Vietnam War was another example of P-R-S and sometimes you don't even need a problem, you just have to kid the people that you have one. President Lyndon "Brown & Root" Johnson, the man who replaced (without an election) the assassinated John F. Kennedy, announced on August 4th 1964 that North Vietnam had attacked American destroyers in the Gulf of Tonkin. The official story claimed a US destroyer on "routine patrol" was targeted by North Vietnamese torpedo boats in an "unprovoked attack" on August 2nd and that this action was repeated against US ships on August 4th. The media, as usual, reported this as fact simply because Johnson and the Pentagon said it was. The truth is, as many studies and investigative books have revealed, there was no second attack on August 4th and the first was not "unprovoked" against a US ship on "routine patrol". The destroyer Maddox was actively involved in intelligence gathering to support attacks on North Vietnam by the South Vietnamese Navy and the Laos Air Force. Two days later there was no repeat attack, it was pure invention to escalate the war. Captain John J. Herrick, the head of the task force in the Gulf of Tonkin, sent cables to Washington that talked of "freak weather effects" and an "overeager sonarman" who was "hearing [his] ship's own propeller beat". Squadron Commander James Stockdale, a famous prisoner of war and later a vice presidential candidate to Ross Perot, was flying over the scene that night. Years later he said that he had "the best seat in the house to watch that event". He said that there was no attack by the North Vietnamese gunboats: "… Our destroyers were just shooting at phantom targets – there were no PT [North Vietnamese] boats there …There was nothing there but black water and American fire power." A year after President Johnson had used this non-existent attack to escalate the conflict into the Vietnam War, he said: "For all I know, our Navy was shooting at whales out there." Tom Wells, author of *The War Within: America's Battle Over Vietnam*,[2] said that the government was able to deceive the American people because of the media's "almost exclusive reliance on US government officials as sources of information" and their "reluctance to question official pronouncements on national security issues". This happens every time and never more so than after 9/11. In *The Uncensored War: The Media And Vietnam*,[3] Daniel C. Hallin writes that journalists had a great deal of information available that contradicted the official version of events, but it was ignored. He said that it was also "… generally known … that 'covert' operations against North Vietnam, carried out by South Vietnamese forces with US support and direction, had been going on for some time". Journalists and media watchers Jeff Cohen and Norman Solomon encapsulate the responsibility of the media in what followed the Gulf of Tonkin:

> "By reporting official claims as absolute truths, American journalism opened the floodgates for the bloody Vietnam War. A pattern took hold: continuous government lies passed on by pliant mass media … leading to over 50,000 American deaths and millions of Vietnamese casualties." [4]

Journalists, or those who pass for them, love to deny responsibility for their actions. They say "we are just the messenger; don't kill the messenger because you don't like the message". But if the messenger accepts the message without question they cease to be some neutral, "independent" courier for information and allow themselves to become an essential tool in the propaganda war against the people. At this point, which was reached a long time ago, they are not "journalists" at all. They are the public relations staff for the official version of life. After President Johnson went on national television to lie about the Gulf of Tonkin and announce "retaliatory air strikes" that became the insane Vietnam War, the media praised his speech and said the North Vietnamese had only themselves to blame. Because of this support only two votes were cast against the Gulf of Tonkin Resolution that went through Congress three days after a US ship was *not* attacked by the North Vietnamese. For the Gulf of Tonkin read Pearl Harbor, Oklahoma, September 11th, and a whole stream of other examples of problem-reaction-solution. Or, in the case of the Gulf of Tonkin, a "no problem"-reaction-solution.

Operation Northwoods

Then there was Operation Northwoods. I mentioned this earlier, but I want to emphasise its manipulation techniques again at this point because they are such a mirror of what happened on September 11th. Northwoods was the plan by the US Joint Chiefs of Staff (and the intelligence network if the truth be told) to organise terrorist attacks against their own people 40 years ago that were to be blamed on Fidel Castro to justify an invasion of Cuba. Recently discovered official documents[5] reveal that the Joint Chiefs of Staff, the same organisation that failed to react when four commercial airliners were hijacked on 9/11, drew up a plan code-named Operation Northwoods that involved civilians being shot, planes being hijacked, boats being sunk, terrorist acts in US cities and innocent people being blamed for it all. The chairman of the Joint Chiefs who pressed ahead with the plans was General Lyman L. Lemnitzer. I think the second syllable of his last name was a secret code for his state of mind. The Northwoods documents talk of developing a communist Cuban terror campaign in the Miami area and other Florida cities and even in Washington.[6] The plan was to stir up so much hatred for Cuba in the United States that the people would support an invasion and even demand that this was done. They intended to explode plastic bombs, arrest Cuban agents and release previously prepared documents substantiating Cuban involvement. The plan included attacks on the now infamous US base at Guantanamo Bay on Cuba where uncharged, untried "terrorists" are kept in disgraceful, inhuman conditions by the land of freedom and morality. The documents speak of "a series of well co-ordinated incidents … in and around Guantanamo to give genuine appearance of being done by hostile Cuban forces".[7] A Memorandum of July 27th 1962 says that the operation would mean an enormous increase in Cuban and American casualties.[8] The techniques to be used included the following: starting rumours; using clandestine radio; landing friendly Cubans in uniform "over the fence" to stage attack on the Guantanamo base; capturing (friendly) Cuban saboteurs inside the base; starting riots near the base main gate using friendly Cubans; blowing up ammunition inside the base and starting fires; burning aircraft on the air base and blaming Cuba; throwing mortar shells into the base; capturing assault teams approaching from the sea or Guantanamo City; capturing a militia group, which storms the base to sabotage a ship in harbour; sinking a ship near the harbour entrance; blowing up an unmanned vessel in Cuban waters … and blaming it on Cuban aircraft that would naturally come and investigate what had happened; issuing false casualty lists to the US media to whip up public opinion against Cuba; conduct funerals for mock victims.[9]

All of this begs the question: who really did blow up the Khobar Towers in the US military complex in Saudi Arabia? Who did blow up the Murrah Building? Who really did target those planes on September 11th? After all, who had easier access to the Khobar Towers, the Murrah Building, and all that was necessary to hijack those planes? Outsider terrorists or the insider US military and civilian authorities? The Northwoods documents call for the use of Soviet Union MIG-type aircraft flown by US pilots to harass civil aircraft, attack surface shipping and destroy US military drone (remotely controlled) aircraft to give the impression it was all done by Communists. "An F-86 properly painted would convince air passengers that they saw a Cuban MIG ..." one document says.[10] It was further planned to stage the mock shooting-down of a US Air Force plane in international waters by simply getting the pilot, using a made-up name, to report that he was under attack and then stop transmitting. He would then fly back to his base where the plane would be repainted with a new tail number and the pilot would resume his real name. A US submarine would dispense aircraft wreckage in the sea and this would be found to confirm the attack and blame it on Cuba. Northwoods also planned the hijacking of civil air and surface craft. Documents say it was possible to create an incident in which people will believe that a Cuban aircraft has attacked and shot down a chartered civil airliner on a flight from the United States to Jamaica, Guatemala, Venezuela or Panama. The destination would be chosen to cause the flight plan route to cross Cuba, and the plan was to replace the civil airliner with an identical one painted in the correct colours and remotely controlled. The real plane would be landed at an Air Force base and the passengers, boarded under aliases, would be taken off. The remotely controlled replacement would be flown over Cuba, send a distress call and then be destroyed by radio signal. All this was planned 40 years ago. Imagine what the technology is like today in comparison?

Remote control?

As we can see from the Northwoods documents, the remote control of large aircraft is not in the least bit new and can be traced back more than four decades. After September 11th George W. Bush called for a system to be developed that would allow controllers on the ground to assume remote control of a hijacked aircraft and direct it to a safe landing at the nearest airport. The *New York Times* quoted him as saying that the new technology, "probably far in the future", would allow air traffic controllers to land distressed planes by remote control.[11] This was a gross misrepresentation of the truth, but then, as I have pointed out many times in my books and talks, Illuminati operatives speak to each other during public speeches and announcements in code that only they understand. In this instance the "we must develop remote control technology" could easily mean, "we used remote control technology". How can Bush say that such technology is "probably far in the future" when the existence of remotely controlled aircraft is publicly known and has been in existence for at least 40 years? A few weeks after 9/11 they were being flown over Afghanistan under the term "surveillance drones". A US Air Force fact sheet available to anyone on the Internet details the capabilities and background of a remotely controlled aircraft technology called the Global Hawk.[12] It says that the Global Hawk Unmanned Aerial Vehicle (UAV) provides Air Force battlefield commanders with near real-time, high-resolution, intelligence, surveillance and reconnaissance imagery flying at extremely high altitudes to survey large areas with pinpoint accuracy. Once the "mission parameters" are programmed into Global Hawk, says the fact sheet, the aircraft can "autonomously taxi, take off, fly, remain on station capturing imagery, return and land". Operators on the ground can alter flying instructions during flight as necessary. *Airman* magazine summarised the control systems of the Global Hawk:

> "The bird's "pilots" stay on the ground. Its flight control, navigation and vehicle management are independent and based on a mission plan. That means the airplane flies itself – there's no pilot on the ground with a joystick manoeuvring it around. However, it does get instructions from airmen at ground stations. The launch and recovery element provides precision guidance for take-off and landing, using a differential global positioning system. That team works from the plane's operating base." [13]

The Global Hawk is 44 feet (13.4 metres) long, has a wingspan of 116 feet (35.3 metres, equivalent to a Boeing 737), and a range of 12,000 nautical miles. It can fly at up to 65,000 feet (19,812 metres) at speeds approaching about 400mph for as long as 35 hours. Global Hawk was developed through the 1990s and the principal contractor is the Illuminati-controlled Northrop Grumman at its Ryan Aeronautical Center, San Diego, California. Communications systems are provided by L3 Com, Salt Lake City, Utah. In June 1999 Global Hawk began tests

and exercises sponsored by US Joint Forces Command. James Roche, the Bush-appointed US Secretary of the Air Force, held many executive posts with Northrop Grumman, including Corporate Vice President and President, Electronic Sensors and Systems Sector, before leaving to join the Bush gang in 2001. Roche, a member of the Illuminati's Council on Foreign Relations and Centre for Strategic Studies, is responsible for the Air Force's "functioning and efficiency, the formulation of its policies and programs".[14] This includes NORAD.

Figure 20: *The Global Hawk remotely-controlled aircraft*

Colonel Wayne M. Johnson became manager of the Global Hawk Programme at the Reconnaissance Systems Program Office, Aeronautical Systems Center at Wright-Patterson Air Force Base at Dayton, Ohio, which assumed total programme control on October 1st 1998. (This is not far in flying terms from the point where Flight 93 was "hijacked" and turned around.) On April 20th 2000 a Global Hawk deployed to Eglin Air Force Base in Florida was flown across the Atlantic to Europe by remote control to take part in NATO exercises and on April 22nd – 23rd 2001, it was flown non-stop the 7,500 miles across the Pacific from the Edwards Air Force Base in California to the Royal Australian Air Force base at Edinburgh, South Australia. This set (officially) new world records for remote controlled aircraft and the plane was deployed in the grotesquely named Operation Enduring Freedom, the mass murder of civilians in Afghanistan. Another remotely controlled aircraft called the Predator, capable of reaching 25,000 feet, was also deployed to Afghanistan and has been used in the former Yugoslavia. The organisation that has been using remote control in many different aircraft during this more than 40-year period of development is NORAD. An article by Alan Staats, first published in *Quill* magazine in February 1998 and posted on the Internet after 9/11, details the history and development of remote control technology. Staats writes:

> "Controlling the aircraft from the ground is nothing new. The military has been flying obsolete high performance fighter aircraft as target drones since the 1950s. In fact, NORAD (the North American Air Defense Command) had at its disposal a number of US Air Force General Dynamics F-106 Delta Dart fighter aircraft configured to be remotely flown into combat as early as 1959 under the auspices of a program know as SAGE. These aircraft could be started, taxied, taken off, flown into combat, fight, and return to a landing entirely by remote control, with the only human intervention needed being to fuel and re-arm them. To this day, drone aircraft are remotely flown from Air Force and Naval bases all over the country to provide targets for both airborne and ground based weapons platforms." [15]

Staats goes on to say that the technology now exists (writing in 1998) that would allow a ground crew to override and direct the flight path of a hijacked plane and that the military has employed this capability since the 1950s. From the engineering point of view, he says, *modifying* and implementing the technology for use on passenger-carrying aircraft in the United States to fly them and land them by remote control *"is a relatively simple matter."* (My emphasis.) In fact, says Staats, "autoland" systems have been in wide commercial use in different parts of the world since the 1980s. Auto landings are routinely performed thousands of times a day throughout the world and Staats continues:

> "It is technically possible to create a system to perform remotely commanded return flights of a hijacked airliner. Onboard digital command, control and display equipment can easily share data with, and accept commands from, ground control stations. Little input beyond the initial command to enter safe return flight and the ultimate destination are needed."

Commercial aircraft are largely flown by computers today anyway and the pilot can have very little to do with flying the plane once it's off the ground. In the Boeing 747-400, for example, the computers are capable not only of landing the aircraft, but also applying the brakes and stopping it, too. A flight plan agreed with the Federal Aviation Administration, or its equivalent around the world, is loaded into the aircraft computer system or Flight Management System (FMS). This can be done through direct programming or a disc. The flight programme includes the planned height and speed of the plane throughout the flight as it makes its way between points in the sky known as waypoints. When the plane has taken off it aims for the first waypoint and then the computer will execute changes to aim for the next point and so on to its destination. Therefore, as Staats points out:

> "Because all the components of controlling the aircraft communicate with each other digitally through a central unit, the FMS, activating such a "safe return" system would be a matter of uploading commands to the FMS to fly the aircraft to the nearest airport. Controlling the aircraft's speed, altitude and course, the FMS would guide it back to land."

In other words, to remotely control any commercial airliner all you need to do is get control of the Flight Management System computers and override the ability of pilots to have an input. Do that and you can fly a plane wherever you like with the pilots in the cockpit unable to do anything about it. You can also turn the transponder off and control the entire system, including blocking the pilot's ability to send the normal hijacking alarm code that, remarkably, none of the pilots on September 11th managed to do. We could, of course, find out if this was the case for sure by listening to the genuine cockpit voice recorders in the black boxes on the four aircraft, but we are not allowed to and, anyway, falsifying the tape or producing an alternative to fit the official line would be child's play. Staats says the data links that could remotely control digital airborne flight control systems in commercial aircraft are already widely used. They are called ACARS (Aircraft Communications Addressing and Reporting System) and these communicate a long list of data including position, fuel consumption, weather and flight plan information to ground stations. ACARS also has the ability to send data to the aircraft from the ground. This link, Staats points out, would allow "both uploading digital control inputs to control the aircraft as well as the potential to download and remotely monitor the digital aircraft displays". Remember that in the secret research and development projects used by the military and Illuminati levels of government, the technology at their disposal is a long, long way ahead of anything we are allowed to see in public use. Could those planes have been hijacked on September 11th by remote control and flown into the World Trade Center and the Pentagon while the pilots on board just looked on in horror? Technically, yes they could, quite easily. Stanley Hilton, the lawyer who has filed a lawsuit against Bush and Co over 9/11, told me he had spoken with a mechanic with United Airlines who personally worked on this remote control system. If you can fly a plane from America to Australia and back without a pilot you will have no trouble directing one into the

World Trade Center. An article by investigator Joe Vialls, a former member of the Society of Licensed Aeronautical Engineers and Technologists in London, claims, like many researchers, that the aircraft on September 11th were indeed taken over by remote control technology. Vialls writes:

> "In the mid-seventies ... two American multinationals collaborated with the Defense Advanced Projects Agency (DARPA) on a project designed to facilitate the remote recovery of hijacked American aircraft. [This] ... allowed specialist ground controllers to ... take absolute control of [a hijacked aircraft's] computerized flight control system by remote means. From that point onwards, regardless of the wishes of the hijackers or flight deck crew, the hijacked aircraft could be recovered and landed automatically at an airport of choice, with no more difficulty than flying a radio-controlled model plane ... [This was] the system used to facilitate direct ground control of the four aircraft used in the high-profile attacks on New York and Washington on 11th September 2001." [16]

Vialls claims, without naming sources, that this technology allows specialist ground controllers to hear cockpit conversations on an aircraft and take over its computerised flight control system by remote means. Vialls refers to the technology as "Home Run" and suggests that these top-secret computer codes were broken on September 11th to allow control of the planes from the ground. He writes:

> "In order to make Home Run truly effective, it had to be completely integrated with all onboard systems, and this could only be accomplished with a new aircraft design, several of which were on the drawing boards at that time. Under cover of extreme secrecy, the multinationals and DARPA went ahead on this basis and built "back doors" into the new computer designs. There were two very obvious hard requirements at this stage, the first a primary control channel for use in taking over the flight control system and flying the aircraft back to an airfield of choice, and secondly a covert audio channel for monitoring flight deck conversations. Once the primary channel was activated, all aircraft functions came under direct ground control, permanently removing the hijackers and pilots from the control loop." [17]

Vialls says that the system began with the best of intentions – to save lives – but "finally fell prey to security leaks, and eventually to compromised computer codes". My own view is that it was sold under the guise of saving lives, but with a very different agenda going on higher up. Vialls says that this technology "piggy backs" on the plane's transponder and this is why, he suggests, the pilots were unable to send the hijack code from any of the many activation points on the aircraft. He says the "takeover" technology locks into the frequency of the transponder's communication channel overriding its use by the pilot. Thus no hijack code is sent because, before the pilot realises there is a problem, there is no transponder channel through which to communicate it. It should be mentioned, however, that the official story has some transponders turned off some time after the planes began to act strangely. Vialls says further that the cockpit listening capability of the "Home Run" technology intercepts the microphones in the cockpit, which normally feed the pilots' conversations to the Cockpit Voice Recorder in a "black box". The voice recorders would therefore be blank, he says, because these microphones would have been de-activated once the remote control took over. He claims that Lufthansa, the German national airline, took action to remove the "Home Run" technology:

> "As long ago as the early nineties, a major European flag carrier [Lufthansa] acquired the information and was seriously alarmed that one of its own aircraft might be "rescued" by the Americans without its authority. Accordingly, this flag carrier completely stripped the American flight control computers out of its entire fleet, and replaced them with a home grown version. These aircraft are now effectively impregnable to penetration by Home Run, but that is more than can be said for the American aircraft fleet." [18]

Andreas Von Bulow, the former Germany Minister for Defence and Minister of Science and Technology, said in his outspoken interview with *Tagesspiegel*: "There is also the theory of one British flight engineer: according to this, the steering of the planes was perhaps taken out of the pilots' hands, from outside. The Americans had developed a method in the 1970s, whereby they could rescue hijacked planes by intervening into the computer piloting. This theory says this technique was abused in this case ..." I called Von Bulow to ask if he could confirm what Vialls claims about Lufthansa, but he said he could not say either way. Brian Desborough, an American conspiracy researcher since the 1960s and a former scientist with the Boeing Corporation, told me:

> "Unlike earlier airliners such as the Boeing 747, which are equipped with conventional hydraulically-operated flight controls, the Boeing 757 and 767 aircraft that were involved in the 9/11 incidents, and the Airbus 300 which crashed at Queens [New York], have fly-by-wire flight control systems as a weight-saving measure. These aircraft types are equipped with a special black box that was developed by the US Department of Defense Research Agency, DARPA. If terrorists attempt to hijack a fly-by-wire aircraft and deviate off course, the black box prevents whoever is piloting the aircraft from sending flight commands to the flight control surfaces and engines. Instead, the aircraft is remotely flown from a land-based covert Federal facility.

> "In all probability, a Global Hawk remote surveillance aircraft was circling at 60,000 feet over New York on 9/11 in order to provide the ground command center a real time image of the aircraft. At 60,000 feet, the surveillance aircraft would be invisible to people on the ground. I'm aware of a very covert research company in California engaged in the development of advanced engines for tanks. A remote surveillance plane circles overhead every day as a security measure, yet is invisible from the ground." [19]

So it was possible to take control of those planes from the ground on September 11th and fly them wherever the controllers wanted them to go. Does this not make more sense than incompetent Dumb and Dumber pilots who had struggled to fly a Cessna at US flying schools? Also, looking at this in another way, if these planes did have "anti-hijack" remote control technology why were they allowed to crash? Why were they not landed safely?

"The enemy within the gates"

Kent Hill, an American Airlines captain on European routes and a life-long friend of "Chic" Burlingame, the pilot of AA Flight 77, is certainly questioning the official story. The two were graduates of the Naval Academy, flew in Vietnam and had flown together with American Airlines for 28 years. Hill could not understand why there was no hijack code sent from any of the planes. He says that they were all trained "on the old type of hijack" where the hijacker is treated cordially, the pilot punches a four-digit code into the transponder to alert ground control that the plane has been hijacked, and then takes hijackers where they wish to go and puts the plane on the ground. "However, this is a totally new situation," he says, "not one of the planes alerted ground control that they were being hijacked. How come?" [20] Hill says he's sure that none of the pilots had control of the aircraft when they crashed because no pilot would do that. "Even if I had a gun at my head, I'd never fly a plane into a building. I'd try to put it in anywhere – a field or a river – and I'd be searing the hell out of them by flying upside down first." [21] How does all this square with the claims that Barbara Olson rang her husband, Bush's Solicitor General Ted Olson, to say that the pilot of Flight 77 was at the back of the plane with her, and to ask what she should she tell him to do?

The question is who or what was in control of the planes during the attacks, "hijacker pilots" or remote control from the ground. Retired Colonel Donn de Grand Pré, a friend of Hill, says he gathered together a group of experienced civilian and military pilots, including combat fighter pilots and commercial airline captains, to discuss what could have happened during what he described as a "so-called terrorist attack [that] was in fact a superbly executed military operation against the United States, requiring the utmost professional military skill in command, communications and control". [22] The group concluded, he said, that "the enemy is within the gates, that he has infiltrated into the highest policy-making positions at the Federal level, and has absolute control, not only of the purse strings, but of the troop build-up and deployment of our military forces, including active, reserve and National Guard units". The colonel reported that the group of highly experienced pilots was not impressed by claims that the four aircraft were flown by hijackers who had trained in planes like the Cessna. He said one officer remarked: "I seriously question whether these novices could have located a target dead-on 200 miles removed from take-off point – much less controlled the flight and mastered the intricacies of 11FR [instrument flight rules] – and all accomplished in 45 minutes." The pilots said that the way the planes were flown ruled out the level of experience and competence reported for the "hijackers". An Air Force officer, who flew more than 100 sorties over North Vietnam, is quoted by the colonel as saying: "Those birds either had a crack fighter pilot in the left seat, or they were being manoeuvred by remote control." Former Special Forces sergeant turned conspiracy investigator, Stan Goff, put it like this in the case of Flight 77:

> "Now, the real kicker. A pilot they want us to believe was trained at a Florida puddle-jumper school for Piper Cubs and Cessnas, conducts a well-controlled downward spiral, descending the last 7,000 feet in two-and-a-half minutes, brings the plane in so low and flat that it clips the electrical wires across the street from the Pentagon, and flies it with pinpoint accuracy into the side of this building at 460 nauts. When the theory about learning to fly this well at the puddle-jumper school began to lose ground, it was added that they received further training on a flight simulator. This is like saying you prepared your teenager for her first drive on I-40 at rush hour by buying her a video driving game. It's horse shit! There is a story being constructed about these events." [23]

I had a long conversation with a pilot who has flown commercial airliners for Lufthansa for 28 years and trained as a military pilot before that. He dismissed immediately the idea that the "hijacker-pilots" could have taken over the controls of the four planes from their computer systems and flown them manually. His view would have been that they would have crashed the planes for sure long before they reached their targets, such is the complex nature of the modern airliner. It is this very complexity, which requires that computers make the calculations, he told me. He did say, however, that hijackers would not need to know how to fly the plane to hit a target. They would only need to know how to reprogramme the Flight Management System to make the computer do it for them. I take the point, but this begs more questions. If that is the way it was done why would the "hijackers" have trained at flying schools on Cessnas and similar small planes when the Lufthansa pilot told me this would be utterly useless and irrelevant to flying a 757 or 767 and equally so for knowing how to reprogram a Flight Management System? This doesn't make sense at all. Although he said the reprogramming could be done pretty quickly by someone who knows what he's doing, Flight 175, the second one to strike the World Trade Center, dramatically changed course only 90 seconds to two minutes after the last communication with air traffic control if we believe those communications were accurate. In that time the "hijackers" would have had to seize control of the cockpit, disable the pilots and reprogramme the computer system. Again this doesn't make sense. But if the plane's controls were suddenly taken over externally and all communications from the cockpit were blocked by the remote control technology these circumstances could be explained. One second you are flying a plane and talking with air traffic controllers, the next the aircraft is flying off course and when you tell air traffic control they do not respond because they can't hear you and you can't hear them.

Were "pilot" hijackers on board?

There is something very strange about the whole "hijackers took over the aircraft" story. It might sound feasible to most people at first hearing and to those who research or question no further. But when you do dig deeper there are many questions. As I have already outlined, around a third of the "hijackers" named have turned out to be still alive. American and United Airlines refuse to confirm that the men named by the FBI even passed through their normal check-in procedures. All it needed was a simple yes or no, but they said I would have to ask the FBI who then said they could not answer any questions because of an "ongoing investigation" and that it may be years before I could find any answers through the Freedom of Information Act, which does not reveal information claimed to be important to "national security" anyway. There were no security video cameras in the departure lounges at Boston Logan Airport so we can't see the "hijackers" boarding Flights 11 and 175. Where there is video surveillance footage at Newark, New Jersey, Washington Dulles and in other areas of the Boston Airport complex, we are not allowed to see it. This is exactly what happened with the video footage of McVeigh and "friends" in Oklahoma. One thing is certain: if the video footage in and around those airports showed the hijackers arriving in their cars, checking in, going through security and boarding the planes it would have been blasted on every television station in the world. They didn't have any problem releasing the footage of "Atta" and "Alomari" rushing to catch the flight from Portland, Maine, that morning or the shots of "Alomari" getting cash the previous night from an ATM machine. Why are they so shy about the real-deal footage that would confirm their story? The fact is that all this time later we still have no proof or independent confirmation that the men named by the FBI were even on the planes. I have given the FBI the chance to provide that, but the bureau refused. Not a single Arab name is on the passenger lists issued by the airlines and while they may say they were not given permission to do so by their families this is yet another of the amazing coincidences that pepper, indeed deluge, the official story. What happened that day, if you believe the official version, is that phone calls were made by passengers describing their plight as it was happening. The UK *Daily Telegraph* reported that "passengers on the hijacked aircraft were ordered to phone their families and tell them they were going to die" and "passengers were ordered at knifepoint to say that their flight had been hijacked and they were going to crash into the White House".[24] Why on earth would hijackers force passengers to call their relatives and give such specific information when the climax of the plan was yet to be completed?

Is it a bird? Is it a plane? Or is it a superscam?

The story of Flight 77 is a catalogue of contradictions. There are two published versions of its route, as I outlined earlier. Both are sourced to the flight tracking company, Flight Explorer, which receives its data from the FAA. The *USA Today* version suggests it took a massive detour off-course in a north to west to south loop over West Virginia before returning to course for a short time, while the other does not include the loop. Both agree that the transponder signal disappeared from the screens of air traffic control near the Ohio border. Even so, NORAD was not alerted according to the official story agreed by NORAD and the Federal Aviation Administration. The plane then completed a 180-degree turn and headed back towards Washington, but still there was no report to NORAD even with two hijacked planes already buried in the World Trade Center. Only at 9.24 was NORAD alerted by the FAA, both organisations told me. This was some 40 minutes after Flight 11 crashed into the World Trade Center; it was at least 35 minutes after air traffic controllers knew that Flight 77 had been hijacked; 24 minutes after the transponder signal was lost; 21 minutes after Flight 175 hit the World Trade Center; and 18 minutes after air traffic control facilities throughout the country knew that Flight 77 had likely been hijacked. Then NORAD says it sent jets from Langley, 130 miles away, instead of alerting Andrews ten miles down the road. The anomalies and contradictions abound with Flight 77 wherever you look.

The Olson story

A *Miami Herald* report of September 14th 2001 says that CNN contributor, Barbara Olson, first rang her husband, the US Solicitor General Ted Olson, at about 9.25 to say the plane had been hijacked. Why wait so long to call when the plane is known to have been hijacked before 9 o'clock? Other stories say she called soon after the hijack in yet another example of the maze of contradictions that surround 9/11 and are designed to muddy the waters. One report says that Olson's office told the media that Barbara "... got on the wrong plane by mistake." [25] If that is correct, it is a very strange thing to say. She had apparently intended to fly the night before, but changed her mind so she could be with her husband on the morning of his birthday, September 11th. This, however, would not explain the statement that "she got on the wrong plane by mistake". Barbara Olson is claimed to have asked her husband what she should tell the pilot, who was, she said, at the back of the plane with her. Two things come to mind. If that is true, it means the pilots allowed themselves to be overpowered and thrown out of the cockpit simply by being threatened with knives and box cutters, and quietly vacated the controls for the hijackers. I don't believe it. Captain Charles F. "Chic" Burlingame III, the pilot of Flight 77, was a graduate of the "Top Gun" fighter pilot school and a Vietnam veteran. Is he going to give up the cockpit that easily? Of course not. Whatever the precise details turn out to be, I have to say that I don't believe the official Olson story as currently presented. There is still a great deal more to know that we are not being told.

No plane?

The way the plane was flown into the Pentagon was fantastic given how it is said to have turned so tightly at such a fast speed and come in so low. Indeed, there have been suggestions that it was not the 757 at all, but a smaller plane or winged missile and, of course, these have been dismissed as crazy and bizarre by the media and the authorities. It has been widely noted that there is remarkably little "aircraft" wreckage

Figure 21: *Most people remember the pictures of the Pentagon after the wall collapsed, but this only happened half an hour after "impact". Before that there was a much smaller impact hole*

at the Pentagon given that it was supposed to have been hit by a Boeing 757. It struck me how many major pieces of wreckage were still visible after a Russian airliner and a DHL cargo plane collided at around 36,000 feet and crashed to the ground in Germany in July 2002. Advocates of the "no plane theory" say that the hole in the Pentagon made by the impact is nothing like big enough for a 757 to have gone through without the wings smashing into the sides of the hole and against the recently reinforced and still standing walls of the Pentagon. A larger section of wall only collapsed some half an hour after the initial explosion and the actual impact hole was far smaller than the one we saw after that wall came down (*Figure 21*). Others have rejected these suggestions with the claim that when the plane struck the building the wings would have collapsed back against the fuselage and slipped through the hole made by the impact from the front of the aircraft. But the no plane advocates point to pictures of a less than 10 foot wide hole made when the object, whatever it was, exited on the other side of three rings of buildings within the Pentagon (*Figure 22*). The official story says that this hole was made by the nose of the 757 or an engine. Those questioning this version say the nose of an aircraft is fragile and between the point of impact and the little hole where the object came out are three rings of buildings in an area of the Pentagon that had just undergone serious reinforcement to protect against terrorist attack. Aerial photographs confirm this, as indeed does Defense Secretary Rumsfeld who said the plane "penetrated three of the five concentric rings of the building".[26] That means the plane had to smash through six outer walls. Could an aircraft not designed structurally to stay intact on impact, the gathering sceptics ask, have been able to score through three reinforced rings of buildings and still be so intact that it could have caused the hole on the other side? The official version is a blaze of apparent contradictions. It says that when the plane struck the building it "pulverised"; the disappearance of the engines and other solid components can be explained by the fact that they "melted"; the absence of 100 tons of melted metal is that the inferno was so hot at more than 2,500 degrees centigrade that everything "evaporated"; the little exit hole, around ten feet across, was caused by the nose or engine of the aircraft, which had penetrated three reinforced buildings despite all of the former.[27] I find it rather difficult to accept that all of those statements can be true! The official tale was summed up by the French website that has highlighted what it sees as the contradictions of the Pentagon crash:

Figure 22: *This is the exit point for whatever struck the Pentagon and the hole is estimated at less than ten feet across. Something ploughed through three rings of buildings and six external walls to cause this damage. What was it?*

"The aircraft thus disintegrated on contact with the Pentagon, melted inside the building, evaporated at 2500°C, and still penetrated two other buildings via a hole 2½ yards in diameter."[28]

Dick Bridges, the deputy manager for Arlington County, was quoted by Associated Press as saying that both the black boxes for Flight 77 were found "… right where the plane came into the building".[29] But if that's the case where was the rest of the wreckage if much of the plane only made it that far and how could it also have scored through those three rings of buildings? The cockpit voice recorder was so badly damaged, it is claimed, that it didn't yield any information – despite the astonishing heat and pressures it was built to withstand. Once again, how convenient. Pentagon spokesman Army Lt. Colonel George Rhynedance said in the Associated Press report that the two black boxes were recovered at 4am, were in the possession of the FBI, and were being examined with help from the National

Transportation Safety Board (what a combination). Dick Bridges said the voice recorder was damaged on the outside and the flight data recorder was charred, but he said the FBI was still confident the data could be recovered from both. So where the hell is the information from the black boxes, then? As I mentioned, some researchers have suggested there was no 757, only a bomb, a small plane, or a missile. Winged missiles are used by the US military and guided to their target by computer (*Figure 23*). Here is an Internet profile of the Cruise missile used by the US military:

Figure 23: *Some suggest that a winged cruise missile (above) was the real cause of the damage at the Pentagon or an unmanned remotely-controlled "drone" like the Global Hawk. Others say it was definitely the Boeing 757*

"Cruise missiles are jet-propelled pilotless aircraft designed to strike distant targets with great accuracy. Travelling at hundreds of miles an hour, cruise missiles use the global positioning system, inertial guidance, optical scenery correlation, and terrain comparing radar to find their targets. Their accuracy makes them especially useful in attacking military targets in urban areas with limited damage to nearby civilian facilities.

"Once airborne, its turbojet engine starts, its wings spread, and it noses over to hug the surface at about 500 miles (800 km) per hour toward its target. Over water, the missile relies on inertial guidance, perhaps also the global positioning system, for navigation. Upon reaching land, the Tomahawk updates its position and corrects its course using TERCOM (terrain contour matching) or DSMAC (digital scene-matching area correlator) – the first system compares radar signals, the second optical images, with a computer-stored map – before closing on the target at an altitude of 100 feet (30 m) or less." [30]

Remember also that there is fantastic technology developed in the secret projects that we never see. One witness, Steve Patterson, said he was watching the World Trade Center coverage on television when he saw a "silver commuter jet" fly past the window of his 14th-floor apartment in Pentagon City. He said the plane was about 150 yards away coming in from the west and about 20 feet off the ground. Patterson said it sounded like the high-pitched squeal of a fighter jet, and came over Arlington cemetery so low that he thought it was going to land on the road. Patterson said it was moving so fast that he couldn't read anything on the side of the "plane", which appeared only big enough to hold 8 to 12 people. [31] Another witness account by Lon Rains, the editor of *Space News*, said: "At that moment I heard a very loud, quick whooshing sound that began behind me and stopped suddenly in front of me and to my left. In fractions of a second I heard the impact and an explosion. The next thing I saw was the fireball. I was convinced it was a missile. It came in so fast it sounded nothing like an airplane ..." [32]

The Northwoods Documents of 40 years ago tell of plans to trick people into believing that were seeing what they were not. One document says "An F-86 properly painted would convince air passengers that they saw a Cuban MIG ..." The account of Danielle O'Brien, an air traffic controller at Washington Dulles Airport, described what appeared to be anything but a 757 commercial airliner on her radar screen as it sped towards Washington:

"I noticed the aircraft. It was an unidentified plane to the southwest of Dulles, moving at a very high rate of speed ... I had literally a blip and nothing more."

She asked her colleague Tom Howell if he had seen it.

"I said, 'Oh my God, it looks like he's headed to the White House.' I was yelling ... 'We've got a target headed right for the White House!' At a speed of about 500 miles an hour, the plane was headed straight for what is known as P-56, protected air space 56, which covers the White House and the Capitol.

"The speed, the maneuverability, the way that he turned, we all thought in the radar room, all of us experienced air traffic controllers, that that was a military plane. You don't fly a 757 in that manner. It's unsafe.

"The plane was between 12 and 14 miles away and it was just a countdown. Ten miles west. Nine miles west ... Our supervisor picked up our line to the White House and started relaying to them the information, [that] we have an unidentified very fast-moving aircraft inbound toward your vicinity, 8 miles west.

"And it went 'six, five, four, and I had it in my mouth to say, three, and all of a sudden the plane turned away. In the room, it was almost a sense of relief. This must be a fighter. This must be one of our guys sent in, scrambled to patrol our capital, and to protect our president, and we sat back in our chairs and breathed for just a second."

Then came the fantastic 360-degree turn at high speed.

"We lost radar contact with that aircraft. And we waited. And we waited. And your heart is just beating out of your chest waiting to hear what's happened. And then the Washington National [Airport] controllers came over our speakers in our room and said, 'Dulles, hold all of our inbound traffic. The Pentagon's been hit.'" [33]

Firefighters say they saw what they believed to be the nose of an aircraft, or as Captain Defina put it: "The only way you could tell that an aircraft was inside was that we saw pieces of the nose gear." [34] Where was the engine that was supposed to have caused the exit hole? He also said, referring to the fuel: "We have what we believe is a puddle right there that the – what we believe is to be the nose of the aircraft." [35] It is also true that some witnesses – the remarkably few that have been reported – have said that they saw an American Airlines commercial aircraft, but there is some interesting analysis of this "evidence" on the San Francisco Bay Area Independent Media Center website that should be read before taking all these accounts on face value.[36]

Now I am not saying that Flight 77 did or did not hit the Pentagon, I am just exploring the arguments of those for and against. I have spoken with other contacts that have friends in the Pentagon and they say it was definitely a commercial airliner and one contact claims he has seen a picture from a surveillance camera that clearly shows the 757. Personally, I would have great reservations about any information that comes out of the Pentagon and if such a photograph exists, and I am not saying it doesn't, it certainly hasn't been shown to the public. I asked former FAA air crash investigator Rodney Stich for his opinion of these "no plane" stories and he was distinctly unimpressed and said they had no validity. He said he has seen many crashes into buildings in which no wreckage could be seen on the outside. Navy Captain Glenn N. Wagner, director of the Armed Forces DNA Identification Laboratory in Rockville, Maryland, said a team of forensic pathologists, odontologists, a forensic anthropologist, DNA experts, investigators and support personnel worked for more than two weeks to identify victims of the attack on the Pentagon had claimed to have identified 184 of the 189 who died in the plane and in the building.[37] You either believe this or you don't, I guess. Surveillance camera stills from the Pentagon have been published, but they were far from conclusive for either argument. Many researchers claimed them to be faked. If, however, clear and conclusive surveillance camera pictures of the plane do exist, as a contact told me, why don't the authorities show them to us and bring an end to the speculation? Let us see them and put an end to all this. The plane/no plane debate is not something that needs to be proved either way to provide the evidence of an insider operation. There is already enough for that. If conclusive pictures do not exist to show the plane we might, legitimately, ask why. In a city awash with surveillance cameras, television crews and tourists there is a remarkable lack of pictures of the "plane" flying across Washington and into the Pentagon. In fact there aren't any that the public has been shown, apart from Pentagon surveillance stills that are so unclear that the "plane" has to be pointed out, and the FBI reportedly confiscated surveillance camera footage immediately after the crash, just as it did after Oklahoma. Given what has been done and planned in the past we would do well not to dismiss anything out of hand before looking at everything very carefully. Could the "757" have been a smaller remotely-controlled "drone" painted in similar colours to the American Airlines jet? Remember how the Operation Northwoods documents include a plan to land a commercial airliner and its passengers at an Air Force base and replace it with a remotely controlled drone aircraft that would have been flown over Cuba and exploded by radio signal:

"An aircraft at Elgin AFB would be painted and numbered as an exact duplicate for a civil registered aircraft belonging to a CIA proprietary organization in the Miami area. At a designated time the duplicate would be substituted for the actual civil aircraft and would be loaded with the selected passengers, all boarded under carefully prepared aliases. The actual registered aircraft would be converted into a drone. Take off times of the drone aircraft and the actual aircraft will be scheduled to allow a rendezvous south of Florida.

"From the rendezvous point the passenger-carrying aircraft will descend to minimum altitude and go directly into an auxiliary field at Elgin AFB where arrangements will have been made to evacuate the passengers and return the aircraft to its original status. The drone aircraft meanwhile will continue to fly the filed flight plan. When over Cuba the drone will be transmitting on the international distress frequency a "May Day" message stating he is under attack by Cuban MiG aircraft. The transmission will be interrupted by destruction of the aircraft, which will be triggered by radio signal. This will allow ICAO [International Civil Aviation Organization] radio stations in the Western Hemisphere to tell the US what has happened to the aircraft instead of the US trying to "sell" the incident."

Many of the world's military leaders are very disturbed people who are emotionally deformed. They would have no problem doing whatever is necessary to bring about the desired end. As General Curtis E. LeMay, a US Air Force Chief of Staff, once said: "There are no innocent civilians … so it doesn't bother me so much to be killing innocent bystanders." [38] If the Pentagon was not hit by Flight 77 then, as the sceptics of the "no-plane" theory have rightly asked, where the hell did it go and what happened to the crew and passengers? One possible answer to the first question is that once the transponder is turned off the controllers can see a blip on the radar screen, but they lose the altitude and identification information from the plane. The Northwoods documents say the take-off times of the remotely controlled drone aircraft and the actual commercial aircraft would be scheduled to allow a rendezvous south of Florida. The rendezvous could have involved both planes flying close enough to each other for both to appear as one "blip" on the radar screen and at that point the drone takes over the flight path of the real passenger plane, which pulls away and lands at an air base. During the period when Flight 77's transponder went off and controllers say they "lost" radar contact for ten minutes, this "switch" could have happened. I am not saying it did, only that it is possible. The pilots on board Flight 77 might have been told by military personnel to land the plane at the nearest Air Force base because of threats from terrorists. Who knows? What would have happened to them in the circumstances would be pretty obvious. But, if you follow the official story, there would not even have been the need to "rendezvous" another aircraft on the radar screen with Flight 77 because it is said that air traffic control lost complete contact with it for that ten minutes after it turned around. Look also at the published maps of the routes taken by the four planes, based on information originating with the FAA. In the case of Flights 11, 175, and 93, they record the course they took even after the transponders were said to be turned off and they were tracked by conventional radar. But with Flight 77 they show only an estimated course because they could not track it. Why? Why only with Flight 77 – the very plane that is the subject of so much speculation over whether it did or did not strike the Pentagon? Why, as some reports suggest, did it take Flight 77 some 15 minutes longer to return to Washington than it took on the outward journey? There is a great deal more to know about Flight 77 that we are not yet aware of and I am certainly open all possibilities. The same goes for each of the planes, in fact, and it is going to take an insider to speak out for the details to be known. One thing to remember is that deception often works best when it is particularly outrageous because most people's minds could simply not comprehend that anyone would do such a thing, and they therefore dismiss the idea as crazy.

What happened to flight 93?

The Pentagon crash has received far less coverage than those involving the World Trade Center and this is even more the case with Flight 93, which crashed about 80 miles east of Pittsburgh in Pennsylvania. By comparison it is hardly mentioned. Flight 93 pulled back from the gate at Newark International Airport at 8.01am bound for San Francisco, but did not take off until 8.42. United Airlines have confirmed this take-off time to me, but could not explain the delay. If the delay was not part of the plan this would have knocked the timings out by up to around 40 minutes. The plane headed west over Pennsylvania and into northern Ohio – home of the military's remote-control aircraft headquarters at Wright-Patterson Air Force Base. The crew apparently received a message from United Airlines warning all pilots of a potential "cockpit intrusion". The pilots confirmed receipt of the message and, because of its late departure, this was the only one of the four planes that had prior warning of possible trouble. It is claimed that Flight 93 was hijacked around 9am. This was some 20 minutes into the flight and after the first plane had crashed into the World Trade Center. *ABC News* reported at the time that shortly before the plane changed direction someone in the cockpit asked the FAA for a new flight plan with a final destination of Washington. I asked the Federal Aviation Administration who made this request, but a media spokesman said he couldn't answer that question. Why would hijackers announce their destination when Flight 77 made no such request? We are told it was 9.16 when the Federal Aviation Administration told NORAD that Flight 93 may have been hijacked, but that it was not until 9.40am that the transponder signal was lost. Both the FAA and NORAD told me they had open lines to discuss what to do about Flights 77 and 93. The official story says that hijackers forced their way into the cockpit wearing red bandanas around their heads, and one of them warned he had a bomb attached to his waist. The hijackers said they were taking the plane to another airport, we are told. Air traffic controllers apparently claim that they heard two short radio transmissions around the time the hijackers "stormed the cockpit" and in one they heard a pilot say: "Get out of here." An unnamed government official quoted in the media said there were at least four radio transmissions in which the phrases "bomb on board", "our demands" and "keep quiet" were heard.[39] *ABC News* claimed to have secured a tape of these transmissions in which a hijacker says: "We'd like you all to remain seated. There is a bomb on board. And we are going to turn back to the airport. And they had our demands, so please remain quiet."[40]

The official version is that passengers attacked the hijackers and the plane smashed into a field at Shanksville, Pennsylvania, at an estimated 575 miles an hour. The time of impact was anything between around 10am and 10.37, again depending on the report you read. NORAD estimated the impact at 10.03 in an e-mail to me. This time window is two hours or more after Flight 11 left Boston and half an hour or more after Flight 77 is said to have struck the Pentagon. What is hard to comprehend is that some seriously big guys could be herded to the back of the plane and guarded by one hijacker, as claimed in phone calls. I understand that he claimed to have a bomb, but that begs the question of why the same claim was not made by hijackers on the other flights to subdue passengers if that was believed necessary. Passenger Mark Bingham was a rugby player who stood six foot four; Jeremy Glick was a rugby player and judo champion; Todd Beamer was over six foot and 200 pounds, and another, Lou Nacke, was a 200-pound weightlifter with a "Superman" tattoo on his shoulder. The hijacker would have had no chance if they had challenged him, and neither would the others probably. The last transmission heard from the cockpit is said to be someone shouting, "Get out of here. Get out of here", followed by grunting, screaming and scuffling, and finally silence. One researcher says he spoke with Deena Burnett, wife of passenger, Tom Burnett Jr, who said that her husband called her on a cell phone to tell her of the hijack. She said he revealed that the hijackers had said in English that they were going to fly the plane into the ground.[41] The media was twisting the story, she is claimed to have said, to make it look like they were trying to save people on the ground when they were trying to save themselves. My question, however, is why hijackers would tell the passengers that they were going to crash the plane when this would clearly trigger a response on the basis of "What do we have to lose"? Why would these "hijackers" want to fly the plane into a field when the three others targeted the very symbols of American power and self-confidence? How does this fit with the official story that the passengers were told by the hijackers that they had a bomb on board and were flying the plane back to the airport? It makes no sense at all.

In April 2002, after months of stalling by the FBI, the families of passengers on Flight 93 were allowed to hear the cockpit voice recording (or what was claimed to be the recording, you can take nothing for granted with these agencies). Tom Burnett, the father of Tom Burnett Jr, said the tape was difficult to follow. "A lot was unintelligible, and a lot of it we couldn't follow very easily, so I don't think it gives us resolution," he said.[42] But he felt he had "learned something, another piece of the puzzle". Burnett's wife, Deena, said they were told that the recording would be played at the trial of Zacarias Moussaoui, the man accused of being an accomplice in the 9/11 attacks. The FBI has only said that the voice recorder includes screaming and sounds of a struggle.[43] *Newsweek* claims to have been given a transcript of the cockpit recorder from FBI sources:

"Beginning at 9.57, the cockpit voice recorder began to pick up the sounds of a death struggle. There is the crash of galley dishes and trays being hurled, a man's voice screaming loudly. The hijackers can be heard calling on each other to hold the door. One of the passengers cries out, 'Let's get them!' More crashing and screaming. In a desperate measure to control the rebellion, a hijacker suggests cutting off the oxygen. Another one tells his confederates to 'take it easy.' The end is near. The hijackers can be heard talking about finishing off the plane, which has begun to dive. The hijackers cry out, "God is great!" The cockpit voice recorder picks up shouting by one of the male passengers. It is unclear whether the passengers have breached the cockpit or are just outside the door. The hijackers apparently begin to fight among themselves for the controls, demanding, 'Give it to me.'"

Mmmm. And then some.

Flight 93 shot down?

I don't think the passengers storming the cockpit caused the plane to crash and the FBI has never confirmed that the passengers got into the cockpit. It is far from impossible that Flight 93 was shot down. The authorities vehemently deny this, but with their track record for telling the truth I'll make up my own mind thank you. I'm sure there is something highly significant about Flight 93 and why that plane was stopped before it reached a target. President Bush did not give the order to intercept and shoot down any commercial airliner that refused instructions to turn away from Washington until after the Pentagon had been hit. He had nearly an hour to give this order to protect Washington after Flight 11 crashed and more than 35 minutes after the crash of Flight 175. But through most of this time he was hearing a story about a pet goat and after he emerged from the classroom he issued no such order until after the Pentagon strike. This was confirmed by Vice President Dick Cheney who told the *Meet the Press* programme: "I wholeheartedly concurred in the decision he made, that if the plane would not divert, if they wouldn't pay any attention to instructions to move away from the city, as a last resort our pilots were authorized to take them out." [44] Flight 93 was only the one in the air when the military were given permission to shoot-to-kill. Had they done so, given what had happened, the vast majority of people would have accepted there was no other choice. Instead the authorities are insistent this did not happen. NORAD told me that F-16s it says were scrambled from Langley to Washington were redirected to check out Flight 93, but when the plane crashed into that Shanksville field they were still 11 minutes, or 100 miles, from making contact. [45] Shucks, missed again. Or did they? Paul Wolfowitz, the Deputy Defense Secretary, said the Pentagon had been tracking Flight 93 and could have shot it down if necessary. [46] Eyewitness reports at the time confirm that Flight 93 was being tracked, but seriously contradict the NORAD claim that the nearest military jet was 100 miles or 11 minutes away at the time of impact. Reports also put in question the claim that the plane came down in one piece. The *Pittsburgh Post Gazette* said:

"Residents and workers at businesses outside Shanksville, Somerset County, reported discovering clothing, books, papers, and what appear to be human remains. Some residents said they collected bags-full of items to be turned over to investigators.

Others reported what appeared to be crash debris floating in Indian Lake, nearly six miles from the crash site." [47]

Six miles from the crash site with only a ten miles an hour wind blowing? Reuters reported Pennsylvania state police as saying that debris from the plane had been found up to eight miles away in a residential community "where local media have quoted residents as speaking of a second plane in the area and burning debris falling from the sky".[48] *Time* magazine for the week of 9/11 reported that the "largest pieces of the plane still extant are barely bigger than a telephone book". Again, look at the very large pieces of wreckage that were left on the ground when the cargo and passenger aircraft collided at 36,000 feet in July 2002. *ABC News* reported that an eyewitness called Linda Shepley had told television station KDKA in Pittsburgh that she "heard a loud bang and saw the plane bank to the side before crashing". Other witnesses said they heard up to three loud booms before the jetliner went down.[49] Danny Butler wrote in the *Herald Sun*: "Witnesses reported eerie sounds from the aircraft as it fell. Some people heard an explosion, and others heard sputtering." [50] A local Pennsylvania newspaper, the *Daily American*, reported the experience of another witness:

"Laura Temyer of Hooversville RD1 was hanging her clothes outside to dry before she went to work Tuesday morning when she heard what she thought was an airplane. 'Normally I wouldn't look up, but I just heard on the news that all the planes were grounded and thought this was probably the last one I would see for a while, so I looked up,' she said. 'I didn't see the plane but I heard the plane's engine. Then I heard a loud thump that echoed off the hills and then I heard the plane's engine. I heard two more loud thumps and didn't hear the plane's engine anymore after that.'" [51]

The National Guard cordoned off the crash area and it was many hours before any television footage was shown and then only from a distance. Lyle Szupinka of the State Police said that one of the large engines from the aircraft was found "at a considerable distance from the crash site". He added:

"If you were to go down there, you wouldn't know that was a plane crash. You would look around and say, 'I wonder what happened here?' The first impression looking around you wouldn't say, 'Oh, looks like a plane crash. The debris is very, very small. The best I can describe it is if you've ever been to a commercial landfill. When it's covered and you have papers flying around. You have papers blowing around and bits and pieces of shredded metal. That's probably about the best way to describe that scene itself." [52]

The Pentagon told the *New York Times* that Flight 93 was being followed by an F-14 with an order from President Bush to shoot down the plane if necessary. The *Telegraph* newspaper that circulates in Nashua and Southern New Hampshire quoted a "Federal Aviation Administration employee who works in the Nashua control facility" as saying that air traffic controllers there had learned through discussions with other controllers that an F-16 fighter stayed in hot pursuit of Flight 93 until it crashed. Although controllers didn't have complete details, they had learned that the F-16 made 360-degree turns to remain close to the plane, the employee said. "He must've seen the whole thing." [53] The first media reports (often the most accurate before the lid goes on) said the plane had been shot down, and *USA Today* reported how local residents said they had seen a second plane in the area, possibly an F-16 fighter, and burning debris falling from the sky. "[FBI Agent] Crowley said investigators had determined that two other planes were nearby but didn't know if either was military," said the paper.[54] Then there was the call taken from the plane by Glenn Cramer, a local emergency dispatcher at the Westmoreland County Emergency Operations Center. He reported that a passenger who said he was in a locked toilet on Flight 93 called the emergency number 911 at 9.58 to say the plane had been hijacked. Cramer said: "He heard some sort of explosion and saw white smoke coming from the plane, and we lost contact with him." [55] Soon afterwards the plane went down. How he saw all this while locked in a toilet is not clear, however. The *Washington Post* reported that FBI agents quickly took possession of the tape of that call and refused to provide any information about the tape's contents or the identity of the caller. Another report said: "[Westmoreland County spokesman] Stephens said the passenger gave the dispatcher information about the situation on the plane, but said the FBI has ordered details not to be released." [56] The idea that this was caused by a hijacker bomb doesn't stand up. Why would the hijackers take such a risk of detection by taking a bomb on the plane, especially when none of the others are suggested to have done so? FBI spokesman Bill Crowley denied that a bomb was involved. He said: "The conclusion of the investigation is that no explosives were used on board the plane." [57] Even CNN noted the discrepancies when correspondent Brian Cabell reported from the scene in Pennsylvania on September 13th:

> "… in the last hour or so, the FBI and the state police here have confirmed that they have cordoned off a second area about six to eight miles away from the crater here where [the] plane went down. This is apparently another debris site, which raises a number of questions. Why would debris from the plane – and they identified it specifically as being from this plane – why would debris be located six miles away? Could it have blown that far away? It seems highly unlikely. Almost all the debris found at this site is within 100 yards, 200 yards, so it raises some questions." [58]

Which were subsequently never asked and never investigated.

The mystery "white jet"

Another aspect of the Flight 93 story that has conveniently been forgotten and ignored is the small white jet seen by residents at the time of the crash. In its edition of September 14th 2001, the *Record* in Bergen County, New Jersey, quoted five people who live and work less than four miles from the crash site. Susan

Custer said she saw a small white jet streaking overhead and then "heard the boom and saw the mushroom cloud". Robin Doppstadt was working inside her family food-and-supply store when she heard the crash and when she went outside she saw a small white jet that "looked like it was making a single circle over the crash site". She said it climbed very quickly and took off. "It's the damndest darn thing," said farmer Dale Browning. "Everybody's seen this thing in the sky, but no one can tell us what it is." Susan Mcelwain of Stonycreek Township said a small white jet with rear engines and no discernible markings swooped low over her minivan, almost clipped the tops of trees, and disappeared over a hilltop. Within a minute, she said, the ground shook and a white plume of smoke appeared over the ridge. "It was so close to me I ducked," Mcelwain recalled, "I heard it [Flight 93] hit and saw the smoke. All I could think of was how close I came to dying." [59] Dennis Decker and Rick Chaney said they heard an explosion and ran outside to see a large mushroom cloud spreading over the ridge. "As soon as we looked up, we saw a mid-sized jet flying low and fast," Decker said. "It appeared to make a loop or part of a circle, and then it turned fast and headed out." They said the plane was something like a Learjet and was white with no markings that they could see. "If you were here to see it, you'd have no doubt," Decker said. "It was a jet plane, and it had to be flying real close when that 757 went down. If I was the FBI, I'd find out who was driving that plane." The FBI did not appear to want to, however, which will surprise no one.

The FBI said it did not rule out a second plane, but then did exactly that. An official at the Cleveland Air Traffic Control Center in Oberlin, Ohio, which tracked Flight 93, said "no comment" when asked if there was any record of a second plane over the crash site. "That's something that the FBI is working on and I cannot talk about," said Richard Kettel, head of tower operations at the Cleveland Center. [60] Small white jets like the one described are used by the US military. One is the T-1A Jayhawk, a medium-range, twin-engine jet trainer, and a military version of the Beech 400A. It is powered by twin rear engines capable of an operating speed of 539 miles per hour and has a range of 2,100 nautical miles. [61] Clearly, as with every other aspect of the 9/11 story, there is a great deal we are not being told and I believe that knowing why Flight 93 crashed in a field while the others were left to complete the job unchallenged will tell us an enormous amount about how these atrocities were organised. A website specialising in the investigation of Flight 93 summarises the situation very well:

"At this point, if a new story comes out – even if it comes with a recording – that shows heroes in the cockpit, I think we all have a right to be skeptical of its accuracy. I have a digital audio studio at home. I, and anyone else familiar with audio these days, can tell you anything can be created. No matter what information is released in the future, skeptics of the hero story have been given all the ammo they need by the FBI to remain skeptical forever. That ammo is silence, time and the failure to discuss witnessed events like the mystery white jet at tree top level before the crash, the wide debris field, the detached engine, the explosions heard by so many and the data recorders." [62]

My own feeling after many months of studying the background is that all the planes were probably supposed to crash much closer in time to each other than they did. If the unexplained delay of 40 minutes between Flight 93 leaving the gate at Newark and actually taking off was not planned for some reason, this could well have scuppered the timeline. NORAD says that Flight 93 crashed at about 10.03 and, if you look at a map, the location is less than 30 minutes flying time from Washington. In fact, at 500miles an hour the 124 miles would be completed in little more than half that time. Let's say it would have taken 20 minutes. Even with its delayed departure that would put Flight 93 over Washington by about 10.25 if it had not crashed. Take away the 40-minute delay before departure at Newark and you would have Flight 93 arriving over Washington in the region of 9.45 to 9.50. Flight 77 (or something) struck the Pentagon at 9.38 and both could easily have been scheduled to strike earlier. It is very possible that Flight 93 and 77 were supposed to hit Washington quite close to each other, as with the two planes in New York that crashed about 20 minutes apart. The target for 93 might have been Capitol Hill, both for its symbolism and because destroying the home of Congress and the Senate would have handed almost complete control to President Bush in that crucial period. But, against that, General Myers, Chairman of the Joint Chiefs of Staff, says he was on Capitol Hill that morning with Senator Max Cleland. If that's true it makes it unlikely that this was the target. The White House is another obvious possibility. If Flight 93 was heading for Washington, and it was genuinely delayed before take off, it would explain why it was the only one not to strike its target. Once Flight 77 hit the Pentagon, or we were told it did, there was no longer a credible story left to explain how a fourth plane, Flight 93, could have arrived some considerable time after that to strike another target without a response from the military. Therefore, it would follow that the best way to solve the problem would be to shoot it down and concoct a cover story that hero passengers challenged the hijacker pilots. I am open to all possibility, but that is certainly one, and I understand there were other events planned that day that didn't happen because of panic and incompetence. However, I think there is something of great significance about Flight 93 that we don't yet know and, until we do, its true background will remain speculation. Maybe Washington was not the target at all and it was following a very different agenda.

"Investigations" you can trust

We cannot hope for the authorities to tell us the truth. That is not what they are there for. The "investigations" into plane crashes, including the Lockerbie bombing quite wrongly blamed on Libya, are fixed to suit the official line and hide what really happened. When TWA Flight 800 crashed shortly after take off from New York on July 17th 1996, the official report by the National Transportation Safety Board claimed it was caused by an explosion in a fuel tank that was traced to a fuel pump. Yes, that's probably partly correct in one sense because fuel tanks do tend to explode when missiles hit them. Jim Sanders, an investigative journalist and the husband of a TWA flight attendant, worked tenaciously to expose the lies of the FBI.

In retaliation, Sanders, his wife and a TWA captain were arrested by the FBI for impeding its "investigation". Sanders went to jail for his trouble, but produced a book and documentary after his release.[63] He acquired samples of seat covers from the plane, which were stained by a reddish residue and when he sent them for analysis to Morton Thiokol and Hughes Aerospace, the laboratories reported that the residue contained 15 chemicals found in anti-aircraft missiles and only one of them – glue – is found in aircraft seat covers.[64] But even though pilots from the Air National Guard reported seeing a missile strike Flight 800, as did some 250 other people, and even though pictures existed of the missile and the remote-controlled flying drone it was supposed to have hit, the FBI, the organisation telling you what happened on September 11th, covered up the whole story with the help of the Navy who took control of the crash scene instead of the usual civilian crash investigators. Richard Russell, a retired airline pilot, acquired the Federal Aviation Administration radar tapes of the incident, which revealed an object travelling at up to 2,000 miles an hour heading directly at the plane. When Russell said he would circulate the tape it was seized by the FBI.[65] Something to ponder here. This means that the FAA knew that Flight 800 was struck by some sort of missile, but kept quiet about it and allowed FBI cover story to become the official "history". That is precisely what has happened in the 9/11 case. The FAA knows the official version is nonsense, but it is keeping quiet again and helping the FBI concoct the Big Lie.

Another interesting point about Flight 800 is the remotely controlled "drone" connection that has not been widely publicised. In the spring of 1997 the *Southampton Press* told the story of Dede Muma, a resident of Riverhead, Long Island, who was mistakenly sent faxes of official documents related to the federal TWA Flight 800 investigation. Her fax number was very close to the one being used for faxes related to the investigation by the FBI and other personnel on Long Island. The cover sheet Dede Muma received indicated it was from a worker at Teledyne Ryan Aeronautical in San Diego to a co-worker helping the FBI on Long Island. Teledyne Ryan Aeronautical is operated by the Illuminati-controlled Northrop Grumman. This is the company behind the Global Hawk remote control aircraft technology. The multiple fax pages detailed the rear structures of the "Firebee" drone aircraft that Teledyne Ryan manufactures for the US military. The FBI claims it was told by the US Coast Guard that the bright orange debris that was found with the debris of Flight 800 was from fishing and boating floats. But here was a fax in May 1997 that revealed how the FBI was asking experts from Teledyne Ryan – makers of a bright orange-red remotely controlled plane for the US military – to identify this mystery debris.[66] Again these official "investigations" are designed to hide the truth, not reveal it.

Controlled demolition?

The major Illuminati player David Rockefeller and his brother Nelson, the four times governor of New York, were the men behind the building of the World Trade Center through the Port Authority of New York and New Jersey. The Rockefellers wanted to name the towers after themselves, but Mayor John Lindsay apparently insisted on the World Trade Center. The twin towers were massive structures. They were 1,368 feet (417 metres) tall and had 110 storeys. Each floor was approximately 210 feet by 210 feet in size. Architect Minoru Yamasaki built the WTC to a revolutionary design with its main supports on the outside. Work began in 1965 and the towers were opened in the early 1970s. Only seven weeks before the 9/11 attacks, the World Trade Center changed hands for the first time when businessman Larry Silverstein, who already owned Building Seven on the site, led a consortium that finalised and celebrated a deal for a 99-year lease on the whole complex, worth $3.2 billion. The deal included new insurance policies with the added benefit of a pay-out in the event of a terrorist attack, and Silverstein will therefore have the money to rebuild on the same site.

One of the most traumatic and defining images of September 11th was the collapse of the twin towers. It led to the biggest loss of firefighters at one incident; the second biggest loss of life on American soil; the first total collapse of a high-rise during a fire in United States history; and the largest structural collapse in recorded history. As *Fire Engineering* magazine said, you would think that this would lead to the biggest fire investigation in world history. But no. Francis L. Brannigan, Glenn P. Corbett and Deputy Chief (Ret.) Vincent Dunn, published an article calling for a proper investigation. All we had been given, they said, is a "series of unconnected and uncoordinated superficial inquiries".[67] There has been no comprehensive "Presidential Blue Ribbon Commission," they wrote, "no top-notch National Transportation Safety Board-like response". Ironically, they went on, we will probably gain more detailed information about the destruction of the planes than we will about the destruction of the towers. "We are literally treating the steel removed from the site like garbage, not like crucial fire scene evidence," said the writers. This is, of course, precisely what happened with the Oklahoma bomb and police even said that some scrap metal from the WTC had been diverted to businesses controlled by the Mob. *Fire Engineering* magazine called on FEMA (you must be joking) to immediately appoint a "World Trade Center Disaster Review Panel" to coordinate a complete review of all aspects of the World Trade Center incident and to produce … :

> "… A comprehensive report that examines a variety of topics including determining exactly how and why the towers collapsed, critiquing the building evacuation procedures and the means of egress, assessing the buildings' fire protection features (steel "fireproofing," fire protection systems) and reviewing the valiant fire fighting procedures employed." [68]

Another publication, *Firefighters Magazine,* also described the destruction and removal of evidence from the World Trade Center site as "a half-baked farce" of investigation.[69] The editorial was written by Bill Manning, editor of the magazine, which often publishes technical studies of major fires. Manning said quite rightly that steel from the site should be preserved to allow proper investigations into the cause of the collapse. He asks:

"Did they throw away the locked doors from the Triangle Shirtwaist fire? Did they throw away the gas can used at the Happy Land social club fire? ... That's what they're doing at the World Trade Center. The destruction and removal of evidence must stop immediately."

Remember what Ben Partin said when they did the same with the Murrah Building in Oklahoma using the same company, Controlled Demolition? *Firefighters Magazine* points out that a growing number of fire protection engineers have suggested that "the structural damage from the planes and the explosive ignition of jet fuel in themselves were not enough to bring down the towers." The *New York Times* reported the frustration of experts from the American Society of Civil Engineers appointed by FEMA to "investigate" the cause of the collapse.[70] They said the decision to immediately recycle the steel columns, beams, and trusses may have cost them some of their most direct evidence to explain what happened. Dr Frederick W. Mowrer, an associate professor in the fire protection engineering department at the University of Maryland, said: "I find the speed with which potentially important evidence has been removed and recycled to be appalling."[71] The office of 9/11 "hero" Mayor Giuliani would apparently not respond to requests to explain why this was happening and instead put forward Matthew G. Monahan, a spokesman for the city's Department of Design and Construction, which was in charge of debris removal at the site. He said: "The city considered it reasonable to have recovered structural steel recycled." The *New York Times* interviewed some of the investigation team, among them some of America's most respected engineers. They said they had at various times been "shackled with bureaucratic restrictions" that blocked them from interviewing witnesses, examining the site and requesting crucial information like recorded distress calls to the police and fire departments. "This is almost the dream team of engineers in the country working on this, and our hands are tied," one team member told the *Times* and they had been threatened with dismissal for speaking to the media. "FEMA is controlling everything," the team member said,[72] and readers of this and my other books will well understand why. Here we go again, massive questions, but no open, public investigation. Wherever you look in every aspect of 9/11 there is suppression of information, questioning and genuine inquiry. Everywhere there is something to hide.

The response of most people as they watched those terrible images of the twin towers falling in on themselves is that they resembled the sort of controlled demolitions that you see on television from time to time. Explosive charges are placed so expertly that enormous buildings, like skyscrapers and football stadiums, are collapsed downward and inward, and so protect the surrounding area from damage. It was not only the public that thought this. Van Romero, the President for Research at the New Mexico Institute of Mining and Technology (known as Tech), said after seeing the towers collapse on television that it appeared to be "too methodical" to be a chance result of airplanes colliding with the structures. "My opinion is, based on the videotapes, that after the airplanes hit the World Trade Center there were some explosive devices inside the buildings that caused the towers to collapse."[73] Romero said the collapse resembled the controlled implosions used to demolish old structures and "it would be difficult for something from the plane to trigger an event like that". If explosions did cause the towers to collapse, he said, the detonations could have been caused by a small amount of explosive placed at strategic points. He said the explosives would likely have been put in more than two points in each of the towers. Why is my mind wandering back to Oklahoma? Romero should know what he is talking about as a former Director of the Energetic Materials Research and Testing Center in New Mexico, which studies the effects of explosions on buildings. Indeed the government must rate him and his organisation highly because on September 11th he and another Tech official were on their way to a building near the Pentagon to discuss defence-funded research. But then, ten days later, after the official story announced that the collapses were caused by heat softening the steel girders, Romero dramatically changed his tune. Now it was the fire and not explosives that was responsible, he said. "Certainly the fire is what caused the building to fail," he told the *Albuquerque Journal*.[74] The intense heat of the jet fuel fires weakened the steel structural beams, which gave way under the weight of the floors above. This set off a chain reaction, as upper floors pancaked on to lower ones. Romero said he still believed it was possible that the final collapse of each building was triggered by "a sudden pressure pulse caused when the fire reached an electrical transformer or other source of combustion within the building". I wonder what happened to Romero in those ten days?

The north tower of the World Trade Center was hit at 8.45 and collapsed at 10.29, an impact-to-fail time of one hour and 44 minutes. The south tower was struck at 9.03 and collapsed at 9.50, an impact-to-fail time of 47 minutes. The tower struck second collapsed first and took almost an hour less to fail than the other one. More than that, the south tower was struck a more glancing blow and, as the world saw, much of the fuel exploded away from the building and not inside. The official story says that this can be explained by the fact that the south tower was struck lower and the damaged section was subjected to greater pressure from the floors above. It is claimed that steel "trusses" holding up the floors failed as they were undermined by the heat, but for the buildings to have virtually imploded like a controlled demolition these trusses would have had to have failed almost simultaneously or one side would have fallen first and caused a topple-over effect. A big topple over would have relieved the pressure on the floors below and they could not have collapsed as they did. With the south tower struck on one side, and thus the most intense fire in that area, would you not expect that this combination would have caused that side to fail first and caused it to topple over much more than it did? It is true that it did topple to a certain extent, but the north tower telescoped straight down and Mark Loizeaux, president of Controlled Demolition, could not explain this. Loizeaux said the south tower, which was hit at about the 60th floor, failed much as you would fell a tree. That is what was expected, he said. But the north tower, struck at about the 96th floor, "telescoped" and failed vertically. Asked to explain this he said: "I don't have a clue." [75]

The official explanation of why the towers came down is that the fire was so hot that the steel became too weak to hold up the weight of the concrete and steel above it. The steel beams then buckled and/or the joints broke. Then the concrete and steel crashed down on to the floor below it, turning the concrete into powder. A chain reaction had started; each floor pulverised the one below it. But we are told that the 47-storey Building Seven on the World Trade Center site also collapsed around 6pm that day because of fire and yet this was not struck by a plane or subjected to an aviation fuel explosion. Also, Lee Robertson, the structural engineer who designed the towers, told an international coalition on terrorism in Frankfurt, Germany, a week before the attacks that they were designed to withstand a hit by a Boeing 707 commercial jet and this carried about as much fuel as a 757 and 767.[76] Another WTC architect, Aaron Swirski, lives in Israel and spoke to *Jerusalem Post* Radio after the attack. He said the buildings were "designed around that eventuality to survive this kind of attack".[77] The melting point of steel is 1,538 degrees Celsius or 2,800 Fahrenheit, and although it would not have had to reach this to fail we are talking a serious temperature in a building of some 200,000 tons of steel. This is significant because when heat is applied it moves outward through the steel and this helps to cool down the source point by carrying heat away. Structural engineer G. Charles Clifton said: "In my opinion, based on available evidence, there appears no indication that the fires were as severe as a fully developed multi-story fire in an initially undamaged building would typically be."[78] Scientist and researcher Brian Desborough makes the following comments on the official story:

"Unlike most high-rise buildings, which possess flimsy curtain walling exterior panels, the outer walls of the twin towers contained a multiplicity of very strong and closely-spaced square-sectioned steel beams. These vertical structural box beams would have absorbed a great deal of the impact energy of the collision.

"An aspect of the 9/11 disaster which I'm well qualified to comment on is the claim that the burning fuel weakened the tower's structural steelwork sufficiently to cause subsequent building collapse. The structural steelwork of a high-rise has to be either encapsulated with concrete or covered with a fire retardant coating. When I was technical director of a chemical company, I personally developed several such coatings. In general, the coating has to prevent the steel from attaining a temperature of 1100 degrees Fahrenheit or it will result in a catastrophic failure. Fire codes vary in different localities, but in general it takes at least one hour for such structural steelwork to attain an elevated temperature of 1100 F.

"Note that the south tower was impacted by the plane at a very oblique angle, causing much of the fuel load to be dumped outside the tower, hence the huge external fireball. This meant that the intensity of the fire inside the building should have been less than in the north tower, yet the south tower was the first to collapse. The burning plastics and jet fuel created a great deal of smoke inside the towers. Although smoke kills people, the carbon particles contained in it in the form of soot, combine with the high-energy free radicals generated by flammable gases, thereby reducing the temperature of the fires and preventing a flashover condition. It is reasonable, therefore, to have expected the Trade Center towers to have maintained sufficient structural integrity to have withstood the aircraft impact and resultant fires." [79]

On August 4th 2002, almost a year after the towers collapsed, the *New York Times* revealed the existence of a tape recording of communications by firefighters who had reached the 78th floor of the south tower. This was just two floors below the main impact and the 78th floor was actually struck by a wing of Flight 175. New York fire officials said they had "delayed listening" to the tape *(what for nearly a year?)* and had continued during that period to say that no firefighter went higher than the 50th floor. The tape is devastating to the official story because the *Times* described how Battalion Chief Orio J. Palmer is heard calmly organising the evacuation of survivors with Fire Marshall Ronald P. Bucca and the extinguishing of only "two pockets of fire" that they could see. Yet we are told that just above them, at the very same time, the building was reaching fantastic temperatures that, the official tale claims, caused the building to collapse shortly after these communications by Chief Palmer. It's fairyland.

We have already seen how expert Romero said that very little explosive would be needed to bring down the towers so long as it was placed in the right locations. Many witnesses at the time reported hearing explosions before the buildings collapsed. Firefighter Louie Cacchioli, who was assigned to Engine 47 in Harlem, said his crew were the first to enter the second tower after it was hit. He said he was taking firefighters in the elevator to the 24th floor to support the evacuation. On his last trip, he said, a bomb went off. "We think there were bombs set in the building," he said. "I had just asked another firefighter to stay with me, which was a good thing because we were trapped inside the elevator and he had the tools to get out." [80] Six months after the attacks in March 2002, CBS broadcast a television documentary of what happened that day using the footage of firefighters taken by two French brothers.[81] They had been shooting their own documentary on September 11th near the World Trade Center featuring the firefighters of the Engine 7, Ladder 1, of the New York Fire Department based a few blocks away from the WTC. Suddenly the film-makers found themselves involved in a very different documentary and it was they who caught the first plane hitting the north tower, which George Bush claimed to have seen live, but could not have done. When the fire crew and cameraman Jules Naudet arrived at the north tower they were astonished to find that the lobby, 96 floors below impact, had suffered widespread damage. This was later explained away by officials who said that burning jet fuel had poured down the elevator shafts and exploded in the lobby. But there was no evidence of burning or incendiary explosion in the lobby area. "The lobby looked like the plane hit the lobby!" one firefighter said.[82] After the event the experts were wheeled out to explain why it was obvious the buildings would collapse because of the fire, but this was clearly not considered a potential problem by the New York fire chiefs who have enormous experience of the potential dangers in the high-rise buildings in that city, none of which have ever failed in this way. Far from clearing the towers in case of collapse they set up their operations command post in the lobby of the north tower. Had that collapsed first they would all have been killed because it was only when the south tower came down that the possibility was even considered.[83] Hundreds of firefighters were sent up the stairways to their deaths because the collapse of the towers was not even taken into consideration. Why was this if, according to the "experts" afterwards, it was so obvious why they collapsed? Then there is the story of the security officer at the World Trade Center, told to Peter Jennings on ABC television. The officer said that after the south tower had collapsed he had received a call from the New York Port Authority Command Center on the 22nd floor asking for a rescue in the north tower.[84] He went there himself with firefighters and they found that the offices were so devastated that they had to "tunnel through debris" to "dig out" the trapped Port Authority employees. Remember these offices were some 70 floors below the impact point of the aircraft. The 22nd, 23rd and 24th floors were also said to contain offices leased to the FBI.[85] It was here, it is claimed, that they are said to have kept the files on the cases against Mobil Oil and James Giffen involving alleged illegal oil swaps between Iran and Kazakhstan and against Federal Reserve chief Alan Greenspan, Morgan and Company, and Goldman Sachs involving gold price fixing. The basements of the World Trade Center contained vast vaults used by the COMEX metals trading division of the New York Mercantile Exchange. Some 3,800 gold bars, weighing 12 tons and worth more than $100 million, were buried under the mountains of rubble left after the attack. I asked the FBI if it had offices on those floors of the World Trade Center, but my question was not answered.

Beam weapons?

It is possible that charges were placed in the buildings at crucial points and exploded by remote control, but we should remember that the Illuminati are not working only with the technology we see in the public domain. They have access to their secret science, and the development of weapons and other technology that is far in advance of anything we see. One example is the energy-particle or "beam" weapon that fires an invisible laser or sound wave so powerful it can turn a building to dust. It has been noted by a number of observers that debris was turning to dust as it fell through the air and not only when it struck the ground. The television evangelist Dr Robert Schuller said after visiting the site that there "was not a single block of concrete in that rubble" [86] Some 425,000 cubic yards of concrete disintegrated, most of it into immense clouds of dust. Dr Charles Hirsch, the Chief Medical Examiner, reportedly told grieving relatives in December 2001 that many bodies had been "vaporized".[87] By then only 500 of the estimated 3,000 had been identified and a report on the BBC in late May 2002 when the clear-up had been completed said only a third of the bodies had been discovered. Dr Hirsch declined to be interviewed, but his spokeswoman Ellen Borakove said he meant that bodies were consumed by blazing fuel or "rendered into dust" when the buildings collapsed. Dr Michael Baden, New York's Chief Forensic Pathologist, had said in September that most bodies should be identifiable because the fires had not reached the 3,200 degrees for 30 minutes necessary to incinerate an entire body. An eyewitness to the collapse told the *American Free Press* that as he stood two blocks from the World Trade Center he had seen "a number of brief light sources being emitted from inside the building between floors 10 and 15". He saw about six of these brief flashes, accompanied by a "crackling sound" immediately before the tower collapsed. This may or may not be relevant. The point I am making is that we need to realise that the technology exists to undermine the buildings using the Illuminati's secret science.

The *American Free Press* interviewed a German physicist who believes a laser beam weapon could have caused the collapse of the twin towers using infrared technology that was first developed in the Soviet Union.[88] The physicist, whom the *American Free Press* does not name, was described as a former East German physicist who studied Soviet infrared technology and plasmoids during the 1960s and 1970s, and was directly involved in the demonstration of a Soviet laser beam weapon for the US Air Force in Weimar in 1991. He was quoted as saying there is evidence that a directed-energy weapon using "deep infrared" radiation was used to bring down the World Trade Center. According to the physicist, the Soviet infrared beam weapon was used during a Soviet dispute with China in 1969 to destroy "a wall" at the Ussuri River, which separates Manchuria from Russia. Infrared radiation employs invisible wavelengths between visible light and microwave on the electromagnetic spectrum and produces enormous heat. It creates a potentially devastating phenomenon called a plasmoid cloud of heated and ionised gas, AFP reported. The rubble of the World Trade Center, which was a steel and concrete construction, burned for more than three months despite having been sprayed with a nearly constant jet of water.[89] The United States has been developing and deploying such weapons for many years, and one of its centres of development has been the Brookhaven Laboratories on Long Island, New York. Lasers are the leading edge of directed-energy weapons. Author Jeff Hecht, wrote in his 1984 book *Beam Weapons: The Next Arms Race*: "The military 'destructor beam' definitely is in our future tactical arsenal." The advanced technology and plasma physics involved in directed-energy weapons give them unprecedented lethal power. They can unleash devastating beams of energy in seconds and less. The German physicist told the *American Free Press*:

> "From my experience as a physicist and research scientist with the GRU [Russia's Central Intelligence Agency] I have enough experience to judge that the World Trade towers have been burning too quickly, too hot, and too completely to have been caused by the kerosene fires that resulted from the crashes. Furthermore, the demolished buildings nearby are an indication that there was a plasmoid cloud involved, which probably affected the buildings nearby."

He said that in 1991 the GRU demonstrated for the US Air Force Electronic Security Command (AFESC) the capabilities of its infrared beam weapon by reducing a ceramic plate to dust from a distance of one mile. He said the demonstration was designed to show the US "how a stealth bomber could be turned into dust in the same way". The plate had been turned into such fine dust, he said, that it was difficult to pick up with a vacuum cleaner. "The plate was not destroyed suddenly as if hit by a bullet, rather it disintegrated in a process taking about 15 minutes." The physicist said that one of the transmitters involved in striking the World Trade Center with a beam weapon could have been located in a high building nearby or on a satellite, plane, or ship.

Keep taking the tablets, Mr President

Soor [...] had the anthrax scare, which was designed to further spre [...] Bush and Co sought to rally public opi [...] at *The Sun* newspaper in Boca Rat [...] other employees tested positive. Let [...] er of prominent people, inc [...] NBC News anchorman Tom Br [...] tested positive for exposure to an [...] two Capitol police officers. C [...] as pushing ahead with his P [...] te House personnel were given C [...] letters began to appear and on the r [...] use Medical Office dispensed ([...] Cheney.[90] That clearly means that [...] White House refuses to discuss [...] Force One was next" Fleischer [...] the security measures including [...] lent ... people who would want to [...] tections are in place and therefore [...] newspeak: "If the White House were [...] g health protections that are in place [...] thrax scare was a sham." [...] where the photo editor died from [...] s to the CIA. Boca Raton, [...] enclave and home to a plant owned [...] y with links to Father George Bush [...] rfare agents exported to Iraq with US [...] of the Gulf War.[92] A man called Peter [...] that he was involved at one time with [...] n and with Ishan Barbouti International [...] al and biological weapons complex in Rabta, Libya.[93] His experience [...] nvestigate what was going on. He said he went to the CIA and FBI, and operated for the US government under a code name. They told him the people he was investigating were international terrorists and they were going to prosecute them. Kawaja said that he continued with his own investigation, however, which included "bugging telephone lines, buildings, and certain other locations throughout the United States."[94] This was when, as I mentioned earlier, he says he intercepted communications to the Commodity Credit Corporation and the Banca Nazionale del Lavorro (BNL), which was publicly exposed as a vehicle for funding Saddam Hussein from the United States. Kawaja said he saw the letters of credit of the BNL, which came from Switzerland, and "a lot of other communications regarding the Gulf War that was to come". He said he recorded calls going to and coming from Baghdad, to and from the United States and London, CIA, FBI, FBI counter-intelligence, US Customs, certain politicians and numerous other individuals. "This is my information," he said in the radio interview. "It is not second-hand." He said that what he found at the Product Ingredient Technology in Boca Raton was "very heinous". He said he found that a strain of hydrogen cyanide called Prussian Blue was being tested on gas mask filters more than a year before the Gulf War and that this information was known to the then President of the United States, Father George Bush. He said that the Gulf War illnesses are actually communicable diseases and they are on gas masks, clothing, weapons and any of the materials that came back from the Gulf War. He said he had reports from several states where civilians have bought some of the clothing and now their entire family are in wheelchairs. Quite a coincidence, therefore, that the anthrax scare should start in Boca Raton.

Senate Majority Leader Tom Daschle told reporters that tests found the letter sent to him contained a very potent form of anthrax that was clearly produced by someone who knew what he or she was doing. It was found to be of the Ames strain of anthrax and the US Army Laboratory was revealed to be the main source of this strain. It was distributed to a handful of laboratories in the United States, Canada and the UK.[95] These included the Defence Research Establishment Suffield, a Canadian biodefence institute; the US Army Dugway Proving Ground in the Utah desert and the Pentagon's leading chemical and biological testing center; the Chemical Defence Establishment at Porton Down, a biodefence institute near Salisbury, England; University of New Mexico Health Sciences Center, a Pentagon-funded Albuquerque research institute; Martin E. Hugh-Jones, an anthrax researcher at Louisiana State University; Northern Arizona University in Flagstaff; and the Battelle Memorial Institute, a major government contractor in Columbus, Ohio. Colonel Arthur Friedlander, senior military research scientist at the US Army Medical Research Institute of Infectious Diseases at Fort Detrick, Maryland, said the Ames strain was distributed by the military for research purposes under strict controls to "legitimate workers in the field".[96] So, yet another coincidence. The strain used in the anthrax scare was the one used by the Pentagon and a few Pentagon-connected laboratories. Funnily enough, after this was revealed, the anthrax scare suddenly ended as fast as it had begun. Oh yes, two other coincidences. Cipro, the drug taken after possible contact with anthrax or as a precaution, is made by the German Illuminati company, Bayer, which was once part of Hitler's I.G. Farben, the chemical giant that ran the concentration camp at Auschwitz. Sales of Cipro obviously soared during the "scare". BioPort, the exclusive producer of anthrax vaccine for the US government, is reported to be closely connected with the Carlyle Group of Father George Bush and its investors, the bin Laden family. In June 2002, Boy George Bush signed new "bio-terrorism" laws that devote $4.3 billion to stockpiling vaccines, food inspections and security for water supplies. One guess whose pockets that is heading for.

Weaving the web

Obviously I can't say in precise detail how the events of September 11th and their aftermath were pulled off. Were there hijackers on the planes? Were they on some and not others? Were they on all of them? Was the Pentagon crash even caused by a plane? Were the aircraft remotely controlled? Were they flown by hijacker-pilots? Were they flown by hijackers who reprogrammed the route via the Flight Management System? At this stage it cannot be said for sure because to know the exact details we need to have someone on the inside who knows the full story and has the courage to speak out. But what we do know is that if hijackers flew those planes they were brilliant pilots and certainly not the ones named by the FBI who attended flying schools in the US. That is a total diversion to take people off the path and has been orchestrated by those who are really responsible. We also know that the official story is a monumental lie at almost every turn and I have identified the structure through which apparently unconnected countries and agencies can be coordinated to work to the same goal, the same "terrorist" attacks and their subsequent "response". That structure is the compartmentalised pyramids I highlighted at the start of this book.

The Illuminati manipulate through these "need to know" compartments to ensure that those necessary for the plan to work are only allowed to know enough for them to make their individual contribution. They have no idea what is happening in the other "compartments". Only the very few at the top, the peak of the Illuminati hierarchy, know how it all fits together. Even people like President Bush will be locked in their particular compartment and won't know the full story. A radio interviewer once asked me: "So you're saying that President Bush organised the whole thing?" I think it was about a week before I stopped laughing. The structure of pyramids inside bigger pyramids, inside still bigger pyramids, makes the coordination possible. The CIA, for example, is a compartmentalised pyramid; so is the FBI; the State Department; the Justice Department; the US Military; al-Qaeda and other terrorist groups; Pakistan intelligence; British intelligence; the UK government; the media; and so on. A tiny few people within these organisations will know what really happened on September 11th and what the Illuminati agenda really involves. Most will have no idea that the Illuminati agenda even exists. They will follow orders from above without knowing where those orders truly originate and why. Only those in the key positions of power and control within those organisations and countries will know anything like the real story.

However, if you go high enough in the CIA pyramid and those of the FBI, US military, government and media, these pyramids are encompassed by a bigger pyramid. At that level a coordinated plan can be operated through all of them while the vast majority of those involved lower down have no idea what they are being

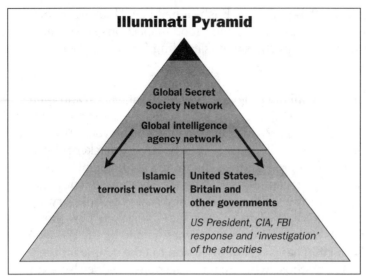

Figure 24: *The Russian doll, pyramid-within-pyramid system that allows one force to manipulate all "sides"*

used for. At this level, the CIA is the FBI is the US government is the controlling level of the US media, etc. This means that the CIA, FBI, US government, military and the media can be coordinated to achieve a common goal. They can hatch and organise the attacks, allow them to happen by thwarting investigations and exposure and then cover up what happened, again by thwarting investigations, destroying evidence and ignoring, jailing or killing witnesses. This is why those genuine FBI agents had their investigations blocked as they always do if they threaten to get in the way of a covert operation by the Illuminati and the FBI leadership. In the same way the Pakistan government and intelligence operation are compartmentalised pyramids, as are al-Qaeda and other terrorist networks; so are German intelligence, Mossad and Saudi Arabia. Again, if you go high enough they are all encompassed by a bigger pyramid, from which one plan can be coordinated through them. Go still higher and there is a pyramid that encompasses the one involving Pakistan, al-Qaeda, and the rest, and the one involving the CIA, FBI, US and UK governments, the US and UK military and the media (*Figure 24*). From this exalted capstone, or master pyramid, it is possible to coordinate actions taken by al-Qaeda, Pakistan and German intelligence, etc. and those governments and agencies in the US and UK. A superb symbolic picture of this hidden hand can be found Michael Mott's book, *Caverns, Cauldrons, and Concealed Creatures*[97] (*Figure 25*). The scene happening on the stage is the "movie" I talk about, the version of events given to us hour by hour by the mainstream media. But the force holding the strings of both "sides" is never exposed and, apart from books like this one, the people are never told where the real power lies and to what end. They keep watching the movie and believing it to be real. This is how it was possible to coordinate and cover up the 9/11 atrocities and the main focus of this operation was not in a cave in Afghanistan, but among shadowy groups in the United States and the Britain who control puppets and lackeys like President Bush.

Some observations

The Illuminati's method of operation would have ensured that the would-be hijackers operated in a compartment of knowledge that led them to believe one thing while a very different scenario was being planned behind the scenes. Once the "hijack" was under way they would have realised that they were not in control of the planes at all, but some external force was – remote control. The external control of the planes from the ground is something virtually every contact I have spoken with is agreed upon. This scenario allowed those really responsible for 9/11 to have Arab men in the right place at the right time to build the cover story of "al-Qaeda

Figure 25: *The Movie. On the stage is what we see every day in the media. Above the stage is what is really going on. Control both "sides" and you control the game*

did it" while behind this compartmentalised smoke screen a very different operation unfolded. People like Zacarias Moussaoui, if he was truly involved, may genuinely believe that they were planning attacks on behalf of al-Qaeda, but all the while a hidden hand would have been using them as a cover for the real deal. I believe the FBI agents who now complain that their investigations were blocked before 9/11 were in danger of exposing, and therefore destroying, the "al-Qaeda" cover story and that is why the higher-ups stepped in. The same with the actions of President Bush to stop FBI agents investigating Osama bin Laden and his family in the months before the attacks. We should not forget either that

we still don't know who these "hijackers" really were because many of those named by the FBI are still alive and we have still not been presented with any credible evidence that the rest of them were on the planes either.

I contacted Monnica Sepulveda, a professional psychic in the United States, who has a very impressive reputation for contacting loved ones that have died.[98] Making this contact is not mumbo-jumbo, it is basic physics. When consciousness leaves the body at "death" it leaves this five-sense frequency range, that's all, because it no longer has a body to operate in this realm of frequency. It simply moves its focus to another frequency state and can therefore be accessed and communicated with by those with the ability to move their psychic "radio dial" to attune with it. I asked Monnica if she could make any contact with those who died on September 11th. She had not followed the 9/11 story much beyond the mainstream media and she was very surprised by much of what she was receiving – including the fact, she said, that she could see an explosion at the Pentagon, but no plane. She said she had made contact with Mohamed Atta, who she was sure was on the "other side":

"Wow, you know what, he's not at all happy with what's happening with him. He doesn't seem to be a happy man about his crossing. There's something about lies. OK, he's making it a little clearer to me … I'm going to use an example because I know you'll understand it. You know how you have members of Freemasons and they have different degrees? That's how he's explaining it to me. It's like people at the bottom don't know everything and they're not privy to knowing what's on the top. That's how I'm getting it from him. God my stomach. And I think that's what bothered him. He thought it was under the guise of one thing, but it's actually something else. So it's big. He says you are already on the right track about knowing the answer. You already know the answer. You just need it validated and you already know the answer. It has to do with a reduction of population, an excuse. He says it's an excuse, whatever that means. It's an excuse. Let me see if I can get clearer than that. Control. Excuse for control. But reduction of population, I wonder why that would be?"

The population reduction policies of the Illuminati have been detailed in my previous books and those of other researchers. I am not saying that this information from the "other side" is right or wrong, that's for everyone to decide for themselves, but what Monnica said certainly fits with the techniques of compartmentalisation at the heart of Illuminati operations. We can see how these people operate from the Operation Northwoods documents, as described by author James Bamford:

"… the plan, which had the written approval of the Chairman and every member of the Joint Chiefs of Staff, called for innocent people to be shot on American streets; for boats carrying refugees fleeing Cuba to be sunk on the high seas; for a wave of violent terrorism to be launched in Washington, DC, Miami, and elsewhere. People would be framed for bombings they did not commit; planes would be hijacked. Using phoney evidence, all of it would be blamed on Castro, thus giving Lemnitzer [the Chairman of the Joint Chiefs of Staff] and his cabal the excuse, as well as the public and international backing, they needed to launch their war."

The other 9/11 scenario, which some contacts close to the Illuminati have claimed to have happened, is even more challenging to our credulity – that there were no "hijackers" on the planes at all. They were simply taken over by remote control and flown to their destinations, end of story. This would mean, of course, that all the "phone calls" from the planes had to have been faked. I would have to see a great deal more evidence to support this before it could even begin to be credibly considered and I certainly have not seen that up to this point. The technology to fake voices apparently exists and false communications of various kinds are frequently used by intelligence agencies. The technology is available to do amazing things with audio and visual, and we must keep this in mind when considering the options. Victor Ostrovsky, a defector from Mossad, Israel's Intelligence Agency, said that a transmitter loaded with pre-recorded messages was planted in Tripoli, Libya, by a Mossad team to beam out fake communications about bombings and attacks planned by Colonel Gaddafi. These were immediately intercepted by the US monitoring network and convinced officials that Libya was behind the 1986 bombing of a Berlin disco in which a US soldier died.[99] In response, President Reagan ordered air attacks on Libya and tried to assassinate Gaddafi. 100 Libyan civilians were killed, including Gaddafi's daughter. Faking phone calls to families is going to be a far more serious challenge, however, and I am not saying for a moment that this is what happened because the logical reaction is that it did not. It would seem to be a very complicated task and, like I say, I would want to see some serious evidence before going there. I pass this on for your information only, as with Monnica's communications. I would, however, add that from my experience "logical" reactions are often not the way to uncover the Illuminati's method of operation. After all, how more fantastic can you get than to convince the world that the US went to the moon in 1969 when it was all faked and the "giant step for mankind" took place on a movie set on Earth? Staggering, yes, but that's what happened, as expert analysis has shown. "Logic" comes from assessing events from the knowledge base that we have. The Illuminati are coming from a much higher level of technological know-how and what may be illogical and far-fetched to us is perfectly "logical" and straightforward to them. What we can say with certainty is that the official story is nonsense and "pilots" who struggled to cope with Cessnas at US flying schools did not fly those aircraft into those buildings. Another point is that many researchers have been looking for a single explanation to cover all four aircraft, but my own feeling is that this was not necessarily the case.

Hide and no seek

Wherever you look in the 9/11 story there are cover-ups, half-truths and, mostly, blatant lies. This is not the behaviour of people who are telling you what really happened on September 11th. It is the behaviour of people who want to sell you a fairytale and make sure you never know the truth. It is for this reason that Bush, Cheney and those who control them, have done everything they can to thwart a legitimate investigation into all elements of 9/11 by whatever source: the CIA, FBI, Congress, everyone. Bush told the United Nations: "Let us never tolerate outrageous conspiracy theories concerning the attacks of September the 11th." What he should have said, more accurately, is: "Let us never tolerate anyone who wants to tell the people the truth of what really happened." Bush and Cheney personally asked Senate Majority Leader Tom Daschle to "limit the congressional investigation into the events of Sept. 11," according to CNN. Cheney met Daschle and "expressed the concern that a review of what happened on September 11 would take resources and personnel away from the effort in the war on terrorism". Daschle confirmed this on the NBC programme *Meet the Press*. Democrat Daschle said Cheney called him on January 24th 2002 to urge that there be no inquiry into September 11th and

Bush had made a similar request on January 28th during a breakfast meeting at the White House. Some 3,000 dead people on American soil and they don't want an inquiry? Bush also called a private meeting with congressional leaders on January 29th 2002 and asked that the House and Senate intelligence committees only look into "the potential breakdowns among federal agencies that could have allowed the terrorist attacks to occur", and not to investigate what actually happened. US National Security Adviser Condoleezza Rice, appearing on *Fox News Sunday*, said the administration opposed any probe outside the congressional intelligence committees because a war against terrorism was still under way. "We worry about anything that would take place outside of the intelligence committees, and indeed, we think the intelligence committees are the proper venue for this kind of review." Yes, and they'll keep the lid on, darlin', eh? As the *International Herald Tribune* put it: "More than seven months into the world's largest criminal investigation, huge uncertainties persist about the most basic aspects of the plot." [100]

The media vilifies individuals who ask the most basic of questions, like the Georgia Democrat representative Cynthia McKinney. She had only asked for an investigation into what the Bush administration knew before September 11th and pointed out that people elected to serve the people were keeping quiet in fear that their "patriotism" be questioned. She wanted an inquiry into reports that warnings by foreign governments to the highest levels of the US government were not acted upon; the profits made in pre-9/11 trading that revealed prior knowledge; the connections between the Unocal oil company and the Taliban rulers of Afghanistan; the connections between the present government and the Carlyle Group of Father George Bush; the suggestion by Bush and Cheney that congressional investigations into 9/11 should not be a full, in-depth inquiry; the enormous profits made by those close to Bush from the vastly increased spending on the military. All highly relevant and legitimate questions in a so-called free country, but she was attacked from all sides and accused of being "crazy" and "treacherous". Bush spokesman Scott McLellan told the *Washington Post*: "The American people know the facts, and they dismiss such ludicrous, baseless views." No they don't, and neither statement is true. A Carlyle Group spokesman called Chris Ullman asked: "Did she say these things while standing on a grassy knoll in Roswell, New Mexico?" No, Mr Ullman, she said them while having the courage to say what her colleagues on Capitol Hill are too gutless to say. Ari Fleischer, the President's Press Secretary, used the same "grassy knoll" (Kennedy assassination) line in seeking to dismiss McKinney. Obviously that was the agreed song sheet. The Democrat Senator for Georgia, Zell Miller, said McKinney's comments were "dangerous and irresponsible". Asking for a proper inquiry into the murder of 3,000 people is "dangerous" and "irresponsible"? Only for Bush and the gang. The orchestrated attacks on McKinney's comments and her character were outrageous, but pathetically predictable. This is how they operate. They reward those who serve them (until they have outlived their usefulness) and seek to destroy those who question. You can judge the right or wrong of your own position by those who oppose you. The *National Review* was founded by the massive Illuminati insider, William F. Buckley, and in the *National Review Online* of April 12th 2002, McKinney was labelled "Representative Awful". Writer Jonah Goldberg said she was suffering from "paranoid, America-hating, crypto-Marxist conspiratorial delusions". Wow, they really are desperate to keep the lid on aren't they?

Blueprints of the mind

The Illuminati know that if they keep telling the people the same thing over and over that most will come to believe it. They also know that even most of those who question parts of the official story will still find it hard to let go of the idea that the foundations of it are true. Adolf Hitler described this technique very well when he wrote:

> "The masses indulge in petty falsehoods every day, but it would never come into their heads to fabricate colossal untruths and they are not able to believe in the possibility of such monstrous effrontery ... The bigger the lie, therefore, the more likely it is to be believed ... Besides, even the most insolent lie always leaves traces behind it, even after it has been nailed down." [101]

Observing the reaction to 9/11, even among many conspiracy researchers, that last sentence has come back to me many times: "Even the most insolent lie always leaves traces behind it, even after it has been nailed down." It is for this reason that some people, even many, are open to the fact that Bush and his cronies were incompetent in their lack of response to warnings of possible attacks, but they cannot get their minds around the idea that those attacks were actually planned by elements within the United States and the "response" to them was already prepared and waiting before they happened. It is too much to handle and, importantly, too much to bear. The thought that people are being ruled and controlled by a force of such malevolence is such an assault on their basic sense of security that they would rather close their minds to it. They don't want to go there. But it is time to have the courage to clear the mind of preconceived ideas and emotional defences and look at the evidence. If we don't do that the global fascist state is staring us in the face. Victor Hugo once said that there is nothing more powerful than an idea whose time has come. It is equally true that there is nothing more imprisoning than an idea we won't let go.

An excellent Internet article was sent to me that was written by Stephen Gowans, a political activist who lives in Ottawa, Canada, in which he applied all this to September 11th. He points out, and I have found this myself over and over in my research, how people take the official story to be basically correct and seek to explain the contractions and anomalies within that story. Gowans gives an example of "muslim extremists" drinking in bars and strip clubs, and how newspapers sought to explain this away by the "hijackers seeking cover" and using the Islamic principle of "taqyya" which "permits Muslims to use all necessary subterfuge to throw suspicion off their real goals". The idea that these men were not "Islamic fanatics" involved in 9/11 is not even explored. Cowans writes: "The underlying thinking goes, 'These were the bad guys, no question, so if they were doing something that's inconsistent with what the bad guys are supposed to do, there must be some reason.'" He also highlights the unexplored inconsistencies between a "brilliantly executed" terrorist attack and the obvious incompetence of those who were supposed to have been involved:

"The same characteristic of being at once both brilliant and crafty but stupid and blundering was attributed to Washington's last hobgoblins – the Serbs. The Serbs were said to be crafty and cunning enough to hide the bodies of the ethnic Albanian Kosovars alleged to have been murdered in the tens of thousands – a story that began circulating when forensic pathologists couldn't find the bodies Washington warned were strewn across Kosovo. At that point, the media, and public, might have said, if the pathologists can't find the bodies maybe there aren't any. Maybe Washington lied. It's not as if Washington hasn't lied before, to provide a pretext for war. But that's not what the media said. Instead, it started grunting, trying to pull size 36-inch waist jeans over a 60-inch waist theory. It said, instead, the reason the bodies couldn't be found is because the Serbs hid them.

"The 'crafty Serbs hid the bodies' cover-up recalls other tortured – and tortuous – explanations. When it was pointed out that the ethnic cleansing of Kosovar Albanians wasn't happening, and therefore bombing couldn't put an end to something that hadn't happened, it was said, 'Ah, but it would have happened, had we not bombed.' In other words, every time one of Washington's stories starts to fall apart, another story is crafted to prop up the first. So, to prop up the story that bodies couldn't be found in Kosovo because the cunning Serbs had hidden them, (again, evading the massive US intelligence apparatus, including its spy satellites that surely would have noticed the disinterment and subsequent reinterment of mass graves), another story had to be told – that the hidden bodies had finally been found. But how were we to know they were actually the bodies of ethnic Albanians?" [102]

I offer some advice for people faced with the daily bombardment of conditioned thought spewed out by the system in all its forms. Instead of getting caught in the irrelevant debates and diversions, take a deep breath, take a step back and look at it again with an open mind free of preconceived thought. Then you will see it in a very different light. "My God, it's all a piece a shit!" Exactly, that's all it is. The 9/11 story is not just partly a piece a shit. Not even mostly. It is *all* a piece a shit. It's time to get a blank piece of paper and look at it again without being influenced by anything the official sources say happened. They're lying to us – lying, lying, lying. End of story.

SOURCES

1   Alexander Litvinenko and Yuri Fel'shtinsky, *Novaya gazeta*, August 27th 2001

2   Tom Wells, *The War Within: America's Battle Over Vietnam* (University of California Press, 1994)

3   Daniel C. Hallin, *The Uncensored War: The Media and Vietnam* (University of California Press, 1989)

4   30-year Anniversary: Tonkin Gulf Lie Launched Vietnam War, by Jeff Cohen and Norman Solomon, July 27th 1994, **http://www.fair.org/media-beat/940727.html** Jeff Cohen also writes some excellent articles about media compliance with the authorities and these can be found at **http://www.fair.org/extra/writers/cohen.html**

5   These can be found at **www.nara.gov** Search for 'Northwoods' and you should find 'Descriptions and Digital Copies added December 7th 1998'. Scroll down to 'Joint Chiefs of Staff Central Files 1962-63' and click on 'NAIL'. Scroll down to 'NAIL Digital CopiesSearch'. Put 'Joint Chiefs Of Staff' in the first keyword box and 'Assassination Records Review Board' in the second and click 'Submit Search'. You should then retrive 99 hits. Click 'Display Results', click 'More hits' and select 'View all thumbnails' on hit 10, 'Northwoods' **www.nara.gov**

6   **nara.gov** Document 140

7   **nara.gov** Document 138, March 9th 1962

8   Document 63

9   Documents 138–142, September 4th 1962

10 Document 141 **nara.gov**

11 Bush to Increase Federal Role in Security at Airports, *New York Times*, September 28th 2001 **nara.gov**

12 **http://www.af.mil/news/factsheets/global.html** See also **http://www.fas.org/irp/program/collect/global_hawk.htm** for more technical details

13 **http://www.af.mil/news/airman/1101/hawk.html**

14 **http://www.af.mil/news/biographies/roche_jg.html**

15 Thwarting Skyjackings from the ground, published in *Quill* magazine February 1998. Posted to Facsnet, October 2nd 2001 **http://www.facsnet.org/issues/specials/terrorism/aviation.php3**

16 Home Run: Electronically Hijacking the World Trade Center Attack Aircraft, **http://www.geocities.com/mknemesis/homerun.html**

17 Ibid

18 Ibid

19 Letter to the author, April 22nd 2002

20 **http://www.masternewmedia.com/issue11/jetsasmissiles.htm**

21 Ibid

22 The Enemy is Inside the Gates, **http://www.geocities.com/mknemesis/colonels.html**

This "world" is only an illusion and we can change it any time we want. It's just a choice right now between fear and love.

23 http://www.narconews.com/goff1.html

24 *Daily Telegraph*, September 12th 2001

25 http://hometown.aol.com/estrellaberosini/httpPage5Analysis911Facts.htlm

26 *New York Times*, September 12th 2001

27 http://www.defenselink.mil/news/Sep2001/n09152001_200109153.html

28 http://www.asile.org/citoyens/numero14/missile/missile_en.htm

29 *Associated Press*, September 14th 2001
    http://www.truthorfiction.com/rumors/pentagoncrash.htm

30 http://americanhistory.si.edu/subs/weapons/armament/missiles

31 *Washington Post*, September 11th 2001, http://www.washingtonpost.com/wp-srv/
    metro/daily/sep01/attack.html

32 http://www.space.com/news/rains_september11-1.html

33 ABCNews.com and National Air Traffic Controllers Association Website,
    http://september11.natca.org/NewsArticles/DaniellOBrien.htm

34 WhatReallyHappened.comhttp://www.nfpa.org/NFPAJournal/OnlineExclusive/Exclusive
    _11_01_01/exclusive_11.01.01.asp" \t "_blank

35 News Conference, September 12th 2001,
    http://www.defenselink.mil/news/Sep2001/t09122001_t0912asd.html

36 http://www.sf.indymedia.org/news/2002/06/131520.php and
    http://www.sf.indymedia.org/news/2002/06/131526.php

37 The Mercury, an Army Medical Department publication, January 2002
    http://www.armymedicine.army.mil/armymed/news/news.htm

38 LeMay was US Air Force Chief of Staff between 1961 and 1965, and a Vice Presidential running
    mate of George Wallace. He was quoted in the *National Journal* of November 26th 1994

39 *Boston Globe*, http://www.boston.com/news/packages/underattack/news/
    planes_reconstruction.htm

40 Ibid

41 http://hometown.aol.com/estrellaberosini/httpPage5Analysis911Facts.html

42 *Washington Post*, Families Hear Flight 93's Final Moments. Most Say Cockpit Recording
    Lifted Their Spirits and Confirmed Victim's Bravery, April 19th 2002, p A03

43 Recorder captures passengers' fight with hijackers, *USA Today*, October 4th 2001, p A3

44 *Meet the Press*, NBC, September 16th 2001

45 NORAD Timeline e-mailed to the author from NORAD media office, May 20th 2002

46 *New York Times*, September 15th 2001

47 Investigators locate 'black box' from Flight 93; widen search area in Somerset crash,
    Pittsburgh Post Gazette, September 13th 2001

48 Reuters, September 13th 2001

49 Outside Tiny Shanksville, a Fourth Deadly Stroke, *Pittsburgh Post-Gazette*, September 12th
    2001, p A13

50 Danny Butler, Passengers Might Have Tackled Hijackers, *Herald Sun*, September 12th p 8

51 **http://www.dailyamerican.com/disaster.html#3**

52 **http://www.blythe.org/nytransfer-subs/2001cov/Flight_93_Brought_Down**

53 Telegraph Online, Nashua and Southern New Hampshire, September 13th 2001

54 *USA Today*, September 14th 2001

55 **http://news.bbc.co.uk/hi/english/world/americas/newsid_1543000/1543466.stm**

56 Mike Wagner & Ken McCall, Pennsylvania Crash Might Yield Important Evidence, *Cox News Service*, September 11th 2001

57 Tom Gibb, FBI Ends Site Work, Says No Bomb Used, *Pittsburgh Post-Gazette*, September 25th 2001, p A1

58 **http://www.newsmedianews.com/wtc.htm**

59 In Rural Hamlet, the Mystery Mounts; 5 report second plane at PA Crash Site, *The Record*, September 14th 2001

60 Ibid

61 **http://www.af.mil/news/factsheets/T_1A_Jayhawk.html**

62 **http://www.flight93crash.com/flight93_heroes.html**

63 Jim Sanders, *The Downing of Flight 800* (Zebra Books, April 1997) **http://twa800.com/pages/sanders_main.htm**

64 *All Fall Down*, p 20

65 Ibid, p 19

66 **http://www.multipull.com/twacasefile/marnews.html**

67 **http://ericdarton.net/afterwords/fireandair.html**

68 **http://ericdarton.net/afterwords/fireandair.html**

69 *Firefighters Magazine* editorial, January 2002

70 *New York Times*, December 25th 2001

71 Ibid

72 Ibid

73 Explosives Planted in Towers, N.M. Tech Expert Says, *Albuquerque Journal*, September 11th 2001, **http://www.abqjournal.com/news/aqvan09/11-01.htm**

74 *Albuquerque Journal*, September 21st 2001.

75 **http://www.civil.usyd.edu.au/wtc_enr.htm**

76 **http://www.eionews.addr.com/psyops/news/wtc_unanswered_questions.htm**

77 **www.rense.com/general17/eyewitnessreportspersist.htm**

78 Elaboration on Aspects of the Postulated Collapse of the World Trade Center Towers, December 13th 2001, Collapse of the World Trade Center Towers; HERA, Manukau City, New Zealand, PDF Files/ Elaboration on WTC Paper, p 5

79 Letter to the author, April 22nd 2002

80 *People* magazine, September 12th 2001

81 CBS, March 11th 2002

82 Ibid

83 Ibid

84 New WTC Evidence Raises Questions of Evidence Destruction by Dick Eastman, October 28th 2001, **http://www.cam.net.uk/home/nimmann/peace/explosions.htm**

85 Ibid

86 Laser Beam Weapons and the Collapse of the World Trade Center, *American Free Press*, February 14th 2002, **http://www.cam.net.uk/home/nimmann/peace/explosions.htm http://americanfreepress.net**

87 *ABC News*, December 4th 2001

88 Laser Beam Weapons and the Collapse of the World Trade Center, *American Free Press*, February 14th 2002, **http://americanfreepress.nethttp://americanfreepress.net**

89 Ibid

90 *Associated Press*, October 24th 2001

91 Ibid

92 **http://www.nypress.com/14/41/news&columns/wildjustice.cfm**

93 Transcribed by Leading Edge Research Group, **http://www.cco.net/~trufax**, and posted at **http://www.alienobserver.com/files/text/kawa2.html**

94 Ibid

95 *Washington Post*, November 30th 2001, p A01

96 Ibid

97 Michael Wm Mott, *Caverns, Cauldrons, and Concealed Creatures* (Hidden Mysteries, Texas, 2000), available through **davidicke.com**

98 Monnica Sepulveda's website is at **http://www.monnica.com**

99 **http://www.geocities.com/CapitolHill/5260/margolis040201.html**

100 *International Herald Tribune*, May 2nd 2002, p 3

101 *Mein Kampf*, pp 180–1, p 231 of the Manheim translation

102 I have not been able to locate an URL for this article, so maybe it has been taken down now

chapter 13

The war on sanity

"Next the statesmen will invent cheap lies, putting the blame upon the nation that is attacked, and every man will be glad of those conscience-soothing falsities, and will diligently study them, and refuse to examine any refutations of them; and thus he will by and by convince himself that the war is just, and will thank God for the better sleep he enjoys after this process of grotesque self-deception."

Mark Twain

When a problem-reaction-solution is being played out there is always prior planning of the "solution" to ensure that it is ready and waiting to be activated once the problem has primed the people. In the case of September 11th, we can expect to find evidence that the invasion of Afghanistan was planned long before those four planes were hijacked. And, of course, we can. On September 18th, before the plan to attack Afghanistan was made public, the former Pakistan Foreign Secretary Niaz Naik told the BBC's George Arney that he had been informed by American officials at a meeting in Germany two months before, in mid-July, that they planned to invade Afghanistan and remove the Taliban before the snows came in mid-October. Arney reported:

"Mr Naik said US officials told him of the plan at a UN-sponsored international contact group on Afghanistan which took place in Berlin. Mr Naik told the BBC that at the meeting the US representatives told him that unless Bin Laden was handed over swiftly America would take military action to kill or capture both bin Laden and the Taliban leader, Mullah Omar.

"The wider objective, according to Mr Naik, would be to topple the Taliban regime and install a transitional government of moderate Afghans in its place – possibly under the leadership of the former Afghan King Zahir Shah. Mr Naik was told that Washington would launch its operation from bases in Tajikistan, where American advisers were already in place." [1]

Naik also said he was told that Uzbekistan would participate in the operation. The UK *Guardian* newspaper followed up the story, confirming its substance and adding more detail on September 22nd. The four-day meeting in Berlin had involved senior officials from the United States, Russia, Pakistan and Iran and was the third in a series of conferences dubbed "brainstorming on Afghanistan".[2] Among the participants besides Naik were Tom Simons, the former US Ambassador to Pakistan; Lee Coldren, who ran Pakistan, Afghan and Bangladesh Affairs in the State Department until 1997; Karl Inderfurth, a former Assistant Secretary of State for South Asian Affairs; Abdullah Abdullah, the Foreign Minister of the Northern Alliance, the Taliban opposition in Afghanistan; Nikolai Kozyrev, the former Russian Special Envoy to Afghanistan; and Saeed Rajai Khorassani, the former Iranian Ambassador to the United Nations. Francesc Vendrell, the Spanish Deputy Chief UN representative for Afghanistan, convened the meeting, which the Taliban had refused to attend.

Niaz Naik said that an American official had told him that an attack on Afghanistan was imminent. "This time they were very sure," he said. "They had all the intelligence and would not miss him this time. It would be aerial action, maybe helicopter gunships, and not only overt, but from very close proximity to Afghanistan."[3] Lee Coldren, head of Pakistan, Afghan and Bangladesh Affairs at the State Department up to 1997, admitted: "There was some discussion of the fact that the United States was so disgusted with the Taliban that they might be considering some military action".[4] This was a rather sudden "disgust", as we shall see, and "considering" military action was hardly the word. Military action was a certainty long before any planes were hijacked. The *Guardian* quoted "senior diplomatic sources" as saying that these threats of invasion were passed to the Taliban by the Pakistan government with the warning that Osama bin Laden must be handed over if war was to be avoided. Naik says that the Taliban had been offered a deal in July 2001 in which they would share power in a government of national unity (i.e. suitable to US oil interests). If they had accepted that, he said, they would have received immediate international aid. Jean-Charles Brisard, the author of a report for French intelligence on the bin Laden network, put the offer in rather starker terms: "At one moment during the negotiations, the U. S. representatives told the Taliban, 'either you accept our offer of a carpet of gold, or we bury you under a carpet of bombs'."[5] What followed these news stories soon after 9/11 was the very invasion of Afghanistan that Naik said he had been informed about in mid-July. NBC also reported that two days *before* September 11th, President Bush was given a "detailed war plan" to dismantle bin Laden's al-Qaeda network. NBC reported that Bush was given a national security directive to sign for a plan that was "pretty much" the same as the one the United States followed after the attacks. The directive was on Bush's desk on September 9th, but he did not have a chance to sign it before the attacks, the report said.

In their own words ...

The idea that the "war on terrorism" is about terrorism or that the invasion of Afghanistan was a reaction to September 11th is cuckoo land. It is part of a long-planned strategy that was laid out by Illuminati strategist Zbigniew Brzezinski in his 1997 book, *The Grand Chessboard*.[6] He said that America was "too democratic at home to be autocratic abroad". This limited the use of US power, especially its "capacity for military intimidation". Never before, he said, had a populist democracy attained international supremacy, but the pursuit of power was not a goal that commanded popular passion ... "except in conditions of a sudden threat or challenge to the public's sense of domestic well-being." (i.e. September 11th). Brzezinski calls Eurasia the centre of world power for some 500 years. This region spans a vast area from the borders of Germany and Poland across to China and down through India and the Middle East. Brzezinski writes that the power that dominates Eurasia would control two of the world's three most advanced and economically productive regions and this would also lead automatically to Africa's subordination. He points out that about 75 % of the world population lives in Eurasia and most of the planet's "physical wealth" is there as well. Brzezinski goes on to say that the strategy for control of this region would lead to a new world order in which nation states would be controlled solely by economic interests as dictated by banks, corporations and ruling elites who would be solely concerned with the maintenance of their power. The Brzezinski (Illuminati) strategy is clear:

"... To put it in a terminology that harkens back to the more brutal age of ancient empires, the three grand imperatives of imperial geostrategy are to prevent collusion and maintain security dependence among the vassals, to keep tributaries pliant and protected, and to keep the barbarians from coming together." [7]

Murder on demand

Afghanistan's new "transitional government" after the Taliban were defeated also fitted the scenario that Niaz Naik said the American officials had presented to him in mid-July. The post-Taliban interim regime was headed by Hamid Karzai, a former Unocal adviser. He has since become head of the new Afghan government. Karsai is the representative of the exiled King Mohammed Zahir Shah, the man named to Naik by American officials months earlier as the possible leader of the country after the Taliban had been violently removed. Zahir Shah reigned from 1933 to 1973 and was living in exile in Rome. He returned to Afghanistan in April 2002 for the first time in 29 years and now lives in the Presidential Palace. Hamid Karzai's interim leadership on behalf of the king was made possible by the highly convenient assassination of Ahmad Shah Massood (also Massoud) who, in late 1999, founded the United Front, later known as the Northern Alliance. Massood led the Mujahadin forces that recaptured Kabul from the pro-Moscow government in 1992. He was assassinated by an "al-Qaeda" suicide bomber on September 9th, just two days before the attacks in America and, very significantly, had he lived he, and not Karzai, would have been the most likely leader of the post-Taliban regime. The Northern Alliance blamed his death on Pakistan's Interservices Intelligence agency (ISI), which is little more than the Pakistan branch of the CIA. Abdul Haq, another Northern Alliance leader, had been talking with American officials in the months before September 11th, but he was apparently not considered "reliable" in pursuing their interests. The Taliban murdered Haq in October 2001 when he returned to Afghanistan from Pakistan with at least one American in his party. The CIA and Pakistan's ISI, which was extremely close to the Taliban, would have known where he was going and when. Haq's death was reported as a "devastating blow" to American efforts to create a post-Taliban regime and he was presented by the American government as "one of us". In fact he was anything but. It emerged after his murder that he was opposing the US invasion of Afghanistan. The *Washington Post* reported that Haq had, in fact, "clashed with the CIA" and that the CIA and the US military had been doubtful about Haq as an Afghan opposition leader.[8] The CIA, said the *Post* article, did not like Haq's independence and felt that he was "not always on message." The real reason why Abdul Haq was manipulated into the hands of the Taliban before the US invasion began was made clear when the UK *Guardian* published the last interview he gave before his death to Anatol Lieven of the (Illuminati) Carnegie Endowment for International Peace. Haq said:

"Military action by itself in the present circumstances is only making things more difficult – especially if the war goes on a long time and many civilians are killed. The best thing would be for the US to work for a united political solution involving all Afghan groups … We have been trying to create a revolt within the Taliban, but the US hasn't given us the chance. They seem to have been determined to attack, even if someone came up with the best proposal in the world to avoid this."

The Illuminati network controlling the governments of the United States and Britain had a plan to invade Afghanistan and that was that. Nothing was going to stop them, whatever was suggested and September 11th was going to be the excuse they needed. Abdul Haq's threat to this plan is obvious from his interview:

"… the US is trying to show its muscle, score a victory and scare everyone in the world. They don't care about the suffering of the Afghans or how many people we will lose. And we don't like that. Because Afghans are now being made to suffer for these Arab fanatics, but all know who brought these Arabs to Afghanistan in the 1980s, armed them, and gave them a base. It was the Americans and the CIA. And the Americans who did this got medals and good careers, while all these years Afghans suffered from these Arabs and their allies. Now when America is attacked, instead of punishing the Americans who did this, it punishes the Afghans." [9]

Is anyone still in any doubt why Haq was killed and who was really behind it? The *Times* of India reported that Haq's fatal expedition was financed by "wealthy American brothers with US intelligence connections", but that "the CIA and other western agencies declined to provide Haq with the arms and air support he asked for".[10] Robert McFarlane, the former National Security Adviser to the Reagan-Bush administration, who was indicted for his role in Iran-Contra, had held meetings with Haq. McFarlane blamed the CIA for its part in Haq's death. He said the CIA had "betrayed" Haq by failing to support his operation into Afghanistan, and leaving him to be captured and killed by the Taliban.[11] When Hamid Karsai was under threat from the Taliban a US helicopter was sent to his rescue.

The set-up

When you put the pieces together it is a clear as can be that the whole Afghanistan operation was planned long before the attacks in the United States. Richard Armitage, the US Deputy Secretary of State and the Illuminati-Bush-CIA operative involved in drug running and political scandals like Iran-Contra, visited India in May 2001. In the same month George Tenet, the head of the CIA, went to Pakistan for "an unusually long meeting" with President Musharraf and also met Lt. General Mahmud Ahmad, the head of Pakistan military intelligence, the ISI.[12] Then you had US officials in mid-July saying they planned to attack Afghanistan by mid-October and that's exactly what happened. They said they wanted a regime to replace the Taliban involving the exiled king, Zahir Shah. On September 9th the Northern Alliance leader, Ahmad Shah Massood, was assassinated in a plot blamed on Pakistan's ISI, a CIA front. The Northern Alliance statement said that: "… a Pakistani ISI-Osama-Taliban axis [was responsible for] plotting the assassination by two Arab suicide bombers … We believe that this is a triangle between Osama bin Laden, ISI, which is the intelligence section of the Pakistani army, and the Taliban."[13] In October, Abdul Haq, another of the anti-Taliban leaders, was killed, "betrayed" by the CIA, said Robert McFarlane, Reagan's National Security Adviser. Through these events the way was opened for the king's representative, Hamid Karzai, the former Unocal adviser, to lead the Afghan government when September 11th had been used to justify the removal of the Taliban.

The Pakistan connection

Mahmud Ahmad, the head of Pakistan military intelligence, or ISI, had arrived in Washington on September 4th for talks with CIA chief George Tenet and other intelligence, Pentagon and government officials and remained there through September 11th. In the wake of the attacks, on September 12th and 13th, he met with Richard Armitage and Senator Joseph Biden, the chairman of the powerful Senate Committee on Foreign Relations that is dominated by the Rockefeller's Council on Foreign Relations. Armitage was fundamentally involved in organising the US government-CIA funding of the bin Laden-Mujahadin networks in Afghanistan via the ISI in Pakistan and was awarded the highest civil honour by Pakistan. After the Armitage-General Mahmoud "discussions", Pakistan, a military state with a long history of sponsoring terrorism (often for the CIA), then joined the "war on terrorism". The US State Department itself, in a document called Patterns of Global Terrorism,[14] confirms the connections between terrorism and the Pakistan military government of President Pervez Musharraf. Secretary of State Colin Powell said in a news conference on September 13th:

> "The United States remains concerned about reports of continued Pakistani support for the Taliban's military operations in Afghanistan. Credible reporting indicates that

Pakistan is providing the Taliban with material, fuel, funding, technical assistance, and military advisers. Pakistan has not prevented large numbers of Pakistani nationals from moving into Afghanistan to fight for the Taliban. Islamabad also failed to take effective steps to curb the activities of certain madrassas, or religious schools, that serve as recruiting grounds for terrorism." [15]

What he didn't say, of course, is that the madrassas were funded by the CIA and Saudi Arabia, and supervised by CIA assets like Sheikh Omar who was later convicted of the 1993 bombing of the World Trade Center thanks to a bomb built by an asset of the FBI. As Powell spoke these words, his deputy Richard Armitage was meeting with the head of Pakistan intelligence at the State Department. This was a staggering piece of mental gymnastics in which a sponsor of terrorism was asked to join the "war on terrorism". This was explained away as US officials seeking cooperation from Pakistan because it was the original backer of the Taliban. Well, on that basis, seek support from the CIA then. To an outsider with no knowledge of the Illuminati, their agenda and methods, this would all appear absurd, but from the Illuminati perspective it's not. They are simply playing their game of global manipulation and control, and that is not played on the basis of logic, as publicly perceived, but on the basis of whatever is necessary at the time to advance the agenda. One day you'll condemn a person, country or organisation to achieve a certain outcome and the next you'll do the opposite. Pakistan and Osama bin Laden are but two examples. The Pakistan intelligence chief Mahmud Ahmad was sent by the CIA and the Pakistan government (same thing) to "negotiate" with the Taliban for the extradition of Osama bin Laden. The "mission" failed, of course, because that is the last thing the Illuminati wanted. If bin Laden was handed over there could be no bombing of Afghanistan and there would never be enough evidence to convict him in a public court anyway. "Go negotiate, Mahmud, so we can claim to be trying to avoid conflict, but for God's sake don't succeed, OK?" "Yes, sir." Just as the bombing of Afghanistan began, the Pakistan government sacked Mahmud Ahmad under the guise of "early retirement" when the *Times* of India reported an alleged connection with Mohamed Atta. This included, said the *Times*, the transfer to Atta of $100,000. The *Agence France Press* also reported that:

"A highly-placed government source told AFP that the 'damning link' between the General and the transfer of funds to Atta was part of evidence which India has officially sent to the US. 'The evidence we have supplied to the US is of a much wider range and depth than just one piece of paper linking a rogue general to some misplaced act of terrorism,' the source said." [16]

The *Times* of India claimed that a guy called Ahmad Umar Sheikh made the transfer to Atta on the orders of the General Mahmud. Ahmad Umar Sayeed Sheikh is a British national and a London School of Economics graduate who was arrested by the police in Delhi following the bungled 1994 kidnapping of four westerners, including an American citizen.[17] The *Times* said its information was based on an official intelligence report sent by the Indian government to the United States. The US indictment against alleged conspirator Zacarias Moussaoui in December 2001 also claims that Atta was involved with a Mustafa Ahmed al-Hawsawi, or "Mustafa Ahmed", from Jeddah, Saudi Arabia, who was based in the months before 9/11 in Dubai, United Arab Emirates. The indictment says that on September 11th Mustafa Ahmed left the United Arab Emirates for … Pakistan. The names of Pakistan and Saudi Arabia continually recur in this story.

The killer question

The US had clearly long planned to launch a war against Afghanistan by mid-October. But here's the key question: how on earth would they ever have justified such a sudden invasion if the September 11th attacks on America had not happened when they did? They would have had no chance of gathering together public and political support for such an invasion, especially in the few months they had between the Niaz Naik meeting with American officials in mid-July and when the attacks were launched on October 7th. Why would they be so confident that they could pull it off, unless they knew that the public justification to do so was going to happen at precisely the right time? Instead of investigating such matters, the *Guardian* turned the revelation that the USA was planning to invade Afghanistan long before September 11th into further support for the official story. The paper suggested that this information meant that Osama bin Laden "far from launching the attacks on the World Trade Center in New York and the Pentagon out of the blue 10 days ago, was launching a pre-emptive strike in response to what he saw as US threats." [18] As I said earlier, there is nothing more imprisoning than an idea you will not let go. In this case, the idea that the official story of 9/11 is basically true and that Osama bin Laden did it. Until people let that go and look at the evidence dispassionately, they will go on trying to make the blatant anomalies and contradictions fit into the official story. I spoke to reporters on the *Boston Globe* and the *New York Post* and saw exactly the same reaction. The *Globe* reporter had seen for himself the clear contradictions in the NORAD story that jets were/were not scrambled. But the suggestion that government involvement in the attacks should be considered simply blew his mind and he would not even begin to go there. The *New York Post* reporter had written a lengthy article about 9/11, but it turned out to be a "clips job". In other words, he took his information from other media articles and had no idea of the sources. When I pointed out contradictions in the government's story he continually tried (and failed) to explain them away within the official version.

Elephant in the living room

The British forces used in the attacks on Afghanistan were based in Oman and here again we have a highly convenient "coincidence". Those forces did not leave Britain for Oman after September 11th, but a week earlier. On Monday, September 3rd, the biggest deployment of Royal Navy and Royal Marines since the Falklands War left the UK for long-planned (like the 9/11 attacks) "exercises" in Oman known as

Operation Swift Sword II led by the aircraft carrier *Illustrious*. This meant that by the time those planes struck the World Trade Center these UK forces were closing in on the very place they needed to be to take part in the subsequent attacks on Afghanistan. Put this together with everything else and red flags abound. I hear people saying "Oh no, these exercises were planned for four years." But as I have been saying in book after book, the major Illuminati problem-reaction-solutions are also planned years, even decades, in advance with a specific date in mind. The "task group" to Oman was led by Rear Admiral James Burnell-Nugent, Commander of the UK Maritime Forces, who said:

> "This is a significant display of maritime power – we are sending 8,500 sailors, airmen and Royal Marines to the Gulf Region. In total the Argonaut task group consists of 40 separate commands, brought together into an integrated, self sustaining joint fighting force." [19]

This is precisely what you need for an attack on Afghanistan and the ongoing war against sanity in the Middle/Near East. Some 23,000 British troops were involved in these "exercises", and also "on station" before September 11th were 17,000 US troops and 23,000 from NATO taking part in Operation Bright Star. These were more "exercises", this time in Egypt. Another location used for the attacks on Afghanistan was the US base at Diego Garcia in the Indian Ocean. This was "given" to the American government in the 1960s by the British Illuminati Prime Minister and Bilderberger, Harold Wilson. The entire population was forced to leave the island by the UK government to allow the US military to move in. Nice people. Stan Goff, a retired Master Sergeant in US Special Forces, studied and taught military science and doctrine. He was a tactics instructor at the Jungle Operations Training Center in Panama and taught military science at the US military academy at West Point, New York. Writing soon after September 11th, he said that, based on his experience in eight conflicts from Vietnam to Haiti, the story he was hearing from the media about the invasion of Afghanistan was simply not believable. "The most cursory glance at the verifiable facts, before, during, and after September 11th, does not support the official line or conform to the current actions of the United States government," Goff wrote. He said that an "elephant in the living room is being studiously ignored". He concluded on October 10th:

> "Given this evidence that a military operation to secure at least a portion of Afghanistan has been on the table, possibly as early as five years ago, I can't help but conclude that the actions we are seeing put into motion now are part of a pre-September 11th agenda. I'm absolutely sure of that, in fact. The planning alone for operations of this scale, that are now taking shape, would take many months. And we are seeing them take shape in mere weeks.

> "It defies common sense. This administration is lying about this whole thing being a 'reaction' to September 11th. That leads me, in short order, to be very suspicious of

their yet-to-be-provided evidence that someone in Afghanistan is responsible. It's just too damn convenient. Which also leads me to wonder – just for the sake of knowing – what actually did happen on September 11th, and who actually is responsible." [20]

Who is bin Laden?

To understand the real background to Osama bin Laden, the CIA asset and stooge, we need to go back more than a decade to the Soviet Union's occupation of Afghanistan between 1979 and early 1989. The major funding for the Mujahadin, the forces in Afghanistan resisting the occupation, came from the CIA and Saudi Arabia, and the channel for this support was Pakistan Interservices Intelligence, or ISI. Not only did the United States fund the resistance to the Soviet occupation, they had worked to make it happen in the first place. It is worth stressing that the Soviet Union did not invade as such because it was asked for help by the then Afghanistan government. Nur Mohammad Taraki, the leader of the ruling Marxist party, had introduced a regime in which women were treated with respect, farming debt had been abolished, there was a minimum wage, and plans were underway for major land reform. These policies were destroyed when the Mujahadin rebels, supported by the CIA, Saudi Arabia and Pakistan, launched a coup in September 1979 in which Taraki was murdered. The Marxists eventually removed the Mujahadin and returned to power, and that was when they asked the Soviet Union for help, and the tanks rolled in. No doubt the Soviet Union had oil and other interests in mind as well. In a 1998 interview with the French publication *Le Nouvel Observateur*, Zbigniew Brzezinski, the big-time Illuminati insider, said that the US had enticed the Soviet Union to invade Afghanistan. Brzezinski was National Security Adviser to President Jimmy Carter and a founder, with David Rockefeller, of the Illuminati's Trilateral Commission. This manipulates the global agenda into being along with other organisations in its network, like the Council on Foreign Relations, Royal Institute of International Affairs, Bilderberg Group, and other far more elite groupings and secret societies (see *And The Truth Shall Set You Free*). Brzezinski was also a founding force behind FEMA, the Federal Emergency Management Agency, which is a 100% Illuminati-controlled operation in the United States. He said:

> "According to the official version of history, CIA aid to the Mujahadin began during 1980, that is to say, after the Soviet army invaded Afghanistan, December 24, 1979. But the reality, secretly guarded until now, is completely otherwise. Indeed, it was July 3, 1979 that President Carter signed the first directive for secret aid to the opponents of the pro-Soviet regime in Kabul. And that very day, I wrote a note to the president in which I explained to him that in my opinion this aid was going to induce a Soviet military intervention."

Brzezinski said that they "knowingly increased the probability" that the Soviet Union would invade, yet at the time the United States government vehemently denied the Soviet claims that they had invaded to challenge the secret involvement of the US in Afghanistan, which had a pro-Soviet regime in power at the time. Brzezinski was asked if he regretted what he did:

> "Regret what? That secret operation was an excellent idea. It had the effect of drawing the Russians into the Afghan trap and you want me to regret it? The day the Soviets officially crossed the border, I wrote to President Carter: We now have the opportunity of giving to the USSR its Vietnam War ..."

The interviewer asked Brzezinski if regretted the support for Islamic fundamentalism and giving arms and advice to future terrorists:

> "What is most important to the history of the world? The Taliban or the collapse of the Soviet Empire? Some stirred-up Muslims or the liberation of Central Europe and the end of the Cold War?" [21]

The truth is that both the Soviet occupation of Afghanistan and the creation of a terrorist network by funding the Afghan resistance were part of the Illuminati strategy. Their agenda is not regulated by national borders or national interest, but by the simple law of cause and effect. It is like a chessboard on which, largely, they have controlled both sides. To hear Brzezinski say he has "no regrets" about goading the Soviet Union into a war that led to the deaths of one and half million Afghans and, through the Taliban, condemned the country and its women to the dark ages, is to understand the regard the Illuminati have for human life. I can't stress enough that if you judge what these guys will do on the basis of what you would do, you will never see what is really going on. The Illuminati do not have the same emotional responses that most of the global population do and they will do things that the rest of us could hardly comprehend. I will elaborate on the reasons for this in the final chapter. Remember, too, that while Jimmy Carter may have signed the first order for covert support of the anti-Soviet Mujahadin in 1979, this was his last year in office. Ronald Reagan and Father George Bush won the November 1979 election and they (Bush) were in power throughout the war between the Soviet Union and the Mujahadin in Afghanistan from the end of 1979 until 1989. During that time, Bush was unofficial president in the Reagan years and became official president in 1988.

Father George funded bin Laden

The funding of the Osama bin Laden terrorist network in Afghanistan during the Soviet occupation was arranged by George Bush, the close friend of the bin Laden family and father of the current President. One of the many reasons for Illuminati interest in Afghanistan has been the enormous opium production over the years. I can see the Bush family drooling from here. This was another motivation behind the CIA involvement in the country and it was through the agency's supply network that the opium was exported to be sold as heroin and destroy still more lives. After the American-backed Mujahadin had ousted the Soviet Union they forced farmers to plant opium in such quantities that Afghanistan became the biggest producer of heroin on the planet and much of it ended up on American streets. Two others involved in the funding of the terror network were the Illuminati operatives George Shultz, Secretary of State under Reagan-Bush, and Richard Armitage, the CIA drug runner who is now Deputy Secretary of State in the "war on terrorism"! For the final years of the invasion, the Soviet Union was led by Rockefeller place man Mikhail Gorbachev, who now runs a "foundation" in the United States calling for a world government, world army, etc., etc. (see *And The Truth Shall Set You Free*). You get the picture.

Al-Qaeda – courtesy of the CIA

One of the foremost authorities on recent Afghanistan history is Ahmed Rashid, the author of *Taliban: Militant Islam, Oil and Fundamentalism in Central Asia*.[22] He doesn't just write about what happened, he lived through it. In 1978 he was in Kabul when a palace coup ousted King Zahir Shah and booked him a ticket to Rome. A year later Rashid was in Kandahar in the south of Afghanistan when the Soviet tanks arrived. He says that the resistance army, the Mujahadin, had their roots in Afghanistan, but as the war continued others were brought in from outside by the CIA and the Saudis. These included Osama bin Laden and those who were to form the foundations of al-Qaeda and later the Taliban. Al-Qaeda emerged from an organisation called Maktab al-Khidamar, or MAK, which bin Laden was running by 1984 for the United States. It was funded and armed by the American government through Pakistan intelligence, the ISI. Rashid says that between 1986 and 1987 the CIA Director William "Iran-Contra" Casey provided 900 Stinger missiles to the Mujahadin along with US advisers. Casey planned, with British and Pakistan intelligence, guerrilla attacks by the Mujahadin in the then Soviet "republics" of Tajikistan and Uzbekistan. Most significantly, given subsequent events, this trio began to support plans by Pakistan intelligence (ISI) and Pakistan's President Zia to bring Muslims from all over the world to join the Soviet resistance groups in Afghanistan. Some 35,000 Islamic militants were trained to fight in Afghanistan. These were the non-Saudis that Michael Springman, the former head of the American visa bureau in Jeddah from 1987 to 1989, talks about. He said he was ordered to provide US visas for such people during the Reagan-Bush and Bush presidencies, and he revealed that they went to the United States for terrorist training by the CIA.

Terrorist training camps in the USA

There are many centres in the USA where foreign terrorists are trained. Among them is the Redstone Arsenal in Huntsville, Alabama. Al Martin, a retired Navy Lt Commander, says that one of the Iranians involved in the bombing of the World Trade Center in 1993 was trained there and completed an explosives course in the guise of a Pakistan officer. The Pakistan connection to 9/11 is extremely important. Martin, author of *The Conspirators: Secrets of an Iran-Contra Insider*,[23] says he was head of accounting for the drug-running operation orchestrated by the Reagan-Bush administration and involving Oliver North. Another CIA terrorist training centre is Fort Benning in Georgia where the School of the Americas has been producing terrorists and dictators to serve US interests in Latin America for decades. Literally hundreds of mass-murdering dictators, military leaders, death squad members, terrorists and human rights abusers have been through the ranks at the School of the Americas or "The School of the Assassins", where training manuals uncovered by the US Intelligence Oversight Board supported terrorism, torture, and human rights abuses. William Thomas writes in his book, *All Fall Down*:

"In training more than 60,000 Latin American and Caribbean government forces, the School of the Americas has spawned the region's most murderous tyrants. Graduates include Manuel Noriega, El Salvador death squad leader Roberto D'Aubuisson, and the former dictators of Argentina, Peru, Ecuador and Bolivia." [24]

There is indeed no shortage of training facilities for the terrorists created by the American and British governments now fighting the "war on terrorism". The Saudi royal family also became heavily involved in the recruitment of non-Afghan fighters and they funded new Islamic fundamentalist schools, or madrassas, in Afghanistan and Pakistan that would spawn the imprisoned, conditioned minds that became the Taliban. Sheikh Omar Abdel-Rahman, the man convicted with associates of the 1993 bombing of the World Trade Center, ran an operation called the Service Office in Peshawar, Pakistan, which recruited Muslim fighters for the CIA, Osama bin Laden, and the Mujahadin in Afghanistan.[25] The name Taliban literally means "students". Afghan writer Ahmed Rashid says that the Saudis took the opportunity to advance the influence of Wahabbism, their preferred form of Islam, which, as I know from my months in Saudi Arabia in the late 1970s, is a sick form of fascism. The Mujahadin were dominated by the Shia expression of Islam, while the Taliban, for the reasons described, would follow the extreme Saudi variety with its violent imposition of Islamic "law" (their version) and the utterly unimaginable abuse of women. Girls were not allowed in schools and women could not work. Public executions happened all the time for "crimes" like homosexuality and adultery. These guys were seriously deranged. While the United States and Britain wheeled out their "first ladies", Laura Bush and Cherie Blair, to condemn the Taliban's treatment of women, the truth is that this happened thanks to Saudi Arabia (which still treats women much the same way) and the governments and intelligence arms of the United States, Britain and Pakistan. The madrassas on the Pakistan border with Afghanistan were a very significant means of Taliban support. They were controlled by the Jamiat-e-Ulema Islam, a Pakistani-based Islamic extremist party. From here they supplied many Taliban recruits and provided a link between the Taliban and Pakistan Interservices Intelligence, the ISI.

Ahmed Rashid says that the ISI wanted a member of the Saudi royal family to join the Islamic mercenaries from around the world in Afghanistan. But there was no way these pampered hypocrites would leave their Saudi palaces for the unforgiving mountains of Afghanistan. The closest they could get was Osama bin

Laden who came from an immensely wealthy Saudi family with extremely strong connections to the "royals". He joined forces with Prince Turki, the Saudi intelligence chief, and General Gul, the head of the ISI. Rashid says these three were in constant contact. In turn, Gul was close to the CIA as the ISI acted, together with the BCCI, as a channel through which billions of dollars from the United States government found their way to bin Laden and the Mujahadin. This CIA money paid Bin Laden Construction to build the very "al-Qaeda" tunnel complexes the US bombed in the "war on terrorism"! Ahmed Rashid wrote of bin Laden:

> "He brought in engineers from his father's company and heavy construction equipment to build roads and warehouses for the Mujaheddin. In 1986, he helped build a CIA-financed tunnel complex, to serve as a major arms storage depot, training facility and medical center for the Mujaheddin, deep under the mountains close to the Pakistan border." [26]

With the end of the war with the Soviet Union in 1989, the battles began between Afghan factions for control of their now "free" country, and the Mujahadin enforced a policy for the mass production of opium and its processing into heroin. This also involved Osama bin Laden according to Michael Ruppert, a former drug investigator with the Los Angeles police. He says that bin Laden worked with Gulbadin Hekmatyar who ran six heroin factories in Afghanistan and Pakistan.[27] We are told that bin Laden returned to construction in Saudi Arabia when the Soviet . Union was ousted. But if he did, and I don't believe it, this was only for a while.

Enter the Taliban

As the generations grew up in Afghanistan who had no education except for the Islamic fundamentalism taught in the Saudi-funded "schools", a very different vision of religion, life and law began to dominate significant swathes of Afghan society, especially in the south. These were generations, says Ahmed Rashid, who had known only war, and many were orphans who had grown up without mothers or sisters, and had never known the unique gift of a woman's company and influence. Life expectancy was only around 44 years and 25% of children died before the age of five. The simple fundamental expression of their religion was the very foundation of their existence. It was all they had, and it was the United States and Britain, as well as the Saudis and the Soviet Union, who had created the circumstances for this. More than that, the USA, Britain and Saudi Arabia also supported the Taliban's campaign of war and terrorism against the Northern Alliance, the consortium of Afghan warlords from the former Mujahadin who were equally violent and dehumanised by the years of never-ending conflict. Mutual hate for the Taliban was pretty much all that held the Northern Alliance together. Ahmed Rashid points out that before the Taliban came to power, Prince Turki, the head of Saudi intelligence and close associate of Osama bin Laden, visited the Pakistan capital Islamabad, the home of the bin Laden-supporting ISI, and the Taliban stronghold of Kandahar.[28] After this visit, the Saudis gave money and arms to support the Taliban's attack on the capital, Kabul. This gave the Taliban control over most of the country in 1996 except for the region in the north that was still held by the Northern Alliance.[29] Far from opposing the Taliban, the United States government, Saudi Arabia, Pakistan, and the US and Saudi oil cartel were delighted with their rise to power. Indeed they were all involved in providing the finance and weaponry that allowed it to happen. From a ragbag of students, the Taliban had, in little more than a year, gathered together an army of some 20,000 men supported by ground and air weaponry. You simply don't do that without massive outside funding and supply. *Newsweek* also reported that Osama bin Laden provided $3 million to the Taliban that was used to bribe opponents to defect and open the route to Kabul in 1996.[30]

The Unocal and Delta-Nimir oil companies, which planned the pipelines across Afghanistan, were particularly pleased with events. Delta-Nimir was Mohamed Hussein Al-Amoudi and Khalid bin Mahfouz, both business associates of the Bush family and named by the US government in the Clinton years as funders of the bin Laden network. The Taliban victory promised the "stability" that would allow the pipelines to carry lucrative oil and gas from the Caspian Sea region across Afghanistan to the Arabian Sea coast of Pakistan. Chris Taggart, a Unocal executive, said that the Taliban victory would make the pipeline project "easier".[31] Ahmed Rashid writes that a US diplomat told him: "The Taliban will probably develop like the Saudis did. There will be Aramco, pipelines, an emir, no parliament and lots of Sharia law. We can live with that." [32] Glyn Davies, another State Department official, said the United States found 'nothing objectionable' in the steps taken by the Taliban to impose Islamic law.[33] He said the Taliban were anti-modern, not anti-western. They were actually anti-life. The war criminal Henry Kissinger, an "adviser" to Unocal, also predictably supported a pipeline deal with the Taliban and it was because of people like him that at no time before September 11th 2001 was Afghanistan named by the US government on its list of states that sponsor terrorism. Mind you, it doesn't list itself or Britain either.

So what if women would now be treated disgustingly and be denied even basic rights? So what if people would be beaten in the street or stoned to death by the Taliban's religious thought police who were nothing more than an "Islamic" SS? So what? We get our pipeline don't we? There were no bleeding hearts in Washington or London, and no demand that the Taliban be removed. Far from being condemned, Taliban leaders were flown to Texas and Washington to be feted by Unocal, the US State Department, and senators like Hank Brown, as negotiations continued for the pipeline deal. The Taliban were even represented by a public relations adviser called Laili Helms, the niece by marriage of Richard Helms, the former head of the CIA. Laili Helms was the Taliban's "unofficial ambassador in the US and their most active and best-known advocate elsewhere in the West".[34] Funny how the Taliban stopped Afghan women from taking careers, but were quite happy to be represented by one in the United States. Richard Helms, by the way, was CIA director in the 1960s, the period of Cuba and Vietnam. He was accused of destroying most of the CIA's secret documents that detailed the agency's own crimes. It was Helms who, as ambassador to Iran, arranged for the training of the notorious secret police of the then Shah.[35] The State Department also lobbied heavily for the Unocal project with both the Taliban and the Pakistan government when the rival offer by the Argentine company, Bridas, threatened to win their approval. Only when women's groups mounted a fierce campaign against the deal and the US government could see that the Northern Alliance resistance to the Taliban made their rule potentially unstable, did Unocal and friends withdraw from the negotiations while announcing that the project could only go ahead when a stable, internationally recognised, regime was in place in Afghanistan. Now, thanks to the "war on terrorism" spawned by 9/11, that's exactly what they have and the pipeline plans have been pulled from the pending file.

The US Republican Congressman Dana Rohrabacher exposed the real force behind the Taliban during Congressional hearings on July 12th 2000. Rohrabacher was an Afghanistan specialist who supported the former king, Zahir Shah. Since September 11th, and with the return to power of the king's supporters, Rohrabacher has gone quiet. But the year before, he had said that he knew the United States only sent "humanitarian aid" to Taliban-controlled areas and the State Department had shown no interest in pursuing information about the location of Osama bin Laden in Afghanistan. This is a constant pattern, as we will see. Rohrabacher said that while the State Department claimed to oppose bin Laden and the Taliban, the US government had been covertly supporting them. He also spoke of the way the United States had manipulated the Taliban into power in Kabul:

"At a time when the Taliban were vulnerable, the top person of this [Clinton] administration, Mr Inderfurth, and Bill Richardson, personally went to Afghanistan and convinced the anti-Taliban forces not to go on the offensive and, furthermore, convinced all of the anti-Taliban forces, their supporters, to disarm them and to cease their flow of support for the anti-Taliban forces. At that same moment, Pakistan initiated a major resupply effort, which eventually saw the defeat, and caused the defeat, of almost all of the anti-Taliban forces in Afghanistan. *[The very same forces the USA and Britain then supported to remove the Taliban after September 11th!]*

"Now, with a history like that, it's very hard, Mr Ambassador, for me to sit here and listen to someone say, 'Our main goal is to drain the swamp' – and the swamp is Afghanistan – because the United States created that swamp in Afghanistan. And the United States' policies have undercut those efforts to create a freer and more open society in Afghanistan, which is consistent with the beliefs of the Afghan people." [36]

Rohrabacher said that not only had the US government acted in a way that kept the Taliban in power, they also showed no interest in acting upon information he had offered the administration on at least three occasions of the precise location of bin Laden's headquarters in Afghanistan. Even in 2001 the Bush administration openly gave the Taliban $124.2 million, and one payment of $43 million was authorised by Secretary of State Colin Powell as late as May.

Bin Laden returns

The official story goes that somehow Osama bin Laden suddenly developed a deep hatred of the United States because of the attacks on Iraq in the Gulf War and their subsequent sanctions. His dramatic conversion to the "I Hate America" movement is supposed to have manifested even though bin Laden was funded and armed during the Soviet occupation by the CIA through the Bank of Credit and Commerce International (BCCI), Pakistan Interservices Intelligence (ISI), and the Saudi royal family; and despite the fact that he supported the victory of the Taliban, which was also funded by CIA-backed sources. I don't buy it myself. Nor do I purchase the claim that he has been "ostracised" by his family. The Bushes are extremely close to the bin Ladens and the Saudi royals, and it was Father George Bush who launched the attack on Iraq in 1991 that was supposed to have made bin Laden hate the United States. It was also during Bush's control of the White House that Osama bin Laden and the al-Qaeda network were funded and armed by the CIA. The "Osama supports Iraq" story doesn't make sense. As researcher Jared Israel points out on his excellent website,[37] there is an enormous difference between the harsh and extreme form of "Islam" that bin Laden claims to support and that of Iraq. The regime may be a dictatorship, but it does not impose Islam in anything like the same way as Saudi Arabia and Afghanistan under the Taliban. When bin Laden was backing the Taliban in their battle for control of Afghanistan, they were fighting a similar religious regime in Kabul to that in Iraq. Afghan writer Ahmed Rashid said of bin Laden: "After Iraq's invasion of Kuwait he lobbied the Saudi royal family to organise civil defense in the kingdom and to raise a force from among the Afghan war veterans to fight Iraq."[38] How does that fit with "Osama supports Iraq and he developed a hatred of the United States because of the Gulf War"? He is supposed to hate the American government because of the Gulf War and yet here he wanted to join in, according to Rashid. Then there is the claim that bin Laden was also incensed by the American military presence in the Islamic "Holy Land" of Saudi Arabia after Saddam Hussein invaded Kuwait. But hold on. As Jared Israel recounts, the bases the US occupied were built in the 1980s at a cost of more than $200 billion in the biggest US military construction project outside the United States.[39] Scott Armstrong, an investigative reporter on the *Washington Post*, told the US television show *Frontline* on February 16th 1993, that the Saudis themselves had provided most of the money, some $156 billion, which, he said, he could document line by line.

> "[The United States has] managed to create an interlocking system that has one master control base, five sub-control bases, any one of which is capable of operating the whole thing, that are in hardened bunkers, that are hard-wired, that is to say, against nuclear blast or anything else. They created nine major ports that weren't there before, dozens of airfields all over the kingdom. They have now hundreds of modern American fighter planes and the capability of adding hundreds more. The Saudis alone have spent $156 billion that I can document line by line, item by item, on weapon systems and infrastructure to support this."[40]

Guess who was a major contractor building these facilities in Saudi Arabia for the "hated infidels" of the United States, the facilities where American troops were located in the Islamic "Holy Land" when the Gulf War was launched? Yes, yes … Bin Laden Construction! This was happening at a time when Osama bin Laden was in Afghanistan and Bin Laden Construction was building the "al- Qaeda" tunnel complexes supported by their family friend and the real power in the White House in this period, Father George Bush.

Bin Laden, Bill Clinton and Kosovo

While Bill Clinton and Tony Blair were using NATO to bomb Serbia and Kosovo for 41 days in 1999, Osama bin Laden was also involved – on Clinton's "side". The Kosovo "Liberation" Army (KLA) and its offshoot, the National Liberation Army (NLA), were still more CIA fronts. They were fundamentally connected to, and financed by, the trafficking of drugs to the United States and throughout Europe. Drug agents in five countries believed this drug cartel to be one of the most powerful heroin smuggling organisations in the world and their operation became known as the "Balkan Route".[41] Greek Interpol said that Kosovo's ethnic Albanians were the primary sources of supply for cocaine and heroin in that country; France's Geopolitical Observatory of Drugs said the Kosovo Liberation Army was a key player in the drugs-for-arms business and was helping to transport $2 billion worth of drugs a year into western Europe; German drug agents said $1.5 billion in drug profits was laundered annually by Kosovo smugglers through as many as 200 private banks or currency exchange offices.[42] The company contracted to supply the US "peacekeeping" troops in the former Yugoslavia is Brown & Root, the drug-running subsidiary of Dick Cheney's Haliburton.

Despite this background, the drug-running, Osama bin Laden-supported KLA was presented in a very different light by Clinton and Blair. They told us the KLA were "freedom fighters" battling to save the ethnic Albanian Muslims in Kosovo from Serbian oppression. Yet, as the *Washington Times* reported, quoting "intelligence documents", members of the KLA were trained in Afghanistan and at Tropoje, Albania, in the terrorist camps run by Osama bin Laden.[43] Britain's *Sunday Times* quoted Fatos Klosi, the head of Albanian intelligence, as confirming that the network of Osama bin Laden sent units into the Serbian province of Kosovo.[44] The *Washington Times* reported that members of the former Mujahadin in Afghanistan were recruited to fight for the KLA, who, I stress, were controlled by the CIA and the United States and British governments. At the same time those same governments were blaming the 1998 US Embassy bombings in Nairobi, Kenya and Dar es Salaam, Tanzania, on Osama bin Laden. The State Department offered a reward of $5 million for his capture (yawn). Clinton had also bombed Sudan and Afghanistan in "retaliation" for the bombings. The same year the US government had condemned the KLA as a terrorist organisation that was funded by the heroin trade and Osama bin Laden. Now here was "NATO" (the US and Britain) supporting this same terrorist organisation with 41 days of bombing against civilian targets in which it was claimed by Serbia that 1,200 people were killed and 5,000 wounded. Once again manipulating behind the scenes in the Balkans on behalf of the Illuminati drug and oil interests was Richard Armitage, the current US Deputy Secretary of State.

"This is Osama bin Laden, CIA, Afghanistan"

The story of bin Laden turning against his former paymasters in America, the Saudi royal dictatorship, and being disinherited by his family, is complete crap. He was a CIA asset and he's still a CIA asset – and stooge. That's why Clinton refused to put him on trial when he had the chance in 1996, as I will explain shortly. That's why they refused a Taliban offer to hand over bin Laden, as French researcher Jean-Charles Brisard revealed in *Bin Laden: The Forbidden Truth*. That's why, as the BBC *Newsnight* programme reported, the present Bush administration told the FBI to back off investigating the bin Laden connection. That's why they didn't "find" him when they invaded Afghanistan despite killing at least 5,000 civilians while "looking" for him. According to Jean-Charles Brisard, the FBI's Deputy Director and head of anti-terrorism John O'Neill resigned in July 2001 because the US State Department was blocking the investigation into the bombing of the *USS Cole* – an attack blamed on the bin Laden network. Brisard said that O'Neill told him: "The main obstacles to investigate Islamic terrorism were US oil interests and the role played by Saudi Arabia in it." O'Neill became head of security at the World Trade Center and died in the attacks of September 11th. Brisard writes that O'Neill told him the US State Department (Powell and Armitage) "explicitly blocked" his investigations into bin Laden's activities. Brisard said: "We now know from different files that the FBI was starting investigations on different aspects of Saudi Arabian support [of bin Laden], and those investigations were all stopped, even under Clinton." [45] The Revolutionary Association of the Women of Afghanistan, which challenged the Taliban's horrific treatment of women, issued a statement on September 14th 2001 condemning the terrorist attacks against the United States. But they also summed up the real story of Osama bin Laden, the "pursuit" of whom, caused thousands of men, women and children, to be murdered by US and British bombing:

> "… the people of Afghanistan have nothing to do with Osama and his accomplices. But unfortunately we must say that it was the Government of the United States who supported Pakistani dictator General Zia-ul-Haq in creating thousands of religious schools from which the germs of Taliban emerged. In the similar way, as is clear to all, Osama has been the blue-eyed boy of the CIA." [46]

You want bin Laden? Er, no thanks

The official bin Laden biography says that he fell out with his former allies over the Gulf War and the US presence in Saudi Arabia, and he began to gather his terrorist reputation after being named as a conspirator in the 1993 bombing of the World Trade

Center (the work of the FBI, the CIA and Mossad). In 1996 he headed for Sudan, but what they don't tell you in the official CV is that in March of that year the Sudan Minister for Defence, Major General Elfatih Erwa, offered to extradite bin Laden to Saudi Arabia or the United States. Both offers were refused. The *Washington Post* reported the story, saying that Sudan had offered either to keep a close watch on him or arrest him for extradition.[47] Ironically, given more recent events, the Clinton administration said they could not put him on trial because they did not have enough evidence against him! They also said they were concerned about a "fundamentalist backlash" if they executed him. Anyway, why kill one of your own? The *Washington Post* said that US officials had told Sudan: "Just ask him to leave the country. Just don't let him go to Somalia." Major General Elfatih Erwa said he told the Americans that bin Laden would go to Afghanistan. He said the American officials replied: "Let him."[48] Here was an opportunity to put bin Laden on trial without a shot being fired, but it wasn't part of the Illuminati strategy so it didn't happen. That's the criteria for everything – is it part of the agenda or not? This is why events that seem so contradictory when you don't know the background make perfect sense when you do. On August 20th 1998, two years after the Sudanese offered to hand over bin Laden to the Clinton administration and were turned down, the same President Clinton ordered the bombing of the El Shifa pharmaceutical plant in Sudan producing 60% of the medicines for a desperate, starving, disease-ridden people. Clinton said the plant in Khartoum was producing chemical weapons and had links with Osama bin Laden, who was accused of involvement in the bombings that year at the US embassies in Kenya and Tanzania. But the United States government later had to admit its "mistake". The plant was not producing chemical weapons, just medicines. Goodness knows how many died and suffered in Sudan as a result of this "mistake". Clinton had been desperate to avert public attention at the time of the bombing from the revelations of his antics with the White House intern Monica Lewinsky.

Cindy's story

Still more confirmation that the authorities had no desire to locate and arrest bin Laden comes with the story of a British couple, Alan and Cindy Thompson, which they told to me after being ignored by everyone they had contacted in officialdom. They drove on their "honeymoon" through 18 countries to Kathmandu and back in a ten-year-old Sherpa van. They covered 22,366 miles over the period of a year and by May 1999 they were in Pakistan on the way home. They had driven through the Khyber Pass with an armed guard and were skirting the border of Afghanistan (*Figure 26 overleaf*). The main road from Dera Ismail Khan (DI Khan) to Quetta was blocked by flooding and they were directed by locals down a dirt track, which turned out to be 80 miles of rough dry river bed. It took them the best part of 11 hours to complete this part of the journey before they reached tarmac at a very small checkpoint just outside the small town of Zhob (formerly Fort Sanderman) and "started to rejoice". However, they found themselves faced with "a rather shady group of armed men, who stood blocking the road ahead". The men turned out to be friendly, but when they reached Zhob, they were surrounded by locals.

Figure 26: *The Pakistan/Afghanistan border towns where Alan and Cindy Thompson found evidence of a secret hideout of Osama bin Laden and visits by American government officials*

Cindy said that two policemen appeared from nowhere demanding to see their passports. They were allowed to go to a small hotel, but Cindy said, "the whole of Zhob followed us and the police insisted that we fill in some forms". She recalled to me:

"We parked our Sherpa in the hotel car park and asked to use one of the showers. We were shown to a room and were followed in by two young men. When we asked what they wanted they told us that they were security! We told them that we didn't need security and to leave us to have a shower. We then asked if we could buy some food. The hotel didn't have any food, but another young man offered to take us somewhere in town who would be able to cook us something to eat. He was calm and gentle natured, explaining that he wanted to be a tourist guide and move out of Zhob.

"His friend who tagged along was very different and took control of the conversation, making his views on politics and religion known to us in a very forceful manner ... 'Osama bin Laden and Islam for the world.' He told us: 'Osama is my hero.' When I started asking him questions about Osama, why was Osama his hero, and what had he done to be given the title hero, he conveniently told us that he was illiterate and couldn't speak English. In fact, his English was very good.

"This guy wasn't friendly and we wanted to leave and were feeling uncomfortable. On the way back to our Sherpa, the second young man was joking with passer's by about our conversation, mentioning bin Laden a number of times. We felt it obvious that he and others in the town knew Osama bin Laden."

Cindy said they knew that bin Laden was a very wanted man and the reward for his capture or location was standing at $5 million. They slept in the van overnight at the hotel in case they needed to move quickly, and left very early the following morning. When they arrived at Quetta, the last main town before they crossed into Iran, they saw a copy of *Dawn*, the English national paper of Pakistan. Inside was an article headed "More Foreigners Visit Afghan Border Areas" and they were shocked to find that they were mentioned, albeit inaccurately:

"Meanwhile, other foreign nationals were also in DI Khan … Mr Alan" [Cindy's husband Alan] "and Ms Cendy" "… passed the night in their vehicle No S176 ESU [it was actually F176, not S] within the Rose Hotel's premises."

The article went on to reveal how "… some intelligence agency people said that somehow the foreigners seem to have discovered the hide-out of Osama bin Laden and a further probe was on." What made this even more relevant is that the article revealed that this location had been visited on May 6th 1999 by "two US consulate officers from Peshawar", where they met the "commissioner and the political agent, South Waziristan". The newspaper also said that Australian High Commissioner, Geoffrey Allen, and his wife, had visited the location at the same time that Alan and Cindy Thompson were there. She said that an Afghani told them that a Swiss Embassy official was also visiting the area. The *Dawn* newspaper reported:

"The Australians all the while stayed in DI Khan and the High Commissioner was seen to [be] under strict surveillance of a secret agency. However, early Friday morning Mr Geoffrey Allen rather surreptitiously left the Circuit House in his car and returned after about 90 minutes … the political agent South Waziristan, Arbab Mohammad Hanif, was also in DI Khan on Thursday and Friday."

Why all this activity by officials of the United States, Australian, and Swiss governments in a remote location that just happened to be an alleged hideout of Osama bin Laden? As the *Dawn* newspaper article said: "… The foreigners in the area had the same destination, Zhob in Balochistan, which is situated near the Afghan border with Pakistan … It is for the first time that such activity has been observed in this area [the road from Zhob to DI Khan], which had virtually remained out of bounds even for the locals." The paper reported official denials of sightings of United States commandoes and a US base in northwestern parts of Pakistan, an area called Waziristan.

Alan Thompson contacted the British Embassy in Islamabad, who did not at first believe they were even in Pakistan. They were advised to take the first flight out, but they couldn't because of their vehicle. Instead, Malcolm Bennett, the British Embassy Warden, was sent to collect them under armed guard and take them to a safe house. While they were there they were invited to a garden party for ex-patriots, hosted by a friend of Malcolm Bennett. Some of the people at the party were aid agency employees, from both America and the UK, who were working on aid projects in Afghanistan and Pakistan. Cindy said that one of the American aid workers told her he had to "move his office in Kandahar because Osama bin Laden had set up office next door"! When they arrived back in the UK, the couple saw an article calling for the capture of bin Laden. They said they phoned the London police headquarters at New Scotland Yard and told their story to an officer with the Anti-Terrorist Squad. Cindy said he told her they would probably be interviewed. They never were. They wrote to the FBI, via the American Embassy in London, but did not receive even an acknowledgement. They followed up with letters to the

Pentagon, but it was the same story. No response. They contacted the BBC and national newspapers, but no one wanted to know. Cindy said that she contacted the foreign editor of the *Observer* newspaper, which was stating that bin Laden might be hiding in Pakistan. "He told me in a most rude manner that, 'Bin Laden didn't hide in Pakistan, but lived in Afghanistan in a cave!' ... then slammed the receiver down before I even had chance to ask when he last visited Pakistan to know such a thing for sure." She said she then posted her story on the CBN news website bulletin board, under the heading: "I found the secret hide out of Osama bin Laden, but no one wants to know. Why?" She said her story "was censored and taken off the website within 10 minutes, stating that it had been censored by the web master ... I re-posted it and it was removed again". After 9/11, the couple re-contacted New Scotland Yard Anti-Terrorist Squad, but still they received no reply. This was Cindy Thompson's summary of their whole experience:

> "We were gobsmacked. We found it incredible that we were offering to give first-hand true information about the most wanted man in the world and the US Embassy couldn't even be bothered to get off their butts and come and interview us! ... We feel that it is about time that this story is told to the world to let the people know the truth to make up their own minds. I believe the truth is: the hunt for bin Laden is a farce. Which makes the $5 billion reward for his capture a farce. Which must make the war on terror a farce. Which in turn makes the governments waging the phoney war a farce. Which of course must make the system that puts the governments into power a farce. It's all such a farce."

That's exactly what it is.

Bin Laden and the Taliban

Bin Laden returned to Afghanistan from Sudan in 1996 and enjoyed great influence with the Taliban and their leader Mullah Omar. Bin Laden ran his "terrorist training camps" from the very caves and tunnel complexes built with Saudi and CIA funds by Bin Laden Construction, and these camps were populated by many of the fanatics brought from all over the world to Afghanistan during the Soviet invasion by the CIA, Saudi Arabia and Pakistan. The United States government had supported these people to achieve one part of the agenda, now they would turn against them to achieve another – the "war on terrorism" that followed September 11th. It is clear that bin Laden, while being accused of terrorism by the United States government and its agencies like the CIA, has, at the same time, been funded and protected by them. This may sound strange, but when people appreciate the nature of the Illuminati agenda and its techniques of manipulation, it makes perfect sense. You need a "baddie" on which to focus public outrage and fear, and this allows you to go about your covert business behind the "baddie" smokescreen. Remember Colonel Gaddafi in Libya? He was a threat to the world at one stage, apparently, the Saddam Hussein of the time, and the "most wanted" terrorist mastermind on earth. Whatever happened to him? He's just another "monster" who has been surpassed by others in the game – the game of mass mind manipulation. Osama bin Laden has never ceased to be an asset and stooge of the CIA and the Saudi royal family. It was even reported by the French daily *Le Figaro*, among others, that bin Laden was visited by a CIA agent at the American Hospital in Dubai, United Arab Emirates, while being treated for a kidney infection between July 4th and 14th 2001, just weeks before September 11th, and members of his family (you know, the ones that ostracised him) were also among the visitors.[49]

Air bin Laden?

The question of how Osama bin Laden and the Taliban leader Mullah Omar escaped from Afghanistan might be answered by the news that in November 2001, soon after the US and British bombing began, leaders of the Taliban and members of al-Qaeda were flown out of the northern Afghan city of Kunduz to safety in Pakistan. How many other similar flights were made we don't know. Seymour Hersh, Defense Correspondent for the *New Yorker* magazine, said a senior intelligence source had confirmed that members of the Taliban and al-Qaeda "accidentally" escaped during the United States-supported evacuation of Pakistan military officials from the town.[50] "Dirt got through the screen", the source is quoted as saying. I think the screen was covered in shit to start with and "Pakistan military officials" were hand in glove with the Taliban and bin Laden anyway. The US military "may" have directly cooperated in the airlifts, the article said, and US central command was ordered to establish a special air corridor to ensure safe passage for the "rescue flights". Alleged targets of the US and British bombing were flown to safety while the men, women and children of Afghanistan and the Taliban foot soldiers were left to their fate. Defense Secretary Donald "aspartame" Rumsfeld had strenuously denied that the flights took place. While the flights were happening in November 2001, Rumsfeld said in typical Illuminati reverse speech: "If we see them, we shoot them down. Any idea that those people should be let loose on any basis at all to leave that country and destabilise other countries is unacceptable." More lies. Decoded, he said: "If we see them we don't shoot them down. Any idea that those people should be let loose on any basis at all to leave that country and destabilise other countries is thoroughly acceptable and suits us perfectly." When faced with the *New Yorker* story, Rumsfeld still denied the airlift took place: "I do not believe it happened. No one that I know connected with the United States in any way saw any such thing as a major air exodus out of Afghanistan into Pakistan." (Because they were looking the other way at the time.) Brajesh Mishra, the Indian National Security Minister, is quoted as saying that as many as 5,000 Pakistanis (Taliban and al-Qaeda among them) were rescued.

Patsy bin Laden

Despite all this funding and support of the Taliban and bin Laden from the United States, and their refusal to arrest or investigate him when the chance was there, he was immediately named as the man behind September 11th. When a problem-reaction-solution is being orchestrated you lay the false blame as quickly as possible to focus public attention on the diversion and ensure that those really responsible remain uninvestigated and unexposed. Bin Laden was named for a number of reasons. These included the fact that as a "Mr Big" terrorist, so the story goes, he has his "network" all over the world. Any country in fact that the US and British Illuminati factions want to demonise, bomb and take over in their open-ended "war on terrorism". More immediately it gave them the excuse to bomb the men, women and children of Afghanistan, remove the Taliban, and ensure that they can build and defend the pipelines that will give them control of the Caspian Sea oil and gas. I don't believe the al-Qaeda "network" is anything like as extensive as we're told and nor that bin Laden is its ultimate controller. I have heard from two separate people with contacts into the intelligence community in the United States that Osama bin Laden was dead before September 11th and everything since relating to him has been a Hollywood movie. What better way to ensure that you have complete control of the story? Amazing, I grant you, but that's what they say.

If bin Laden was planning the brilliantly organised attacks that we saw on September 11th, the idea that the CIA and connected agencies would not have known about it is ludicrous. Bin Laden has moved around Afghanistan with a huge entourage and could have been located any time, just as David Koresh could have been arrested again and again when he left the Waco compound without the need to murder men, women and children, as they did so coldly and deliberately in 1993. These guys can read your licence plate from space and yet they could not track bin Laden, either in the years before 9/11 or since? What a laugh. The infamous Echelon surveillance network, operated by the United States from locations like Menwith Hill in Yorkshire, England, constantly monitors telephone, fax, and e-mail communications around the world by using "key words" and voice identification technology to pick out those of most interest to the intelligence agencies. Particular targets, like suspected terrorists, are directly monitored through this system. Echelon appears to have been designed by the National Security Agency (NSA) based at Fort Meade, between Washington and Baltimore, and it is connected with "collecting" stations around the world that monitor Internet, fax, phone calls, databases, and e-mails, together with "all telexes carried over the world's telecommunications networks, along with financial dealings: money transfers, airline destinations, stock information, data on demonstrations or international conferences, and much more".[51] A former Defense Intelligence Agency official told United Press International (UPI): "It's a pretty awesome capability." Echelon can also intercept all the messages carried by the communications satellites positioned above the equator and each of them can process hundreds of thousands of e-mails, phone calls and telexes as well as monitoring undersea cables. Days after September 11th the German daily newspaper, *Frankfurter Allgemeine Zeitung* (FAZ) reported that US and Israeli intelligence agencies had received warning signals at least three months earlier through the Echelon system that Middle Eastern terrorists were planning to hijack commercial aircraft to use as weapons to attack important symbols of American and Israeli culture. British intelligence agencies also had advance warning, the paper said, quoting German intelligence sources.[52]

They knew exactly where bin Laden was, before and after, but they did nothing because that was not the idea. The *Baltimore Sun* reported five months before the attacks that National Security Agency officials "... have sometimes played tapes of bin Laden talking to his mother to impress members of Congress and select visitors to the agency".[53] Richard Sale, the UPI International Terrorism Correspondent, reported seven months before September 11th how a US government case against bin Laden in the United States District Court in Manhattan was "based mainly on National Security Agency (NSA) intercepts of phone calls between bin Laden and his operatives around the world – Afghanistan to London, from Kenya to the United States".[54] Khalid Al Fawwaz, who was on trial, allegedly ran bin Laden's "media information office" in London and provided bin Laden with a satellite phone, the indictment said, "to facilitate communications". Instead, said the UPI report, it allowed the US and British authorities to listen in on bin Laden's conversations. Sale wrote that when UPI wanted to send information to a former CIA official about Ayman al-Zawahiri, a senior bin Laden military commander and organiser, the CIA man exclaimed: "My God, don't put that in an e-mail," and indicated that the worldwide listening system would "light up". "NSA has huge watch lists," he said. Ben Venzke, the Director of Intelligence, Special Projects, for iDefense, a Virginia information warfare firm, said that since 1995, bin Laden has tried to protect his communications with a "full suite of tools", but "the codes were broken", US officials said.[55] I thought these 9/11 attacks were being planned by bin Laden for years? How did he do this without, it seems, mentioning it in any of the communications monitored by the national security apparatus of the United States with an annual budget of more than $30 billion? Did he organise it by telepathy or what? *Village Voice* journalist Russ Kick in his article detailing the prior warning of the 9/11 attacks described the situation perfectly:

"The US has the Central Intelligence Agency, the Federal Bureau of Investigation, the National Security Agency, the Defense Intelligence Agency, the National Reconnaissance Office, the Secret Service, and a host of other intelligence and security agencies. These agencies employ Echelon, which monitors the majority of electronic communication in the world; Carnivore, which intercepts email; Tempest, a technology that can read a computer monitor's display from over a block away; Keyhole satellites that have a resolution of four inches; and other spy technologies, probably most of which we don't know about. In 2001, the US spent $30 billion on intelligence gathering and an additional $12 billion on counterterrorism. With all of these resources, and more, we're supposed to believe that the government didn't have the slightest inkling that terrorists were planning to attack the United States, much less hijack planes and send them careering into major landmarks." [56]

Stan Goff, a former US Special Forces Master Sergeant, trained troops in the art of planning and warfare. This is his view:

"This cartoon heavy they've turned bin Laden into makes no sense, when you begin to appreciate the complexity and synchronicity of the attacks. As a former military person who's been involved in the development of countless operations orders over the years, I can tell you that this was a very sophisticated and costly enterprise that would have left what we call a huge 'signature'. In other words, it would be very hard to effectively conceal." [57]

Unless, of course, those who should have been defending America from such attacks were the ones who were planning them. Bin Laden's first reaction to the coordinated and pre-arranged allegations against him was to deny involvement. He told the Karachi-based *Ummat* newspaper:

"I have already said that I am not involved in the 11 September attacks in the United States. As a Muslim, I try my best to avoid telling a lie. I had no knowledge of these attacks, nor do I consider the killing of innocent women, children and other humans as an appreciable act. Islam strictly forbids causing harm to innocent women, children and other people. Such a practice is forbidden even in the course of battle. It is the United States which is perpetrating every maltreatment on women, children and common people." [58]

The latter is quite obviously true and it may well be correct that he knew nothing about the attacks, unless the CIA told him, but the rest of it does not fit the bin Laden profile in Afghanistan, Kosovo and elsewhere. I just can't see him going about his business never telling a lie or worrying about the effect on "innocent women, children, and other humans". What about the torture and murder of innocent women by the Taliban regime that he helped to fund, arm, and maintain in power? It's bollocks Osama, absolute bollocks. But was he the "mastermind" behind the September 11th attacks? You must be joking. Journalist Robert Fisk has met bin Laden in both Sudan and Afghanistan, and he wrote in the UK *Independent* the day after the attacks: "If Mr bin Laden was really guilty of all the things for which he has been blamed, he would need an army of 10,000." [59] Fisk went on:

"His supporters would gather round him with the awe of men listening to a messiah. And the words they listened to were fearful in their implications. American civilians would no more be spared than military targets. Yet I also remember one night when Mr bin Laden saw a pile of newspapers in my bag and seized them. By a sputtering oil lamp, he read them clearly unaware of the world around him. Was this really a man who could damage America?"

Bin Laden is a CIA stooge, manipulated to his bootstraps, should he wear them. He was used to front up the Afghanistan war with the Soviet Union and he's been used to front up the terrorist camps full of CIA-trained Islamic fanatics from around the world. These misguided, mind-controlled, pawns like bin Laden and his followers, are used as diversions and convenient villains to hide those who are really behind the terrorist attacks of the last decade. These attacks have advanced the Illuminati agenda of centralised control and the dismantling of basic freedoms, and never more so than since 9/11. It could well be that bin Laden, if he's still alive, is largely unaware that he is a carefully created fall guy and it is far from impossible that he may actually believe that operatives connected to his network were responsible. It may be that he knows he's a patsy. He may even be a willing one and that is why he was allowed to escape from Afghanistan and the US and British governments suddenly lost interest in finding him. It may be that he is already dead and that we have been treated to a series of clones or look-alikes since September 11th. Nothing is worth dismissing in this high-tech Alice in Wonderland without investigating the evidence first. Personally, I would not trust for a second the Al-Jazeera TV station in Qatar, the "Arabic CNN", which has been the source of bin Laden's video statements about the attacks and their aftermath. Qatar is an American puppet state and home to the biggest storage base for the US military outside of America.[60] Al-Jazeera was launched in 1996 and financed by the Emir of Qatar, Sheikh Hamad Bin-Khalifah Al Thani. After an approach from Vice President Cheney, the Emir ensured that Al-Jazeera did not broadcast a video interview with bin Laden in October 2001. Are we really supposed to believe that an Emir and a state so close to the US government is going to be allowed to broadcast information that really harms the interests of those controlling the American administration? Of course not. What they broadcast is largely what suits the Bush crowd to broadcast – including the "video statements" by the man claimed to be Osama bin Laden after September 11th. We don't even know if it is, that is only what we are told. How do we know? Through these Al-Jazeera statements by bin Laden he has sung a rather different tune to his initial claims of not wanting to harm innocent civilians. He has welcomed and gloried in the attacks, while never actually claiming responsibility for them. In one pre-recorded statement, broadcast when the bombing of Afghanistan began, he said:

"God Almighty hit the United States at its most vulnerable spot ... When Almighty God rendered successful a convoy of Muslims, the vanguards of Islam, He allowed them to destroy the United States. I ask God Almighty to elevate their status and grant them Paradise." [61]

Not coincidentally, these "statements" came at just the right time to boost the Bush-Blair campaign that was seeking support for the bombing and invasion of Afghanistan. Osama bin Laden was not the mastermind behind the attacks on September 11th and so Bush, Blair and their criminal conspiracy have never been able to produce the evidence that he was. Instead they have had to reply on lies, bluff and manipulation, and the knowledge that people have short memories and succumb very easily to the conditioned reality that results from simple repetition.

SOURCES

1   US 'Planned Attack on Taleban', BBC News Online, September 18th 2001

2   *Guardian*, September 22nd 2001

3   Ibid

4   Ibid

5   *Bin Laden: The Forbidden Truth*

6   Zbigniew Brzezinski, *The Grand Chessboard, American Primacy and it's Geostrategic Imperatives* (Basic Books, 1997)

7   Ibid, p 40

8   How CIA Tried to Save Afghan Guerilla, *Washington Post*, October 29th 2001

9   *Guardian*, November 2nd 2001, full transcript at **http://www.ceip.org/files/Publications/lievendispatch-haq.asp?from=pubdate**

10   *Times of India*, October 29th 2001

11   The Tragedy of Abdul Haq, How the CIA betrayed an Afghan freedom-fighter, by Robert McFarlane, *Wall Street Journal*, November 2nd, 2001 **http://www.opinionjournal.com/editorial/feature.html?id=95001406**

12   The Indian SAPRA news agency, May 22nd 2001

13   Statement released on September 14th 2001

14   **http://www.state.gov/s/ct/rls/pgtrpt/2000**

15   Answer to journalist's question to Secretary of State Colin Powell, State Department Briefing, September 13th 2001

16   *Agence France Press*, October 10th 2001

17   India Helped FBI Trace ISI-terrorist Links, *Times of India*, October 12th 2001

18   *Guardian*, September 29th 2001

19   Royal Navy press release, September 2001

20   **http://www.narconews.com/goff1.html**

21   *Le Nouvel Observateur*, January 15th – 21st 1998, p 76

22   Ahmed Rashid, *Taliban: Militant Islam, Oil and Fundamentalism in Central Asia* (Yale University Press, January 2000)

23   Al Martin, *The Conspirators: Secrets of an Iran-Contra Insider* (New Improved Entertainment Corporation, August 2001)

24   *All Fall Down*, p 70

25   **http://www.thenewamerican.com/tna/1997/vo13no05/vo13no05_assets.htm**

26   How a Holy War Against the Soviets turned on US, by Ahmed Rashid, *Pittsburgh Post-Gazette*, September 23rd 2001, Two Star edition, p A-12

27   *The Truth and Lies of 9/11*, video recording of Michael Ruppert speaking at Portland State University, November 28th 2001

28   *Taliban: Militant Islam, Oil and Fundamentalism in Central Asia*, p 166

29   Ibid, p 201

30   *Newsweek*, October 13th 1997

31   *Taliban: Militant Islam, Oil and Fundamentalism in Central Asia*, p 166

32   Ibid, p 179

33   How America Courted the Taliban, by Ishtiaq Ahmad, *Pakistan Observer*, October 20th 2001

34   Richard Helms's Afghani Niece Leads Corps of Taliban Reps and the Accidental Operative by Camelia Fard and James Ridgeway, **http://www.villagevoice.com/newsletter/popup.php**

35   Ibid

36   Hearing of the House International Relations Committee on Global Terrorism and South Asia, July 12th 2000

37   **http://emperors-clothes.comhttp://emperors-clothes.com**

38   How a Holy War against the Soviets Turned on US", by Ahmed Rashid, *Pittsburgh Post-Gazette*, September 23rd 2001, Two Star edition, p A-12

39   **http://www.tenc.net/news/probestop-i.htm**

40   *Frontline*, show number 1112, The Arming of Saudi Arabia, February 16th 1993

41   KLA Rebels Train in Terrorist Camps, *Washington Times*, May 4th 1999

42   Ibid

43   Ibid

44   Reported in the *Charleston Gazette*, November 30th 1998, p 2A

45   **http://www.salon.com/politics/feature/2002/02/08/forbidden/print.html**

46   Press statement, September 14th 2001

47   *Washington Post*, October 3rd 2001

48   Ibid

49   *Le Figaro*, November 1st 2001

50   *New Yorker*, January 21st 2002

51   NSA Listens to bin Laden, *UPI*, February 13th 2001

52   Echelon Gave Authorities 3 Month Warning Of Attacks – German Paper, **Newsbytes.com**, September 13th 2001

53   *Baltimore Sun*, April 24th 2001

54   NSA listens to bin Laden, UPI, February 13th 2001

55   Ibid

56   Russ Kick, *Village Voice*, September 2001

57   **http://www.narconews.com/goff1.html**

58   *Ummat*, September 28th 2001

59   Robert Fisk, Is the World's Favourite Hate Figure to Blame?, *Independent*, September 12th 2001

60   **ArabicNews.com** Qatar-USA, Politics, November 24th 1998

61   BBC News Online, October 7th 2001

chapter 14

"Bin Laden did it"

"The whole aim of practical politics is to keep the populace alarmed and hence, clamorous to be led to safety, by menacing it with an endless series of hobgoblins – all of them imaginary."

Henry Louis Mencken

O sama bin Laden is not considered guilty of the September 11th attacks because of the evidence against him. How could he be? None worth a dime in a court of justice has been presented. He is, instead, guilty by repetition – the repetition of the claim that he is guilty. That's it. But then, as we have seen, Adolf Hitler said:

> "The masses indulge in petty falsehoods every day, but it would never come into their heads to fabricate colossal untruths and they are not able to believe in the possibility of such monstrous effrontery ... The bigger the lie, therefore, the more likely it is to be believed ... Besides, even the most insolent lie always leaves traces behind it, even after it has been nailed down." [1]

What a summary of September 11th and its aftermath. The Nazi techniques are being used today because the same mentality and network is in power. When the Taliban were told by Bush to hand over bin Laden ("please don't, we want to bomb you") they asked for important little details from the US, like the evidence that he was responsible. President Bush's reaction encapsulates the fascist state unfolding before our eyes: "There's no need to discuss innocence or guilt, we know he's guilty." [2] Secretary of State Colin Powell said that bin Laden was definitely to blame and they would be producing compelling evidence to prove it. But they never did. When the time came to reveal this "evidence" Powell said he could not make the information public because it was "classified". Yes and filed under "piece of crap". But the Illuminati agenda demanded brutal attacks on the Afghan people and they had to generate public and political support for the invasion. To do that they needed people to believe that the Afghanistan-based bin Laden was responsible for 9/11 and it was left to Tony Blair, the UK's Illuminati Prime Minister, to try to kid the public with the "evidence" that never was.

The Blair "dossier"

Blair read a "dossier" to a compliant House of Commons on October 3rd 2001, watched by the non-researching, unquestioning, "leaders of the opposition" in the Conservative and Liberal Democrat parties. If either really thought it was a scam (no evidence that they did) they would not have had the guts to say so because of the perceived effect on their political prospects. The opening sentence of this "dossier of evidence" against bin Laden was a classic: "This document does not purport to provide a prosecutable case against Usama bin Laden in a court of law." No, Mr Blair, but it is more than enough to justify the murder of at least 5,000 Afghan men, women and children, who had nothing whatsoever to do with bin Laden, isn't it? Blair and Bush are war criminals and to a far greater extent than those they condemn and put on show trials like the former Serbian leader Slobodan Milosevic, who may not be a nice man to say the least, but he is not in the class of Blair and the Bush family when it comes to the slaughter of the innocent. The 21-page document that claimed to show that bin Laden was responsible was summed up in an article by former US Special Forces Master Sergeant Stan Goff:

> "The so-called evidence is a farce. The US presented Tony Blair's puppet government with the evidence, and of the 70 so-called points of evidence, only nine even referred to the attacks on the World Trade Center, and those points were conjectural. This is a bullshit story from beginning to end. Presented with the available facts, any 16-year old with a liking for courtroom dramas could tear this story apart like a two-dollar shirt. But our corporate press regurgitates it uncritically. But then, as we should know by now, their role is to legitimize." [3]

This Blair "report" was compiled by such trustworthy organisations as MI5 and MI6, with their drafts going to Washington and the CIA for approval. Would these people lie to you? Surely not. As you would expect, the "report" is full of mind games to hide the simple fact that the hard evidence it produced to support the "bin Laden did it" campaign was, er, zilch. Instead of that, we have lines like: "The clear conclusions reached by the government are: Osama bin Laden and Al Qaida, the terrorist network which he heads, planned and carried out the atrocities on 11 September 2001." The bigger the lie the more will believe it and the more you repeat the lie the more effective it will be. The Blair "evidence" document says that: "Usama Bin Laden [was] … linked to the attack on the *USS Cole* on 12 October 2000, in which 17 crew members were killed and 40 others injured".[4] What he doesn't say is that the FBI was blocked by Bush from investigating that involvement. The document is page after page of old information not related to the events of September 11th and the brief references to those attacks are unsubstantiated allegations with no sources presented. At one point Blair said that three of the 19 hijackers had been "positively identified as associates of Al Qaida" and one had been "identified as playing key roles in both the East African embassy attacks and the *USS Cole* attack". First of all what is meant by an "associate" and second, as we have seen, the head of the FBI has admitted that he cannot prove who the "hijackers" really were. Look at how many the FBI named – and continues to name – who are still alive. The man Blair links to the embassy and *Cole* attacks is supposed to be Khalid al-Midhar or Mihdhar. But, as the UK *Guardian* reported, this man's identity is the subject of much confusion because it was believed that he was using several aliases and, the paper said, American investigators "are not even certain that his name is really Khalid al-Mihdhar." [5] How can the FBI be so certain that Khalid al-Mihdhar was on Flight 77 and make a link between him and bin Laden? In fact, according to *Arab News*, a young Saudi computer programmer called Khalid Al-Mihammadi had "the shock of his life when he saw that his picture was among the suspects who had hijacked American Airlines Flight 77 that crashed into the Pentagon in Washington on Sept. 11". [6] The picture was claimed by the FBI to be al-Mihdhar, but it appears to have been Al-Mihammadi, who had studied English in the United States for nine months and returned to Saudi Arabia earlier that year.

Blair also said in his statement of "evidence" that they had learned since September 11th that bin Laden "himself asserted shortly before 11 September that he was preparing a major attack on America". He gave no source as usual, but this "evidence" would appear to be the claim that bin Laden telephoned his mother in Syria the day before the attacks to say there was going to be some "big news" and he might not be contactable for some time. Can you really imagine him doing that on the day before the attacks were due to take place? Are we to believe that the CIA was not tapping the phones of bin Laden's family and associates if they really were trying to catch him? Why didn't they know of the call before the attacks, then? Bin Laden's mother, Alia Ghanem, said in a newspaper interview that he had not called her in six years for the very reason of preventing his location being traced. [7] The get-out clause for Blair and Powell when they were asked for real evidence was always the same. Blair told the House of Commons: "There is evidence of a very specific nature relating to the guilt of bin Laden and his associates that is too sensitive to release." Oh, so we just have to trust you then, Tone? Don't think so mate. This nonsense was supported by Lord Robertson, the Secretary General of NATO, Bilderberger, and former Defence Secretary in the Blair government. Perhaps the most laughable statement by Blair, and it had plenty of competition, was when he claimed, "No other organisation has both the motivation and the capability to carry out attacks like those of the 11 September – only the Al Qaida network under Usama bin Laden." What about the United States national "security" network with its $30 billion a year official budget, plus all the profits from drugs and other covert operations? This has fundamental connections with the vast US military and government machine and other intelligence networks like British intelligence, German intelligence and Mossad. It is a grouping with the power, money, and technology both to carry out the attacks and to block the normal security response that allowed them to happen. Are they more likely to be able to pull off such a highly professional operation, or a guy in a cave of whom journalist Robert Fisk wrote: "… Mr bin Laden saw a pile of newspapers in my bag and seized them … By a sputtering oil lamp, he read them clearly unaware of the world around him"?

Three months before 9/11, Tony Karon took the same line in his analysis of bin Laden in *Time* magazine:

"… The media's picture of Bin Laden sitting in a high-tech Bat cave in the mountains around Kandahar ordering up global mayhem at the click of a mouse is more than a little ludicrous. Yes, the various networks of Islamist terror have made full use of the possibilities presented by technology and globalization. But few serious intelligence professionals believe Bin Laden is the puppet-master atop a pyramid structure of terror cells. It's really not that simple, but personalizing the threat – while it distorts both the nature of the problem and the remedy – is a time-honored tradition. Before Bin Laden, the face of the global terror threat against Americans belonged to the Palestinian radical Abu Nidal. Or was it Colonel Ghaddafi? Ayatolla Khomeini, perhaps? And does anyone even remember the chubby jowls of Carlos the Jackal, whose image drawn from an old passport picture was once the icon of global terror?" [8]

Wag the "bin Laden" video

With more and more questions being asked about the lack of evidence to justify attacks on Afghanistan, a stone-age country in the middle of a famine, the Bush-Blair terrorism network had an amazing piece of good luck. Just when they needed it, the bin Laden "confession" video turned up. Phew, what a relief. The "confession" is like a scene from the 1998 movie *Wag The Dog*,[9] which is so close to the truth. A US president is about to face an election for a second term when his aides realise that the story of a sexual affair is about to hit the press. They hire a Hollywood producer played by Dustin Hoffman to create a non-existent US war with Albania to take news of the affair off the front pages. They pick Albania because they figure no one in America would even know where it was or certainly nothing about the place. There is no actual war; they just kid the people that there is. It all takes place in a movie studio where interviews and "war footage" are created and then handed to the television news networks as "footage from the front." If you haven't seen the movie, I would recommend you give it a look. In the end, with the "war" won and the president re-elected, the Hoffman character threatens to spill the beans. He is then led away by large men to a blacked-out car never to be seen again. It is so close to what really happens even though it is portrayed as a comedy.

Hollywood or "holy-warred"

Hollywood and the Illuminati have always been hand in hand and the place of "magic" has been used from the start as a massive weapon in global propaganda and mind conditioning. Let's be fair, it is from Hollywood that most people get their "history", an outrageous distortion most of it, but extremely beneficial to the agenda. After September 11th, Bush dispatched Karl Rove, his chief political adviser, to meet 45 of Hollywood's top players, including executives from all the main studios, at the Peninsular Hotel in Beverly Hills. There they formed the

Hollywood 911 committee to tell the world the Gospel according to Washington. The movie-makers were told they could have access to military sites, aircraft carriers, almost anything they wanted, so long as their productions did not criticise the government.[10] Bush adviser Mark McKinnon told the BBC's *Newsnight* programme without once bursting into laughter:

> "We don't want to, or intend to, turn Hollywood into a propaganda machine. It's not in the long-term interests for the effort, Hollywood, or this administration. This administration is very first-amendment minded. This President has no interest in telling people what to do, what to say, or how to say it."[11]

So they want to use Hollywood as a propaganda machine and tell people what to do, what to say and how to say it, then? Gotcha. Jack Valenti, President of the Motion Picture Association of America, said: "We are at war. If I was in the White House, I'd reach out to the most powerful persuaders on earth, the movie industry, and ask, "What can you do to help?" What can they do? What Bush wants them to do, of course, is to tell lies like they have since Hollywood was founded, although there are honourable exceptions that have tried to turn the tide. Among them is Larry Gelbart, the creator of *M*A*S*H*, the brilliant series about the Korean War. He said of the government's overtures to Hollywood: "It is easy to talk out of the other side of your mouth when you are two-faced. You have got this extra mouth. They want it all ways."[12] Yes they do, and some big players in Hollywood from studio owners and down through the various disciplines are working to advance the Bush propaganda. All this brings me to the bin Laden "smoking gun" video.

With the evidence non-existent to pin the rap on bin Laden, and with an invasion of Afghanistan to justify, it was no surprise that the bin Laden "confession" would drop from the heavens. It is said by official Pentagon statements to have been shot at a "guest house in Kandahar" and was "found in an abandoned private house in Jalalabad". By whom, pray? Well that depends on which official spokesman you listen to. In fact most of the story of 9/11 depends on that. We have been variously told that the bin Laden tape was found by the US Navy, the US Army, the "United Front" (Northern Alliance), the "military" and the CIA. More details, please? Er, sorry, classified. The video is claimed to have been shot on November 9th 2001. President Bush is said to have viewed the tape on November 30th, the *Washington Post* "broke" (officially leaked) the story of its existence on December 9th, and the rest of us saw bits of it on December 13th. The tape is around 40 minutes long and of very poor quality, which suits the manipulation perfectly. It includes shots of a downed helicopter in Ghazni province and two sections of a man claimed to be bin Laden talking to a Saudi cleric and others at a "dinner". Strangely, the tape had the first part of the "bin Laden" conversation at the end of the tape, the end of the conversation at the start, with the helicopter footage in between. Maybe Afghan video cameras whirl the other way, like Chinese writing. Or perhaps they shot the end of the conversation

Figure 27: *"Fatty bin Laden" on the CIA home video*

last, then went out and filmed the helicopter, before returning to shoot the start of the conversation. Yep, that must be it. We were told that the US government used the latest voice and face identification techniques (to check it or make it?), and a team of Arabic translators, none of them familiar with the Saudi language, spent days listening to the tape to make sure the conversations were accurately translated. Why didn't they succeed then? It is not accurately translated, as confirmed by State Department consultant Christopher Ross, and if that is the face of the "Osama bin Laden" we have been seeing elsewhere then he must have placed a very large order with the Kandahar Cream Cake Company and been visited by a doctor from the Jalalabad Nose Job Clinic – "cave visits a speciality" (*Figure 27*). But we shouldn't mock, they are doing their best, and after all President Bush said:

"This is bin Laden unedited. It's preposterous for anybody to think that this tape is doctored. That's just a feeble excuse to provide weak support for an incredibly evil man."

Quite right, George, and I would ask your dad to pass that on next time he visits the bin Laden family. British Foreign Secretary, Jack "straw man" Straw, said there was "no doubt it is the real thing" and this is perhaps the final confirmation that it isn't. A German television programme called *Monitor*, on the Das Erste channel, asked two independent translators and an expert in oriental studies to analyse the US government translation. They found it to be "inaccurate" and "manipulative". One of the programme's translators, Dr Abdel El M. Husseini, said that he had carefully examined the Pentagon's translation and found many problems with it. "At the most important places where it is held to prove the guilt of Bin Laden, it is not identical with the Arabic," he said.[13] Oh goodness, I am surprised. He said that in Arabic the word "previous" does not appear in the sentence in which the official translation claims to say: "We had notification since the previous Thursday that the event would take place that day." Dr Murad Alami, another translator on the programme, said the alleged statement that the attacks would take place "on that day" cannot be heard in the original Arabic version. Garnet Ratter, professor of Islamic and Arabic Studies at the Asia-Africa Institute at the University of Hamburg, told the programme: "The American translators who listened to the tapes and transcribed them apparently wrote a lot of things in that they wanted to hear but that cannot be heard on the tape no matter how many times you listen to it." Bin Laden's mother was quoted by Britain's *Mail on Sunday* as saying the tape was a fake. "The voice is unclear and uneven. There are too many gaps and the statements are very unlike him", she said.[14] On the tape the "bin Laden" figure appears to say, according to the official translation, that most of the hijackers did not know the details of the operation until just before they boarded the planes:

> "The brothers, who conducted the operation, all they knew was that they have a martyrdom operation and we asked each of them to go to America but they didn't know anything about the operation, not even one letter. But they were trained and we did not reveal the operation to them until they are there and just before they boarded the planes … (inaudible) … Those who were trained to fly didn't know the others."

Are we to believe that after "years of planning" most of those involved were only given the essential details in the few minutes before they boarded the planes for a "brilliantly executed operation"? "Hey, Abdul, quick, we don't have much time. You know those two big towers in New York? Well …" What trash. Where is the video footage at Washington Dulles and Newark New Jersey of these "hijackers" being told the plan? Nowhere. It couldn't have happened like that and yet here is "bin Laden" saying that it did. The tape translation has the bin Laden figure saying that he had been informed of the date of the attacks in advance. Well I guess as the "mastermind" he would have to be told it was happening. The figure says it was 5.30pm when he heard the news on the radio that the first plane had hit the World Trade Center and he had told the people with him that they should be patient, the implication being that he knew there would be others. The "bin Laden" figure then says that he continued to listen to the radio. What happened to his satellite television that visiting journalists have talked about? Would he not on that of all days have made sure CNN was switched on and ready? Or at least tuned to that when the events began? Instead he sits listening to the radio while the rest of the world watches live what he is supposed to have orchestrated.

The translation also has "bin Laden" saying that he did not expect the two towers to collapse as they did. He thought that the fire would undermine the iron structure of the building and that three or four storeys would collapse. Isn't it strange that a man who comes from one of the biggest construction families in the Middle East should not think that three or four storeys falling on those below would threaten the whole building if that was how it is supposed to have happened? Why would he "confess" on tape? Why take that chance? It has been suggested that it was done as a recruitment video, but (a) that means the "confession" would have been widely circulated and a copy would eventually have fallen in the wrong hands, and (b) why would they record a "recruitment video" on such a crap camera with such crap quality when we are told he has limitless funds? None of this makes any sense because it isn't true. By the time the video is said to have been shot on November 9th, the Taliban were in serious trouble. The country was being carpet-bombed by the US and Britain, and on that day the Northern Alliance claimed to have won the battle for the strategic town of Mazar-e-Sharif. The capital, Kabul, would fall within days. Yet at no time in the whole tape does bin Laden or anyone else mention the US invasion, the bombing, the Taliban's retreat, or the alleged pursuit of the man himself. Once again – uh?

"Bin Laden" is also claimed to say on the tape that Mohamed Atta was the leader of the hijackers, but he does not say that at all. He speaks only of Mohamed, hardly a rare name among Muslims, and bin Laden would have said that name many times in recorded conversations. The name "Atta" did not leave his lips. The bin Laden figure says: "Mohamed from the Egyptian family was in charge of the group." The name "Atta" only comes in the translated subtitles on the broadcast version, which says: "Muhammad (Atta) from the Egyptian family (meaning the Al Qa'ida Egyptian group), was in charge of the group." The translation is peppered with these in-bracket comments that are not on the soundtrack. The term "inaudible" appears over and over on the subtitles when they could not understand what was said even after playing the tape back dozens of times and later another 50 times more. Significantly, many of these "inaudibles" come at the start of sentences. It is all a manipulator's dream. A skilled editor can take someone's words and change the order to make them say what they didn't say before. An audiotape of George W. Bush was sent to my website in which he openly declares his intentions for a fascist state. What he said was true, but he didn't actually say it like that. His words from other speeches and statements had been re-edited to make it sound as if he had said that. The result was amazingly good, and imagine what Hollywood could do. In fact, Hani Al Sibaei, a specialist in Islamic affairs, told Al-Jazeera television that the congratulatory wishes on the tape and bin Laden's happy expression were taken from a tape of bin Laden being congratulated on the marriage of one his children, which happened four years earlier. Al Sibaei described the "bin Laden confession" as "fabricated and a scandal for the greatest democratic country in the world".[15] Not sure about the last bit, but you get his drift. With voice recognition technology they would have another means of mimicking the sound of the voice and with the Arabic audio so poor and difficult to hear this would be very straightforward for an expert. There are no close-ups of lips on the video, making it even easier to manipulate.

Seeing is believing?

I remember watching the movie *Stuart Little* with my son a few years ago. It is a story about a mouse living with a human family. The cats in the neighbourhood, real ones not animations, speak to each other like humans and it struck me watching the mouths move so perfectly with the words that the days of believing what you are seeing, even with an apparent television interview or statement, are long over. If they can do that with cats, what could they do with humans? When the actor Oliver Reed died during the filming of the movie *Gladiator* he was replaced in the rest of the film by a computer-generated image of himself. We have also seen in advertisements and movies like *Forrest Gump* how actors today can be seen chatting and shaking hands with people long dead. Sean Broughton, a director of Smoke and Mirrors, one of Britain's top visual effects companies, said it would be relatively easy for a skilled professional to fake the video of bin Laden. First they would transfer the original video images on to film tape, he said. The distortion, or "noise" and graininess, would be removed and a "morphing package" would be used to manipulate the image on a computer screen. It would be possible to change the person's mouth and expressions to fit whatever soundtrack they chose and finally the "noise" and graininess would be returned and the whole thing transferred back to videotape.[16] Smoke and Mirrors used this technique to put Bill Clinton's head on an actor for an advertisement for a United States insurance company. Broughton said there were perhaps 20 people in America who would be good enough to fool everybody, but "to find someone that good and make sure they kept quiet would probably be pretty difficult".[17] Not for the Illuminati it wouldn't. Philip Taylor, Director of the Institute of Communications at Leeds University in England and the author of *Munitions of the Mind, a History of Propaganda*, said US military leaders had once suggested to him intercepting a live broadcast of Saddam Hussein "and morphing a blonde on one arm and a bottle of scotch on the other".[18] They decided against doctoring the video, he said, because of its extraordinary potential price – ruining US credibility forever if they were found out. Greg Strause, the Visual Effects Supervisor at Pixel Envy, a company involved with special effects on the movie Titanic, said: "That's how we make our money, kind of faking things to convince everyone else it's real. We just did some Nike commercials where half the people are digital. You wouldn't be able to pick them out." [19] Henry Hingson, a former President of the National Association of Criminal Defence Lawyers, said that in this day and age of digital wizardry, many things could be done to alter the video.[20] Bob Crabtree, Editor of the magazine *Computer Video*, said it was impossible to judge whether the video was a fake without more details of its source. "The US seems simply to have asked the world to trust them that it is genuine." [21]

There are some other puzzling aspects of the tape. The Pentagon says it was shot in mid-November, although reports say it carries a date of November 9th. The cleric with "bin Laden" says he journeyed to the location on a night of a full moon, but the full moons at that time were on October 31st and November 30th, long before and even longer after the tape was supposed to have been recorded. The cleric, who was a paraplegic, would have had to make his alleged journey of some five hours or more from Kabul to Kandahar while the intensive US bombing and the anti-Taliban forces of the Northern Alliance were sweeping the country. Pakistan Commander Ghamsharik apparently reported on November 23rd that bin Laden dined with Pakistanis in Jalalabad on November 9th and stayed there until the 13th .[22] If that is so, how could he also be in Kandahar on the 9th making his video "confession"? "Bin Laden" appears to have a ring on his right hand in the video while in his other appearances he only wore a watch and the left-handed bin Laden is seen to be gesturing a lot and making notes with his right hand in the "confession".

A *Daily Telegraph* story two months after the attacks claimed the existence of a video in which bin Laden "admitted that his al-Qa'eda group carried out the attacks on the World Trade Center and the Pentagon".[23] In the alleged video interview with Pakistani journalist Hamid Mir, "shot in the Afghan mountains at the end of October", a "smiling bin Laden goes on to say that the World Trade Center's twin towers were a 'legitimate target' and the pilots who hijacked the planes were 'blessed by Allah'". The deaths of thousands of people were justified by bin Laden, the *Telegraph* claimed, because they were "not civilians" and were working for the American system. "If avenging the killing of our people is terrorism then history should be a witness that we are terrorists," bin Laden is quoted as saying. "Yes, we kill their innocents and this is legal religiously and logically." The *Telegraph* report says that in the video bin Laden also claims responsibility for an "unspecified terrorist outrage in Riyadh, Saudi Arabia, which he claims was sparked by secret messages in one of his videos". He admits for the first time, said the *Telegraph*, that he was using public statements on video to "whip up terrorism" and this was "a danger about which the British and American governments have warned broadcasters." A few things come to mind here. If this video is so damning, why haven't we seen it everywhere? How strange that bin Laden would be denying involvement in the attacks in one interview and then admitting them in another and allowing it all to be videoed. The *Telegraph* noted that bin Laden had publicly issued four previous videos since September 11th and always denied carrying out the atrocities. Why would he admit that he was using some kind of code on his videos to communicate to terrorist cells? What would be the point of making this public and alerting people to what you were doing, thus preventing any further use of the technique? What a coincidence that he should "say" this after the US and British governments had used the claim that he was doing this to pressure broadcasters into limiting the footage of bin Laden that the public is allowed to see.

Then there was the September 11th "hijacker" "confessing" to the attacks in a tirade to camera that is said to have been recorded on March 6th 2001, some six months before 9/11. Guess who "released" the tape? Al-Jazeera television, the "Arab CNN", based in US-controlled Qatar. The station claimed to have "received" the tape in April 2002, but would not say from what source. The "hijacker" was named as Ahmad al-Haznawi al-Ghamdi. This "hijacker" speaks to camera on good-quality footage as if he is sitting in a television studio and, most bizarrely, behind him are images of the burning World Trade Center. This was supposed to have been shot six months before the attacks! So, if that is correct, Al-Jazeera has electronically added the background of the burning WTC. Why? They claimed it was the "first proof" that al-Qaeda was behind the attacks, so why doctor this "proof" in such a bizarre manner? Why not give us the original footage? Why would this guy record a video six months before the attacks warning that the fight against the United States would be taken to American soil? "The time has come to prove to the whole world," he says, "that the United States put on a garb that was not tailored for it when it had the mere thought of resisting the Mujahadin." The United States did not resist the Mujahadin, it funded and armed them, and why would a carefully planned and secret operation to attack targets in the United States be revealed by one of the hijackers on tape six months before the day? Crazy. But most people believe it and to the Illuminati that is all that matters. On the same Al-Jazeera tape is claimed to be the al-Qaeda second in command, Ayman al-Zawahri, and a silent Osama bin Laden. The alleged Zawahri calls the September 11th attacks a "a great victory" and adds: "This great victory was achieved only thanks to the grace of God the Almighty, not due to any skill or competence on our part." At least the last bit is true. There will, no doubt, be other "finds" when the Illuminati operatives in government and the military want to manipulate the public mind to support the agenda, and there will certainly be other "terrorist attacks" for the same reason, not least with chemicals and disease.

Suffer the little children ...

It was on the non-existent "evidence" detailed here that the world allowed the mentally disturbed leadership in the United States and Britain to launch their merciless attacks on Afghanistan civilians. What a statement about the human condition and how easy it is for the few to control and dictate to the many. Richard Lloyd Parry wrote in the UK *Independent* of the death and suffering that he witnessed in Afghanistan. He told of Sami Ullah who was asleep when the brave boys from the "war on terrorism" bombed a residential area of Tarin Kot. Parry wrote: "In the 11 hours between the explosion and the moment when he finally regained consciousness, the bodies of Mr Ullah's wife, his four children, his parents, and five of his brothers and sisters had been lifted from the rubble of their home and buried." [24] So it went on across the country. They even dropped what passed for "food aid" in yellow packets that were the same colour and shape as the cluster bombs with which they were killing indiscriminately. How many died because they thought a cluster bomb was the food they were so desperate for after the normal supplies had been stopped by the bombing campaign? All this in a country that already had half a million widows and half a million orphans with limbs lost to wars and the more than ten million landmines that pepper the landscape. The people who are running your world and the stupid juveniles who do their bidding from the skies are deeply, deeply disturbed and require some serious mental, emotional and spiritual healing. Major General Smedley Butler was twice awarded the Medal of Honor while serving for more than 30 years in the United States Marine Corps. He encapsulated the real nature of war in a speech in July 1933 in which he said that war is just a racket conducted by the very few at the expense of masses and that only a small group on the inside knows what it is really all about. He went on:

> "Like all the members of the military profession, I never had a thought of my own until I left the service. My mental faculties remained in suspended animation while I obeyed the orders of higher-ups. This is typical with everyone in the military service. I helped make Mexico, especially Tampico, safe for American oil interests in 1914. I helped make Haiti and Cuba a decent place for the National City Bank boys to collect revenues in. I helped in the raping of half a dozen Central American republics for the benefits of Wall Street. I helped purify Nicaragua for the international banking house of Brown Brothers in 1909–1912. I brought light to the Dominican Republic for American sugar interests in 1916. In China I helped to see to it that Standard Oil went its way unmolested." [25]

It is sobering to consider as the military go about their deadly business with their "faculties in suspended animation", the kind of weaponry and destructive power they have at their fingertips whenever a drug-running, child-abusing, psychopathic family like the Bushes tells them to go slaughter some unarmed population of men, women, and children, who are terrorising no-one and just wish to live in peace. These uniformed, unthinking, "Yes sir" pawns in a game they don't understand, have at their disposal, for instance, the fuel-air bombs described earlier by Wade Frazier:

"The bomb works thus: there are two detonations; the first spreads a fine mist of fuel into the air, turning the area [about the size of a football field] into an explosive mix of vast proportion; then a second detonation ignites the mixture, causing an awesome explosion. The explosion is about the most powerful 'conventional' explosion we know of.

"At a pressure shock of up to 200 pounds per square inch (PSI), people in its detonation zone are often killed by the sheer compression of the air around them. Human beings can typically withstand up to about a 40-PSI shock. The bomb sucks oxygen out of the air, and can apparently even suck the lungs out through the mouths of people unfortunate enough to be in the detonation zone. Our military used it on helpless people [in the 1991 Gulf Slaughter]." [26]

Yes, and they used it in Afghanistan and they will use it anywhere they choose until the human herd puts a spiritual rocket up its collective arse. Instead we allow into power intellects like the UK Foreign Secretary Jack Straw who said on September 28th 2001 that "the most fundamental civil liberty is the right to life and preserving that and sustaining that must come before others" (when he was justifying the removal of basic freedoms); and then on October 8th he confirmed that UK and US strikes against Afghanistan had caused "considerable damage" and warned they could continue for weeks (when he was supporting the slaughter of men, women, and children). How this man remembers to breathe has always been beyond me, but look at him, look at Bush, and ask what having them as "leaders" says about the people they dictate to. These are the kind of "leaders" the people of this planet have allowed to take the world into a war – the mass murder of whoever they chose – that in the words of Dick Cheney may not end in our lifetimes. The *Concise Oxford Dictionary* defines terrorism as: "One who favours or uses terror-inspiring methods of governing or coercing government or community, hence terrorism." A United States army manual says that terrorism is: "The calculated use of violence or the threat of violence to attain political or religious ideological goals through intimidation, coercion, or instilling fear." [27] Under either definition, George Bush and Tony Blair are classic terrorists along with all those who support their insane campaign of mass slaughter.

The "war" game

The word "war" slips from the lips of politicians so easily, yet the people who have never experienced it forget what that word really means. As the Japanese leader Shogun Tokugawa said: "If you have to go to war you have already lost." War is not some sanitised news report about "smart bombs" and cities "falling". It is about dead children, dead mothers and fathers. It is about kids seeing the dismembered limbs of their mums and dads splattered all around them; it is about mums and dads seeing their children in the same state. It is about waking up to find every member of your family is dead. My father was in the medical corps during the Second World War and he told me of the endless times they filled coffins with ballast to give loved ones the impression there was a body inside when it was just the bits and pieces that were left. He told me how young soldiers in agony and afraid to die would be brought to the makeshift medical centres screaming for their mothers thousands of miles away. Simon Weston, the British soldier who suffered horrendous burns in the Falklands War thanks to the stupidity of his commanders, presented an excellent BBC documentary about that war in 2002. In it he said that there was no glory in war. When they killed you, he said, they were killing some mother's son. When you killed them you were doing the same. In Afghanistan, which is only the start of the "War on Sanity" being waged by the disturbed minds of Bush, Blair and their masters, there were many more dead mothers' sons and daughters, and there were thousands of dead kids and their mums and dads. That's the reality that Bush and Blair are seeking to sell the world as "fighting for freedom". A point that should never be lost is that they both know that's what they are really doing.

I say this to those "journalists", the intellectual prostitutes who sell their souls and their minds to the official line, refusing to investigate the lies while arrogantly dismissing as "wingnuts" those who do: look at all the dead and maimed children, and their mums and dads in Afghanistan, Iraq, Bosnia and elsewhere, the victims of the wars and agenda that you close your eyes to because you don't have the guts or the desire to expose what is really going on. Then look in the mirror and face one of the people responsible for these horrors. Yeah, you. I say to all those in the global population who cheer, look the other way, or refuse to make their voices heard: do the same. You are all as responsible in your own way as Bush, Blair and the Illuminati and those brave little boys in their flying machines playing virtual reality games with real people whenever their masters say "jump".

The big lie

The official fairy story has been compiled from blatant lies and "evidence" that was so obviously planted and manufactured. The bin Laden "confession" tape is but one example. There was also the "hijacker's passport" "found" near the World Trade Center; Mohamed Atta's "letter" and "baggage" that somehow failed to make it on to Flight 11; and a long, long list of other nonsensical "evidence" detailed throughout this book. The UK *Guardian* reported that journalists had described how they were directed to buildings in Kabul and other locations in Afghanistan to "find" apparent proof of al-Qaeda's involvement in the hijackings. This included, the paper said, new box cutters still in their packaging and a freshly torn page from an American magazine detailing Florida flying schools.[28] How juvenile and obvious. Yet the media still reported these "discoveries" as if they were genuine. A simple question comes from this. If the official story is true, why have they had to manufacture so much "evidence" and tell so many provable lies to hold it all together? How can you believe anything these guys say given their life-long commitment to lying by reflex action? The Pentagon even set up an "Office of Strategic Influence [Lies]" after September 11th to "help the United States get its story over," said Defense Secretary Rumsfeld.[29] Why they thought they needed to do that when the mainstream media overwhelmingly reports their story without question says something about the ridiculous nature of their claims. The Office of Strategic Lies was closed when it was revealed to be proposing to use the Internet and other sources to spread disinformation. They do that anyway without any need for a new organisation.

The manipulators know that most people do not retain details of events and statements, only an image, a feeling. They know that people are mostly short on memory and long on retaining an image. They are well aware that they can get away with contradictions so long as the drip, drip, drip, of false information feeds the image in people's minds of what happened. They did not need to substantiate the authenticity of the bin Laden "confession" tape and that's good because they knew they couldn't. It was just used for a few days to feed the "image" at a crucial time when they needed the propaganda to justify bombing Afghanistan. Note that after the initial release of the tape, nothing has been heard of it or reported about it or investigated further. There is only silence. The same with the hijacker "passport", the anthrax scare, and all the other lies and manipulations. Play them to feed the public's image of events and then forget they ever happened. It is only when they are listed in books like this that the scale of the contradictions can be seen because, understandably, most people have forgotten most of the detail they have been told about 9/11 and they retain only the image of what happened: bin Laden did it.

It is quite a statement about the current mental, emotional and spiritual state of the human family when you consider the basis on which those thousands of Afghan men, women and children, were slaughtered by the mentally deranged terrorists and cowards running the United States and British governments and their military. No evidence worthy of a court of justice was produced to prove that Osama bin Laden and the Taliban were involved in the attacks of September 11th; not one of the alleged "hijackers" was an Afghan or has been connected to the Afghan people; and some seven of the "hijackers" named by the FBI were found to be still alive anyway. With the United States and British governments having no evidence to support their long-planned intention to bomb the shit out of Afghanistan, their front men, Bush and Blair, merely repeated over and over the pre-rehearsed mantra of lies and unsourced allegations. Their "target", bin Laden, has been a CIA asset and stooge for 20 years and the Taliban were funded, armed and manipulated into power by the CIA, Pakistan intelligence and the Saudi royal family, all of which suddenly claimed to oppose them. Afghanistan was in the middle of a horrendous drought and famine with average life expectancy little more than 40. For a child to make it to adulthood was a serious achievement in itself and it was, and is still more so today, a country of widows and orphans after the seemingly endless external and internal conflicts.

Ladies and gentlemen of planet earth, those were the circumstances in which the brave boys and girls of the United States and British military flew over Afghanistan at heights well beyond the range of the pop-gun Afghan air defences and unleashed state-of-art technology of mass destruction on a stone-age country in the middle of a famine. Yet most people just sat around and watched without protest, many even cheered. That is the level to which we have sunk, the cesspit in which we continue to drown. People sat there, even cheering, when the fascist bombs of America and Britain were wiping out desperately poor and hungry Afghan families, and everyone who did that is responsible for what happened and continues to happen.

Excuse me a moment, I need a fucking drink.

SOURCES

1   Adolf Hitler, *Mein Kampf*, pp 180–1, p 231, of the Manheim translation

2   Statement at the White House, October 14th 2001

3   **http://www.narconews.com/goff1.html**

4   **http://www.newsmedianews.com/wtc.htm**

5   UK *Guardian*, October 7th 2002

6   *Arab News*, September 27th 2001

7   Interview by Saudi journalist and bin Laden family friend Khalid Batarfi, the editor of the Saudi newspaper, *Al Medina*, reported in the UK *Mail on Sunday*, December 23rd 2001

8   **Time.com** June 20th 2001

9   *Wag The Dog*, New Line Cinema, released January 9th 1998

10   BBC *Newsnight*, January 30th 2002

11   Ibid

12   Ibid

13   **http://www.rense.com/general18/inac.htm**

14   Interview by Saudi journalist and bin Laden family friend Khalid Batarfi, the editor of the Saudi newspaper, *Al Medina*, reported in the UK *Mail on Sunday*, December 23rd 2001

15   **http://www.americanfreepress.net/12_21_01/Bin_Laden_Video/bin_laden_video.html**

16   UK *Guardian*, December 16th 2001.

17   Ibid

18   Knight Ridder Service, December 16th 2001

19   Ibid

20   UK *Guardian*, December 16th 2001

21   Ibid

22   **http://www.worldmessenger.20m.com/video.html**

23   *Daily Telegraph*, November 12th 2001

24   UK *Independent*, October 25th 2001

25   *All Fall Down*, p 113

26   Wade Frazier, **http://home1.gte.net/res0k62m/iraq.htm**
     Highly recommended for Iraq background

27   *All Fall Down*, p 66

28   UK *Guardian*, December 14th 2001

29   *The Province*, Vancouver, February 27th 2002
     http://www.worldmessenger.20m.com/video.html

chapter 15

Behind the movie

"The interests behind the Bush Administration, such as the CFR, the Trilateral Commission – founded by Brzezinski for David Rockefeller – and the Bilderberg Group have prepared for and are now moving to implement open world dictatorship within the next five years."

Dr Johannes Koeppl, former official of the German Ministry for Defence and adviser to NATO

What happened on September 11th, its consequences and cover-up, is not some isolated, one-off nightmare that will eventually pass from our lives as the years progress and memories fade. The deaths of 3,000 people in the United States and thousands more already killed and maimed in the "war on terrorism" are part of a coldly calculated plan for a global fascist state in which people will be no more than micro-chipped pawns for a tiny cabal in need of psychiatric help. This plan has been unfolding for at least thousands of years in our version of "time" and I will explain how that is possible in due course. The horror of 9/11 is not "it", just another step on the road to "it" – a global fascist state.

I have been researching and communicating this information since the early 1990s and warning of the very society now unfolding before our eyes. Thousands of others have been doing the same and far-sighted researchers were revealing the agenda decades ago. Most people ignored the warnings and others just laughed. But slowly at first, and now rapidly, there is a gathering body of people across the world from a vast diversity of backgrounds that are waking up to what is now becoming the obvious. My website alone attracts some million visits a week and this number is growing all the time. The reason for this is not only that more and more people have been researching the conspiracy and uncovering an enormous library of evidence, it is also that when the time comes for secret manipulation to install its long-planned agenda, there is a point where it has to break the surface, where it can be seen. It is one thing to predict the micro-chipped society, quite another when micro-chips are being introduced. We are now at that stage when day after day the changes predicted years ago in my books and those of other researchers are becoming reality. As this has progressed, more of those who have witnessed the agenda on the "inside" are confirming the plan from their own experience. One such man is Dr Johannes Koeppl who was an official of the German Ministry of Defence and worked at NATO in the late 1970s as an adviser to former NATO Secretary General, the Bilderberger, Manfred Werner. He met many of the Illuminati's important political players, people like Zbigniew Brzezinski, the founder of the Trilateral Commission with David Rockefeller, and National Security Adviser to Jimmy Carter. Koeppl made presentations to meetings of the Illuminati's Bilderberg Group and to different subsections of the Trilateral Commission. Eventually he had seen enough to realise that the conspiracy was no mere theory. These guys really did intend to take over the world and Brzezinski was right at the heart of it. Koeppl said:

> "In 1983–4, I warned of a take-over of world governments being orchestrated by these people. There was an obvious plan to subvert true democracies and selected leaders were not being chosen based upon character but upon their loyalty to an economic system run by the elites and dedicated to preserving their power. All we have now are pseudo-democracies." [1]

Bush and Blair are wonderful examples of this. Koeppl said he realised he was dealing with a "criminal society". His articles warning of the conspiracy were eventually blocked by mainstream publications like *Newsweek* and his career in politics going back 30 years was destroyed.[2] Like anyone with a brain on active duty, Koeppl can see what September 11th and the "war on terrorism" are really about. This was more than a war against terrorism, he said, it was a war against the citizens of all countries. The "current elites" were creating so much fear that people didn't know how to respond. But they must remember, he said, "This is a move to implement a world dictatorship within the next five years. There may not be another chance." [3]

Different masks, same face

Divide and rule is obviously the basis of any attempt by the few to control the many and in the Illuminati strategy this happens at all levels. They operate through all races while playing those races off against each other. They operate through all religions and do the same. The technique is identical wherever you look – keep them divided so they can be ruled. This extends even to those people and groups who are, in their different ways, challenging parts of the Illuminati agenda. I mean those who campaign against globalisation; additives in food; genetically modified food; lethal chemicals sprayed on crops; fluoride in the water; radiation from nuclear facilities; the dangers of vaccinations; the global drug-running network; the banking scam; "third world" debt and poverty; the destruction of rainforests; the explosion in surveillance and the dismantling of civil liberties; and a whole long list of other campaigns by pressure groups and "pressure people". What 95% of them don't realise, however, is that they are all challenging the same force. These apparently unconnected expressions of injustice and abuse are different strands in the same strategy – Illuminati control of the planet and its population (*Figure 28*).

The Pyramid of Manipulation

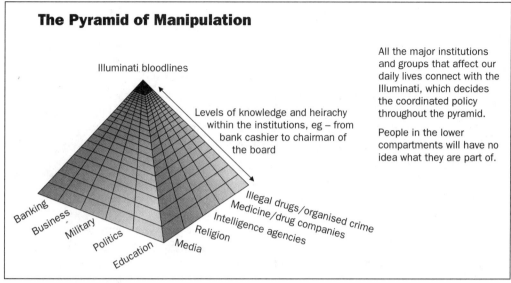

Illuminati bloodlines

Levels of knowledge and heirachy within the institutions, eg – from bank cashier to chairman of the board

All the major institutions and groups that affect our daily lives connect with the Illuminati, which decides the coordinated policy throughout the pyramid.

People in the lower compartments will have no idea what they are part of.

Banking
Business
Military
Politics
Education
Media
Religion
Intelligence agencies
Medicine/drug companies
Illegal drugs/organised crime

Figure 28: *Pyramids of Manipulation*

The human being in fully awakened consciousness is genius incarnate. That may sound funny when you look at the world today, but then you are not looking at fully awakened consciousness. You are often observing consciousness operating at a capacity only slightly beyond the point where it can remember to breathe. But that is not what we are, it is what we have allowed ourselves to become. Awakened, vibrant consciousness expressing itself through the physical body is a nightmare to control and deceive, and the Illuminati know that. For this reason the human being is subjected to a second-by-second bombardment of conditioning, disconnection and "dumbing down" through an "education" system designed only to indoctrinate; a media that is there to do the same and put consciousness to sleep with an endless diet of soaps, game shows, and the official story; chemicals added to food (like Rumsfeld's aspartame); chemicals in the water like fluoride; chemicals that fall from the sky with the chemtrails dispersed by military aircraft all over the world, causing health effects on the population, as now widely documented;[4] vaccinations that scramble the body's natural chemistry and assault the immune system;[5] radiation released in the atmosphere; electromagnetic pollution and extremely low frequency (ELF) waves, and goodness knows what is hitting us from space these days.

I mentioned the mental effects of aspartame earlier and fluoride is another example of the assault on humanity's ability to think straight. Fluoride is a major intellect suppressant that is being added to water supplies and toothpaste. Sodium fluoride is a common ingredient in rat and cockroach poisons, anaesthetics, psychiatric drugs and military nerve gas. It is one of the basic ingredients in the mind drug Prozac and the Sarin nerve gas used in the attack on the Japanese subway system. Independent scientific evidence says that fluoride causes various mental disturbances and makes people stupid, docile, and subservient. This is besides shortening life span and damaging bone structure. The first use of fluoridated drinking water was in the Nazi prison camps in Germany thanks to the Illuminati's pharmaceutical giant I.G. Farben. This was the company that ran camps like Auschwitz and it still exists as its constituent parts like Bayer. Did the Nazis do this because they were concerned about the teeth of the inmates? This mass medication of water supplies with sodium fluoride was to sterilise the prisoners and force them into quiet submission. Charles Perkins, a chemist, wrote the following to the Lee Foundation for Nutritional Research, Milwaukee, Wisconsin, on October 2nd 1954:

> "... in the 1930s, Hitler and the German Nazis envisioned a world to be dominated and controlled by a Nazi philosophy of pan-Germanism. The German chemists worked out a very ingenious and far-reaching plan of mass control, which was submitted to, and adopted by, the German General Staff. This plan was to control the population in any given area through mass medication of drinking water supplies. By this method they could control the population in whole areas, reduce population by water medication that would induce sterility in women and so on. In this scheme of mass control sodium fluoride occupied a prominent place." [6]

That's worth thinking about when you use fluoride toothpaste that is not even beneficial to your teeth (see *Children Of The Matrix* and the medical archives at davidicke.com). If you think you are safe because fluoride is not added to your local drinking water, what about that beer you're drinking or that can of soda? Where did that water come from? Just imagine the effects of a daily intake of mind suppressants for someone eating and drinking aspartame foods, drinking fluoride water, and cleaning their teeth with fluoride toothpaste. The cumulative affect of all this could make people so stupid they would vote for George Bush or Tony Blair. Or even vote at all. Or believe the official story of 9/11. That explains it then. Genetically modified food is designed to genetically modify the body, rewrite the DNA. So are vaccines, crop chemicals and food additives. The DNA rewrite is aimed at reducing the ability of consciousness to manifest its genius through the brain and I'll go into more about this later. GM food is being promoted by Monsanto, an Illuminati corporation notorious among researchers and campaigners, and the company that bought Rumsfeld's Searle Pharmaceuticals, the producers of aspartame. The Bush administration is awash with Monsanto placemen and women.

The onslaught on body and mind is orchestrated by the same people who manipulate the financial system and entice the population into ever greater debt. The financial system is legalised theft, which lends people money that doesn't exist and charges them interest on it. It is designed to make us dependent and ensure that we serve and obey the system if we are to survive, let alone prosper. The goal is the control of choice, control of the body, control of the mind, control of the emotions, control of perception. It is important for those who challenge these apparently diverse problems and injustices to realise that they are all manipulated by the same group to the same end: mass control. This, and the cabal behind it all, is the thread that connects globalisation, additives in food, genetically modified food, lethal chemicals sprayed on crops, fluoride in the water, radiation from nuclear facilities, the dangers of vaccinations, the global drug running network, the banking scam, "third world" debt and poverty, the destruction of rain forests, the explosion in surveillance, the dismantling of civil liberties, and all the rest.

No need for prophets

Exposing the agenda is no longer about predicting what will be. It is here with us now. In my first book on these subjects in the early 1990s I wrote about the coming of the human micro-chip and how the plan was for everyone to be chipped and connected to a global computer. The chipping of domestic animals, I wrote, was merely the forerunner to the human chip and this was preparing the public mind to accept micro-chipping as part of everyday society. Most dismissed this as nonsense and the ravings of a nutcase. Now all over the world people are being micro-chipped in "trials" for a micro-chipped population. In *Children Of The Matrix*, I featured a chip-making company called Applied Digital Solutions Inc., and the chip technology it planned to introduce across American society and around the world. Months after the book was published, the company announced human trials for its "VeriChip". It said it would soon have a prototype of a "much more complex device, one that is able to receive signals from Global Positioning System satellites and transmit a person's location".[7] The chips make people "scannable just like a jar of peanut butter at the supermarket checkout line".[8] Well, given this is all we are to the Illuminati, I guess that's appropriate. A signal from the chip transmits a verification number to a scanner and this number is cross-referenced in a central computer with all the person's personal details. If you read *And The Truth Shall Set You Free*, the first edition of which was written in 1994, you'll find all of this predicted. At first Applied Digital appeared to withdraw the technology in the face of opposition, but after September 11th it began promoting the chip with renewed vigour and the "trials" began. Marc Rotenberg, the executive director of the Electronic Privacy Information Center, said: "Parents will decide that their kids should be implanted, or maybe their own aging parents."[9] The idea is that government agencies will eventually decide who gets chipped and they plan to decide, in the interests of "national security", that everyone will. This includes babies at birth.

The "trials" of the VeriChip were given massive publicity in the American media, just as similar "trials" had been in the UK. Jeffrey and Leslie Jacobs and their teenage son, Derek, from Boca Raton (that place again) in Florida, were given their chips on national television. They had accepted the whole manufactured excuse for the micro-chip and became unknowing pawns and promoters of an agenda designed to imprison the human population. Leslie Jacobs hoped it would make her feel more secure in an insecure world. The Illuminati hope that others feel the same way because that's the idea. The signs are certainly good. Applied Digital said soon after the launch publicity that it had a waiting list of 4,000 to 5,000 people for the VeriChip and planned to operate a "chipmobile" that will visit Florida's senior citizen's centres.[10] The company is charging $200 for the chips and a $10 monthly fee to store the information, but you watch the price come down to something like zero when the mass chipping is designed to start. I love the idea of the "chipmobile". Good thinking. They could have them touring the neighbourhoods playing catchy little tunes like ice cream vans. "Hey dad, can I have a micro-chip, oh pleeease, dad, my friends are all having one." If you want to be a good parent, if you really love your children, you will secure their safety by connecting them to a global positioning satellite. Go on, you know it makes sense.

All the things they now say about parents who question the appalling effects of vaccines on their children will be used with the imposition of the micro-chip. Schools run by idiots in the United States are refusing to allow children to attend if they are not vaccinated and parents are being told they will go to jail if they don't let their kids be injected with vaccines that wage war on their bodies and immune systems. Yep, it's the Land of Free for sure. What greater definition of dictatorship can you have than losing the right to decide what is injected into your own body and those of your children? The chip is just the next step. The opening emphasis in the VeriChip campaign was the "medical benefits" of having your health records and medicine details implanted on the chip – just as I predicted it would be years ago on the basis of information from people who had been involved in meetings planning the chip. The campaign was also especially targeting an estimated four million people in the United States who have Alzheimer's disease and the idea was being sold as a caring, helpful way of ensuring they don't get lost. Illuminati agendas always target the most vulnerable groups first to get people familiar with something, and then the plan is expanded to the rest of society. In the same way, such technology is introduced as a "voluntary" free choice to start with and then made compulsory once it is established. Alzheimer's patients are one of the fastest-growing groups in the United States. Why? The Illuminati agenda is to introduce a step-by-step plan, which will mean that people will not be able to have school meals, buy food, receive state benefits, board a plane, drive a car, etc., etc., unless they are micro-chipped and/or subjected to eye scans, face scans, thumbprint scans, and all the other Big Brother technology now in circulation. In May 2002, the Bush government (the private "US" corporation) introduced legislation that mandates drivers' licences issued by the states to carry a computer chip and include a "unique identifier" like a fingerprint. The Driver's License Modernization Act, sponsored by Virginia Representatives Jim Moran (Democrat) and Tom Davis (Republican), also directs that the chip must be capable of accepting software for other applications, including those of private companies. They claim the objective is to stop identity fraud and support "national security". You know, I think there could just be another reason myself. The bill would release $315 million in "federal funds" (money from the American people) to help to pay for the new licences and link up state computer systems, which is exactly what the agenda demands. There's now also a tooth implant that has been developed to put micro-chip technology in our teeth.

What they don't tell you

That's some of the bullshit behind the micro-chip campaign, but what's the truth? As I have been saying all these years, the technology the public are allowed to see is light years behind that which exists in the shadows, the secret research projects funded by the Illuminati profits from the global drug trade, banking scams and all the rest. I was invited in 1997 to meet a scientist who was working against his will for the CIA. He had joined the agency believing he was serving his country, but he soon realised they did not want his genius to serve or help anyone or anything. They wanted his knowledge to advance the Illuminati agenda for the Big Brother state that he soon understood was very real indeed. When I asked him why he continued to work for the CIA when he was so sickened by how his work was being used, he told me the story of what happened when he began to rebel and refuse to cooperate. He left his home one day and remembers nothing until he woke up in a room. As he recovered his faculties he realised there was something attached to his chest. He opened his shirt as he told me the story and I saw a sort of see-through shampoo-like sachet with an orangey-golden liquid inside. These are called "patches" in the CIA. He said that his body had been manipulated to need the drug in the sachet to survive and the "patch" had to be replaced every 72 hours. If he did not do what the CIA demanded, he was told, the patch would not be replaced and he would start to die an agonising death. Later when he rebelled again he learned how true this was as they allowed his health to deteriorate painfully until he agreed to do what they wanted. The scientist said he was withholding knowledge that he had from his CIA bosses because he knew that once they thought a scientist had contributed all he could to their plans the patches are not replaced and they are allowed to die to ensure that their secrets die with them. He told me that large numbers of people in the secret projects are "patched" in this way.

The scientist said that the technology to cure cancer, provide pollution-free and cost-free energy, and create abundant growth in deserts without water (by stimulating the energy field of the plants), had been known for a long time. It was kept secret because the Illuminati did not want the people to have the freedom, choice, benefits and abundance this would provide. Instead they used the technology in a different way, to enhance their control. But he stressed more than anything the Illuminati agenda for micro-chipping the population. He said to me in 1997 that the micro-chips already developed and waiting to be introduced were so small they could be inserted by hypodermic needle during vaccination programmes. The question is therefore legitimately asked about how many people are already micro-chipped without their knowledge. Look how easy it would be. The only thing you would need to do is ensure that the chips were in the vaccine dose. Once that was done the doctors and nurses all over the world would insert the chips without any idea that were doing so. What is happening now with the VeriChip and suchlike is just the beginning. The VeriChips are not even nearly the state-of-the-art. The scientist told me that "electronic tagging" and keeping people constantly monitored from satellite (one of the real reasons for the "Star Wars" space technology) was only a part of the micro-chip agenda and not even the most important. He said it was not the signals going from the chip to the computer and satellite that was foremost in the agenda, but the signals going the other way. He said that once people were micro-chipped the computer-satellite system could program the chips, either individually or en masse, to make people docile or aggressive, sexually stimulated or sexually suppressed, kill them from a distance, give them diseases, scramble their minds and emotions, anything at all. That's the real agenda of the micro-chip. I remember years ago when I had satellite television I called the provider's office at the opposite end of the United Kingdom to ask to take another channel. I thought they would send me another programmed card for my receiver equipment, but no. The guy asked me to watch my screen and tell him what was happening, and the new channel came up before my eyes. I asked him the obvious question: "How did you do that?" He said he had just sent a signal to the card in the machine in front of me and reprogrammed it to accept the new channel. That's the plan for micro-chipped people. It is the ultimate goal of the Illuminati because then they can create a situation in which every child born is micro-chipped and under their control mentally, emotionally and physically from the day they arrive in this "world".

If you want to see the kind of technology available over the counter to manipulate mind and body just search around the Internet. I came across a device called Sonic Nausea, a small electronic device which can, says the website blurb, "really turn one's stomach".[11] It "generates a unique combination of ultra-high frequency sound waves which soon leads most in its vicinity to queasiness". It can also cause headaches, intense irritation, sweating, imbalance, nausea or even vomiting, says the website. Hiding the device in your neighbour's house might put an end to their late-night parties or it could be used in a bureaucrat's office, the executive lunchroom … "the possibilities are endless for that small portion of inventive payback". The bigger version, the Super Sonic Nausea, "provides serious, substantial capability to disrupt and disperse gatherings … Speeches, demonstrations, crowd dynamics – this device has been used to 'influence' more of these in recent years than you might suspect." Also, according to the promotional blurb, "if planted near the podium, you might just have a case of a speaker with diminished clarity and concentration, or perhaps is even unable to complete his presentation 'due to illness'". This "illness", says the blurb, "might even be contagious, as some of the VIPs up there with him also seemed to have caught the same bug". Imagine what they could do through a micro-chip in your body connected to a computer system.

Freedom to exploit

Wherever you look, the centralisation of power is moving on at tremendous speed in all areas of society and, of course, the more you centralise power the more power you have to centralise even quicker. Political power is moving further and further from the people. First national governments took over the central control of previously diverse, self-governing regions and peoples, and now massive

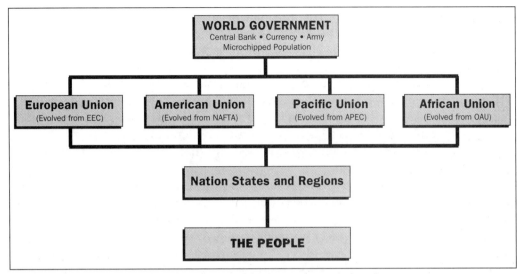

Figure 29: *The Illuminati world government structure that is planned to control the global fascist state*

superstates controlled by bureaucrats are dictating to national governments. We are only one step from the structure that has been the Illuminati goal for so long – world government, army, bank, and currency (*Figure 29*). We have the European Union that passes laws and issues bureaucratic dictates that override and supersede anything decided by national parliaments. This was manipulated into being step by step from the European "free trade area" that the people were "sold" after the Second World War. (See *And The Truth Shall Set You Free* for how this was done and by whom.) The European Union has a single currency, the euro, which is a stepping-stone to the world currency, and a European Central Bank in Frankfurt dictates financial policy to the subservient nation-states. While I was writing this book, the President of the European Commission, the Bilderberger, Romano Prodi, was demanding a centralised EU policy on foreign affairs, defence and law, and the power to dictate to "nations" their tax and spending policies. He also called for a European tax to fund these increased powers. Using classic newspeak and reverse meaning, he said that the EU can be turned into a "grand political project" (turned into?) and pave the way for a "supranational democracy" (centralised dictatorship).[12] I predicted all of this in my previous books because the agenda is so transparent. The same is planned in the Americas, Africa and Asia-Australia. In *And The Truth Shall Set You Free*, I wrote that the NAFTA "free trade area" in the United States, Canada and Mexico would be extended to the whole of the Americas and then turned into a mirror of the European Union. Soon after George W. Bush came to power he attended the Summit of the Americas in Quebec, Canada, at which this was agreed. The Canadian dollar is being artificially suppressed to encourage Canadians to replace it with the US dollar, the preferred stepping-stone currency for the Americas. The pressure has also begun since September 11th to impose a "common security zone" and the Massachusetts "Democrat" Ted Kennedy and Kansas "Republican", Sam Brown, have proposed the

Enhanced Border Security Act. This seeks to "harmonise" US and Canadian immigration and Bush has called for the same. "The secretary of state, in coordination with the secretary of the treasury and the attorney general, shall promptly initiate negotiations with Canada and Mexico to assure maximum possible compatibility of immigration, customs, and visa policies," Bush said.[13] This is exactly what happened in Europe, as nations were drip, dripped into a centralised superstate. Africa now has an African Union and in Asia-Australia the Trojan horse "free trade" zone is called Asia Pacific Economic Cooperation (Control) or APEC. Nation states are becoming administrative units for these centralised bureaucracies and we have seen nothing yet.

In every facet of society the centralisation of power can be seen, as giant corporations merge with giant corporations throughout business, banking and media ownership. What has been the case secretly for so long is now on public display as the Big Brother society becomes manifest. We have the orgasmic situation for the Illuminati in which "free trade" (free for them) and the dropping of "trade barriers" (protecting your own people from exploitation) means that the Illuminati transnationals can make their products for next to nothing by abusing people in the poorest countries, often ruled by vicious dictatorships, and paying them a pittance for working horrendous hours. Then these companies ship their products to the rich countries and sell them at an enormous profit. The people in the poor countries lose because of their criminal exploitation and the people in the rich countries lose because they are exploited in another way, and these imports destroy companies and jobs at home. The only people who win are the Illuminati and their transnational network, but then that's the idea. The Illuminati, incidentally, want to destroy small business because it represents the diversity they despise so much and this is why business law is rigged in favour of the biggest corporations. The world army that would enforce the decisions of the world government (currently known as the "war on terrorism") has been forming before our eyes for decades. The idea is to fuse the powers of NATO and the UN forces into a world army in which foreign troops would police other countries. This is because troops from one country are far more likely to carry out orders to strike against a foreign population rather than their own.

Globalised fascism

As I keep stressing, if there are a few who want to impose total control on the many then power has to be centralised. The fewer people making decisions affecting the many, the more power the few will have, obviously. We have seen the excuse of 9/11 constantly exploited to achieve this. One example in America is the Office of Homeland Security, and in Europe we are seeing ever more Europe-wide laws and policing. The European Union (EU) introduced a European arrest warrant and people arrested in one country can be handed over to another without extradition procedures. The EU is setting up "joint investigation teams" (stepping-stone to the long-planned European police force, currently known as Europol) and it has pledged to "improve cooperation and exchange of information" between the national intelligence agencies within the Union (stepping-stone to the long-planned European intelligence agency). The EU also wants greater cooperation with agencies in the United States (stepping-stone to the long-planned world intelligence agency to go with the world government, army, central bank and currency).

A Europe-wide definition of a terrorist has also been introduced to underpin the European arrest and extradition warrants. A terrorist group is defined as a "structured organisation … of more than two persons, acting in concert to commit terrorist offences". A better definition of the Bush family I have yet to see. But what constitutes a "terrorist" is so widely defined on both sides of the Atlantic that it could be used – and will be – to imprison, and worse, those who are simply challenging and exposing the Illuminati agenda and corruption through circulating information and peaceful protest. The UK Home Secretary David Blunkett plans to introduce ID cards – a stepping-stone to the micro-chip – just as they are in the United States and they will be proposed eventually by the European Union. British governments have been trying to introduce ID cards for a long time, but the resistance from civil liberties groups has thwarted them. Now that they have 3,000 dead people to use to press their case, we are seeing ID cards proposed with renewed vigour along with the outrageous invasions of phone and e-mail privacy I mentioned earlier. We are also having eye-reading technology introduced at airports and it is all designed to ensure that the global population is followed and tracked wherever they go 24 hours a day. John Wadham, director of the civil rights organisation, Liberty, was correct when he said: "As with all governments, other illiberal measures are being smuggled in under the cover of proposals to deal with the events of 11 September." [14] What kind of mind uses the horrors of September 11th to advance its own agenda? The very minds behind 9/11 and the "war on terrorism".

Hitler revisited

People say they wonder how the concentration camps of Nazi Germany could have been allowed to happen. Why didn't people see what was going on and do something about it? It is an irony beyond belief to know that while they are asking these questions the very same situation is being introduced in their own society. What happened in Nazi Germany couldn't happen again? It *is* happening. "Civilian Holding Areas" or "Internment Camps", what we know as concentration camps, are in place across the United States, for instance. Congressman Henry Gonzales of Texas confirmed years ago what researchers and local people had been claiming for so long: these camps do exist. He said: "… the truth is yes – you do have these stand-by provisions, and the plans are here … whereby you could, in the name of stopping terrorism … evoke the military and arrest Americans and put them in detention camps." [15] According to one report, the US Army's Director of Resource Management confirmed the legitimacy of a memorandum which came to light that talked of the military's inmate labour programme for civilians. The memo says: "Enclosed for your review and comment is the draft Army regulation on civilian inmate labor utilization" and the procedure to "establish civilian prison camps on installations".[16] If you search the Internet you can see many articles and pictures of these camps, with lists and maps of their locations according to researchers and local people. You will also see the ten regions of the United States planned to be introduced after the final takeover.[17] The concentration camps are for the "dissidents" and those who seek to expose or resist the Illuminati global fascist state. The people arrested without charge or public knowledge and jailed indefinitely since 9/11 are part of the policy of preparing the public to accept such things as a necessary step to win the "war on terrorism". In the same way that countries are demonised when the Illuminati want to bomb their population, so people within the countries of the "West" are demonised if they challenge that policy, expose the conspiracy and highlight its inhuman insanity. This is what happened to those Germans who challenged Hitler and the Nazis, and to Russians who would not bow to the Stalin dictatorship. The very same is being planned across the "West" today because this is due to happen on a large scale once the "war on terrorism" has been escalated still further. The Iran-Contra investigation revealed that there were plans to round up dissidents and immigrants during a possible US invasion of Nicaragua and to hold them in emergency prisons at US military bases and other locations. This was all claimed to be lawful because of secret Executive Orders and National Security Decision Directives introduced in the name of "national security". This technique is being used to intern American civilians in their own country.

The proposed Model State Emergency Health Powers Act gives "public health officials" the right to close roads and airports, herd people into stadiums, and quarantine entire cities in the event of a "bio warfare attack" or contagious disease. Such attacks are planned by the Illuminati. The proposed law originates from the Centers for Disease Control and Prevention in Atlanta, and was drafted by lawyers and public health professors at Georgetown University in Washington and Johns Hopkins University in Baltimore. It would give states immense power to control their populations. James Lee Witt, the former head of the Illuminati's Federal Emergency Management Agency (FEMA), said that orders from the Centers for Disease Control and a state's Governor would be implemented by military units of the National Guard. The bill's leading author, Lawrence Gostin, said that Congress "should give public health authorities strong powers to be able to isolate or quarantine people if necessary for the public health,"[18] Asked if this would include a National Guardsman shooting a grandmother trying to evade such quarantine, he said: "You have to use all reasonable force. Sometimes that could mean lethal force."[19] All the authorities need to invoke the powers covered by the bill is a "bio attack" or contagious disease and that's no problem for them. Civilian internment camps have been law at least since the late 1940s when J. Edgar Hoover, the notorious head of the FBI and a seriously disturbed being, developed a plan codenamed "Security Portfolio". This allowed the FBI to put up to 20,000 Americans in security detention camps at a time of "emergency" and these people would not have the right to a court hearing – exactly what has been happening since September 11th.[20] Although these laws were removed in 1971, a new phase was about to start. In December 1975, Senate hearings produced "Intelligence Activities, Senate Resolution 21", which revealed through documents, memos and government informants, that the government had plans to intern a vast number of American people using so-called Master Search Warrants and Master Arrest Warrants. The latter give the FBI permission from the Attorney General to:

> "Arrest persons whom I deem dangerous to the public peace and safety. These persons are to be detained and confined until further order. [The FBI also has permission to] "… search certain premises where it is believed that there may be found contraband, prohibited articles, or other materials in violation of the Proclamation of the President of the United States." [21]

These laws give the Attorney General, currently John Ashcroft, the right to decide who can be interned indefinitely and what constitutes, for instance, "prohibited articles". The President only needs to impose the state of emergency to activate these powers and plans, and Nazi Germany will be visited on America. We are already seeing this happen and similar plans will be in place in Europe, too. On August 2nd 1990, just ahead of the Gulf War, President Father George Bush signed two executive orders, 12722 and 12723, that involved martial law in the United States and suspending the Constitution. Professor Diana Reynolds of the Fletcher School of Diplomacy at Boston's Tufts University said that when Bush announced a national emergency he "activated one part of a contingency national security emergency plan".[22] This plan involves a series of laws passed since the presidency of Richard Nixon, which Professor Reynolds says give the president boundless powers. She says that the Defense Industrial Revitalization and Disaster Relief Acts of 1983 "would permit the president to do anything from seizing the means of production, to conscripting a labor force, to relocating groups of citizens", and the cumulative effect of these laws is to suspend the Constitution whenever the President decides to invoke them. She says that they "permit the stationing of the military in cities and towns, closing off the US borders, freezing all imports and exports, allocating all resources on a national security priority, monitoring and censoring the press, and warrantless searches and seizures".[23]

Heeere's FEMA – again

The paramount agency at the heart of all this is the Federal Emergency Management Agency (FEMA) of Zbigniew Brzezinski and Oliver North. Professor Reynolds said that the stimulus for the centralisation of vast powers in FEMA came from the actions of Father George Bush in 1976 when he was director of the CIA. She said that Bush assembled a group called Team B, which released a report claiming that the CIA had underestimated the dangers of a Soviet nuclear attack. The report advised the development of elaborate plans for "civil defence" and a post-nuclear government, and three years later FEMA was given overall responsibility for these plans. Bush signed Executive Order 12681 on July 6th 1989, which gave FEMA, a supposedly "emergency response" agency, the right to spy on

Americans. Bush declared as law without Congressional debate that FEMA's National Preparedness Directorate would "have as a primary function intelligence, counterintelligence, investigative, or national security work".[24] Note the term "primary function". When a "national emergency" or "martial law" is invoked by the President, FEMA already has the power to make people work wherever it dictates; have every person registered; commandeer their homes and make them live where FEMA demands; take control of food and power supplies; radio and television stations and frequencies; health care, education, and all transportation including aircraft and airports. The military takeover of airports since September 11th is just the first step in the control by the US military of its own people. Louis Guiffreda, a cousin to the Bush family, I am told, was head of FEMA and became Deputy Attorney General of California. (See *Children Of The Matrix* for a strange story about Guiffreda.)[25] He was a close associate of the then Governor of California Ronald Reagan, who, as US President, appointed him head of FEMA. Guiffreda was the man who said that anyone who attacks the state, even with words, becomes, by definition, a revolutionary and enemy. While he was head of FEMA he said "legitimate violence is integral to our form of government, for it is from this source that we can continue to purge our weaknesses".[26] For "weakness" read those who know what is going on. Guiffreda has also written that "Martial Rule comes into existence upon a 'determination' [note not a public declaration] by the senior military commander that the civil government must be replaced because it is no longer functioning anyway." He adds: "Martial Rule is limited only by the principle of necessary force."[27] According to Professor Diana Reynolds, it is possible for the President to make declarations concerning a national emergency secretly through a National Security Decision Directive. Most such directives are classified as so secret that "researchers don't even know how many are enacted".[28]

Ben Bradlee Jr writes that FEMA's 1984 REX 84-ALPHA exercises involving Oliver North were designed to test its ability to take authority from the Department of Defense, the National Guard in every state, and "a number of state defense forces to be established by state legislatures".[29] REX 84 was similar to a plan secretly adopted by Reagan when he was governor of California together with Edwin Meese, who later became US Attorney General, and … Louis Guiffreda, the FEMA director in 1984 when the North "exercises" were happening.[30] Part of the plan when FEMA assumes command in an "emergency" is that the military would then be "deputised" by FEMA to overcome the law forbidding military involvement in domestic law enforcement. The 1878 law of Possee Comitatus forbids the federal US military to be involved in law enforcement on American soil that involves arrests, searches, seizure of evidence and other activities performed by the police and civilian law enforcement. However, moves are being made to change this so the military state can roll on. Paul Wolfowitz, the Deputy Defense Secretary, agreed during testimony to the Senate Armed Services Committee in October 2001 that it might be desirable to give federal troops more of a role in domestic policing to prevent terrorism. "In certain cases we can do more than anyone else in the country because of the special capabilities that we have," he said. What did Clinton call for after Oklahoma? An easing of restrictions on the military's involvement in domestic law enforcement.

The *Washington Post* reported soon after 9/11 that top military authorities wanted to appoint a four-star commander to "coordinate federal troops used in homeland defense, part of a broad reorganization that Pentagon officials say could change some forces' primary mission from waging war overseas to patrolling at home".[31] The *Post* said that the attacks of September 11th and the "war on terrorism" have "... blurred the distinction between foreign wars and domestic crimes and prompted a rethinking of the Pentagon's command structure and force assignments". Problem-reaction,-solution. Boy George announced in April 2002 the formation of Northern Command, or NORTHCOM, headed by a four-star general, which will "coordinate" with the Office of Homeland "Defense". The first head of NORTHCOM was widely predicted in the media to be Ralph Eberhart, the head of NORAD and Space Command at Cheyenne Mountain, which failed to react in time when four airliners were hijacked in North American airspace. NORTHCOM will coordinate "homeland defence" for North America and for the first time Mexico comes under a Pentagon command. Bush also called in June 2002 for a new cabinet department to take control of "homeland defence" and make sure the failings of intelligence before 9/11 did not happen again (problem-reaction-solution). At the same time, Britain announced plans to create a 6,000-strong military "rapid-reaction force" to react to "possible terror attacks". Bush clone Robert Mueller, who became head of the FBI just two weeks before 9/11 and has since "led" the "investigation", also announced to the media on May 15th, 2002, a plan for an FBI "supersquad" that would lead all major "terrorism investigations" worldwide.[32] This would involve hiring hundreds of agents and analysts, and the creation of an Office of Intelligence, headed by a former CIA official. Well that fills me with confidence. This is an example of what I said about the publicly exposed incompetence of an organisation, in this case the FBI, being used to increase its power through problem-reaction-solution. The FBI "super squad" is another organisation with centralised power designed to cover up the people behind the orchestrated terrorism that is planned in the future. We don't want those naughty genuine agents actually investigating these atrocities, so we'll create our own operation and fill it with our guys. Job done. FBI special agent Coleen Rowley said in her letter of complaint to Mueller in May 2002:

"Your plans for an FBI Headquarters' 'Super Squad' simply fly in the face of an honest appraisal of the FBI's pre-September 11th failures. The Phoenix, Minneapolis and Paris Legal Attache Offices reacted remarkably exhibiting keen perception and prioritization skills regarding the terrorist threats they uncovered or were made aware of pre-September 11th. The same cannot be said for the FBI Headquarters' bureaucracy and you want to expand that?!"

The logic or otherwise of an action depends on where you are standing and what you wish to achieve. From Coleen Rowley's point of observation, Mueller's proposal is crazy, but from the Illuminati's point of view it makes perfect sense in their desire for control. The Illuminati agenda is not hiding any more, such is the magnitude of the advances made as a result of September 11th. It is unfolding all around us and yet, as in Nazi Germany, if it doesn't directly affect people immediately they don't want to know and don't want to speak out for those who are being targeted. The Reverend Martin Niemöller, a pastor in the German Confessing Church, spent seven years in a Nazi concentration camp and what he said about the progression to tyranny should hang on the wall in every home:

> "First they came for the communists, and I did not speak out because I was not a communist. Then they came for the socialists, and I did not speak out because I was not a socialist. Then they came for the labour leaders, and I did not speak out because I was not a labor leader. Then they came for the Jews, and I did not speak out because I was not a Jew. Then they came for me, and there was no one left to speak out for me."

Human race, please note.

FEMA and Hurricane Andrew

I have spoken with survivors of Hurricane Andrew, which struck South Dade County, Florida, in 1992 and anyone who wants to know what the world will be like under organisations like FEMA and their masters should listen to what they say. The horror stories they tell about the actions of FEMA beggar belief. Far from helping the hundreds of thousands of homeless and injured victims, FEMA cordoned off the area and left the people to fend for themselves. They were given no food, no water, no medical supplies, no shelter and no help whatsoever when the disaster struck. One of the victims was K.T. Frankovich who suffered serious injuries in the hurricane. She tells of her horrific experiences in her book, *Where Heavens Meet* [33] About three days after the hurricane had devastated the region, she said a long line of police cars, about 12 to 15, arrived in her area. Each car was driven by a man dressed in a dark police uniform and they had three other plain-clothes men riding as passengers, she said. K.T. had a broken jaw, eight teeth knocked out and huge pieces of glass were embedded in her body that only a scalpel could remove. She begged this FEMA convoy for help and this was the exchange that followed, as described by K.T. in *Where Heavens Meet*:

> "'Please, sir, I need medical help,' I begged, barely able to speak. The officer sitting behind the wheel sighed heavily. He turned his head away from me and gazed out his windshield. The other three men in the car quietly looked at me. 'Sir, please, I need to get to a hospital,' I begged frantically. The officer took his time about reaching over to turn off the engine. With another sigh, he slowly opened the door and climbed out. He then proceeded to close the door and stood there with his legs spread astride.
>
> "'Lady, do me a favour,' he answered. 'Find yourself a piece of paper and a pencil. Write down your name and social security number next to the telephone number of your

nearest living relative. Tuck the piece of paper in your pocket so tomorrow, when I find your body, I'll know who to contact.'

"'No! No!' I cried out. 'You don't understand. I need to get to a hospital. I've been badly injured.'

"'No! You're the one who doesn't understand,' he hissed back.

"With that, he reached over to his holster and took out his gun. He grabbed me, forcing me up against the side of the car, and proceeded to put the barrel of the gun against my temple. I heard the hammer cock. From the position he had pushed me into, I could see directly into the car. The man sitting in the front passenger seat looked away from me immediately, glancing down at the floor. The two passengers in the back seat turned their heads quickly, staring out the window on the opposite side of the car. My son and the other survivor watched as the officer had pulled back the hammer on the gun. So shocked out of their minds by what they were witnessing, neither one could move!

"'You don't belong here!' the officer growled, pressing the barrel into the side of my head. 'Now you get the hell outta here before I blow away your ass!'

"He shoved my face into the car window and then released me. Someone grabbed me from behind and whirled me around so fast, I didn't have time to think! Before I knew it, I was being thrown over a shoulder. My rescuer took off running as fast as he could! I caught a brief glimpse of my son running next to me. With one gigantic leap, he and the survivor who carried me dove behind a pile of debris. All three of us crashed on top of each other in one tangled-up heap.

"'I'll shoot your damn asses!', the officer's voice rang out." [34]

This is the mentality behind FEMA, the US military, the Office of Homeland "Security" and leaders of government. That mentality would not orchestrate what happened on September 11th to advance its agenda? The official death toll in Hurricane Andrew was 26,[35] but K.T. Frankovich says she saw at least 71 bodies taken away from one small area alone. She estimates the dead to have numbered thousands. But how many people know that? Only those involved and no one is listening to them. As always the media told us what the official sources told them and they had no inclination to investigate further because life's easier that way. When you consider how 8,230 mobile homes and 9,140 apartments disappeared in the wake of 200–300 miles-an-hour winds, it is obvious that the official dead toll of 26 is insane. K.T. Frankovich recalls:

"The National Guard along with the Coast Guard, the Army, FEMA, Metro Dade Police, state police and local police removed dead bodies and body parts as quickly as possible during those first ten days of the aftermath. Horrified survivors watched as both uniformed and civilian-clothed men searched the rubble and filled body bags, which they then stacked in military vehicles or huge refrigerator trucks normally used to transport food, only to drive off and leave the stranded injured to fend for themselves.

"Not until I managed to escape the aftermath did I discover that the 'thermo-king' sections of these same refrigerator trucks, jam-packed with wall-to-wall body bags, ended up being stored at Card Sound Navy Base, located in an isolated area just above the Florida Keys. The inside temperature was kept cool by portable generators until the bodies were either incinerated or just plain dumped into huge open grave pits.

"Those working on the body pick-up operation were forced to take what is known as the Oath of Sworn Secrecy, which is strictly enforced by the government. Many of them plunged into shock, once exposed to the ghastly devastation and countless mutilated bodies. The horrors were way beyond human comprehension. I can vouch for this, as I accidentally stepped on the severed hand of a young child when I initially crawled out of the debris, only to witness shortly thereafter two dead teenagers and the decapitated body of a baby girl." [36]

K.T. says that when she lectured at the Clearwater Convention in Florida in 1999, a man in the audience introduced himself as Chief Petty Officer Roy Howard and said he had spent nine weeks on active duty working in South Dade County amid the devastation. He said he learned that at least 5,280 people had died and that the bodies had been "confiscated" by the National Guard and secretly disposed of in incinerators in a joint operation with FEMA. At least another 1,500 bodies were "confiscated" from lakes and other water.[37] This is the America that the population doesn't see, but it soon will if people don't wake up fast. FEMA, the organisation behind all this and with all those fascist powers to takeover America, is a 100% Illuminati creation funded by the profits from the CIA-Bush family drug operation. It is no surprise to learn, then, that it was during Father George's time at the CIA and in the White House between 1980 and 1992 that this "emergency management" network was established in the name of fighting terrorism and … drug trafficking![38] You have got to admire their cheek if nothing else.

"We will not tolerate civil disobedience …"

The training of troops for the planned military coup on the United States, and the conditioning of the population to accept it for their own safety, is well under way in the form of "urban warfare exercises" known as "Urban Warrior". These have been happening all over America and often involve foreign troops for the reasons outlined earlier. They are coordinated by the US Marine Corps Warfighting Laboratory, based in Quantico, Virginia. One of these "exercises" was at Monterrey Bay on Saturday, March 13th 1999, when hundreds of marines landed in amphibious landing craft from ships five miles offshore. They swarmed into the city of Monterrey, patrolling the streets to "practise" counterterrorist operations among American people. It was planned and agreed by local and federal authorities, and local people were given no choice. S. Brian Willson, who challenged the decision, wrote:

> "It seems that this "Urban Warrior" exercise is part of a national effort, still virtually under wraps after years of preparation, to utilize the armed forces to counter the much talked about increased threat of "terrorist" activities in the United States. It is conceivable that this Urban Warrior exercise, as a counter-"terrorist" operation, will have as suspects and adversaries US residents considered unpopular or undesirable based on convenient political demonizing." [39]

That was written in 1999 and the attacks of September 11th have given those behind Urban Warrior the perfect excuse to expand what has been happening for years already. Footage I saw of one these Urban Warrior invasions in Oakland, northern California, included soldiers pointing guns at civilians in their own streets and one shouted "attention, attention, attention, American forces are here to help, keep calm, we will not tolerate civil disobedience". [40] In Kingsville, Texas, the black helicopters (which are not supposed to exist) of the elite Delta Force suddenly descended on the population for an "exercise" in the streets of their town. Delta Force was created during the Carter administration as a counterterrorist unit within the US military. These are the guys preparing to be used in the military coup on America and they were present at Waco. Delta Force took over San Antonio in Texas for an "exercise" despite opposition for two years by local law enforcement against them doing so. Marines took control of the city hall at Swanboro, North Carolina, and set up a checkpoint directly in front of the police station where they posted a sign that read, "Military Checkpoint Ahead". [41] Deli owner Marty Proctor had Marines outside his shop and he concluded: "This is training for urban warfare against the American people … they're just preparing for when people get pissed off enough to start saying 'enough's enough.'" He said that a man and woman pulled up outside his deli and were too afraid to get out of their car:

> "They had little kids. Of course they don't want the kids walking up and down the street with people in camouflage gear carrying M-16 machine guns. We saw a guy today that was carrying an M-60. One guy was there with an M-60 in the prone position aiming it down the street." [42]

Proctor said that some residents told him the Marines at checkpoints had pointed automatic weapons at them, though the soldiers claimed they were not loaded. Marines lay behind sandbags pointing machine guns at cars approaching the checkpoint and there were military vehicles mounted with automatic weapons. One Marine questioned by reporters from the WorldNet Daily website told them: "Most people see police officers on a day to day basis and think nothing of it. They're not intimidated, as they should be. When we're seen, it's an intimidation thing more than anything." He was asked if residents should be concerned about the military acting as a police force and he said: "It's a new world. It's a new world." [43] That's for sure. Some of these "exercises", like one in Austin, Texas, have not told the population what is happening until it is over because the idea is to observe the reaction of people who believe the military have taken over their town.

You can trust me children, I have a nice car ...

These "exercises" have also included using children to find out where the legal gun owners live. The targeting of children and young people, and the general use of the people to spy on each other on behalf of the state is at the heart of the policy, as it is in any fascist society. You see many references to high-tech surveillance in children's television programmes as the conditioning continues. A plan called Capital Area Campus Crime Stoppers in Austin, Texas, offers rewards for those reporting fellow students to the authorities. "The mission of the Campus Crime Stoppers program is to assist the AISD Police Department and the Travis County Sheriff's Office in the fight against crime on school campuses," says its website. [44] Students are urged to call the number 499-TIPS and if their report leads to an arrest they will qualify for a reward of $200. Each year since it was launched in 1995, says the website, student participation has increased. Students can also become members and get discounts at Highland Lanes, Showplace Lanes, Westgate Lanes, Dart Bowl, Fiesta Texas, Music Mania, and Chaparral Ice. Hey, and don't miss the exciting fundraising events of Capital Area Crime Stoppers, Inc., including Crime Stoppers: Fight Back Austin and the annual jail-a-thon. A few can only control the many if the many control each other. Children and young people are being especially targeted so that they come to accept the constant surveillance and control as part of life because they have known no different. Schools are becoming fortresses with cameras everywhere and in the United States fingerprint scanners are being introduced for children to pay for school lunch. Walter Curfman, Superintendent of the Tussey Mountain School District in western Pennsylvania, said: "You always have your finger with you, unless you cut it off." [45] How observant. The scanning system was developed in response to a federal regulation requiring that cafeterias hide who is getting free or reduced-price lunches, Curfman said (problem-reaction-solution). The company behind the scheme now wants to expand the system for use in recording attendance and on school door locks. Thumbprints are now also being introduced for rental car hire and even buying food in the local store – exactly as predicted in my books in the mid-1990s. [46] The reason that most people are accepting Big Brother schools is to protect their children from harm. Fear, the big F, is the Illuminati's prime vehicle for manipulation. This has been fuelled by students going crazy with guns, as in the mass killing at the Columbine (Columba, Semiramis) School on April 20th 1999. Note the date again – April 19th and 20th are the Satanic days dedicated to the god Baal and demand blood sacrifice. Same as Waco, same as Oklahoma. See also the information in my books on mind control.

Good job it's only a theory, eh?

There remain billions of people today who still say there is no evidence of the conspiracy and it's just a theory. There are many reasons for this. Among them are a lack of research; not wishing to admit they have been duped all their lives; and solid, virtually impenetrable denial because they don't want to face the situation we are in. Head in the sand, as it is known. Meanwhile the military fascist state rolls on with tracking systems for cars and cellphones connected to global positioning satellites that can spot them, the authorities claim, down to a few feet. (So why did they not find bin Laden then?) There are proposals to implant electronic devices into "non-violent" offenders to ensure they don't go outside a designated area and the devices can be programmed to trigger shocks until the person goes back to where the authorities have told him he must be. The United Nations continues to take control of enormous tracts of land in the United States and elsewhere in the name of "protecting the environment" when the forces behind the UN are the ones behind the pollution and environmental degradation. Now, thanks to September 11th, the explosion of legislation I detailed earlier has demolished what was left of civil liberties and basic freedoms. Watch also for the China connection. Insiders, including the CIA scientist with the "patch" on his chest, have told me for many years that China is planned to play a major role at some point in this agenda.

Back to Iraq? They've never been away

As I complete this book, the Bush and Blair governments are trying to persuade people it is a good idea, and perfectly legitimate, to invade and mass bomb Iraq in the "war on terrorism". This is not for any alleged connection between Saddam Hussein, the attack on America and Osama bin Laden, because they do not want to focus any attention on the members of the Iraqi Republican Guard that were settled in Oklahoma and elsewhere in the United States by Father George Bush after the Gulf War. Perhaps it was with this in mind that the CIA said in February 2002 that there was no evidence that Iraq has engaged in any terrorism directed at the United States or its allies. Instead they want to invade Iraq because of Saddam's "threat to the world with his weapons of mass destruction". National Security Adviser Condoleezza Rice told *New Yorker* reporter Nicholas Lemann that the policy was not just to stop terrorism, but to prevent the accumulation of weapons of mass destruction in "the hands of irresponsible states." [47] What, like the US and Britain? The weapons they said were owned by Iraq are those that Scott Ritter, one of the weapons inspectors in Iraq, said did not exist. He told *Arms Control Today* that the threat from Iraq was basically zero. He said: "Iraq no longer possessed any meaningful quantities of chemical or biological agent, if it possessed any at all, and the industrial means to produce these agents had either been eliminated or were subject to stringent monitoring." [48] The same was true of Iraq's nuclear and ballistic missile capabilities and Ritter said it was possible as early as 1997 to determine that, from a qualitative standpoint, Iraq had been disarmed. Meanwhile Pakistan, a country with deep connections to 9/11, was allowed to possess nuclear weapons with no consequences from the United States once it agreed to join the "war on terrorism". As always, the Illuminati change the rules to fit the desired goal. If the agenda is threatened by the agreement of the Taliban to hand over bin Laden or Iraq allows new weapons inspections, the very actions you demand to avoid an invasion, you just say sorry, changed our mind, and think of another excuse. Asked if it would make a difference to US invasion plans if Iraq gave in to US demands, Secretary of State Colin Powell told CNN that "even then the United States believes the Iraqi people would be better served with a new kind of leadership".[49] Not to mention America. Or, as Bernard Lewis of Princeton University said in his Middle East briefing of senior White House staff: "... in that part of the world, nothing matters more than resolute force and will".[50]

The Iraqi people have lost some one million children to bombing, hunger and disease caused by sanctions demanded by the United States and Britain since 1991. This is a country in which babies are being born with unbelievable deformities because of the radioactive material contained in the bombs that have devastated the lives of the people. Cancer rates have soared and Iraq has developed the world's highest rate of childhood leukaemia. Some 70% of Iraqi women are now anaemic, and two coordinators of the so-called "oil-for-food" programme, which provides the oil cartel with cheap Iraqi oil, have resigned and spoken out against the genocidal affects of the sanctions. Now, as I write, Bush and Blair are trying to overcome opposition around the world, and justify the mass bombing of these people and the occupation of their country. Why? I will let President Bush answer in his own reversed and coded message:

> "The hijackers were instruments of evil who died in vain. Behind them is a cult of evil that seeks to harm the innocent and thrives on human suffering. Theirs is the worst kind of cruelty, the cruelty that is fed, not weakened, by tears. Theirs is the worst kind of violence, pure malice while daring to claim the authority of God. We cannot fully understand the designs and power of evil; it is enough to know that evil, like goodness, exists. And in the terrorists evil has found a willing servant."

This is why those in power spend trillions of dollars on war and destruction when a fraction of that would bring an end to hunger and avoidable disease across the world. It doesn't have to be like this, it is just a choice. The world is the way it is because the forces behind those in political, military and media power want it to be this way and the rest of the people allow it to be this way. While the planet is being taken over more and more every day by the Illuminati military state, the mainstream media creates a diversion for the public mind with its game shows, its obsession with sport and celebrity gossip, and "news" programmes that are largely propaganda arms of the official version of life. The agenda is introduced virtually without challenge while the people focus on the latest football game for Manchester United or the Miami Dolphins, drool over the Oscar ceremony, or speculate on the father of a movie star's "love child". Having served the Illuminati by producing the diversion (largely, at the lower levels, through ignorance) the media completes its crucial contribution by seeking to ridicule or discredit those who do have the foresight and passion to investigate and expose the conspiracy. As Andreas von Bulow, the former German Defence Minister, said: "Journalists don't even raise the simplest questions and those who differ are labelled crazy."[51] There's a guy on

British television called Jon Ronson who produced a book called *Them: Adventures With Extremists* [52] that purported to offer insight into people like conspiracy researchers. Note the implication in the title that if you talk about the conspiracy you are an "extremist". What does that make those who orchestrate the mass murder of thousands of civilians in Afghanistan and Iraq then – "moderates"? I found Ronson depressingly, though predictably, uninformed and I was not alone. You have seen how much information is presented in this single book, never mind the thousands of pages in my previous publications and the 5,000 pages on my website. Yet in an interview promoting his book in 2002, Ronson said of my information: "I think he made it up." [53] I would like to say that Ronson is an exception, but sadly he is not. If we are going to bring an end to the Illuminati agenda, and we are, everyone has to take responsibility for researching and communicating what is happening. If people expect the mainstream media to do it for them, they may as well put their hands in the air now, get in line for a micro-chip, and prepare for a global version of Nazi Germany.

But then all this is only a theory, so no worries; and those of us who expose it are just crazy nutters, right?

Zzzzzzzzzzzzzzzzzzzzzzzzzz. Knock, knock.

SOURCES

1   http://www.fromthewilderness.com/free/ww3/zbig.html. Dr Johannes Koeppl has a German language website at www.antaris.com. He also wrote a book in 1989 entitled *The Most Important Secrets In The World*

2   http://www.fromthewilderness.com/free/ww3/zbig.html

3   Ibid

4   There's some good background on chemtrails at http://www.trufax.org/research3/contrails.html The Space Preservation Act of 2001, HR 2977 IH, presented to the 107th Congress by Congressman Dennis Kucinich on October 2nd 2001, describes chemtrails as an "exotic weapons system". This act can be found at http://www.carnicom.com/hr2977.htm

5   See http://www.sickofdoctors.addr.com/articles/vaccinesandautism.htm

6   http//www.davidicke.net/medicalarchives/badmed/stupidfluoride.html – see the medical archives at davidicke.com for a library of articles and information on these subjects

7   First Humans to Receive ID Chips, *Los Angeles Times*, May 9th 2002

8   Ibid

9   Ibid

10   Ibid

11   http://www.spyproducts.com/SonicNausea1.html

12   *Daily Mail*, May 23rd 2002

13   http://usinfo.state.gov/topical/rights/law/01103003directive2.htm

14   http://news.bbc.co.uk/hi/english/uk_politics/newsid_1653000/1653142.stm

15   http://www.hermes-press.com/gonzalez5.htm

16   *Cherith Chronicle*, June 1997

17   A good start is http://www.mt.net/~watcher/fema.html

18   Vast Quarantine Role Advocated for States, *Free Press Washington*, November 7th 2001,
     http://www.freep.com/news/nw/terror2001/quar7_20011107.htm

19   Ibid

20   David Burnham, *Above The Law*

21   http://www.federalobserver.com/archive.php?aid=753

22   *Guardian*, January 16th 1991 (This *Guardian* is an independent weekly based at 33 West
     17th St., New York, NY 10011)

23   Ibid

24   Ibid

25   *Children Of The Matrix*, p 247

26   http://www.federalobserver.com/archive.php?aid=753

27   *Guardian* (New York) January 16th 1991

28   Ibid

29   Ben Bradlee Jr, *Guts and Glory: The Rise and Fall of Oliver North* (Donald I. Fine, June 1988)

30   Ibid

31   Military Favors a Homeland Command, Forces May Shift to Patrolling US, *Washington Post*,
     November 21st 2001

32   *Washington Post*, May 15th 2002, p AO1

33   K.T. Fronkovich, *Where Heavens Meet* (Language of Souls Publications, Florida, 1999)

34   http://www.nexusmagazine.com/hurricane.html

35   http://www.usatoday.com/2000/century/weather/stories/wandrew.htm

36   http://www.nexusmagazine.com/hurricane.html

37   Ibid

38   http://www.mt.net/~watcher/fema.html

39   Veterans for Peace Inc., February 8th 1999, http://www.mbay.net/~jenvic/vfp/feb8.htm

40   *9/11 – The Road to Tyranny*, available from **Infowars.com**

41   Marines on Main Street, by David M. Bresnahan, **WorldNetDaily.com**
     http://www.worldnetdaily.com/bluesky_bresnahan/20000414_xex_marines_main.shtml

42   Ibid

43   Ibid

44 **http://www.austincrimestoppers.org/campus.htm**

45 ABC News, January 18th 2001,
    http://abcnews.go.com/sections/scitech/DailyNews/fingerprint_kids010118.html

46 New system lets Kroger Shoppers Pay with Fingerprint, *Houston Chronicle*, May 15th 2002

47 The Next World Order, the Bush Administration May Have a Brand-New Doctrine of Power, *New Yorker*, April lst 2002

48 *Arms Control Today*, June 2000

49 **http://www.foreignpolicy-infocus.org/commentary/2002/0205cabal_body.html**

50 Ibid

51 *Der Tagesspiegel*, January 13th 2002

52 Jon Ronson, *Them: Adventures With Extremists* (Simon & Schuster Trade, January 2002)

53 **http://www.salon.com/people/conv/2002/03/14/ronson/index2.html**

Finally, the most important chapter of all ...

chapter 16

From here to eternity

An eye for an eye makes the whole world blind

Mahatma Gandhi

"Just look at us. Everything is backwards; everything is upside down. Doctors destroy health, lawyers destroy justice, universities destroy knowledge, governments destroy freedom, the major media destroy information and religions destroy spirituality"

Michael Ellner

Throughout most of this book I have been referring to the world as perceived by the five senses. Therefore, although the information has been very challenging and fundamentally contradicts the conditioned view of life, the overwhelming majority of readers will no doubt be persuaded by the vast body of interconnected evidence and "coincidences" that, at the very least, there is another agenda going on that they are never told about. Others will have dismissed the whole idea of a conspiracy from the start, but then the price of sand is quite cheap at the moment, apparently, and those people will have long put the book down to catch the latest from CNN.

At this point, however, I am about to part company with the credulity of a number of those who have been with me thus far. Nothing like as many as you would think, given where I am going from here, but a good number for sure. That's fine and as it should be. I am not trying to persuade or convince anyone of anything. My only desire is to see that all people have access to all information and, that done, they should be free to make up their own minds about what to make of it. But I would stress that in our five-sense prison we are denied an infinity of knowledge about the nature of life and to consider possibility only from the five-sense perspective, especially one constantly and massively conditioned and programmed by Illuminati propaganda, is an exercise in fundamental self-delusion. What we are not being told about 9/11 is infinitesimal compared with what we are not being told about life itself – who we are, where we come from, and the nature of reality. For the vast majority of the six billion incarnate spirits on this planet the ability to see and feel and "know" beyond the five senses is the land of the cuckoos and fairies. They live in the "real world". They have no truck with that airy-fairy nonsense. Can I see it, hear it, touch it, smell it, and taste it? Oh, it exists then. But in fact their "real world" is the world of the Illuminati illusion.

I am me – and shall always be

I am guided by information and intuition, and I will go wherever that takes me, no matter what anyone else may think. What people make of my information is none of my business, but what I make of it is very much my business and no one else's. I will decide how I view reality because I have that infinite divine right and nothing and no one is going to deflect me from that, not by ridicule, condemnation, nor any other means. I make this point because most research into the global conspiracy is compiled and written from the five-sense perspective. It is about names, dates, places, agendas and connections. That's fine and necessary. I do the same myself, as you can see, but that's only part of the story, the point where the conspiracy interacts with the physical senses and the world that we see, hear, touch, smell and taste. The conspiracy, however, is much bigger than that; *we* are much bigger than that. But when I go beyond the five-sense prison, beyond the conditioned reality, most conspiracy researchers dismiss me because I am "not credible". What they mean is that I am prepared to go in my search for truth far beyond where their minds are prepared to explore. Often this is because they cannot comprehend of phenomena at work beyond the range of the five senses, but in other cases it is because they fear that if they do venture outside the accepted "norms" their "credibility" will be threatened. They are still allowing the conditioning of others to dictate where they will go and what they will say. They are still controlled by the fear of what other people think, still operating in the five-sense prison, and so still under the control of the Illuminati agenda, albeit much less so than the majority of the population.

Tent pitching

When we arrive in this five-sense "world" we begin to walk our journey of experience. I have likened it to carrying a tent in a backpack, walking down the road and looking for somewhere to pitch it, settle down, and find our comfort zone. Where we choose to stop decides the way we see the world because this is the point, the perspective, from which we observe people and events. Here are some of the "camp sites".

- **Base Camp:** Most people don't choose to walk very far. A few strides and out come the pegs at a point where they believe what the media tells them and accept that they are ordinary and powerless or that they know all they need to know (same thing). They are happy to drift through life guided by accepted "norms" and conditioned "thought". They include the atheists and the fanatical religious believers, those who think this world is all that exists and those who think that if they do whatever their religion tells them they might get a ticket to the afterlife in paradise. I will call these the "Base-Campers" and they represent by far the greatest number of humankind.

- **Radical Camp:** Others walk a bit further until they find an acceptable spot. These are the "Radical-Campers", and they have begun to see that there is more to know than we are told. They may be "greens" and "environmentalists" or campaigners against the arms trade, "third world" debt, globalisation and other five-sense injustices. The Base-Campers who pitched their tents back down the road see these Radical-Campers as extreme and "loony" because we judge everything and everyone from our own point of observation – where our tent is pitched. What is perfectly sensible to one person or group will be extreme or crazy to another. In the same way, our conditioning, background and accumulated "knowledge" lead us to see the same event from very different perspectives. If a guy came out of the sea with a crab clinging to his bum someone might shout, "Hey, there's a crab's claw stuck to your bum." But a fellow crab might say, "Hey, you've got a man's bum stuck to your claw." Depends on your point of observation.

- **Conspiracy Camp:** Those who are still not satisfied with the perspectives and beliefs of the Radical Camp decide to walk some more before they pitch the tent. These "Conspiracy-Campers" realise that the injustices the Radical-Campers acknowledge are not random, but part of a coldly calculated global injustice, the Illuminati conspiracy. They will see the connections and the game plan within the five-sense reality – the names, dates, coordination and so on. The Radical-Campers see these Conspiracy-Campers as extreme in the same way that Base Campers see them. The Radical-Campers may, and indeed many do, condemn the Conspiracy-Campers as "racist" and "Nazis". Did you know that a global fascist state is unfolding all around you? What? You're a Nazi – condemn him, ban his meetings, ban his books. You think I'm joking? If only I was. Back down the road in the tent city of the Base Camp, they see the Conspiracy-Campers as crazy, loony "conspiracy theorists" akin to members of the Flat Earth Society.

- **Infinity Camp:** There are others, the "Infinity-Campers" I will call them, who continue to walk on past the point where the five-sense conspiracy researchers are banging in their pegs. They have no desire to pitch a tent and they don't even carry one because there is never enough time to put it down before something draws them further down the road of inner and outer discovery. By now the road is quiet with not many people about, but those who venture this far start to realise that the world we see, hear, touch, smell and taste, is an illusion and only a very tiny frequency range that those senses can perceive. Beyond its vibrational walls is infinity, where all possibility exists. They see that the five-sense "human bodies" of the Illuminati leaders are only a physical vehicle for entities operating beyond the five senses to control the "physical" world and turn humanity into a giant battery, an energy source. To conventional five-sense conspiracy researchers, Infinity-Campers are extreme and doing great harm to their efforts to persuade people through names, dates, places, etc., that the conspiracy is real. To the Radical-Campers they are lunatics, but dangerous ones if "naïve" people believe what they say. To the Base-Campers they should be locked away in a psychiatric institution because they are clearly mentally ill. In short: anyone who moves beyond the point where you have pitched your tent is seen as extreme and the further they wander down the road the more extreme you perceive them to be. Their points of observation are so different, and this puts them, literally, on different "wavelengths".

Of course, this is a simplistic outline of what happens and there are many subgroups and cross-matches, but the theme I have laid out here is very true and can be observed every day. My friend Guylaine Lanctot, a former Canadian doctor and author of two brilliant books, *The Medical Mafia* and *What The Hell Are We Doing Here Anyway?*,[1] refers to the Base-Campers as the white sheep and the Radical and Conspiracy-Campers as the black sheep. The white sheep are the masses that blindly accept the official version of reality while the black sheep rebel against that to a larger or lesser extent. But they are all still sheep, still caught in the five-sense "fly trap". What they think they see is what they think they get. I can understand, given this situation, why many people will find this last chapter challenging to their sense of reality, but so be it. It's just a choice and we should not be looking at differing perspectives as right or wrong. I would say "different" is a far more appropriate description. Anyway, if you are new to this information, I should strap in.

"World" of illusion

We don't live in a "world" at all. We live in a frequency range, the one that our five senses can access and perceive, and the five-sense range of perception is tiny. Infinite creation is not structured like a tower block. "Heaven" is not in the sky. The sky is in the sky. Infinity consists of infinite frequencies sharing the same space in the same way as all the radio and television frequencies broadcasting to your area now are sharing the same space that your body is occupying. Those broadcast frequencies are not just around your body, they are sharing the same space. They can do this because they are operating on a different frequency range or wavelength to your body and to each other. Only when the frequencies are really close do we get "interference", otherwise all are oblivious to each other's existence because they literally operate in different frequencies, different "realities" or "worlds". When you tune your radio to a station, say Radio 1, that is what you get. You don't hear Radio 2, 3, or 4 because they are not broadcasting on the wavelength to which your radio is tuned. Move the dial from the frequency of

Radio 1 to Radio 2 and now, obviously, you hear Radio 2. But Radio 1 did not cease to broadcast when you moved the dial from its wavelength. It goes on broadcasting – existing – while your focus, your consciousness, is tuned to something else. This is precisely the principle on which infinite creation operates. When people say that infinity is within you or, symbolically, the Kingdom of Heaven is within you, that is correct. All infinity is within us because all of infinity shares all space. The point is, however, that we cannot see all of infinity with our five senses, just as you cannot hear all the radio stations available by tuning to one of them. We see only that tiny part of infinity that is vibrating to the frequency of those senses – what we see, hear, touch, smell and taste. This is what I call the five-sense prison because most people are so trapped in its manufactured and manipulated illusions that they believe that this is all that exists. It is their only reality. This is further ingrained and conditioned by the "education" system, the media and "science", all of which are dominated by the belief that the "world" of the five senses is all that there is. Why is this? Because that's what the Illuminati want us to believe for reasons I will explain shortly.

Vibrations in the mind of "God"

Everything is vibrating energy. When energy is vibrating slowly it appears to us to be "dense" and "solid", but look at it under a microscope and no matter how "solid" something seems to be it is still vibrating energy. If it were not vibrating it could not exist. As the speed of vibration increases the energy becomes less and less dense, just as ice becomes water becomes steam, becomes "invisible". Heat raises the speed of vibration, as with this ice-water-steam example. When something gets hotter its vibration increases and it becomes less "solid". Apply enough heat to a "solid" substance like metal and it melts because its vibrational state has dramatically changed. In the same way, when a vibration increases so does the temperature. As I have been writing in my books since 1991, the vibration of this planet is getting faster and look at what has happened to the temperature. We have the phenomenon of "global warming", which has been wrongly blamed on industrial pollution. I am not, I stress, saying that pollution is a good thing, only that it is not the cause of the rising temperature. That is down to the quickening frequency or vibration of the planetary energy field, and it has hardly started yet.

Another dimension

If you change the vibration of something its physical expression will change. An opera singer can break a wine glass merely from the sound of her voice because of the vibrational connection between the sound vibration of the voice and the vibrational field of the glass. For a split second the voice vibration becomes the same frequency as the glass, it tunes into it, you might say, and dismantles its vibrational stability. So it smashes. Our five senses can perceive only the denser vibrational fields that reflect light. As the vibration increases it eventually reaches a point where we can no longer see it because it has gone beyond the frequency range of the five senses. At this stage, to our five-sense reality, it "disappears". It has done no such thing; it has merely left the frequency range of our five-sense prison. It hasn't "disappeared" any more than Radio 1 "disappears" when you retune to Radio 2.

Bands of frequencies have become known as dimensions. For simplicity I will refer to the frequency range accessible by the five senses as the "Third Dimension" or "Physical Dimension". But even then we cannot perceive most of what exists in this one universe alone. According to the latest research, apparently, some 99.5% of it we cannot see. Our eyes can only see matter that reflects light, what science calls luminous matter. This is why, when you are in complete darkness, you can't see anything. Only when you introduce light to reflect from the objects around you can they be seen. Some 99.5% of mass in this universe is called "dark matter" because it does not reflect light. Therefore we can't see it. A friend of mine, the Italian physicist Giuliana Conforto, explains all this in simple terms in her superb books, *Man's Cosmic Game* and *Giordano Bruno's Future Science*.[2] In the first book she gave the figure of less than 10% of mass can be seen, but new evidence now suggests that we can see only 0.5%. We have people making definite judgements and proclaiming certainties about the nature of life and creation when we can't even see 99.5% of our own universe! It is like spending your entire life in a tiny prison cell on some little isolated island and then telling everyone there what the rest of the world is like. We would say that was the height of stupidity, arrogance and self-delusion, but that is precisely what official "education", "science" and "media" etc., (and those who accept that version of reality) are doing every day. So are those conspiracy researchers who say that I must either be crazy or working for the Illuminati when I take the conspiracy beyond the five-sense level and into the unseen realms. Well if such people want to stay in jail, they should be my guest, but I ain't keeping them company.

When people find it hard to comprehend or understand each other we say they are not on the same wavelength. That is exactly the case. People stuck at "tent camps" one, two, or three, are not on the same wavelength as each other and so, as with radio stations, never their minds shall meet. The Infinity Camp is on such a different wavelength to those groups still tuned to the various levels of the five-sense prison that most people simply cannot comprehend where they are coming from or what they're saying. I remember being "interviewed" by a BBC radio host in England called Steve Wright and two others whose reason for being there I never did work out. Anyway, it was hilarious to watch them. Their faces, particularly Wright's, were a picture of total incredulity. It was so funny. Afterwards I had letters from listeners to the programme who understood clearly the information that Wright and friends could not even begin to fathom. Why? Different wavelengths, different point of observation, different reality. But my most memorable encounter with a different wavelength was a lady called Christine Smith from the UK *Daily Mirror*. After five minutes of talking with this lady and hearing her constant repetition of "yeeaahhh" whenever I completed a sentence, I realised that nothing was going in, not least because I could see no evidence that there was anything for it to go in to. Not even the simple suggestion that the five senses can't see everything produced a glimmer of discernable neuron activity, and it all sailed way over her head. Mind you, it didn't have to be very high to do that. I decided that if I had a conversation with the wall behind her I would definitely glean a more intelligent response. I couldn't work out if we were actually on different wavelengths or if, in fact, she was not on one at all. Then the stunning realisation hit me. She was a feature writer on the second biggest selling newspaper in the UK, and sitting at that crucial point between what is happening in the world and what the people are told is happening. Wow. Deep intake of breath, move on.

Parallel universes

The official scientific explanations of life are so blatantly absurd that they have left the scientific establishment in a maze of dead-end streets. When it came to the big questions, the contradictions and anomalies, they have nowhere to go unless they change their foundation beliefs and misconceptions. Thankfully, at last, this is beginning to happen among more and more scientists. An edition of the BBC science series *Horizon* in 2002 was devoted to the gathering acceptance among scientists of the existence of parallel universes or parallel realities, as I prefer to call them. The opening narrative to the programme said:

> "For almost a hundred years science has been haunted by a dark secret, that there might be mysterious, hidden worlds beyond our human senses. Mystics have long claimed there were such places. They were, they said, full of ghosts and spirits ... but ever since the 19th century physicists have been trying to make sense of an uncomfortable discovery. When they tried to pin point the exact location of atomic particles like electrons, they found it was utterly impossible. They had no single location ... The only explanation that anyone could come up with is that the particles don't just exist in our universe. They slip into existence in other universes, too, and there are an infinite number of these parallel universes, all of them slightly different. In effect, there's a parallel universe in which Napoleon won the Battle of Waterloo; in another the British Empire held on to its American colonies; in one you were never born ... they are even stranger than Elvis being alive."

Although this was not mentioned in the programme, the reason the particles "appear" and "disappear" is because they are changing frequencies. One scientist told *Horizon* that different "universes" had different laws of physics, and Alan Guth of the Massachusetts Institute of Technology said: "... one found that the reality was far stranger than anybody would have invented in the form of fiction. Particles really do have the possibility in some sense of being in two different places at the same time." This may be a scientific "revelation" today, but mystics and their like have known it for thousands of years, and they have been ridiculed and burned at the stake for having the audacity to share what they know. When I made these points years ago I was labelled a "nutcase". The Illuminati have had this knowledge since their creation and they have done everything they could to suppress this understanding among the people while using it themselves to manipulate, control and delude. They have used both their religions and their "science" to do this, but the dam is now collapsing. Science still has a long way to go, however, to match the understandings that existed in what we call ancient history, and the parallel universe theory will have to encompass one day an even more amazing fact: we are all "parallel universes" – every single one of us.

The great illusion

What is reality? It is whatever we decide to make it. We all live in our own individual, unique, universe. There are points of agreement where our universes meet and we may, for instance, look out of the window and all agree that we see trees, houses and cars. Beyond that, however, we see the world in subtly different, or even completely different, ways. We may agree that we see a car, but one person may think it's lovely and another may think it's horrible. We may agree that we are looking at a man or a woman, but one will think the person to be beautiful while another thinks otherwise. This is because we are on different wavelengths, observing from a different universe. You could gather together a thousand people to consider a topic of debate and you would have, in various forms, a thousand different perceptions of that subject. They would see the same thing in a thousand different ways because they are observing from a thousand different universes … universes of the mind and spirit. Billions of incarnate universes on this planet believe that what the five senses perceive is all that exists. To others that range of perception is such a fraction of all that exists that it would be impossible to measure. Like I say, we are not talking right and wrong here, just different. What arrogance and delusion it is for one person, one universe, to seek to impose its reality on another. It is psychological fascism.

What we call reality is simply the wavelength or wavelengths to which we are connected. Those who can only perceive possibility within the five senses will have a dramatically different reality to those that can perceive beyond and into the Great Infinity. One who can accept only the illusions of the five senses will believe that what they see is all there is; that we are born as some kind of random accident; and that we have anything from a few seconds or 100 years in some kind of chemically created "consciousness" before we cease to exist. Others may believe that after "death" they go to some other part of this five-sense reality, some eternal paradise or eternal hell. But those that can perceive beyond the five-sense prison, however, can see that we are all one infinite consciousness; that all energy is consciousness; and that therefore all that exists in whatever form is part of one unified whole, one infinite mind-spirit. We are all one; we are each other. While the five senses present us with the illusion of division and "empty" space between us, beyond the walls of this prison of perception is all consciousness and, by definition, all energy. There is no "empty" space, between us or anything else; it is energy vibrating to a frequency outside the range of the five senses. Those who have retained or regained their higher senses, their "psychic sensitivities" you might say, can feel this energy. We sense it as "atmosphere", good and bad "vibes", and as feeling, not thought. Those who have expanded beyond the five senses will begin to understand that divine infinity is an ocean of consciousness vibrating to different wavelengths and that we are a droplet within that ocean. Our droplet manifests itself as our own unique universe within the infinite. We can choose to disconnect from the infinite and become an isolated droplet and this is what happens when we accept the five-sense illusion. Our incarnate consciousness becomes so mesmerised by the illusions of the five senses that it disconnects from the ocean and lives within an infinitesimal fraction of its infinite potential. But we can choose to open our hearts and minds to reconnect with all that we are and then we realise that we not only a droplet in the infinite ocean, we *are* that ocean. You can pick up a droplet of water in your hand on the seashore and you can look at it in isolation. When we do so we are looking at a symbol, a profound symbol, of most people on planet earth today and for a long time "past". They are isolated, disconnected, and with no idea that the ocean exists never mind that they are part of it, indeed they *are* it. These are the people manipulated to believe in the five-sense reality and that alone. If you turn your hand and let the droplet fall back into the water, it is no longer part of the ocean, it *is* the ocean, for it is connected to every other droplet. That is our true state. We are infinity. We are all that exists, has existed, and ever will exist. When we break free of the five-sense prison, we begin to access greater and greater levels of infinity and our point of observation changes dramatically.

In the world, but not of it

As we progress through the process of deconditioning from the programmed illusions of a lifetime or lifetimes we start to move the focus of our consciousness from within the five-sense prison to beyond it. At this point we are observing the prison from outside of its walls. We begin to see what we have been part of and deluded by in our five-sense state. We can see the symbolic bars, warders, fences, surveillance cameras and the tiny little cell we have been sitting in while thinking we were free. We can see the "electric chairs" – all the manipulated abuses of our mind and body that lead us to kill the physical vehicle that allows us to experience this "world". When we connect with this level of our consciousness beyond the physical illusion we are *in* this "world" in a physical sense, but we are no longer *of* it. The vast majority at this time who remain imprisoned by the five senses are so deeply deluded by their constantly conditioned reality that they believe that spending a lifetime in a mental, emotional and, increasingly, physical prison cell is living in a free world. They are so caught in the illusion that they cannot see the bars. They sit there, unquestioning, unchallenging and oblivious of their plight. If you were the Illuminati and your desire was to control the people of this planet and manipulate them to build a world in your image in line with your agenda for a global dictatorship, what state of being would you like your targets to express? Would it be easier to control people mesmerised by the five-sense illusion? Or would it be easier to try to control incarnate consciousness still connected to levels beyond this "world" – consciousness that could look into this prison from outside and see it for what it is? The question answers itself.

Curse of ignorance

It is for this reason that throughout what we call history there has been an onslaught against the knowledge that reveals the nature of reality and those who communicate it. This is what the inquisitions were really all about, taking the knowledge out of circulation. Hundreds of thousands of "witches" were hung and burned because they carried knowledge of life beyond the five-sense prison, and how to communicate with it. As the Illuminati manipulated over thousands of years, especially through the Roman Empire and those that followed in Europe, they used the cover of Christianity to destroy the knowledge of who we are, where we come from and the nature of life. When these empires went into Asia, Africa, the Americas and elsewhere they sought to destroy the knowledge held in those ancient societies. They slaughtered the shamen and others who were the carriers and communicators of the knowledge across the generations. This is why the esoteric, the "occult", or "paranormal" is dismissed as either crazy or evil. As I have detailed in previous books, the Illuminati not only infiltrated what we call the "scientific establishment", they created it. They introduced the very version of the this-world-is-all-there-is "science" that is taught as unquestionable fact in the schools and universities. To progress in science is virtually impossible unless you promote, or at least do not expose, this ludicrous vision of the world and creation. "Science" is policed by this mindset because official science is not overwhelmingly about discovery; it is about selling a lie to hide the truth from the people. Ask a scientist who has challenged the official version, and let him or her tell you what happens to their career. When Galileo had the audacity to say that the earth was a sphere and not flat he was put under house arrest for the last eight years of his life. The same happens today, it's just a little more subtle that's all. Well, most of the time it is. Control of science and scientists is essential to the Illuminati agenda because if we had free-thinking science the human race would have been aware long ago of the nature of reality. In fact without the suppression it would never have forgotten.

The Illuminati have used two apparent "opposites" to control the reality of people: official science and the greatest form of mind control ever invented – religion. These are seen as opposites, as polarities, but they are oppo-sames. They are the same outcome by a different route. "Science" has basically told us that the world that we see is all that exists and that what happens to us in our few years of consciousness is as random as life itself. Religion tells us that if we do as it says we will go to paradise as a chosen one. If we do not do as it says we shall spend our eternity in the fires of hell. Both "opposites" have a common theme. You are not in control of your life; you are either a random accident or the pawn in the game of some dictator god who is so loving he will condemn you to an eternity of suffering for having the nerve not to do what the men in frocks tell you. The common theme is that you are ordinary and powerless, and you must look outside of yourself, to others, to tell you what you should think, do and say.

The five-sense prison

It is clear why the Illuminati have spent so much time and effort destroying and suppressing the knowledge of reality, consciousness and creation that would set us free of the five-sense illusion. The last thing they want us to have is the knowledge that we are all that exists and that whenever we choose we can access an infinity of love, wisdom, understanding and intuitive "knowing" from our higher levels of consciousness. The foundation of the Illuminati control of this planet is the control of our reality and our imagination of ourselves. It is designed to so disconnect incarnate consciousness from its multi-dimensional, infinite self that it becomes an isolated droplet in a five-sense prison. When we concede to that conditioning we cease to be the ocean. This disconnected droplet, imprisoned in a physical body, then looks to the five senses for a fix on itself and reality. And from what sources do those five senses gather their "information" and "guidance"? From the eyes and the ears – the "information" that bombards those senses minute by minute through the "education" system, politics, "science" and the media. All these sources are controlled and created by the Illuminati to condition the population to believe in a five-sense reality. The technique is so simple. You thought-police the five-sense prison and you destroy, suppress, ridicule or demonise the knowledge of who we really are and the infinity beyond the lower senses. You say that psychics who are connecting with some of these other levels of consciousness are mad, deluded or in league with the "Devil". People who have experiences that cannot be explained by the laughable limitations of five-sense reality are similarly dismissed and discarded. Once you have created this structure, anyone born into it is immediately subjected to a lifetime of constant conditioning to mould a reality that suits the agenda and maintains the target in mental, emotional and spiritual enslavement. Only a few in these circumstances have the wisdom and determination to seek their own truth and not the one dictated to them by those that control the flow of what is bravely called "information". It is to hold our focus in the five senses that we are subjected to a minute-by-minute onslaught of five-sense stimulation through advertising, the media, movies, food, drink and sex. There is nothing wrong with such stimulation because it is one level of experience, but the aim is to so addict the five senses that this becomes our only level of experience and perception. I must say they have done a bloody good job so far, but we are now entering a very different era.

We can talk about secret societies and Bilderberg Groups and all these other name, date, people, expressions of the conspiracy, and we should because that awareness is important. But all the countless aspects of this conspiracy are designed to one end: the manipulation of humanity's imagination of itself and the conditioning of our reality. How we see ourselves and the world dictates our behaviour and our perception of others. Control the sense of reality and you control the person completely. A brilliant American comedian called Bill Hicks used to say:

"Matter is merely energy condensed to a slow vibration. We are all one consciousness experiencing itself subjectively. There's no such thing as death, life is just a dream, and we are the imagination of ourselves."

The Illuminati conspiracy can be summed up in one sentence: the manipulation of humanity's imagination of itself. The events of September 11th have had a massive effect on the human perception and sense of reality – exactly as planned.

Mirror, mirror, on the wall …

The five-sense realm does not really exist as a physical "world". It is a mirror, a reflection, of our inner state of being. If you stand in front of a mirror you see a reflection of yourself. It's not you, it's not real, it's a reflection. You are in control of that reflection because the image in the mirror cannot move, open and close its eyes, or wave its arms around unless you choose to do that. If you imagine your consciousness to be you looking in the mirror and you imagine the reflection to be the world that you see through your eyes and experience as your "life", then perhaps you can appreciate what I mean when I say that five-sense reality is an illusion. As Albert Einstein put it: "Reality is just an illusion, albeit a persistent one." When we look through our eyes at the five-sense mirror we are looking at a reflection of ourselves, both individually and collectively. We cannot hide from ourselves, much as we would like to, because we are looking ourselves in the face every waking second of every day. Indeed that is the very point in being here – so consciousness can observe itself. If we are consumed by inner conflict and insecurity, if we are full of fear, anger and frustration with no love for ourselves, this will reflect in the "mirror" I call the five-sense "world". A war is the outer conflict reflecting the inner conflict. The Illuminati know that if they can manipulate and stimulate inner conflict, the outer one will be easy to manifest. If we feel ourselves to be insignificant, powerless and ordinary that will reflect in the five-sense mirror as a life experience that is without power. We will be just another sheep in the pen considered by ourselves and others to be insignificant and expendable. In truth we are none of those things. We are genius incarnate, infinity incarnate, if we choose to be. But when our isolated, disconnected, droplet of consciousness is programmed to *believe* that negative version of ourselves, we reflect that state of being into the five-sense mirror and "live" that imagination of ourselves, that reality. We are what we believe ourselves to be and the Illuminati's most important goal is to tell us what to believe ourselves to be. Once you reconnect to the infinite ocean you begin to understand that nothing and no one is powerless, ordinary or insignificant. To claim so is to say that divine infinity is all of those things. You start to realise that if we change our imagination of ourselves we can live our lives as the incarnate ocean and not as a disconnected droplet; as infinity and not only as far as our eyes can see. Then we can tap into and express the full magnitude of who we really are and the Illuminati's juvenile game will be over.

Seeing is believing

The Illuminati are desperate for us to believe that the mirror is real. That way we will spend our lives trying to change the reflection from inside the reflection. Impossible. The only way to change a reflection is to change what is being reflected – our inner state of being. When we change, the world must change, but not until. The Illuminati know this and they have no problem with the Far Left attacking the Far Right and so on. For goodness sake, they are manipulating that division and conflict. They want people believing that to affect the five-sense prison you have to take action with the five senses – condemn, protest, "fight" for what you believe in. But unless the inner changes, the outer cannot. It doesn't matter if you are a Far Right fascist who wants to impose his will and fight the hated Left; or if you are a Far Left Communist who wants to impose his will on others and fight the hated Right; or if you are from the Extreme Centre and wants to impose your will on others and fight the Far Right and the Far Left. There is a common theme that unites them all and they need each other to go on "fighting". If the inner wants to "fight" for anything – for control, for dictatorship, for freedom, for justice and all the other endless things that people "fight for" – what are they all doing? They are adding their contribution to the "fight", the conflict. We don't have to fight for freedom, we just have to be free. If the inner decides to be free, the outer expression will reflect that freedom. If the inner decides that it needs to "fight" for freedom, it's outer reflection will be the experience of "fighting." Don't fight for it. Don't hope for it. Don't campaign for it. Just be it.

Billions of people are spending their lives thrashing around in a reflection and getting more and more frightened, angry, stressed and frustrated that nothing is changing and things are only getting worse. But of course nothing is changing as they would wish. How can it? It's getting worse because the more frightened, angry, stressed, and frustrated people become at aimlessly thrashing around in a reflection while thinking it's real, the more their mental and emotional state "gets worse" and so must reflect in the mirror as the world "getting worse". It is a vicious circle that can only be broken when we realise that five-sense reality is an illusion and we are creating it. We can have a five-sense illusion that is a prison because inner prisons must become outer prisons; or we can have an illusion that is a paradise. It's our choice, our decision, but whatever we choose, the five-sense "world" will still be an illusion, a reflection, because that is what it is meant to be: a mirror through which consciousness can observe itself.

Playing with our minds

This knowledge of consciousness held in the secret society networks for thousands of years has allowed the Illuminati to manipulate the minds of an ignorant humanity and never more so than today. I feel for people who live in the United States because they are subjected to some of the fiercest reality conditioning anywhere on the planet. I would suggest that there is a reason for this – the United States (a private corporation) was set up from the start as a mind-control experiment. Americans are seen as the most powerful nation on earth and technologically the most advanced. It is even believed, shock of shocks, that the USA is the home of freedom. I remember my own experience in 1996 when I travelled the United States for three months and found it to be one of the most controlled, dictatorial societies I had ever seen. But because of the mantra of "this is the land of the free" most people don't realise what a dictatorship they live in. People complain that "American culture" is taking over the world because McDonald's, Burger King and all the other symbols of American society are everywhere. Hollywood, television and advertising are dominated by American settings and influences. But this is not "American culture" that we are seeing exported to every corner of the world, it is those experiments to suppress the human body, mind and emotions that have been seen to have the desired effect within the experimental human laboratory known as the United States. When it has been shown to work there, the rest of us get it. From America has come the fast-food onslaught on human physiology; "soundbite" journalism in which substance is sacrificed to the superficial; the obsession with material symbols and trinkets as a measure of human "success" and achievement. Americanisation is Illuminatisation. That's why I feel for Americans because they are at the sharpest end of all of this conditioning of human perception. What applies to individuals in the Illuminati mind-control programmes also applies to the population as a whole. In the UK the psychologists, social workers and police, glean their knowledge of Multiple Personality Disorder or Dissociative Identity Disorder (used to create mind-controlled slaves) from the Illuminati Tavistock Group (see *The Biggest Secret*). Dr William Sargant, a psychiatrist with Tavistock, wrote in his 1957 book, *The Battle For The Mind*:

> "Various types of belief can be implanted in people after brain function has been deliberately disturbed by accidentally or deliberately induced fear, anger, or excitement. Of the results caused by such disturbances the most common one is temporarily impaired judgement and heightened suggestibility. Its various group manifestations are sometimes classed under the heading of "herd instinct", and appear most spectacularly in wartime, during severe epidemics, and all similar periods of common danger, which increase anxiety and so individual and mass suggestibility.

> "... We would be advised not to underestimate the effect on the collective psyche in terms of fear and a desire for the authorities to 'protect people' from that fear." [3]

When the Illuminati unleash their wars, Wacos, Oklahoma bombs and 9/11s, they are using trauma-based mind control on the population because they know that a traumatised mind is a suggestible one. This fits the goals of problem-reaction-solution perfectly because once you have created the event and gleaned the reaction of fear, the minds of the people are suggestible to the "solutions" the perpetrators offer. Proposing the slaughter of thousands of civilians and their children in Afghanistan would have caused outrage among many if it had been suggested without September 11th. But after those attacks in New York and Washington there was no problem. For this reason we are going to see more "terrorist attacks", not least involving chemicals and disease, to keep the people traumatised and open to future stages of the "war on terrorism". Once again we have the common theme here – the control and manipulation of reality.

Who controls the controllers?

Only by understanding the nature of reality can we answer the obvious question that comes from the information I present about the bloodlines and how long they have been manipulating this five-sense reality. The question of why would people dedicate their lives to the plan for global domination when they knew they would be dead long before the goal was reached. How about if the entities controlling the bodies of those in power through the ages have largely been the same ones all along? What if they operate just beyond the frequency range of the five senses and use apparently "human" physical bodies to manipulate the five-sense world? What if when one body gives up on them at "death" they just move into another and continue the manipulation, the long-term agenda, for another period of "time"? The area of my research that people find most difficult to comprehend is that the bloodlines placed in the positions of power throughout the world are not "human" in the sense that we understand that term. I appreciate why people find that so difficult because being caught in the five-sense illusion includes being subconsciously programmed to believe that if you can't see it, it doesn't exist. I have revealed in considerable detail in my last two books, *The Biggest Secret* and *Children Of The Matrix*, the staggering number of people, both ancient and modern, who have told of the same experience – seeing an apparently human being, often people in power, transform in front of their eyes from a human body to that of a reptilian entity. Others have seen the same transformation, a phenomenon known as "shape-shifting", involving other non-human entities and not only reptilian. But the reptilian form is by far the most common theme among the endless people I have spoken with around the world. This also appears to be the case with the ancient accounts from all over the planet detailing the same experience. I am not going into all that again here because I have covered this at great length already in previous books. But I want to emphasise why this phenomenon is possible. To the conditioned five-sense reality the idea is crazy, bizarre and ludicrous. If people wish to believe that, go ahead, it makes no difference to me either way. But are those people saying that only that which they have seen with their eyes or has been accepted as real by official sources can exist?

People will just have to believe what they want to believe and I have no desire whatsoever to convince anyone of anything. It really doesn't matter to me either way if people accept what I say or not. But after all these years of full-time research, which has taken me to 40 countries, thousands of people and countless ancient and modern accounts, it is clear that this "world" or frequency range, the five-sense prison, is manipulated from outside by non-human entities that take over or "possess" the apparently "human" bodies of the Illuminati bloodlines. You can read the detailed background in *The Biggest Secret* and *Children Of The Matrix*, but in summary this is the situation we face. Between dimensions, in this case between the third dimension (the five-sense prison) and the next one, the fourth dimension, are little "crevices" of frequency. The Italian physicist Giuliana Conforto, author of *Man's Cosmic Game*, calls them "inter-space planes" and they lie between the dimensions or, as the scientists called them in the *Horizon* programme, parallel universes. It is in the inter-space plane, Giuliana suggested to me, that these reptilian and other entities reside. This is the realm of the "demons" of folklore that have been frightening and manipulating humans for as long as ancient accounts go back. In *Children Of The Matrix* I quote the work of Maurice Doreal who says that in 1925 he recovered ancient tablets tens of thousands of years old that had been placed under a Mayan Temple of the Sun God in the Yucatan, Mexico, and it is said that the tablets originated in the continent known as Atlantis that was lost to enormous geological cataclysm a long time ago. They have become known as the Emerald Tablets of Thoth, and Doreal's translations refer to the inter-space planes of Giuliana Conforto as "spaces and planes unknown to man".[4] The translations also say that in these spaces and planes are the serpent beings that manipulate this world. In South Africa, Credo Mutwa, the famous Zulu Sanusi (shaman) and official historian of the Zulu nation, recounts the same story. He told me that in ancient African accounts passed down through the ages, they called the inter-space planes the "heavens between heavens" and this, he said, was where the reptilian beings reside that manipulate our world. In frequency terms, the inter-space plane is very close to the range of the five senses, but just outside, just beyond the range that our eyes can see. However, if someone with psychic sight can extend their vibrational range a little they can connect with that frequency range and see some of these entities – and they do. People who have taken mind-altering drugs that break through the vibrational walls of the five senses and allow consciousness to see beyond it have had the same experience. Also, if these entities lower their vibration only slightly to enter the five-sense range they become visible to us here and people from all walks of life all over the world have told me a stream of accounts detailing this very experience (see *Children Of The Matrix* and *The Biggest Secret*). Those who have experienced Illuminati blood and sacrifice rituals have also told me many stories of seeing this "shape-shifting" transformation from "human" to reptilian among the participants. As the *Horizon* science programme about parallel universes said:

> "The only explanation that anyone could come up with is that the particles don't just exist in our universe. They slip into existence in other universes, too, and there are an infinite number of these parallel universes, all of them slightly different."

It is possible for particles to move between "universes" or "realities" and "dimensions" and so it is possible for entities, consisting of particles, to do the same. This is a major reason why the Illuminati bloodlines have taken part in these rituals from ancient times to the present day. The rituals allow them to connect with their masters in the inter-space planes, not least because human blood and the vibrational fields created by the rituals produce the frequency environment in which the reptilian and other entities can manifest in the five-sense frequency range. Credo Mutwa has described to me how he witnessed rituals decades ago at which people in the room shifted from a human to a reptilian form, but there have been countless other people from very different cultures and backgrounds who have described the same experience of what happens once the blood begins to flow. Maurice Doreal's translations of the ancient Emerald Tablets reveal:

"Far in the past before Atlantis existed, men there were who delved into darkness, using dark magic, calling up beings from the great below us. Forth came they into this cycle, formless were they, of another vibration, existing unseen by the children of earth-men. Only through blood could they form being, only through man could they live in the world.

"In ages past were they conquered by the Masters, driven below to the place whence they came. But some there were who remained, hidden in spaces and planes unknown to man. Lived they in Atlantis as shadows, but at times they appeared among men. Aye, when the blood was offered, forth they came to dwell among men."

This brings us to the reason why the Illuminati are obsessed with bloodline.

The bloodlines

Thousands of years ago, indeed aeons probably, a non-human race interbred with humans to create hybrid bloodlines and this story is told in every native culture. Such sources retain far more of the true history of human existence than the manipulated and mendacious "history" taught in today's schools and universities. We even see an expression of these accounts in that amalgamation of ancient writings, some real, some added much later, that we know as the Old Testament. This tells of the Sons of God (sons of the *gods* in the true translation) who interbred with the daughters of men to create the hybrid race, the Nefilim. The accounts say that the Nefilim caused mayhem wherever they went. Different versions of the Nefilim story with the same common theme can be found all over the world and South African shamen like Credo Mutwa, for example, refer to the Nefilim as the Chitauri – the "Children of the Serpent" or "Children of the Python" because this non-human race takes a reptilian form. Such accounts are featured in detail in *Children Of The Matrix* and *The Biggest Secret*, as are the modern accounts of insiders who have confirmed to me that the world is indeed controlled by bloodlines that are not in fact "human", but reptilian-human hybrids. By "insiders" I mean those who work for this network against their will; those who have experienced its privileges and diabolical rituals before turning against it; and those who have been victims of its grotesque agenda and mind-control projects. The ancient idea of the Divine Right to Rule, the right to rule because of your bloodline, originates from this interbreeding. The "divine" does not relate to "God", the Infinite Spirit, but to the "gods", the non-human entities involved in the interbreeding. They became known as the "dragon bloodlines" and the symbol of the dragon comes from these reptilian "gods". Chinese emperors claimed the right to rule through their genetic connection to the serpent gods and still today we have "royal" families around the world who come to the throne only because of their DNA and for no other reason. In more recent times these bloodlines have moved out of the overt positions of "royal" power and dictatorship because people would no longer stand for that form of rule. Now they dominate the population in another way, through politics, banking, business and media ownership.

The bloodlines that manipulate the world today are genetically connected through this hybrid DNA, a genetic fusion caused by the interbreeding of humans with the "gods", as the ancients perceived this non-human race. This interbreeding continues to the present day as thousands of accounts around the world confirm. If you are hearing this for the first time, I know how bizarre and crazy it sounds to the conditioned view of reality. But you will see in my other books the scale of the evidence to support this apparently ridiculous story and how it explains a stream of ancient and modern 'mysteries'. So many things that later turn out to be true appear at first hearing to be impossible and insane. That's because people only hear the opening line and don't read on to see the detailed evidence to support it, and also because most people are conditioned to believe that anything beyond their perception cannot, by definition, be true. When people first suggested the earth was round, they were called crazy because it was thought that those living on the bottom would have fallen off. The critics dismissed the idea at this point and walked away convinced that the earth had to be flat. Yet when you introduce the law of gravity, what seemed at first to be crazy suddenly became far more credible. So it is with the fact that a non-human race is controlling and manipulating humanity through hybrid bloodlines – the same bloodlines that have been placed in positions of power since ancient times. The supporting evidence is there if only people are prepared to open their minds and remove their backside from the furniture.

These bloodlines have what has been described to me by insiders as a "corrupted DNA", corrupted by the interbreeding, and you find similar stories among the ancient accounts also. The DNA is the body's genetic blueprint and can have a massive effect on behaviour. One consequence of this corruption is that these bloodlines do not have the same emotional responses as the rest of the earth people. We have an emotional "fail-safe" mechanism in which the consequences of knowing what our actions would do to others act, most of the time, as a defence against extreme behaviour like torture, mass murder, abusing children and so on. However, when, as in the case of these bloodlines, you are not subject to such emotional responses then you can do anything to any number of people without experiencing the emotional fall-out. Killing thousands in the World Trade Center or Afghanistan is no emotional challenge for you. It is just another day's "work", another step on the road to global domination. To you the human population is seen in the same way as most humans see cattle. We see constant examples of this "cold-blooded" DNA in action among today's world leaders. The corrupted DNA has a vibrational sympathy with the reptilian entities of the inter-space plane. This allows them to possess these bodies far more easily than those with non-corrupted DNA. The Emerald Tablets, as translated by Maurice Doreal, describe how the serpent entities of another frequency possessed the bodies of those in power in this five-sense reality:

"In the form of man moved they amongst us, but only to sight, were they as are men. Serpent-headed when the glamour was lifted, but appearing to man as men among men. Crept they into the councils, taking form that were like unto men. Slaying by their arts the chiefs of the kingdoms, taking their form and ruling o'er man. Only by magic could they be discovered, only by sound could their faces be seen. Sought they from the kingdom of shadows to destroy man and rule in his place."

The five-sense "world" has been manipulated by these inter-space reptilian and other entities for at least thousands of years and it is done by possessing the hybrid bloodlines and taking over their mental processes. This means that if the Illuminati, the reptilian network in human form, can manipulate these bloodlines or bodies with the corrupted DNA into the positions of power they are putting the reptilian entities into those positions. Here you have the reason why United States presidents are so genetically connected and why they go back to the royal and aristocratic families of Europe who, in turn, descend from the ruling royal families of the ancient world going back to when the interbreeding began. You also have the reason why the Illuminati families are obsessed with interbreeding: it is to protect the corrupted DNA that can be quickly diluted if it is bred with DNA that is not corrupted. The Illuminati have arranged marriages on the basis of genetics and most of them are sham relationships to produce the children. They also use artificial breeding programmes to pass on the genetic "purity" they so desperately desire to maintain. To them the "human body" is only a vehicle for them to operate in this five-sense frequency range. What you see is their five-sense human body. What you don't see is what is looking through its eyes from the inter-space plane. If you saw the movie, *The Matrix*, you will recall how the "agents", who were manipulating the masses and controlling the computer-generated illusion, could come in and out of that "world" by moving in and out of different "human" bodies. The same principle applies to the reptilians and other entities in the five-sense reality that we live in. According to the translations of the Emerald Tablets the reptilian influence was acknowledged and dealt with in the distant past, but the tablets warned:

"Yet, beware, the serpent still liveth in a place that is open at times to the world. Unseen they walk among thee in places where the rites have been said; again as time passes onward shall they take the semblance of men."

And they have. The major players in the Illuminati and those behind 9/11 and the "war on terrorism" are reptilian inter-space entities occupying human form within the five-sense world and they are not "American" or "British" or "Chinese", they are entities manipulating through those physical forms and have no allegiance to the people they "lead". They could not care less if an American dies for their cause or a Chinese because they identify with neither. The reptilian connection is the reason for the explosion of reptilian symbolism among Illuminati organisations. (See *The Biggest Secret* and the symbolism archive at *davidicke.com* for more.) The inter-space reptilians have an undeveloped emotional level, which allows them to cause death and destruction while feeling no emotional consequence for the suffering they cause. They are beings of thought and ritualistic instinct, not feeling. More than that, their whole aim is to cause slaughter and pain because of the energy that this generates.

Reptilians Inc.

Physicist Giuliana Conforto tells me that inter-space planes do not have a natural energy source like a dimension. Any entities operating there would need to create an energy source for themselves and they have – fear. When we feel fear it generates a vibration, an energy field. Every time we think and feel, no matter what our state of being may be, we are sending out "broadcast" waves that vibrate to the frequency of the particular thought or emotion. We feel these frequencies coming from people in what we call "vibes". The low vibration of fear and its associated emotions like anger, aggression, stress and guilt produce frequencies that pour into the inter-space plane and this has become the energy source of these reptilian and other entities. The more humanity feels fear in all its forms the more energy – power – the reptilians have to sustain them and use back against us. The entire Illuminati system has been designed to generate the energy of fear and turn the human population into an inter-space energy source. Appropriately, in the movie, *The Matrix*, the character called Morpheus holds up a battery and says: "The Matrix is a computer-generated dream world built to keep us under control in order to change the human being into this." The recent major children's movie called *Monsters Inc.* had the same theme. The "monster" world did not have an energy source and so they walked through "doors" (interdimensional gateways) into children's bedrooms in the human world. There they would frighten children and when the kids screamed with fear the monsters would capture that energy and take it back through the door to power their world. This is one major aspect of September 11th and its aftermath that is not acknowledged because it is so far from conditioned reality. But imagine the fear generated as a result of 9/11. Imagine how much has been generated by two world wars, the "war on terrorism", and a political, financial, business, military, and media system that is specifically designed to maintain humanity in a constant state of fear, worry, stress, and anger. Take another look at the micro-chipping programme from this perspective. Once people are micro-chipped they can be externally triggered through the chip to produce fear on demand. Get a micro-chip and be a battery, you know it makes sense. In the light of all this, take another look at that coded speech by George W. Bush after 9/11:

"The hijackers were instruments of evil who died in vain. Behind them is a cult of evil that seeks to harm the innocent and thrives on human suffering. Theirs is the worst

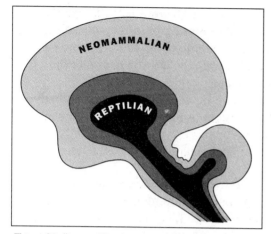

Figure 30: *The reptilian brain or "R-complex" is an ancient part of the human brain. From here we get the character traits of cold-blooded behaviour, the desire for top-down hierarchy, and an obsession with ritual. These are balanced by other parts of the brain in humans, but not in the full-blown reptilians, which manipulate this planet*

kind of cruelty, the cruelty that is fed, not weakened, by tears. Theirs is the worst kind of violence, pure malice while daring to claim the authority of God. We cannot fully understand the designs and power of evil; it is enough to know that evil, like goodness, exists. And in the terrorists evil has found a willing servant."

The cruelty that is "fed, not weakened, by tears". Exactly.

Reptilian brain

The more we understand the reptilian mind the more we can understand both the behaviour of the Illuminati across the centuries and the global society they are creating. They have distinct character traits and they are seeking to make humans the same.

These reptilian characteristics and their connection to the human brain are fundamental to the perpetuation of the illusions of the five-sense world that I call the Matrix. The most ancient part of the human brain is known by scientists as the R-complex or "reptilian brain" (*Figure 30*). It is the most obvious remnant of our reptilian genetic history, along with those people around the world still being born with tails (see *Children Of The Matrix*). This reptilian brain is vital to understanding the ways in which the Illuminati manipulate human thinking and perception. Most people have no idea of the reptilian heritage of the human body and its influence on our behaviour. Scientists say that the reptilian brain represents a core of the nervous system, and look at the character traits of the reptilian brain as agreed by scientists. I quote here from an Internet article by Skip Largent:

"At least five human behaviours originate in the reptilian brain ... Without defining them, I shall simply say that in human activities they find expression in: obsessive compulsive behaviour; personal day-to-day rituals and superstitious acts; slavish conformance to old ways of doing things; ceremonial re-enactments; obeisance to precedent, as in legal, religious, cultural, and other matters ... and all manner of deceptions." [5]

Add other traits of the reptilian brain such as "territoriality" (this is mine, keep out); an obsession with hierarchical structures of rule and control; aggression; and the idea that might is right, winner takes all, and you have the very characteristics displayed by the Illuminati and their agents for thousands of years. You simply could not describe them better than to list the traits of the reptilian brain. Racism comes from the reptilian brain, also, and the aggressive, violent sex that the Illuminati bloodlines indulge in big time – ask Father Bush, Cheney, President Gerald Ford, and other Illuminati names I expose in my books. Can it really be a coincidence that the Illuminati manifest the classic traits of the reptilian brain while, at the same time, the evidence mounts that they are reptilian bloodlines? Cosmologist Carl Sagan, who knew far more than he was telling, wrote a book called *The Dragons of Eden*[6] to highlight the reptilian influences on humanity. He said: "… It does no good whatsoever to ignore the reptilian component of human nature, particularly our ritualistic and hierarchical behaviour. On the contrary, the model may help us understand what human beings are really about." Other areas of the human brain balance the extremes of the reptilian characteristics in most people, but they can still be seen, for example, in those who live their lives as a daily ritual, such as going to the same supermarket at the same time every week and having the same meals on the same days. The Illuminati have sought to turn society into a clock-watching, ever repeating daily cycle, because that locks the people who succumb to this into their reptilian level of perception and further activates the reptilian brain. They have also created a society in which most people are focused on physical or financial survival, and the survival mentality is a reptilian instinct. The whole Illuminati agenda is based on the terror of not surviving and they equate control with survival. Their survival where they currently reside in the inter-space plane is also dependent on humans continuing to be their energy source. Their horrific agenda is based on survival in their reptilian minds. Those with the most dominant reptilian genetics, the Illuminati, obviously express more of the characteristics associated with the reptilian brain and this is why, as detailed at length in my other books, the Illuminati are utterly obsessed with ritual.

They also know better than anyone how to manipulate the reptilian brain or R-complex of humans and it is through that part of the brain that humanity is most controlled and directed. The human brain is in two parts, or hemispheres, the right brain and the left-brain, connected by a mass of nerve fibres. The left side is rational, logical, and "intellectual". It works closely with the physical senses and can be summed up by can I touch it, see it, hear it, smell it or taste it? It communicates through spoken and written words. The right brain is where we manifest imagination, intuition, instincts, dream-states, the subconscious. It is the artist, musician, creative inspiration. It communicates through images and symbols, not words. This right side is closely related to the reptilian part of the brain. Reptilians communicate through imagery and symbols – just like the Illuminati secret society network. They have an entire secret language based on symbols. This brings us to the most effective form of human conditioning by the Illuminati – movies and television. As Skip Largent writes:

"All movies and television are a projection of the reptilian brain. How so? Movies and television (video games etc.) are all undeniably dreamlike, not only in their presentation of symbolic-reality, but also in that humans experiencing movies, etc., have the same brain wave patterns as when they are dreaming. And guess where dreaming originates in your head? In the reptilian brain (although other parts of our brain are involved) ... The "language" of the reptilian brain is visual imagery. All communications transferred by reptiles are done so by visual symbolic representations, each having specific meaning." [7]

This is precisely what the Illuminati do through their symbolism. The movie and television industries are not only owned by the Illuminati – they created them. They understand how visual images can be used to condition the population. In normal circumstances, the reptilian-dominated right brain receives images through the eyes or the imagination, and the left brain decodes those images into thoughts and conclusions. The Illuminati have intervened in this process, however, to control human perception. Their aim is to disconnect the functions of these two distinct parts of the brain so we can be manipulated through the right brain while only being conscious of the left. They plant images into the right brain (the dream-state, the non-conscious) using symbolism, subliminal imagery and pictures, while often telling the left-brain how it should interpret those images. This is done through "education", "science" and the media. Television news is a classic. The right brain is shown pictures and the reporter's voiceover tells the left brain what they mean. During the Kosovo conflict we were shown pictures of refugees fleeing across the border and the voiceover said they were actually fleeing Serbian atrocities. This "explanation" (this sense of reality) increased public support for NATO bombing of the Serbs. What later emerged is that many of the refugees were fleeing the effects of NATO bombing. Same images, but a very different reality. What is happening all the time is that the left brain is being told by external sources how to decode right-brain images. What we urgently need to do is regain control of our left brains and decide for ourselves what we are seeing.

You will find that words like imagination, imagine, dream and suchlike are used constantly in advertising. They know that if they can use those trigger words that encourage the right-brain, non-conscious, daydream state, they can access your mind with imagery and then tell your left brain how to decode that into conscious language – "I want that car"; "I think the police should be given more powers to stop crime"; "I need Viagra to be a real man again"; "We need a world government to solve our problems". Television and movies are producing a fantasy world of make-believe to open up the unconscious right brain and allow the Illuminati secret access through that to the conscious mind. Children are most at risk from this and they are being bombarded by fantasy images to this end. In early childhood the mental state is controlled almost exclusively by the reptilian brain and the purveyors of children's "entertainment", like Disney, exploit this knowledge. I was also interested to find an article in the *Los Angeles Times* while writing this chapter that highlighted another trait of the reptilian brain – greed and excess. The article was headed "Living Ever Larger; How Wretched Excess Became a Way of Life in Southern California". French anthropologist G. Clotaire Rapaille is quoted as saying:

"... the desire for excess comes from the 'reptilian brain,' the earliest, most primitive structures in our mental evolution. The reptilian wants to grab as much food as possible, to be as big and powerful as possible, because it's focused on survival. When it comes to a choice between the intellect and the reptilian, the reptilian always wins.

"Satisfying that inner lizard has its downsides. Our insatiable appetites have left Americans 9 pounds heavier, on average, than we were two decades ago, and more vulnerable than ever to heart disease and diabetes. We're racking up mountains of debt (the late fees we pay on credit cards have more than tripled since 1996, to $7.3 billion a year) and burning up fossil fuels like crazy. We demand things that, deep down, we don't really want or even use ..." [8]

The "American culture" that is being exported across the world by the day is the culture of the reptilian brain and that's exactly what it was designed to be from the start when the Illuminati based in Britain and other European centres confiscated the lands of the Native Americans and set up their "New Atlantis", as the initiate Francis Bacon called it. I am convinced the "Old Atlantis" went the same way before it collapsed amid cataclysmic events. Readers of my other books will know the emphasis I place on the Illuminati's obsession with blood rituals and human sacrifice. Stories like that of Bram Stoker's shape-shifting, blood-drinking *Dracula*, are not just fantasies. They are based on what is actually going on in the world every day (see *The Biggest Secret* and *Children Of The Matrix*). I was interested to come across an article in a 1999 Bram Stoker Society Newsletter about the reptilian nature of the *Dracula* character:

"... even writers of the century that has seen Dracula's redemption are not blind to the old creature's inhuman, threatening nature. Valdine Clemens writes of 'Dracula: The Reptilian Brain at the Fin de Siecle,' contrasting the novel's extensive use of modern technological devices (typewriter, phonograph, telephone, hypodermic injection, blood transfusion) with Dracula's reliance on a literally 'reptilian' way of thinking. Vampires and reptiles share not only the traits of not caring for their young, lack of sexual bonds, and lack of the mammalian capacity for play, but the primitive 'reptile brain's' reliance on instinct and habit. Amanda Fernbach, in 'Dracula's Decadent Fetish,' explicates another of ... Dracula's ... threats: '[Dracula] offers a decadent deconstruction of gender, presenting images of feminized men and masculinized women under the sign of vampirism.' In 'Corruption Becomes Itself Corrupt' Marion Muirhead shows Dracula as a vehicle of entropy, a Victorian-era answer to the late twentieth century phenomenon of the serial killer." [9]

Again, all the traits you find in the Illuminati are there. As the article says: "vampires and reptiles share not only the traits of not caring for their young, lack of sexual bonds, and lack of the mammalian capacity for play, but the primitive 'reptile brain's' reliance on instinct and habit". This lack of caring for their young is how the Illuminati families can put their children through horrendous rituals to bring them into line. Look at the British royal family, the reptilian Windsors, and consider how they have brought up their children in such an emotionless way. So many families of the aristocracy are the same. There are many more evolved reptilians that have moved beyond these base reptilian instincts, but they are not the ones behind the Illuminati.

Activating the bloodline

The major and ancient Illuminati families know who they are and their hybrid nature, but there are many other offshoots within societies all over the world who have no idea that they carry the hybrid corruption. Nor are they trying to manipulate anyone. From what I have learned over the years the DNA corruption lies dormant unless it is activated and until that point it has no effect on the person. Such people go through life oblivious of their bloodline. However, if they come into contact with the vibrational code that activates the corruption then that is a very different story. They become seriously open to possession by the inter-space entities. This vibrational code or key is generated at the secret society rituals of the Illuminati network and this is another reason why they have performed the same basic rituals since ancient times. They are designed to produce the vibrational code that activates the DNA corruption and opens the vibrational door to the inter-space entities. The children of Illuminati families are put through the rituals by their parents in the full knowledge that they are being opened to possession so the baton can be passed on to the next generation. Talk to anyone who has been involved in Satanism and they will tell you that its hierarchy is decided by the power of the demonic entities that you allow to possess your body during the rituals designed for this end. The theme of "selling your soul to the Devil" is a valid one in the sense that Satanists allow their bodies to be possessed in return for power in the five-sense world. The same applies to the Illuminati and in fact Satanism is one of the strands in their web.

The story for those who are not born into the Illuminati families and have no idea of their bloodline is rather different. The Illuminati keep detailed records of who has the dormant DNA corruption. They have used genealogical libraries like the one at the Illuminati-controlled Mormon Church in Salt Lake City, Utah, to do this in the past, but the preferred method today is a global DNA database that they are now manipulating into being under the guise of stopping crime and terrorism. What happens to these unknowing "corruption carriers" is that they are targeted by the Illuminati in the knowledge of who they are. They might be making a career in politics, the law, the military, the media and so on, and they will find that their careers suddenly take off and some powerful people begin to support them. At this stage they are under the impression that this sponsorship by influential people is because of their ability or, in the case of politics, because the supporters believe in what the target stands for. But in truth it is because of their DNA. At some point the target is invited to join the secret society network as a good career move and they are put through the rituals that activate the DNA corruption. Still they will have no idea of what is going on, just as 99% of Freemasons have no idea what their bizarre initiation rituals really mean and are structured to achieve. Once the target's DNA possession code is triggered by the rituals the process of possession by the inter-space entities begins to unfold. The person's thoughts, emotions and attitudes begin to change until they are a fully possessed being. How many times do we hear former friends and colleagues of those in power say that they are not the same people they once knew? We are led to believe that these changes of personality are due to the influences of power – "power corrupts and absolute power corrupts absolutely". Of course, there is some validity in this, but the main reason for the personality change is quite simply that are no longer the same being, let alone the same character.

With this knowledge, the apparently complex, mysterious and contradictory begins to come into clear focus. People think that Americans would not slaughter Americans, for example, and government agencies could not have been involved in the planning of 9/11. But the leaders are not American; they are reptilian entities possessing a "human body" that was born in America. It is the same with the leaders in Britain, Saudi Arabia, Pakistan, China, Germany and all the rest. These "leaders" have no allegiance to the people of these nations, their only allegiance is to themselves as reptilians that have been manipulating this world for aeons to create a global centralised fascist state through which they can control a micro-chipped, constantly monitored, population. Their allegiance is to a long-planned conspiracy to create a structure in which every child born into this five-sense world is immediately micro-chipped and turned into an externally manipulated and controlled battery to provide an energy source for the inter-space entities that are running the show by occupying physical bodies.

If you look at *Figure 31 (overleaf)* I have symbolised the structure of reptilian control. The Illuminati manipulate their bloodlines (in other words the inter-space entities) into the positions of power across the world through their secret society web in each country. Most of these leaders in the various countries are working to the same goal and they only appear to be in conflict for the purposes of deluding the people into a false reality. There is also great rivalry on one level between different elements of the Illuminati because as one researcher told me years ago: "They are like a gang of bank robbers. They all agree on the job, but then argue about how the spoils are shared out". Those who are so consumed by the desire for power and control are not going to switch that off when it comes to having power over those on the same side. But they all depend on the agenda for their collective power over humanity and that is the cement that holds the warring factions together. The reptilian leaders of the various countries play out a pre-arranged plan that appears to the public to be the random result of random events. But in fact, as the Illuminati puppet Franklin Delano Roosevelt said: "Whatever happens in politics you can bet it was meant to happen." The leaders of the United States, Saudi Arabia, Pakistan, Russia, China etc., are not American, Arab, Pakistani, Russian, and Chinese except in their outer five-sense form. They are reptilian-possessed beings working to the same agenda. The interaction between them is just the movie. The Li bloodline in China, for example, is one of the major Illuminati bloodlines on the planet and this has been bred into other races over thousands of

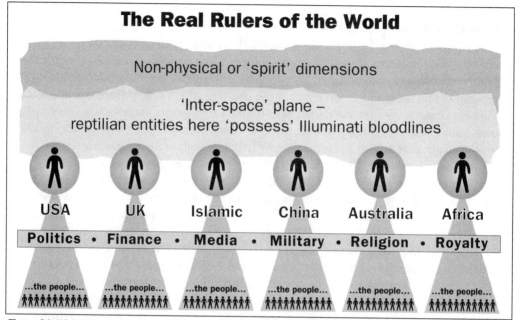

The Real Rulers of the World

Non-physical or 'spirit' dimensions

'Inter-space' plane –
reptilian entities here 'possess' Illuminati bloodlines

| USA | UK | Islamic | China | Australia | Africa |

Politics • Finance • Media • Military • Religion • Royalty

...the people...   ...the people...   ...the people...   ...the people...   ...the people...   ...the people...

Figure 31: *While those in power in different countries appear to be different "races" with an allegiance to their "nation", they are mostly reptilian-possessed entities working to the same goal – a global fascist state. Many of them may not like each other and there may be much infighting, but their overall agenda is the same.*

years to the point where it does not manifest as a "Chinese" body, but still maintains the corrupted DNA. As I was writing this book, a fellow researcher contacted me to say that he had an excellent Chinese source that claimed to have seen the Illuminati Li family "tree" and saw that it connected to Bill Clinton and the Bush family. The reptilian bloodlines do not relate to an earth race, they have infiltrated all races and cultures. These reptilian leaders manipulate "their" nations to fight with other nations to advance their collective agenda, but of course they rarely if ever see a gun fired in anger. George W. Bush ordered an invasion of Afghanistan, but he didn't go there and fight, he sent pawns from the people. His father ordered the war against Iraq, but he didn't go there and fight, he sent pawns from the people. The reptilian entities in the positions of power manipulate the peoples of the world to fight each other in the five-sense prison and in doing so advance their structure of global centralisation while producing vast quantities of fear to feed their own "world". The human race has been duped all this time and never more so than now. The conditioned reality they are programmed to accept prevents them from seeing the malevolent game that is being played out all around them. The idea of reptilian entities controlling their lives by hiding within human form is beyond most people's comprehension because it is so far from their conditioned sense of possibility. They have never been told the vibrational truths or had access to the ancient and modern evidence and information that would tell them a very different version of reality. Because of this, even when most people are presented with the truth they laugh in its face.

Operation infinite freedom

What we call "life" on this planet – the "three score years and ten" between "birth" and "death" – is only a short experience within the five-sense frequency range. It is a short and challenging experience of the dense vibrations of this five-sense reality to allow our consciousness to look itself in the face. The body is the five-sense vehicle for our consciousness to do that. Unfortunately this "world" has become so manipulated that humans now identify who they are and what they can do by the nature of their physical bodies. Racism is just one expression of this ludicrous misunderstanding. It is like an astronaut judging who and what he is by the nature of his space suit. We would think that was stupid. "You are not your spacesuit", we would say, "you are what is inside your spacesuit". Exactly. But that's how most humans judge themselves and the world every single waking second. I have a body, therefore I am. Is my body black, white, yellow, brown, male, female, fit, fat, tall, small, old, bald, souped up or fucked up? These are judgements we make about ourselves and others in relation to who we are, and who and what other people are. These judgements are added to those made on the basis of what we do for a "living" and how much money or fame we may or may not have. If you observe the world, those two criteria – the body and the bank balance – are the foundations on which most people judge themselves and others in terms of success and failure. You can have a fat body and lots of money, and the money tips the balance when the judgements are made. You are successful. But if you are fat and broke, wow, what a friggin' failure. If you are broke and beautiful, then beauty tips the balance when the judgements are made. He's got no money, but he's gorgeous. If you are beautiful and wealthy you've hit the jackpot and the paparazzi will follow your every move so the failures can see what they're missing. All the time we are judging success in these ways, and the Illuminati love that and have worked so hard to achieve it. The more we make judgements on success and failure based on five-sense reality – beauty and the bank – the more we become entranced by the illusions and delusions of this "world". We become trapped in the web and forget who we are – infinite consciousness having a physical experience. That's the last thing the Illuminati want us to know and they have created a society based on stimulating the five senses, making them objects of addiction and worship, and suppressing the connections between our incarnate self and our infinite self: the ocean. As John Lennon used to sing:

> Keep you doped with religion and sex and TV.
> And you think you're so clever and classless and free.
> But you're still fucking peasants as far as I can see.

We face a daily onslaught of stimulation and manipulation of the five senses to keep us imprisoned in five-sense reality and to hold the focus of our consciousness and perception at that level of our infinite self. They want to keep us in the eggshell, or the egg cell. "Would you like to open your mind to infinite possibility?" "No thanks, I'd rather have me dick rubbed." Food additives, vaccines and the explosion of chemicals that are consumed every day as "food", "drink" and "medicine" are also designed to disconnect the pathways from five-sense reality to infinite self. So are the wars, conflicts, terrorist outrages and financial manipulations. They want us so focused on power and survival (reptilian brain) and fear in all its forms that we never even consider the basic questions of life: who are we and what the hell are we doing here? "Look mate, I can't think about all that stuff, I have a living to earn and a family to feed." "Look mate, I can't think about all that stuff, I have a career to build." Hello? Knock, knock, anyone in there? You are infinite consciousness and you are in control of your reality whenever you choose to be. You can live life or, like most people, let life live you. It's your call. Do you want suppression and control, or infinite freedom? You have the power to choose and don't let anyone kid you otherwise.

What is reality? Whatever you want it to be

If you sit in a room with a group of people and you all choose to attack and condemn each other you will have a deeply unpleasant experience and so will they. The responsibility for that experience is not down to some outside force. It is you and the others choosing to attack and condemn each other. You will have created your own reality and while you may blame this person or that person for "starting it", the truth is that you are all responsible for what happened because you all took part. This is what is happening to the human race collectively every day. We are all responsible for what is happening in the world and in our lives, but we blame each other for it. That same group of people could sit in that same room and make a different choice, so creating a different reality. They could love each other, be nice to each other, and respect everyone's different opinion. In doing so they would create a pleasant experience, a pleasant reality. We are in control of what we experience. The difference between the "world" being a prison or a paradise is merely the choices we make. The world we see though our eyes in people, places and events, is just a mirror of our inner self. The "outer" world we see is the reflection of the "inner" self that we don't see and don't wish to acknowledge is responsible. Change that and we change the reflection in the mirror – our lives, the "world". If we don't change ourselves the reflection can't change no matter how much we may cuss and blame, pass "laws" and thrash around in five-sense reality. Stage one, the first step in bringing down the vibrational walls built by the Illuminati, is to start, from this moment, to take responsibility for what is happening in our lives and the world in general. The Illuminati may be the driving force behind the global fascist state, but we are just as responsible if we sit on our arses and let them do it. I am not advocating mass protest or stockpiling weapons. That approach cannot change anything because it is operating on the same vibrational level as the Illuminati – five-sense reality – and they are experts at controlling those realms of perception. You shoot at them with a rifle, they'll shoot at you with a tank. You mass protest at their meetings and they'll put agents provocateurs in the crowd to justify sending in the helmets to knock the living shit out of you. If we try to change five-sense reality with the weapons and illusions of five-sense reality we are just adding still further to the control of perception by five-sense reality. Round and round and round we go in an ever-descending spiral, deeper and deeper into five-sense illusion. We are bigger than that.

Five-sense reality, the Illuminati's home ground, is an energy field, a dense energy field, currently ablaze with low-vibrational disharmony and chaos. The events of 9/11, and those that have followed, have added massively to that, exactly as planned. Symbolically we are living our daily lives in a raging sea of energy, whipped up into vast hurricanes, whirlwinds, and waves by the fear, anger, frustration, and hatred that, second by second, spew from human consciousness across the world. Each one has its own disharmonious wavelength and the sum total has created the reality we experience – disharmony. Imagine trying to think straight if you were stood in a raging torrent, and you were using all your strength just to remain standing and survive. That is what our minds and emotions are coping with every minute as we move through the energy field of planet earth – the violent, turbulent sea of energy that human thought has manifested, and the Illuminati has constantly encouraged and manipulated. This makes it almost impossible for most people to hold a connection with their infinite self on the other side of this turbulence, and generates the very fear and disharmony that feeds the reptilians and other entities in the inter-space plane. To turn machine guns on the Illuminati and to hurl bile and hatred at them would not change anything. It would just add to the disharmony that disconnects and imprisons us. There is another way. When faced with a problem you can either find a "solution" or remove the cause. Solutions are usually not solutions at all and lead only to more problems. For instance, going to war against the Illuminati might be seen as a "solution", but all it does is create another war, more death, conflict and disharmony, and the world would be in a worse state than it was before. It is the same with our health. Stress-related illness is treated with pills that use chemicals to target the symptoms of the stress. These cause other chemical reactions in the body – known as "side-effects" – and another chain reaction of consequences begins. The only way to cure stress-related illness is to remove the cause of the stress. The mature and sensible way to remove a problem is to remove the cause. When you observe the problems of the world, you are not, in general, looking at causes, but symptoms. Starving children in a world of plenty is not a cause, it's a symptom. War is the same and all the other problems we so wish would be no more. Their causes, I would suggest, are the following:

1. We have given our power and responsibility away (same thing) and so allowed a few to dictate events in the world.

2. We have made judgements based on "What's in it for me, how does this affect me?" rather than "What is the right and decent thing to do?"

3. Most people have become so entranced by the addictions of the five senses that they can perceive no other reality and judge all possibility by the world that we see, hear, touch, taste and smell.

4. We have, as a result, become disconnected from our infinite self, the ocean of love, wisdom and knowing that is waiting to rejoin us whenever we choose to broadcast the invitation.

5. We have become mesmerised by five-sense reality and allowed the Illuminati's manipulated wars and divisions to cause us to project the wavelengths and vibrations of so much fear, conflict, hatred and disharmony that we have turned the energy field in which we live into a raging torrent of chaotic and conflicting energy. This holds us in five-sense disconnection.

What's the answer? We love ourselves and we love each other.

From that will come all things. When we love ourselves and respect ourselves for what we are, infinite consciousness having a physical experience, our whole sense of perspective changes. The irrelevant details and petty conflicts, fears and frustrations of five-sense reality become meaningless to a spirit that knows it is all that exists. There is no we, just one infinite "I". We are not part of "God", together we *are* "God". Now, still worried about the price of beer or what the boss thinks of you? Still concerned about getting that promotion or what the "future" might bring? You are the beer; you are the boss; you are everyone in every job; you are the "future"; the "past"; the "present"; the infinite Now; you are all that is, ever has been or ever will be. Yeah, you sweeping the streets and picking up the garbage, you considered a "failure" by conditioned minds – you, too. Yes, and George Bush, father and son; and Cheney, Powell, Kissinger, Blair and all the rest of them. They are "God" also. They are just observing reality from a different place and a different perspective, one dominated by fear and the survival mentality. Their desire to control everything and everyone is founded on that very survival instinct: "If I control everything, I will control my survival." Relax guys; you will survive because consciousness cannot be destroyed, only transformed into another state. The Illuminati need to be loved more than any of us, and to change this world from a prison to a paradise we need to love them as much as we need to love ourselves. Indeed by loving ourselves, we are loving them and vice versa.

I can hear the macho men with the surplus-store uniforms and the gun-show weaponry screaming from here. "Fucking love 'em? You New Age wanker. We need to blow their fucking asses into the fires of fucking hell." Mmmm. That'll make it a better world; I'll look forward to that with those guys in charge. On second thoughts, when does the next spaceship leave for a faraway galaxy? Get me a ticket, quick. It is not the physical body in the positions of power that matters, except to the Illuminati, it is the consciousness that is deciding its behaviour. Minds controlled by the belief in some angry, vicious, fire and brimstone "God" are actually the same mentality as the Illuminati they say they oppose. The only difference is how they manifest that mentality. The Christian gun-toters are also full of fear, and also express the survival mentality. That's why they stockpile guns, food and water for when their version of Armageddon comes. They say they believe in freedom, but listen for long enough and that's the last thing they want. They don't want freedom for all, they want the freedom to replace a system of control that they don't like with a system of control that they do – theirs. They want to replace rule by the Illuminati with rule by the conflicting "laws" of a book that out-contradicts and out-fairytales even the official story of 9/11. That's not freedom, that's just another prison. The fact is, I would suggest, that most people who talk about freedom don't want that in truth. They couldn't cope with its responsibilities and the thought that the days of imposing their will and beliefs on others, including their children, were over. Freedom is to freely express your uniqueness while respecting the freedom of others to do the same. "Are you saying people should be free to kill each other then?", I hear the sceptics cry. Of course not. How can you disrespect another's freedom more than to destroy their ability to freely experience this world by taking their means to do so away from them? Freedom of self and respect for the freedom of others are one and the same. Without respecting another's right to freedom we cannot be free. This is why to look the other way at the treatment of people at Guantanamo Bay and in the exploited lands of Africa, South America, the Middle East, Asia and elsewhere, is to deny our own right to be free. While one person on this planet is not truly free to express his or her uniqueness of thought, view, and lifestyle, none of us can be truly free. How come? Because they are us and we are them. We are each other. When we love ourselves and love all things the causes of our plight in this five-sense reality will disappear without a gun being fired. This is why:

1. When you love yourself and respect yourself you will never give away to anyone your power and responsibility to perceive and act. You will not be told what to do and what to think.

2. When you love and respect all things, you will not make judgements based on "How does this affect me?", but only on the basis of what you believe to be right.

3. When you open your heart to love of self and all things, you immediately connect with the infinite ocean that is also love. If you express the vibration, the frequency of love, in its true, unconditional sense, you must connect with that same frequency out in the infinite, beyond the five-sense illusion. The infinite will then become your point of observation, and not five-sense reality. You will be in this "world" physically, but your consciousness will not be of it. Addiction over.

4. When you express love for self and others you no longer project the disharmonious, chaotic vibrations, of fear, conflict, hatred and aggression, and instead broadcast harmony – love – into the raging sea around us. We become the vehicle to bring love out of the infinite and into the energy field of five-sense reality. When we do so, and more and more do the same, we transform the chaos into harmony, the raging sea into a pool of tranquillity.

As this process begins to unfold it becomes easier and easier for incarnate consciousness in five-sense reality to reconnect with infinite self as the chaotic vibrations around us subside and allow the connection with the infinite to be received unpolluted once again.

With people thinking for themselves and taking responsibility for their thoughts and actions; with people doing what they believe to be right without thinking of the consequences for themselves; with people reconnecting with infinite self and disconnecting from the illusions of five-sense reality; with people living in a harmonious energy field that is not constantly undermining their mental and emotional state; with all of these things, all manifesting from love, the Illuminati game will be over, their energy source will be gone, and they will have to wake up and move forward in their infinite journey also. The prison will be a paradise.

Love is the answer.

Love is seen by so many as a weakness when it is the ultimate power. Love in its true expression is without fear. Love does not lie down in the face of threats and fear of the consequences; it always does what it believes to be right. It knows there are no consequences, only infinite experience. Enlightened people for thousands of years have talked of "thinking" from the heart. This is not the physical heart, but the spiritual one, the heart vortex, or "chakra", in the centre of the chest that connects us from the five-sense frequencies through to the infinite ocean of love. You know where it is because when you feel love that's where you feel the physical and emotional sensation. The symbol of the physical heart became associated with love when this truth was lost. Through this same vortex point comes our inspiration and intuition because that also originates at higher levels of ourselves, out in the infinite.

What changed my life in the late 1980s/early 1990s was when I decided that if my head and intuition (heart) were ever in conflict I would always go with the intuition. It can appear to get you into trouble in the short term and the head screams "I told you so – see what happens when you don't listen to me?" But stick with it and wonders manifest. Eventually the head observes this and realises that following your heart is the way. At that point what you think and what you feel become the same, and the internal war between thoughts and feelings that ravages the lives of so many comes to an end. The Illuminati want us to close our hearts and they work constantly to make this happen. They know that when we close our heart vortex, our connection with the infinite also closes. They want us to be dominated by the five-sense head, not the infinite heart. A physicist friend told me that the ingredients of some vaccines affect the para-thyroid gland in the throat in a way that suppresses the connection between the heart vortex and the throat vortex through which we communicate with language. Communication then becomes dominated by the flow of thought from the five-sense brain and lower mind. I know this may sound far-fetched to many, but this is the level of detail to which the Illuminati go to hold us in five-sense reality. More than that, they have to go to these levels of detail because being imprisoned by the five-senses is not our natural state. Humans are like a ball in a tank of water – its natural place is floating on the top. If you want to change that you have to hold the ball on the bottom of the tank and keep holding it there. The moment you let go, whoosh, it's floating on the top again. Our natural state is multidimensional connection and so the Illuminati have to work constantly to hold us in disconnection through an onslaught of mental, emotional, and physical means – mind manipulation, stress and fear, and food additives, vaccines, etc. But all of these are useless if we "think" and feel from the heart and view the world from that perspective. It overrides all attempts to disconnect us and we make very different decisions to those dictated from the conditioned, five-sense head. Love is the answer. It always has been, is, and ever will be.

I love you George Bush

Any other "solution" is avoiding the point and kidding ourselves that the answers and the blame lie "out there". The human race as a whole is as responsible for 9/11 in its own way as those who actually did it. For if people had made different choices earlier and had not given away their minds and responsibility, it would never have happened. While we go on cooperating with our own imprisonment there will be more manufactured outrages until we decide to wake up and grow up, and start manifesting the true infinite magnitude of who and what we really are. I have exposed the actions of those in power in relation to September 11th and so many other horrors, but to focus all responsibility on those people is to deny our own. Despite appearances, the aim of this book has not been to apportion blame, either to the Illuminati or the human race in general. It may appear to be about that in the earlier chapters as I detailed the events of 9/11 from the perspective of five-sense reality and it is important that those directly responsible are identified or these horrors will go on. But as I have indicated from the start, that is only one level of observing that day and its aftermath. The one highlighted in this chapter is far more relevant, I would suggest, because it offers a way home, a way to turn back from the vibrational abyss. This book is primarily about offering another vision of reality and possibility, not apportioning blame; for blame is a five-sense perspective. From this higher point of observation, those responsible for 9/11 are not to "blame" any more than humanity's dereliction of responsibility is to "blame". These were choices that led to consequences and those consequences can lead to learning and enlightenment if only we choose to observe from that level of maturity. But will we? Some 3,000 dead civilians in America are met by at least 5,000 dead civilians in Afghanistan. How the hell does that move the world on? On that basis, only when we are all "dead" and the world is a wasteland, will we have peace. What nonsense, what utter bollocks. As Gandhi said: "An eye for an eye makes the whole world blind." In the same way, the answer to the Illuminati is not to blow them away or inflict the "justice" of capital punishment because that will only add to the mental state that leads them to continue the manipulation of this reality to feed their own desperation to "survive". Yes, they need to be removed from the positions of power and prevented from continuing their genocide, but until they can see the nonsense of their actions, not least for the effect on themselves, they will continue in what we call the future to manipulate this "world" by taking over other "bodies". At some point we have to talk.

The only way to dismantle the Illuminati web of control is to think and feel it out of existence – to love it into a higher state of reality, beyond survival and into the infinite. As scientist and philosopher Buckminster Fuller put it: "You never change things by fighting the existing reality. To change something, build a new model that makes the existing model obsolete." When the Illuminati let go of the fear of survival they will see what they have been missing and they will be seriously pissed off to realise how long they have been missing it. So I say to them, I am not a threat to your survival. No one is. You are infinite consciousness that has nothing and no one to survive. I love you George Bush, father and son; I love you Cheney and Powell and Kissinger and Carlucci and the Illuminati High Council and the reptilian hierarchy in the inter-space plane. I love you. If I don't love you I don't love myself. Everything is everything and so if I don't love you I can't love myself. This is a very different perspective to the one you have read throughout most of this book, but both perspectives are true. They are just different levels of looking at the same events. September 11th was a terrible day, one of endless such days on this planet over thousands of years. But the greatest opportunities are often brilliantly disguised as your worst nightmare. This one has presented an opportunity to wake up and see beyond the illusion. September 11th can add to the nightmare or it can help to free us from it.

Many people across the planet, far more than the Illuminati could have believed, are not buying the fairytale and they are asking questions about what happened that day and what is happening in the world in general. More and more are going through this process of awakening to a new reality and amid the apparent darkness the light is beginning to shine. This book is the end of an era for me and the start of a new one. I think we have enough publications now about the conspiracy from the five-sense perspective. My books on these subjects alone run to thousands of pages and in them and other works there is enough information about the names, dates, places and techniques of manipulation. It is important to know these facts to be streetwise within five-sense reality, but that's only one level of the game. Changing reality from "I can't" to "I am", from small horizon to no horizon, is where my journey takes me now. From exposing the conspiracy, to thinking and feeling it out of existence. As the Morpheus character says in the movie, *The Matrix*: "You have to let it all go, Neo; fear, doubt, disbelief. Free your mind."

If you remember only one thing from this book, I would rather it not be about NORAD or Bush or Mohamed Atta. I would prefer it to be simply this. You have created your "life" and we have created the "world" we collectively experience. That means we can change it anytime we want. It's a just choice right now between fear and love. You are not your body or your family or your job or your religion or your bank balance. You are all that has been, is, or ever will be. You are all love, all hate, all fear, all freedom. You are everyone and everything.

Don't think you are. Know you are.

SOURCES

1   Guylaine Lanctot, *The Medical Mafia* and *What The Hell Are We Doing Here Anyway?* (Here's the Key Inc., PO Box 113, Coaticook, QC, Canada, JIA 2S9, and available at **davidicke.com**)

2   Giuliana Conforto, *Man's Cosmic Game* and *Giordano Bruno's Future Science* (Edizioni Noesis, Italy, 1998)

3   Dr William Sargant, *The Battle For The Mind: A physiology of Conversion and Brainwashing* (New York: Harper & Row Publishers, Inc., 1957)

4   Maurice Doreal, *The Emerald Tablets* (Source Books, Nashville, Tennessee), or see **http://www.crystalinks.com/emerald.htmlhttp://crystalinks.com/emerald.html**

5   **http://www.telepath.com/skipsll/trirept.htlm**

6   Carl Sagan, *The Dragons Of Eden* (Ballantine Books, New York, 1977)

7   **http://www.telepath.com/skipsll/trirept.htlm**

8   *Los Angeles Times*, June 9th 2002

9   *Bram Stoker Society Newsletter* (Dublin, Ireland, July 1999)

"I have no power, so what can I do?"

If a million people who know the score put this information in front of ten others every week, hardly an enormous task, it means that ten million new people will hear another version of the world every seven days. And if those ten million do the same, the following week the one million will have become 100 million. If they all do the same, the next week the one million will be a thousand million. All this achieved simply by everyone who knows the story telling it to ten new people.

So the answer to the question: "What can I do?", answers itself. You can change the world.

We have the power to transform what is happening, but we won't do it by talking only to those who already know the basic agenda. We will do it by constantly expanding the numbers who have access to this information and we all have the power to do that.

It's just a choice.

Questions faxed to the FBI on May 8th 2002

Was Flight 93 delayed before leaving the gate? Could you confirm the actual departure time and explain why it was delayed?
Refused to respond

Where are the cockpit/air traffic control communication tapes for the four aircraft? Why are the public not allowed to hear them?
Refused to respond

Can I talk to the air traffic controllers involved with the four flights?
Refused to respond

At what time was it known that flights 11, 175, 77 and 93 had been hijacked? What time was it known that something could be wrong on each of the flights?
Refused to respond

Why were the seat numbers for the hijackers given by the FBI for Flight 11 different to those given by attendants Madeline Amy Sweeney and Betty Ong in calls from the plane?
Refused to respond

Can you confirm that the people you name as hijackers passed through all normal check-in and security procedures on all flights?
Refused to respond

Why are there two conflicting time codes on the video footage of Mohamed Atta as he went through airport security at Portland, Maine? Why is one time code in the centre of the screen?
Refused to respond

Which passengers used seat-back phones and which used cellphones to make their calls from the planes?
Refused to respond

How did you know so quickly who the hijackers were when apparently no passengers mentioned that they were Arabic or Middle Eastern hijackers? Can you confirm that no passenger mentioned the Middle Eastern or Arabic nature of the hijackers they described?
Refused to respond

Why were the men the FBI says were the hijackers not on the official passenger lists released by the airlines?
Refused to respond

Which hijacker did the passport belong to that was found near the WTC? Who found it? Can I talk to him/her?
Refused to respond

How do you explain the massive discrepancy between the flying skills apparently displayed by the hijacker-pilots and the way their flying instructors said their ability was extremely limited or virtually non existent?
Refused to respond

What happened to the eight black boxes on the four aircraft, and what do they reveal?
Refused to respond

Why does the FBI continue to name the same list of 19 hijackers when some seven of those named have been found to be still alive? Which of those named has the FBI established are still alive?
Refused to respond

Were your offices in the WTC empty on September 11th as some sources report?
Refused to respond

Can I speak with the staff at Boston Logan, Washington Dulles and Newark Airports who checked in the hijackers?
Refused to respond

Can I have a complete list of all the passengers on the plane and their seat numbers?
Refused to respond

Can I see the phone company statements detailing the calls made by attendants Madeline Amy Sweeney and Betty Ong from Flight 11?
Refused to respond

Can I see the phone company statements relating to the calls made by passengers from the hijacked planes?
Refused to respond

What evidence is there that Mohamed Atta is connected to al-Qaeda?
Refused to respond

If Atta is connected to Al Qaeda, why was he allowed to move around the United States so freely using his own name and credit card?
Refused to respond

How do you equate "Islamic fundamentalists" with reports of them drinking alcohol?
Refused to respond

Do you believe that the "Middle Eastern man" who is said to have walked into the Boston air traffic control room on September 8th was Mohamed Atta?
Refused to respond

Atta returned his car to Warrick Car Rental in Florida on September 9th. How did he travel from Florida to Boston? If by air, what flight and airline did he take?
Refused to respond

Why did Mohamed Atta drive from Portland, Maine, the night before September 11th?
Refused to respond

When and how did Mohamed Atta book and pay for his ticket on Flight 11?
Refused to respond

How and when did the other named hijackers book and pay for their tickets on the hijacked flights?
Refused to respond

When and how did Mohamed Atta and Abdulaziz Alomari book and pay for their tickets from Portland, Maine, to Boston?
Refused to respond

Can I see copies of the paperwork relating to the above transactions?
Refused to respond

Who was the man you name as Alomari and show on video camera footage, when the real Alomari has been found to still be alive in Saudi Arabia?
Refused to respond

Where were Mohamed Atta's bag, his Koran and videos found? How many bags did he have?
Refused to respond

Which plane did Mohamed Atta's bag fail to board? Was it the Portland flight to Boston or Flight 11? Why did the bag not make it on to the plane?
Refused to respond

Did other hijackers check in bags?
Refused to respond

Boston Logan Airport parking garages have surveillance cameras, although the departure lounge does not. So what does the security video footage in the garages show of the hijackers arriving in their white Mitsubishi at around 7:15am on September 11th and the argument they are said to have had with someone about a parking space?
Refused to respond

Can I see that video footage and have the name of the man who had the argument with them?
Refused to respond

Can I speak to him?
Refused to respond

Where is the video footage of the hijackers in the departure lounges at Dulles and Newark, and what does it show? Can I see that video footage?
Refused to respond

How did the hijackers arrive at Dulles and Newark airports that morning?
Refused to respond

Where is the video security footage of the "Middle Eastern men" who are said to have arrived at Boston Logan parking garage from Portland, Maine. What does it show? Can I see it?
Refused to respond

Where did these other Boston hijackers stay on the night of September 10th?
Refused to respond

Where is the security video footage of the "Middle Eastern men" said to have visited the parking garage at Boston Logan in the white Mitsubishi five times in the week before September 11th? What does it show? Can I see it?
Refused to respond

Boston police say Mohamed Atta's red 1989 Pontiac Grand Prix was also found at Boston Airport parking garage. How did it get there and why did he therefore rent the Nissan Ultima to drive from Boston to Portland, Maine, on September 10th?
Refused to respond

Can you tell me exactly where and when the Algerian pilot Lotfi Raissi, who was arrested in the UK on the orders of the FBI, is alleged to have trained some of the hijackers to fly and over what period?
Refused to respond

Why would an alleged "Islamic fanatic" like Lotfi Raissi be married to a white Roman Catholic?
Refused to respond

When did Robert Mueller officially become head of the FBI?
Refused to respond

Did Mohamed Atta or anyone of that name ever attend training at Maxwell Air Force Base in Montgomery, Alabama, or anywhere else in the USA?
Refused to respond

Is it correct, as reported by the Times of India, that Mohamed Atta was sent $100,000 on the orders of the then head of Pakistan Interservices Intelligence, the ISI?
Refused to respond

Official reply to FBI questions

Fugitive Publicity
and Special
Services Unit

FBI FAX

O   P   C   A

To: Mr. David Icke

From: Ernest J. Porter   Office of Public and Congressional Affairs
           Voice: (202) 324-9858   Fax: (202) 324-3525

Subject: FOLLOW-UP ON YOUR REQUEST

Date: May 10, 2002

Dear Mr. Icke:

Rex Tomb asked me to look at your letter to him of May 8 in which you pose a
number of questions about the terrorist attacks of 9/11/01 and the subsequent
investigation.

As much as I regret to be the bearer of disappointing news, I am sorry to report
that it will not be possible to grant an interviews or provide information at this
time. As Mr. Tomb may have mentioned, our investigation into the attacks
still is very much in progress, and it has been FBI policy for many decades to
decline comment in such circumstances.

It will be some time, perhaps years, before the FBI's investigative files on this
case may be available through vehicles such as the Freedom of Information
Act. The answers to your questions may be found in the files at that time.

Nonetheless, your interest in contacting us is indeed appreciated.

TOTAL P.01

Questions sent to Fraser Jones

Media spokesman for the Federal Aviation Administration (FAA)

In his reply on June 6th 2002 he said he had given all the information he had for questions one to five, and for six: "The FAA monitors prohibited airspace and would be aware if a pilot blundered into such an area. Our mission is not civil defense. We would help coordinate the appropriate response given the circumstances."

1. I have been going through the timeline you sent me and I have some more questions. I asked when there was first known to be a problem with the four flights and in answer to that you gave me the times that the FAA informed NORAD. These are not the same times as when a problem was first identified. Could I have the times when problems were first identified?
No answer

2. Flight 11 failed to respond to the air traffic controller at 8.13 and yet both the FAA and NORAD say that the FAA did not inform NORAD of a problem until 8.40. Why a delay of 27 minutes?
No answer

3. Flight 77 failed to respond to air traffic control at 8.50am and six minutes later the transponder was turned off ... yet both NORAD and the FAA say that the FAA did not inform NORAD of a problem until 9.24. Why the delay of 34 minutes, especially when, by 9.03am, two planes had crashed into the World Trade Center?
No answer

4. Before Flight 77 turned around it made a detour off course in a north-west-south loop over West Virginia [according to USA Today] before returning briefly to its agreed route. Why was this ignored?

5. At what time exactly did the FAA and NORAD establish open lines to the discuss Flight 77 and Flight 93?
No answer

6. NORAD has told me that the FAA is responsible for policing No Fly Zones like the ones over Washington and New York. What is the procedure that the FAA has for doing this, what aircraft does it use and where are they based, and what happened on September 11th when there was no response? If the FAA doesn't have planes, then who does? What is the point of a No Fly Zone if there is nothing to defend it? *See above*

Communications transcript

This is a transcript obtained by the *New York Times* of the alleged radio communications between air traffic controllers and American Airlines Flight 77 from Washington Dulles International Airport to Los Angeles on September 11th.

8:12:29 AAL77: Good morning ground American seven seven is off of dixie twenty six with information tango.

8:12:36 Ground Control West: American 77 Dulles taxi to runway three zero.

8:12:39 AAL77: Taxi three zero American seven seven.

8:16:01 Local Control West: American 77, Dulles tower. Runway three zero taxi into position and hold you'll be holding for landing traffic one left and for spacing wake turbulence spacing behind the DC 10.

8:16:29 AAL77: And American ah seven seven is ready.

8:16:32 Local Control West: American 77, Dulles tower. Runway three zero. Taxi into position and hold you're holding for wake turbulence landing traffic one left and you need to be fifteen in trail of that DC 10.

8:16:41 AAL77: Position and hold three zero, American seven seven.

8:19:20 Local Control West: American 77 your departure frequency will be one two five point zero five. Runway three zero cleared for take off.

8:19:27 AAL77: One two five oh five. Runway three zero cleared for takeoff, American 77.

8:20:26 Local Control West: American 77, turn left heading two seven zero contact departure.

8:20:31 AAL77: Two seventy heading departure, American 77. Good day.

8:20:38 AAL77: Is with you passing one decimal one for three.

8:20:43 North Departure: American 77, Dulles departure radar. Contact climb and maintain five thousand.

8:20:47 AAL77: Five thousand, American 77.

8:22:05 North Departure: American 77 climb and maintain one one thousand eleven thousand.

8:22:08 AAL77: up to one one thousand American 77.

8:23:23 North Departure: American 77 (whistling sound) cleared cleared direct linden contact Dulles one one eight point six seven.

8:23:28 AAL77: direct linden eighteen sixty seven American 77 good day.

8:23:28 North Departure Low: O.K. O.K. O.K.

8:23:34 Radar Control: Got the board there already.

8:23:36 North Departure Low: All right we got normal frequencies all the way around nothing hot at this time. Ah, traffic where is this where is this go one twenty-eight where the hell is that? O.K., O.K.

8:23:43 AAL77: American 77 with you passing nine decimal one for eleven one one thousand.

8:23:47 North Departure: American 77 Dulles approach climb and maintain one seven thousand.

8:23:50 AAL77: one seven thousand American 77.

8:23:55 North Departure Low: O.K., alright. Point outs at this time you got seven lima vector direct dc a seven thousand november zero nine romeo is at five thousand he's already talking to north north sees the traffic, he's going to climb do whatever he has to do. American 77 is direct linden climbing to eleven switched and gone one tango seven is a point out to manassas seven nine x-ray's been pointed out to west he's at six thousand on going to join victor one sixty eight other than that that's all you have.

8:24:23 Radar Control: I got it.

8:25:33 NH: American 77 contact Washington center one two zero point six five good luck.

8:25:37 AAL77: point six five American 77 thank you ma'am good day.

8:25:49 AAL77: center American 77 with you passing one three decimal zero for one seven thousand.

8:25:57 Controller 5: American 77 Washington center roger climb and maintain flight level two seven zero.

8:26:00 AAL77: two seven zero American 77.

8:30:38 Controller 5: American 77 contact Washington center one three three point two seven.

8:30:42 AAL77: ah thirty three twenty seven American 77.

8:31:08 AAL77: (unintelligible) American 77 passing two five decimal one for two seven oh.

8:31:23 Controller 3: American 77 ah climb climb and maintain flight level two niner zero sir.

8:31:30 AAL77: two niner zero American 77.

8:34:16 Controller 3: American 77 turn twenty degrees right vector for your climb.

8:34:17 Controller 3: American 77 turn twenty degrees right vector for your climb.

8:34:19 AAL77: turn twenty right American 77.

8:37:33 Controller 3: American 77 recleared direct Charleston climb and maintain cor correction recleared direct Henderson sir climb and maintain flight level three niner zero.

8:37:39 AAL77: direct Henderson out of two nine for three nine oh requesting three five zero for a final American 77.

8:37:57 AAL77: center American 77 you copy request for three five zero as a final.

8:38:03 AAL77: three five zero for a final American 77 thank you sir.

8:39:30 Controller 3: American 77 amend your altitude maintain flight level three three zero for traffic.

8:39:36 AAL77: American 77 stop at three three zero.

8:39:52 Washington Air Route Traffic Control Center in Leesburg,Virginia: So who wants to talk to American 77 Bobcat or Henderson?

8:40:03 Controller 3: American 77 contact Indy center one two zero point two seven.

8:40:06 AAL77: twenty five seven American 77 thanks sir good day.

8:40:14 AAL77: center American 77 with you level three three zero.

8:40:16 Indianapolis Control, Henderson Sector Radar: American 77 Indy center roger squawk three seven four three.

8:40:18 AAL77: three seven four three American 77.

8:43:52 Indianapolis Control, Henderson Sector Radar: American 77 climb and maintain flight level three five zero.

8:43:54 AAL77: thirty three for three five oh American 77.

[At about 8:45 American Airlines Flight 11 crashed into the World Trade Center and was known to be hijacked for some 25 minutes before that.]

8:47:20 Indianapolis Control, Henderson Sector Radar: American 77 turn ten degrees to the right vectors for traffic.

8:47:23 Indianapolis Control, Henderson Sector Radar: American 77 turn ten degrees to the right vectors for traffic.

8:47:23 AAL77: ten right American 77.

8:47:33 AAL77: ten right American 77.

8:50:48 Indianapolis Control, Henderson Sector Radar: American 77 cleared direct um Falmouth.

8:50:51 AAL77: uh direct Falmouth American 77 thank you.

8:56:32 Indianapolis Control, Henderson Sector Radar: American 77 Indy.

8:56:46 Indianapolis Control, Henderson Sector Radar: American 77 Indy.

8:56:53 Indianapolis Control, Henderson Sector Radar: American 77 American Indy radio check how do you read.

8:57:12 Indianapolis Control, Henderson Sector Radar: American 77 American Indy radio check how do you read.

8:57:28 Indianapolis Control, Henderson Sector Radar: American alt 77 American radio check how do you read.

8:57:35 Indianapolis Control, Henderson Sector Radar: override beeping.

8:57:35 Indianapolis Control, Dacos Radar: this is uh   Indianapolis Control, Dacos.

8:57:38 Indianapolis Control, Dacos Radar: this is uh   Indianapolis Control, Dacos.

8:57:55 Indianapolis Control, Henderson Sector Radar Associate: override line beeping.

8:57:59 Controller 3: American 77 roger maintain flight level three five zero show that as your final.

8:58:08 Indianapolis Control, Henderson Sector Radar Associate: outside line ringing.

8:58:14 AAL: American dispatch Jim McDonnell.

8:58:19 Indianapolis Control, Henderson Sector Radar Associate: this is Indianapolis center trying to get a hold of American 77.

8:58:23 AAL: uh Indys hang on one second please.

8:58:25 Indianapolis Control, Henderson Sector Radar Associate: what?

8:58:26 AAL: hang on one second sir.

8:58:28 Indianapolis Control, Henderson Sector Radar Associate: all right.

8:58:30 AAL: who ya trying to get a hold of.

8:58:31 Indianapolis Control, Henderson Sector Radar Associate: American 77.

8:58:32 AAL: O.K.

8:58:33 Indianapolis Control, Henderson Sector Radar Associate: on frequency one two zero point two seven.

8:58:35 AAL: one two zero.

8:58:36 Indianapolis Control, Henderson Sector Radar Associate: point two seven we were talking to him and all of a sudden it just uh –

8:58:38 AAL: O.K., all right we'll get a hold of him for ya.

8:58:40 Indianapolis Control, Henderson Sector Radar Associate: all right.

8:58:41 Indianapolis Control, Henderson Sector Radar: American ah 77 Indy ah center how do you read.

8:58:51 Indianapolis Control, Henderson Sector Radar: American 77 Indy radio check how do you read.

9:00:25 Indianapolis Control, Henderson Sector Radar: American 77 Indy

9:00:29 AAL2493: center American ah twenty-four ninety-three.

9:00:31 Indianapolis Control, Henderson Sector Radar: American twenty four ninety-three go ahead.

9:00:33 AAL2493: yeah we uh sent a message to dispatch to have him come up on twenty twenty-seven is that what you want em to do.

9:00:41 Indianapolis Control, Henderson Sector Radar: yeah we had em on west side of our airspace and they went into coast and ah don't have a track on em and now he's not talking to me so we don't know exactly what happened to him. We're trying to get a hold of him we also contacted you company so thanks for the help.

9:00:51 AAL2493: all right.

9:01:50 Indianapolis Control, Henderson Sector Radar Associate: over ride line beeping.

9:02:00 Indianapolis Control, Henderson Sector Radar Associate: outside line ringing

9:02:07 AAL: American dispatch Jim McDonnell.

9:02:09 Indianapolis Control, Henderson Sector Radar Associate: yeah this is Indianapolis center we uh I don't know if I'm talking to the same guy about American 77.

9:02:13 AAL: yeah I cell called him but I did not get a reply back from him.

9:02:17 Indianapolis Control, Henderson Sector Radar Associate: we uh we lost track control of the guy he's in coast track but we haven't we don't where his target is and we can't get a hold of him um you guys tried him and no response.

9:02:26 AAL: no response (background noise).

9:02:28 Indianapolis Control, Henderson Sector Radar Associate: yeah we have no radar contact and uh no communications with him so if you guys could try again.

9:02:35 AAL: we're doing it.
9:02:37 Indianapolis Control, Henderson Sector Radar Associate: all right thanks a lot.
9:02:38 AAL: we're doing it thank you.
9:03:07 Indianapolis Control, Henderson Sector Radar: American 77 Indy.
[Around this point United Airlines Flight 175 crashed into the World Trade Center.]
9:06:20 Indianapolis Control: override line beeping.
9:06:21 Indianapolis Control, Dacos Radar Associate: Falmouth Decos.
9:06:22 Indianapolis Control, Henderson Sector Radar Associate: this is Henderson American seventy seven do you guys have radar on him is he over Falmouth or –
9:06:25 Indianapolis Control, Dacos Radar Associate: no we just moved the track there we never you know.
9:06:27 Indianapolis Control, Henderson Sector Radar Associate: O.K. all right you just have the track out there.
9:06:29 Indianapolis Control, Dacos Radar Associate: you guys never been able to raise him at all.
9:06:31 Indianapolis Control, Henderson Sector Radar Associate: no we called company they can't even get a hold of him so there's no no uh no radio communications and no radar.
9:06:36 Indianapolis Control, Dacos Radar Associate: and his last clearance as far as you know is on course to Falmouth and then jay one thirty four right well we're just gonna treat him like non radar and we've already told the next sector they're gonna have to sterilize for him until we find out.
9:06:49 Indianapolis Control, Henderson Sector Radar Associate: O.K. thanks.
9:06:50 Indianapolis Control, Dacos Radar Associate: ID.
9:08:43 Indianapolis Control, Henderson Sector Radar Associate: override line beeping.
9:08:54 Indianapolis Control, Henderson Sector Radar Associate: line ringing.
9:09:27: AAL: and it was a Boston–L.A. flight and 77 is a Dulles–L.A. flight and uh we've had an unconfirmed report a second airplane just flew into the World Trade Center.
9:09:00 AAL: American dispatch Jim McDonnell.
9:09:02 Indianapolis Control, Henderson Sector radar associate: Indianapolis Center did you get a hold of American 77 by chance?
9:09:05 AAL: no sir but we have an unconfirmed report the second airplane hit the World Trade Center and exploded.
9:09:10 Indianapolis Control, Henderson Sector Radar Associate: say again
9:09:11 AAL: you know we lost American eleven to a hijacking American was off … Boston to Los Angeles flight.

[Despite this, we are still about 16 minutes from the FAA informing NORAD of a problem with Flight 77 according to official timeline.]

9:09:17 Indianapolis Control, Henderson Sector Radar Associate: it was all right I can't really I can't hear what you're saying there you said American eleven.

This "world" is only an illusion and we can change it any time we want. It's just a choice right now between fear and love.

9:09:23   AAL: yes we were hijacked.

9:09:25   Indianapolis Control, Henderson Sector Radar Associate: and it –

9:09:27   AAL: and it was a Boston–L.A. flight and 77 is a Dulles–L.A. flight and uh we've had an unconfirmed report a second airplane just flew into the World Trade Center.

9:09:42   Indianapolis Control, Henderson Sector Radar Associate: thank you very much good bye.

9:10:30   Indianapolis Control, Henderson Sector Radar Associate: calls Indianapolis Control, Dacos Radar Associate line beeps.

9:10:32   Indianapolis Control, Dacos Radar Associate: Indianapolis Control, Dacos.

9:10:34   Indianapolis Control, Henderson Sector Radar Associate: all right this is Henderson there was an American eleven departed off of uh New York going to L.A. got hijacked American 77 departed off of Dulles is going to L.A. dispatch doesn't know where he's at and confirmed that two airplanes have been uh they crashed into uh the World Trade Center in New York so as far as American 77 we don't know where he is but they say uh American eleven was hijacked off of a New York airport going to LAX [Los Angeles] and uh

9:11:07   Indianapolis Control, Dacos PA: but we don't have a track on him.

9:11:07   Indianapolis Control, Henderson Sector Radar Associate: affirmative.

9:11:10   Indianapolis Control, Dacos Radar Associate: you mean like they just took off without a clearance.

9:11:13   Indianapolis Control, Henderson Sector Radar Associate: no you mean American eleven.

9:11:14   Indianapolis Control, Dacos Radar Associate: yep.

9:11:15   Indianapolis Control, Henderson Sector Radar Associate: he he's depart well I guess he did because he was going to L.A.

9:11:17   Indianapolis Control, Dacos Radar Associate: but nobody ever tracked American eleven is what I'm asking.

9:11:20   Indianapolis Control, Henderson Sector Radar Associate: don't know that I don't.

9:11:22   Indianapolis Control, Dacos Radar Associate: oh O.K.

9:11:23   Indianapolis Control, Henderson Sector Radar Associate: know just where he left from or uh.

9:11:25   Indianapolis Control, Dacos Radar Associate: there's no flight plan in the machine right now and –

9:11:28   Indianapolis Control, Henderson Sector Radar Associate: yeah I just looked at that, too.

9:11:29   Indianapolis Control, Dacos Radar Associate: I'm …

9:11:30   Indianapolis Control, Henderson Sector Radar Associate: as far as what we know that's all we know I talked to dispatch and that's what they relayed and they confirmed it here that I guess two airplanes about crashed into the Trade Center.

9:11:37   Indianapolis Control, Dacos Radar Associate: huh?

9:11:39   Indianapolis Control, Henderson Sector Radar Associate: all right.

9:11:40 Indianapolis Control, Dacos Radar Associate: oh.

9:13:54 Indianapolis Control, Henderson Sector Radar Associate: override line beeping.

9:14:04 Indianapolis Control, Henderson Sector Radar Associate: line ringing.

9:14:37 AAL: American dispatch Jim McDonnell.

9:14:39 Indianapolis Control, Henderson Sector Radar Associate: Indy center here.

9:14:40 AAL: yes sir.

9:14:42 Indianapolis Control, Henderson Sector Radar Associate: American eleven you guys said he departed off of uh New York.

9:14:45 AAL: Boston.

9:14:46 Indianapolis Control, Henderson Sector Radar Associate: Boston he was going to L.A. and it was a hijacked airplane.

9:14:49 AAL: yes.

9:14:50 Indianapolis Control, Henderson Sector Radar Associate: and you, have you heard anything from American 77.

9:14:52 AAL: no.

9:14:52 Indianapolis Control, Henderson Sector Radar Associate: O.K. and if.

9:14:53 AAL: I talked to a winder in the center up there and I gave em them the information I got.

9:14:55 Indianapolis Control, Henderson Sector Radar Associate: O.K. thanks a lot.

9:14:56 AAL: O.K.

9:14:57 Indianapolis Control, Henderson Sector Radar Associate: all right.

[Despite these exchanges it would be another ten minutes before NORAD was informed about Flight 77 by the Federal Aviation Administration, according to the official timeline.]

bibliography

Bamford, James: *Body Of Secrets* (Doubleday, April 2001)

Beaty, Jonathan and Gwynne, S.C.: *The Outlaw Bank: A Wild Ride Into The Secret Heart Of The BCCI* (Random House, New York, 1993)

Bradlee Jr, Ben: *Guts And Glory: The Rise And Fall Of Oliver North* (Donald I. Fine Inc., 1988)

Brzezinski, Zbigniew: *Between Two Ages: America's Role In The Technetronic Era* (The Viking Press, 1970)

Brzezinski, Zbigniew: *The Grand Chessboard, American Primacy And Its Geostrategic Imperatives* (Basic Books, 1997)

Conforto, Giuliana: *Giordano Bruno's Future Science* (Edizioni Noesis, Italy, 2002)

Conforto, Giuliana: *Man's Cosmic Game* (Edizioni Noesis, Italy, 1998)

Dempsey, James X. and Cole, David: *Terrorism And The Constitution: Sacrificing Civil Liberties in The Name Of National Security*, available from the First Amendment Foundation, 3321–12th St NE, Washington DC 20017

Doreal, Maurice: *The Emerald Tablets* (Source Books, Nashville, Tennessee), or at *http://crystallinks.com/emerald.html*

Dugger, Ronnie: *The Politician: The Life And Times Of Lyndon Johnson* (Norton, 1982)

Evanzz, Karl: *The Judas Factor: The Plot To Kill Malcolm X* (Thunder's Mouth Press, 1993)

Fletcher, Prouty, Leroy: *JFK, The CIA, Vietnam And The Plot to Assassinate John F. Kennedy* (Birch Lane Press, 1992)

Griffin, Michael: *Reaping The Whirlwind* (Pluto Press, January 2000)

Hallin, Daniel C.: *The Uncensored War: The Media And Vietnam* (University of California Press, 1989)

Helsing, Jan van: *Secret Societies And Their Power in the 20th Century* (Ewertverlag, Gran Canana, Spain, 1995)

Hopsicker, Daniel: B*arry And The Boys: The CIA, The Mob, And America's Secret History*, available through *http://www.barryandtheboys.com*

Ide, Dr Arthur F.: George W. Bush: *Portrait Of A Compassionate Conservative* (Monument Press, Texas, September 2000)

Keith, Jim: *Casebook On Alternative 3* (IllumiNet Press, USA, 1994)

Lanctot, Guylaine: *The Medical Mafia* (Here's the Key Inc., PO Box 113, Coaticook, QC, Canada, JIA 2S9, and available at *davidicke.com*)

Lanctot, Guylaine: *What The Hell Are We Doing Here Anyway?* (Here's the Key Inc., PO Box 113, Coaticook, QC, Canada, JIA 2S9, and available at *davidicke.com*)

Marrs, Jim: *Crossfire: The Plot That Killed Kennedy* (Carrol and Graf Publishers, New York, 1989)

Mencken, Henry Louis: *The American Language* (New York, 1919)

Morgenstern, George: *Pearl Harbor, The Story Of The Secret War* (Costa Mesa, USA, 1991 edition). First published in 1947

This "world" is only an illusion and we can change it any time we want. It's just a choice right now between fear and love.

Mott, Michael Wm: *Caverns, Cauldrons, And Concealed Creatures* (Hidden Mysteries, Texas, 2000), available through the David Icke website, *davidicke.com*)

Mullins, Eustace: *The World Order, Our Secret Rulers* (self-published, USA, second edition, 1992)

North, Oliver: *Under Fire* (HarperCollins, 1991)

Orwell, George: *1984* (Dutton/Plume, 1983). First published in 1949

Perloff, James: *The Shadows Of Power: The Council On Foreign Relations And The American Decline* (Western Islands, Appleton, Wisconsin, USA, 1988)

Powell, Colin: *My American Journey* (Random House, 1995)

Rashid, Ahmed: *Taliban: Militant Islam, Oil And Fundamentalism In Central Asia* (Yale University Press, January 2000)

Reed, Terry and Cummings, John: *Compromised: Clinton, Bush, And The CIA* (SPI Books, New York, 1994)

Sagan, Carl: *The Dragons Of Eden* (Ballantine Books, New York, 1977)

Sanders, Jim: *The Downing Of Flight 800* (Zebra Books, April 1997)

Shaw, Jim: *The Deadly Deception* (Huntington House Inc., Lafayette, Louisiana, 1988).

Stich, Rodney: *Unfriendly Skies*. This book can be ordered through *http://www.unfriendlyskies.com*

Stinnett, Robert: *Day Of Deceit: The Truth About FDR And Pearl Harbor* (Simon & Schuster May 2001)

Thomas, William: *All Fall Down, The Politics Of Terror And Mass Persuasion* (Essence Publications, 2002)

Various contributors: *The Day That Shook The World* (BBC Worldwide Ltd, 2001)

Wells, Tom: *The War Within: America's Battle Over Vietnam* (University of California Press, 1994)

index

C

Other work by David Icke

THE BIGGEST SECRET $29.95   £16.00

More than 500 pages of documented, sourced, detail that exposes the forces that really run the world and manipulate our lives. He reveals how the same interconnecting bloodlines have been in control for thousands of years. Includes the background to the ritual murder of Diana, Princess of Wales, and the devastating background to the origins of Christianity. A highly acclaimed book that broke new ground in conspiracy research.

CHILDREN OF THE MATRIX $29.95   £16.00

The companion book of *The Biggest Secret* that investigates the reptilian and other dimensional connections to the global conspiracy and reveals the world of illusion – the "Matrix" – that holds the human race in daily slavery.

... AND THE TRUTH SHALL SET YOU FREE $24.95   £13.95

Icke exposes in more than 500 pages the interconnecting web that controls the world today. This book focuses on the last 200 years and particularly on what is happening around us today. Another highly acclaimed book, which has been constantly updated. A classic in its field.

I AM ME • I AM FREE $21.95   £10.50

Icke's book of solutions. With humour and powerful insight, he shines a light on the mental and emotional prisons we build for ourselves…prisons that disconnect us from our true and infinite potential to control our own destiny. A getaway car for the human psyche. A censored sticker is available for the faint-hearted!

FROM PRISON TO PARADISE – video $59.95   £32.00

A six hour, profusely illustrated presentation on three videocassettes recorded in front of 1,200 people at the Vogue Theatre, Vancouver, Canada. It will make you laugh, it may even make you cry, but for sure it will blow your mind as endless threads and strands throughout history and the modern world are connected together to reveal the hidden hand, the hidden web, that has controlled the planet for thousands of years.

LIFTING THE VEIL $6.95   £6.95

Compiled from interviews with an American journalist. An excellent summary of Icke's work and perfect for those new to these subjects. This title is available from Bridge of Love UK and the Truthseeker Company, San Diego, USA.

THE REAL AGENDA BEHIND 9/11 $59.95   £32.00

A new three-video package in which David Icke explains the unreported background to the horrific events of September 11th 2001 and offers a road to freedom from the emerging global prison cell.

TURNING OF THE TIDE – video $24.95 £12.00

A two-hour presentation, funny and informative, and the best way to introduce your family and friends to Icke's unique style and information.

SPEAKING OUT – video $19.95 £15.00

A two-hour interview with David Icke.

THE FREEDOM ROAD – video $59.95

Another triple video by David Icke in which he presents the story of global manipulation. What has happened? What is happening? What will happen? All are revealed in this eye-opening, heart-opening, mind-opening video package. Not available in UK.

David Icke's earlier books are published by Gateway. See back page for contact addresses where all these books and tapes are available.

The Reptilian Agenda

with Credo Mutwa

David Icke has produced
video packages totalling more than six hours,
with the Zulu Sanusi (shaman) Credo Mutwa, who David describes
as a genius and the most knowledgable man he has ever met.

The Reptilian Agenda, part one • (3 hours 30 minutes)

Credo Mutwa reveals a stream of astonishing and unique knowledge that, up to now, has only been available at the highest level of initiation in the African shamanistic stream. But, Credo says, the world must know the truth. He tells of how a reptilian extraterrestrial race has controlled the planet for thousands of years. Fantastic confirmation of *The Biggest Secret* and *Children Of The Matrix*.

The Reptilian Agenda, part two • (2 hours 45 minutes)

Credo takes the story on from ancient times and explains how the reptilians have taken over the world and what we can do about it.

Reptilian Agenda is a three tape set in the US for $59.95 *(not available separately in the US)*

Both are available from Bridge of Love USA, UK, Australia and Africa.
See back page for contact addresses.

The Arizona Wilder interview

Revelations
of a
Mother Goddess

Arizona Wilder conducted human sacrifice rituals for some of the most famous people on Earth, including the British Royal Family. In this three-hour video with David Icke, she talks at length about her experiences in an interview that is utterly devastating for the Elite that control the world.

This astonishing video is available for **$39.95** and is a two tape set
in the United States or
£15 (plus **£1.50** p&p) in the UK.

See back page for contact addresses.

Other books available from Bridge of Love ...

The Medical Mafia

The superb expose of the medical system by Canadian doctor, Guylaine Lanctot, who also shows how and why 'alternative' methods are far more effective. Highly recommended.

Trance Formation Of America

The staggering story of Cathy O'Brien, the mind controlled slave of the US Government for some 25 years. Read this one sitting down. A stream of the world's most famous political names are revealed as they really are.
Written by Cathy O'Brien and Mark Phillips.

What If Everything You Knew About AIDS Was Wrong?

HIV does NOT cause Aids, as Christine Maggiore's outstanding book confirms. Concisely written and devastating to the Aids scam and the Aids industry.

What The Hell Are We Doing Here Anyway?

Guylaine Lanctot brilliantly exposes the mental and emotional prisons that trap the people in a daily illusion and offers the keys to multi-dimensional freedom.

For details of prices and a catalogue of all Bridge of Love books, tapes and videos, please send a self addressed, stamped envelope to one of the contact addresses on the back page.

Ordering David Icke books and tapes online

David Icke's books and tapes and most of those listed
in the bibliography, are available via
www.bridgeoflove.com
www.davidicke.com

The David Icke website also includes the Hidden Mysteries
bookstore with its excellent list of rare and unique
books on the subjects discussed in David's books.
Hidden Mysteries can also be contacted via:

Hidden Mysteries
22241 Pinedale Lane
Frankston, Texas 75763

Phone ordering: **903-876-3256**

info@hiddenmysteries.com
http://www.hiddenmysteries.com

www.davidicke.com

One of the world's most visited websites on conspiracy material with more than a million visits per week.

5,000 webpages of detailed information on all the subjects covered in this book – and more. The site is updated with current information every day and includes the award-winning *Reptilian Archives*, a library of ancient and modern information, and personal experiences of the reptilian connection.

Many attempts have been made to close down *davidicke.com* and hack into the system to disrupt this site. But we're still here. See for yourself the information they are trying to block.

Bring David Icke to your city or conference

If you would like David Icke to speak at your conference or public meeting, contact: _
email: *davidicketalks@aol.com*
tel/fax (England): 01983 566002

Can you help?

If you have any information you think will help
David Icke in his research, please write to, or email, him at
davidicketalks@aol.com

Please source the information wherever you can and
it will be held in the strictest confidence.

To order David Icke's books and tapes, contact one of the following:

UK & EUROPE	**Bridge of Love Publications UK**
	PO Box 43
	Ryde
	Isle of Wight
	PO33 2YL tel/fax: **01983 566002**
	England email: **dicke75150@aol.com**

USA	**http://www.bridgeoflove.com**
	Bridge of Love Publications USA
	c/o TGS Services
	22241 Pinedale Lane
	Frankston, Texas 75763
	Toll Free in the US: 888-609-5006
	Others call: 903-876-3416

Visit the David Icke website:

www.davidicke.com

For details of books, videos, talks and new information – constantly updated